T0397178

The Cambridge Handbook of Identity

While identity is a key concept in psychology and the social sciences, researchers have used and understood this concept in diverse and often contradictory ways. *The Cambridge Handbook of Identity* presents the lively, multidisciplinary field of identity research as working around three central themes: (i) difference and sameness between people; (ii) people's agency in the world; and (iii) how identities can change or remain stable over time. The chapters in this collection explore approaches behind these themes, followed by a close look at their methodological implications, while examples from a number of applied domains demonstrate how identity research follows concrete analytical procedures. Featuring an international team of contributors who enrich psychological research with historical, cultural, and political perspectives, the handbook also explores contemporary issues of identity politics, diversity, intersectionality, and inclusion. It is an essential resource for all scholars and students working on identity theory and research.

MICHAEL BAMBERG is Professor of Psychology at Clark University, USA, and the 2021–2022 President of the Society for Qualitative Inquiry in Psychology (APA Division 5). During 2020 he was the Fulbright Distinguished Chair at Adam Mickiewicz University, Poland.

CAROLIN DEMUTH is Associate Professor for Cultural and Developmental Psychology and co-director of the Centre for Cultural Psychology at Aalborg University, Denmark. She is also the 2021–2024 President of the Association for European Qualitative Researchers in Psychology (EQuiP) and Associate Editor of *Frontiers in Psychology: Cultural Psychology*.

MEIKE WATZLAWIK is Professor for Development, Education, and Culture at Sigmund Freud University in Berlin, Germany, where she is also the Head of the Psychology Department and leads the clinical Master's program. She is a Humboldt Fellow and the editor of several books, such as *Capturing Identity* and *Educating Adolescents around the Globe*.

The Cambridge Handbook of Identity

Edited by

Michael Bamberg
Clark University, Massachusetts

Carolin Demuth
Aalborg University, Denmark

Meike Watzlawik
Sigmund Freud University, Berlin

CAMBRIDGE
UNIVERSITY PRESS

University Printing House, Cambridge CB2 8BS, United Kingdom

One Liberty Plaza, 20th Floor, New York, NY 10006, USA

477 Williamstown Road, Port Melbourne, VIC 3207, Australia

314–321, 3rd Floor, Plot 3, Splendor Forum, Jasola District Centre,
New Delhi – 110025, India

103 Penang Road, #05–06/07, Visioncrest Commercial, Singapore 238467

Cambridge University Press is part of the University of Cambridge.

It furthers the University's mission by disseminating knowledge in the pursuit of
education, learning, and research at the highest international levels of excellence.

www.cambridge.org
Information on this title: www.cambridge.org/9781108485012
DOI: 10.1017/9781108755146

First published 2022

A catalogue record for this publication is available from the British Library.

Library of Congress Cataloging-in-Publication Data
Names: Bamberg, Michael G. W., 1947– editor. | Demuth, Carolin, editor. |
 Watzlawik, Meike, 1975– editor.
Title: The Cambridge handbook of identity / edited by Michael Bamberg,
 Clark University, Massachusetts, Carolin Demuth, Aalborg University, Denmark,
 Meike Watzlawik, Sigmund Freud University, Berlin.
Description: Cambridge, United Kingdom; New York, NY: Cambridge University Press,
 2022. | Series: Cambridge handbooks in psychology | Includes bibliographical
 references and index.
Identifiers: LCCN 2021020784 (print) | LCCN 2021020785 (ebook) |
 ISBN 9781108485012 (hardback) | ISBN 9781108719117 (paperback) |
 ISBN 9781108755146 (epub)
Subjects: LCSH: Identity (Psychology) | BISAC: PSYCHOLOGY / Social Psychology
Classification: LCC BF697 .C258 2021 (print) | LCC BF697 (ebook) | DDC 155.2–dc23
LC record available at https://lccn.loc.gov/2021020784
LC ebook record available at https://lccn.loc.gov/2021020785

ISBN 978-1-108-48501-2 Hardback
ISBN 978-1-108-71911-7 Paperback

Contents

Part V Where Is Identity?

Figures

Tables

Contributors

MATS ALVESSON is a professor at Lund University, Sweden, at the University of Queensland Business School, Australia, and at City University, London. He has published *The Stupidity Paradox*, with A. Spicer (2016), *Reflexive Leadership*, with M. Blom and S. Sveningsson (2016), and *Return to Meaning: For a Social Science with Something to Say*, with Y. Gabriel and R. Paulsen (2017).

MICHAEL BAMBERG held teaching positions in sociology at the Free University of Berlin, Germany, in linguistics at the University of York, UK, and in foreign languages at Tongji University, China, before being appointed professor of psychology at Clark University, USA. His scholarly interests are in narrative, identity, and qualitative methodology.

DAVID BECKER is a professor of social psychology at the Sigmund Freud Private University in Berlin, Germany. He is also a consultant to the German Agency for International Cooperation and other multistate bodies with reference to psychosocial work in geographical areas of conflict and crisis, specifically the Middle East.

KEITH BERRY, PhD, is a professor and graduate director in the Department of Communication at the University of South Florida, USA. His research concerns how relational communication, culture, and identity intersect with each other. Much of Dr. Berry's recent research has focused on youth bullying, reflexivity in autoethnography and ethnography, and LGBTQ issues.

MARIE-CÉCILE BERTAU, PhD, is an associate professor and director of the PhD Program at the Department of Psychology, University of West Georgia, USA. Her psychological language research is pursued in a pragmatic–dialogic framework, encompassing interpsychological and intrapsychological activities, to better understand the workings of language in human life.

ISHWAR BRIDGELAL is a PhD student in educational psychology at Temple University, USA. His research interests focus on college students' identities, motivation, and development. His scholarship employs narrative methods to study identity processes in naturalistic contexts, with particular interest in interventions that aim to advance equity and identity exploration.

SVEND BRINKMANN is a professor of psychology in the Department of Communication and Psychology at Aalborg University, Denmark, where he serves as director of the Center for Qualitative Studies. His research is particularly concerned with philosophical, moral, and methodological issues in psychology and other human and social sciences.

OCTAVIA CALDER-DAWE is a critical health psychologist based at Victoria University of Wellington, New Zealand. Her research explores sociocultural dimensions of health and well-being. Much of her work examines the interrelationships between identity, embodiment, and inequality, with a particular focus on gender, emotion, and, most recently, disability.

DAVID CANTER, PhD a professor emeritus at the University of Liverpool, UK, was formerly head of the Psychology Department at the University of Surrey, UK. He has published widely on many aspects of crime, growing out of his earlier work developing the field of environmental psychology and the study of civic, social, and governmental actions in emergencies.

CARLA CUNHA, PhD, is an associate professor in the Department of Social and Behavioral Sciences at the University Institute of Maia, Portugal, where she coordinates the Master's Program in Clinical and Health Psychology. Her scholarly interests include the dialogical self and process-outcome psychotherapy research. With Min Han, she co-edited *The Subjectified and Subjectifying Mind* (2017).

MARTIN DEGE is an assistant professor of narrative inquiry at the Pratt Institute, USA. His scholarly interests include narratives, concepts of crisis and how they shape our everyday lives, the historical emergence of psychology as a discipline, and, on an institutional level, concepts of digital humanities and how digitalization changes both research and teaching.

CAROLIN DEMUTH is an associate professor in cultural and developmental psychology in the Department of Communication and Psychology at Aalborg University, Denmark. Her work is located within discursive, narrative, and cultural psychology. At present, she is president-elect of the Association for European Qualitative Researchers in Psychology (EQuiP).

ADRIENNE EVANS is a reader in media at the Center for Postdigital Cultures, Coventry University, UK. She examines how gender organizes personal, social, and intimate relationships, and their manifestations in media culture.

She is the author of *Technologies of Sexiness* (2014), *Postfeminism and Health* (2018), and *Postfeminism and Body Image* (forthcoming).

ALESSANDRA FASULO is a senior lecturer at the University of Portsmouth, UK. Her research interests include conversation analysis, narrative studies, atypical interaction, and autism. She also edited (with Roberta Piazza) *Marked Identities* (2014).

HANOCH FLUM is an associate professor emeritus and former head of the Department of Education, Ben-Gurion University of the Negev, Israel. His research interests focus on career and identity development within cultural and social contexts. His scholarship combines educational and developmental perspectives with an emphasis on qualitative modes of inquiry and educational applications.

MARK FREEMAN serves as distinguished professor of ethics and society in the Department of Psychology at the College of the Holy Cross, USA. His works include *Rewriting the Self* (1993), *Hindsight* (2010), and *The Priority of the Other* (2014). He also serves as editor for the Oxford University Press series Explorations in Narrative Psychology.

JOANNA K. GARNER is a research associate professor and executive director of the Center for Educational Partnerships at Old Dominion University, USA. Her research interests focus on creating sustainable, collaborative research–practice partnerships across formal and informal educational settings, with an eye to educators' and learners' identity development and change.

ALEX GEORGAKOPOULOU is a professor of discourse analysis and sociolin-guistics at King's College, London, UK. She has developed the concept of small-stories research, a paradigm for studying identities within the narratives of everyday life. Her latest publications include (with Stefan Iversen and Carsten Stage) *Quantified Storytelling: A Narrative Analysis of Metrics on Social Media* (2020), and (co-edited with Anna De Fina) *The Cambridge Handbook of Discourse Studies* (2020).

KORINA GIAXOGLOU is a lecturer in applied linguistics and English at The Open University, UK. Her research monograph, *A Narrative Approach to Social Media Mourning: Small Stories and Affective Positioning* (2020) was featured in the Routledge Book series Research in Narrative, Interaction, and Discourse.

ALEX GILLESPIE is an associate professor in social psychology at the London School of Economics, UK, and an editor of the *Journal for the Theory of*

Social Behaviour. His research focuses on disruptive experiences, using a wide range of naturally occurring data, including letters, diaries, social media, news, and documents.

SUSANN GJERDE is an associate professor at the University of South-Eastern Norway and a researcher at Lund University, Sweden. Her research interests include leadership, management, identity, and values, and role and leadership development. Before joining academia, Susann spent eighteen years as a management consultant specializing in leadership development.

RAMIRO GERMAN GONZALEZ RIAL is a postdoctoral researcher at the Institute of Psychology, University of São Paulo, Brazil. He was an assistant professor at the Pontifical Catholic University of Chile, and an assistant professor at San Sebastián University, Chile. He works within the fields of social and cognitive psychology, with an emphasis on collective memory and cultural, ethnic, and indigenous identity.

DANILO SILVA GUIMARÅS is a professor at the Institute of Psychology, University of São Paulo, Brazil, working with theoretical and methodological issues concerning the cultural construction of senses, from a semiotic-cultural and constructivist perspective in psychology. His investigations focus on the process of dialogical multiplication with respect to tensional boundaries between cultural meanings and indigenous psychology.

TILMANN HABERMAS teaches psychoanalysis and clinical psychology at Goethe University, Frankfurt am Main, Germany. His recent work focuses on narrative and life-story identity in the sixteen-year Longitudinal Study of Life Narratives (MainLife), and on the role of narration in coping with emotional experiences.

LARS-CHRISTER HYDÉN received his PhD in psychology from Stockholm University, Sweden. His current position is full professor of social psychology at Linköping University, Sweden, and director of its Center for Dementia Research. His research explores how people with dementia interact, use language, and tell stories.

AVI KAPLAN is a professor of educational psychology at Temple University, USA. His research interests focus on motivation and identity development in educational contexts, and his scholarship emphasizes research–practice partnerships and applications. He holds fellowships within the Association of Psychological Science and the American Psychological Association.

NINA KEMPER is a graduate student in psychology at Goethe University, Frankfurt am Main, Germany. Working at the interface between narrative identity and social context from a psychoanalytic perspective, she is especially interested in how life stories are influenced by significant others, and the broader social context of these stories.

THEO KLIMSTRA is an associate professor in the Department of Developmental Psychology, Tilburg University, The Netherlands. His research focuses on various aspects of identity development, including formation processes and narrative aspects, and on personality development.

JANE KROGER, PhD, is a professor emerita at the University of Tromsø, Norway. She is the author *of Identity Development: Adolescence through Adulthood* (2000) and *Identity in Adolescence: The Balance between Self and Other* (2004), the editor of *Discussions on Ego Identity* (1993), and has published more than seventy investigations of identity development during adolescence and adulthood.

ABIGAIL LOCKE is a professor of critical social and health psychology at Keele University, UK. Her research interests concern gender, parenting identities, and health, and much of her work focuses on societal constructions of "good" motherhood and "good" fatherhood, typically applying a qualitative, discursive lens to her work.

JAMES E. MARCIA, PhD, is a professor emeritus of psychology at Simon Fraser University, Canada, and has a private practice in psychodynamic psychotherapy. He is an author of *Ego Identity: A Handbook for Psychosocial Research* (1993). With students, he has developed measures of Erikson's stages of psychosocial identity (Industry vs. Inferiority through Integrity vs. Despair), with an emphasis on identity.

CRISTINA MARINHO is currently working as a teaching fellow at the University of Edinburgh, Scotland, in the School of Philosophy, Psychology, and Language Sciences. With Professor Michael Billig, she has investigated political discourse at the Parliamentary Commemoration of April Revolution in Portugal. Their collaborative work resulted in *The Politics and Rhetoric of Commemoration: How the Portuguese Parliament Celebrates the 1974 Revolution* (2017).

MAREE MARTINUSSEN is a McKenzie postdoctoral fellow within the Melbourne Graduate School of Education, University of Melbourne, Australia. Her research traverses the sociology of everyday life, gender studies, identity studies, and critical studies of higher education, prioritizing people's active problem-solving in their embodied, routine, and strategic sense-making practices.

TUI MATELAU-DOHERTY is a PhD graduate from Auckland University of Technology and a Senior Lecturer at Unitec Institute of Technology, New Zealand. Her research uses multimodal (inter)action analysis to explore the relationship between creative practice and ethnic identity.

LUCAS B. MAZUR holds a PhD from Clark University, USA, and is an assistant professor at the Jagiellonian University in Krakow, Poland. He also teaches at the Sigmund Freud University in Berlin, Germany.

JANE MONTAGUE is head of psychology at the University of Derby, UK. Her research focuses on relationships, gender, and physical/mental health. She has published with colleagues in the areas of breast cancer, infertility, and compassionate mind training. She applies a qualitative approach, generally using the principles of interpretative phenomenological analysis to explore experience.

OANA NEGRU-SUBTIRICA is a senior lecturer in the Department of Psychology, Babes-Bolyai University, Cluj-Napoca, Romania, investigating personal, parental, and social factors in identity formation, and how motivation and goals are shaped by educational and occupational strivings.

SIGRID NORRIS is a professor of multimodal (inter)action and director of the AUT Multimodal Research Center at Auckland University of Technology, New Zealand. She is the author of *Analyzing Multimodal Interaction* (2004), *Identity in (Inter)action* (2011), *Systematically Working with Multimodal Data* (2019), and *Multimodal Theory and Methodology* (2020), and editor of the journal *Multimodal Communication*.

SARAH RILEY is a professor in critical health psychology at Massey University, New Zealand. She works across psychology, sociology, cultural, and media studies, exploring issues of gender, health, and digital subjectivity. Her books include *Critical Bodies* (2008), *Technologies of Sexiness* (2014), *Postfeminism and Health* (2018), and *Postfeminism and Body Image* (forthcoming).

MARTINE ROBSON is a lecturer in psychology in the Center for Critical Psychology at Aberystwyth University, Wales. She uses poststructuralist theory to examine how people adopt, resist, and transform health discourses. Publications include, using Deleuzian frameworks for health promotion, *Postfeminism and Health* (2018), and *Postfeminism and Body Image* (forthcoming).

ONNIE ROGERS, PhD, is an assistant professor of psychology at Northwestern University, USA. She studies identity development, stereotypes, and inequalities, and the experiences of racially and ethnically diverse youth. She is an editor for the *Journal of Adolescent Research*, and directs the Development of Identities in Cultural Environments (DICE) research team at Northwestern University.

DAVID ROWLANDS recently completed a PhD exploring the application of narrative approaches to understanding and addressing criminological and addiction issues, following a long career of clinical practice working with substance misusers. He has published widely on the narrative aspects of criminality and addiction.

JOÃO SALGADO is an associate professor and director of the Laboratory of Psychotherapy Research at the University Institute of Maia, Portugal, and a full research member of the Center of Psychology at the University of Porto, also in Portugal. He is a psychotherapist and Director of the Psychotherapy Service of his university. The focus of his current research is psychotherapy.

SUSAN A. SPEER is a senior lecturer in the School of Health Sciences, Division of Psychology and Mental Health, at the University of Manchester, UK. She uses conversation analysis to examine clinical communication, identity, and prejudice, and to study research methods "in action."

STEFAN SVENINGSSON is a professor of business administration at Lund University, Sweden. His research focus includes leadership, managerial work, and organizational change. Recent books include *Managerial Lives: Leadership and Identity in an Imperfect World,* with Mats Alvesson (2016), and *Managing Change in Organizations*, with Nadja Sörgärde (2019).

MOIN SYED, PhD, is an associate professor of psychology at the University of Minnesota, Twin Cities, USA. His research is broadly concerned with identity and personality development among ethnically and culturally diverse adolescents and emerging adults. He is co-editor of the *Oxford Handbook of Identity Development* (2014) and former editor of the journal *Emerging Adulthood*.

MEIKE WATZLAWIK is professor of development, education, and culture at the Sigmund Freud University in Berlin, Germany, and head of the university's Psychology Department, as well as director of the clinical master's program. Her scholarly interests include identity development in adolescence, diversity, and theoretical approaches to culture.

SUE WIDDICOMBE is a senior lecturer at the University of Edinburgh's School of Philosophy, Psychology, and Language Sciences, UK. She has been published in the *British Journal of Social Psychology*, *Discourse Studies*, and

Social Science and Medicine on topics including categories and identities, social interaction, and discursive psychology. With Charles Antaki, she was co-editor of the book *Identities in Talk* (1998).

JULIE WILKES is a postgraduate researcher in the School of Health Sciences, Division of Psychology and Mental Health, at the University of Manchester, UK. She uses discursive psychology and conversation analysis to investigate identity in kinship care.

DONNA YOUNGS, PhD is a chartered forensic psychologist, a consultant in private practice, and was formerly a reader in investigative psychology at Huddersfield University, UK. Her studies of psychological processes differentiating styles of criminal action led to her framework for distinguishing the psychological narrative forms that underpin a person's life story and identity.

TANIA ZITTOUN is professor of sociocultural psychology at the University of Neuchâtel, Switzerland. She studies development in the lifecourse and imagination, and has used diaries, longitudinal documentaries, archival material, and ethnographic work as data in her research. With Alex Gillespie, she is the author of *Imagination in Human and Cultural Development* (2016).

1 Identity: With or Without You?

Perspectives and Choices Guiding This Handbook

Meike Watzlawik, Carolin Demuth,
and Michael Bamberg

The conception of this handbook goes way back, taking us more than five years until completion.[1] It all began with an early plan to organize a symposium for the 31st International Congress of Psychology (ICP) for July 2016 in Yokohama, Japan. The intention was to bring together a group of international identity researchers, from within psychology and from neighboring disciplines, to see whether there were any new developments in identity theory and empirical research, and whether they had a common center or were drifting pieces moving in all kinds of directions (cf., for example, Nochi, 2016, or Watzlawik, 2016). This was the original idea. So, in the summer of 2015 we started contacting researchers we knew (and whom we did not know up to that moment), asking whether they would be interested in joining us for the symposium. Preparing the symposium was as stimulating as the actual gathering that took place on the afternoon of July 28 one year later under the header *Identity and Identity Research in Psychology and Neighboring Disciplines*. Janka Romero, the Commissioning Editor for Psychology at Cambridge University Press, had contacted us beforehand with the offer to talk about the potential to turn this into a book project, and we, the symposium participants, started following up the same night over dinner – not knowing that this would keep us busy for the next five years. We went through the usual editorial routines: developing a proposal, revising the proposal, and contacting old and new colleagues in the field, up to the point of delivering the full set of manuscripts in January 2021.

This is the brief story of the book's conception. Its emergence, the process from conception to print, is telling. First, we started out with the – what we thought *original* – idea of seriously bringing together different theoretical frameworks and different conceptualizations of how to do empirical identity work. What had guided us was our own recognition that the use of the term identity, even in our own work, had been not only fuzzy but often confusing, probably mystifying important phenomena rather than elucidating and yielding research in a rather straightforward and fertile way. Thus, it was

---

[1] Victor Krusborg Olesen has played a central role in the finalization of this book (e.g., by formatting the manuscripts and creating the index). We would like to take this opportunity to say thank you, the support was greatly appreciated!

our intent to thoroughly assess whether (and if so, how) current research on identity centered around one or a small number of key notions, or at least whether it could be organized around a number of different centers which may point in different directions for empirical work and applications. Our second incentive to take on a handbook of this magnitude was, in our conviction, that identity theory and research over the last ten years had taken a turn – a turn that had been inspired by the theoretical and editorial work of Margaret Wetherell (2009; see also Wetherell & Mohanty, 2010) with summaries ten years ago of how the field of identity studies had been reshaped and where it seemed to be headed for the next decade. This handbook here and now is where we feel we are, ten years later, in the form of a new synopsis and a new outlook that had been called for. It was our conviction that psychology was turning more toward the realms of cultural, contextual, and socially relevant work, and away from traditional information processing and experimental work. This is what we originally had hoped to capture and convey, but also document and illustrate.

The advice we received from reviewers of our first proposal presented the first hurdle, but turned out ultimately to be extremely helpful. Basically, we were advised to put together a collection that was more balanced and gave voice to traditional approaches and quantitative empirical methodologies as well. So, there went the original impetus to be avant-garde and keen on new directions and developments. With a revised proposal six months later, we struck a compromise; something we now, retrospectively, view as a fortunate turn of events: the volume has become rounder and readers are better positioned to judge for themselves where possibilities lie for innovation and progress in theorizing identity and turning it into empirical studies.

We also have to realize that the world over the last decade has changed – and probably even more so from when we started this volume, and definitely, and most profoundly, in the year 2020. If we consider the question of *who-we-are* – or more concisely, *Who-am-I?* – as forming the core around which identity studies revolve, this question has undergone deep scrutiny, and new identity categories have emerged. Ten years ago, national identity, gender and sexuality, as well as immigrant identity had settled as the kinds of themes/ categories through which identities were navigated and investigated. By 2018, immigration had transformed into a new topic (again) that had to deal with new dimensions of massive uprootedness – especially by refugees and asylum seekers in Europe, and globally. While it may be fair to say that ethnicity and race have surely been themes covered by identity researchers in the past, they have taken on radically new proportions and a different depth over the last five years, but particularly in 2020: race and ethnicity have experienced a transposition to systemic issues of equity, inequality, and injustice. Newly emerging discussions around the histories of colonialism and indigeneity propel the who-am-I question with new force and intensity. Again, while Asian identity *under a header of collectivism* has been on the horizon of identity research for a while, particularly in contrast to so-called Western *individualistic* identity, a recent shift to black, brown, and indigenous identities has transformed former research on race and ethnicity and moved it into the vicinity of critical issues regarding inclusion and diversity, and again equity and justice. Finally, whiteness, by and large ignored in identity studies, and lingering only on the very fringe of interest to identity researchers, has charged, again especially in the year 2020, into the frontline of principled and urgent identity matters.

All this is not to mention a virus that posed the who-am-I (and collective who-are-we) question in the form of a worldwide experience of uncertainty – a continuous identity threat for which the answers are yet to be determined (cf. Bamberg, 2021a). Civil unrest, food insecurity, and unemployment, topics only on the horizon for identity research in underprivileged populations and nation-states with a less developed industrial base and more authoritative infrastructure, suddenly struck "much closer to home" in 2020 in Europe and North America. A number of additional, brand-new and pressing identity challenges – and we will return to them in our concluding section to this handbook – are emerging in the face of disinformation, cybersecurity, and surveillance. For us as authors, taking together the impact of these rather new and drastic challenges to our social consciousness and our sense of who we are, as individuals, as organizations, and as collectives, constituted one of the driving forces to join and pursue bringing together a new collection of thoughtful investigations of identity matters.

When surveying the contemporary field of traditional developmental takes on how identities form and change over the lifespan, we came to the conclusion that not too much had changed over the last two decades. Surely, identity research has contributed to deeper and better insights into how to conceptualize change (and constancy) during childhood, adolescence, adulthood, and aging. Some even may claim that since the turn of the century a new kid on the block (Arnett, 2000) has joined the ranks of well-established identity stages in life.[2] The covering of developmental identity status work and neo-Eriksonian expansions will have to be covered in a volume like ours. One aspect of developmental approaches that stood out to us from early on was an assumption that seems to run in the blood of developmental stage theories: once a new phase or stage has been achieved and its identity finalized, the next – often *higher* and more accomplished – stage becomes the built-in theoretical implication for what changes and how change takes place. Transformation and change are the foci of empirical developmental identity research; and, as such, *having* a certain identity, e.g., *being* an accomplished adolescent or emerging

---

[2] It may be noteworthy that Arnett questioned the meaningfulness of stages when it comes to describing individual developmental trajectories. Arnett (2016, p. 290) proposes "the idea of life stages as *master narratives* . . ., as a way of explaining how life stages provide the raw material for individuals to construct a personal identity narrative."

adult, is the presupposition to *becoming* what comes next. Doing the actual work it takes to remain *adolescent*, or *adult*, including its claims and contestations, navigations, iterative practices, negotiations, and all the relational work to maintain these identities, becomes backgrounded, if not hidden. Collecting and putting contributions together in this handbook, we decided to balance these issues carefully against more recent developments in other identity domains that seemed to be at least equally if not more compelling.

Another important aspect for our original plan for the 2016 ICP symposium in Yokohama was to check deeper into Foucauldian approaches to identity and subjectivity and see how they could be bridged with traditional approaches. Here again, one of the few who had already tried to test these waters, i.e., differentiate certain aspects and integrate others of Foucault's approach to discourse with critical discourse analysis (cf. Fairclough, 2013) and with social identity psychology (which was emerging out of the Loughborough School), was Margaret Wetherell (1998, 2001). Our attempt for our symposium was to focus more strongly on the role of the subject and subjectivity, a discussion that had come out of sociology under the header of subjectification, and had entered psychology with Henriques et al. (1984), Venn (2002), and a new journal, *Subjectivity* (see Blackman et al., 2008). Alongside this tradition, the subject had been theorized as on one side of the coin being subjected to social, cultural, and contextual forces (*socially* constructed), but also on the flip side as being an agent *in the world* (self-constructed). This dimension of how to theorize identity and make it relevant for empirical investigation, when compared with developmental identity formation processes and issues of social relatedness, i.e., the integration/differentiation of individual, organizational, and collective identities, had traditionally been given short shrift. Although there had been attempts to conceptualize agency as one dimension of self-construals with the two end poles autonomy and heteronomy (the second dimension being interpersonal distance, with the two end poles separation and relatedness) in cross-cultural psychology (Kagitçibasi, 2005), developments over the last ten years in social theory in general, and in cultural psychology more specifically, offer a different and wider examination of agency, especially in terms of a research orientation that integrates the world-to-person dimension of experience in identity formation processes, and no longer simply juxtaposes it with self-discovery or self-construction. To us, it seemed as if a wider integration of the being-subjected dimension into identity research could have particularly positive repercussions when confronted with new identity challenges such as inequality and social justice.

When we drafted this handbook and were looking back at identity studies over the first decade of the twenty-first century, a theoretical shift became apparent that had made its way into identity studies, and was to a large degree still in full swing: identity had been decentered – or better, destabilized – and was undergoing a number of reconceptualizations. Most identity research appeared to be still reminiscent of and committed to some form of core, from where stability and constancy to persons or organizations was radiating. However, it seemed to us that considerations of change – or at the very least adaptations to the experience of a changing world – had started to penetrate the center stage of identity concepts. At the same time, identity was blurring more and more with self, subjectivity, and other neighboring concepts, and terms such as self-identity (cf. Widdicombe & Marinho, this volume), role identity (cf. Kaplan et al., this volume), voices (cf. Bertau, this volume), or identity as a form of self-interpretation (cf. Brinkmann, this volume) mirrored this blurring. Even in our own writing, we started referring to people as having a *sense* of self or *identity* – a further softening of identity, pushing it to where self and identity were used almost interchangeably (Bamberg, 2011). All this had led to what some outside the discipline of psychology had referred to earlier as a *crisis* of identity (cf. Hall & du Gay, 1996). Stuart Hall (1996) himself – like many others (e.g., Brubaker & Cooper, 2000) – had called into question whether we actually still need the term/concept of identity. However, almost all – in the same breath – answered that the current use and popularity of the concept, and the ways it had ensued inquiry, had made it close to *indispensable* (cf. Wetherell, 2010).

Alongside and in concert with the slow process of decentering identity over the last three decades ran a process of opening psychology to theorizing and a closer investigation of culture – in one way in the form of studies of crosslinguistic/cross-cultural variation (cf. Demuth & Keller, 2011; Markus & Kitayama, 2010), paralleled by in-depth descriptions and explications of single cultures (cf. Lutz, 1988; Schwartz, White, & Lutz, 1992), especially by use of ethnographic in combination with other qualitative methodologies. It is noteworthy that this clearly signaled a move away from aggregating and comparing large-scale data sets on people's assumed shared beliefs or attitudes toward more fine-grained and in-depth studies of shared repertoires that people actually put to use in their everyday routines and practices. Simultaneously, it juxtaposed assumptions about identity as something fixed, inalienable, and inherent to persons with something that was enacted and performed, and at the same time situated in contexts that mostly were rela-tional and interactional. Similarly, this was paralleled in the role that was attributed to language, including how to analyze language. While traditional identity studies would view language as a window on what is *behind* perform-ance and how beliefs and attitudes are *represented*, culturally context-sensitive studies started to turn to investigate bodily practices with which people are assumed to make sense of each other – and in doing so, make sense of themselves. Language practices became focal points as practical concerns in ways the relational business between people as a different kind of identity business was viewed as coordinated and navigated.

When contrasting these two kinds of positions this way, we realized that we basically had four principled strategies for identity research at hand that we wanted to collect in this handbook, and – as far as that was possible – have to speak to one another. The first consists of assuming identity as (metaphorically) located and accessible inside the person, requiring methodological tools to mine and pull out what is hidden from clear sight. An alternative view locates identity as external to the person – as surfacing and empirically discernible in *identity work*, the way it is performed by people (or organizations, for that matter) in actions taken (cf. Sveningsson, Gjerde & Alvesson, this volume). The third position would be to assume identity as both: located – and by the researcher locatable – inside the person as well as outside, in their performance/behavior (Bertau, this volume, takes this point of departure). The fourth way would be to characterize the interior–exterior distinction as unfounded, if not false, and approach identity without any claims toward interiority and/or exteriority.

Facing the task of outlining and representing positions that display the spectrum of centering and decentering identity the way we tried to frame recent research trends in identity studies in the previous paragraphs, when more concretely designing the substance and new perspectives we wanted to offer with this handbook, we faced a second important and ongoing transformation that has impacted the field of identity studies. Methodologically, over the last decade, we have experienced a tremendous increase in, together with a much more widespread acceptance of, qualitative research in identity studies (cf. Watzlawik & Born, 2007). With the integration of qualitative guidelines into the *Publication Manual of the American Psychological Association* (2019 – see also Levitt et al., 2018), qualitative methodologies have moved away from the status of an underground or subversive methodology and entered the recognition of researchers who had thus far been invested in experimental or large-scale survey research (Demuth, 2015b, 2015c; Demuth & Schjødt Terkildsen, 2015). Recent calls have emerged that consider qualitative methodologies as better situated to go beyond the integration of new and thus far underserved populations and pursue issues of social inequity and justice (cf. Bamberg, 2021a, 2021b). It was these trends that we were hoping to collect and give voice to – originally with the Yokohama symposium, and now that these issues had become more pressing, within our role as editors of this handbook.

With the imperative to promote what runs under the header *qualitative methods*, and to integrate it into a handbook that attempts to call attention to newly emergent trends as well as to a broad representative methodological spectrum, the question emerged: Which ones should we select (and which ones should we omit), especially in regard to the broad range of newly (qualitative) methodologies making an appearance in psychology? In addition to biographical identity research (see Habermas & Kemper, this volume), we decided to include a number of methods that thus far have had little exposure to identity studies but are committed to capturing the microgenetic aspects of identity as unfolding under the microscopic looking glass of identity researchers. Under the umbrella of discursive studies, these approaches comprise a wider scope of methods such as conversation analysis (Wilkes & Speer, this volume), research that can be broadly located within the Loughborough School of discursive psychology (Locke & Montague, this volume), as well as Foucauldian-informed discourse analysis (Riley, Robson & Evans, this volume), and critical discursive psychology (Calder-Dawe & Martinussen, this volume). We have also included narrative approaches (Berry, this volume; see also Hydén, this volume) comprising newer developments that stress the performing nature of storytelling (Giaxoglou & Georgakopoulou, this volume). Some of the chapters represent the recent developments of turning away from discourse (alone) as the predominant way to produce identity (Calder-Dawe & Martinussen, this volume, see also Freeman, this volume) and away from an individualistic conception of identity (e.g., Norris & Matelau-Doherty, this volume).

1.1 Organization of the Book

The book is divided into five parts.

Part I: *The Origin and Development of the Concept of Identity*
Part II: *New Perspectives and Challenges*
Part III: *Methodological Approaches*
Part IV: *Current Domains*
Part V: *Where Is Identity?*

The individual parts are presented below to give insight into the structure and logic of the book.

Part I: The Origin and Development of the Concept of Identity

As mentioned, lining up the first three chapters for the handbook, we intend to introduce readers to the complexities that identity studies are facing. All three chapters in this section circle around three central themes:

(i)   temporal identity: how we as persons or organizations claim to exist throughout time, i.e., claim to be the same in the face of change, and claim to undergo change in the face of permanence;
(ii) sameness/difference: how people and organizations align and disalign vis-à-vis others, i.e., claiming to be the same as others and simultaneously being different, if not unique; and
(iii) agency: being a product of the world and simultaneously making and producing the world.

Michael Bamberg and Martin Dege in their chapter on **decentering histories of identity** start with an investigation of where the notion of identity came from – its history and the way it found entrance into late-modern use in American English. They sidestep the challenge any historiography faces, namely not having a clearly established and accepted definition of what to look for in history books or historical records, and therefore start out by probing into the way identity is being used in contemporary everyday English language. Delineating meanings of identity – in contrast to and as partially overlapping with what they call *neighboring terms* (e.g., self, subject, individual, and conscious/conscience) – they condense identity into five aspects that they subsequently subject to historical scrutiny, i.e., how these aspects took on shades of meaning over time and became what they identify as central to identity. In their tour de force through the histories of how this conglomerate term *identity* came into usage in late-modern English, they pick apart and interrogate its Eurocentric origin and contemplate its constrictions and potential occlusion of alternative theories and empirical methodologies for the field of identity studies.

Sue Widdicombe and Cristina Marinho in their chapter on **challenges in research on self-identity** follow suit and document the repercussions for each of the above three key aspects of self-identity. They prefer the term self-identity, owing to the slippage and partial intersection between identity and self, and rename the three realms for identity maneuvering identified in the previous chapter by Bamberg and Dege, respectively: (i) continuity, (ii) uniqueness, and (iii) agency. They cycle through ways researchers – coming from different theoretical and methodological perspectives – have taken these three domains and rendered them researchable. For each aspect they summarize and to a degree juxtapose exemplars of traditional, positivist approaches with a social constructionist perspective and a poststructuralist perspective, showing how the three constructs (continuity, uniqueness, and agency) are differently defined in those respective approaches, and how they lead to different kinds of questions and, for obvious reasons, result in highlighting different outcomes and relevancies for practical purposes. Weighing carefully the pros and cons of approaching identity from different perspectives, Widdicombe and Marinho equip readers of the subsequent chapters of this handbook as well as their own research with tools to distinguish more clearly between the assumptions and decisions that inform us – and, if at all possible, to consider what alternatives could have been chosen, and reflect on the reasons why those have been ruled out.

Mark Freeman, in his concluding chapter of the three that are aiming to interrogate the concept of identity from different angles, introduces **the mystery of identity** with a profound challenge: identity, he argues neither has a "firmly agreed-upon conceptualization of the phenomenon" nor does it bespeak "a singular phenomenon" (**p. 77**). He raises what he calls **fundamental questions, elusive answers** and demonstrates strikingly well, in a section entitled "Excursion: Coming to Terms with the Mystery," how impossible it is to give a sensible answer from a personal experiential point of view to the who-am-I question. Instead of helping to develop strategies to make what is unknown about identity known, he calls for making the little we know about our identities *unknowing*. What Freeman clarifies in his chapter are the seemingly unsurmountable difficulties when engaging in identity studies, especially when attempting to address temporal identity issues (what Widdicombe and Marinho call *continuity*) and sameness/difference, for which Freeman employs the term *otherness* (*uniqueness* – for Widdicombe and Marinho).

As such, it is telling how all three introductory chapters seem to zoom in on and tackle very similar issues, but having started from different points of departure, and employing vocabularies that have different implications. Another aspect that is equally elucidating is that all three introductory chapters interrogate identity by using different rhetorical styles: while Bamberg and Dege present a mix of semantic and historical analysis, Widdicombe and Marinho employ the genre of summary reports of contemporary identity studies (aiming for methodological classifications). In contrast, Freeman's chapter resembles an essayist writing style that is embraced methodologically by identity researchers who proceed autoethnographically (see Berry, this volume). Overall, opening the handbook with these three introductory chapters serves the function of a first attempt – and from a rather general angle – to sort through developments, commonalities, and differences between research traditions within the broad field of identity studies.

Part II: New Perspectives and Challenges

While Part I offers general reflections on the construct of identity and takes up some theoretical approaches by way of example, these are explored in greater depth in the second part. Part II thus aims to provide an overview of different (theoretical) approaches to identity – in many cases starting with their historical roots and taking specific cultural contexts into account.

Svend Brinkmann opens this part by introducing **identity as moral** as well as ethical **self-interpretation**, showing that individuals continuously interpret themselves in light of values and moral commitments, which leads the author to contrast his approach with the striving for value-*neutrality* often found in psychology and the social sciences. For Brinkmann, identity "implies both morality and narrative and is never purely individual, but intertwined with various layers of society" (**pp. 101–102**). Octavia Calder-Dawe and Maree Martinussen stress the same when describing identity as a potential *interdisciplinary* meeting point for scholars striving to understand identity at the interface of social formations and individual psychologies. While Brinkmann emphasizes the moral and ethical aspects of identity, Calder-Dawe and Martinussen explore the *affective* turn in identity research, introducing an **affective discursive practice approach**. With the help of an empirical example, the authors show how, while still maintaining focus on the individual's active meaning-making processes in a certain societal and cultural framework,

(i) affect and emotion can enter analysis, and (ii) the discursive as well as the embodied can be examined in the same analytic frame. On this basis, the authors give an outlook on future research agendas that may focus on the individual *and* (not only *Western*) collectives, more explicitly potentially connecting the dots between the pushes and pulls of socio-historical regimes and the more idiosyncratic play of personalized affective patterns and situated practices.

Following this idea, a non-Western perspective is then introduced in Ramiro Gonzalez Rial and Danilo Silva Guimarães's chapter. The cisgendered men,[3] both psychologists/researchers from Brazil and Chile, invite the readers to reflect on their roles when examining the identities of others by introducing an ethnographic **identity study of indigenous Mapuche women weavers in southern Chile**. The example is used to demonstrate (i) how societal power relations constitute identities as well as lead to the emergence of identity formation (and/or survival) strategies that allow the individual to negotiate change and consistency, and (ii) how certain theoretical convictions of what identity is (not) can blind us to alternative approaches.

Marie-Cécile Bertau also stresses the latter in her chapter, in which she presents a **language-dialogical take on identity**. She advocates a fundamental opening to plurality, to dynamics with incessant change as well as to context-ualizing any phenomenon – potentially leading to the decolonization of psychological science. She lays out two potential paths or *logics* to reach this goal: (i) *adding* others, emotions, bodies, contexts, etc. to the individual-focused take on identity, and (ii) reformulating the self-other-related self as *mediated* by language-as-activity, thereby allowing for the analysis of dialogical, dynamic, sociocultural practices in and through which identities emerge. From her perspective, we need to give up on the traditional understanding of homogeneity (sameness) to be able to assess internal differences as well as contradictions (polyphony of voices). In this regard, "[o]therness is crucial to [the] self who is in constant negotiations with others' voices in order to form. Hence, identity as matching with oneself is neither assumed, nor necessary" (**p. 190**) – a conclusion Gonzalez and Guimarães draw as well.

Bertau vividly shows that identity is nothing static, but something that is constantly constructed and negotiated, an understanding of identity that also appeared in the psychoanalytic framework, as Tilmann Habermas and Nina Kemper show in their chapter. They argue for a **narrative** and co-narrative conception of **identity from a psychoanalytic perspective**, providing an overview of historical changes that lead to its emergence. After briefly describing the work of Freud and Erikson, they move to more clinically oriented analysts before describing changes that occurred in the 1990s. By returning to Erikson,

---

[3] Cisgender (from Latin *cis*, meaning *on the same side*) refers to a person who identifies with the gender they were assigned at birth. Being cisgender (non-transgender) is an aspect of a person's gender identity.

they present a concept of narrative identity "which is enriched by psychoanalytic developments of the past fifty years" (**p. 194**).

Erikson also plays a major role in the final chapter of this section, since he is a key figure in the history of Jane Kroger and James E. Marcia's **identity status approach.** Kroger and Marcia give an overview of the approach's historical roots, its key concepts, (methodological) elaborations over time, empirical findings, and current developments in this field. They also discuss the gains and losses when approaching identity with the help of the variables exploration and commitment as well as possible implications for (clinical) practice and future research (e.g., establishing integrative approaches that are able to capture the relationship between "psyche, soma, and society" when assessing identity formation processes). The identity status approach will be followed by concrete empirical examples provided in Negru-Subtirica's and Klimstra's chapter in the next section. In addition, the attempt is made to link theoretical perspectives presented in Part II with methodological chapters in Part III, so that the reader can understand the empirical implications and see concrete examples of how they can be implemented.

Part III: Methodological Approaches

Part III aims at presenting a variety of methodological approaches that capture current trends in the fast-developing field of identity research. Different theoretical approaches to how identity is conceptualized will obviously bring about different methodological approaches to studying this construct, and this variety is also reflected in this part of the handbook. All chapters provide a theoretical introduction to their methodological approach, as well as hands-on practical examples to illustrate how analysis is done in practical terms.

The section starts with the contribution of Korina Giaxoglou and Alexandra Georgakopoulou, who address the three central themes mentioned above in terms of constancy and change, uniqueness and conformity, and agency and construction in the **analysis of small stories and positioning**. They enhance existing small story approaches by adding a visual dimension to analysis and going beyond face-to-face encounters. They demonstrate in an example of an online vlog by a young woman diagnosed with brain cancer how identity can be studied in digital contexts drawing on a range of modalities (e.g., text, image, sound, and video) and how practices of affective positioning in storytelling serve as acts of modulating proximity or distance from the illness, the viewing audiences, and the emotional self as an integral part of identity performance and the staging of authenticity.

Julie Wilkes and Susan Speer present an **ethnomethodological** and **conversation analytic** (CA) **approach** to identity research, drawing on a study on how *kinship carers* (close relatives taking over the parental role from parents who are unable to care for children) manage their (parental) identity in peer support group meeting discussions. They contrast this to how studies in this field have traditionally theorized identity, and clarify the advantages CA can offer to identity research, i.e., by microanalytically investigating how people negotiate and manage identity in the sequential unfolding of the interaction. By doing so, they demonstrate that identity needs to be understood as situated and interactionally *worked up* in social interaction rather than as an internal cognitive phenomenon that is expressed through language. While CA usually sticks strictly to situated social interaction and speaker's orientation within this interaction, the chapter argues that CA also offers insights in which *macro* social phenomena contribute to identity constructions by studying concrete language practices in situated social interaction.

Sarah Riley, Martine Robson, and Adrienne Evans take a poststructuralist approach in their **Foucauldian-informed discourse analysis**. Identity in this approach is primarily understood in terms of power relations that underlie broader societal discourses that produce specific subjects. Accordingly, the focus is less on how identity is constructed in situ but rather on what societal discourses enable this sense-making. This is in line with a more decentered view of identity, making a link between personal identity and society – both understood as fluid and dynamically changing. The authors illustrate their approach with examples from a study on how couples in long-term relationships navigated lifestyle advice after one of them received a diagnosis of coronary heart disease.

Sigrid Norris and Tui Matelau-Doherty likewise present an approach that decenters the individual, however, from a somewhat different perspective: they consider identity neither as something that is produced only as individuals, nor only through the social, nor only or even predominantly through talk, but as something that is produced through mediation in *every* action in everyday life, and people may engage in more than one action at a time, producing several identities simultaneously. In their **multimodal (inter-)action analysis (MIA),** they aim at studying the processes underlying this continuous and complex negotiating of identity in everyday lives. Drawing on a recent study on how a Māori creative artist navigates her identity in everyday life, they exemplify the individual steps of analysis.

Keith Berry's chapter on **autoethnography** takes us back to the inner perspective of self-understanding and self-interpretation through reflection on lived experience. In line with its theoretical underpinnings, the chapter is written in a style autoethnographers embrace to study identity. Identity here is views. While autoethnography conceives of identity as an inherently social and cultural process, and is itself a relational approach in that it investigates the relationship between selves and others as one moves through life, the analytical focus lies on self-interpretation and self-reflection in a very intimate way. Of all the methodological approaches presented in this handbook, auto-ethnography is probably the one that allows for most creativity and experimentation, which does not mean, however, that "anything goes," as the author shows when discussing criteria for the evaluation of autoethnography. The chapter also points to the potential therapeutic effect (for oneself and for others) and possible transformation of subjectivity/identity that may result from deep engagement with one's self-narratives. The author illustrates one way of doing autoethnography by concrete examples of a study on youth bullying.

Two chapters in this section take a more explicit cultural psychology approach to the study of identity. Tania Zittoun and Alex Gillespie, drawing on semiotic mediation as the main driving force for human psychological functioning, locate the dynamics of identity at two levels: microgenesis operating in seconds and minutes within social interaction, and ontogenesis operating at the level of days, months, and years. They illustrate how **diary studies** allow the study of identity dynamics and processes of continuity and change over time on both levels. The authors consider diaries not merely as reflecting identity dynamics, but as being part of these, as a sociocultural tool for mediating one's relationship to oneself and thus participating in, or constituting, the dynamics of identity. They illustrate their approach with concrete examples from an analysis of the diary of a young English woman during World War II.

João Salgado and Carla Cunha, in their chapter, advocate **positioning microanalysis** from dialogical self theory. Identity here is seen a dynamic process and a product of the tensional relation between multiple perspectives or positions of the self. The dialogical dynamics established by these different I-positions are a core element for understanding how identity works. Accordingly, analysis aims at laying open how these dynamics develop over time both by studying microgenetic movements of self-positions from moment to moment and over longer periods of time. The five phases of analysis are illustrated by an example from the first psychotherapy session of a woman diagnosed with major depression.

With the chapter written by Oana Negru-Subtirica and Theo Klimstra on **identity status research methods**, we return to the theme that was introduced by Kroger and Marcia in Part II. The authors here show that, also within this approach, the question of how *processes* of identity formation can be depicted has played a central role in recent times. Taking up criticisms that statuses only provide a *static* image of identity development unable to tell us much about the *dynamic* processes involved, they introduce approaches that aim to fill this gap. They themselves focus on a person-centered approach. Drawing on questionnaire data on identity processes, they show how **cluster analysis** and **latent class/profile analysis (LCA/LPA)** can be applied to depict how multiple variables are configured within persons – also capturing the *classic* (cf. Kroger & Marcia, this volume) but also more nuanced identity statuses. The chapter provides a detailed comparison of cluster analysis and LCA/LPA results based on the same data set, so that researchers who want to work with large samples and want to apply this method know what the (dis)advantages of each procedure are. The authors end the chapter with a discussion of the approach's limitations (e.g., not being able to depict the temporal sequence or order of different identity processes with cluster-analytic studies using cross-sectional designs), but also of potential ways to overcome them (e.g., adapting LCAs/LPAs for longitudinal research purposes).

Donna Youngs, David Rowlands, and David Canter also start their chapter with identity studies that are based on questionnaire data. They introduce the **narrative roles questionnaire (NRQ)**, which assesses "how well role statements describe offenders' experiences during crime commission, allowing quantitative exploration of criminal identity at the episodic level of the criminal act" (p. **414**). Moving from a more static to a more dynamic perspective, they then present the **life as a film (LAAF) procedure**, which examines identities revealed in personal narratives as elicited in interviews on the larger scale of life trajectories. LAAF allows for the analysis of inherent identity conflicts as "characteristic of criminals" (e.g., when longing for supportive relationships, but seeing material goals as dominant) from an unfolding perspective, leading to implications for how individuals can be supported in reassessing and reconstructing their personal narratives.

In the last chapter of Part III, Lucas B. Mazur examines the role of **experimentation within the social identity approach**. He critically discusses how experimental methods shape but also limit our understanding of identity within this specific tradition, inviting the reader to reflect on theoretical and methods-based biases from which no one is immune – regardless of perspective.

The chapters in this section thus cover a vast range of different methodological approaches each rooted in somewhat different theoretical conceptions of identity: some represent the recent developments of turning away from discourse (alone) as the predominant way to produce identity and toward the inclusion of affective embodied aspects of identity construction; others stress the dialogical nature of the individual. The material to be analyzed also varies greatly from mundane conversations to therapy sessions, diary entries in writing or in a digital context, questionnaire data, self-storytelling and writing, everyday actions, and societal discourses.

All these approaches have in common, however, that identity is not conceived of as anything (any longer) that is contained within an individual or that emerges from an individual alone. They all try to find ways to capture and depict the dynamic nature of identity development – acknowledging the multitude of possible influences. The studies that serve as examples to illustrate the respective methodological approaches in the various chapters also make clear how vast the field of possibilities is in which identity research is applicable and relevant. This becomes even clearer in the next section when we discuss current domains of identity research in various fields.

Part IV: Current Domains

We are writing this chapter at the end of 2020, while two of the editors are in Europe (Germany and Denmark, respectively) and one in the United States. Starting in the middle of December, a stricter lockdown was imposed both in Germany and Denmark that most likely will be extended until at least the end of January 2021. The Governor's Orders in Massachusetts also became stricter by, e.g., limiting indoor gatherings to ten individuals. Since March 2020, we have been facing a global pandemic. One of the contributors to this volume has been affected by Covid-19 herself while finishing the final version of her chapter. On the one hand, people have lost loved ones, have become seriously ill, have been faced with economic losses, and have struggled with physical distancing – not to mention social distancing. On the other hand, technical advances that probably would have taken a very long time to implement under different, more *usual* conditions, became possible – allowing for meeting and teaming up with people who seemed so far away before.

These technical advances were taken advantage of when Martin Dege and Irene Strasser initiated an online conference on *The Psychology of Global Crisis* in May 2020.[4] The authors of this handbook as well as the editors participated as keynote speakers, members of the organizing committee, and discussants. Keith Berry, for example, who introduces autoethnography in this handbook (Part III) as a possible methodological approach to identity, talked about "Communicating Crisis: The Potent Symbols of Covid-19" from an autoethnographer's perspective.[5] Danilo Silva Guimarães, who – together with Ramiro Gonzalez Rial – points out the shortcomings of Western perspectives on identity in Part I of this handbook, talked about "Amerindian Paths through Recurrent Sociocultural Crises"[6] at the conference. Alessandra Fasulo, who discusses identity in a clinical context with regard to autism in this volume, talked about the changes of lifestyle the pandemic brought about in families with children, particularly in terms of space and time,[7] and Marie-Cécile Bertau, who introduces a language-dialogical approach to identity in this handbook, focused on "Time, the Other, and the Collective Voice"[8] in her keynote. Scientists from all over the world came together to discuss these and related topics to better understand crises and be able to more effectively help individuals who are faced with them.

Why mention this here? It shows that *current* or *hot* topics change over time – sometimes unexpectedly fast. They challenge, among others, the question of identity – what identity is, was, and can(not) be (anymore). Addressing

---

[4] All talks and discussions of the conference can be watched online on the YouTube channel *The Psychology of Global Crises #PGC2020*.

[5] www.youtube.com/watch?v=OUE0QReuJbU.

[6] www.youtube.com/watch?v=gwNdRcOQ8UY.

[7] www.youtube.com/watch?v=1sZCVceBwlQ.

[8] www.youtube.com/watch?v=nWj0SeAWfWw.

these challenges quickly and jointly seems to be a necessary endeavor in sciences, nowadays facilitated by technical advances (the latter being a challenge to identity themselves). What we must not forget, though, is that even if some topics are *hotter* than others, or more pressing, there are still others that need to be discussed and that (should) shape the current landscape of identity research.[9] At the abovementioned conference, David Becker and Nimisha Patel pointed this out when talking about "War, Conflict and Human Rights: Responding to Psychosocial Issues Arising from Covid-19."[10] For individuals in war regions, for example, Covid-19 will not be the biggest threat they are facing.

In this part of this handbook, "Current Domains," we will thus turn to current topics, other than Covid-19, as exemplars that look at identity and identity research from different angles; one of them being the chapter of David Becker, who represents the field of **political psychology** and focuses on identity development in traumatic environments, stressing that "trauma is not a mental illness, but a social and political reality in many parts of the world" (p. **582**). This reality and its effects on identity development need to be understood to work with and for traumatized individuals. Fragmentation and ambiguities are key elements in his chapter, and he advocates for their recognition – in research and practice – stating in the end that if we are "willing to understand that people who have suffered extremely throughout their lives are both healthy and ill, fragmented and whole, and thus fundamentally contradictory, then possibly they can establish a relationship in which these people can flourish and develop" (p. **582**).

Along a similar line of argument, Abigail Locke and Jane Montague stress the "enacted, situated, relational and embodied nature of identities" (p. **508**) in their chapter, which represents the field of **health psychology** in this handbook. After a brief overview of the field and its historical development, the authors turn to two identities specifically: maternal identities and potentially challenged identities when cisgendered women are faced with the diagnosis of and treatment for breast cancer – examples Locke and Montague use to underscore the complex nature of identity.

Lars-Christer Hydén, whose chapter was assigned to the field of **geronto-psychology**, adds to the complexity by demonstrating that our understanding of identity is easily challenged when we focus on individuals with dementia. He shows that even if these individuals might increasingly be challenged as conversationalists and storytellers, they are still active meaning-makers, so

---

[9] Just a side note to stress this point: One of the editors is working at the Sigmund Freud University in Berlin. The university is located in the old Tempelhof airport, and members of the university can look into the hangars that are no longer used for air traffic. In 2016, the hangars became one of the biggest refugee camps in Berlin; currently, they are being transformed into a vaccination center. Not only in the media or in personal discussions, but also in the actual shaping of the environment, certain topics are more prominent than others.

[10] www.youtube.com/watch?v=Uy16nY1tTww.

that, indeed, we have to look beyond what people are able to *tell* us about themselves when we want to understand identity in the making (e.g., stressing *embodied* identities as Locke and Montague, this volume, do as well).

Alessandra Fasulo, representing the field of **interactional studies and cultural psychology**, points out another blind spot in identity theory and research. While Hydén challenges the assumption that people lose their identities when they do not have access to, for example, autobiographical memories anymore, Fasulo points out that identity, understood as something that is established in the exchange with others, might not be straightforward to achieve for someone who does not experience satisfactory control of ordinary social practices. She critically discusses the topic of autistic identities from three different research strands: autism as collective identity or 'groupness,' processes of autism identifications, and autistic identity as self-understanding. She comes to the conclusion that identity studies will largely benefit from drawing on the "work of autistic scholars and those with a critical disability approach [to] promote innovative research paradigms that, starting from what autistic people have to say about their own condition, can build an understanding of autism in its own sake, and also develop instruments for lifelong support" (p. **481**).

All of these authors show quite vividly that micro (e.g., individual role-taking or positioning) and macro levels (e.g., social representations of a *good mother* or an *autistic person*) have to be jointly taken into account when we really want to understand identity development, since it is embodied, enacted, and constructed in relation to the specific requirements of a certain sociocultural, institutional/organizational, historical, and political context.

The institutional/organizational context in particular is the focus of Stefan Sveningsson, Susann Gjerde, and Mats Alvesson's chapter, which represents the field of **organizational psychology** in this handbook. The authors, on the one hand, stress the benefit of identity studies for a better understanding of contemporary organizational life – especially when identity is considered to be not something static but a phenomenon in flux, which they characterize by referring to *identity work*. On the other hand, the authors also take a critical stance toward the concept of identity by advocating for a restriction of the concept's scope to be able to respond to the challenges of the field in a more differentiated way, and to avoid "a (re)production of unwanted narcissism in our already narcissistic time of age" (p. **586**).

While Sveningsson et al. thus criticize the inflationary use of the construct of identity, pointing out that it might not even be relevant when looking at certain jobs and/or situations (*exit* strategies in some areas of interest), Avi Kaplan, Hanoch Flum, Ishwar Bridgelal, and Joanna K. Garner describe the rather recent *entry* of the term into a specific field of research: **educational psychology**. Nevertheless, they also come to the conclusion that the term is used in diverse ways with various implications for how to approach it methodologically, leading to their differentiation of perspectives that foreground (1) identity content, (2) identity structure and formation processes, or (3) the role of culture in identity and its formation. Within the framework of this differentiation, a link to the chapters of the second and third parts of this handbook is established, e.g. by referring to identity status theories (cf. Kroger & Marcia as well as Negru-Subtirica & Klimstra, this volume).

Kaplan et al. arrive at the conclusion that integrative perspectives are needed to – at least partially – overcome the limitations of the different perspectives. For this purpose they introduce the dynamic systems model of role identity, in which they define role identity as the unit of analysis (see also Locke & Montague, this volume). After pointing to current *hot topics* of the field that need to be addressed from this – and other – integrative perspectives, they stress the need for *identity education* to better support students in their repeated identity exploration in times of "increased volatility, uncertainty, complexity, and ambiguity" (p. **552**). Although they state that the impact "of these trends on structures and practices in public education has been relatively minor," they foreshadow new developments in light of the current pandemic, which, in a matter of weeks, "dramatically reshaped all aspects of life, including education" (p. **552**). The latter statement shows that Covid-19, with which we started this paragraph, or crises that impact whole societies or even the world are not the hot topics per se, but they potentially influence *all* areas of identity research which we looked at so far. Systems are interconnected and need to be analyzed in concert when we address identity issues, as Locke and Montague and others explicitly stress in their chapters.

The need to acknowledge the complexity of human phenomena in identity theory and research will therefore be the topic that we conclude our overview of this part with: Leoandra Onnie Rogers and Moin Syed discuss the multiple levels of identity and **intersectionality**; the chapter was *not* assigned to a specific domain, since it addresses an issue relevant across (sub-)disciplines. The authors point out that intersectional research is engaged in its own identity struggles, when the question arises what counts as such, but they then turn to an example of how it *can* be used to better understand systemic oppression and inequality, and, with that, identity as a psychosocial process that unfolds within specific contexts, as mentioned above.

In Part V, the conclusion of this handbook, we pose the general question: **Where is identity?** The question is addressed from different angles: Where is identity *located*? Where (and when) is it (made) *relevant*? Where is identity when looking *beyond Western theories*? And finally: Where lies the *future* of identity research? The possible answers to these questions are diverse in nature and show how slippery, blurred, and confusing the term can be. Identity thus could be, as Valsiner (2019) puts it,

> a perfect example of a *non-existing object* . . . – an important invention of our minds that subsists in our ideational domains, giving us all kinds of psychological troubles. We search for it, we try to build it, we contrast it with that of the others, we worry about "losing" it – identity is in the middle of

most of our self-reflexivity and – not surprisingly – occupies a central place in the discussions in ... psychology.   (p. 436)

We contend that this holds for other disciplines in the same way. The conclusion of the article from which the above quote is taken is that identity may be considered to have a similar motivating effect as "the efforts to reach the horizon in our moving outwards in space." In the analogy, this would make identity the *inner* horizon "toward which we strive but which cannot be reached as it 'moves away' from us while we try to reach it" (p. 437). We, the editors, also think that the term has *motivational* function (e.g., inspiring researchers to study phenomena), but instead of looking at it at the horizon, we put it under the magnifying glass: we will demonstrate that it can be a useful umbrella term – under whose protection light can be shed on the confusion of various related constructs (Bamberg & Dege, this volume). In addition, the reader will find different organizing principles throughout the book that aim to bring order to the various definitions and theoretical approaches to identity – with the challenge to reflect on what these definitions accomplish for those who establish(ed) them. While definitions usually include specific aspects but exclude many more, all authors in this handbook nevertheless seem to agree on the need for definitions (as well as methodological approaches) that are able to capture the dynamic and complex nature of this *multifaceted* object (see Part V) – which in light of a changing society will remain a challenging endeavor, but one that is definitely worth tackling.

Through the storm, we reach the shore ...[11]
from the song "With or without you" (U2, 1987)

References

American Psychological Association. (2019). *Publication Manual of the American Psychological Association, 7th Ed.* Washington, DC: American Psychological Association.

Arnett, J. J. (2000). Emerging adulthood: A theory of development from the late teens through the twenties. *American Psychologist, 55*(5), 469–480.

Arnett, J. J. (2016). Life stage concepts across history and cultures. Proposal for a new field on Indigenous life stages. *Human Development, 59*, 290–316.

Bamberg, M. (2011). Who am I? Narration and its contribution to self and identity. *Theory & Psychology, 21*(1), 3–24.

[11] Probably the most famous U2 song, "With or without you" (see the title of this chapter) originated from a demo recorded in 1985 that the band worked on continuously before it was released on their album *The Joshua Tree*. What at first appears to be a love song had, on closer inspection, various sources of inspiration; one of them was Bono's (lead vocalist as well as primary lyricist) sometimes seemingly impossible effort to reconcile his *identities* as musician and married man.

Bamberg, M. (2021a). Positioning the subject. In S. Bosančić, F. Brodersen, L. Pfahl, L. Schürmann, T. Spies, & B. Traue (Eds.), *Following the Subject. Grundlagen und Zugänge empirischer Subjektivierungsforschung* [Following the subject. Foundations and approaches of empirical research on subjectivation] (pp. 114–132). Wiesbaden: Springer.

Bamberg, M. (2021b). Narrative in qualitative psychology. In P. Camic (Ed.), *Qualitative Research in Psychology. Second Edition: Expanding Perspectives in Methodology and Design.* Washington, DC: American Psychological Association.

Blackman, L., Cromby, J., Hook, D., Papadopoulos, D., & Walkerdine, V. (2008). Creating subjectivities. *Subjectivity*, *22*(1), 1–27. doi:10.1057/sub.2008.8.

Brubaker, R. & Cooper, F. (2000). Beyond "identity." *Theory and Society*, *29*(1), 1–47.

Demuth, C. (2015a). New directions in qualitative research in psychology. *Integrative Psychological & Behavioral Science*, *49*(2), 125–133.

Demuth, C. (2015b). Erratum to: New directions in qualitative research in psychology. *Integrative Psychological & Behavioral Science*, *49*(2), 134.

Demuth, C. (2015c). "Slow food" post-qualitative research in psychology: Old craft skills in new disguise? *Integrative Psychological & Behavioral Science*, *49*(2), 207–215.

Demuth, C. & Keller, H. (2011). Culture, learning, and adult development. In C. Hoare (Ed.), *The Oxford Handbook of Reciprocal Adult Development and* Learning, *2nd Ed.* (pp. 425–443). Oxford: Oxford University Press.

Demuth, C. & Schjødt Terkildsen, T. (2015). The future of qualitative research in psychology – A discussion with Svend Brinkmann, Günter Mey, Luca Tateo, and Anete Strand. *Integrative Psychological & Behavioral Science*, *49*(2), 135–161.

Fairclough, N. (2013). *Critical Discourse Analysis. The Critical Study of Language*, *2nd Ed.* Abingdon: Routledge.

Hall, S. (1996). Introduction: Who needs "identity?" In S. Hall & P. du Gay (Eds.), *Questions of Cultural Identity* (pp. 1–17). Thousand Oaks, CA: Sage.

Hall, S. & du Gay, P. (Eds.). (1996). *Questions of Cultural Identity.* Thousand Oaks, CA: Sage.

Henriques, J., Hollway, W., Urwin, C., Venn, C., & Walkerdine, V. (1984). *Changing the Subject: Psychology, Social Regulation and Subjectivity.* London: Methuen.

Kagitçibasi, Ç. (2005). Autonomy and relatedness in cultural context: Implications for self and family. *Journal of Cross-Cultural Psychology*, *36*, 403–422.

Levitt, H., Bamberg, M., Cresswell, J. W., Frost, D. M., Josselson, R., & Suarez-Orozco, C. (2018). Journal article reporting standards for qualitative primary, qualitative meta-analytic, and mixed methods research in psychology: The APA Publications and Communications Board task force report. *American Psychologist*, *73*, 26–46.

Lutz, K. (1988). *Unnatural Emotions: Everyday Sentiments on a Micronesian Atoll and Their Challenge to Western Theory.* Chicago, IL: University of Chicago Press.

Markus, H. R. & Kitayama, S. (2010). Cultures and selves: A cycle of mutual constitution. *Perspectives of Psychological Science*, *5*, 420–430.

Nochi, M. (2016, July). *The "snap-shot" approach to identity research: Investigating self-narratives of a person with a severe language problem.* Paper presented at the 31st International Congress of Psychology, Yokohama, Japan.

Schwartz, T., White, G. M., & Lutz, C. A. (Eds.). (1992). *New Directions in Psychological Anthropology.* Cambridge: Cambridge University Press.

U2 (1987). With or without you. *The Joshua Tree* [LP]. London: Island Records.

Valsiner, J. (2019). *Culture & Psychology*: 25 constructive years. *Culture & Psychology, 25*(4), 429–469.

Venn, C. (2002). Narrative identity, subject formation, and the transfiguration of subjects. In W. Patterson (Ed.), *Strategic Narrative: New Perspectives on the Power of Personal and Cultural Stories.* Lanham, MD: Lexington Books.

Watzlawik, M. (2016, July). *The concept of "identity capital" – A contradiction to identity "in flux"?* Paper presented at the 31st International Congress of Psychology, Yokohama, Japan.

Watzlawik, M. & Born, A. (2007). *Capturing Identity: Quantitative and Qualitative Methods.* Lanham, MD: University Press of America.

Wetherell, M. (1998). Positioning and interpretative repertoires: Conversation analysis and post-structuralism in dialogue. *Discourse & Society, 9*, 387–413.

Wetherell, M. (2001). Themes in discourse research: The case of Diana. In M. Wetherell, S. Taylor & S. J. Yates (Eds.), *Discourse Theory and Practice – A Reader* (pp. 14–28). London: Sage.

Wetherell, M. (Ed.). (2009). *Theorizing Identities and Social Action.* Basingstoke: Palgrave Macmillan.

Wetherell, M. & Mohanty, C. T. (Eds.). (2010). *The Sage Handbook of Identities.* London: Sage.

PART I

The Origin and Development of the Concept of Identity

2 Decentering Histories of Identity

Michael Bamberg and Martin Dege

The individual, as the basic social unit from which other social organizations and social relations form, is another system of ideas which needs to be understood as part of the West's cultural archive. Western philosophies and religions place the individual as the basic building block of society.

(Linda Tuhiwai Smith, 1999, p. 49)

What if we were to see modernity differently – as a dispersed experience based on exchange rather than transmission, happening everywhere simultaneously, even if to different degrees and with different effects?

(Geoffrey Batchen, 2014, p. 7)

The following three assumptions frame this chapter.* First, we fully affirm Linda Tuhiwai Smith's assertion from the above epigraph that identity is central to "the West's cultural archive." Here, identity is not a single entity or concept. Rather, it overlaps and intersects with related concepts such as self, the individual, subjectivity, and consciousness – to name a few of the many labels used when speaking about issues of identity. They in concert coalesce in a signification of a sense of who *we* are – *we* as individuals and as members of collectives; with a sense of agency and belonging; and an idea of temporal stability and change. Second, we hold that moving into an unfolding of how people historically have talked about identity, and over time have come to configure a sense of who they are, will help us better understand how people talk about and make sense of themselves in contemporary discourse. In tandem, and third, we argue that a contemporaneous and historical understanding will both serve the larger and strategic purpose of this chapter to *decenter* what we call modern European discourses around identity and related denominations – the way they emerged as sense-making strategies over the last five centuries in metropolitan Europe, resulting in what might be called a *new* European sense of self. In summary, the goal is to examine

* We would like to express our gratitude to Carolin Demuth, Luke Moissinac, Meike Watzlawik, and Nancy Budwig for their comments on previous versions of this chapter. For a section that intended to compare the English terms *identity, self, subject/subjectivity, individual/individuality/individualism*, and *awareness/consciousness/conscience* with their counterparts in Japanese and Māori we had enlisted consultation from Masahiro Nochi and Yas Igashari for contemporary Japanese, and Pita King from Massey University for Māori. We appreciate their assistance and hope to work with them on this topic in a separate publication.

historiographies of modern European identity discourses for implied chronologies that feed a Eurocentric superiority vis-à-vis – and even at the expense of – others. To accomplish this goal, we will continuously try to scrutinize whose discourses made it into the history books of a modern Europe, and whose discourses were left on the margins. We further seek to follow Geoffrey Batchen's advice (above) in trying to show the emergence of European identity discourses as a product of new contact and exchange between people across boundaries – between people in emerging cities, across regions, nation-states, and different languages in Europe – and simultaneously globally between and across already existing cultures and societies.

We claim that the shape of a contemporary European understanding of identity is constituted through interactions across differences within an emergent Europe. Simultaneously, what may have originated in metropolitan Europe, and what is viewed as having slowly diffused from there outward into the periphery, is fundamentally shaped by what it diffused into. As such, the making of modern identity not only needs to be viewed as framed through experiences of regionally and transnationally coming up against Otherness, but also by and through global encounters *with* Otherness in newly *discovered* continents (cf. Alpert, 2019). Taking this perspective, colonialism and its settler-colonial varieties are as essential and foundational for emerging identity discourses in Europe as the local and particular conditions in European metropolises. We expect that considerations like these will motivate alternative ways of talking and thinking about identity and identity research. It is our hope to inspire students and scholars of identity to be able to more critically and confidently sort through the wide range of definitions of identity, self, and their corresponding terms in psychology, and examine this complex body of work by considering alternative strategies.

In this chapter, we interrogate identity from three angles. We start with an analysis of how an understanding of identity as a complex meaning system circulates in contemporary (English) language use. Next, we turn to how this meaning complex evolved within the history of what is widely understood as European modernity. In a third step, we address how this kind of European understanding made it into a particular understanding of the discipline of psychology in the United States and, from there, looped back into what we started with, i.e., our current contemporary (English) language use. In the hope of having sufficiently decentered dominant Eurocentric identity discourses and opened them to closer analytic scrutiny, we end our chapter with the question for alternatives.

To start with, and seemingly paradoxically, to historically scrutinize identity discourses in order to better understand contemporary discourses, we need to have an understanding of what we are scrutinizing, irrespective of how preliminary this understanding is. Here, rather than giving a clear-cut and expert definition of identity, we begin by charting a course for approaching identity in the complex and multifaceted interpretations of how it surfaces in contemporary language use. In other words, we start by taking identity discourses out of the realms of philosophy, psychology, and neighboring academic disciplines and attempt to follow how the term *identity* is implemented in contemporary English by everyday people. This exercise, at this point rough and provisional, is meant to provide a general sense of the complexities and tentativeness involved when the term *identity* surfaces. In addition, it conceivably sensitizes hidden meanings and associations implied in ways it is used in daily practices rather than by academic experts.

In this first section then, we will consider the lexical item *identity* and neighboring and overlapping (and potentially competing) terms, such as *self*, *subject/subjectivity*, *individuality/authenticity*, and *consciousness/conscience*. To outline upfront what identity discourses in contemporary English language use have in common will help us crystallize a meaning complex that suggests that identity relies on a *sense of interiority* that can be accessed by way of *reflection*, serving as a compass for direction in three realms: (i) to navigate a sense of temporal stability and change, (ii) to integrate a sense of who we are and where we belong in relation to others, but also being able to differentiate from them, and (iii) to navigate a sense of agency – as on the one hand being subjected to seemingly uncontrollable forces, but on the other impacting on the world through our human actions and activities.

After this preliminary analysis of everyday discourse, we turn to an assessment of the historicity of this agglomerate. Here, we will focus on the specifics of European history and its historiographies, i.e., how specific historical predispositions and accidents have arguably resulted in what has been termed the New Age of modernity. This section builds on the assumption that underneath any historical changes leading to what has been termed *modernity* were (and still are) general possibilities for societal development. With modern discourses on identity at its center, the European emergence of modernity came about in parallel and partly intersecting with other discourses outside of Europe, though with these European discourses as some of the first. As such, this impacted contemporaneous and subsequent societal developments elsewhere, and ultimately globally. This attempt to write identity history requires evaluation and critique. More specifically, we will rely on the notion of contemporaneous identity discourses from our first section and examine the discursive conditions of its genesis across the last four or five centuries within the emerging European nation-states and the emergence of new forms of communication across them. Here, we will build on and add to a large body of historiographies that have attempted to establish genealogies of European modernity by investigating the products of literate elites, typically philosophers and fiction writers. To do this effectively, we would have preferred a historical determination of how discourses around the term identity had evolved in the talk of commoners, i.e., across the social boundaries of slaves, plebeians, peasants, aristocrats, bourgeois citizens, civilians, and members of the working class, as well as across gender and age lines – and this historically across the centuries. Knowing well that such testimonies are sparse, we will nevertheless attempt to outline the historical emergence of a European, modern, common discourse around identity and bring in more than philosophical testimonies, scrutinizing the broader material with regard to its representation of, and relevance for, a common awareness across socially diverse strata and class differences.[1]

In the third section, we will review how the newly emerging discipline of psychology adopted and transformed identity discourses as they were originally circulating around the middle of the nineteenth century in Europe. We will follow two strands of theorizing identity in psychology (experimental and psychoanalytical), and how they migrated from Europe to North America, with our focus on the second. Here, we attempt to document how the emergence of a private and self-controlled individuality (Elias, 1939) paved the way for a new (psycho)-analytic identity discourse that looped back from the emerging discipline of psychology into the unfolding of what is currently running under the header of a therapeutic culture/ethos (Illouz, 2008, 2012), proliferating in its clone of what is commonly referred to as the self-help industry.

In our final section, we will ask the key question of whether the way we lay out the historical changes in identity discourses can be imagined otherwise. More specifically, we broach the question of whether at any point in their European trajectories – or in partnership with other historically arising (Indigenous) identity discourses[2] – it may have been possible to arrive at different discourses that would have allowed alternative ways of defining and framing identity, potentially also resulting in alternative ways of investigating identity methodically. Although it is suggestive and relies more on asking questions than conclusive statements, we hope that this section provides an overarching orientation that readers can use as coordinates for approaching identity and identity research when reading handbook chapters – but also as a necessary springboard to pursuing their own line of identity research.

---

[1] Attempts along these lines have been made in the past – and from at least two kinds of perspectives: one coming from what Linda Tuhiwai Smith called "Western critiques of Western research ... that enabled systems of self-critique" (1999, p. 164), of which Pelz (2016) presents an excellent starting point. The other presents itself in a more general project of *decolonizing methodologies* – as suggested by the title of Smith's book (1999), to which we owe a good deal of our inspiration.

[2] Indigenous/Indigeneity, apart from its definitions under domestic and international laws, to us has three different connotations relevant for identity. In this chapter we will try to keep them separate and point to their differences in meaning when using these terms: (i) Indigeneity as a particular (historical and) local discourse; (ii) Indigeneity as local discourse that has its own Indigenous history, i.e., language and cultural tradition of myths, rituals, beliefs, and relational practices; (iii) Indigeneity as discourses that are marked by power differentials, and as such have the tendency to deprive people of their traditions and subject them to inhumane, unequal, and exclusionary treatment. We capitalize the terms Indigenous and Indigeneity throughout this chapter to declare our recognition and general alignment with the third definition.

From the very start, we need to point out two limitations we are facing. The first is that by fixating our ordinary language analysis on English, followed by a historical genealogy of identity within the territorial space of Europe, i.e., a Eurochronology, one automatically runs the risk of an endorsement of an ethnocentric European exceptionalism. This suggests that we must continuously reflect on and relativize any judgment or generalization that may point in this direction. The second limitation comprises the dilemma that our approach to historical change is prone to transporting certain ideologies into how we approach identity, interiority, and reflection and what we make of them. Consequently, before beginning our discussion, we need to emphasize the relevance of recognizing and reflecting on what we, as authors, bring to the analysis in light of our own historical and social situatedness. We acknowledge and reflect on our background as white, male, middle-class Germans. Each of these categories brings a certain baggage that conveys our obligation to consider the historical situatedness that impacts the conceptions put forward here. In particular, having been raised against the backdrop of racist histories that brought about the Holocaust and two World Wars, we acknowledge that our own backgrounds and historical situatedness impact our conceptions. We will thus simultaneously try to display our conceptual provisions of identity discourses that are grounded in contemporary (English) language use and their historiographies and open them up to how they could be otherwise. With this in mind, we do not attempt to sweep our positionality into a footnote but make it central to the attempt to decenter the project of European identity discourse development and open up possibilities for alternative conceptualizations of identity – alternatives that may help clear the ground for how to investigate identity in different forms and methodologies.

2.1 Contemporary Identity Discourses

Historiographies of the body (Ruberg, 2019), sexuality (Foucault, 1978). or emotions (Plamper, 2015; Rosenwein & Cristiani, 2018), as well as work that presents histories of self and identity (Barresi & Martin, 2011; Rose, 1989; Taylor, 1989), have become flourishing fields. And as exemplified by the entries in this handbook, the concept of identity is found across disciplines and fields. However, identity can also be considered a new concept. As James Fearon's (1999) and Philip Gleason's (1983) analyses of the everyday use of the term identity in contemporary (American) English usage show, identity was only recently introduced into Western discussions, and here first as part of academic terminology – from where it seemed to have quickly spread into popular contemporary discourses. Fearon (1999) stated that this recent development goes back to Erik Erikson's theoretical claim that each person forms their own identity (Erikson, 1968). Thus, the question arises of how this relatively new, and culturally specific, concept can be utilized as a guide for transcultural and transhistorical inquiry into how people, organizations, or institutions come into being and maintain (or change) a sense of who they are, i.e., their identities.

The way psychologists, sociologists, political theorists, and others have utilized this concept to theorize (and empirically investigate) individuals and collectives across time and societies constitutes a very diverse, if not confusing, spectrum. Norbert Elias's (1993) and Erik Erikson's (1958) respective works on Wolfgang Amadeus Mozart and Martin Luther may serve as captivating examples for transhistorical and transcultural analyses of two individuals' personal identities. Investigations into peasants' identities during the "Great Peasants' War" (1524/5) (Blickle, 2006; Habermas, 1976) and Polish peasants around the turn of the twentieth century (Thomas & Znaniecki, 2018–2020) offer fascinating transcultural approaches to the identities of collectives. Simultaneously, a closer look at these investigations shows that the theoretical assumptions and analytic procedures guiding this kind of work differ considerably. In this handbook entry, we build on Fearon's (1999) original investigation of the common, everyday language use (cf. Austin, 1962; Searle, 1971; Wittgenstein, 1994) in which the term *identity* is embedded and put to use. Starting from more common usage, rather than pondering how identity has been configured in theoretical (and empirical) work by experts, may offer ways to disentangle what is notable about *identity* among competing terms such as *self*, *subjectivity*, and *individuality*. In the sections to come, we start with a brief outline of how identity is made use of in the English language, followed by other terms: (i) *self* (sense of self), (ii) *subjectivity*, (iii) *individuality* (and its modification of an *authentic individuality*), and (iv) *awareness* (alongside *consciousness* and *conscience*). The purpose of comparing these terms is to capture some differences in usage but simultaneously carve out how they work together by assuming specific types of *interiority* and *reflexivity*, from where more particular terms find their application in everyday English. We intend to capture the most common terms. However, this analysis could easily be extended to include *character, personality, independence, freedom*, and *autonomy*, to name a few – which all similarly intersect with identity, assuming a built-in and seemingly reflective organization of interiority. Confining our discussion to this limited set of terms and how it intersects with identity, we provide a foundation for the section to follow, consisting of how identity with a presumed internal nucleus could emerge historically and become a new subject for factual and empirical inquiry.

Approaching ordinary language terms as representatives of ideas or certain kinds of consciousness is not unproblematic. *Words* (including the minutiae of their phonological pronunciation), *terms, concepts, metaphors, ideas, narratives, discourses, backgrounds*, and even *ideologies* have been isolated and scrutinized as in one way or another reflecting a certain collective stance or affiliation of speakers. And arguments have been made for what actually is (and what is not) being analyzed when decontextualizing parts of speech and using them to make assumptions about collective consciousnesses.[3] In the following, although we cannot make these discourses explicit in the way they deserve, we appropriate the notion of discourses as units of analysis from where a certain kind of collective understanding can tentatively be assumed as given. As such, we aim to illuminate certain aspects of the lexical, pragmatic, and discursive usages of *identity* (and its neighboring terms) in everyday common use of American English.

2.1.1 Identity

Rooted in the Latin attribute *idem* (same), later nominalized as *identitas* (sameness), identity came to designate the particular temporal quality of constancy across time – denoting repeated recognitions of a person or entity to form the characteristics by which they become recognizable. In other words, aspects of temporal stability are taken to create a foundation for a singular entity's recognizability, thereby constituting its identifiable features. This, in turn, makes it possible to differentiate it from (vis-à-vis) other entities. This essential kind of temporal semantic foundation is what makes two (or more) different objects identical, such as identical twins or two identical copies of a document. Fearon (1999, p. 36) goes on to distill two further denominators out of the everyday ways identity is put to use in contemporary US English: (i) as something "that a person takes pride in, or views as, unchangeable but socially consequential," and (ii) thereby providing particular social categories. He argues that these categories are "defined by membership rules and allegedly characteristic attributes or expected behaviors" (ibid.). Thus, to judge from a first and preliminary examination of the etymological roots and the common, everyday use of the term, *identity* connotes (personal) characteristics that are embraced as stemming from a sense of temporal continuity (i.e., a particular contour of temporal change), and that those characteristics distinguish this person or entity from (vis-à-vis) other entities in terms of generalizable membership categories. We will return to these two characterizations of identity (change and distinguishability) after considering other related terms.

2.1.2 Self

Self, in English, is used to place emphasis on the person referred to – as in "I my*self* am responsible," emphasizing the subject *I*. In addition, if used as a reflexive pronominal form to mark the syntactic object, English splits the agentive subject (e.g., *I* or *we* as subject), and marks the receiving or

---

[3] Reflecting on our own engagement in these debates (cf. Bamberg, 1997; Bamberg & Lindenberger, 1984; Bamberg & Wipff, 2020; Wierzbicka, 1997), we acknowledge that these issues basically remain unresolved.

undergoing object by a case (*me*), to which -*self* (*myself*) needs to be added – as in "I hurt myself" or plural, "they hurt themselves." English does not allow dropping the post-fix "*I hurt me*" or "*they hurt them.*" Thus, -*self*, initially, is not nominalized. Rather, self designates the recipient/target of an action that originated from the same entity/person. *Self*, as a nominalized entity, captures this reflective concession and yields it to the subject who reflects on *their self*. To clarify: the self, to *be* a self, requires an agentive *I* that looks at and reflects on itself, as if looking through a looking glass (cf. Carroll, 1871; Cooley, 1902) and taking this perspective for the purpose *of making sense* of oneself – or, to gain *a sense of self*. It is this self-reflective aspect that makes it possible (in English) to form compounds such as self-awareness, self-control, and the like.[4] Turning oneself into the object of reflection, i.e., subjecting self to introspection (*subjectifying self*), opens the person to interrogation, critique, and judgment – potentially even in ways that enable suspending judgment (cf. Butler, 2003, 2005). Nominalizing the self – in conjunction with turning the self into its object – implicates the person as conceivably *having* (owning) a self, so that it can actually be inspected and interrogated as part of a person's interiority. This split of the self into a subject and a simultaneous object position provides English-speakers with the option of detaching the self as agent from (vis-à-vis) the self as object/undergoer, as, for instance, in denials of responsibility. *Allowing oneself* to engage in questionable activities (cf. John Edwards, 2008; Edison Chen, 2010 – both quoted and analyzed in Bamberg 2010 and 2020, respectively), or *convincing oneself* that "normal rules don't apply" (to quote Tiger Woods from his press conference, February 09, 2010) are discursive devices – typically utilized in apology accounts – that illustrate this kind of split of the same person into an agentive *allower* and a subjected *allowee*. In short, it seems that the original emphasis of a person's agency, when combined with a self-reflective underpinning, has filtered into William James's (1890/2007) *I*–*me* distinction and G. H. Mead's (Miller, 1982) subsequent elaboration of a *me* as the object of an *I*, and a presumed *me*/*self* as the socialized object that is acquired through language in interaction. Below, we will revisit how this distinction is further split when discussing Sigmund Freud's use of ego, id, and superego.

2.1.3 Subjectivity

There are two ways in which the terms subject and subjectivity are put to use in English: the first appears as a concept of the person, who (i) is agentive in

---

[4] Last updated on February 12, 2020, Wiktionary (2020) (Category: English words prefixed with *self-*) lists 387 English words that are prefixed with *self-*, including twenty that figure heavily in psychology texts: self-knowledge, self-esteem, self-concept, self-perception, self-schema, self-awareness, self-consciousness, self-appraisal, self-evaluation, self-assessment, self-categorization, self-image, self-control, self-realization, self-worth, self-love, self-respect, self-defense, self-verification, self-preservation.

the world (e.g., the *subject-as-agent* = with a person-to-world direction of fit as in *Leslie climbed the mountain*) and (ii) is being subjected to forces seemingly out of control of the self (*subjected-as-undergoer/experiencer* = with a world-to-person direction of fit as in *Leslie was attacked*).[5] Both directions of fit bring to the fore a focus on *agency* but disregard the dimension of temporal continuity and recognizability (cf. *identity*) as well as the reflective focus of an I → self or self → other differentiation (cf. self/sense of self). A second and partly overlapping meaning of the terms subject and subjectivity unfolds in their semantic contrast to object and objectivity. As such, subjectivity calls up a personal, individualized, and experiential way of giving meaning to experience, in contrast to depersonalized, objective, *true* ways of sense-making. Within this subjectivity–objectivity contrast, subjectivity and *the subject* configure aspects that not only differentiate the person from others but heighten their potential uniqueness – the utmost differentiation within the self–other dimension, which, as we will argue below, is even more heightened when we turn to individuality and authenticity.

The two connotations of subjectivity, (i) providing the subject with agency and (ii) marking experiential uniqueness, do not square with each other and are potentially confusing. For our purpose here, and to clear some ground for the historicity of identity, it may suffice to be cognizant that the two rather different connotations of subject/subjectivity both heavily rely on the concept of interiority, i.e., recognizing one's capacity for agency and uniqueness implies having choices that go along with appropriations of freedom, rights, ownership, duties, and liabilities (cf. Bamberg, 2021; Harré, 2015). More interestingly, no other English term of the identity-self-subjectivity spectrum orients as much and as clearly with a focus on agency as bidirectional, i.e., from person to world *and* from world to person. As explained in more detail elsewhere (Bamberg, 2021), this bidirectionality lends itself to following up empirically by the use of positioning theory and positioning analysis (see also the chapters by Bertau; Calder-Dawe & Martinussen; Giaxoglou & Georgakopoulou; Locke & Montague; Riley, Robson, & Evans; Salgado & Cunha; Wilkes & Speer, all this volume).

2.1.4 Individuality and Authenticity

The term *individual* refers to a single member that stands out as separate from other members of the same species or category. When mapped onto a singular person or entity, its derivative *individuality* calls up aspects of the reflective self, and an experiential subjectivity touched on in the previous sections. It also presupposes a sense of a certain temporal continuity and, according to

---

[5] The two opposing kinds of *directions of fit* capture particularly well the person at the two opposing ends of a direction of action: the person as originator of an action (as subject) versus the person as target (object) of others' (including nature's) actions.

Fearon (1999), even pride, that emerged in our discussion of the defining characteristics of identity. Individuality, then, denotes a self-reflective *I* who intends to grasp reality, makes decisions, and acts accordingly; an individual who emphatically and determinedly decides to stand out as different – typically vis-à-vis the norms of collective others.[6] To act and to be authentic implies having *original* authorship over one's actions and requires an assessment of, and alignment with, one's presumed inner feelings and attitudes. This is typically pitted against that which is considered to confine externally and to impose on the self in the form of (social) conventions and protocol. To *be* individual and *act* authentically, thus seems to necessitate reliance on a most inner core, often considered to be the *true* self, that serves as a guidepost for acting within a certain continuity and recognizability of both standing out and fitting in with regard to intimate and less intimate social relations. Individuality and authenticity as relatives of identity, self, and subject/subjectivity sharpen two essential ingredients of the mix we intimated earlier, namely an unabatedly positive sense of the person's interiority as a morally worthy guide, and the self as an isolated but potentially thoroughly agentive subject – foreshadowing a concept of a conscience as its interior compass.

2.1.5 Aware(ness), Conscious(ness), Conscientious, Conscience

In common English, *being aware* typically means being aware of something; this presupposes being *awake*, i.e., not asleep or unconscious. Furthermore, it requires an agency (typically in the form of a self or a mind) that directs and orchestrates the senses toward a particular object or locus of attention. Although *conscious* (adjective), *conscientious* (adjective), and *conscience* (noun) are derivatives of the same Greek verb *to know*, they differ in what they connote: While *being aware* suggests at the very least some minimal form of reflection, *consciousness* connotes a higher state of awareness – one that regulates, controls, and even, to a degree, integrates the direction of senses. *Conscientious* and *conscience* signify an even higher degree of self-reflection – one that inserts a moral orientation and can differentiate right from wrong. As such, a person's conscience can gain its own agency and function as an inner voice – one that, when consulted, can tell the person *the right thing* to do. Interestingly, this can range from a seemingly shallow level of self-reflective awareness to a deep and value-laden moral consciousness (represented in a person's conscience) that is able to contrast one's own individualistic actions based on one's egotistical urges and desires vis-à-vis a sense of social responsibility, and potentially even altruism. Grounded in *knowledge*, the guidepost in the form of individuals' conscience is ultimately rational, i.e., it is ultimately open to reasoning discourse about what is right and what is wrong; and as

---

[6] We purposely neglect that individuality, the characteristic of *standing out*, can of course also be assigned by others – without having it claimed for themselves by *the individual*.

such, this kind of moral reasoning contributes in an important way to a sort of *moral compass* that is central to how identity is configured in common English.

2.1.6 Returning to Identity

To clarify, working through the ways identity and the intersecting discourses about self, subjectivity, individuality/authenticity, and consciousness compare and contrast in contemporary English usage, where and how they are situated and also overlap, but also accentuating slightly different shades of meaning, was not intended to result in clear-cut definitions. Instead, in working through terms that relate to and are often used as synonyms or proxies for identity, we aimed to indicate that we are entering a complex and nuanced territory. This, nevertheless, can provide guidelines that allow a closer look, in the next section, at how this rather complex conception of identity discourses came into being over time. To serve this purpose, we would like to distill five principles that have crystallized in our discussion thus far:

(1) Identity as the site of the management of temporal change (stability, continuity, and also discontinuity) in order to provide recognizable characteristics that are maintainable (and changeable) across time.
(2) Identity as the site where these characteristics are managed to demarcate differences (and sameness) between self and others – their belonging and separateness.
(3) Identity as the site where the self seems to be able to agentively manage these characteristics (with a person-to-world direction of fit), in spite of being subjected to forces that appear to be out of direct control (a world-to-person direction of fit).
(4) Identity as the site for a self-reflective rationality, i.e., where it is possible to (critically) interrogate and manage (1)–(3) in a coordinated fashion (cf. Bertau, this volume).
(5) The site of identity as located inside, i.e., within the interiority of a self; where it seems to be given the status of an authentic command center – for navigating one's own actions and activities; and this command center is also assumed to provide a compass for what is held to be right and wrong.

To summarize and condense the relationship between these five principles, when speaking of identity, modern English conveys a narrative of the following kind. First, there is something like an interior central navigation bridge to a person's self. From this command center, three kinds of decision territories are navigated: (i) temporal stability and change; (ii) how to blend in and differentiate from others (e.g., other people, animals, nature); (iii) how to engage as agentive subject or as recipient, i.e., subjected to forces in the world (for further discussion of these three principles, see Widdicombe & Marinho, this volume). Finally, and accordingly, this narrative ends with the assumption that this internal command bridge is accessible by and to the self – using (self-)

reflective means; and, that if these reflective means are employed rationally, we may get it, i.e., identity, right. The next step in refining our understanding of this identity narrative and its kinds of concomitant identity discourses involves examining the sociogenesis of this kind of identity narrative.

2.2 A European History of Identity Discourses

The attempt to assemble a historiography of becoming self-reflective and, in this process, establishing an internal navigation bridge from where to steer oneself in terms of the three identity territories suggested above, strongly resembles a project that has been attempted many times before. It is the project of laying out the contributing factors that arguably resulted in *the history of modernity*. And we will sketch this project below from two angles, though intending to open it to alternative points of departure. First, we review the material changes that occurred across a particular territory (metropolitan Europe) over several centuries. In a second step, we illuminate the history of discursive changes that went alongside these changes. However, we feel the need first to discuss the limitations and problems of this attempt, because this project itself can be viewed as grounded in modern assumptions from where there may be no return, i.e., from where conceptions of alternative histories may be difficult to excavate, and from where cultural traditions that formed alongside the unfolding project of European modernity were pushed aside by elites who claimed those other traditions to be more primitive and less legitimate projects. To avoid this pitfall, we will start from the assumption that a presentation of the unfolding history of modern European identity discourses is precisely the sociogenesis of conditions that enabled a certain Indigenous, local consciousness – one that is best characterized in terms of a particular type, namely as *European* modernity. This historical unfolding we view as running parallel with *other modernities*. We shall return to integrating European modernity into the more global construct of Indigenous historiographies after we sketch the changes that took place within European traditions. This will help pave the way in the next section of this chapter to depict how identity-theoretical assumptions in the discipline of psychology could emerge in the particular academic constellations of a socio-historical (and political) context of teaching, learning, and research – first in Europe, and then diffusing outward into North American identity discourses.

2.2.1 Problems with Modern Projects of Identity Histories

First, the claim that identity/self or subjectivity/consciousness and conscience (as well as constructs like mind, emotions, agency, character, and personality) are subject to historical changes and large-scale cultural diversity may be hard to swallow. For instance, psychology students we teach are baffled (though this may be due to teaching at small liberal institutions in the US): Aren't these (identity, subjectivity, consciousness) human dispositions that are universally shared – and definitive of what makes us humans (in contrast to other life forms)? Furthermore, aren't what ontogenetically unfolds across the life course (and across different societies) in regard to these dispositions simply individual or cultural differences – but all grounded in the center of human sense-making, i.e., in a deep and internalized sense of who we are as humans? While this argument by no means only reflects students' and laypeople's folk psychologies, this way of conceptualizing identity is also deeply woven into experts' theories, as documented in traditional handbooks on the topic of identity (e.g., Barresi & Martin, 2011; McLean & Syed, 2015; Schwartz, Luyckx, & Vignoles, 2011). More pertinently, it shows how deeply the concepts of interiority and reflection are already woven into a common European and US American consciousness, as alluded to in our opening quotation from Linda Tuhiwai Smith, leaving little room to take a critical and historical look at them.

In addition, there are further issues specific to the writing of a history of identities, and particularly with drafting a European identity project. In this chapter, we shall occasionally touch on them. First, whose histories are incorporated (i.e., who are *the natives* in a European sociogenesis), and what are these histories supposed to accomplish? Second, what counts as evidence for the moments and events that are picked out and arranged into a plot that is assumed to feed the emergence of what can conceivably be considered the current state of (modern) identity discourses? And third, whose values are written into this way of doing historiography? Alongside these questions (which we will follow up briefly in the next paragraphs) inextricably travel assumptions about the good of any history-writing – ranging from conservatively justifying the status quo to drafting progressionist goals for a better future. This final question will be taken up in our concluding summary in this section and later in our opening for potential alternatives.

First and foremost, historiographies that span centuries typically feature conceptual changes in elites or the ruling classes, and their analyses at best offer insight into how the discourses of formerly underprivileged populations changed in the process of overthrowing old and gaining access to new power relations. Our sketch of European modernity discourses will start from there as well. However, recognizing that we know little, for instance, of the *state of self-awareness* of women and slaves, including foreigners, in the slave societies of Athens and Rome, or to what degree they were credited within the ruling male ideology, and whether they credited themselves, with a personal consciousness, a sense of self or subjectivity, we face an insurmountable conundrum. To give another example: We know equally little about the life of peasants in the medieval "Dark Ages," until European peasants launched a number of collective revolts against the nobles and landlords (1381 in England, 1431/1467 in Galicia, and 1524/25 in Germany), after which peasants again seemed to have disappeared from documenting a shared and conscious interest in articulating their experiences of subjugation. In contrast to the slave revolts in Rome, of interest for the peasants' demands for rights and freedom was their reported invocation of divine laws,[7] mirroring aspects of the religious liberation of the Reformation that also enabled nobilities to begin to exert their independence from the fetters of the Catholic Church. This interest in the identities of oppressed and marginalized individuals and collectives emerged only sporadically, such as in the wake of activist women's groups in the early twentieth century, and more recently in a worldwide outcry against the visible persistence of colonialism and systemic racism – and here particularly in the face of contradictions to the liberal promise as apparently anchored in most constitutions of *modern* nation-states.

Second, when it comes to what historiographers can rely on in terms of testimonies that bespeak the subjectivity and identity discourses of people in previous centuries, assuming we had access to verbal conversations – or, at the very least, more writings – of, for instance, women and slaves in Athens or Rome, and of peasants in medieval times, or of members of the working class during the Industrial Revolution,[8] we would be able to analyze those records in light of suggestions made in the chapters of this volume (and elsewhere). Instead, the data that are available and typically made use of are writings of literate, privileged men, philosophers and theologians, joined later by male (and increasingly female) novelists, who in their writings had started thematizing issues of reflection and interiority – either as existential issues of being human, in the face of God – or, later on, as internal struggles in fictional characters. However, apart from, and in addition to, theological, philosophical, and literary testimonies, attestations date back to Hammurabi's legal code from Mesopotamia and early Egyptian dynasties that lay out and define the duties of (government) officials. These codifications of behaviors resemble the codes and restrictions of behaviors laid out in the writings of Confucius (551–479 BCE), and much later in the form of the courtesy books by Baldassare Castiglione (1528/1959) and Erasmus van Rotterdam (1530/ 1974). These works were later reinvestigated, starting with the groundbreaking work by Norbert Elias (1939), as reflecting aspects of the developing psychological changes in the conceptions of European upper- and, later on, increasingly middle-class identities, which in sociological research over the last fifty years also provided a look into the probable social causes of such psychological changes. In our sketch of the history of European modernity discourses, we start with a brief historical summary of socio-political and

---

[7] As documented in the writings of Thomas Müntzer (1988), a theologian leader of the peasant uprising.

[8] Notable exceptions are James Myles's fictional autobiography of *Frank Forrest*, which first appeared in ten chapters of a weekly newspaper between January 3 and March 7, 1850; and recent editions of *Memoirs of Victorian Working-Class Women* by Florence S. Boos (2017).

economic changes, followed by the discursive changes resulting in what we call a *new* consciousness.

Third, we consider any sketch of the emergence of European modernity bound to comprise a value stance that, in one way or another, is arguably, and simultaneously, the result of this same emergence. For once, as Homi K. Bhabha (1986) explicates concisely, "there is no master narrative or realist perspective that provides a background of social and historical facts against which emerge the problems of the individual and collective psyche" (p. xiii). Besides, reducing European modernity somewhat, and taking *liberté, égalité, fraternité* as the core values of its modern consciousness, it can be argued that, as abstract and ideal as these values are, they were only secured over a history of struggles and reforms against, and emancipated from, the ruling classes that existed (and kept existing) in the form of aristocracies, nobles, courts, and the Church. They mirror values at the hearts of other liberation movements, such as feminist, anti-slavery, and anti-colonial action orientations. However, maintaining our previous commitment to a critical lens, this realization requires an even more in-depth consideration of the inhumane and exclusionary consequences of modern Eurocentric (and, particularly later on, US American) exceptionalism. This resulted in new forms of patriarchy and slavery, colonialism, and the global expansion of capitalism, with an increase or, at the very least, a shift in inequality and injustice in their wake. To conclude, we see it as our primary task to bracket temporarily our own deep-seated values of <personal> freedom, <personal> autonomy, democracy, liberty for all, the right to vote, etc. – with the ultimate aim of opening our historiography to alternative views; and to avoid the dangers of repeating and naturalizing "the order of Western historicism" (Bhabha, 1986, p. xi).

2.2.2 The European Identity Project as a History of Material and Socio-Political Conditions

Enlightenment (rational) and Romanticism (emotional) debates certainly provided important impulses for the identity concept as it plays out in academic debates and everyday life today. Yet, the traditional study of how Jean-Jacques Rousseau influenced Immanuel Kant, for example, tells us little about how identity played out *on the ground* and how the self-concept of the everyday person changed during the settle time (Koselleck, 2004). As we mentioned before, there is obviously no way to go back and interview peasants, bondsmen, industry workers, and the like. Such material simply cannot be acquired. However, there is much concrete material about tremendous socio-political changes in Europe between 1750 and 1850, and even further into the early twentieth century, with strong influences on the concepts of identity and self that we can draw on. These changes played out in the arenas of science, new forms of production and global trade, and the newly emerging public sphere.

With the scientific revolution (from the Renaissance through the eighteenth century), a new generation of thinkers interested in the newly emerging natural sciences – the so-called scientific materialists – began to dominate intellectual discourses. Instead of philosophical speculations about human autonomy (Kant), the corrupting effect of society on the individual (Rousseau), the immortality of the soul (Hume), and the relation of the self to God (Descartes), an ontological leveling occurred. With the rise of the empirical sciences, humans became conceptualized as part of nature in the same way as plants and animals and thus as following the same laws. Forces previously separable by kind were now seen as similar. An energetic model of input and output and measurable growth emerged first in physics, and later in the economy and the human sciences. The number of academic journals increased during the settle time from a mere handful in central Europe to several hundred by the 1850s (Mabe, 2003). Ludwig Büchner, one of the first successful authors of popular science books, quotes in his 1855 bestseller *Kraft und Stoff* (Force and Matter) famous intellectuals of his time, such as the German pathologist Rudolf Wirchow and the Italian neurologist Carlo Matteucci, and praises their success and advanced understanding of the human body as a complex mechanical system regulated by chemical reactions and energy flow. Hermann von Helmholtz, in 1847, presented a version of the first law of thermodynamics at the Physical Society of Berlin (Helmholtz, 1889). This law insists that energy is at a constant level in the universe and is neither created nor destroyed; it merely changes form. The conserved energy of which nature is composed operates in a transcendental though not a metaphysical way, and serves as the basis of all manifestations of both matter and force.

This scientific revolution went hand in hand with advanced technological changes during the First and Second Industrial Revolutions. From roughly 1760 to 1820, the first period was characterized by mechanization, population growth, urbanization, and a steady rise in average income and living standards, all primarily driven by the textile industry in Great Britain. Before the Industrial Revolution, the gross domestic product per capita in Europe had been mainly stable. The newly emerging industries, however, initiated a capitalist economy that focused on constant expansion and growth. Notably, Great Britain formed a global trading empire and inaugurated an intensification of colonization. The Second Industrial Revolution (1870 until the outbreak of World War I) amplified these processes with the development of production lines, standardization, and electric power, eventually resulting in modern consumer capitalism. This newfound power through mass production also changed how human beings, as the motor (Rabinbach, 1990) of this process, were regarded. Medieval Christian dogma considered idleness as a sin, a failure of character (Wenzel, 1960). By contrast, the new energetic model allowed for speculations about human nature in terms of ability, that is, usability, employability, and controllability of (other) human beings in the interest of production, progress, and profit.

The new capitalist order redistributed wealth and generated further distinctions between the state and the social polity that created its own sphere. James Donald (1996) characterizes the new citizen's consciousness in terms of a "citizenship that demands not absolute loyalty and obedience to the monarch (subjection) but a new capacity for self-determined agency (subjectification) and so new forms of intersubjective and intrasubjective relationships" (p. 178). Jürgen Habermas describes these changes in *The structural transformation of the public sphere* (1989). He claims that with the end of feudal societies, a distinction between the private and public emerged and that, within this distinction, the private allowed for a space of critique and self-reflection. International trade and the processes of industrialization and democratization in the emerging European nation-states went hand in hand with an increased need for (self-)critical debates to exchange economic, scientific, and cultural knowledge and form public opinion. These debates mostly took place in newly emerging coffee and tea houses and among the emerging bourgeoisie. The influx of tea, particularly in Britain, drastically reduced alcohol consumption, one of the pressing social issues of the time (Sournia, 1990) – and thus allowed for more (rational) debate. Improvements in printing press technology likewise allowed for more conversation and debate in written form and rising educational levels. God and the Churches became less influential; instead of an *annus domini*, an ever-repeating year of God, development toward a better life with more income, more available products, more education and knowledge, increased communication, and heightened democratic participation became desirable and reachable for an increased number of people. Freud's psychoanalysis rests on this energetic understanding of the self as split and the need for self-control as much as seemingly rational approaches to self-regulation. The self is drastically reoriented toward a developmental trajectory fixed on what is to come in the future. In the words of Eva Illouz (2012), new forms of uncertainties emerged, where "the shaping of the modern individual was at one and the same time emotional *and* economic, romantic *and* rational" (p. 9, our emphasis), where the private sphere and the newly gained domain of interiority could become "a space for ourselves" (ibid.) – a shelter for the cultivation of an authentic self, to which only the I had (privileged) access for a retreat into myself.

This new, mechanistic, energetic model of a human being that turns inward to understand themselves and outward to offer (self-)critique, self-control, and self-awareness consists of a regulation of an interior energy flow to maximize productivity and minimize unproductive expenditure. It also depends on continuous development in the accumulation of ability and knowledge within ever-increasing social networks of the *other*. The formation of these social networks, especially within and across the boundaries of principalities and emerging nation-states, is best described in terms of developmental processes with an integrative and simultaneously differentiating function (cf. Werner, 1980/1948). On the one hand, meeting, connecting, and trading with others who do not belong to the same network community enforced the recognition of differences – differences in appearance, languages spoken, or in interaction rituals and communicative behavior. On the other, this push toward differentiation comes with the necessity of communicating across these differences – and as such an opening-up to, if not embracing of, commonalities and sameness.[9] Thus, the emerging sense of a European identity – across national, regional, local, and individual boundaries – presupposes some form of acknowledgment of an inevitable interdependency. This acknowledgment of an interdependency within and between communicative networks is an essential predisposition for the constitution of regional dialects and national languages, and simultaneously for a national and a *new* European consciousness – and, as we will argue below, also for the potential vision of a *new* global identity.

2.2.3 The European Project as a History of Identity Discourses

A radical transformation to the *new* consciousness of modern times is commonly held to have taken place between medieval times (also called the *Middle Ages*, which were assumed to have started under the problematic label *Dark Ages*) and modernity (the *Enlightenment*). When exactly this radical change took place and what its precursors are thought to be is subject to theoretical and empirical debate; we will touch only briefly on these debates below. However, the time frame from 1750 to 1850 is said to constitute the settle time for this rather sizable transformative project to resolve (cf. Koselleck, 2004). As noted above, the testimonies previous historiographers of a modern European identity have relied on to construct their theories are predominantly those from elites, i.e., typically men who had been educated within dominant discourses within the Church, and increasingly at the courts of emerging European nobilities. Their access to languages such as Latin and Greek, as well as their growing abilities to read, write, and interpret texts available to them, distinguish these elites from the common people, including women, peasants, and members of the emerging working class. In addition, being situated within the discourses of royals/nobilities (and within the hierarchy of the Church) implies the cultural expectation of differentiating and buffering dominant hegemonic discourses from newly emerging counternarratives of the lower castes and classes such as peasants and wage earners, as well as those of women. Thus, the documents and testimonies that are typically used to outline a history of European modernity have to be read against the grain of their tendency to, if not legitimize, then nevertheless assume the hegemonic discourses within the class structures of their times as shared background. It is against this background that we consider the construction of a continuity of

---

[9] It should go without saying that we do not mean to imply that this recognition of mutuality and interdependence automatically results in the erosion of power relations or power balance.

identity discourses – starting in Athens, carried on throughout Rome and the Early Church Fathers, rediscovered during the Renaissance, and feeding the Enlightenment – as more than problematic.

Two streams of a new kind of discourse can be marked as keystones for what was at stake during this time of settlement (roughly 1750–1850): for one, the turn to a rational and reflective attitude toward nature and social life, called the Enlightenment period. This period is said to overlap and be followed by a time period best characterized as one in which revising this reflective attitude to include self-reflective dimensions, paired with a subjective and affective engagement with all realms of life, including nature, others, and selves, took place. This new and inwardly directed sensitivity, labeled Romanticism (1770–1848), also served as a critical response to an economic and cold rationality that had brought about a focus on mechanistic causal explanations of (human) life, together with a strong interest in the body (as a biological object) and the psyche (as a psychological system). The emergence of Corpuscularianism in the works of Enlightenment rationalists and empiricists such as Thomas Hobbes, John Locke, Robert Boyle, Isaac Newton, René Descartes, and other intellectuals of the time allowed for a distinction of primary (outer, visible) and secondary (inner, hidden) qualities. Galileo (1914/1638; 1909/1842, pp. 33ff.) famously insisted on a distinction between an objective world describable in mechanistic terms and subjective experience. The consequences of these intellectual developments also influenced the newly emerging narrative of self and identity, and, as such, paved the way for a modern, post-Enlightenment, post-industrialization rationality.

Out of the group of Enlightenment thinkers, David Hume (1888, p. xix) first envisioned psychology as a science, and he indeed thought of it as the foundation of all other sciences. Hume's work exemplifies contemporaneously emerging debates: He discussed identity in the face of change and the place of human beings in the entirety of nature. Like Kant after him, Hume turned away from speculative metaphysics in favor of reason. Kant, who primarily unfolded his theory of self and identity in response to Hume, can be taken to provide the grounds for a stronger emphasis on subjectivity among the Romanticist thinkers. While Enlightenment rationalists had largely become dogmatic and the empiricists had largely fallen for skepticism, Kant provided a new synthesis. Most importantly, he discussed identity in relation to a unity of consciousness, stability over time, and as the source of agency. Kant's noumenal self (1998, p. 369), and the distinction of a noumenal world that stands in opposition to the phenomenal world that we experience, forms the base of modern concepts of *interiority*. This inner world, for Kant, also meant that the mind does not merely receive sensations from the world, as the empiricists would have it, but actively structures sensations. As such, every experience comes with an *I think* that *attributes* intention and agency (Kant, 1998/1787). The unifier of these thoughts is the self; a self that is an autonomous meaning-maker. It is at this point that Kant borrows from French

Romanticism and specifically Rousseau. Through reading Rousseau's *Emile*, Kant reflected on human nature and "to honor human beings" (Kant, 2011/ 1764, p. 96). The notions of a self as individual, innocent, and benevolent, a self that stands in contrast to a corrupting society, all relate to Rousseau's Romanticism. Drawing from this, Kant develops his liberalism that posits all human beings as fundamentally equal. One of the quintessential tensions in modern democracy – that between equality and individuality – is reflected in this debate. Post-Kantian German philosophers extended this new notion of individuality and equality. However, they were less concerned with science than their Enlightenment predecessors (including Kant) and instead showed a heightened interest in religion and the social aspects of the self. The play-wrights and poets Friedrich Schiller and Johann Wolfgang von Goethe were at the forefront of this movement known as *Sturm und Drang* (Storm and Stress). From the young Goethe's writings springs a self that is haunted by opposing forces. Struggling with the allures of life and death, the only escape from this is finding your true self, and failure to do so may lead to suicide. The publication of *The sorrows of young Werther*, a coming-of-age *Bildungsroman* of unrequited love in 1774, brought instant fame to Goethe and allegedly led to several cases of suicide among the readership, emulating Werther's behav-ior in the novel. Schiller collaborated closely with Goethe and shared many of his views. Yet, he was more focused on the social world and thereby further bridged the gap between Rousseauian Romanticism and Kantian rationalism and empiricism. In accordance with Rousseau (2002/1762), Schiller (1795), too, believed in society's corrupting effects on the individual. However, he insisted that it was not society per se but the particular turn it had taken during the Enlightenment. Like so many philosophers to follow, Schiller believed in the power of art and aesthetics as the path to human flourishing and inner wholeness.

As we argued above, the material and socio-political changes that are taken as having prepared for changes in the conceptualizations of personal and collective identities in the writing elites, and in the consumption of their writings feeding new collective European identity discourses, started to happen long before Enlightenment and Romanticism. The construct of a Renaissance (stretching roughly from the twelfth/fourteenth to the seventeenth century and coinciding with the so-called Age of Discovery and Colonialization) served to portray the changes as a more continuous develop-ment relating to more global processes of integration and differentiation. We have already mentioned the problematic concoction of a continuous line of a reflective agency construct stretching from Athens via Rome and early Christianity into the Enlightenment as one of the credits of the Renaissance. Nevertheless, in concert with an increase of dense and durable communicative networks across European territories and languages, this suggests a more gradual transformation in consciousness that could spread among the newly emergent classes in Europe. However, we should keep in mind that two contradictions riddle these constructs of epochal changes. First, although the descriptions of changes in consciousness point toward freedom, equality (collective and personal), and progress as (new) ideals, they clash with European colonialization, rapaciousness, and slavery in the new colonies, and freshly emerging inequalities, inequities, and injustices between the newly emerging classes, advanced weaponry and warfare, and exploitation of environmental resources. Second, descriptions of changes in consciousness can be viewed as, and often are, serving to legitimize these new structural conditions. Nonetheless, both of these may also help provide points of critique and departure for options in designing alternatives.

2.2.4 Decentering European Modern Identity: Alternative Modernities, Indigeneity, and the Global Transformation

We have already cautioned that taking a European development of modernity as the paradigmatic universal (and imperialistic) mode of discourse on identity has resulted in a reference to a sense of self as exceptional and superior to other historical and geopolitical sense-making strategies. Nonetheless, at least two other choices exist.

First, we can treat the European strand of sociogenesis as one variant among other developments of modernity. Following this line of argument, a subject-centered form of reason that emerged as European modernity was always paralleled by other emerging sociogenetic sense-making strategies of societies at different historical times and locations. The concept of *multiple modernities*, developed initially by Shmuel Eisenstadt (2001, 2003) and elaborated by Peter Wagner (2011) (see Delanty, 2013 for a critical review), effectively challenges attempts to universalize and essentialize the European model, with its discourse of exceptionalism and hegemony vis-à-vis other modernization projects in the rest of the world. We also need to take into consideration that this European project took place in a global context. What we claimed above as a project of differentiation and integration, where traders between different emerging nation-states and across different languages had learned to communicate across their differences, and thereby learned to constitute themselves as same-*and*-different within a newly defined European territory, applied equally to the world outside, i.e., vis-à-vis the peoples of the new languages and cultures beyond European borders.[10] Avram Alpert (2019), borrowing from Edward Said and Raymond Williams, and following their claim, argues constructively that "the modern world and those in it were 'constituted' by colonial encounters" (p. 4).

---

[10] D. T. Suzuki stretches and claims for the European concept of enlightenment, "when one is enlightened, he does not stand out from the rest of the world, but embraces it ... The very moment of enlightenment experience takes in the world and its totality" (Suzuki, 1952, cited in Alpert, 2019, p. 2).

A second way of decentering the hegemonic European sociogenetic model of a new consciousness in relation to other sense-making strategies of identity and self would be to explicitly mark the European variant as local and native and as an indigenous strand of sociogenesis. Following this line of reason, a European strand would become easier to set in relation to other indigenous cultural traditions. First, this view would potentially lend itself better to critical interrogation of the assumption of the individual as the basic building block of society (Smith, 1999, p. 49), and the modern European wisdom of pitting human *nature* against *nature in the natural world* (ibid., p. 48). Second, setting particular indigenous discourses and their sociogenesis in relation to European indigenous discourses forces a sorting through of how the latter has threatened, and in some cases eliminated, the maintenance and reclaiming efforts of the former. Third, it would be of interest to the topic of identity and self-consciousness to lay out the potential benefits of non-European indigenous identity discourses. We will return to this argument below when discussing budding alternatives to dominant European identity discourses.

To sum up, it should be noted that attempts to decenter the project of European identity formation will undoubtedly open up considerations about the consequences of adopting historiographies that wrestle for authenticity and legitimization. Probably more important, it may enable discussions about newly emerging identity discourses – discourses that emerge as a function of particular historical moments, particular places, and particular social forces. To follow up on and deepen how identities and identity projects can be theorized along these dimensions would open up debates about postcolonial and subaltern theories of identity, as well as identity projects emerging from marginalization and oppression, and embed them in historical and experiential contexts – debates that are outside the scope of this chapter but worth following up on elsewhere.

2.3 Identity and Modern Psychology

In the preceding section, we have proposed the case for a historical emergence of European modern identity discourses that projected itself into sense-making strategies of identity and sense of self within a modern European collective consciousness. This leads to the question of how this particular kind of consciousness could expand from here into shared contemporary expressions of identity, self, subject, individual, and conscious/conscience, the way they surface in our contemporary use in US English. The line of reason we pursue in the following is that our current, everyday usage of identity discourses emerged over centuries in Europe and extended into configurations of identity discourses in contemporaneous US English through the newly emerging discipline of psychology. More concretely, we claim that psychology in Europe emerged as an academic discipline that took basic tenets of modern identity and made them the center of scholastic and educational endeavors. From there, these moved into newly emerging strands of psychology in the US – from where, in turn, psychology became a global discipline, providing sense-making strategies for self and identity for common, everyday discourses across the languages around the globe.

To start with, there were large numbers of conceptual ponderings on issues of identity and sense of self before the dawn of European modernity, surfacing not only in emerging European nation-states and national languages but in different spheres in the world. Within the European schools of thought, a sense of identity with a self-reflecting interiority can be traced back to the emerging academic disciplines of theology and hermeneutic text critique, and then, during the second half of the nineteenth century, beginning to take off within European philosophy as the exploration of the human soul/mind. Two particular European traditions, one surfacing under the header of experimental psychology, the other in the form of psychoanalysis, are claimed to have served as two relatively smooth bridges that shaped psychology in the US. Kurt Danziger (1997) has summarized one of them in terms of how a science-grounded psychology was able to define its subject matter by tracing the scholastic experiences of US psychologists in mainly German laboratories from the mid-1800s onward. Matching the unfolding of these new traditions within US academia with shifts in methodologies that dominated the conduct of psychological research around the globe is another contribution, summarized in Danziger's *Constructing the subject: Historical origins of psychological research* (1990). A second tradition, exceptionally well outlined by Illouz (2008), and the one that we will follow up in more detail here, credits Freud's visit to Clark University in 1909, and the enthusiastic reception of his lectures by a newly emerging free-spirited, upper-middle-class, humanistic audience. These two traditions remained separate within the American Psychological Association (APA) that was founded at Clark University thirteen years before Freud's visit.

According to Illouz (2008, 2012), Freud's adoption of the modern discourse of an interiority that can be turned to for the examination of one's own authentic wishes and desires, but that can also serve as a refugee,[11] was met by a sentiment that had long been endorsed by the highly educated, emerging American secular and liberal elites. Freudian ideas were viewed as taking the Enlightenment two steps further: into deeper levels of self-exploration and in a more rigorous secular direction of personal independence and freedom. A second direction opened up more radical possibilities of self-advancement with the hope of a cleaner and better moral conscience. Although there had

---

[11] "The energetic and successful man is he who succeeds, by dint of labor, in transforming his wish fancies into reality. Where this is not successful in consequence of the resistance of the outer world and the weakness of the individual, ... the individual takes refuge in his satisfying world of fancy" (Freud, 1909, fifth Clark Lecture).

been pre-Freudian anticipations of an unconscious level of interiority, typically attributed to literary fictional characters (cf. Vallins, 2011), Freud's division into the ego/*I*, the *superego*, and a more deep-seated level of hidden memories and formerly uncontrollable desires and drives, the *id*, opened up new techniques of self-interrogation and surveillance (for more detail, see Habermas & Kemper, this volume).

The assumption of an inner self that is monitored by itself requires a shift from the public as monitoring and judging what is right and wrong toward individuals' internalized interpretative frames such as shame and embarrassment (cf. Elias, 1939) as authoritative corrective. In other words, conversations between communally anchored social actors are assumed to turn inwardly into conversations held by the ego with its interiority. Through the emergence of psychology, it takes center stage in academic and public probing. First, it should be noted that this process of self-monitoring is modeled after the rational discourse of an early bourgeois type of reasoning discourse, i.e., that irrational or repressed desires, and disruptive emotions, can be identified, scrutinized, and ultimately kept in check. This early formulation of the therapeutic dialogue has been elaborated and refined in what is currently investigated under the headers of *voices* and *dialogicality* (cf. Bertau; Gonzalez Rial & Guimarães; Salgado & Cunha, all this volume) and in motivational enhancement approaches to therapy. Second, this kind of tracking of and reasoning with oneself is thought to be productive only if it is performed in the form of an authentic disclosure, i.e., in ways that truly engage the psychodynamic entities of ego, superego, and id in identifications of what is right and what is wrong – following the basic principles of therapeutic interviewing (cf. Illouz, 2006). In this respect, therapeutic disclosure as authentic relates directly to the scientific materialists' attempts to uncover the body's inner workings and the mind as a function of energy flow.

A number of recent inquiries have taken up Elias's pioneering thesis of the historical changes from a social and public navigation of a hetero-controlled identity to a private and self-controlled individuality (Elias, 1939). Illouz's (2008, 2012) spearheading scrutiny of the emergence of the therapeutic ethos since Freud's Clark Lectures in 2009 in particular has documented how a therapeutic psychological culture could loop back from psychology as an academic discipline into mainstream common sense-making in popular discourses about self, identity, subjectivity, and individual worthiness over the last decades. Ole Jacob Madsen (2020) gives an illuminating exposition of how psychology as a discipline ultimately fed into what he calls "the permanent triumph of the therapeutic" (p. 23), and he showcases how therapeutic culture could develop into a global phenomenon. Others (summarized in Nehring, Madsen, Cabanas, Mills & Kerrigan, 2020) have developed a body of research highlighting several ways in which the therapeutic ethos has resulted in a boom in self-help products. These products are successfully promoted by a happiness and wellness industry that promises to respond to people's problems but in practice "largely deflects, distracts, and pacifies social subjects in the neoliberal era that promotes the ruthless pursuit of domination, power, and capital" (Rimke, 2020, p. 47), thereby producing new forms of oppression covering up even more subtle exploitation.

Now, having arrived at a seemingly rather dark side of where our historical pursuit of the marriage between new European identity discourses and a modern psychology with its own identity discourses has taken us, we return to our original question: Is there space for alternatives or counternarratives to European identity projects? More specifically, can we delineate mechanisms for discerning the value and merits of alternative approaches to identity and identity research? We share Heidi Rimke's (2020) assessment that the triumph of the therapeutic across the globe is not homogenous, and neither is it total. Madsen (2020) also concludes that the therapeutic threat "does not mean that it becomes a hegemonic ideology that necessarily produces uniformity" (p. 22). Rather, he and Rimke (2020) both maintain that local traditions, with their own particular values and norms, will most likely develop their own unique blends "of regional peculiarities" (Madsen, 2020, p. 23). In this context, it would be particularly interesting to follow up on how (other) Indigenous approaches to psychology and identity research have emerged as contrastive and potentially new collaborative frameworks (cf. Smith, 1999).

2.3 Alternatives?

Finally, as we cautioned initially and throughout this chapter, historiographies are typically meant to legitimize the present, and often also particular future orientations, including their underlying assumptions and values; alternatively, they can be critical of the present, its desirability and moral/ethical implications. Our aim in tracing the historical conditions that enabled an emergence of European modern discourses about identity, self, and its neighboring concepts was to show ways of decentering these discourses, i.e., stripping them of their privilege in serving as Eurocentric reference culture (cf. Delanty, 2015). However, taking this critical position quasi from the outset does not strip us of our own positionality, and neither does it result in a direct and demonstrable road to alternatives. Nevertheless, we would like to end our chapter with a few takeaways from our excursion into the histories of identities, as we promised in our opening section. These are framed in the form of questions rather than suggestions and will end with a brief excursion into alternative Indigenous identity discourses.

Without a doubt, identity research that works with a conceptualization of an internal subject who reflects on their interiority has motivated ingenious questionnaires and innovative interview techniques that attempt to unearth deep-seated cognitive and psychoanalytic inferences that people arguably rely on when reflecting their sense of self. Chapter 3 in this volume by Sue

Widdicombe and Cristina Marinho presents paradigmatic types of this sort of research. But what about alternatives? Do they need to negate the concepts of interiority and reflexivity as cornerstones for identity work and identity formation processes? Or, is it possible to *simply* bracket the interiority–exteriority distinction – as well as the reflective versus non-, un-, or pre-reflective distinctions? And what would a pursuit of research look like along the lines of identity displays in people's actions and interactions – without banking on their conscious, self-reflective awareness as empirical evidence? Furthermore, are there any consequences concerning the role attributed to language in identity formation processes and how language can be approached analytically? We believe this is where personal identity research can learn from organizational identity theories, where the navigation of affinities and differences between organizations and temporal stability and change are investigated empirically as actions taken and communicated. There, typically, any recourse to something like an interiority (e.g., the *heart* and *soul* of a company) is clearly understood metaphorically as anthropomorphism. Also, a number of contributions to this handbook seem to steer clear of investigating interiorities. Interestingly, these contributions position themselves within traditions that originated in neighboring disciplines – e.g., symbolic interactionism, discursive psychology, ethnography, and conversation analysis (cf. Becker; Brinkmann; Giaxoglou & Georgakopoulou; Hydén; Kaplan, Flum, Bridgelal, & Garner; Locke & Montague; Norris & Matelau-Doherty; Riley, Robson, & Evans; Wilkes & Speer, all this volume). It is also worth noting that language is investigated here in its interactional and relational function, rather than in its role in reflecting on internal representations.

Our second set of questions concerns the status of what we had termed *sites* for identity management, i.e., constructions of temporal (stability and change), synchronic (differentiation and integration vis-à-vis others), and agentive (versus subjectification) senses of identity. Concerning these three sites, we can ask which of them are considered central to approaching identity theoretically – in this volume or elsewhere: Some investigations center on one, others focus on two, but rarely are the intersections of all three central to identity theory and their empirical investigation. Starting, for instance, with the navigation of identity as maneuvering temporal constancy/stability and change, it may be of interest that constancy, i.e., no change, is often characterized and, we would argue, mischaracterized in terms of *continuity*. Widdicombe and Marinho (this volume), for instance, chose this course of action. Similarly, Tilmann Habermas and Nina Kemper (also this volume) take continuity in contrast to breaks, disruptions, and ruptures as most relevant for the construction of personal temporality. What is under consideration here are two different change trajectories that are juxtaposed: one in the form of a positive and preferable continuous form of change, the other as discontinuous and disrupting the preferred form of change. The former is controlled by an agentive steering toward (continuous) progressive self-development; the latter is experienced as a disruptive world-to-person direction of agency constellations. Note that there is nothing wrong with this particular way to coordinate constancy and change as directions of fit for agency navigation. However, these kinds of considerations easily feed attributions of beneficial worth to a continuous self, especially if under the aegis of self-agency. In contrast, change becomes more of an antagonistic force – especially if not under the control of self-agency. What is noticeable here is how seemingly innocent sites of being-in-the-world are theorized and become empirically invested with what we had identified earlier as a hegemonic European way of modern identity construction – raising again the question of whether or how there are ways to do this differently.

An interesting alternative with regard to the terrain of self–other identity relations is offered in the form of a relational counter-discourse that radically questions interiority and reflection as the central place from where individuals differentiate and integrate their sense of self vis-à-vis others. In a relational ontology, as Anne Salmond (2012, p. 125) demonstrates with respect to Māori values and their traditions, for example, a sense of self is fundamentally embedded in the world, rooted within a position of situatedness, and inhabiting and navigating places from there. It does not require a center in the form of a command bridge from where the *out-there* is navigated and conquered, because relations and relationships are always already given, and a sense of self is given or taking off from there. This relational perspective challenges European modern discourses of the self as outside of, and often in contrast, to nature (cf. Smith, 1999) and questions assumptions about inner consistency and self-actualization as striving for inner consistency and coherence (Salmond, 2012). This is where, according to Smith (1999), "Indigenous peoples' ideas and beliefs about the origins of the world, their explanations of the environment, often embedded in complicated metaphors and mythic tales are now being sought as the basis for thinking more laterally about current theories about the environment, the earth and the universe" (p. 159). Overall, since relational counter-discourses are considered eco-friendlier, more sustainable, and more productive than current European modernity discourses (cf. Sillitoe, 1998), they have become better positioned and more accentuated to be heard. For example, reviewing the seemingly context-free and universally accepted model of (modern) biomedicine in its own European Indigenous traditions (Sax, 2014) opens perspectives on its limitations. But even more so, other Indigenous medicines of what are typically called traditional healing methods can be newly evaluated in terms of their contributions to healing and well-being. A renewal of European sense-making strategies in terms of a deeper appreciation of identity projects grounded in a close human–environment connection can be another consequence. This could result, though not simply or straightforwardly, in a deeper awareness of environmental conditions and connectivity with the natural world and its inhabitants – and lead to, as Smith (1999) points out for Māori identities, an example of local sense-making: "Māori knowledge represents the body of knowledge which, in today's society, can be extended, alongside that of existing Western knowledge" (p. 175). And as suggested by Margaret Bruchac (2014), researchers working within other traditions may be able to "gain information and insight by consulting Indigenous traditions; these localized knowledges contain crucial information that can explain and contextualize scientific data" (ibid., p. 3814).

References

Alpert, A. (2019). *Global Origins of the Modern Self, from Montaigne to Suzuki.* Albany, NY: State University of New York Press.

Austin, J. L. (1962). *How to Do Things with Words.* Cambridge, MA: Harvard University Press.

Bamberg, M. (1997). Culture, words and understanding. *Culture & Psychology, 3*(2), 183–194.

Bamberg, M. (2010). Blank check for biography? Openness and ingenuity in the management of the "who-am-I" question. In D. Schiffrin, A. De Fina, & A. Nylund (Eds.), *Telling Stories: Language, Narrative, and Social Life* (pp. 109–121). Washington, DC: Georgetown University Press.

Bamberg, M. (2020). Narrative analysis: An integrative approach – Small stories and narrative practices. In M. Järvinen & N. Mik-Meyer (Eds.), *Qualitative Analysis – Eight Traditions* (pp. 243–265). London: Sage.

Bamberg, M. (2021). Positioning the subject. In S. Bosančić, F. Brodersen, L. Pfahl, L. Schürmann, T. Spies, & B. Traue (Eds.), *Following the Subject. Grundlagen und Zugänge empirischer Subjektivierungsforschung* [Following the subject. Foundations and approaches of empirical research on subjectivation] (pp. 114–132). Wiesbaden: Springer.

Bamberg, M. & Lindenberger, U. (1984). Zur Metaphorik des Sprechens. Mit der Metaphorik des Sprechens zu einer Alltagstheorie des Sprechens [On the metaphorics of speaking. With the metaphors of speech toward an everyday theory of language]. *Sprache und Literatur, 53*, 18–33.

Bamberg, M. & Wipff, Z. (2020). Re-considering counter narratives. In K. Lueg & M. Wolf Lundholt (Eds.), *The Routledge Handbook of Counter Narratives* (pp. 71–84). Abingdon: Routledge.

Barresi, J. & Martin, R. (2011). History as prologue: Western theories of the self. In S. Gallagher (Ed.), *The Oxford Handbook of the Self* (pp. 33–56). Oxford: Oxford University Press.

Batchen, G. (2014). Local modernisms. *World Art, 4*(1) 7–15.

Bhabha, H. K. (1986). Foreword: Remembering Fanon: Self, psyche and the colonial condition. In F. Fanon, *Black Skin, White Masks* (pp. vii–xxvi). London: Pluto Press.

Blickle, P. (2006). *Der Bauernkrieg: Die Revolution des Gemeinen Mannes* [The Peasant War: The revolution of the common man, 3rd ed.]. Nördlingen: C. H. Beck.

Bruchac, M. (2014). Indigenous knowledge and traditional knowledge. In C. Smith (Ed.), *Encyclopedia of Global Archaeology* (pp. 3814–3824). New York, NY: Springer.

Boos, F. S. (2017). *Memoirs of Victorian Working-Class Women: The Hard Way Up.* Cham: Palgrave Macmillan.

Büchner, L. (1867). *Kraft und Stoff. Empirisch-naturphilosophische Studien. In allgemein-verständlicher Darstellung* [Force and substance. Empirical-natural-philosophical studies. In a generally understandable presentation, 9th ed.]. Leipzig: Theodor Thomas.

Butler, J. (2003). What is critique? An essay on Foucault's virtue (2000). In J. Butler & S. Salih (Eds.), *The Judith Butler Reader* (pp. 302–322). Malden, MA: Blackwell.

Butler, J. (2005). *Giving an Account of Oneself.* New York, NY: Fordham University Press.

Carroll, L. (1871). *Alice through the Looking-Glass.* London: Macmillan.

Castiglione, B. (1528/1959). *Il cortegiano* [The book of the courtier], translated by C. S. Singleton. New York, NY: Doubleday.

Cooley, C. H. (1902). *Human Nature and Social Order.* New York, NY: Scribner's.

Danziger, K. (1990). *Constructing the Subject: Historical Origins of Psychological Research.* Cambridge: Cambridge University Press.

Danziger, K. (1997). *Naming the Mind. How Psychology Found Its Language.* London: Sage.

Delanty, G. (2013). *Formations of European Modernity: A Historical and Political Sociology of Europe.* London: Palgrave.

Delanty, G. (2015). Europe and the emergence of modernity. The entanglement of two reference cultures. *International Journal for History, Culture and Modernity, 3*(3), 9–34.

Donald, J. (1996). The citizen and the man about town. In S. Hall & P. Du Gay (Eds.), *Questions of Cultural Identity* (pp. 170–190). London: Sage.

Eisenstadt, S. N. (2001). The civilizational dimension of modernity. *International Sociology, 16*(3), 320–340.

Eisenstadt, S. N. (2003). *Comparative Civilizations and Multiple Modernities: A Collection of Essays by S. N. Eisenstadt (Volumes 1 and 2).* Leiden: Brill.

Elias, N. (1939). *Über den Prozeß der Zivilisation. Soziogenetische und psychogenetische Untersuchungen* [On the process of civilization. Sociogenetic and psychogenetic studies], Volumes I and II. Basel: Verlag Haus zum Falken.

Elias, N. (1993). *Mozart: Portrait of a Genius*, translated by E. Jephcott; edited by M. Schröter. Berkeley, CA: University of California Press.

Erasmus of Rotterdam (1530/1974). *The Collected Works of Erasmus.* Toronto: University of Toronto Press.

Erikson, E. H. (1958). *Young Man Luther: A Study in Psychoanalysis and History.* New York, NY: Norton.

Erikson, E. H. (1968). *Identity: Youth and Crisis.* New York, NY: Norton.

Fearon, J. D. (1999). What is identity (as we now use the word)? Mimeo, Stanford University, last accessed February 14, 2020 at https://web.stanford.edu/group/fearon-research/cgi-bin/wordpress/wp-content/uploads/2013/10/What-is-Identity-as-we-now-use-the-word-.pdf.

Fanon, F. (1986). *Black Skin, White Masks*, translated by C. L. Markmann. London: Pluto Press.

Foucault, M. (1978). *The History of Sexuality. Volume 1: An Introduction*. New York, NY: Pantheon Books.

Freud, S. (1909). About psychoanalysis. 5 lectures given at the 20th Anniversary Celebration of the founding of Clark University in Worcester, Mass., September 1909, last accessed March 24, 2020 at www.rasch.org/over.htm.

Galilei, G. (1909/1842). *Opere Complete di G. G., Vol. IV*. Florence: G. Barbera.

Galilei, G. (1914/1638). *Dialogues and Mathematical Demonstrations concerning Two New Sciences*. New York, NY: McMillan.

Gleason, P. (1983). Identifying identity: A semantic history. *Journal of American History*, *69*(4), 910–931.

Goethe, J. W. (1774). *Die Leiden des jungen Werthers*. Leipzig: Weygand'sche Buchhandlung.

Habermas, J. (1976). Legitimationsprobleme im modernen Staat. *Politische Vierteljahresschrift 17*(7), 39–61.

Habermas, J. (1989). *The Structural Transformation of the Public Sphere: An Inquiry into a Category of Bourgeois Society*. Cambridge, MA: MIT Press.

Harré, R. (2015). Positioning theory. In K. Tracy (Ed.), *The International Encyclopedia of Language and Social Interaction*. Hoboken, NJ: Wiley-Blackwell.

Helmholtz, H. V. (1889). *Über die Erhaltung der Kraft* [On the conservation of power]. Leipzig: Wilhelm Engelmann.

Hume, D. (1888). *A Treatise of Human Nature*. Oxford: Clarendon Press.

Illouz, E. (2006). *Cold Intimacies: The Making of Emotional Capitalism*. Oxford: Polity Press,

Illouz, E. (2008). *Saving the Modern Soul: Therapy, Emotions and the Culture of Self-Help*. Berkeley, CA: University of California Press.

Illouz, E. (2012). *Why Love Hurts. A Sociological Explanation*. Cambridge: Polity Press.

James, W. (1890/2007). *The Principles of Psychology (Vol. 1)*. New York, NY: Cosimo.

Kant, I. (1998/1787). *Critique of Pure Reason*. Cambridge: Cambridge University Press.

Kant, I. (2011/1764–1765). Remarks in the observations on the feeling of the beautiful and sublime. In *I. Kant, Observations on the Feeling of the Beautiful and Sublime and Other Writings* (pp. 65–204). Cambridge: Cambridge University Press.

Koselleck, R. (2004). *Futures Past: On the Semantics of Historical Time*. New York, NY: Columbia University Press.

Mabe, M. (2003). The growth and number of journals. *Serials*, *16*(2), 191–198.

Madsen, O. J. (2020). Therapeutic cultures. Historical perspectives. In D. Nehring, O. J. Madsen, E. Cabanas, C. Mills, & D. Kerrigan (Eds.), *The Routledge International Handbook of Global Therapeutic Cultures* (pp. 14–24). Abingdon: Routledge.

McLean, K. C. & Syed, M. (Eds.). (2015). *The Oxford Handbook of Identity Development*. New York, NY: Oxford University Press.

Miller, D. L. (Ed.) (1982). *The Individual and the Social Self: Unpublished Work by G. H. Mead*. Chicago, IL: University of Chicago Press.

Müntzer, T. (1988). *The Collected Works of Thomas Müntzer* (edited by P. Matheson). Edinburgh: T&T Clark.

Myles, J. (1850). *Chapters in the Life of a Dundee Factory Boy. An Autobiography*. Edinburgh: Adam & Charles Black.

Nehring, D., Madsen, O. J., Cabanas, E., Mills, C., & Kerrigan D. (Eds.) (2020), *The Routledge International Handbook of Global Therapeutic Cultures*. Abington: Routledge.

Pelz, W. A. (2016). *A People's History of Modern Europe*. London: Pluto Press.

Plamper, J. (2015). *The History of Emotions: An Introduction*. Oxford: Oxford University Press.

Rimke, H. (2020). Self-help, therapeutic industries, and neoliberalism. In D. Nehring, O. J. Madsen, E. Cabanas, C. Mills, & D. Kerrigan (Eds.), *The Routledge International Handbook of Global Therapeutic Cultures* (pp. 37–50). Abington: Routledge.

Rabinbach, A. (1990). *The Human Motor: Energy, Fatigue, and the Rise of Modernity*. New York, NY: Basic Books.

Rose, N. (1989). *Governing the Soul: The Shaping of the Private Self*. London: Routledge.

Rosenwein, B. H. & Cristiani, R. (2018). *What Is the History of Emotions?* Cambridge: Polity.

Rousseau, J.-J. (2002/1762). *The Social Contract and the First and Second Discourses*. New Haven, CT: Yale University Press.

Ruberg, W. (2019). *History of the Body*. London: Red Globe Press.

Salmond, A. (2012). Ontological quarrels: Indigeneity, exclusion and citizenship in a relational world. *Anthropological Theory, 12*(2), 115–141.

Sax, W. S. (2014). Postscriptum: The futures of indigenous medicine: Networks, contexts, freedom. In N. Uddin, E. Gerharz, & P. Chakkarath (Eds.), *Futures of Indigeneity: Spatiality, Identity Politics and Belongings* (pp. 294–314). Oxford and New York, NY: Berghahn Books.

Schiller, F. (1795). Briefe über die ästhetische Erziehung des Menschen. *Die Horen*, 1–3.

Schwartz, S. J., Luyckx, K., & Vignoles, V. L. (Eds.). (2011). *Handbook of Identity Theory and Research*. New York, NY: Springer.

Searle, J. (Ed.). (1971). *The Philosophy of Language*. Oxford: Oxford University Press.

Sillitoe, P. (1998). The development of indigenous knowledge: A new applied anthropology. *Current Anthropology 39*(2), 223–252.

Smith, L. T. (1999). *Decolonizing Methodologies: Research and Indigenous Peoples*. Dunedin: University of Otago Press.

Sournia, J.-C. (1990). *A History of Alcoholism*. Oxford: Wiley-Blackwell.

Thomas, W. I. & Znaniecki, F. (1918–1920). *The Polish Peasant in Europe and America (5 Vols.)*. Chicago, IL: University of Chicago Press.

Taylor, C. (1989). *Sources of the Self: The Making of the Modern Identity*. Cambridge: Cambridge University Press.

Vallins, D. (2011). 1775–1825: Affective landscapes and Romantic consciousness. In D. Herman (Ed.), *The Emergence of Mind. Representations of Consciousness in Narrative Discourse in English* (pp. 187–214). Lincoln, NE: University of Nebraska Press.

Wagner, P. (2011). From interpretation to civilization – and back: Analyzing the trajectories of non-European modernities. *European Journal of Social Theory, 14*(1), 89–106

Wenzel, S. (1960). *The Sin of Sloth: Acedia in Medieval Thought and Literature.* Chapel Hill, NC: University of North Carolina Press.

Werner, H. (1980/1948). *Comparative Psychology of Mental Development, Revised Ed.* New York, NY: International Universities Press.

Wierzbicka, A. C. (1997). Response to Michael Bamberg. In S. Niemeier & R. Dirven (Eds.), *The Language of Emotions* (pp. 227–229). Amsterdam: John Benjamins.

Wiktionary. (2020). Category: English words prefixed with self-, last accessed February 22, 2020 at https://en.wiktionary.org/wiki/Category:English_words_prefixed_with_self-.

Wittgenstein, L. (1994/1953). *Philosophical Investigations*, translated by G. E. M. Anscombe. Oxford: Blackwell.

3 Challenges in Research on Self-Identity

Sue Widdicombe and Cristina Marinho

In this chapter, we focus on what have been described as three key aspects of self-identity: continuity, uniqueness, and agency. We use the hyphenated term "self-identity" because some of the researchers whose work we discuss talk about the self, others about identity, and there is often some slippage in the two terms (see Oyserman, Elmore, & Smith, 2012, who refer to "self and identity" for this same reason). Our aim is not to provide a systematic review of the literature in order to draw conclusions about what we know about these topics. Instead, we want to explore conceptual and epistemological questions about how these intangible qualities have been translated into objects of research and knowledge, and the assumptions that researchers make in the service of that translation. We have chosen to focus on these aspects because, as we will show, they have been the focus of decades of research from a diverse range of theoretical and methodological perspectives. They are therefore useful for our broader aim to exemplify the correspondence between theoretical assumptions and the rationale for asking certain kinds of questions, and between assumptions made about the ontology of each phenomenon and the methodology used to render it researchable. We begin our discussion with the concept of continuity. We conclude by highlighting some of the issues and challenging decisions that, often implicitly, underlie research on self-identity.

3.1 Continuity

The terms stability, continuity, and consistency are often used interchangeably to evoke the idea of being the same over time and/or contexts. Some researchers have conceptualized continuity or stability as an interesting and challenging puzzle. Bamberg, De Fina, and Schiffrin (2011, p. 178), for example, formulate this puzzle as follows: how can we "claim to be the same in the face of constant change," and how can we "claim to have changed in the face of still being the same"? Similarly, Oyserman et al. (2012, p. 13) present stability as a "conundrum": "even if self and identity change, people can still have an experience of stability." These approaches share the assumption that both continuity and change are relevant to people, and that this duality is somehow contradictory or incompatible. Nevertheless, despite superficial similarities in framing the question, there are significant differences in how the question is conceptualized and therefore researched. An initial observation is that Bamberg et al. juxtapose two seemingly contradictory claims and seek to describe how people negotiate them (assuming this dilemma is one that people do address), whereas Oyserman et al. refer to experience and seek to resolve the question theoretically and empirically (thus treating the dilemma as the researcher's). This makes continuity a good starting point for our examination of the role of our taken-for-granted assumptions in defining and therefore creating the constructs we seek to understand.

As noted above, Oyserman at al. (2012) observe that many theories assume that, once developed, self-identity is relatively stable (indeed, it has been proposed that a key task in the transition from adolescence to adulthood is the achievement of a stable identity; Erikson, 1968). From a lay perspective, too, it can be taken for granted that people experience stability or a "core essence" of self-identity. However, they also note that a stable self would not be effective and that there is an important benefit to self-identity being sensitive to and thus varying according to the specific situation. Two key questions follow from these assumptions. First, there is the question of whether self-identity is *really* stable or not. Second, assuming that, in fact, consistency in self-identity is apparent rather than real, the question becomes what accounts for the perception or experience of continuity? What makes our self-identity *seem* stable? In the first case, the researcher's role is to discover the truth (of whether self-identity is or is not stable); in the second case, the researcher's role is one of explaining this taken-for-granted experience.

Let's take the first question. It makes sense within a traditional scientific (positivist) framework in which there is a "right" or "true" answer to questions relating to stability. These questions, expressed as hypotheses or statements, require researchers to operationalize stability or turn it into something that can be observed directly or inferred from observable behavior. For example, stability is inferred from the observation that people resist feedback that contradicts their previously given self-ratings in experimental settings, for example by ignoring it or discrediting the source (see Oyserman et al., 2012).

More commonly, researchers have sought to make stability directly observable. One way of doing so stems from Erikson's (1968) theory of development in which stability is conceptualized as a process of commitment to an identity. Building on this theoretical assumption, stability is operationalized using self-report scales of the extent of exploration and engagement in identity (Crocetti, Rubini, & Meeus, 2008). A different development of these theoretical ideas is found in the concept of "self-concept clarity" (or SCC). This is described as a "metacognitive" construct relating to whether the content of identity (self-views) is confidently defined, stable, and consistent (Campbell et al., 1996). More specifically, stability here is operationalized as the composite of twelve items or statements which include statements about consistent beliefs or personality, a sense of identity or feeling of genuineness (e.g., having a clear sense of who and what I am; feeling I am the person I appear to be). Some statements invoke a temporal dimension through reference to frequency, or "day by day" (e.g., my beliefs about myself seem to change frequently). In other words, it is a summary term for a range of different meanings or judgments which are all considered manifestations of an underlying "consistency" in self-identity. In their study, Campbell et al. compared this scale with participants' ratings of traits (as me or not-me) administered four months apart. They found that the SCC measure explained 22 percent of the variance in those ratings, which they interpreted as good enough statistical evidence of its validity (although this could also have been interpreted as indicative of difference). In a further development, Schwartz et al. (2011) argue that change and stability in self-identity should be conceptualized as happening on a daily as well as longer term basis, and that at the micro level a single item measure of SCC is sufficient, specifically, "Today I had a clear picture of who and what I am." To ensure the validity of this single statement as a measure of SCC, they compared it with the full scale. They report that although reliability coefficients and convergent and divergent validity for the scale were somewhat low, they decided that their significance could be discounted as probably due to considerable daily fluctuations.

The point is that once we examine more closely the concept of "continuity," we see a variety of interpretations of what it means, and the significant role of researchers' decisions about what counts as equivalent. Our argument is not that the practice is wrong or inaccurate, but that interpretation is a necessary part of doing scientific research. However, following the initial efforts to create a way to measure the psychological construct as described above, the scale is of interest not solely for what it enables researchers to say about self-identity but for how it relates to something else (see Kroger & Marcia, this volume; Negru-Subtirica & Klimstra, this volume). That is, in later work, the primary aim is not the exploration of consistency in self-identity per se, but its relation to other variables. For example, Lodi-Smith et al. (2017) and Crocetti et al. (2016) look at how SCC is linked to transitions from adolescence to adulthood. Schwartz et al. examine the effects of SCC on anxiety and depression. They also build a model of the associations between SCC and identity commitment in the educational sphere.

Continuity has been conceptualized and operationalized in other ways too, such as consistency in ratings of specific self-descriptive traits over a period of time. English and Chen (2011), for instance, use this approach. They also distinguish two meanings of consistency: being the same over time and being the same person in different situations. They assessed the "across contexts" kind of consistency by asking participants to rate the self-descriptiveness of eighteen attributes for three relationship contexts. They then created a "score" of inconsistency by taking the average standard deviation of each attribute across the three contexts. In practice, then, consistency equates to little variation in judgments of the self-relevance of a limited set of traits, and this clearly differs from the feelings and beliefs of continuity discussed above. The measurement of consistency across time is achieved by administering the same inventory twice, about thirty-four days apart, and calculating the index of consistency in the same way. It is worth noting that in defining consistency in practice through this statistical index, the details or content of the specific dimensions through which consistency is displayed are treated as irrelevant. The meaning of consistency is simply "the same over time," not how or in what ways someone experiences stability.

An important point is that these conceptualizations of consistency are not constructed in isolation: they depend for their significance on a web of background theories and further assumptions. For English and Chen (2011), consistency is linked to adjustment and well-being (following Erikson and others), so it is a normative feature of well-adjusted individuals, at least in Western cultures, and a valued achievement rather than a (false) experience (and the alternative, inconsistency or malleability, is considered potentially problematic). On the other hand, working within an "interactionist" framework, they assume that self-identity is a product of the interaction between the person and the situation. These perspectives are reconciled by producing a theoretical explanation for consistency within a situation. Specifically, they argue that self-concept stability may be derived from global, cross-situationally consistent self-views or it can be based on an "if–then" form of consistency within contexts or relationships. These depend on cultural values (the latter is more relevant in Eastern cultures). This study, then, treats stability as a cultural fact, operationalizes it as a statistical correlation, and provides an account for situational variation.

We discussed earlier a second set of questions. These begin with the assumption that people are not *really* stable, so that the relevant question becomes one of accounting for why we think we are. Oyserman et al. (2012) suggest three kinds of answers to this question; practical, methodological, and conceptual. First, they propose that one reason we seem to be consistent may be that we tend to stick to similar situations and similar interactions and these create the impression of stability. Second, apparent stability is a result of the methods used in its investigation (e.g., repeated assessment using the same measure in the same situation). In addition, much evidence relies on people's reports of or judgments about consistency. If people experience stability even when self-identity changes, they are likely to report this (self-report may not therefore be the best way to address questions of stability and change; Oyserman et al., 2012). Third, the status of stability is reconceptualized as a belief rather than a given fact about self-identity. Thus, rather than try to access consistency directly, researchers focus on conceptualizing and researching people's *belief* in self-consistency. By way of an example, Dweck (2008) conceptualized two types of implicit theories or beliefs about stability and argued that people could be differentiated accordingly. Some people have fixed ("entity") theory beliefs (believing that qualities such as intelligence are fixed traits); others have a malleable ("incremental") theory, believing that their most basic qualities can be developed through effort and education. These beliefs can be general or relate to specific domains such as personality and morality. They are made accessible by asking people to rate their disagreement or agreement with general statements such as "I am a certain kind of person, and there is not much that can be done to really change that" or "I can always change my personality" (Dweck, 1999). In contrast to formulations of consistency we discussed earlier, it is about the possibility of change in self-identity rather than the absence of change over time or situations. Nevertheless, as we saw above, after the initial efforts toward conceptualizing and operationalizing implicit theories of consistency, it becomes of more interest in relation to the role it may play with respect to other psychological phenomena rather than being of interest in itself. For example, Ward and Wilson (2015) test the idea that people's implicit beliefs (about their stability or malleability) play a moderating role in appraising the self in the distant past and help thereby to create the illusion that their present self is better.

We noted above that another way of addressing the coexistence of stability and change in self-identity is to regard it not as something to be resolved but as a phenomenon to be described. So, for Bamberg et al. (2011), consistency in the context of change is conceptualized as a dilemma that people manage, negotiate, or seek to reconcile. Where and how they do this is related to a further set of assumptions, specifically that self-identity is constructed through narratives or the stories we tell about ourselves, so language plays a key role (we can see this in the framing of the puzzle in terms of our *claims* to be the same or changed). There is also a significant epistemological difference in that Bamberg et al. adopt a social constructionist perspective, assuming that self-identity and consistency are done, made, or constructed rather than awaiting discovery through the right measures. The focus thus shifts to the processes through which self-identity is made through engagement in discursive practices. Moreover, "this process of active engagement in the construction of identity ... takes place and is continuously practiced in everyday, mundane situations, where it is open to be observed and studied" (2011, p. 178). This approach is not scientific in the sense of hypothesis testing to discover the conditions in which people really are or believe themselves to be consistent, but it is empirical, because it aims to observe consistency by collecting instances of discursive activities or narratives where it is done. By assuming that language is the site and means of construction and negotiation, phenomena like stability are treated as observable in language as people interact, rather than hidden within the person.

These assumptions about consistency make it appropriate to collect and examine narrative talk and identify instances in which a person engages in discursive activities by using phrases that construct self-identity as "the same" or as different to how they were previously. By way of an example, Bamberg (2010) examined a narrative generated through an ABC News interview in which US presidential candidate John Edwards is asked about an extramarital affair. Bamberg focuses on three excerpts, one of which is a response to the question "How could you do that?", and another of which is a response to a question about how his supporters would see him now. Bamberg argues that this question challenges the sense of continuous identity and thus invites Edwards to address constancy and change directly. He observes that Edwards refers to "being the same back then," having the "same thoughts or views," and being "no different from the person they knew" (2010, p. 117), thereby portraying consistency. It is also worth noting that the questions are not treated as a neutral means of generating an assessment of consistency, as might be the case with a questionnaire; instead they are regarded as an integral part of its production. In other words, the interviewer's question co-constructs the narrative, and this provides a further "layer of construction" (indeed, Bamberg notes that narratives are rarely produced spontaneously).

Similar ideas about consistency and change being managed dilemmas brought about through questions can be seen in Nikander's (2009) work. She also assumes that language is the means of and medium for addressing such dilemmas, but her focus is on turn-by-turn talk in interaction rather than narrative, and her analysis draws on discursive psychological and conversation analytic techniques. So, rather than pick out phrases, or the components of narrative, she assumes that negotiating dilemmas becomes observable through paying attention to the sequential detail of talk produced through interaction with an interviewer or interlocutor. She adopts the assumptions of discursive psychology and conversation analysis, namely that identity is produced in and through talk, through the use of tacit skills (ethno-methods), and that identity production has an action-orientation (see Calder-Dawe & Martinussen; Locke & Montague; Wilkes & Speer; Riley, Robson, & Evans, all this volume). These assumptions are reflected in the way she analyzes consistency and change, by identifying discursive skills or know-how via patterns observed in the talk, and by showing what they achieve. Specifically, she analyzes a sequence of turns in interviews on aging conducted with middle-aged participants. She shows how the people she interviewed (i) rejected aging in relation to their own identity, (ii) acknowledged the possibility of change, and (iii) then reiterated their initial claim about the contemporary irrelevance of age. She calls this a "provisional continuity device." It is produced in the context of questions (and the assumptions built into the questions) about age. She observes (2009, p. 873) that a similar device was found in Widdicombe and Wooffitt's (1995) work on change in relation to subcultural style. Identifying sequential and other patterns in researcher's own and others' data may be used to suggest its character as a tacit skill or practice for accomplishing continuity (or dealing with challenging assumptions relating to change).

These analyses have in common the assumption that consistency is achieved through language. However, Bamberg treats language as narrative, whereas Nikander treats it as interaction, and the view of language dictates where they look for moments in which consistency is being done. With this in mind, let us consider two further approaches in which language is conceptualized in part as Discourse which has an ideological character. The clearest exposition of these ideas can perhaps be found in the psycho-discursive (Wetherell, 1998, 2015; see also see Calder-Dawe & Martinussen, this volume) and narrative-discursive approaches (Taylor, 2012, 2015; Taylor & Littleton, 2006, see also Giaxoglou & Georgakopoulou; Hydén; Berry, all this volume). Within these approaches, Discourses provide culturally available resources which may be used by people to construct their self-identities in talk. It is proposed that when a person uses the culturally available terms, metaphors, and statements which constitute a particular discourse to talk about themselves, they position themselves within that wider discourse. Since these discursive resources incorporate history, culture, politics, and ideology, this framework provides a way of understanding the relationship between autobiographies or the stories people tell about themselves and the wider context within and through which those stories are produced. As people tell stories about themselves on a particular occasion, and they use terms or phrases from a succession of Discourses, they position themselves momentarily within each of those discourses, building a self-identity that is multiple, fragmented, and fleeting. The problem with this view is that it seems to contradict the experience of continuity. Their conceptualization of continuity is thus developed as a solution to this problem: to reconcile theory and taken-for-granted experience. Both Wetherell and Taylor argue that we tend to position ourselves in similar contexts using a limited set of discursive resources and accumulate a pool of resources, or anecdotes which are told and retold on subsequent occasions and supplemented through use. Consistency is thus understood as the accumulation of the discursive resources which are built through use in similar contexts over someone's lifetime (or, as Wetherell puts it, the "sedimentation" of discursive positions), and Taylor and Littleton (2006) conceptualize the experience of continuity as a "meta-narrative" that ties these repeated narratives together. Consistency is made researchable through observing the repeated use of terms that derive from particular discourses and interpretation of what is said in terms of wider discourses (Taylor & Littleton, 2012; Wetherell, 2015). In comparison to Bamberg's approach outlined earlier, there consistency was to be found in the narratives themselves, whereas here consistency lies in the interpretation of these narratives as coming from the wider discourses that govern the person's life.

Before we leave our discussion of consistency, there is one more approach we want to consider, in part because it shows that an interest in narratives is not exclusive to researchers adopting a social constructionist approach (see also Habermas & Kemper, this volume). To access stability and change directly, Dunlop, Gou, and McAdams (2016) asked respondents to talk about life transitions or "turning points" (in general or related to moving to university or becoming a parent). This method treats language as a means of representing those experiences or turning points. The narratives were coded according to two narrative master themes (redemption and contamination) as well as for agency and emotional tone. This coding permitted the researchers to inspect and compare frequencies and determine the statistical relation between the narratives used at different points in time, enabling the quantification of change and stability. Sengsavang et al. (2018) adopt a similar conception in their longitudinal approach. In their research, numerical scores are given by judges to narrative themes, to allow statistical analysis. This in turn assumes that the question of whether self-identity is stable or malleable can be addressed by quantifying the degree to which this is the case in relation to particular narratives.

3.2 Uniqueness

There are many ways in which uniqueness could be conceptualized. The Oxford English Dictionary (n.d.), for example, defines it as the fact of being one of a kind, or the quality of being very special or unusual. In the social-psychological literature on self-identity, it is conceptualized as being or constructing oneself as unique or different from others. Independently of the specific definition adopted, it is frequently conceptualized in relation to its supposed opposite, that of sameness to others. This notion of uniqueness as "opposite to" is manifested in different ways. For example, Bamberg (2010, p. 112) conceptualizes it as a dilemma to be negotiated or managed in self-narratives: he asks "whether it is possible to consider oneself as unique in the face of being the same as every other person (and vice versa)." In practice, it involves identifying terms, phrases, and grammatical forms in self-narratives which are interpreted as manifesting uniqueness or sameness in relation to others. For example, in his analysis of John Edwards' interview, the sense of being special and the same as everyone was picked out by identifying a shift from "I" to the generalizing pronoun "you," and through descriptive terms and membership categories used to describe the self as an exceptional lawyer, as someone with a lawyer's ego, or as a national public figure. To this "microanalysis" Bamberg added an additional layer of analysis, which identifies Edwards' self-presentation of being the same as everyone as part of a master narrative, namely "the master narrative of politics and publicity as corrupting otherwise noble characters" (2010, p. 115). This sort of analysis is attached to ontological positions about the nature of the object of study, some of which are driven by direct observations (namely that self-narratives about being unique/different and similar to others occur in real interactions and that people adjust the content of their self-narratives to the interaction), and others by theory (such as the assumption that this self-narrative format originates outside the individual) (see Bamberg & Dege, this volume, for more detail; Bamberg, 2011; Bamberg et al., 2011).

The idea of being unique or different from others in opposition to being the same as others is also worked up by Brewer (1991; Brewer & Pickett, 2014) and Snyder and Fromkin (1980). Here the ontological position adopted by the researchers is that uniqueness (as well as similarity) is an inner phenomenon. Specifically, they conceptualize differentiation from others (or uniqueness) as a human need, in the sense of a biological drive. Furthermore, the researchers assume (either theoretically or via interpretation of previous studies) that this need arises through comparison with others and in tension with an opposite human need, the need to be similar (or identify with) and feel close to others. For instance, Snyder and Fromkin (1980) postulate that the need for uniqueness works in opposition to the need for similarity in that the satisfaction of one of these needs threatens the intensity of the other (see also Lynn & Snyder, 2002). In order to make the need for differentiation researchable, it has to be turned into an object of research. One problem is, of course, that needs are not directly observable, but can perhaps be investigated as manifested via thought and behavior. The challenge here is then to turn the need for differentiation from others into something that can be observed. The solution to this challenge is found in a further key assumption: that these needs must be balanced. In particular, it is proposed that people are motivated to reach a *moderate* level of distinctiveness or, to use the authors' own words, to achieve an "optimal balance" between the two opposing needs or a state of "optimal distinctiveness" (Brewer, 1991; Brewer & Pickett, 2014; Slotter et al., 2014; Snyder & Fromkin, 1980). Taken together, these assumptions mean that the existence of the need can be ascertained by *disrupting the balance* and seeing whether participants *act or think (in a particular way) to restore the balance* when given the opportunity. In practice, extreme disruptions and their consequences for participants' reactions and thinking are most often investigated.

In this line of research, researchers have invented different ways of creating an imbalance and measuring how the balance is restored. Each of these ways has different implications for what is meant by being different from others. It is worth stressing, before we describe these ways, that the focus of the researchers moves away from investigating differentiation from others per se, to investigating how people's need for differentiation from others (and similarity to others) is restored cognitively.

In these experimental studies, an internal imbalance between the needs is thought to be achieved by manipulating participants' self-perceptions in terms of *extreme* similarity or *extreme* differentiation in relation to "everybody else" (Brewer & Pickett, 2014), "other students" (Brewer & Pickett, 2014; Snyder & Fromkin, 1980), or romantic partners (Slotter et al., 2014). One way of creating an internal imbalance was by asking one group of participants to recall (and write down) recent situations in which they had felt extremely similar to others, and another group to recall when they had felt extremely different from others (Brewer & Pickett, 2014; Slotter et al., 2014). A second way was by telling some participants, via false feedback, that their personality traits were atypical, and some other participants that their personality traits were extremely similar to others (Brewer & Pickett, 2014). A third way was by telling some participants, also via false feedback, that their personality traits, as well as their attitudes, values, beliefs, abilities, and interests, were highly similar to others, and by telling other participants that they were slightly similar (Fromkin, 1970). It is then hypothesized that participants led to perceive or feel *extremely* similar to others (in comparison to those who were led to perceive or feel extremely different from others) will seek to re-establish a balance between the needs by stressing their difference from others.

In these studies, participants are provided with different (observable) opportunities to re-establish the balance between the two needs. Brewer and Pickett (2014) propose that a balance can be re-established via group identification or self-descriptive traits, and thus asked participants to indicate the importance for their self-concept (i.e., for how they think about themselves) of thirty-two different social categories. Participants in the extreme similarity manipulation can re-establish a balance by showing higher identification with generic social categories (e.g., "men," "women," "young adults") than those in the other manipulation. Generic social categories were assumed by the researchers to "allow" differentiation. A second way of restoring a balance between the two needs was advanced by Fromkin (see Snyder & Fromkin, 1980, for more detail). Here, participants were asked to generate as many different uses they could think of for a specific object. Those in the extreme similarity manipulation could restore the disrupted balance by generating more ideas (judged by researchers as more creative) than those in the other manipulation. A third way was proposed by Slotter et al. (2014), who advocated that seeking autonomy enables romantic partners to restore a balance between their needs for distinctiveness and identification with the other. Participants were asked about, for example, their intention to spend time with their partners in the following week. According to the researchers, participants in the extreme similarity manipulation could re-establish a balance by indicating their intention to spend less time with their partners (than those in the other manipulation). For Slotter et al., such an answer corresponds to a manifestation of the need for distinctiveness – or to feel autonomous.

In the studies mentioned above, the implicit need to be different from others (as well as its counterpart, that is, to be similar to others) is assumed to be "manifested in" or associated with: personality traits; a combination of personality traits, attitudes, interests, abilities (etc.); a general feeling; identification with generic groups; showing creativity; and seeking autonomy. The point here is that uniqueness or differentiation can take different forms, depending on researchers' definitions and their focus of interest (e.g., their focus on individuals vis-à-vis "general others," group members, or romantic partners).

Another way to make being unique (or different from others) researchable is by asking people directly. In this line of research, some researchers define being unique as a need (e.g., Snyder & Fromkin, 1977, 1980; Lynn & Harris, 1997), while others conceptualize it as a stable and well-defined self-perception (e.g., Şimşek & Yalinçetin, 2010). Despite this difference, both positions propose to study uniqueness using individual-differences scales. It is worth noting that Snyder and Fromkin (1980) sought to reconcile research using scales with experimental research (mentioned above). According to the authors, it is "logical to speculate" (1980, p. 77) that the need for uniqueness is as much influenced by specific situations (such as situations of extreme similarity) as by individual differences.

Snyder and Fromkin (1980) define uniqueness as a universal need or motive and then introduce a second assumption, namely that individuals differ in their need or desire for it. In practice, this means that researchers use scales and thus treat this need as an individual disposition (i.e., personal or personality characteristic) the intensity of which varies from one individual to another. Researchers often develop their own scales, each of which is claimed to reflect a different aspect of the same construct. By looking at their items, it is possible to capture the meaning of uniqueness that each scale is proposing to get at.

Snyder and Fromkin (1977) developed the first of many "need for uniqueness" scales (NUS). In their scale, participants are asked to provide their agreement with thirty-two statements. The need for uniqueness is here operationalized via a variety of items or statements that tap into different meanings (dimensions) of "need for uniqueness" and spheres (e.g., career, personal, or societal), which combined are claimed to capture individuals' general level of need for uniqueness. The items and statements of this scale reflect an amalgamation of different psychological constructs; they are feelings, attitudes (evaluations and behaviors), and beliefs about non-conformity to rules or others (e.g., "I tend to express my opinions publicly, regardless of what others say"), standing out in different situations (e.g., "Being a success in one's career means making a contribution that no one else has made"), and assertiveness (e.g., "I sometimes hesitate to use my own ideas for fear they might be impractical"). Based on all the items of the scale, a total score is computed and compared to baseline results in order to find out whether it corresponds to a high, moderate, or low need for uniqueness. Lynn and Harris (1997) also created a need for uniqueness scale, the Self-Attributed Need for Uniqueness Scale (SANU). This scale was developed in order to capture another dimension of the need for uniqueness which, according to the authors, captures a more common conceptualization of the need than that proposed by Snyder and Fromkin. In Lynn and Harris' scale, the need for uniqueness is operationalized via a more limited number of items (four), which together are meant to reflect a more *unified* (which was also confirmed statistically) and *general* conception of the need. It includes items about general preferences for being unique/different (e.g., "I have a need for uniqueness") and behaving differently from others (e.g., "I intentionally do things to make myself different from those around me").

Other researchers, also working within an individual-differences frame-work, have developed other scales aiming to measure *people's sense* of unique-ness. Here, too, uniqueness is treated as a personal characteristic, but it is not defined as a need. It is rather conceptualized as a stable and well-defined perception about the self. Şimşek and Yalinçetin (2010) developed the Personal Sense of Uniqueness (PSU) scale to capture "personal perceptions of self as unique to the individual and different from others" (2010, p. 576). This scale contains five general uniqueness items, which combined appear to reflect a *unified* meaning: it captures general feelings ("I feel unique") and general perceptions about personal and unique characteristics (e.g., "I think that the characteristics that make me up are different from others; as people get to know me more, they begin to recognize my special features"). It is worth stressing that this scale is claimed to reflect a unidimensional meaning (which was confirmed statistically) about feeling and perceiving oneself as unique or different from others. Another example of investigating a person's sense of uniqueness was proposed by van Doeselaar et al. (2019), who sought to investigate two measures of distinctiveness, namely general and comparative distinctiveness. General distinctiveness was measured via the PSU scale, whereas the comparative distinctiveness measure was developed by the authors. The latter sought to capture a more comparative meaning of distinct-iveness, that is, distinctiveness between self and important others on defining characteristics or personality traits. The authors asked participants to list important others (and say who they were) and disliked others, and to rate themselves and these others on, for instance, a Big Five personality scale (namely, the Ten-Item Personality Inventory-revised). Deviations of each profile (profiles from each participant and each "other") from a general profile (or normative profile) were then calculated. The deviation of the participant was then correlated with the deviations of each "other." The key point is that these correlations represent the degree of "distinctive similarity" between the self and each "other" – or, more specifically, "the degree to which two profiles are similar in the ways they diverge from the average profile" (ref. to Rogers et al., 2018, p. 126). Participants' average q-correlations between self and "others" were then multiplied by −1 so that higher scores reflected higher comparative distinctiveness. As can be seen, in this study, the authors worked with two different measures of distinctiveness, which they presented as two measures of the same construct: a more general measure of sense of unique-ness, and a more specific measure of distinctiveness, which is operationalized via differentiation from specific others.

Research with individual-differences scales often uses different scales of the same construct in order to capture its different dimensions or meanings (e.g., van Doeselaar et al., 2019; Lynn & Harris, 1997). These scales can be merged into one scale and used to test a model (e.g., Lynn & Harris, 1997). To be able to merge different scales, researchers rely on statistical tests (e.g., Cronbach's coefficient alpha). Another aspect to note about this sort of research is that scales for different constructs (such as the NUS and PSU) are expected to be statistically different via weak or non-significant correlations (e.g., Şimşek & Yalınçetin, 2010), whereas those for the same construct (such as the PSU and the comparative distinctiveness measure) are meant to show positive and significant correlations – although this might not occur (see van Doeselaar et al., 2019, for an example). Also, once a specific scale is validated, researchers then seek to establish the relevance of the scale by investigating how the scale *predicts* or *relates* to other constructs, such as psychological well-being variables (van Doeselaar et al., 2019; Şimşek & Yalınçetin, 2010) or desire for scarce products (Lynn & Harris, 1997). Another line of research with individual-differences scales is to explore *antecedents* of the need for uniqueness or sense of uniqueness. For example, Hall et al. (2015) investigated self-guides (ought and ideal self-guides) as possible antecedents of the need for uniqueness (measured via different need for uniqueness scales).

3.3 Agency

Similar themes can also be observed in relation to the final aspect of self-identity we consider. In Bamberg et al.'s chapter (2011, p. 178), agency is conceptualized as a dilemma between "the person, the *I-as-subject*, who constructs the way the world is," and "the *me-as-undergoer* [who] is constructed by the way the world is." These dual aspects of agency are treated as manifest in the descriptions of self that are to be found in narratives in two ways: through person descriptions and grammatical form. In the analysis of John Edwards's testimony referred to above, Bamberg (2010) picks out references to willpower, and "agentic self-constructions" such as descriptions of the self being strong, in control, or self-determined. The converse is displayed through phrases such as "being swept away," through the construction of a victim role, and in ascriptions of blame or credit to self or others. These construct the person as agentic or non-agentic within the situations described. Agency is also shown through grammatical forms used, such as the use of the first-person pronoun in conjunction with a verb and intentionalist terms such as "wants to." These assume that agency can be found or observed in the enactment of agency rather than through descriptions of what the person is like. This distinction between constructions of being agentic and of enacting agency can be seen in other approaches, too.

As we noted above, Bamberg's conceptualization of agency is driven by the assumption that self-identity is constructed through narratives, so these are the appropriate place to seek instances of agency-constructions. By contrast, Brooks (2009) adopts a discursive psychological approach and assumes that language has an action-orientation; linguistic terms and devices are used in ways that accomplish some action. These assumptions are reflected in her analysis of agency in radio phone-in calls where the topic was eating disorders.

In particular, she looked at how agency was constructed in different ways for a purpose, analyzing how speakers' non-agency was constructed in three ways: through use of terms that constructed the eating disorder as separate from the individual; through grammatical structures which gave agency to the illness; and through metaphors, like "slip into" eating problems, which portrayed the individual as not in control of their actions. She then argued that the function of these constructions that shifted agency from the speaker is that they help deal with potential moral blame for the eating disorder. We see here, then, how the analyses and conclusions are shaped by assumptions about the nature of language.

The same point can be made about Archer and Parry's (2019) analysis of TV/radio interviews in which two different celebrities are questioned over particular transgressions. They adopt a conversation analytic perspective and thus assume that language is interaction in which actions are co-produced through the turn-by-turn structure of talk (see also Wilkes & Speer, this volume). They treat issues of accountability and therefore agency as worked up between people and thus to be found in adjacent turns in interaction. In keeping with these assumptions, they examine the delicacy with which inter-viewers make the transgressions relevant and elicit the subsequent accounts. They then focus on how the celebrities use descriptive terms that reduce the severity of or camouflage their actions, or that implicate others as jointly responsible. In this analysis, agency is conceptualized in terms of accountabil-ity for specific actions and the claims people make about their own (lack of) responsibility for those actions within an interactional context in which the speaker is held to account (e.g., through an interviewer's questions).

There are also examples of research which conceptualize agency in terms of how interactants enact agency or produce "a sense of control and choice." This work assumes that agency "is inevitably a public and interactional event not a psychological state (which would be hard to assess and observe). It requires the exchange of talk between the individual and those around her or him (who may encourage or frustrate their initiatives)" (Antaki & Crompton, 2015, p. 646). We will discuss briefly three examples. In each, researchers have located agency in interactions in an institutional setting in which there is some asymmetry in roles, knowledge, or power. In our first example, Antaki and Crompton (2015) examine (and contrast) interactions between staff and people with learning disabilities in two service environments. They identify instances in which staff promoted (or not) a "discourse of agency" through verbal practices which portray the service user's joint engagement in activities as willed and driven by a shared purpose. These include using requests and suggestions, rather than directives, which treat the service users as knowing and competent to answer; and using terms which indicate joint purpose or investment in the activity.

Our second example is provided by Backhaus's (2018) study of encounters between staff and residents during the morning rounds in a home for the elderly. His conceptualization of agency in its doing draws on work in conversation analysis on the organization of turn-taking. He uses this to identify a mechanism through which care workers and (in a few cases) residents take control of the routine care interactions. Specifically, he takes the view that conversations are organized into "adjacency pairs" or pairs of actions in which a first pair part (FPP) requires a corresponding reaction or second pair part (SPP; Schegloff, 1968). So, one way of making agency researchable is by looking at how it is "worked out in the give and take of the turn-taking system itself." Backhaus thus looks at how access to or control of the first position is crucial in directing the care routine interaction, and that normally the care workers take the FPP in their initial summons and greetings, leaving the resident to react in the SPP. As the care worker and resident take alternating turns in the encounter, taking the first turn gives the care worker control of all the FPPs in the series of conversational actions which direct the care routine, with the resident left to produce the reactive SPPs. In this way, the care workers exercise control over, and therefore agency in, directing routine care. However, in a small number of cases Backhaus shows that the resident summons the care worker through the nurse call and thereby occupies the first and subsequent FPPs. This enables the resident to put forward *his* reason for calling, requesting what he wishes to be done. In this conceptualization, agency is not a property of the person but related to what a person does through a series of contingent actions (Koenig, 2011) and to the patterns of asymmetry found in communication which can be observed as they unfold (Backhaus, 2018).

As a third example, Koenig (2011) conceptualizes agency as done through resistance to a prior turn in interaction. In the doctor–patient interactions he studies, he shows how patients can resist recommendations and thereby assert agency by not responding or by questioning the recommendation until their treatment preferences and concerns are addressed. He looks at how doctors pursue acceptance in response (e.g., through reassurance or proposing alternative treatment). So, for these researchers studying interaction is one way of examining agency "in the doing." Here, it is assumed that the back and forth flow of conversation is the primary site for demonstrating agency and for treating others as agents. Such conversations are situated within a particular context, so the aim is to find how the sense of agency is done through the linguistic, semantic, and grammatical features afforded by talk (assuming that this is an important context for understanding self and other psychological phenomena).

Discursive psychology and conversation analysis are not the only approaches that aim to capture agency in its doing. Damen et al. (2015) define agency as a "personal sense of causation." They operationalize this sense using the theory of "apparent mental causation" (Wegner & Wheatley, 1999) to explain this sense and turn it into something that can be researched. This theory proposes that the sense of agency is derived from a process of cognitive inference as our minds try to make sense of our actions after we have performed them. When effects or outcomes are consistent with our prior thoughts and quickly follow our actions and there is an absence of other potential agents, we are likely to experience a sense of agency. Thus, making people think about future actions (i.e., planning or intending) will influence the sense of agency, so agency-sense can be manipulated by getting participants to plan or not to plan ahead of actions, and it is measured by asking participants to indicate on a 100-point scale the degree to which they felt they had caused a tone to occur. Damen et al.'s work thus makes "agency as action" researchable by creating the opportunity to act in a laboratory in a way that simulates the sense of agency that is tied immediately to actions.

3.4 Challenges

In this chapter, we examined three aspects of self-identity: continuity, uniqueness, and agency. Our aim was to highlight diverse ways in which each seemingly intangible phenomenon was made researchable. Our purpose in doing so was to show that the operationalization of these constructs was dictated not by some intrinsic quality of the phenomena but by the web of epistemological, theoretical, and ontological assumptions which inform the kind of object that is conceptualized and how it is made researchable, where researchers assume it to be located, and the kinds of questions it is appropriate to ask about it (see also Mazur, this volume).

Our point is that research is always done within a set of background assumptions about what we can know and about the nature of the world. Our review of work on consistency, uniqueness, and agency has highlighted several of these: a traditional or positivist approach which assumes that the world works in an orderly way and that we can discover "psychological laws" and "psychological objects" that explain how and why we behave the ways we do; social constructionist perspectives which assume that our worlds and ourselves are constructed through social processes and that, using the right kinds of discursive or narrative lens, we can identify these constructive processes; and a poststructuralist perspective concerned with the discourses which bring into existence the psychological objects, terms, and knowledge through which our subjectivity is effectively shaped, but which are themselves products of history, politics, and culture (see Riley, Robson, & Evans, this volume). The concepts of consistency, agency, and uniqueness are defined and make sense within these different overarching perspectives. For example, validating measures of consistency depends on the assumption that it is a real thing, existing independently of our research, and if there is a problem in accessing it, this is a technical or methodological problem rather than an ontological one. Alternatively, identifying discursive practices through which people construct themselves as agents makes sense within a discursive constructionist framework, and so on. These overarching assumptions determine the kinds of questions that researchers ask, and we highlighted throughout the close connection between epistemology and research questions or, conversely, how research questions presuppose certain states of affairs. For example, questions about why we think we are stable or how we balance needs for uniqueness and sameness, or how agency can be found in planning, presuppose that stability is merely a perception, or that we are biological or cognitive beings. Furthermore, the different epistemological assumptions determine what kind of object is researched, for instance, an object that can be measured, a discursive practice, an experience, or something beyond discourse. They also determine where it is located, whether that is within the person, in narratives or interactions, or beyond the discourse.

Setting these assumptions side by side brings into sharp relief the important subjective element in researching self-identity in terms of the choices we have available and the decisions we make. These decisions include how to bridge the gap between the phenomenon we are interested in and the object of research. This inevitably involves decisions about what we take to be a reasonable "stand in" for the elusive features of self-identity, whether this is a set of statements designed to "catch" the phenomenon, discursive practices which produce it, or apparently contradictory claims in small stories.

Thus, one challenge is to make explicit the assumptions and decisions that inform the study, perhaps reflecting on other possibilities. Researchers tend not to look much beyond their immediate theoretical framework, and so the status as decisions of theories and methods adopted may not be immediately obvious. Indeed, one of the challenges we had in writing this chapter was that research adopting one perspective tended not to refer to work on the ostensibly similar concept from other perspectives and, hence, views remain unchallenged. (Work in the discursive fields may be a partial exception to this; the psycho-discursive and psycho-narrative approaches are explicitly presented as dealing with questions that other discursive approaches leave unanswered).

A further challenge relates to decisions about whose interests drive research, and in whose terms the phenomena make sense. Much of the research we have been discussing is driven by the interests and assumptions of the researcher rather than the individuals who are the subject of the research. Thus, we have examined how the researcher sets up the puzzle or conundrum as such and therefore in need of investigation, or who is motivated to reconcile stability and change or uniqueness and sameness. It is the researcher rather than the participant who worries about continuity in the context of their theoretical view of self as positioned in Discourse. To an extent, discursive psychology and conversation analysis stand out in this respect, in that they begin from the question of where consistency matters to people in their course of living their everyday lives, in what situated contexts of their lives, and how people 'do' agency in the moments when they do. In other words, this tries to get as close as possible to the contexts in which consistency, agency, and uniqueness are relevant to people. This has the advantage of minimizing the "interpretative gap" (Edwards, 2012, p. 425) between "phenomena, data, analysis, and conclusions that all research must manage" by focusing on how people make relevant and deploy continuity, make claims to uniqueness, and enact or claim agency within talk or text, and what they thereby accomplish. The price is the loss of the scientific status of the resulting research, with its attractive assumption that researchers are in the privileged position of telling us why we think we are consistent, when uniqueness matters, and how we enact agency. On the other hand, given the rich possibilities afforded by a conceptualization of aspects of self-identity as an everyday, practical, social concern, this may be a price worth paying.

References

Antaki, C. & Crompton, R. J. (2015). Conversational practices promoting a discourse of agency for adults with intellectual disabilities. *Discourse & Society*, *26*(6), 645–661.

Archer, W. & Parry, R. (2019). Blame attributions and mitigated confessions: The discursive construction of guilty admissions in celebrity TV confessionals. *Discourse & Communication*, *13*(6), 591–611.

Backhaus, P. (2018). Reclaiming agency in resident–staff interaction: A case study from a Japanese eldercare facility. *Discourse Studies*, *20*(2), 205–220.

Bamberg, M. (2010). Blank check for biography? Openness and ingenuity in the management of the "who-am-I" question. In D. Schiffrin, A. De Fina, & A. Nylund (Eds.), *Telling Stories: Language, Narrative, and Social Life* (pp. 109–121). Washington, DC: Georgetown University Press.

Bamberg, M. (2011). Who am I? Narration and its contribution to self and identity. *Theory & Psychology*, *21*(1), 3–24.

Bamberg, M., De Fina, A., & Schiffrin, D. (2011). Discourse and identity construction. In S. J. Schwartz, K. Luyckx, & V. L. Vignoles (Eds.), *Handbook of Identity Theory and Research* (pp. 177–199). New York, NY: Springer.

Brewer, M. B. (1991). The social self: On being the same and different at the same time. *Personality and Social Psychology Bulletin*, *17*(5), 475–482.

Brewer, M. B. & Pickett, C. L. (2014). The social self and group identification. In T. R. Tyler, R. M. Kramer, & O. P. John (Eds.), *The Social Self: Cognitive, Interpersonal and Intergroup Perspectives* (pp. 71–87). Hoboken, NJ: Taylor and Francis Group.

Brooks, S. (2009). Radio food disorder: The conversational constitution of eating disorders in radio phone-ins. *Journal of Community & Applied Social Psychology*, *19*(5), 360–373.

Campbell, J. D., Trapnell, P. D., Heine, S. J., Katz, I. M., Lavallee, L. F., & Lehman, D. R. (1996). Self-concept clarity: Measurement, personality correlates, and cultural boundaries. *Journal of Personality and Social Psychology*, *70*(1), 141–156.

Crocetti, E., Moscatelli, S., Van der Graaff, J., Rubini, M., Meeus, W., & Branje, S. (2016). The interplay of self-certainty and prosocial development in the transition from late adolescence to emerging adulthood. *European Journal of Personality*, *30*(6), 594–607.

Crocetti, E., Rubini, M., & Meeus, W. (2008). Capturing the dynamics of identity formation in various ethnic groups: Development and validation of a three-dimensional model. *Journal of Adolescence, 31*(2), 207–222.

Damen, T. G. E., van Baaren, R. B., Brass, M., Aarts, H., & Dijksterhuis, A. (2015). Put your plan into action: The influence of action plans on agency and responsibility. *Journal of Personality and Social Psychology, 108*(6), 850–866.

Dunlop, W. L., Guo, J., & McAdams, D. P. (2016). The autobiographical author through time: Examining the degree of stability and change in redemptive and contaminated personal narratives. *Social Psychological and Personality Science, 7*(5), 428–436.

Dweck, C. S. (1999). *Self-theories: Their Role in Motivation, Personality and Development.* Philadelphia, PA: Psychology Press.

Dweck, C. S. (2008). Can personality be changed? The role of beliefs in personality and change. *Current Directions in Psychological Science, 17*(6), 391–394.

Dweck, C. S., Chiu, C. Y., & Hong, Y. Y. (1995). Implicit theories and their role in judgments and reactions: A word from two perspectives. *Psychological Inquiry, 6*(4), 267–285.

Edwards, D. (2012). Discursive and scientific psychology. *British Journal of Social Psychology, 51*(3), 425–435.

English, T., & Chen, S. (2011). Self-concept consistency and culture: The differential impact of two forms of consistency. *Personality and Social Psychology Bulletin, 37*(6), 838–849.

Erikson, E. H. (1968). *Identity: Youth and Crisis.* New York, NY: Norton.

Fromkin, H. L. (1970). Effects of experimentally aroused feelings of undistinctiveness upon valuation of scarce and novel experiences. *Journal of Personality and Social Psychology, 16*(3), 521–529.

Hall, D. L., Blanton, H., & Prentice, D. A. (2015). Being much better and no worse than others: Deviance regulation, self-guides, and the motive to be distinct. *Self and Identity, 14*(2), 214–232.

Koenig C. J. (2011). Patient resistance as agency in treatment decisions. *Social Science & Medicine, 72*(7), 1105–1114.

Lodi-Smith, J., Spain, S. M., Cologgi, K., & Roberts, B. W. (2017). Development of identity clarity and content in adulthood. *Journal of Personality and Social Psychology, 112*(5), 755–768.

Lynn, M. & Harris, J. (1997). The desire for unique consumer products: A new individual differences scale. *Psychology & Marketing, 14*(6), 601–616.

Lynn, M. & Snyder, C. R. (2002). Uniqueness seeking. In C. R. Snyder & S. J. Lopez (Eds.), *Handbook of Positive Psychology* (pp. 395–410). Oxford: Oxford University Press.

Nikander, P. (2009). Doing change and continuity: Age identity and the micro–macro divide. *Ageing and Society, 29*(6), 863–881.

Oxford English Dictionary (n.d.). Uniqueness, last accessed October 4, 2020 at www-oed-com.ezproxy.is.ed.ac.uk/view/Entry/214714?redirectedFrom=uniqueness+#eid.

Oyserman, D., Elmore, K., & Smith, G. (2012). Self, self-concept, and identity. In M. R. Leary & J. P. Tangney (Eds.), *Handbook of Self and Identity, 2nd Ed.* (pp. 69–104). New York, NY: Guilford Press.

Rogers, K. H., Wood, D., & Furr, R. M. (2018). Assessment of similarity and self–other agreement in dyadic relationships: A guide to best practices. *Journal of Social and Personal Relationships, 35*(1), 112–134.

Schegloff, E. A. (1968), Sequencing in conversational openings. *American Anthropologist, 70*(6), 1075–1095.

Schwartz, S. J., Klimstra, T. A., Luyckx, K., Hale III, W. W., Frijns, T., Oosterwegel, A., van Lier, P. A. C., Koot, H. M., & Meeus, W. H. J. (2011). Daily dynamics of personal identity and self-concept clarity. *European Journal of Personality, 25*(5), 373–385.

Sengsavang, S., Pratt, M. W., Alisat, S., & Sadler, P. (2018). The life story from age 26 to 32: Rank-order stability and mean-level change. *Journal of Personality, 86*(5), 788–802.

Şimşek, Ö. F. & Yalınçetin, B. (2010). I feel unique, therefore I am: The development and preliminary validation of the personal sense of uniqueness (PSU) scale. *Personality and Individual Differences, 49*(6), 576–581.

Slotter, E. B., Duffy, C. W., & Gardner, W. L. (2014). Balancing the need to be "me" with the need to be "we": Applying optimal distinctiveness theory to the understanding of multiple motives within romantic relationships. *Journal of Experimental Social Psychology, 52*, 71–81.

Snyder, C. R. & Fromkin, H. L. (1977). Abnormality as a positive characteristic: The development and validation of a scale measuring need for uniqueness. *Journal of Abnormal Psychology, 86*(5), 518–527.

Snyder, C. R. & Fromkin, H. L. (1980). *Uniqueness: The Pursuit of Human Difference.* New York, NY: Plenum Press.

Taylor, S. (2012). "One participant said …": The implications of quotations from biographical talk. *Qualitative Research, 12*(4), 388–401.

Taylor, S. (2015). Discursive and psychosocial? Theorising a complex contemporary subject. *Qualitative Research in Psychology, 12*(1), 8–21.

Taylor, S. & Littleton, K. (2006). Biographies in talk: A narrative-discursive research approach. *Qualitative Sociology Review, 2*(1), 22–38.

van Doeselaar, L., Klimstra, T., Denissen, J. J. A., & Meeus, W. H. J. (2019). Distinctiveness as a marker of identity formation. *Journal of Research in Psychology, 78*, 153–164.

Ward, C. L. P. & Wilson, A. E. (2015). Implicit theories of change and stability moderate effects of subjective distance on the remembered self. *Personality and Social Psychology Bulletin, 41*(9),1167–1179.

Wegner, D. M. & Wheatley, T. (1999). Apparent mental causation: Sources of the experience of will. *American Psychologist, 54*(7), 480–492.

Wetherell, M. (1998). Positioning and interpretative repertoires: Conversation analysis and post-structuralism in dialogue. *Discourse & Society, 9*(3), 387–412.

Wetherell, M. (2015). Tears, bubbles and disappointment – New approaches for the analysis of affective-discursive practices: A commentary on "researching the psychosocial." *Qualitative Research in Psychology, 12*(1), 83–90.

Widdicombe, S. & Wooffitt, R. (1995). *The Language of Youth Subcultures: Social Identity in Action.* New York, NY: Harvester Wheatsheaf.

4 The Mystery of Identity: Fundamental Questions, Elusive Answers

Mark Freeman

Despite the wealth of research and scholarship on identity, in psychology, sociology, and beyond, there is no firmly agreed-upon conceptualization of the phenomenon. Indeed, there really is no singular phenomenon: while the psychologist might conceive of identity in terms of a dawning sense of "who one is" emerging during the adolescent years, the sociologist might look toward the broad categories by which one is identified – as male or female, straight or gay, for instance. There is also the memoirist, the historian, the philosopher, and any one of a number of others, all of whom may see their respective undertakings as being in the service of understanding identity. What exactly is one to do in the face of this welter of perspectives?

In order to gain a foothold on what I am here calling the "mystery" of identity, it may be useful, first, to specify what I mean by this elusive term in the context of the present inquiry. In speaking of identity herein, I am speaking of that particular, and particularized, "sense of self" that has at its source the fundamental question "Who am I?" There are, of course, multiple ways of beginning to answer this question. I could turn to basic social indicators, that is, ways in which I might be identified: I am a man. I am white. I am a 64-year-old college professor who writes chapters on identity. (And so forth and so on.) I could also turn to a personality trait inventory or a questionnaire, and thereby see how I fare in relation to others. Finally, for now, I could turn in more microscopic or discursive fashion to the various episodes or conversational exchanges scattered throughout my life and see what kind of identity work is being done, after which time I might, if so inclined, see what they all "add up to," if only for the time being. In the present context, however, I am after something different – something more explicitly *psychological* (in the sense of moving beyond the aforementioned social indicators, experientially relevant though they may be); something more *intra-subjective* (in the sense of encompassing the famous "I–me" relation [James, 1950/1890], wherein "I" take stock of those aspects of my life I consider to be self-defining [Singer, 2004]); and something more *long-range* (in the sense of reflecting the "big story" [Freeman, 2006, 2011] of my life, across the many and varied situations I have lived through across some significant swath of time).

Qualifications are in order for each of these. In referring to the psychological, nothing whatsoever is being said about the *extra*-psychic (social, cultural, historical, etc.) sources of identity (Freeman, 1999, 2002). Indeed, as I have suggested elsewhere, however much there is a felt "my-ness" both to my identity and to the story I tell about the movement of my life, "what is 'mine' is, at one and the same time, permeated by what is 'other,'" which in turn means that "any and all attempts to separate selfhood from its sociocultural surround must fail" (Freeman, 2010a, p. 137). In addressing the mystery of identity, it will therefore be imperative to acknowledge this sociocultural situatedness and also to determine the extent to which it can be made available to reflection.

In referring to the intra-subjective, nothing whatsoever is being said about the inter-subjective sources of identity. However much my own coming to terms with the story of my life is an internal process, there is no separating who I am either from the myriad relationships within which my life takes shape or from the myriad ways in which I am seen by others (Freeman, 2007, 2013b). Along the lines being drawn, "it might plausibly be said that, while the proximal source of one's story is the self, the distal source is the Other" (Freeman, 2014a): other persons, most notably, but also those "objects" outside the perimeter of the self – for instance, nature, art, God – that give form and meaning to my life and identity.

In referring to the long-range dimension of identity, finally, nothing whatsoever has been said about the decidedly shorter-range dimension of identity that is part and parcel of the "small stories" (Bamberg, 2006, 2011; Bamberg & Georgakopoulou, 2008; Georgakopoulou, 2006, 2007) comprising my day-to-day life. Here, I simply wish to note that, however heated the big story/small story debate has sometimes appeared, there is no reason to see these perspectives as fundamentally at odds with one another. On the contrary, they bespeak two distinct temporal "moments" in the formation of identity, each of which speaks, cogently, to the overarching question of who I am (Freeman, 2011, 2015).

Speaking of Bamberg's work, in particular, I have come to find his tripartite framework for understanding identity (Bamberg, 2011; see Bamberg & Dege, this volume) to be useful in framing some of my own ideas. At a most basic level, personal identity brings forth the issue of personal continuity (or lack thereof), that is, the question of what persists across the course of time (see also Widdicombe & Marinho's comments on the related idea of consistency, this volume). In addition, there is the question of one's difference from (or similarity to) others (see Widdicombe & Marinho's comments on uniqueness). Finally, both Bamberg and Widdicombe and Marinho underscore the importance of attending to the question of agency, which Bamberg interestingly refers to in terms of person-to-world and world-to-person "fit"). Bamberg refers to these three dimensions as "dilemmatic territories." One might also think of them as "axes" on which these three dimensions of identity may be placed. Whatever else "I" may be, my continuity in time, my singularity, and my agency (or lack thereof) are constitutive of my distinctive identity.

In some of my own work on narrative identity (Freeman, 2013a, 2013b), I have suggested that there are two additional axes, which I conceptualize as two interrelated "triads," that bear upon identity. Drawing especially on the work of Paul Ricœur (1981, 1991), I referred to the first of these as *spheres of temporality*, suggesting that "narrative identity emerges in and through the interplay of past, present, and future in the form of remembering, acting, and imagining" (Freeman, 2013b, p. 223). Drawing on the work of such varied thinkers as Martin Buber (1965, 1970), Emmanuel Levinas (1985, 1994), and Charles Taylor (1989, 1991), I referred to the second triad as *spheres of otherness*, suggesting that "this temporal interplay is itself interwoven with our relation to other people, to the non-human world and to those moral and ethical 'goods' that serve to orient and direct the course of human lives. By thinking these two triadic spheres together," I offered, "my aim is to arrive at a picture of narrative identity appropriate to the complexities entailed in its formation" (Freeman, 2013b, p. 223).

Taking together Bamberg and Dege's work, Widdicombe and Marinho's, and my own, we have a quite comprehensive multidimensional scheme with which to locate personal identity. We also have a large challenge that bears mentioning at this juncture, and in many respects it lies at the very heart of the "mystery" before us. Here, I am referring to the fact that the process of discerning one's identity – at least in the psychological, intra-subjective, long-range manner being considered – is irrevocably *interpretive*. "Reflection," Ricœur has written, "must become interpretation because I cannot grasp the act of existing except in signs scattered in the world" (1970, p. 46). Following Ricœur, there is no "short-cut" to self-understanding. "There is no direct apprehension of the self by the self, no internal apperception or appropriation of the self's desire to exist through the short-cut of consciousness but only through the long road of the interpretation of signs" (1974, p. 170). So it is that Ricœur came to speak of the "vanity" of the Cartesian *cogito*, partly owing to the primacy of interpretation, but also because of the inevitable "hiddenness" and indeed opacity of much of the inner life, moored as it is in the mischievous machinations of the unconscious. We thus encounter a "wounded *cogito*, which posits but does not possess itself, which understands its originary truth only in and by the confession of the inadequation, the illusion, and the lie of existing consciousness" (1974, p. 173).

These are strong words, indeed, and how significant we take them to be depends in part on how much credence we give to the Freudian view of selfhood, as set forth by Ricœur and others. But there is a more fundamental mystery involved in discerning one's identity, one that is intimately and intricately bound up with the history of the very idea of identity (see especially Izenberg, 2016; also Giddens, 1991; Seigel, 2005). As Gusdorf (1980/1956) points out in his classic essay "Conditions and limits of autobiography," the turning-inward that is involved in the I–me relation itself bespeaks what he refers to as an "involution" of consciousness:

> The truth is that one is wonderstruck by everything else much sooner than by the self. One wonders at what one sees, but one does not see oneself. If exterior space – the stage of the world – is a light, clear space where everyone's behavior, movements, and motives are quite plain on first sight, interior space is shadowy in its very essence. The subject who seizes on himself for object inverts the natural direction of attention; it appears that in acting thus he violates certain secret taboos of human nature ... The image is of another "myself," a double of my being but more fragile and vulnerable, invested with a sacred character that makes it at once fascinating and frightening. Narcissus, contemplating his face in the fountain's depths, is so fascinated with the apparition that he would die bending toward himself. According to most folklore and myth, the apparition of the double is a death sign.   (p. 32)

One significant aspect of the mystery of identity, therefore, is this very self-encounter, bound up as it is with seeking to see that which, strictly speaking, cannot – and perhaps should not – be seen. "Mythic taboos underline the disconcerting character of the discovery of the self. Nature did not see the encounter of man with his reflection, and it is as if she tried to prevent this reflection from appearing" (Gusdorf, 1980/1956, p. 32).

It is true: "You are the only one who can never see yourself except as an image" (Barthes, 1989, p. 36). "One cannot really see one's own exterior," Bakhtin (1986) adds, "and no mirrors or photographs will help." In fact, "our real exterior can be seen and understood only by other people, because they are located outside us and because they are *others*" (p. 7). In encountering our own selves, we must therefore emulate these others in a way, and thereby see "oneself as another" (Ricœur, 1992). The task is a daunting one. But this is only part of the mystery at hand. For, in addition to this epistemological dimension of the mystery, there is the ontological dimension – which is to say, that dimension of our own self-encounter which is always and inevitably suffused with our own "pre-understanding" (Gadamer, 1975, 1976), as well as always and inevitably constrained by both the irreducible heterogeneity and the sheer elusiveness of the interior life. There is no escaping any of this, either. In seeking to come to terms with some aspect of my identity, I bring my language, my storehouse of culturally-fashioned understandings and narrative patterns, and, not least, my current psychological situation, with its sundry wishes and needs, both conscious and unconscious. As for the "text" of my interior life – the particular aspect of Me I am seeking to understand at this particular moment in time – it is itself suffused with all of this prejudicial matter as well. That is because this very text, far from being some "thing" outside of me (like an actual text, sitting on my bookshelf), is something that, in a distinct sense, I myself have created; it is a memorial image, as it were, issuing from the present moment, and will likely be a more or less blurry montage comprising elements of both "then" and "now," firsthand material and secondhand material, memory and fantasy.

Given this positively fraught state of affairs, it might be argued that there is no possibility of arriving at anything even close to an "objective" account of identity; that consequently, any account we come up with can only have subjective validity; and that, in the end, all that really matters is that this account is tolerably acceptable, at least for the time being, and allows us to get on in the world. Isn't this enough?

4.1 Excursus: Coming to Terms with the Mystery

Let me now try to put some flesh on the issues being considered by turning briefly to a recent occasion in which I found myself doing some concentrated identity work. During the course of a bicycle ride I took a while back, I arrived at the realization that I had been living under a cloud for some time. Not surprisingly, I also began to muse about why that might be. What had been going on in my life that may have led me to this state? Then again, was this even the right question to ask? What was the proper time frame for launching my search? I had fallen into this sort of funk before, a number of times, actually. Times like these are reminiscent of the "black moods" my father would sometimes suffer from. Where did *his* come from, though? Were they genetic in some way? Had I gotten some of those genes? Then there was my mother; she herself had a reputation for being a "Pollyanna," but there had been some serious darkness on her side too – a bipolar brother; a nephew, my cousin, who had put a gun to his head (and fired it); another cousin, someone I spent a lot of time with as a kid and whom I searched for once, on an island near Seattle, and couldn't find, only to learn not long after that she too had found the world too much to bear. Could this stuff be in there too? Was I the recipient of some weird genetic double-whammy? Perhaps. Oftentimes, moody phases like the one I just described seem to arrive unbidden. They are often difficult to control too, difficult to move; I just need to wait them out, hope they pass quickly. Perhaps, therefore, they are just part of "who I am." Should I just go with this scenario? It's the easiest option, in a way; I can spare myself the burden of searching further and just get on with it as best I can.

Then again, maybe this wasn't a matter of biology at all. I can remember the deep frustration and anger my father sometimes felt about aspects of his station in life – the job he had as a traveling salesman, the trunk of his car filled with samples, so tedious, all for the sake of making a decent living. (I have a memory of him looking into that trunk and visibly bemoaning his fate.) Boys often identify with their fathers. I had certainly taken on some of his traits, both good and not-so-good. Was this one? Had I somehow "learned" to deal with my own challenges and disappointments in life by unwittingly mimicking his rather dark way of dealing with them? He has been gone more than forty years, though. Was grief involved, unfinished and unfinishable? Speaking of grief, I should also mention that my mother died just a few years ago after a decade or so suffering from dementia. In her final years, she lived in a nursing home right in Worcester, where my family and I live. We saw her often; even when she was barely there, she remained a big part of our life. How did all of this figure in? It didn't make sense to consider her passing the "cause" of my malaise; again, I had gone through comparable phases in the past, before her dementia arrived. But it could certainly be a contributing factor. In fact, it probably had to be. One doesn't just "get over" the death of a parent, especially not in circumstances like this one. Was I still in mourning?

It's certainly possible, but it didn't feel like I was. What else might I look toward to try to get hold of what was going on? Where do I begin? And on what basis can I justify doing so? I could, and perhaps should, go back to the trials and tribulations of childhood. There is no question but that there were some complications back then, but I can't recall what they were with any clarity, and, whatever they were, I don't think they were particularly exceptional. Much of my childhood, in fact, is downright foggy; add up all the minutes I can remember with any vividness at all – up until age seven, say – and there are precious few of them, virtually none of them sharp and clear. Do early experiences, or early phases of experience, "cause" things to emerge later on, in ways unbeknownst to us? Presumably, they do – fraught though the idea of "causation" surely is. But how can we possibly know how? Can we?

As far as I could tell, childhood was probably not the best place for me to explore in this instance in any case. Whatever was going on – if indeed there *was* something going on beyond those more visceral sources referred to earlier – seemed, felt, more recent. I was about to step down as chair of my department. Our oldest daughter would soon be getting married. Our other daughter had landed back at home, after having been away for a spell, and that would no doubt create some significant challenges. Things could sometimes be difficult with my wife. Two of my closest friends had suffered mightily around this time, and I had been alongside them, or had at least tried to be, in whatever way I could. I am finding the professorial life more alienating these days, and I have begun to think about retirement. The wider world – especially the one created by our lunatic president and his sycophantic acolytes – often seems utterly bathed in bizarre and downright bad stuff, surely enough in itself to make one scream or weep. It couldn't be any one of these things – or at least I don't think it could. Was it all of them, conspiring with one another in some sort of unconscious behind-the-scenes psychic stew, their collective weight having fallen upon me? Or was something else altogether going on? (*What?*)

I should also ask: Where are all of these questions coming from? What kind of person asks them? Among other places, they are coming from a modern Western self, the kind of self who asks just these sorts of questions, seeing in the twists and turns of his or her history the surest sources of being (Freeman, 1998;

Weintraub, 1975). Does this mean that, in the end, all we have are sense-making devices – biophysical, psychoanalytic, Eriksonian psychosocial speculations (etc.) – and that, consequently, it's culturally constructed interpretation and narrative "all the way down," pick the one(s) that suit you best?

4.2 Narrative, Identity, and the Problem of Fictionality

There are some versions of narrative knowing that might hold to this idea: the past is what we make it, it might be said, and the force of events can only be gleaned as a function of what one believes. "The significance of autobiography," Gusdorf (1980/1956) writes,

> should therefore be sought beyond truth and falsity, as those are conceived by simple common sense. It is unquestionably a document about a life, and the historian has a perfect right to check out its testimony and verify its accuracy. [But] it is of little consequence that the *Mémoires d'outretombe* should be full of errors, omissions, and lies, and of little consequence also that Chateaubriand made up most of his *Voyage en Amérique*: the recollection of landscapes that he never saw and the description of the traveller's moods nevertheless remain excellent. We may call it fiction or fraud, but its artistic value is real: there is a truth affirmed beyond the fraudulent itinerary and chronology, a truth of the man, images of himself and of the world, reveries of a man of genius, who, for his own enchantment and that of his readers, realizes himself in the unreal.   (p. 43)

For Gusdorf, "The literary, artistic function is thus of greater importance than the historic or objective function in spite of the claims made by positivist criticism both previously and today" (p. 43). The fact is, the person who sets out to answer the "Who am I?" question "does not surrender to a passive contemplation of his private being. The truth is not a hidden treasure, already there, that one can bring out by simply reproducing it as it is." No; discerning the past "realizes itself as a work in the present: it effects a true creation of the self by the self." The implication: "The creative and illuminating nature thus discerned in autobiography suggests a new and more profound sense of truth as an expression of inmost being, a likeness no longer of things but of the person" (p. 44). And this likeness, one can presume, is that which the auto-biographer posits between his or her self-image and the story told; "it does not show us the individual seen from the outside in his visible actions but the person in his inner privacy, not as he was, not as he is, but as he believes and wishes himself to be and have been" (p. 45). Much the same, it might be held, can be said of identity more generally. In the end, it is a self-fashioned self-image; and, like autobiography, its significance should be sought "beyond truth and falsity," as Gusdorf had put it.

This basic mode of thinking about identity has become familiar fare, particularly in those quarters of theory in which the very act of interpreting and narrating oneself is seen to entail an inevitable measure of distortion and falsification. Consider the perspective offered by Michael Gazzaniga in his (1998) book *The Mind's Past*, when he discusses "the illusion of self." According to Gazzaniga,

> Reconstruction of events starts with perception and goes all the way up to human reasoning. The mind is the last to know things. After the brain computes an event, the illusory "we" (that is, the mind) becomes aware of it. The brain, particularly the left hemisphere, is built to interpret data the brain has already processed. Yes, there is a special device in the brain, which I call the *interpreter*, that carries out one more activity upon completion of zillions of automatic brain processes. The interpreter, the last device in the information chain in the brain, reconstructs the brain events and in doing so makes telling errors of perception, memory, and judgment. The clue to how we are built is buried not just in our marvelously robust capacity for these functions, but also in the errors that are frequently made during reconstruction. Biography is fiction. Autobiography is hopelessly inventive.   (p. 2)

Hopelessly. Strange word, that one. What exactly is the role of this "interpreter" about which Gazzaniga speaks? "It is really trying to keep our personal story together." And,

> To do that, we have to learn to lie to ourselves ... We need something that expands the actual facts of our experience into an ongoing narrative, the self-image we have been building in our mind for years. The spin doctoring that goes on keeps us believing that we are good people, that we are in control and mean to do good. It is probably the most amazing mechanism the human being possesses.   (pp. 26–27)

In sum: "The interpreter tells us the lies we need to believe in order to remain in control" (p. 138). As for the conclusion, "Sure, life is a fiction, but it's our fiction and it feels good and we are in charge of it" (p. 172). Putting aside the question of whether these "fictions" always "feel good," what we have in Gazzaniga and others of his ilk is a modern, neuroscientifically inspired version of Gusdorf's thesis, the latter's portrait of the autobiographer spinning yarns in accordance with what "he believes and wishes himself to be and have been" having been transformed into the former's interpreter-based fiction-and-feel-good liar, whose very identity is grounded in "the illusion that we are something other than what we are" (p. 175).

There is, of course, an element of truth to this way of conceptualizing identity: as noted earlier, in seeking to answer the "Who am I?" question, I do not encounter some object in the world, set apart from my own interpretive belonging; I encounter a "me" that, on some level, I myself have fashioned. It therefore stands to reason that some might consider the process "hopelessly inventive," hopelessly mired in my own subjective designs and desires as well as the various cultural narratives from which I inevitably draw as I seek to make sense of my own life. Moreover, it is also true that the narratives I tell about and to myself, whether in the privacy of my own mental home or the public arena of dialogue, are, in part, constitutive of my identity and that this is so irrespective of their truth value. However false Binjamin Wilkormirski's (1996) "memoir" of his childhood in a concentration camp may have been (it turned out that the story of his life was unwittingly based on erroneous assumptions about his origins), there is a very real sense in which he became the subject of his imaginings (Freeman, 2010a). And however much we ourselves may embellish or elevate or flat-out lie about our pasts, these too are partially constitutive of who we see ourselves to be.

Owen Flanagan (1996) has some useful things to say about these issues. On his account, it is important to distinguish two different aims tied to the process of self-representation:

> First, there is self-representation for the sake of self-understanding. The is the story we tell ourselves to understand ourselves for who we are. The ideal here is convergence between self-representation and an acceptable version of the story of our actual identity. Second, there is self-representation for public dissemination, whose aim is underwriting successful social interaction. The two are closely connected. Indeed, the strategic requirements of the sort of self-representation needed for social interaction, together with our tendencies to seek congruence, explain how self-representation intended in the first instance for "my eyes only," and thus, one might think, more likely to remain true, could start to conform to a false projected social image of the self, to a deeply fictional and far-fetched account of the self.   (pp. 68–69)

As Flanagan (1996) goes on to suggest – rightly, I think, if controversially – "Self-represented identity, when it gets things right, has actual identity (or some aspect of it) as its cognitive object." Why controversially? We have already seen some of the difficulties inherent in the idea of "getting things right." In a related vein, it is no simple task to speak of one's "actual identity." One might even ask: *Is* there such a thing? It might be possible to speak of one's actual "personality," i.e., that which might be measured or observed by others in some sort of "objective" way. But insofar as my identity is *mine*, it is not entirely clear whether a comparable move can be made. In the end, again, aren't I just whatever I make myself out to be, however distorted and deranged my own self-representation may be? Isn't this notion of self-making (Bruner, 1987, 1991) ultimately what identity, especially "narrative identity" (McAdams & McLean, 2013; Ricœur, 1992; Singer, 2004), is all about?

The answer is clear: Yes and no. As already noted, the narratives I tell about and to myself are, in part, constitutive of my identity. This is true, Flanagan (1996) tells us, in two senses:

> First, even considered as a purely cognitive activity, self-representation involves the activation of certain mental representations and cognitive structures. Once self-representation becomes an ongoing activity, it realigns and recasts the representations and structures already in place. Second, the self as represented has motivational bearing and cognitive effects. Often,

this motivational bearing is congruent with motivational tendencies that the entire system already has. Sometimes, [however], especially in cases of severe self-deception, the self projected for both public and first-person consumption may be strangely and transparently out of kilter with what the agent is like. In such cases, the self as represented is linked with the activity of self-representation but with little else in the person's psychological and behavioral economy. Nonetheless, such misguided self-representation helps constitute ... the misguided person's actual full identity.   (p. 69)

Has the aforementioned dilemma been resolved? Not yet. As Flanagan (1996) himself acknowledges,

To conceive of the self as a fiction seems right for four reasons: it is an open-ended construction; it is filled with vast indeterminate spaces, and a host of tentative hypotheses about what I am like, that can be filled out and revised post facto; it is pinned on culturally relative narrative hooks; and it expresses ideals of what one wishes to be but is not yet.   (pp. 72–73)

At the same time, he quickly adds, the self-as-fiction idea is "misleading" too. For one,

The author of a true piece of fiction has many more degrees of freedom in creating her characters than we have in spinning the tales of our selves ... There are, after all, the things we have done, what we have been through as embodied social beings, and the characteristic dispositions we reveal in social life.   (p. 73)

As such, "Third parties will catch us if we take our story too far afield." And, if we are truly forthright in our self-encounters, "We may also catch ourselves." In short: "There are selection pressures," as Flanagan calls them, "to keep the story one reveals to oneself and to others in some sort of harmony with the way one is living one's life." Secondly, "some people ... are massively self-deceived." And, "self-deception only makes sense if selves are not totally fictive, that is, only if there are some facts constraining what is permitted in our self-narrative. So real selves are fictional to a point. But they are less fictional than fictional selves because they are more answerable to the facts. The self," therefore, "can be a construct or model, a 'center of narrative gravity,' a way of self-representation, without being a fiction in the problematic sense" (p. 73).

One could quibble with Flanagan's reference to "the facts." One could also quibble with his recourse to the language of "representation." But let us not quibble. Instead, let us dive deeper into the dilemma before us. On the one hand, insofar as the self is an "open-ended construction, ... filled with vast indeterminate spaces, and a host of tentative hypotheses about what I am like, that can be filled out and revised post facto," and is also "pinned on culturally relative narrative hooks," expressing "ideals of what one wishes to be but is not yet," we would appear to be far (far) away from considering the "truth" of identity as anything but an (utterly) subjective one. On the other hand, however, we are, on Flanagan's account, "constrained" by the fleshy particulars of our lives, and it is patently clear that, even if there is no promised identity-land of unvarnished truth, there is an all too vast landscape of falsity, self-deception, which, in turn, would seem to imply that there must also be a condition of *un*-self-deception – a "region" of truth, as one might call it (Freeman, 2010b).

The narratives we tell about ourselves, and to ourselves, are extremely important, to be sure. They are indeed constitutive of who and what we are, formative of our very identities. This is precisely why it might be argued that who and what I am, as a self, is what I take myself narratively to be. But we – or at least I – cannot rest comfortably with this position. In what follows, therefore, I want to restore the mystery of identity – the kind of mystery that characterized my own earlier attempt to come to terms with that puzzling funk I was in. And I want to do so not just because I have a thing for the unknowable but because I think it is a more truthful rendition of the situation at hand.

It's not that I can't tell a story about this phase of my life, or at least certain aspects of it. I also think that some insights, even truths, might issue from the process. But more and more, I have come to see just how fragile this process is. I have also come to see what a profound challenge it is to discern who and what we are and how we might have become that. Alongside the narrative we might consciously bring to mind based on what we know and believe about our past, there is another, deeper narrative – or would-be narrative, tied to unspeakable events like fathers' early deaths, or "spectacular" (as the newspaper put it) car crashes like the one I was in at age 17, or loves gone south – not to mention, of course, all of the Freudian dark matter circulating through the nether reaches of our childhoods, resonating in ways we might barely acknowledge, if at all.

I don't mean to suggest that only negative or painful experiences are the ones with lasting but difficult-to-discern consequences. There are positive ones too, and ordinary ones that happen our way during the course of a day or month or year. These, too, seep into the psychical bloodstream, in ways largely unbeknownst to us. There is no reconstructing them in any definite way, no charting them. In addition, there are dimensions of our lives that are rooted in history and culture and are part of the deep, largely unconscious backdrop of being. So it is that I have written elsewhere of the "narrative unconscious" (Freeman, 2002, 2010b), by which I mean those culturally rooted aspects of our histories that have yet to become – and may never become – an explicit part of our stories. There is thus no "solving" the mystery of identity. All we can do is interpret and narrate. But how?

4.3 Erosion and Creation

The novelist Karl Ove Knausgaard addresses this very question in his little book *Inadvertent* (2018). "We live in an ocean of time," he writes, where events, things, and people are continually succeeding one another, but we cannot live with such boundless complexity, because we disappear in it, and therefore we organize it into categories, sequences, hierarchies. We organize ourselves – I am not nameless, my name is such and such, my parents were like this and that, I went to school in such and such a place, I experienced this and that, by character I am like this and like that, and that has caused me to choose this and that. And we organize our surroundings – we don't just live on a plain with some grass, bushes, roads, and houses, we live in a particular place in a particular country with a particular culture, and we belong to a particular stratum within that culture.

All of us sum up our lives in this way, that is what we call identity; and we sum up the world we inhabit in similar ways, that is what is called culture. What we are saying about ourselves fits, but no more than if we had said something entirely different, thought something entirely different about ourselves and our place in the world – if, for example, we had lived during the Middle Ages and not in the early twenty-first century – and it too would have fit and seemed meaningful.   (pp. 10–11)

What is the implication here? One implication is that the "fit" between our identity and our understanding of the world is, on some level, "arbitrary." I don't think Knausgaard is right about this. That the kind of story I tell myself now couldn't have been told in the Middle Ages is surely so. But that doesn't make it arbitrary. On the contrary, this story has a kind of necessity, tied to the lifeworld I have come to inhabit, the kinds of selves that are born into this world, and the kinds of understandings, and misunderstandings, that circulate through it.

This is where the interpretive challenge begins. For Knausgaard, it is also where *writing* begins. The reason is "that literature by its very nature always seeks complexity and ambiguity" and thereby rejects "monologic claims of truth about the world" (p. 11) – including, especially, the world of identity. The point is an important one. If Knausgaard is right, the most appropriate inroad into discerning our own identity, in all of its mystery and multiplicity, is through literature, literary *poiesis* – and, I would add, those other modes of *poiesis* found throughout the various arts (Freeman, 2018, 2020).

The challenge at hand is a massive one – one, in fact, that cannot ever fully be met. For, even amidst the inevitable cultural-historical situatedness and saturatedness that characterizes the stories we tell about ourselves, it is imperative, still, to find language that, on some level, transcends this very condition. "Writing," Knausgaard asserts, "is precisely about disregarding how something seems in the eyes of others, it is precisely about freeing oneself from all kinds of judgments and from posturing and positioning. Writing is about making something accessible, allowing something to reveal itself" (p. 27). "Thoughts," therefore – or at least those thoughts that are rooted in these conventionalized judgments – "are the enemy of the inadvertent, for if one thinks about how something will seem to others" – or, I would add, to *oneself* – "if one thinks about whether something is important or good enough, if one begins to calculate and to pretend, then it is no longer inadvertent and accessible as itself, but only as what we have made it into" (p. 28).

Knausgaard adopts something of a "method" to counteract all this – a method in which

> I simply wouldn't have time to think, to plan or to calculate, I would have to go with whatever appeared on the screen in front of me. This method came about because I had set out to write about myself, and since we know more about ourselves than about any other subject, it seemed important to avoid the established versions and to seek instead the complexity that lies beneath our self-insight and self-image and which can be accessed only by not thinking about how our thoughts and feelings will seem to others, how it will look, who I am if I think and feel these things.
>
>   This form made it possible to see how closely interwoven the "I" is with the "we," how language, culture, and our collective notions course through us, how common even our most secret and solitary emotions are. I hadn't realized that before, nor did I expect to as I set out to write these books, for then my idea was to write about the most private of matters, that which was only my own, while what the form I had chosen enabled me to say turned out in the end to be the very opposite.   (pp. 37–38)

The ultimate goal: "to erode my own notions about the world, allowing whatever had been kept down by them to rise to the surface. The only way I could accomplish this was to abdicate as king of myself and let the literary, in other words writing and the forms of writing, lead the way" (pp. 38–39). Hence the importance of the idea of the inadvertent:

> I have to hit upon it inadvertently, or it has to hit upon me. It is one thing to know something, another to write about it, and often knowing stands in the way of writing. *Make it new*, Ezra Pound said—and is there any other way to do that than to let everything we know about something fall away and regard it from a position of defenselessness and unknowing?   (p. 40)

Following Knausgaard in broad line, it would appear that we have before us both a large challenge and a quite radical opportunity to rethink and reimagine the project of exploring and discerning identity. On his account, who and what we are is inevitably bathed in obscurity, partly because our own "notions about the world" cannot help but constrain our capacity to discern what is really there, and partly because our own defensive, ego-driven designs cannot help but intrude on our own capacity to truly know ourselves. We therefore arrive at what may appear to be a very odd premise for an inquiry into identity: in order to fathom the mystery of identity, it is imperative that we "unself" ourselves, as Iris Murdoch (1970) might put it, in such a way as to allow whatever we may have "kept down," whether wittingly or unwittingly, to "rise to the surface." What's more, the most appropriate vehicle for doing so, on this account, is *literature*, art-ful writing that seeks to disclose or "unconceal" (Heidegger, 1971) that in ourselves which had heretofore been obscured or opaque. Those adhering to a more traditionally science-based view of inquiry into identity may find this perspective entirely too imprecise, unwieldy, subjective. But it may be that moving toward this more art-ful rendition of things bears within it a view of identity more adequate to the human condition, in all of its messy mystery.

4.4 Unknowing Identity

Let me briefly review the territory we have covered thus far in the form of three large, interrelated ideas.

First, while the stories we tell about ourselves, and to ourselves, are not arbitrary, the process of telling these stories is, as I put it earlier, extremely "fragile," in the sense of being highly susceptible to conventionalized under-standings. This susceptibility is all but inevitable. As Ernst Schachtel (1959) has stated,

> In the course of later childhood, adolescence, and adult life, perception and experience ... develop increasingly into the rubber stamps of conventional clichés. The capacity to see and feel what is there gives way to the tendency to see and feel what one expects to see and feel, which, in turn, is what one is expected to see and feel because everybody else does. Experience increasingly assumes the form of the cliché under which it will be recalled because this cliché is what conventionally is remembered by others.   (p. 288)

The same is true of memory, which "is even more governed by conventional patterns than are perception and experience" (p. 291). And, most important for present purposes, the same is true of the stories we might ultimately tell about our lives. Along these lines, Schachtel, not unlike Knausgaard, notes that "the greatest problem of the writer or the poet" – or the person seeking to discern his or her identity – "is the temptation of language. At every step a word beckons, it seems so convenient, so suitable, one has heard or read it so often in a similar context" – an already *known* context. It is imperative, therefore, "to fight constantly against the easy flow of words that offer themselves" and to thus enter the unknown. Ultimately, Schachtel acknow-ledges, there is no way to fully move beyond the culturally, and linguistically, articulated world we inhabit. "Like the search for truth, which never reaches its goal yet never can be abandoned, the endeavor to articulate, express, and communicate an experience can never succeed completely" (p. 296). And yet, one must move in this direction as best one can. Following Knausgaard and Schachtel, the first and perhaps most basic challenge of exploring and discern-ing identity is precisely to find language that somehow counteracts our sus-ceptibility to those narrative identity scripts and schemes that inevitably "beckon" us, luring us into the too-comfortable confines of predigested modes of thinking, feeling, and writing. It is a tall order, indeed.

Second, the stories we tell about ourselves, and to ourselves, are also susceptible to the consolations, and, at times, outright illusions, of consciousness, of rational "understanding." And by virtue of this rationalizing process, aiming as it does toward comprehension, grasping, our deeper corridors are, to a greater or lesser extent, occluded. They thus warrant hermeneutic "suspicion" (Ricœur, 1970, 1974), and call for strategies of laying bare, or at least more bare, these deeper corridors. Having said this, we ought not operate under the further illusion that we can reach transparency. There *is* no making the unconscious conscious – not fully, at any rate. The mystery, the irreducible mystery, thus remains. Freud seemed to recognize this too. There is a wonderful little passage in *The Interpretation of Dreams* (1953/1900) in which he says as much when he writes,

> There is often a passage in even the most thoroughly interpreted dream which has to be left obscure; this is because we become aware during the work of interpretation that at that point there is a tangle of dream-thoughts which cannot be unraveled and which moreover adds nothing to our knowledge of the content of the dream. This is the dream's navel, the spot where it reaches down into the unknown.   (p. 525)

This is quite remarkable, especially given Freud's penchant for using the more explanatory language of archeology. Interpretation – narrative interpretation – is inevitable, unsurpassable. He is only talking about dream interpretation here. But this idea goes well beyond the domain of dreams. Our origins, in their vast multiplicity, reach down into the unknown. And strictly speaking, there is no getting to them, no means by which we can reach the rock bottom of transparent understanding. This is not to be seen as some sort of interpretive "failure," however. On the contrary, it is simply an avowal of what might be termed "hermeneutic humility," a willingness to say the words, "I don't know."

I am reminded here of the poet Wisława Szymborska's Nobel Lecture from 1996, "The Poet and the World," when she discusses the idea of inspiration. "Whatever inspiration is," she writes, "it's born from a continuous 'I don't know.'" Poets, in particular, must keep repeating this commitment. "Each poem marks an effort to answer this statement, but as soon as the final period hits the page, the poet begins to hesitate, starts to realize that this particular answer was pure makeshift that's absolutely inadequate to boot." For this reason, Szymborska concludes, "It looks like poets will always have their work cut out for them." And so too for those of us seeking to plumb the depths of identity.

None of this means that we can't, or shouldn't, try to make psychological sense of our lives. What it does mean is that we might do more recognize what I am here calling the mystery of identity. Too often, in psychology and the other social sciences, we have tried to erase this mystery, or at least subdue it. But in the end, it really can't be done. And this, far from being a matter of failure, instead underscores what an incredible challenge, and privilege, it is to begin to fathom who and what we are and how we might have gotten that way.

Third, for Szymborska, along with Knausgaard, the process of writing – artful writing, what I earlier referred to as *poiesis* – is key. This doesn't mean writing that's filled with adornment and literary flourish. Rather, it means writing that is non-monologic and that "allows something to reveal itself," as Knausgaard had put it. This idea has informed much of my recent work on what I call "a poetics of the Other" (Freeman, 2007, 2019). For years, I tried to formulate a more capacious and expansive conception of psychological science, my assumption being that, for political reasons especially, I had to stay within the confines of the scientific game. I therefore conjured up oxymoronic ideas like "poetic science" (Freeman, 2011, 2014b). That idea still has its place. More and more, however, I have come to think that the scientific project, when brought to the deeper reaches of the human realm, is misconceived and that, consequently, a radical shift – a "post-scientific" shift, as I recently put it (Freeman, 2019) – is called for. In this respect, poetically inspired writing about identity and about the human condition more generally ought to be considered primary, foundational even, in the sense of coming *before* the various rationalizing schemes social scientists, especially, tend to foist onto experience.

Heidegger's (1977) essay "Science and reflection" speaks cogently to this idea. "Regarded in terms of its essence," he writes, "the reality within which man of today moves and attempts to maintain himself is, with regard to its fundamental characteristics, determined on an increasing scale by and in conjunction with that which we call Western European science" (p. 156). Put (too) simply, reality essentially became coextensive with the factual, with that which could be secured and encapsulated through scientific knowing. According to Heidegger, this represented a severe constriction and diminution of the very idea of reality. The result is that the "more primordially fundamental characteristic" (p. 163) – out of which the factually real stands forth, becoming available for observation and manipulation – progressively becomes relegated to the background of things. And so, to make a long story short, the very ground out of which there emerges the "objectness" of reality – the kind of objectness so near and dear to much social science – becomes obscured. Marilynne Robinson (2012) puts the matter simply and well: "We live on a little island of the articulable, which we tend to mistake for reality itself" (p. 21). The challenge is thus to move off this little island and to thereby encounter reality in its fuller measure.

Gabriel Marcel's (1950) distinction "presence" and "object" may be helpful in this context. As he explains,

> [W]hen we say that a presence must not be thought of as an object, we mean that the very act by which we incline ourselves towards a presence is essentially different from that through which we grasp at any object; in the case of a presence, the very possibility of grasping at, of seizing, is excluded in principle.   (p. 255)

Grasping is something that *I* do. In the case of presence – including that specific form of it where "I" encounter "me" – something quite different happens: "a presence is something which can only be gathered to oneself or shut out from oneself, be welcomed or rebuffed" (p. 255) – in short, allowed to reveal itself. Moreover, "In so far as a presence, as such, lies beyond the grasp of any possible prehension, one might say that it also in some sense lies beyond the grasp of any possible comprehension" (p. 256). We are therefore talking here about a different kind of knowing, one which is not a grasping but is instead a kind of *unknowing*, as Knausgaard had put it. This unknowing, I want to suggest, is critical to the project of exploring and discerning identity.

4.5 Coda: In the Aftermath

So, what was that funk I was in? I have some ideas. And with time and distance, I may have more. Finally, however, *I don't know*. And strictly speaking, I *can't* know. Instead, I need to "erode my own notions about the world," as Knausgaard put it, and see what emerges. This, we have seen, means "[abdicating] as king of myself" – unselfing – and "[letting] the literary, in other words writing and the forms of writing, lead the way." But what exactly does this mean? And is there anything that might be done, by way of an interpretive "strategy" of some sort, to gain some traction into addressing the mystery of identity?

Using my own aforementioned experience as an example, I might have followed Bamberg and Dege's or Widdicombe and Marinho's leads and looked toward issues of the interplay of continuity/consistency, difference/ uniqueness, and agency to gain some headway into the problem at hand. In addition, following the ideas introduced earlier regarding what I called "spheres of temporality" and "spheres of otherness," I might have looked toward the interplay of my past, present, and future. All were surely operative in some way; the challenge was to gather some sense of how – how, for instance, my childhood might have entered the picture, or the current circumstances of my life, or my images of, and plans for, the future. I also might have looked toward the relational sphere – for instance, the deaths of my parents, or the changing realities of family and friends and colleagues, or, more fundamentally, my changing sense of what's most real and significant. I actually did a variant of both of these inquiries at the time; I took a kind of inventory of these two spheres to see what I might learn. But I might have done so more methodically, systematically, in the hope of arriving at a picture of my own identity "appropriate to the complexities entailed in its formation," as I put it earlier.

Even with this more methodical approach, however, I would not, and could not, have arrived at clear and clean answers to the questions I might have posed – especially the overarching question: Who am I? One reason, again, is that my identity, rather than being an object in the world, may be better understood as a kind of "presence," as Marcel had put it, an ungraspable reality calling for a different mode of apprehension than objects permit. But even this may not be quite right. The reason, as we noted earlier, is that, strictly speaking, when "I" encounter "me," there is nothing truly *there* – save the somewhat gauzy, ethereal, boundary-less image I myself fashion as I seek to come to terms with this or that aspect of my life. It is precisely this element of self-fashioning that brought with it the idea that, in the end, we are what we make of ourselves. Partially true though this idea may be, it isn't quite right either. If there is anything to be learned from that brief psychological excursion we went on a while back, it is that "[W]e do not make ourselves. We cannot remake ourselves through memory." Ultimately, therefore, "We are not self-constituting beings. We are constituted through the vast movement of history, of which we are the largely quiescent effects … Symptoms of a millennia-long malaise whose cause escapes us." Indeed, "Memory theater," as Simon Critchley (2015) calls it,

> cannot be reduced to my memory, but has to reach down into the deep immemorial strata that contain the latent collective energy of the past. The dead who still fill the air with their cries. The memory theater would have to immerse itself in the monumentally forgotten. Like a dredging machine descending down through the lethic waters of the contemporary world into the sand, silt, and sludge of the sedimented past.   (p. 83)

If we are to speak of "presence," therefore, it is a ghostly one at best, an absent presence, as it were, something that is at once eminently real and yet wholly ungraspable.

That psychologists, among others, have sought to "contain" identity in one way or another stands to reason; it is important, at times, to get hold of what we can. But it is equally important, I think, to recognize and avow the existence of phenomena that resist this getting-hold and that therefore require something else, something better suited to the phenomena in question. In the case of identity, as we have come to understand it, this something, I have suggested, is literature, broadly conceived. In offering this perspective, I make no claims at all about the coherence or continuity of identity. Nor, in turn, would I want to specify what form of literature is required. Some identities may lend themselves to comparatively smooth beginning-middle-end tales; others, to more modern or postmodern forms; others still, perhaps, to the free verse of poetry. It all depends on the questions one asks, the person doing the questioning, and, not least, the "vast movement of history" that precedes us, uncontainable and unnameable though it is. Whatever else identity may be, it remains something of a mystery. Rather than this being cause for despair, however, it is cause for celebration – quiet celebration, founded in the unending inspiration of what we do not and cannot know about our own deepest strata.

References

Bakhtin, M. M. (1986). *Speech Genres and Other Late Essays*. Austin, TX: University of Texas Press.

Bamberg, M. (2006). Stories: Big or small – Why do we care? *Narrative Inquiry, 16*, 139–147.

Bamberg, M. (2011). Who am I? Narration and its contribution to self and identity. *Theory & Psychology, 21*(1), 3–24.

Bamberg, M. & Georgakopoulou, A. (2008). Small stories as a new perspective in narrative and identity analysis. *Text & Talk, 28*, 377–396.

Barthes, R. (1989). *Roland Barthes*. New York, NY: Noonday Press.

Bruner, J. (1987). Life as narrative. *Social Research, 54*, 11–32.

Bruner, J. (1991). Self-making and world-making. *Journal of Aesthetic Education, 25*, 67–78.

Buber, M. (1965). *Between Man and Man*. New York, NY: Macmillan.

Buber, M. (1970). *I and Thou*. New York, NY: Charles Scribner's and Sons.

Critchley, S. (2015). *Memory Theater*. New York, NY: Other Press.

Flanagan, O. (1996). *Self Expressions: Mind, Morals, and the Meaning of Life*. New York, NY: Oxford University Press.

Freeman, M. (1998). Mythical time, historical time, and the narrative fabric of the self. *Narrative Inquiry, 8*, 27–50.

Freeman, M. (1999). Culture, narrative, and the poetic construction of selfhood. *Journal of Constructivist Psychology, 12*, 99–116.

Freeman, M. (2002). Charting the narrative unconscious: Cultural memory and the challenge of autobiography. *Narrative Inquiry, 12*, 193–211.

Freeman, M. (2006). Life "on holiday"? In defense of big stories. *Narrative Inquiry, 16*, 131–138.

Freeman, M. (2007). Narrative and relation: The place of the Other in the story of the self. In R. Josselson, A. Lieblich, & D. McAdams (Eds.), *The Meaning of Others: Narrative Studies of Relationships* (pp. 11–19). Washington, DC: APA Books.

Freeman, M. (2010a). The space of selfhood: Culture, narrative, identity. In S. R. Kirschner & J. Martin (Eds.), *The Sociocultural Turn: The Contextual Emergence of Mind and Self* (pp. 137–158). New York, NY: Columbia University Press.

Freeman, M. (2010b). *Hindsight: The Promise and Peril of Looking Backward*. New York, NY: Oxford University Press.

Freeman, M. (2011). Stories, big and small: Toward a synthesis. *Theory & Psychology, 21*, 114–121.

Freeman, M. (2013a). Axes of identity: Persona, perspective, and the meaning of (Keith Richards's) *Life*. In C. Holler & M. Klepper (Eds.), *Rethinking Narrative Identity: Persona and Perspective* (pp. 49–68). Amsterdam: John Benjamins.

Freeman, M. (2013b). Storied persons: The "double triad" of narrative identity. In J. Martin & M. H. Bickhard (Eds.), *Contemporary Perspectives in the Psychology of Personhood: Philosophical, Historical, Psychological, and Narrative* (pp. 223–241). Cambridge: Cambridge University Press.

Freeman, M. (2014a). *The Priority of the Other: Thinking and Living beyond the Self*. New York, NY: Oxford University Press.

Freeman, M. (2014b). Qualitative inquiry and the self-realization of psychological science. *Qualitative Inquiry*, *20*, 119–126.

Freeman, M. (2015). Discerning oneself: A plea for the whole. In K. C. McLean & M. Syed (Eds.), *The Oxford Handbook of Identity Development* (pp. 182–191). New York, NY: Oxford University Press.

Freeman, M. (2018). Living in verse: Sites of the poetic imagination. In O. V. Lehmann, N. Chaudhary, A. C. Bastos, & E. Abbey (Eds.), *Poetry and Imagined Worlds* (pp. 139–154). London: Palgrave Macmillan.

Freeman, M. (2019). Toward a poetics of the Other: New directions in post-scientific psychology. In T. Teo (Ed.), *Re-envisioning Theoretical Psychology: Diverging Ideas and Practices* (pp. 1–24). London: Palgrave Macmillan.

Freeman, M. (2020). Psychology as literature. Narrative knowing and the project of the psychological humanities. In J. Sugarman & J. Martin (Eds.), *A Humanities Approach to the Psychology of Personhood* (pp. 30–48). London: Routledge.

Freud, S. (1953/1900). *The Interpretation of Dreams. Standard Edition, Vols. 4 & 5*. London: Hogarth.

Gadamer, H.-G. (1975). *Truth and Method*. New York, NY: Crossroad.

Gadamer, H.-G. (1976). *Philosophical Hermeneutics*. Berkeley, CA: University of California Press.

Gazzaniga, M. S. (1998). *The Mind's Past*. Berkeley, CA: University of California Press.

Georgakopoulou, A. (2006). Thinking big with small narrative and identity analysis. *Narrative Inquiry*, *16*, 129–137.

Georgakopoulou, A. (2007). *Small Stories, Interaction and Identities*. Amsterdam: John Benjamins.

Giddens, A. (1991). *Modernity and Self-identity: Self and Society in the Late Modern Age*. Stanford, CA: Stanford University Press.

Gusdorf, G. (1980/1956). Conditions and limits of autobiography. In J. Olney (Ed.), *Autobiography: Essays Theoretical and Critical* (pp. 28–48). Princeton, NJ: Princeton University Press.

Heidegger, M. (1971). *Poetry, Language, Thought*. New York, NY: Harper Colophon.

Heidegger, M. (1977). *The Question Concerning Technology and Other Essays*. New York, NY: Harper Torchbooks.

Izenberg, G. (2016). *Identity: The Necessity of a Modern Idea*. Philadelphia, PA: University of Pennsylvania Press.

James, W. (1950/1890). *The Principles of Psychology, Volume One*. New York, NY: Dover.

Knausgaard, K. O. (2018). *Inadvertent*. New Haven, CT: Yale University Press.

Levinas, E. (1985). *Ethics and Infinity*. Pittsburgh, PA: Duquesne University Press.

Levinas, E. (1994). *Outside the Subject*. Palo Alto, CA: Stanford University Press.

Marcel, G. (1950). *The Mystery of Being, Vol. 1: Reflection and Mystery*. Chicago, IL: Henry Regnery.

McAdams, D. P. & McLean, K. C. (2013). Narrative identity. *Current Directions in Psychological Science*, *22*, 233–238.

Murdoch, I. (1970). *The Sovereignty of Good*. London: Routledge.

Ricœur, P. (1970). *Freud and Philosophy: An Essay on Interpretation*. New Haven, CT: Yale University Press.

Ricœur, P. (1974). *The Conflict of Interpretations*. Evanston, IL: Northwestern University Press.

Ricœur, P. (1981). Narrative time. In W. J. T. Mitchell (Ed.), *On Narrative* (pp. 165–186). Chicago, IL: University of Chicago Press.

Ricœur, P. (1991). Life in quest of narrative. In D. Wood (Ed.), *On Paul Ricœur: Narrative and Interpretation* (pp. 20–33). London: Routledge.

Ricœur, P. (1992). *Oneself as Another*. Chicago, IL: University of Chicago Press.

Robinson, M. (2012). *When I Was a Child, I Read Books*. New York, NY: Picador.

Schachtel, E. G. (1959). *Metamorphosis: On the Conflict of Human Development and the Problem of Creativity*. New York, NY: Basic Books.

Seigel, J. (2005). *The Idea of the Self: Thought and Experience in Western Europe since the Seventeenth Century*. Cambridge: Cambridge University Press.

Singer, J. A. (2004). Narrative identity and meaning-making across the adult lifespan: An introduction. *Journal of Personality*, *72*, 437–459.

Szymborska, W. (1996). The poet and the world (Nobel Lecture), last accessed April 13, 2021 at www.nobelprize.org/prizes/literature/1996/szymborska/lecture/.

Taylor, C. (1989). *Sources of the Self: The Making of the Modern Identity*. Cambridge, MA: Harvard University Press.

Taylor, C. (1991). *The Ethics of Authenticity*. Cambridge, MA: Harvard University Press.

Weintraub, K. (1975). Autobiography and historical consciousness. *Critical Inquiry*, *1*, 821–848.

Wilkormirski, B. (1996). *Fragments: Memories of a Wartime Childhood*. New York, NY: Schocken.

PART II

New Perspectives and Challenges

5 A Moral Perspective: Identity as Self-Interpretation

Svend Brinkmann

There is a significant tradition in philosophy of conceiving of human identity in ethical or moral terms.[1] To be someone – to have an identity – is from this perspective to be committed to certain values and goods without which one would not be the same person. This way of thinking goes back to the ancient Greeks, and it was rejuvenated in the twentieth century by philosophers and psychologists who rehabilitated the notion of virtue ethics (most centrally MacIntyre, 1985).

In this chapter, I shall articulate this tradition by first tracing its historical background and then arguing that a hermeneutic idea of identity as self-interpretation is a useful starting point for moral approaches to identity. In this light, identity is a task of continuously interpreting oneself in light of values and moral commitments.

In the main sections of the chapter, I argue that identity as self-interpretation has two dimensions, which I refer to as morality and narrative, respectively. These should not be understood as opposite poles, but rather as mutually connected dimensions: The moral dimension in our lives typically finds expression through narratives, and life narratives are almost always saturated with morality. I draw on the work of Charles Taylor specifically to argue that human self-interpretation necessarily takes place within inescapable frameworks of ethical values, and I also refer to the virtue ethics of Alasdair MacIntyre and the hermeneutic philosophy of Paul Ricœur, the latter stressing how the commitment to an identity project of "self-constancy" is a necessary condition for the realization of ethical values in our lives.

Finally, I discuss how a contemporary consumer society in fragments now challenges human moral identity, when it focuses more on subjective self-realization than on normative values, and I refer to sociologists such as Hartmut Rosa and Axel Honneth to back this claim. In short, my goal is to approach identity as moral self-interpretation by showing that it implies both

---

[1] I use the terms "ethical" and "moral" interchangeably here. "Ethics" comes from the Greek *ethos* (character) and "morality" from the Latin *mores* (which also means character, custom, or habit). It is immensely difficult to provide a precise definition of these terms, but I use them to refer to *the oughtness of life*, i.e., to the idea that human life is not just one factual state of affair after another, but centrally involves nonarbitrary and nonconventional normative demands (to act, think, feel, and be in required ways).

morality and narrative and is never purely individual, but intertwined with various layers of society.

5.1 Historical Background

The concept of identity has not always been central to human self-understanding. This, however, does not mean that individuals were without resources for self-interpretation in earlier times. When recorded human history began – in the imagined hemisphere of the West, with the Greeks – the key concept was character rather than identity (Brinkmann, 2010). In the writings of Aristotle (1976), for example, the goal of human life is to flourish (*eudaimonia*) by acquiring the virtues (*arēte*) that enable individuals to engage in activities that are intrinsically valuable. Such activities include ethics, politics, and philosophical contemplation. Aristotle's ethics was thus centered on character, since one had to develop a virtuous character in order to realize the proper life for human beings. Simply put, the goal was not a modern one of realizing one's unique potentials as an individual, but rather to perfect the character that enables one to realize a virtuous form of human life.

Not just the Greek culture of honor and virtue emphasized character, but also early Christianity functioned along these lines. The questions that framed people's subjectivities were "Who are *you*?", addressing God as the great Other, and "How can I build the character that enables me to obey your command?" In order to understand oneself as a subject and interpret one's own life, the person should understand the purposes and meanings that God had cast unto the universe. Life was lived within the confines of an *ontic logos* (Taylor, 1989), a meaningful cosmic order, which defined the direction of a meaningful life.

Later with modernity, related to the rise of capitalism, urbanization, industrialization, and individualism, the question of individuality shifted from one of character to one of personality. A key existential question became: "What am I?", following the birth of the individual as an agent with discrete, measurable properties. One could now be understood, and understand oneself, as an individual in relative isolation from larger social and cosmological contexts. New psychological practices concerned with measurements of individuals' characteristics emerged, and also a romantic ethos of individualist expressionism (Berlin, 1999) supported the personality-oriented self-interpretation. Psychology was born as a science and a set of practices that took an interest in individual differences concerning personality, which became important in the industry, mass education systems, and the military (Rose, 1999).

Finally, in a postmodern consumer culture, the central question of subjectivity became "Who am I?", concerned not so much with discrete personal(ity) characteristics as with finding one's place in fluid, changing communities and subcultures. This paved the way for the notion of identity, especially after World War II and the rise of countercultures from the late 1960s onwards. Perhaps 1968 can be singled out as the (mythological) year of emancipation of identities, witnessing both the many cultural revolutions that were to set identities free across the West and also the publication of Erik Erikson's (1968) seminal *Identity: Youth and crisis.* To the extent that we today live what Zygmunt Bauman has called "the consuming life," we live a life that "is not about acquiring and possessing ... It is instead, first and foremost, about being on the move" (Bauman, 2007, p. 98). Living with a consciousness of being on the move makes identity a problem: How can I be someone when I am constantly changing? Thus, an explosion in identity discourse has been the result after the problematization of identities in the emerging consumer society in the postwar era.

Identity, in short, has become a central problematic for human subjects today, in a way that character and personality were in earlier times. However, identity has at the same time seemingly lost the moral connotations that were originally attached to character, and this can be seen as a significant problem for human beings, at least if living a self-interpreting life is unavoidably a moral affair, as I shall argue below. With this, we arrive at the next question of this chapter: What does it mean to say that identity is a form of self-interpretation?

5.2 Identity as Self-Interpretation

The hermeneutic tradition in psychology and the social sciences claims that we should understand human identity in terms of self-interpretation (for an overview of this tradition in psychology, see Richardson, Fowers, & Guignon, 1999).[2] This tradition goes back at least to Wilhelm Dilthey's (1977) descriptive psychology, which conceived of mental life as an ongoing process of interpretation (de Mul, 2004). Following Dilthey and also Heidegger (1927), Charles Taylor has argued that we are essentially self-interpreting animals. Seeing the human being as a self-interpreting animal "means that he cannot be understood simply as an object among objects, for his life incorporates an interpretation, an expression of what cannot exist unexpressed, because the self that is to be interpreted is essentially that of a being who self-interprets" (Taylor, 1985b, p. 75). In this perspective, *who I am* cannot simply be determined by citing a collection of objective facts about me (e.g., my height, kinship relations, or personality traits). An answer to the question "Who am I?" must refer to the agent's self-interpretation, i.e., to "an understanding of what is of crucial importance to us. To know who I am is a species of knowing where I stand"

---

[2] The following sections of this chapter rework material that has previously been published in a journal article (Brinkmann, 2008).

(Taylor, 1989, p. 27). And "knowing where I stand," in this regard, means concerning important issues, i.e., those we conventionally refer to as moral.

According to Taylor's thesis, my identity is thus determined by what matters to me, by what I find valuable, by my commitments. And these are not simply given, but rest on self-interpretations that must be articulated in words and images within one or more interpretive traditions – including what Taylor refers to as *social imaginaries* (Taylor, 2004). Our individual self-interpretations (and thus our identities) derive their contents and legitimacy from the self-interpretations of society and from the social imaginary. Taylor defines social imaginary as:

> the ways people imagine their social existence, how they fit together with others, how things go on between them and their fellows, the expectations that are normally met, and the deeper normative notions and images that underlie these expectations.   (Taylor, 2004, p. 23)

The social imaginary does not just consist of mental representations in people's heads, but is lived and constituted in shared social practices. It is not simply the cluster of intellectual ideas we employ when we think about social relations. It is not an explicit social theory, but rather what determines how we formulate such social theories. It determines which questions we can meaningfully ask about our social existence (and which we cannot ask), and it affects the explicit ideas we form of society and ourselves.

Taylor uses the term "imaginary" because his focus "is on the way ordinary people "imagine" their social surroundings, and this is often not expressed in theoretical terms, but carried in images, stories, and legends" (Taylor, 2004, p. 23). Taylor's hermeneutic approach is part of the "practice turn" in recent social theory, which identifies social life with practices (Schatzki, 2001), and the social imaginary should be understood as that common understanding that makes possible shared practices in the first place (Taylor, 2004, p. 23). Our practical background understandings, our implicit knowledge of what to do in different situations, would not be possible without "a wider grasp of our whole predicament: how we stand to each other, how we got to where we are, how to relate to other groups, and so on" (p. 25).

In this sense, the concept of social imaginary resembles Foucault's (2001) notion of *epistēmē*, which notably figured in the early parts of his work. But while Foucault understood the episteme as something like an unconscious cultural code to be made explicit by structural analysis, Taylor rejects the idea that the social imaginary can be fully expressed in explicit doctrines. It is lived rather than thought, and based on habitual, bodily practices rather than underlying social rules. In short, the social imaginary is our "implicit grasp of social space" (Taylor, 2004, p. 26). And it is within such social space that self-interpretation becomes possible.

If our identities, our understandings and interpretations of ourselves, are dependent upon moral traditions and social imaginaries that frame certain things and projects as meaningful, worthy, and valuable, then it follows for Taylor that identities themselves are embedded in practices: "Certain moral self-understandings are embedded in certain practices, which can mean both that they are promoted by the spread of these practices and that they shape the practices and help them get established" (Taylor, 2004, p. 63). This hermeneutic way of thinking about human identity does not dissolve individual human identity in a sea of discursive practices, but invites us to look first and foremost to the constitutive background of history, practices, and the social imaginary that enables humans to have self-understanding and thus identity.

When answering the question "What is self-interpretation?", Taylor puts great weight on the human capacity to articulate the frameworks, horizons, and social imaginaries that constitute our identities. Articulations are constitutive of identities and life meanings (Taylor, 1989, p. 18), for an identity is related to the agent's explicit identifications (p. 27). Having an identity means knowing where one stands with regards to important questions, and this involves the capability of "answering for oneself" (p. 29). This is so because the human agent "exists in a space of questions. And these are questions to which our framework-definitions are answers, providing the horizon within which we know where we stand, and what meanings things have for us" (p. 29).

Without wanting to deny the importance of being able to verbalize, give accounts, and answer for oneself (Butler, 2005), I believe we also need to focus on those dimensions of self-interpretation that are not easily verbalized. Much interesting hermeneutic theory, including much of Taylor's own work, was developed under the influence of the linguistic turn in philosophy and social theory, but, as the recent practice turn has tried to make clear, we should also look at self-interpretation and other psychological processes in light of the social practices in which we participate as embodied agents. A self-interpretation does not always exist in people's minds or biographies in clear-cut forms that can be easily expressed verbally, for self-interpretations are dispersed across bodies, persons, practices, and society, and are often vague, ambiguous, and full of contradictions. And although we live within what Taylor calls "webs of interlocution" (Taylor, 1989, p. 36), not all dimensions and levels of self-interpretation lend themselves to explicit articulation.

5.2.1 The Moral Dimension of Identity as Self-Interpretation

As we have seen, Taylor argues that human identity is defined by the person's commitments and identifications, which enable one to take a stand (Taylor, 1989, p. 27). In this sense, identity is the moral side of the self: "identity largely is a matter of the extent to which we care about being a certain kind of person. Our identities are shaped by deliberating over what matters to us. And what matters is worked out through accepted interpretations of moral goods and standards" (Sugarman, 2005, p. 797).

What does this mean more concretely? Let me introduce an example, which is something of a classic in philosophy, viz. the story Jean-Paul Sartre tells in *L'Existentialisme est un humanisme*. The story is about a young man during World War II who approaches Sartre with a difficult dilemma. He can either remain in France with his ailing mother or go away to join the Resistance and plan for the liberation of occupied France. Sartre, the existentialist, is unable to offer advice to the young man, because in his view the issue has to be settled by radical choice. There can be offered no genuine reasons in favor of either option, and the young man should therefore just choose one option in the face of this existential absurdity. What Sartre wants to communicate is that the young man's dilemma is not simply one between A and B, but is about choosing the values that make A and B important. This is what is meant by radical choice – it is a choice *of* values, not simply *between* values. Radical choice is a choice that is not grounded in any reasons, but simply willed.

In his seminal paper "What is human agency?" Taylor (1985c) discusses Sartre's example and critiques his notion of radical choice. What Sartre forgets, Taylor argues, is that the situation as depicted is only a dilemma for the young man because he is faced with two rival moral demands that are unchosen. His mother might die if he leaves her, and at the same time the enemy is about to destroy the foundation of ethical life in the young man's country, and he cannot just sit passively and watch that; "it is a dilemma only because the claims themselves are not created by radical choice," says Taylor (p. 30). If the values that give rise to the dilemma were in fact the result of a choice, then the young man could at any moment dissolve the dilemma by declaring one of the claims invalid. The fact that he cannot do so brings out the ludicrousness of the idea that values are created by our choices: "if serious moral claims were created by radical choice, the young man could have a grievous dilemma about whether to go and get an ice cream cone" (p. 30). What confronts us as valuable and what does not, is not determined by our subjective decisions. In a sense, these issues "resist" our dealings with them and "object" to us. Even Nietzsche's wish to remake the table of values, his attempt to redefine what is of worth, presupposed a horizon of moral issues that he did not himself invent or choose. Remaking the table of values, Taylor observes dryly, means "redefining values concerning important questions, not redesigning the menu at McDonald's, or next year's casual fashion" (Taylor, 1991, p. 40).

Thus, the moral questions and commitments that are identity-defining do not come from individual minds, but from shared practices and the social imaginary. This is where we find the moral frameworks that are presupposed in our everyday lives when we explain ourselves to others and answer questions such as "What did you do?" and "Why did you do that?" When we give accounts of our actions, we offer descriptions and justifications in the light of our motives in the situation and try to show that the situation justifies our acting in a certain way (Butler, 2005). Sometimes we explain ourselves by saying "I did this, because I wanted to!", although, as Louch (1966) has demonstrated, such explanation is vacuous (and a likely reaction is: "Of course you want to – otherwise you wouldn't be doing it!"); the only context in which such an "explanation" is informative is when others may not have expected the action or suspect that it was done under pressure.

To explain and deliberate about one's actions in light of one's desires and preferences ("What do I want the most?"), is what Taylor (1985c) calls weak evaluation. A paradigm example of weak evaluation is when we go to a restaurant and try to determine which meal to order. One scans the menu and finally decides to go for the fish. When asked the reason why, there is rarely anything more to say than "Because I felt like it!" One weighs one's desires and determines which is the quantitatively strongest one. In weak evaluation, all one's motivations, desires, and preferences are put on a par. They are considered as commensurable and put on the same scale. But if the model of weak evaluation were the only model a person had recourse to in deliberating and explaining herself, we would find that this person led an extremely impoverished and inhuman life. All she could do would be to act on her strongest desire at any given moment. Such a person could never articulate a genuine reason for her actions, for she could not refer to any moral frameworks; all she could say would be that she did something because her strongest desire made her. In that sense, she could only refer to causes and not to reasons. If acting means acting for a reason, such an individual could not act at all, and she could not have an identity in the sense discussed in this chapter. The young man's deliberations in Sartre's example did not just concern his strongest desire in a quantitative sense, for in that case he could simply have tried to measure or weigh his preferences, and there would be no need to consult an older and more experienced person such as Sartre. The deliberations were about which of two desires he *ought* to realize, regardless of their subjective strength. This is what Taylor calls strong evaluation, and which Sartre missed entirely with his notion of radical choice.

As persons, we not only have desires, but also desires about which desires to have (so-called second-order desires). Perhaps I find that every time I meet the Salvation Army, my miserliness makes me walk by without donating any-thing, but when I come home, I regret it and decide that the next time I meet them, I would like to have the desire to give away some money. So we have the capacity for evaluating our desires. But in light of what? If we could only evaluate desires in the light of other desires, as in the restaurant example above, it would merely be a matter of determining which desire were strongest. Then we could never have a genuine reason to change our desires, and this runs counter to our everyday moral experience, where we in fact are often concerned with changing our desires for moral reasons, and not just because other desires are quantitatively stronger. This is where Taylor's notion of strong evaluation is relevant. Strong evaluation is when the goods in question are not seen as constituted as good by the fact that we desire them, but rather are seen as normative for desire (Taylor, 1981, p. 193). In strong evaluation we are concerned with the qualitative, indeed *moral*, worth of our motivations, desires, and ways of life. The quantitative strength of our desires does not matter here, but rather the issue of whether what we desire is *worth* desiring; whether it is qualitatively desirable. Taylor's fundamental argument in *Sources of the Self* (1989) is that our strong evaluations are constitutive of our identities. This is quite clear in the example from Sartre: The young man can be said to learn who he is by discovering the values that give rise to his dilemma. His orientation to these values defines who he is.

Taylor argues that moral values or strongly valued goods are real. They are not subjective or illusory. His argument rests on the following two points: "1. You cannot help having recourse to these strongly valued goods for the purposes of life" and "2. What is real is what you have to deal with, what won't go away just because it doesn't fit with your prejudices" (Taylor, 1989, p. 59). What he means by the first point is that strongly valued goods are a transcendental condition for the existence of acting human beings and their identities, as we know them. If we could not refer to properties of the world that are perceived to be morally valuable independently of our subjective desires and motivations, then we could not conceive of human action or identity. This is so because identifying human action implies identifying reasons, and these in turn refer to moral properties, i.e., issues of value and worth that stand or fall independently of my personal inclinations.

The other point made by Taylor is that what is real is what we have to deal with. As seen in Sartre's example, we have to deal with morality in our lives, and we need the kind of understanding of the world that can only be expressed by moral concepts: "What better measure of reality do we have in human affairs than those terms which on critical reflection and after correction of the errors we can detect make the best sense of our lives?" (Taylor, 1989, p. 57). And further:

> Suppose I can convince myself that I can explain people's behavior as an observer without using a term like "dignity." What does this prove if I can't do without it as a term in my deliberations about what to do, how to behave, how to treat people, my questions about whom I admire, with whom I feel affinity, and the like?   (Taylor, 1989, p. 57)

If this is true, then we must say that value-terms are indispensable to us, and we should therefore not try to remove them or purify them in psychological studies of human life, for they are an essential part of the language we need to act and live. The task of psychology is to study mental life, and if mental life is normative in a moral sense – since there are better and worse ways of acting, feeling, and thinking that can even be said to define actions, feelings, and thoughts as such – then psychology ought to take this normativity seriously (see Brinkmann, 2018). As humans, we cannot do without some sense of moral orientation or strong value (Smith, 2002, p. 93). As one of Taylor's exegetes says, "no one could conceivably choose to live a 'care-free' life in the sense of a life led without background distinctions of worth" (p. 100). We cannot as humans do without an orientation to supposedly uncreated and unchosen values, for without such an orientation we could have no identity.

5.2.2 The Narrative Dimension of Identity as Self-Interpretation

The idea that our identities are formed by our commitments to issues of non-subjective moral worth does not imply that identities are therefore fixed once and for all. On the contrary, having an identity, living a life, should be seen as a quest, as a kind of craving to be rightly placed in relation to the good (Taylor, 1989, p. 44). A quest is about moving, and in order to understand this temporality of our lives, we need narratives (Ricœur, 1992). Our identities are framed by our relations to values, and the crux of our biographies is how we move and develop in relation to these values: "It only makes sense to ascribe direction to a life if we can distinguish between more or less significant moments, events or experiences. But in doing this we are articulating a changing relation to the good" (Smith, 2002, p. 98).

Narratives make sense of our movements in the space of moral values, and the study of human identity thus becomes connected to moral inquiry and to narrative studies: "In order to have a sense of who we are, we have to have a notion of how we have become, and of where we are going" (Taylor, 1989, p. 47). The self-interpretation of who I am is thus dependent not just on what we could call a structural dimension (i.e., related to the structures of the moral traditions of which I am a part), but also on a temporal dimension related to the stories of how I have become – and of how we have become, as a community of self-interpreters. With reference to Heidegger (1927), we can say that a human being is not an object or a substance, but rather a happening or an event that unfolds in time (Richardson, Fowers, & Guignon, 1999, p. 211), and such happenings or events are not to be grasped in a causal framework citing universal laws, but in a normative framework citing interpretive structures, values, and reasons for action (Brinkmann, 2006).

In his seminal work *Oneself as Another*, the French hermeneutic philosopher Paul Ricœur (1992) tried to show that people can only be moral in the strict sense if they are able to relate to their lives as a whole, or as something that threads its way through time as a continuum and is best understood as a story, a coherent narrative. He asks, rhetorically: "How, indeed, could a subject of action give an ethical character to his or her own life taken as a whole if this life were not gathered together in some way, and how could this occur if not, precisely, in the form of a narrative?" (p. 158). Why is "life as a narrative whole" a prerequisite for morality? Because, Ricœur argues, if others cannot be sure that I will be the same tomorrow as I am today and was yesterday, then they have no reason to trust me or that I will do what I promise and otherwise live up to my obligations. And if I do not know my own past or feel committed to trying to establish a link between yesterday, today and tomorrow, then others have no reason to trust me. If I do not have what Ricœur calls "self-constancy," then neither others nor I will be able to count on me. Self-constancy – which in this case means identity – is a basic precondition for trust between people – and hence for ethical life.

We can thus say that Taylor's arguments are about how moral values (and strong evaluations) constitute our identities through our autobiographical storytelling, and, in a way, Ricœur approaches the same problem from the opposite direction and argues that there can only be morality (in the sense of commitments to ethical values) because of a certain kind of identity or self-constancy. We can only make promises and commit to actions together over time because we (and others) understand ourselves as being the same over time – because we have a more or less coherent identity. And we only have this because we are able to view our lives as a single narrative – as a story that stretches from birth to death.

Like Taylor, Ricœur belongs to the hermeneutic tradition, but it is significant that also Alasdair MacIntyre – who has been one of the most influential moral philosophers in recent decades – reaches similar conclusions based on Aristotelian virtue ethics. Concerning the narrative dimension, MacIntyre (1985) claims that "Stories are lived before they are told" (p. 212), but the way they are lived is not just up to individuals. We are not sole authors of the narratives of our lives, for "We enter upon a stage which we did not design and we find ourselves part of an action that was not of our making" (p. 213). This is his way of pointing to practices and the social imaginary. MacIntyre continues:

> [T]he key question for men is not about their own authorship; I can only answer the question "What am I to do?" if I can answer the prior question "Of what story or stories do I find myself a part?" We enter human society, that is, with one or more imputed characters – roles into which we have been drafted – and we have to learn what they are in order to be able to understand how others respond to us and how our responses to them are apt to be construed.   (MacIntyre, 1985, p. 216)

MacIntyre's view implies that "the characters in a history are not a collection of persons, but the concept of a person is that of a character abstracted from a history" (MacIntyre, 1985, p. 217). The modern view of individuals, persons, or selves as something primary in history and social life is pure fiction, according to MacIntyre. In reality, we live our lives according to scripts that are drafted beforehand. The practices in which I am engaged – as a father, husband, academic, etc. – are not of my own making, and the ways I orchestrate my participation in such practices owe much to narrative forms that precede my own life. This, however, does not mean that humans are not responsible or accountable:

> To be the subject of a narrative that runs from one's birth to one's death is . . . to be accountable for the actions and experiences which compose a narratable life. It is, that is, to be open to being asked to give a certain kind of account of what one did or what happened to one or what one witnessed at any earlier point in one's life than the time at which the question is posed.   (MacIntyre, 1985, pp. 217–218)

To be someone, to have an identity, means to be accountable, and accountability is indeed a fundamental moral virtue across practices.

5.2.3 Levels of Self-Interpretation and How They Clash in Consumer Society

I began this chapter by connecting self-interpretation and thus identity to the social imaginary and larger social practices. After reviewing the significance of morality and narrative for human identity, it is time to return once more to the overarching frameworks of self-interpretation to address those aspects that are not purely individual. Self-interpretation is also a social, collective, and indeed societal affair. Building on the work of Taylor, German sociologist Hartmut Rosa poses the following question:

> Where and what is the self-interpretation of a society? How can it be identified? Who can claim to have the "correct" form of that self-interpretation (which always is, at the same time, an understanding of the world), given that different social and political groups give divergent accounts of their self-understanding, and different languages and meaning-systems obtain in different spheres of society (as, for example, economy, science, art, religion, politics)?   (Rosa, 2004, p. 692)

For a social theorist, it is clear that self-interpretation is not just something conscious and reflective, but must include elements of taste, body practices, and emotions. Bourdieu's (1977) studies of the habitus should alert us to this fact. It is also clear that self-interpretation is not just something belonging to individuals qua individuals, but also to "society" or social processes. In order to help us think more clearly about self-interpretation, Rosa (2004) outlines a basic model of the matter. It distinguishes first between societal and individual levels of self-interpretation, and second between implicit and explicit levels of self-interpretation. Given these distinctions, we get the following taxonomy of four levels of self-interpretation:

A Societal and explicit self-interpretation: Society's self-descriptions (shared self-understandings expressed in laws, media, institutional texts, etc.).
B Societal and implicit self-interpretation: Social institutions and practices (the tacit understandings embedded in educational, work, and family practices, for example).

C Individual and explicit self-interpretation: Reflective self-image (persons' self-concepts).

D Individual and implicit self-interpretation: Pre-reflective sense of self (bodily habits, feelings, habitus).

These levels are not hierarchically ordered, but should be understood as divided by two axes with changes and adaptations being able to occur in all directions (Rosa, 2004, p. 697). Many psychologists and social scientists have argued for the primacy of one level over the others. For example, historical materialists have argued that social change in principle always emanates from B to all other levels. Political communitarians put emphasis on A and want to align the other levels with it, while liberalists put emphasis on C and on the rights of individuals to live in accordance with one's self-images. Methodological individualists claim that social change always begins with C and/or D, whereas collectivists point to A and/or B. Many psychological theories of identity focus on C, and although most of the theories that are concerned with psychological development (e.g., cultural-historical psychology) focus on how C is influenced by B in particular (i.e., through socialization and educational processes), and sometimes also note the influence from A and D, some such theories claim that identity becomes autonomous and can be studied in relative independence from A, B, and D.

Finally, some psychological theories of identity focus almost exclusively on D. Notably, the theories of humanistic psychology (e.g., Maslow, Rogers) work with a notion of an authentic inner self that can be thwarted by cultural processes resulting in a "false self" and a distrust in one's own organismic evaluation of situations and events. The process of self-realization or self-actualization was conceived by the humanistic psychologists as a way of aligning not just the individual reflective concept of the self (C), but also to some extent society and social institutions (A and B), with the authentic and personal inner sense of self, rooted in early childhood experiences or perhaps even in innate structures (as in some trait theories).

The important lesson to learn from Taylor, MacIntyre, and Ricœur is that identity – conceived as moral and narrative self-interpretation – involves all four levels. And identity problems may appear in different ways, whenever conflicts arise between the levels. As Rosa says, pathologies can arise when the discrepancies between levels "have grown beyond the horizon of possible reintegration via mutual, creative adaptations and partial, context-dependent reconciliations or compromises and when they lead to consistently contradictory impulses on the level of action" (Rosa, 2004, p. 699). Schematically put, a conflict between levels A and B can obviously lead to ideological or institutional crises, when there is a mismatch between society's self-descriptions and its dominant institutional self-understandings. A conflict between A and C could be called legitimation crisis (when what we think about ourselves as individuals is out of touch with our society's self-definitions). Here the social imaginary is detached from the way I imagine myself and my own life course as an individual. On the other hand, counternarratives may also come from C and influence A. Conflicts between B and C could be interpreted as alienation (when people are unable to recognize themselves in the institutions in which they participate), and a conflict between B and D would emerge as clinical pathologies and deviant behavior (p. 700). That is, when people's unreflective habits and patterns of emotional response do not fit with the practices and institutions of society, we tend to label their behaviors as pathological and normatively condemn them. Finally, a conflict on the individual side between levels C and D would be what psychologists have traditionally called identity problems. That is, when our explicitly articulated ideas about our lives do not match with our pre-reflective feelings and habits; if, for example, a person's ideals of heterosexual love (which, of course, are intertwined with cultural and societal norms) clashes with that person's sexual feelings for others of the same sex.

On the basis of such a model of identity as self-interpretation, we can move on to throw light on significant contemporary identity problems. Today, and to an increasing extent since the rise of consumer cultures after World War II, we tend to imagine our lives through a self-realization discourse. In this sense, we have come to think of ourselves as individuals in a new way. This, of course, does not mean that we have liberated ourselves from a social embedding; we still "learn our identities in dialogue, by being inducted into a certain language. But on the level of content, what we may learn is to be an individual" (Taylor, 2004, p. 65). And the kind of individual we learn to be is one that continually develops and realizes her own true self. In the years after World War II, "members of Western societies were compelled, urged, or encouraged, for the sake of their own future, to place their very selves at the centre of their own life-planning and practice" (Honneth, 2004, p. 469). We have been taught to think of individual identity "as being the stuff of experimental self-discovery" (p. 470), and thus perhaps to ignore the larger social wholes from which we derive our self-understandings. Today, as Rose has observed, "each individual must render his or her life meaningful as if it were the outcome of individual choices made in furtherance of a biographical project of self-realization" (Rose, 1999, p. ix). A principal material foundation for this development and extension of practices of self-realization across strata and classes is "the extreme growth of income and leisure time" which has been able to "extend the space available for individual decision and, on the other hand, to reduce the formative influence of the social milieux particular to the different classes" (Honneth, 2004, p. 468).

Self-realization has thus become a central feature of current institutionalized expectations inherent in social reproduction (cf. level B above), where many social arenas from family life to education and work today are organized in accordance with a self-interpretation stressing self-realization. In the case of work life, this has been explored by Richard Sennett (1998, 2006).

Teamwork, networking, flexibilization, personality development practices, and the destruction of bureaucracies and hierarchies in contemporary organizations all have positive sides, but the downside is a "corrosion of character," a lack of a sense of belonging, a growing threat of being useless, and a reduction of loyalty and informal trust (Sennett, 2006).

If one is continually forced to engage in projects of subjective self-discovery and self-development, then social bonds and commitments easily become less important. The crucial moral and narrative dimensions of identity easily become downgraded. The "new spirit of capitalism" that has arisen with the societal transformation from industrial to consumer society has manifested itself in new practices and institutions that increasingly present themselves as "networks," which threaten to "destroy the social fabric," according to several leading sociologists (Boltanski & Chiapello, 2005, p. 377). Networks are less stable than bureaucracies as institutional forms, and participation in fluid and flexible networks appears to be insufficient to secure both a coherent life narrative and also a moral framework within which to understand oneself – both of which were central dimensions of identity, according to Taylor's theory recounted above. Living with a pure "network sociality" (Wittel, 2001), where one should continually develop and learn to connect in new ways, makes it difficult to achieve what Ricœur (1992) called self-constancy.

As I previously argued, self-interpretation is not a single, monolithic thing, and we should bear in mind that not everyone in the Western world subscribes to a simple version of the idea articulated by the humanistic psychologists, for example, that each of us has a private, inner self that that can be developed and realized. There are many other forms of self-interpretation, including religious and, to an increasing extent, scientific ones. In his book on *The Politics of Life Itself*, Rose argues that the deep interior psychological space, through which human beings came to understand themselves in the first half of the twentieth century, "has begun to flatten out, to be displaced by a direct mapping of personhood, and its ills, upon the body or brain, which then becomes the principle target for ethical work" (Rose, 2007, p. 26). According to Rose, we are witnessing a "geneticization of identity" (p. 112), and biomedical identity claims in general are finding a noteworthy place among competing self-interpretive resources. In spite of this, however, I agree with Rose that our basic interpretation of the dynamics and structure of human development remains largely unaffected by the discursive shift from "the inner self" to "the brain," from psychotherapy and self-development books to Prozac and Ritalin. Like the humanistic ideal of becoming oneself, also the recent "somatic ethics" with its idea of "the neurochemical self" is bound up with fundamental ideas about self-fulfillment, an "ethic of authenticity," and "a realization of the true self" (p. 100). I mention this just to indicate that what I refer to as "self-realization" here is one pervasive aspect of our self-interpretation that turns up in many guises, including a recent biological and medical variant (and many emerging religious practices could possibly be counted among self-realization practices as well).

The central contradiction inherent in the current aspects of self-interpretation that are based on self-realization is that what was once an idea that promised an increase in qualitative freedom, autonomy, and individual decision-making has been "altered into an ideology of de-institutionalization" (Honneth, 2004, p. 467), and, according to Honneth's harsh verdict, the result is "the emergence in individuals of a number of symptoms of inner emptiness, of feeling oneself to be superfluous, and of absence of purpose" (p. 467). The ideas of the liberation movements of the 1960s, aiming to secure a foundation for individual decision-making through self-realization, have been trans-formed into a vehicle for social reproduction of the consumer society, resulting less in freedom than in a constant demand to change and develop in accord-ance with inner experiences, which perfectly suits a flexible consumer econ-omy, but without much concern for morality or self-constancy. The paradox of self-realization as a dominant self-interpretation is that "the identity of the autonomous, self-determining individual requires a social matrix" (Taylor, 1985a, p. 209), viz. one in which people care about public deliberation and the lives of others. The freedom to realize one's true self is only possible in a society where "the free individual who affirms himself as such already has an obligation to complete, restore, or sustain the society within which this iden-tity is possible" (p. 209). But if society is becoming deregulated, partly in response to the demand for individual self-realization, and if people feel less loyalty, trust, and commitment toward a shared moral order, then the social conditions of self-realization are in fact paradoxically threatened. Self-realization discourse – in its many forms – serves as a legitimizing factor in the deregulation of consumer society, and the paradox of self-realization, as one aspect of the contemporary Western self-interpretation, seems to be that a unique and relentless demand to be oneself makes self-realization impossible. We could also say that there is a deep contradiction between the demands to "Be yourself!" and "Change and adapt all the time!"

I believe that the best understanding of the paradox is obtained by being sensitive to the contradictions between different levels of self-interpretation. In Rosa's (2004) model, the paradox is explained by looking at the emerging discrepancy between levels B and D. If one claims, like the humanistic psychologists, that life does or should revolve around a pre-reflective sense of self (level D) that should be allowed free rein to the largest possible extent, then what ensues when institutions from families and schools to work organ-izations (level B) are organized in accordance with this claim is a disappear-ance of a stable social matrix in which to realize oneself. Honneth believes that this is indeed today's situation:

> the ideal of self-realization pursued throughout the course of a life has
> developed into an ideology and productive force of an economic system that

> is being deregulated: the expectations individuals had formed before they began to interpret their own lives as being an experimental process of self-discovery now recoil on them as demands issuing from without, so that they are explicitly or implicitly urged to keep their options regarding their own decisions and goals open at all times.   (Honneth, 2004, p. 474)

In his eyes, this is a significant source of "social discontent and suffering which Western societies throughout their history have not previously known on a massive scale" (Honneth, 2004, p. 474). The ideal of self-realization can be seen as an ideological response in a deregulated society, and at the same time as serving further deregulation and "free choice" above all else. Furthermore, it seems to be the case that the increasing societal deregulation (on level B) and an explicit ideology of neoliberalism (on levels A and C) in Western societies have created a growing class of permanently superfluous people, who do not receive those forms of societal recognition that are needed to develop an integrated sense of identity. Moreover, those individuals who are unable to keep up with the pace of social acceleration (Rosa, 2003) and the demands for continual self-development, i.e., those who are insufficiently "self-entrepreneurial" and cling to a sustaining life narrative (Sennett, 2006, p. 5), increasingly suffer from mental exhaustion, resulting in "a rapid rise in the frequency of depression" (Honneth, 2004, p. 475).

5.3 Conclusions

In this chapter, I have tried to articulate a perspective on identity as moral self-interpretation. I began by arguing that identity as a concept with which we understand ourselves is a child of late or postmodernity, with earlier concepts being character and personality that were previously employed by individuals to understand themselves. The question of identity is "Who am I?", and following in particular the work of Taylor, but also MacIntyre and Ricœur, I argued that an answer to this question involves references to moral values and the narrative structure of a life. Thus, morality and narrative are two key – and mutually supporting – dimensions of identity as self-interpretation.

Finally, I used the work of Rosa to develop a view of self-interpretation as being both implicit and explicit, and having both individual and societal aspects. Human moral identity is thus not a single, monolithic thing, but rather a complex form of self-understanding that draws on various resources. The different levels of self-interpretation can be in tension or downright contradictory, leading to various social and psychological problems, and I tried to show that the individualistic call for "self-realization" may lead to identity problems, when it severs the bonds of persons to issues of non-subjective values. If the philosophical sources invoked in this chapter – Taylor, MacIntyre, and Ricœur – are valid, then it is such values that are constitutive of human identity.

Readers may wonder why the sources of this chapter are primarily philosophical. Why has it been philosophers rather than psychologists who have developed these perspectives on identity? Although there are exceptions within psychology (e.g., Richardson et al., 1999), the answer is probably that psychology in large parts has attempted to provide value-neutral descriptions and analyses of its subject matter. But if identity is a matter of orienting to moral values that cannot be reduced to neutral notions like "beliefs" or "desires," then this phenomenon comes to sit uneasily with psychology. We can hope that psychologists now and in the future begin to study identity as the phenomenon it in fact is, viz. a moral kind of self-interpretation that does not lend itself to value-neutral analysis. Just as one cannot study a field such as logic in a value-neutral way, since logic is a normative field (concerned with correct inferences), so it seems impossible to study identity in a value-neutral way, if this is also a normative phenomenon related to moral values and the quest for narrative coherence or self-constancy.

References

Aristotle. (1976). *Ethics*. London: Penguin.

Bauman, Z. (2007). *Consuming Life*. Cambridge: Polity Press.

Berlin, I. (1999). *The Roots of Romanticism*. London: Chatto & Windus.

Boltanski, L. & Chiapello, E. (2005). *The New Spirit of Capitalism*. London: Verso.

Bourdieu, P. (1977). *Outline of a Theory of Practice*. Cambridge: Cambridge University Press.

Brinkmann, S. (2004). The topography of moral ecology. *Theory & Psychology*, *14*(1), 57–80.

Brinkmann, S. (2005). Human kinds and looping effects in psychology: Foucauldian and hermeneutic perspectives. *Theory & Psychology*, *15*(6), 769–791.

Brinkmann, S. (2006). Mental life in the space of reasons. *Journal for the Theory of Social Behaviour*, *36*(1), 1–16.

Brinkmann, S. (2008). Identity as self-interpretation. *Theory & Psychology*, *18*(3), 405–423.

Brinkmann, S. (2010). Character, personality, and identity: On historical aspects of human subjectivity. *Nordic Psychology*, *62*(1), 65–85.

Brinkmann, S. (2018). *Persons and Their Minds: Towards an Integrative Theory of the Mediated Mind*. London: Routledge.

Butler, J. (2005). *Giving an Account of Oneself*. New York, NY: Fordham University Press.

Cushman, P. (1990). Why the self is empty: Toward a historically situated psychology. *American Psychologist*, *45*(5), 599–611.

de Mul, J. (2004). *The Tragedy of Finitude: Dilthey's Hermeneutics of Life*. New Haven, CT: Yale University Press.

Dilthey, W. (1977). *Descriptive Psychology and Historical Understanding*. The Hague: Martinus Nijhoff (first published 1894).

Erikson, E. (1968). *Identity: Youth and Crisis*. New York, NY: Norton.

Foucault, M. (2001). *The Order of Things: An Archeology of the Human Sciences.* London: Taylor & Francis (first published 1966).

Heidegger, M. (1927). *Being and Time.* New York, NY: HarperCollins Publishers (this ed. published 1962).

Hogg, M. A. & Vaughan, G. M. (2005). *Social Psychology, 4th Ed.* Harlow: Pearson Education.

Honneth, A. (1996). Pathologies of the social: The past and present of social philosophy. In D. M. Rasmussen (Ed.), *Handbook of Critical Theory* (pp. 369–396). Oxford: Blackwell.

Honneth, A. (2004). Organized self-realization. *European Journal of Social Theory, 7* (4), 463–478.

Louch, A. R. (1966). *Explanation and Human Action.* Christchurch, New Zealand: Cybereditions Corporation (this ed. published 2000).

MacIntyre, A. (1985). *After Virtue,* 2nd ed. with postscript. London: Duckworth.

Richardson, F. C., Fowers, B. J., & Guignon, C. B. (1999). *Re-Envisioning Psychology: Moral Dimensions of Theory and Practice.* San Francisco, CA: Jossey-Bass.

Ricœur, P. (1992). *Oneself as Another.* Chicago, IL: University of Chicago Press.

Rosa, H. (2003). Social acceleration: Ethical and political consequences of a desynchronized high-speed society. *Constellations, 10*(1), 3–33.

Rosa, H. (2004). Four levels of self-interpretation. *Philosophy and Social Criticism, 30* (5–6), 691–720.

Rose, N. (1999). *Governing the Soul: The Shaping of the Private Self.* London: Free Association Books.

Rose, N. (2007). *The Politics of Life Itself: Biomedicine, Power, and Subjectivity in the Twenty-First Century.* Princeton, NJ: Princeton University Press.

Schatzki, T. R. (2001). Practice theory. In T. R. Schatzki, K. Knoor Cetina, & E. von Savigny (Eds.), *The Practice Turn in Contemporary Theory* (pp. 1–14). London: Routledge.

Sennett, R. (1998). *The Corrosion of Character.* New York, NY: Norton.

Sennett, R. (2006). *The Culture of the New Capitalism.* New Haven, CT: Yale University Press.

Smith, N. H. (2002). *Charles Taylor: Meaning, Morals and Modernity.* Cambridge: Polity Press.

Smith, R. (1997). *The Norton History of the Human Sciences.* New York, NY: Norton.

Sugarman, J. (2005). Persons and moral agency. *Theory & Psychology, 15*(6), 793–811.

Taylor, C. (1981). Understanding and explanation in the Geisteswissenschaften. In S. M. Holtzman & C. M. Leich (Eds.), *Wittgenstein: To Follow a Rule* (pp. 191–210). London: Routledge & Kegan Paul.

Taylor, C. (1985a). Atomism. In *Philosophy and the Human Sciences: Philosophical Papers 2* (pp. 187–210). Cambridge: Cambridge University Press.

Taylor, C. (1985b). Self-interpreting animals. In *Human Agency and Language: Philosophical Papers 1* (pp. 45–76). Cambridge: Cambridge University Press.

Taylor, C. (1985c). What is human agency? In *Human Agency and Language: Philosophical Papers 1* (pp. 15–44). Cambridge: Cambridge University Press.

Taylor, C. (1989). *Sources of the Self: The Making of the Modern Identity.* Cambridge: Cambridge University Press.

Taylor, C. (1991). *The Ethics of Authenticity*. Cambridge, MA: Harvard University Press.

Taylor, C. (1999). Two theories of modernity. *Public Culture, 11*(1), 153–174.

Taylor, C. (2004). *Modern Social Imaginaries*. Durham, NC: Duke University Press.

Wittel, A. (2001). Toward a network sociality. *Theory, Culture & Society, 18*(6), 51–76.

6 Researching Identities as Affective Discursive Practices

Octavia Calder-Dawe and Maree Martinussen

In this chapter, we outline what an affective discursive practice (ADP) view offers the field of identity research, and make a case for the particular utility of such an approach for identity studies, including theorization and analysis of the social-psychological subject. Margaret Wetherell's (2012) ADP approach builds on her earlier breakthroughs in discursive research in critical social psychology, "pull[ing] on a large number of threads germane to critical psychology and the study of the psychosocial and subjectivity more broadly" (Wetherell, McConville, & McCreanor, 2019, p. 3). With ADP, Wetherell demonstrates the centrality of affect and emotion when analyzing identities. Additionally, creativity and innovation are encouraged, while remaining firmly oriented to clearly defined theories of power and agency. It offers a generous interdisciplinary view of what is recruited in the service of identity construction and everyday identity work: a rich spectrum of body states and practices entwined with personal meaning-making, habits, and histories, unfolding through overlapping regimes of feeling and knowledge. Affective discursive identity practices range from the strained rehearsal of a cheery smile to the complex conversational "working up" of oneself in light of prevailing regimes of good personhood. ADP draws across scales to offer a fresh perspective on familiar debates regarding agency and structure, while illuminating productive ways forward for the field of identity studies, as well as affect and emotion research more generally.

We begin in Section 6.1 with an overview of the development of affective discursive practice, pointing to continuities with and divergences from other forms of critical social psychology, including *critical discursive psychology* (CDP), also developed principally by Wetherell (e.g., Wetherell, 1998, 2007, 2008). From here, Section 6.2 explores ADP in detail, introducing it as a highly productive intervention into the current "turn to affect" that is sweeping the social sciences. We outline how some of the most influential lines of such thinking were motivated by a turn away from discourse, coupled with a turn toward the body and feelings; we suggest that in many respects this was also a turn away from people's daily business of negotiating identities in interaction with their social worlds. We outline the strengths of ADP and discuss its particular utility for approaching thorny issues of agency in identity research. In Section 6.3, we flesh out our key lines of argument in relation to

ADP with an empirical example, and demonstrating its potential to extend and advance the empirical investigation of identities and identifications.

6.1 The Development of Affective Practices and Critical Social Psychology

One of the most common ways to understand identity in social psychology is to theorize it as having two discrete but interrelated components, personal identities and social identities (Reicher, Spears, & Haslam, 2010). In contrast, discursive research within British social psychology was predicated upon finding ways to bring social and personal identities, or the "inside" and "outside" of identity work, into closer alignment. Influences contributing to these discursive approaches in critical social psychology were diverse and included postmodernism, social constructionism, psychoanalysis, Bakhtinian dialogism, Wittgensteinian philosophy, conversation analysis, and ethnomethodology, where language and narrative are given primacy in the process of constructing identity. Through critiques of mainstream behaviorist psychology in the 1970s onwards (Parker, 1999), a range of discursive approaches built a blueprint for understanding identity as more seamless, and not neatly divided into group-based and personal identities that individuals switched between. Critical social psychologists questioned dominant, cognitivist traditions in psychology that treat identities as relatively stable and measurable through attitudes, mental states, cognitions, motivations, dispositions, and so forth, represented in language (Taylor, 2015). In these conventional understandings of language, realities inside people's heads are treated as separate from words, which neutrally convey aspects of their identities. In contrast, interventions from critical social psychologists illuminated how communicating through discourse does more than simply convey meaning; rather, this is how we make meaning. The constant telling and retelling of memories, histories, or relationships, both individual and collective accounts, produces discursive resources for people to use when constructing their identities, over and above simply communicating them. Moreover, the way we talk about social objects and identities affects how they are organized hierarchically, making some identities more valuable and/or available than others. Meanings about, for example, how to be a good mother, friend, or worker may become more dominant than others in particular socio-historical contexts.

In more recent developments in the social sciences, the turn to language is often presented as being eclipsed by a turn to affect, sparked by a perception that discursive methods are inadequate in capturing fleeting and unpredictable affect and emotion (e.g., Anderson, 2009; Clough, 2008; Sedgwick, 1997). However, the study of emotion has been an element of critical forms of social psychology from the outset, predating the contemporary swell of interest.

For example, within *discursive psychology*, which draws on micro, ethnomethodological insights and conversation analysis, emotions are studied as conventions of language use and social interaction (Edwards, 1999). Far from being mysterious and ineffable, emotions are shown to be ordered and normatively intelligible – or unintelligible, if people do not use the "correct" emotion (Campos, Ramos, & Bernal, 1999). Emotions are treated as conventions of social order, and are translated into technical knowledges to study identities. This does, however, leave discursive psychology open to charges of being inattentive to meanings that flow from sensing bodies. From this perspective, discursive psychology takes an overly techno-rational view of the power of emotions, losing an opportunity to feel with participants and to attend to the subjective experience, including how particular constructions of self and identity become meaningful to people over a life course.

In contrast, critical social-psychological approaches informed by psychoanalysis, now often referred to as *psychosocial research* (Taylor, 2017; Walkerdine, 2008), could be characterized as deprioritizing empiricism. These lines of enquiry developed via Lacanian psychoanalysis, systems theory, feminist theory, and phenomenology (Blackman et al., 2008; Frosh, 2014). Here, the discursive realm remains a significant analytic resource, but identities are theorized in relation to people's psychic lives and the dynamic unconscious. Although contested (Hollway & Jefferson, 2005; Spears, 2005), a certain primacy is assigned to the "inner" and the development of one individual's psychobiography (this emphasis is also evident in Chapter 9 where Habermas and Kemper outline additional psychoanalytic perspectives on identity). The specifics of one individual's unique account and sense-making tends to be the focus, rather than collective identity practices (Emerson & Frosh, 2004). Similarly, building up a knowledge of the conventions in constructing identity in talk is deprioritized.

We have provided a very brief sketch of the emergence of critical social psychology and outlined two divergent paths forged as a result, discursive psychology and psychoanalytic psychosocial research. Although our detailing of these two schools of identity theory simplifies many nuances and tensions, we have illustrated the stark differences between the poles of critical social psychology, to explain how CDP sits between them and resolves the issues of each. Indeed, as can be gauged from Wetherell's productive exchanges with both discursive psychologists (Wetherell, 1998, 2007) and psychosocial analysts (Wetherell, 2003, 2005b), the positioning of CDP as a middle-ground approach within this spectrum was evident throughout its development. In common with psychosocial studies, CDP leans toward a feminist ethics where understanding the felt experience of living out certain identities is paramount, including identities that are routinely othered (Wetherell, 2006, 2008). In a similar vein, attention to how affecting experiences become meaningful to people over time and layer to form deep investments stays in the frame (Wetherell & Edley, 1999). Simultaneously, however, the tools of discursive psychology may also be drawn on. The study of people's interactions at the micro level are also an important constituent part of a flexible kitbag of tools, offering identity analysts much choice in how to study identity practices across scales, the personal, interactional, cultural, and historical. This flexibility also informs how identities are defined within CDP, where different orders of identity are delineated. Some orders of identity are smaller units of analysis. Discursive psychology, for example, typically examines the *identity positions* people make use of from one moment to the next in social interactions. While in CDP the identity positions people take on briefly may be relevant, their significance comes through linking them to broader ideologies outside the immediate conversation, which is avoided in discursive psychology. Thus, it should be noted that although CDP analysts often borrow the analytical tools of discursive psychology, they use them more flexibly. The implicit, ideological aspects of identity that may not be directly referred to by participants in the immediate interactional context are often integral components of CDP analysis. Indeed, analogous to identity positions are *imaginary positions* (Wetherell & Edley, 1999) and *subject positions* (Davies & Harré, 1990) in which the ideological force of positions is emphasized. A way of thinking about how identity positions are treated in CDP is as characters that we populate our stories with, and which come loaded with meanings (Seymour-Smith, 2002). Depending on their positive or negative connotations, which are also affected by the context in which they are deployed, we may choose to distance ourselves from them rather than identify with them. As such, occupying identity positions that are dynamic and variable involves active processes of meaning-making.

Within a CDP approach, analyzing these identifications allows an examination of what positions are available, intelligible and evaluated as "good" in any cultural moment or setting. Although identity positions may be taken on temporarily, lightly, or ambivalently, evaluations of such positions as they are put to use (as positive, negative, both, or something in between) often point to deeper identity investments (Wetherell, 2003), that is, durable identities that people have attached meaning to over a longer period of time, akin to the order of identities that psychosocial analysts are interested in. Despite not relying on psychoanalytic theory as psychosocial research typically does, the concept of *psycho-discursive practices* brings attention to the continuity of particular identity positions. Wetherell argues that an individual's sustained use of identifications has implications for their psychology; this is how a vocabulary is acquired that comes to define "motives and a character with particular emotions, desires, goals and ambitions" (Wetherell & Edley, 1999, p. 353). An illustrative example that we touch on later is the naturalization of an ideal working mother, a "supermom." The analogy with a superhero is reflective of the commonsense notion that being a supermom is inherently good. But as we will show in our data example, the supermom identity position can be used flexibly – to account for potential failings relating to the cleanliness of one's house, success as a wife, or as a host for visiting friends. Through a relatively brief social interaction, a supermom position is variously identified with and distanced from. With this ideal position, certain aptitudes are expected and desires and tensions become routinized (and gendered), but they require personalization and become meaningful in the flow of social interaction. It becomes clear also that the process of sustaining supermom performances becomes a materially affecting process, intensifying the rhythm of daily life. In this sense, the affective work entailed in everyday identity practices is a form of practical engagement with the world (Scheer, 2012). Embodied, layered, intersecting affective performances get the business of identity work and organizing social life done. Further, although psycho-discursive practices need to be continually performed, they often "stick" through becoming entwined with other durable identities. Meanings of durable identity positions such as "wife" or "employee" may be relational to a supermom position, for example. In this way, individuals can be thought of as sites of practice where, through psycho-discursive practices, meanings become organized in predictable ways and a personal style emerges. This *personal ordering* might be posited as "personality" in conventional social-psychological approaches, but within a CDP framework there is always orientation to continuing and open-ended identity work, along with the active struggles that emerge as people are faced with different cultural resources, interactions, and relations (Wetherell, 2007). Again, underscoring the flexibility in a CDP approach, while the uniqueness of an individual's biography might be the unit of analysis, it is also possible to account for how less durable identities nudge personal orders in different directions.

So far, we have discussed the advantages of CDP in relation to more fine-grained discursive methods and psychoanalytic-informed psychosocial approaches in critical social psychology. As we begin to move toward discussing the implications of the development of critical psychology in the context of the affective turn, it is worth outlining a few other staples that make up the CDP analytic toolkit, which, as we shall see, can be extended to incorporate an affective lens.

A foundation of critical discursive psychology is that identities are organized in and through *interpretative repertoires*, recognizable routines of descriptions and evaluations, such as familiar anecdotes or clichés (Seymour-Smith, Wetherell, & Phoenix, 2002) that represent "common knowledge" (Billig, 1991; Wetherell & Potter, 1992). The making and remaking of identities through commonsense assumptions requires tailoring for specific social contexts, and because they are ideological, social power differentials provide the logic behind them. Assumptions about who has the right or aptitude to behave in certain ways are rhetorically organized and presented as logical rationale (common sense), but what often goes unnoticed in the flow of interaction is the moral and affective aspects of these logics. For instance, we have seen a changed political party landscape in many Western nations in recent years, carried through on the basis of overt claims linking purported decreases of living standards to "invasions" of immigrants. Often, however, as the rhetorical context demands, claims about improving public housing and health care systems become the vehicle for this messaging. Although minority groups are the targets, they may not feature explicitly, and we can still access these parts of the argumentative chain and their moral force. As Sara Ahmed (2004) notes, emotions "do things," giving the imagined position of migrant and refugee a "sticky" quality, where some forms of sense-making and emoting become hegemonic (Wetherell, 2015b).

Another useful analytic tool in the CDP toolkit is the notion of *trouble* as it relates to identity practices. CDP rests on practice theory, where attention is drawn to the logic of situated human action. This may be highly patterned and habitual, while also flexible and open to customization (Reckwitz, 2002). Identifying what becomes troubled, or remains untroubled, in social interactions can be useful in working out where the boundaries of particular fields of practice lie. When feelings of hesitation, the wish to guide interactions into another territory, or a flicker of confusion enter the interactional fray, they indicate more than just interactional trouble. Interactional repairs, the practical adjustments people make when speakers smooth out or self-right interactions gone awry, also signals social-psychological trouble (Wetherell, 2005a). The categories we identify with (woman, manager, person of color, etc.) are associated with particular social-psychological dispositions, emotional routines, levels of authority, etc. that we routinely make part of narratives of self, and psychobiography. Breaching interactional rules is also frequently a breaching or questioning of these personalized associations, and therefore implicates psychology. Further, the analysis of interactional or identity troubles is associated with *contradiction*, and moments where people become engaged in *ideological dilemmas* (Wetherell & Edley, 1999). Theorization of contradiction and ideological dilemmas in CDP draws on the work of Michael Billig (1991), who argued that discourse is primarily organized in conflicting ways, as a perpetual argument. Every position has a counterposition, and switching back and forth between them is part and parcel of answering everyday-life questions. While in conventional social psychology contradiction in accounts might be problematic where the accuracy of accounts is important, from a CDP perspective, they are analytically useful and highlight that identity performances are contextual.

In summary, pressing contemporary questions that have emerged in the social sciences about how to study the relationship between the identity groups to which people belong, associated emotional practices, and issues of ideology and social power bear a striking resemblance to earlier debates that occurred as forms of critical social psychology were developing. Then, as now, the central question is, how can we study the deeply felt, the seemingly inchoate sensations in being "moved" by something, in methodical and evidence-based ways? By revisiting the emergence of CDP, the predecessor of affective discursive practices, it is apparent that there has been a long-standing impulse in Wetherell's work to disrupt dichotomies between thinking and feeling that blight emotion studies, which are relevant for identity research. In this context, it is unsurprising that ADP theory has developed in the form of intervention, questioning some of the assumptions propelling the turn to affect. As we shall see in Section 6.2, ADP draws on and extends CDP, providing a stronger identities studies response to affect and emotions scholars, whose work, while immensely generative, might otherwise offer little to the empirical study of identity.

6.2 Identity, Affect, and Affective Discursive Practices

6.2.1 Fleshing Out the "Turn to Affect"

For more than a decade, the humanities and social sciences have been humming with new theoretical work foregrounding affect as a way into understanding the social world. Emphasizing feeling and embodiment and with a distinct interest in the affectivity of bodies, places and objects, this "affective turn" (Halley & Clough, 2008) opens up tantalizing questions and possibilities for exploring identity. Affect and emotion scholarship is wide-ranging and transdisciplinary (Ahmed, 2004; Brown & Stenner, 2009; Burkitt, 2014; Cromby, 2015; Everts & Wagner, 2012; Laurier & Philo, 2006; Massumi, 2002; Reddy, 2001; Sullivan, 2018). Instead of attempting to review this disparate field in its full breadth, we take a sharper focus and consider two highly influential currents within the affective turn. Both of these currents of work entail a turn away from discourse and meaning-making (Wetherell, 2012, 2015b), precipitating a break with the empirically oriented CDP tradition outlined above. They also raise some serious red flags for identity scholars.

The first line of scholarship we turn to is linked to Eve Kosofsky Sedgwick and Adam Frank. Sedgwick (2007) has been well known for her critique of paranoid discursive analytic strategies that produce "all or nothing" (p. 631) accounts of social life and leave little room for questions of feeling, embodiment, and agency. It was Sedgwick's contention that the majority of the humanities and social sciences had become stuck in a rut, where the formula for providing research conclusions was to deem any social object as good *or* bad. By disregarding feelings in their analysis, researchers could not reach nuanced conclusions where social objects could be both good *and* bad. As part of a broader movement toward the embodied and experiential, Sedgwick and Frank (1995) have taken up the work of psychologist Silvan Tomkins, breathing new life and authority into his basic emotion paradigm (Sedgwick & Frank, 1995). Tomkins (1995) is well known in psychological circles for theorizing the existence of a set number of innate basic emotions or "affect programs" evolved to guide our responses to what he saw as universal human predicaments. Following Tomkins' theorization of a neat and fixed correspondence between neurophysiological activation and bodily registration of feeling (and despite their advantageous starting point of a clearly embodied account of affect), Sedgwick, and Frank (1995, as cited in Wetherell, 2012) advanced an agenda in which affects "unfold in an automatic, clunk-click, sequential manner" (p. 37). When an appropriate prime is presented, a predefined emotion is felt. Furthermore, basic emotional states unfold prior to processes of cognition and evaluation, and are thus (somewhat ironically) outside the sphere of human agency. Critics have identified a range of issues with Sedgwick and Frank's arguments, including the Anglophone framing (assuming that bodies "speak English" and emote according to the "basic emotions" of the Western cultural canon; see Wetherell, 2015b) and its mismatch with cutting-edge psychobiological thinking (Leys, 2011). Moreover, a basic emotions standpoint is problematic insofar as it privileges a depersonalizing, biological account that closes off social justice-oriented questions pertinent to identity studies: How do power, privilege and perceptible identity categories organize affective experience, and affectively charged interactions?

A second cluster of work, associated with Brian Massumi (2002) and Nigel Thrift (2008), proceeds from a very different understanding of the nature of affect and emotion, but reaches similar conclusions concerning the division between thinking and feeling. For these scholars, affect is a form of excess, an instinctive, precognitive force that both precedes and exceeds the disciplining domains of language and discourse. Affect strikes preconsciously and moves through the material world indiscriminately. It is a series of flows "moving through the bodies of human and other beings" (Thrift, 2008, p. 236), a kind of electricity, entraining what it hits into a particular kind of response. Smells, objects, places and atmospheres pulse with affect just as fleshy bodies and body parts do. Rather than an interest in thoughts, interpretation, and meaning, our attention turns instead to a different plane of preconscious movement, sensation, transmission, and contagion. Once again, we arrive at a series of binary differentiations that cleave the discursive from the affective: bodies versus words, non-conscious activation versus conscious action. As Wetherell (2012, 2015b) has argued, the abandonment of discourse and meaning-making evident in Massumi's and Thrift's work obfuscates how cultural conditions of possibility and personal histories are profoundly entwined with our bodies' sensing and sensual capacities. It is also a turn away from identity and subjectivity. Curiously, in attending to the biological body, these theorists seem to lose their grasp of figuring, feeling personhood. As a corollary, they rule out a consideration of the role of identity process and identifications in how we are moved by events, scenes and people; but we will return to this point more fully later. Suffice to say that these binaries, and the analytic losses they precipitate, demand a response from identity researchers.

6.2.2 Theorizing Identity: An Affective Discursive Approach

Encountering these new theories, identity scholars (particularly those affiliated with psychology) might be excused for eyeing the turn to affect with a twinge of unease. But this would be a mistake; for, as we will demonstrate, the turn to affect presents a generative and useful opportunity to clarify and refine the study of identity in a manner that explicitly takes account of domains that might more usually have been left to one side: for example, embodied experience, material objects, sounds and places. There are several exciting lines of work taking up this challenge (Cromby & Willis, 2016; McGrath, Mullarkey, & Reavey, 2019; Sullivan, 2018; Taylor, 2015) and finding ways to broaden the scope of identity-based inquiries without relinquishing the strengths and benefits of discourse and narrative-based approaches. We focus in particular on Margaret Wetherell's important theoretical work on *affective discursive practices* (Wetherell, 2012, 2013, 2015a; Wetherell, McConville, & McCreanor, 2019) which we argue offers a flexible and fruitful way forward for identity scholars.

Wetherell's work on ADP arises in conversation with the affective turn and some of the knotty problems that follow from the "rubbishing of discourse" (Wetherell, 2012, p. 19). In particular, ADP helps to articulate and make visible the role that identifications play in the affective dimensions of social life. Arguably, ADP personalizes affect and emotion, where the affect theory of Thrift, Sedgwick, and others leaves it depersonalized. Building from her highly influential work in CDP, Wetherell makes a persuasive argument for a social practice approach to affective phenomena that considers thinking alongside feeling, meaning-making alongside embodiment. Rather than a delineating a rigid analytic process, Wetherell's practice approach is "a way of thinking" about affect and emotion, one which spurs analysts to "traverse the body, the discursive, social contexts, histories, personal stories and affect's movement" (Wetherell, 2012, p. 26). Thus, an affective discursive practice approach makes space for a truly expansive theorization of identities and identity practices across multiple scales. This mode of analysis is sensitive to the way identities cohere and change through the enactment of an array of affective discursive practices over the life course. At the same time, analyses are attentive to the histories and resonances of these personally staged and inflected, affective discursive identity practices. In this sense, an affective discursive approach recognizes identities (and the processes of identification that give rise to them) are always already social, indexing the self as well as the social world as they are produced in practice. As a consequence, Wetherell (2008) dispenses with conceptual divisions between the social discourses and norms that provision identities, and the subjective working up of these social identities in particular, individual lives, terrain sometimes referred to as "subjectivity."

The approach Wetherell (2012) outlines has strong continuities with CDP, and shares many of its tools, tenets and strengths. The fundamental unit of interest – identity practices – remains constant, as does the accompanying interest in balancing attention to habit, history, and past identity practice alongside creativity and customization. Vitally, for those concerned with affect, meaning-making, and identity, Wetherell brings an interest in everyday and routine experiences to the study of affect and emotion, alongside the jolting, uncanny affective phenomena favored by others (Sedgwick & Frank, 1995; Thrift, 2008). Thus, affect and emotion are made amenable to empirical investigation as practical knowledges that are constructed through experience and guide us through social life. These patterned, often familiar practices are the bread and butter of our affective lives – and, Wetherell contends, they must have a place in our inquiries, if we are to make the most of what feeling, affect, and emotion have to offer us conceptually.[1]

Alongside these continuities are some important points of divergence and extension. Enriched through engagement with transdisciplinary thinking about the nature of affect and emotion, Wetherell's ADP approach brings new vocabularies and new realms of experience to the attention of identity scholars. Familiar concepts in discourse studies are stretched in new directions. For example, we are invited to explore how identity work unfolds within a generational "regime" of emotions (Reddy, 2001), and a shared "structure of feeling" (Williams, 1977) guiding everyday practices. From here, we might explore how prevailing "canonical emotions," familiar and orthodox procedures for emoting (McConville et al., 2017), scaffold and privilege particular affective identities and performances. As we write, scholars are beginning to experiment with this new conceptual wardrobe, pushing identity studies in attractive and compelling new directions (Chowdhury & Gibson, 2019; Martinussen, 2019; Scully, 2015; Van Der Merwe, 2019).

An affective discursive practice approach also dares discursively-minded identity researchers to broaden their understanding of what counts as data, and what matters for identity work. Drawing inspiration from multimodal work on affect and emotion in human geography and cultural studies (see Wetherell 2015a), ADP positions the material world – objects, places, sounds, smells – within the purview of identity studies. In part, this is enabled by ADP's stronger orientation toward the synchronic, in-the-moment dimensions of identity, such as claiming a "victim" or "expert" identity position during a quarrel, alongside the "usual diachronic concerns" (Wetherell, 2015a, p. 85) with broader and more stable social formations. To concretize what this broadened view might look like in the context of an empirical research project, we find Bille and Simonsen's (2019) theoretical work on atmosphere particularly helpful. Where places and artifacts are often cast as "affect generators"

---

[1] We understand feeling, affect, and emotion to gesture toward the same broad territory, albeit with different connotations. Feeling conjures subjective experience, emotion invokes discrete cultural categories such as "pride" and "disgust," while affect is the more general term and is most favored in recent theoretical work.

that radiate atmosphere in and of themselves, Bille and Simonsen (2019) argue that atmosphere "is not only something humans *feel*, or that conditions perception, but it also simultaneously positions the felt space as something humans *do*" (p. 10). Thus, atmospheric practices arise in the coming together of the affective potentials of particular bodies, places, and objects. In relation to the study of identity, this theorization not only orients us to the potential of specific scenes, sights, and sounds to invoke and act on identities, but also points out the active participation of figuring, feeling bodies in the structuring and perception of atmospheres. For example, in Wetherell and colleagues' (2019) analysis of ANZAC Day commemorations,[2] the multimodal artifacts assembled for the event – a hushed crowd, the civic building "red-draped by floodlights" before dawn (p. 10), the lingering notes of *The Last Post* – combine differently for/with participant Juliet than the crowd at large. Juliet herself becomes a site of identity practice; her dissent goes against the grain of the larger system of solemn reverence in which she is situated. Kaupapa Māori researchers (Moewaka Barnes et al., 2017) have also shown how indigenous ways of being, knowing, and feeling – often represented as primitive superstition in Western/settler knowledge systems – can be productively explored alongside multimodal discursive affect theory. This is a challenge to researchers to widen interpretations of what counts as data, and to acknowledge how diversity in the identity positions that researchers hold can advance studies of identity and affect. Taking up this challenge might result in more researchers bringing "the gift of spirit into the heart of the academy" (Moewaka Barnes et al., 2017, p. 11), and a decolonizing research agenda for identity studies in the "West."

This understanding of atmospheres as a social practice entangled with the work of identity practices and the material world of objects, sounds, smells, places, and spirit has, we believe, much to offer identity studies and identities studies researchers, as a field where the spiritual and material worlds as well as synchronic concerns have, historically, taken a back seat. Attention to atmospheric practices as part and parcel of the study of identity also plugs the field of scholarship into cutting-edge conversations that are unfolding in other disciplines exploring the intertwining of the spatial and the social.

6.2.3 Identity, Emotion, and Agency

We conclude our discussion of what affective discursive practice approaches have to offer identity researchers with some specific reflections on where this analytic strategy sits in relation to ongoing debates in identity studies concerning the nature of agency. In some identity scholarship, the question of agency is posed as a conflict between internal energies and the external forces that act

---

[2] ANZAC Day commemorates the Australians and New Zealanders who served and died in all wars and armed conflicts, with a particular emphasis on World War I and II. The principal activity is a highly ritualized "dawn service" held at war memorial sites across the country.

to channel and constrain them. This sets up what we consider to be a rather unhelpful binary notion of the individual versus the social: inside versus outside. Unsurprisingly given Wetherell's impatience with "either–or" thinking, an ADP approach sidesteps this binary and focuses instead on the imbrication of the psychological and the social. In doing so, it offers particular advantages for thinking through questions of identity, agency, and the entanglement of our so-called "inner" and "outer" lives.

Identity is therefore an obvious site for ADP analyses precisely because it is the meeting place of the "micro and macro, the exterior and interior" (Taylor, 2010, p. 3); a site where broader social formations are refracted through individual lives. In line with earlier CDP thinking and more contemporary psychosocial approaches, an ADP perspective rejects so-called "discourse determinism" (Wetherell, 2012; see also Wetherell, 2005b) arguing that broader cultural figurations and the subject positions they make available are not automatically or uniformly stamped onto people. Rather, identity practices are complex, intersectional, and actively negotiated, reformulated, and enacted by reflexive subjects in light of personal and social orders combined with the particular material and interactional possibilities at hand (Wetherell, 2012). At the same time, Wetherell's approach is wary of a heavy-handed focus on the voluntaristic and synchronic elements of practice, considering it to be similarly unpromising. As we have seen in relation to affect and emotion scholarship more broadly, a focus on the present moment risks obscuring the influence of personal and social histories, leaving analysts struggling to account for pattern and continuity.

An emphasis on practice allows ADP to find a middle ground between these two perspectives on questions of agency and structure. Elsewhere, we have characterized ADP as an approach that probes what Sedgwick (2007) terms the "middle ranges" of agency (Martinussen & Wetherell, 2019). Analytic attention explores *relative* power as evident in choices, capacities, and contingencies, alongside the constitutive qualities of the broader affective discursive terrain. ADP is distinctive in its capacity to work across these registers, inviting attention to how identities are actively crafted, while also exploring the histories and resonances of the materials and resources that are being put to work. Rather than seeking to differentiate between "inner" and "outer" lives in a manner that privileges either agency or passivity, analysts can take up the tools of ADP to investigate identities and identifications as simultaneously personally negotiated, embodied, and often deeply felt, *as well as* thoroughly social (Wetherell, 2012).

This stance on agency and identity makes a helpful intervention into broader investigations of affect and emotion, which, as we have seen, can become unhelpfully depersonalized and deterministic. In seeking to understand collective action, for example, dominant accounts from outside psychology and identities studies have theorized the transmission of affect and emotion as a form of interpersonal contagion. For instance, in the work of

Nigel Thrift (2008), affect moves as an undifferentiated series of flow, sliding from one object/person to the next in a precognitive manner, and entraining bodies together into joint action, as a flock of starlings in flight. While undoubtedly beguiling, Thrift's notion flounders when brought to bear on social life, as it entirely bypasses any agentic, individual figuring of collective emotions (see, for example, Sullivan, 2015). Wetherell herself (2015b, p. 154) is quick to point this out:

> analogies which compare the shared affective action of humans en masse with flocks of starlings are obfuscating. Worse still, these approaches close off promising lines of enquiry, and render processes of "affective engineering" uncanny and deeply obscure. A key advantage of an affective practices approach to the social psychology of affect is that this approach can join together what is divided in Thrift's work.

As Wetherell (2015b) makes clear, an inattention to identity and meaning-making risks a kind of affective determinism, wherein contagious affect works on and passes through us irrespective of our identities, personal history, and habit. The briefest reflection on one's own life demonstrates that this under-standing of crowd psychology is implausible in the extreme (see Reicher, 1996, 2001). Passers-by are not automatically, preconsciously enlisted into jubilant celebration of a World Cup won, nor are they necessarily pulled into a fervent "Pro-Life" demonstration, or a homophobic attack. Affect and emotions may be shared by members of a group, but not necessarily. In some circumstances, the affective discursive practices in evidence may be highly coordinated; more often, we suggest, the practices crowd members take up are likely to vary considerably in form and intensity. To examine and explain such variation, we need tools that allow us to study how affect becomes personalized, and identity theory that can account for the crucial role of agency, identifications, and affiliations in parsing the "hit" of affect. This is precisely what an affective discursive mode of analysis offers.

6.3 Identities and Affective Discursive Practices: An Illustration

In this final section, we aim to demonstrate the potential of affective discursive analyses to illuminate identifications and invigorate identity studies. To do so, we will focus on a single interview extract drawn from our current research investigating young women's negotiations of positivity practices and "positive" identities in Aotearoa, New Zealand. As part of this project, we interviewed twenty-four women aged between 18 and 35, drawn from three groups whose regular activities demand considerable emotional work: service and hospitality workers; mothers of young children; and Instagram influen-cers. Members of these groups are often expected to conform to a fairly constrained emotional repertoire for the benefit, approval, and pleasure of others. Interviews lasted between one and two hours, and covered a range of topics including personal experiences with emotional management and positivity. The centrality of feeling and emotion in our discussions of personal, professional, and maternal identities makes this work an ideal forum for showcasing affective discursive analyses of identity work (see, for example, Chowdhury & Gibson, 2019; Gill & Organ, 2018; Scharff, 2016).

After a brief orientation to the interview in question, we will work our analysis up in three directions, in order to illustrate three angles or entry points into affective discursive analysis of identity practices that, we find, offer particularly compelling and useful insights into identity. The first, and broadest, of these angles investigates identities, subject positions, and identifications in light of structures of feeling (Williams, 1977), prevailing emotion regimes (Reddy, 2001), and feeling positions and the dominant discursive formations they articulate with(in) (Wetherell, 2012). The second angle interlocks with and personalizes the first, asking how particular identities, identifications, and investments take shape in context, and concretize or wither over time. Taken together, these two analytic entry points highlight different identity "chronologies" or timescales, offering a vocabulary for macro societal and generational influences on affective identity processes, while also inviting attention to personal identity investments and affiliations, and the moment-to-moment positioning work of the interview itself. The third angle orients toward dimensions of experience that, while undoubtedly implicated in the construction of identities, have tended to fall outside traditional investigations of identity within psychology: objects, places, sounds, and images.

Before proceeding any further, a note to readers: the three entry points we identify are not discrete or mutually exclusive analyses, but angles that can, and should, be productively worked together to inform a single analysis. As we hope to illustrate below, a multifaceted analysis of the phenomenon of interest has potential to produce a rich and complex account of identity work that cuts across the embodied, the contextual, the interactional, the spatial/material, and the socio-political.

6.3.1 Interviewing Mia

Our interview with Mia took place on University campus,[3] in a private room with a view of the Auckland harbor, hot drinks, and biscuits. The interview was audio-recorded and subsequently transcribed. It began with the interviewer, Octavia, inviting Mia to talk about "your experiences of being a mom, how it came about and how it has been for you." Taking up this invitation with considerable gusto, Mia talked largely unprompted for the two-hour interview. At the time of the interview, Mia was pregnant and

---

[3] Mia is a pseudonym selected by the participant. Some details of this interview have been generalized or altered to maintain confidentiality.

anticipating the imminent arrival of her second child. Raised in a South Asian country, Mia had moved with her husband to New Zealand several years earlier, prior to the birth of her first child. A full-time working Mom, Mia had opted to begin her maternity leave in advance of her due date, which, she explained, allowed her some breathing space at home as well as free time to join the research.

A salient feature of the interview with Mia was her reflections on her initial difficulties in adjusting to the arrival of her first baby. The timing of this interview, and Mia's late-pregnancy embodiment, lent a particular affective intensity to our conversation. As Mia talked over maternal identity and experiences (and sipped on a very weak coffee), her posture and movements, as well as her baby's kicks and flutters, could draw our attention toward the newborn-to-be at any moment. In what follows, we draw on this interview to examine affective discursive identity work across multiple chronologies, making use of multiple lines of evidence. While informed by our knowledge of Mia's interview as a whole, we focus our discussion on the single transcript extract presented below.[4] This talk came roughly 15 minutes into the interview, as Mia was responding in detail to the initial prompt noted above (talk about your experience of being a Mom).

MIA   Um (.) as I said it was a very funny situation for me you know (.) for someone who is really confident I I was pushed into a place where I wasn't confident at all.

INT   *A huge yeah (.) shift [Mia: Yeah] for you?*

MIA   And for someone who was (.) who was working for 12 years and then took a year break (.) so again another external factor you know where .hhh at work it's pretty logical you're used to .hhh meeting targets you're used to meeting goals and stuff and (.) With a baby (.) you (.) none of that is possible (.) you know there there is no goal there's just surviving it (.) And you know that mental shift you know like to draw you a comparison like for example at work you are able to do five things (.) whereas at home you'll you'll be like I need to cook (.) I need to do my laundry I need to clean the house and (.) whatever you know fold the laundry up (.) but but with a baby none of those four things happen (.) so you're this new mom who's just sitting (.) there looking at all the stuff (.) that has not happened .hhh And that sort of really um works on your mind [Int; mmm] because you're used to success in in some small ways you know small things and you know that feeling of ah achievement (.) oh I've achieved this. And I think um (.) achieving a happy baby is amazing (.) *I I think the society does not understand

---

[4] A note on transcription notation: we use (.) to mark a brief pause, .hhh to indicate an audible out-breath, underlined text to indicate emphasis, and * * signs around a passage of text to show that it was spoken with a "laughing" voice. Interviews were audio-recorded but not video-recorded.

how difficult that is (.) **[Int: yeah]** just having a <u>healthy</u> baby (.) a <u>healthy</u> (.) mindset a <u>dirty</u> house (.) all good you <u>know</u>* and having that sort of <u>acceptance</u> like .hhh like you feel oh god people are going to come over to see me and the baby (.) and you'd really want them to come over because you are craving for that adult stimulation you really are <u>I</u> was. And then you're like oh god the house is a <u>mess</u> (.) maybe we shouldn't. And so you start sort of judging and isolating yourself (.) Um (.) I wasn't one of those people *I was like you know if you are a friend of mine you will come home and (.) load the dishwasher you <u>know</u>* because <u>I</u> would do that for you sort of thing.

6.3.2 Feeling Positions and Affective Discursive Formations

A range of affective discursive identity positions are evident in this short passage. In Mia's talk, we can see the "professional achiever" [lines 5–9] giving way to the "overwhelmed Mum" [lines 6–12] surviving the demands of new motherhood. A little later, the latent figures of the "failing Mum" and the "supermom" set the scene for the arrival of the "balanced Mum" [lines 14–17], who adjusts successfully to motherhood by recalibrating her expectations.

To make sense of the appearance of these figures within Mia's talk, we might usefully examine prevailing and affectively charged cultural resources that entwine with, and help to scaffold, these dominant identity positions (e.g., latent figures of the failing mum and the supermom). Such macro-level cultural resources, including structures of feeling (Williams, 1977), canonical emotions (McConville et al., 2017), and emotional styles (Reddy, 2001), are tuned to the broad emotional registers that lend particular generations, institutions, and social groups a "distinctive affective flavor" (Wetherell, 2012, p. 103). In current Westernized contexts, the affective flavor of young women's meaning-making and identity work is often heavily inflected with neoliberal, postfeminist, and "psy" discourses (Chowdhury & Gibson, 2019; Gill & Kanai, 2018; Scharff, 2016). These discourses are animated by a shared affective discursive circuitry wherein confidence, resilience, and an affective orientation toward self-management and self-improvement are leading and preferred emotional styles (Gill & Orgad, 2017, 2018). In turn, this circuitry makes a feeling of personal responsibility for one's successes and failures a powerful emotional common sense, or "structure of feeling," which undergirds a great deal of meaning-making work.

This "responsibilized" structure of feeling and the winning emotional style it validates are evident in Mia's workplace disposition, the "professional achiever" [lines 5–9]. This identity position centers on a confident affective discursive orientation to the world around her, wherein she formulates goals, meets targets and is rewarded with success and 'that feeling of [. . .] *achievement*' [line 14]. Mia's loss of confidence after the birth of her child is thus comprehensible as a serious problem, one entangled with her initial struggle to translate an efficient, successful disposition into her new home life (as evidenced through "mess" [line 20] and tasks left incomplete [lines 9–13]). Mia addresses this identity trouble by invoking an affective repertoire stemming from psy discourses: the "journey of emotional growth." Through insight into the sources of her low confidence [lines 1–6], rejecting unhelpful social expectations and reaching "acceptance" of her messy house [lines 15–17], Mia describes herself as able, now, to confidently prioritize her own and her baby's needs in a manner compatible with the affective discursive position of the "professional achiever" while also affirming her alignment with balanced, confident motherhood.

6.3.3 Identifications, Investments, and Identity Work

While the analysis above offers a broad picture of the meaning-making resources Mia has to hand to build and negotiate identities, it has less to say about how and why these particular affective positions and the emotional styles associated with them might have come to have particular meaning and resonance. To shed light on these matters of personalization, so crucial to the study of identity, we return to Wetherell's (2012, 2013) concept of affect as practice.

While a theory of practice clearly underscores affective discursive modes of analysis as we have discussed them so far, some elements of practice theory are particularly useful for articulating the processes through which we are physically and discursively recruited into the kinds of broader social patterns of feeling, action, and response outlined above. Practice, at once noun and verb, delineates a social phenomenon while also gesturing toward possibilities for repetition and revision, habit and innovation, pattern and specificity. Over a lifetime, particular habits of feeling are formed, re-enacted, laid down, and concretized, shaped by highly specific contexts and resourced by a broader social material. Thus, a personal order is built, embodied, carrying with it particular affective discursive dispositions while retaining enough elasticity to move – and be moved – in new directions.

In the interview with Mia, we can see traces of precisely this kind of patterning. Mia describes how, over her 12-year career, she became "used to success" [lines 13–14], comfortable in the pleasurable affective rhythms of professional goal-setting and achievement and the "professional achiever" favored in neoliberal social orders. Mia paints a picture of how her everyday achievements prompted regular, satisfying moments of self-evaluation – "oh I've achieved this" [line 14]. Over time, these small moments of interpellation sediment into a prevailing feeling position for Mia as a capable, successful person, an identity she can carry forward. In other words, we can see how emotion and affect become personalized through psycho-discursive practices. Yet, these familiar patterns are always at risk of meeting with competing interactional demands, or more sustained forms of trouble. In attempting to transpose this disposition onto her new life with a newborn, Mia's goals (cooking, laundry, cleaning, folding) are unachieved; she implies that, like other mothers, she is left "just sitting (.) there looking at all the stuff" [lines 11–12]. A focus on the affective discursive dimensions of this extract tunes us in to the "affective clout" (Sointu, 2016) of the original experience and its retelling in the interview, as Mia loses her grip on a familiar, valued identification.

Shifting our gaze from personal histories to the interpersonal present, we can see that a considerable degree of active figuring and identity crafting is also evident, as Mia asserts that "achieving a happy baby is amazing," articulating an alternative, more livable vision of successful mothering in the form of a revised checklist: "a healthy baby (.) a healthy (.) mindset a dirty house (.) all good" [lines 15–17]. Finally, Mia's feeling position of humor and reasonableness, conveyed jointly through her ironic checklist and her laughing vocal tone, work to affirm her interactional positioning as balanced and genuine. Thus, an analysis of the affective discursive is capacious enough to examine the texture of long-term identity investments, as well as more locally oriented identity projects such as appearing reasonable, generous, or just.

6.3.4 Objects, Places, Sounds, Images

To conclude this section, we turn to domains that are less frequently considered in analyses of identity and identity practices: objects, places, sounds, and images. We are interested, in particular, in demonstrating how one or several of these elements combine with social and personal histories to produce *affective atmospheres* (Anderson, 2009; Duff, 2016; Wetherell et al., 2019) that entrain and engage particular identifications and feeling positions. We draw particularly on Bille and Simonsen's (2019) theorization outlined in the previous section, wherein atmosphere is theorized as a relational practice that arises "between people, places and things."

We can trace one such affective atmosphere in Mia's account. In the short extract we present, Mia references the "stuff" of her home life repeatedly: unwashed laundry, uncooked food, house cleaning, unfolded laundry, dirty house, mess. When Mia and these objects come together, a particular atmosphere seems to result: one of failure and shame. Although Mia concludes by distancing herself from "those people" who judge and isolate themselves because of household mess, the prominent role of unruly household objects in her talk nevertheless suggests their potential to trouble her performance of a nonchalant, confident maternal identity. Indeed, the affective atmosphere entrained between Mia and these objects appears to intensify at the prospect of a visit from friends: "oh god the house is a mess."

While we rely on the analysis of audio transcript data in this analysis, Mia's use of affective discursive resources demonstrates the expansive reach of discourse and its capacities to mobilize in ways that exceed common sense understandings of thinking and speaking, into broader affective domains. This understanding of atmosphere – and its affective intensification when others assemble as witnesses – illuminates the specific affective potential of household mess, disorder and dirtiness to unsettle "good" feminine and maternal identities. It also suggests why mothers, but not other participants, routinely warned interviewers and apologized for the "state" of their houses before we visited. The gendered address of everyday household objects, and their capacity to reproach women, perhaps mothers especially, is a neat illustration of the imbrication of objects, identities, and atmospheres. Again, although relying on the analysis of words, the difficulty of separating out meanings that have multimodal and embodied effects comes into view. As women excuse themselves, they become sites of practice for the interplay of politicized organization of meanings of household objects.

This understanding may, in turn, help us answer questions about how and why particular objects and scenes affect social groups differently, without reference to the purely physiological or biological. Atmosphere does not reside in a particular physical environment, nor is it fixed in a particular object; it is instead the relational assembling of people, discursive regimes, and the material world. As people move through an affecting field, they practice an affective atmosphere (Bille & Simonsen, 2019) differently. Returning to Mia, it becomes evident later in the interview that stray socks, grimy basins, and piled-up dishes do not produce the same feeling of failure and shame with/on her husband. An understanding of affective atmospheres might thus offer a richer account of heterosexual men's purported "dirt blindness" (Ruppanner & Churchill, 2018). An affective discursive attention to objects, places, sounds, and images underscores the value of multimodal inquiries to identity studies, as bodies, investments, and artifacts come together to interpellate, and in doing so, become part of the identity "infrastructure" or resources (Döveling, Harju, & Sommer, 2018) of everyday life.

6.4 Conclusion

Affect and emotion scholarship presents new opportunities and challenges for the study of identity. In this chapter, we have argued for the value of an affective discursive practice approach for the advancement of the field of identity research. Firstly, we have demonstrated how ADP provides a roadmap for identity researchers to capitalize on the wide-ranging, multimodal interests of affect and emotion literature while maintaining focus on people's active meaning-making and practice. Remaining attentive to the co-construction of meanings about what can be felt by whom, and patterning in their forms, allows identity scholars to better track the ideological effects of affective practices. Additionally, ADP gets around the binaries of discourse and practice or words and bodies, by treating affect as a form of social practice that gets done and redone through identity work.

Secondly, through building on the discursive study of identity found in critical discursive psychology, ADP becomes a comprehensive toolkit for the empirical study of identity alongside studies of affect and emotion, which continue to develop at pace. While apprehending identities – with all of their embodied, narrative, and historical richness, across and modalities and scales – ADP helps us to keep hold of the complexities of identifications. Pulling apart the mobilization of meaning as turbulent or searing affects are registered is not an easy task, but one that is likely to be increasingly expected of identity scholars in the turn of affect in the social sciences. An affective discursive practice approach points a way forward for surveying the discursive and the embodied through the same analytic frame, providing a set of practical tools with which to realize this ambition.

Thirdly, an affective discursive practice approach can help the field of identity studies advance future research agendas that orient to questions of collective feelings, actions, and responsibilities. Current events punctuated with terror and political fragmentation, where violent, divisive, and hateful feeling positions and identifications seem to be gaining new ground, highlight the urgent need to ask how affect mobilizes and recruits through processes of political identifications (Wetherell, 2019). Identity scholars entering this territory will need the kind of capacious toolkit affective discursive practice offers: one that invites analysis of identities through the prisms of personal attachments, bodywork, and atmospheric practices. At the same time, lastly, ADP provides new lines of enquiry for investigating longer-standing political issues and inequalities. We have demonstrated how the gendering of affective practices associated with pervasive mandates to be responsible for the self can elide structural sexism in the home. We have pointed out also how colonial histories are being examined through indigenous lenses with the aid of ADP, both inside and outside the academy. As we work toward more hopeful and decolonized futures, ADP might, in the right hands, offer an assemblage of tools flexible enough to bend outside the contours of "Western" emotional canons toward a broader territory of identification, feeling, and spirit.

References

Ahmed, S. (2004). *The Cultural Politics of Emotion*. Edinburgh: Edinburgh University Press.

Anderson, B. (2009). Affective atmospheres. *Emotion, Space & Society*, 2(2), 77–81.

Bille, M. & Simonsen, K. (2019). Atmospheric practices: On affecting and being affected. *Space and Culture*, 24(2), doi:10.1177/1206331218819711.

Billig, M. (1991). *Ideology and Opinions: Studies in Rhetorical Psychology*. London: Sage.

Blackman, L., Cromby, J., Hook, D., Papadopoulos, D., & Walkerdine, V. (2008). Creating subjectivities. *Subjectivity*, *22*(1), 1–27. doi:10.1057/sub.2008.8.

Brown, S. D. & Stenner, P. (2009). *Psychology without Foundations*. London: Sage.

Burkitt, I. (2014). *Emotions and Social Relations*. London: Sage.

Campos, G. P., Ramos, C. S., & Bernal, J. J. Y. (1999). Emotion discourse "speaks" of involvement: Commentary on Edwards. *Culture & Psychology*, *5*(3), 293–304. doi:10.1177/1354067X9953002.

Chowdhury, N. & Gibson, K. (2019). This is (still) a man's world: Young professional women's identity struggles in gendered workplaces. *Feminism & Psychology*, *29*(4), 475–493, doi:10.1177/0959353519850851.

Clough, P. T. (2008). The affective turn: Political economy, biomedia and bodies. *Theory, Culture & Society*, *25*(1), 1–22, doi:10.5565/rev/athenead/v13n3.1060.

Clough, P. T. & Halley, J. O. (Eds.). (2008). *The Affective Turn: Theorizing the Social*. Durham, NC: Duke University Press.

Cromby, J. (2015). *Feeling Bodies: Embodying Affect*. Basingstoke: Palgrave.

Cromby, J. & Willis, M. E. H. (2016). Affect – or feeling (after Leys). *Theory & Psychology*, *26*(4), 476–495, doi:10.1177/0959354316651344.

Davies, B. & Harré, R. (1990). Positioning: The discursive production of selves. *Journal for the Theory of Social Behaviour*, *20*(1), 43–63. doi:10.1111/j.1468-5914.1990.tb00174.x.

Döveling, K., Harju, A. A., & Sommer, D. (2018). From mediatized emotion to digital affect cultures: New technologies and global flows of emotion. *Social Media+ Society*, *4*(1), 1–11.

Duff, C. (2016). Atmospheres of recovery: Assemblages of health. *Environment and Planning A: Economy and Space*, *48*(1), 58–74. doi:10.1177/0308518X15603222.

Edwards, D. (1999). Emotion discourse. *Culture & Psychology*, *5*(3), 271–291, doi:10.1177/1354067X9953001.

Emerson, P. & Frosh, S. (2004). *Critical Narrative Analysis in Psychology: A Guide to Practice*. Basingstoke: Palgrave Macmillan

Everts, J. & Wagner, L. (2012). Guest editorial: Practising emotions. *Emotion, Space & Society*, *5*, 174–176.

Frosh, S. (2014). The nature of the psychosocial: Debates from studies in the psycho-social. *Journal of Psycho-Social Studies*, *8*(1), 159–169.

Gill, R. & Kanai, A. (2018). Mediating neoliberal capitalism: Affect, subjectivity and inequality. *Journal of Communication*, *68*(2), 318–326. doi:10.1093/joc/jqy002.

Gill, R. & Orgad, S. (2017). Confidence culture and the remaking of feminism. *New Formations*, *91*, 16–34.

Gill, R. & Orgad, S. (2018). The amazing bounce-backable woman: Resilience and the psychological turn in neoliberalism. *Sociological Research Online*, *23*(2), 477–495.

Hollway, W. & Jefferson, T. (2005). Response: But why did Vince get sick? A reply to Spears and Wetherell. *British Journal of Social Psychology*, *42*(2), 175–180, doi:10.1348/014466605X37503.

Laurier, E. & Philo, C. (2006). Possible geographies: A passing encounter in a café. *Area*, *38*(1), 353–363.

Leys, R. (2011). The turn to affect: A critique. *Critical Inquiry*, *37*(3), 434–472.

Martinussen, M. (2019). Critical social psychology and interdisciplinary studies of personal life: Greater than the sum of its parts. *Social and Personality Psychology Compass*, *13*(1), 1–13.

Martinussen, M. & Wetherell, M. (2019). Affect, practice and contingency: Critical discursive psychology and Eve Kosofsky Sedgwick. *Subjectivity*, *12*(2), 101–116, doi:10.1057/s41286-019-00071-y.

Massumi, B. (2002). *Parables for the Virtual: Movements, Affect, Sensation*. Durham, NC: Duke University Press.

McConville, A., McCreanor, T., Wetherell, M., & Moewaka Barnes, H. (2017). Imagining an emotional nation: The print media and Anzac Day commemorations in Aotearoa New Zealand. *Media, Culture & Society*, *39*(1), 94–110.

McGrath, L., Mullarkey, S., & Reavey, P. (2019). Building visual worlds: Using maps in qualitative psychological research on affect and emotion. *Qualitative Research in Psychology*, *17*(1), 75–97, doi:10.1080/14780887.2019.1577517.

Moewaka Barnes, H., Gunn, T. R., Moewaka Barnes, A., Muriwai, E., Wetherell, M., & McCreanor, T. (2017). Feeling and spirit: Developing an indigenous wairua approach to research. *Qualitative Research*, *17*(3), 313–325, doi:10.1177/1468794117696031.

Parker, I. (1999). Critical psychology: Critical links. *Annual Review of Critical Psychology*, *1*, 3–18.

Reckwitz, A. (2002). Toward a theory of social practices: A development in culturalist theorizing. *European Journal of Social Theory*, *5*(2), 243–263.

Reddy, W. (2001). *The Navigation of Feelings: A Framework for the History of Emotions*. Cambridge: Cambridge University Press.

Reicher, S. (1996). The battle of Westminster: Developing the social identity model of crowd behaviour in order to deal with the initiation and development of collective conflict. *European Journal of Social Psychology*, *26*, 115–134.

Reicher, S. (2001). The psychology of crowd dynamics. In M. A. Hogg & S. Tindale (Eds.), *Blackwell Handbook of Social Psychology: Group Processes* (pp. 182–208). Oxford: Blackwell.

Reicher, S., Spears, R., & Haslam, S. A. (2010). The social identity approach in social psychology. In M. Wetherell & T. C. Mohanty (Eds.), *The Sage Handbook of Identities* (pp. 45–62). London: Sage.

Ruppanner, L. & Churchill, B. (2018). Sorry, men, there's no such thing as "dirt blindness" – you just need to do more housework. *The Conversation*. Retrieved April 20, 2021 from https://theconversation.com/sorry-men-theres-no-such-thing-as-dirt-blindness-you-just-need-to-do-more-housework-100883.

Scharff, C. (2016). The psychic life of neoliberalism: Mapping the contours of entrepreneurial subjectivity. *Theory, Culture & Society*, *33*(6), 107–122, doi:10.1177/0263276415590164.

Scheer, M. (2012). Are emotions a kind of practice (and is that why they have a history?) A Bourdieuan approach to understanding emotion. *History & Theory*, *51*(2), 193–200.

Scully, M. (2015). The problem of a subjective authenticity and the articulation of belonging among the Irish in England: A psychosocial approach. *Qualitative Research in Psychology, 12*(1), 34–44. doi:10.1080/14780887.2014.958369.

Sedgwick, E. K. (1997). Paranoid reading and reparative reading; or, you're so paranoid, you probably think this introduction is about you. In E. K. Sedgwick (Ed.), *Novel Gazing: Queer Readings in Fiction* (pp. 1–37). Durham, NC: Duke University Press.

Sedgwick, E. K. (2007). Melanie Klein and the difference affect makes. *South Atlantic Quarterly, 106*(3), 625–642.

Sedgwick, E. K. & Frank, A. (1995). *Shame and Its Sisters: A Silvan Tomkins Reader.* Durham, NC: Duke University Press

Seymour-Smith, S., Wetherell, M., & Phoenix, A. (2002). "My wife ordered me to come!": A discursive analysis of doctors' and nurses' accounts of men's use of general practitioners. *Journal of Health Psychology, 7*(3), 253–267, doi:10.1177/1359105302007003220.

Sointu, E. (2016). Discourse, affect and affliction. *The Sociological Review, 64*(2), 312–328, doi:10.1111/1467-954X.12334.

Spears, R. (2005). Commentary: Where did Vincent's van go? *British Journal of Social Psychology, 44*(2), 165–168. doi:10.1348/014466605X39628.

Sullivan, G. (2015). Collective emotions. *Social and Personality Psychology Compass, 9* (8), 383–393. doi:10.1111/spc3.12183.

Sullivan, G. (2018). Collective emotions: A case study of South African pride, euphoria and unity in the context of the 2010 FIFA World Cup. *Frontiers in Psychology, 9*, 1252, doi:10.3389/fpsyg.2018.01252.

Taylor, S. (2010). *Narratives of Identity and Place.* New York, NY: Routledge.

Taylor, S. (2015). Discursive and psychosocial? Theorising a complex contemporary subject. *Qualitative Research in Psychology, 12*(1), 8–21, doi:10.1080/14780887.2014.958340.

Taylor, S. (2017). Psychosocial research. In B. Gough (Ed.), *The Palgrave Handbook of Critical Social Psychology* (pp. 225–241). London: Palgrave Macmillan.

Thrift, N. (2008). *Non-representational Theory: Space, Politics, Affect.* London: Routledge.

Tomkins, S. S. (1995). *Exploring Affect: The Selected Writings of Silvan S. Tomkins.* Edited by E. V. Demos. Cambridge: Cambridge University Press.

Van Der Merwe, H. (2019). Emotional labour and the practicing psychologist: When the psychologist's professional emotions go awry. *European Journal Qualitative Research in Psychotherapy, 9*, 27–40.

Walkerdine, V. (2008). Contextualizing debates about psychosocial studies. *Psychoanalysis, Culture & Society, 13*(4), 341–345. doi:doi.org/10.1057/pcs.2008.31.

Wetherell, M. (1998). Positioning and interpretative repertoires: Conversation analysis and post-structuralism in dialogue. *Discourse & Society, 9*(3), 387–412.

Wetherell, M. (2003). Paranoia, ambivalence, and discursive practices: Concepts of position and positioning in psychoanalysis and discursive psychology. In R. Harré & F. Moghaddam (Eds.), *The Self and Others: Positioning Individuals and Groups in Personal, Political, and Cultural Contexts* (pp. 99–120). Westport, CT: Praeger.

Wetherell, M. (2005a). Methods for studying intersectional and multiple identities: Troubled and untroubled subject positions and the macro/meso and micro. Paper presented at the ESRC Seminar Series, Methods in Dialogue, 18–20 May, Cambridge.

Wetherell, M. (2005b). Unconscious conflict or everyday accountability? *British Journal of Social Psychology*, *44*(2), 169–173, doi:10.1348/014466605X39619.

Wetherell, M. (2006). Formulating selves: Social psychology and the study of identity. *Social Psychological Review*, *8*(2), 62–72.

Wetherell, M. (2007). A step too far: Discursive psychology, linguistic ethnography and questions of identity. *Journal of Sociolinguistics*, *11*(5), 661–681, doi:10.1111/j.1467-9841.2007.00345.x.

Wetherell, M. (2008). Subjectivity or psycho-discursive practices? Investigating complex intersectional identities. *Subjectivity*, *22*(1), 73–81, doi:10.1057/sub.2008.7.

Wetherell, M. (2012). *Affect and Emotion: A New Social Science Understanding*. London: Sage.

Wetherell, M. (2013). Affect and discourse – What's the problem? From affect as excess to affective/discursive practice. *Subjectivity*, *6*(4), 349–368, doi:10.1057/sub.2013.13.

Wetherell, M. (2015a). Tears, bubbles and disappointment – New approaches for the analysis of affective-discursive practices: A commentary on "Researching the psychosocial." *Qualitative Research in Psychology*, *12*(1), 83–90, doi:10.1080/14780887.2014.958399.

Wetherell, M. (2015b). Trends in the turn to affect: A social psychological critique. *Body & Society*, *21*(2), 139–166, doi:10.1177/1357034X14539020.

Wetherell, M. (2019). Understanding the terror attack: Some initial steps. *New Zealand Journal of Psychology*, *48*(1), 6–9.

Wetherell, M. & Edley, N. (1999). Negotiating hegemonic masculinity: Imaginary positions and psycho-discursive practices. *Feminism & Psychology*, *9*(3), 335–356, doi:10.1177/0959353599009003012.

Wetherell, M., McConville, A., & McCreanor, T. (2019). Defrosting the freezer and other acts of quiet resistance: Affective practice theory, everyday activism and affective dilemmas. *Qualitative Research in Psychology*, *17*(1), 13–15, doi:10.1080/14780887.2019.1581310.

Wetherell, M. & Potter, J. (1992). *Mapping the Language of Racism: Discourse and the Legitimation of Exploitation*. New York, NY: Columbia University Press.

Williams, R. (1977). *Marxism and Literature*. Oxford: Oxford University Press.

7 The Negotiation of Continuity and Change of Mapuche Women Weavers in Chile and Its Implications for (Non-Eurocentric) Identity Research

Ramiro German Gonzalez Rial and
Danilo Silva Guimarås

This chapter reviews an ethnographic study by one of the authors (González, 2014) of indigenous women weavers living in the Araucanía Region of Chile. We present a theoretical reflection on identity under construction, one that includes indigenous perspectives on the topic. The term *perspective* can refer to specific meaning-making processes shared by communities. Similar terms are "communities of interpretation" (see, for example, Pfeifer, 2016) or "master narratives" (see Bamberg & Andrews, 2004, for further reading), both of which present shared and accepted ways of meaning-construction. Nevertheless, our understanding of the notion of perspective, as discussed here, is also related to the anthropological theory of Amerindian perspectivism, which emphasizes the role of the body in the construction of the person, identities, and alterities (cf. Lagrou, 2007; Lima, 1996, 1999, 2005; Morais, 2017; Pierri, 2018; Pissolato, 2007; Vilaça, 2006; Viveiros de Castro, 2006).

In the framework of Amerindian perspectivism, the issue of body manufacturing in the core of communitarian life is central to understanding the process of construction of identities and alterities, as we will observe in our ethnographic study focused in this chapter. The notion of perspective that we focus on here refers to more than the individual positioning within lived experience,[1] allowing some views about others and things in the world, while preventing alternative views. It implies the inclusion and exclusion of different objects available to phenomenological first-person embodied experience toward

---

[1] We have articulated the Amerindian Perspectivism Theory within cultural psychology through the notion of dialogical multiplication addressing the construction of an indigenous psychology (cf. Guimarães, 2010, 2011, 2013, 2015, 2018, 2019, 2020; Jensen & Guimarães, 2019; Kawaguchi & Guimarães, 2018; Nigro & Guimarães, 2017; Valsiner, 2019).

others and the world. For each perspective, concretely lived at a specific moment, the I, the other, and the world are accounted as different.

Our approach initially departed from an analysis of data – excerpts of dialogues with Mapuche weaver-women and their textile products – construed in accordance with Eurocentric notions of self and identity (a differentiation of these terms will follow below, **pp. 153–55**). For this chapter, we also introduce reflective elements in pursuit of further nuances reflecting the complexity of indigenous positions vis-à-vis issues imposed by religious, economic, and psychological traditions. These are, for the most part, foreign to indigenous individuals, but in the face of a process of persistent colonization and coloniality they have led to the construction of a range of creative solutions.

In this chapter, we as researchers are observing Mapuche weaver-women at both the collective and individual levels – in conjunction with culture – to understand identity-building processes. This entails *human subjectivity*, which always reflects personal engagement with society (cf. Hermans, Konopka, Oosterwegel & Zomer, 2017, p. 510), while, at the same time creating the possibility of *personal distancing* from the immediate situation through semiotic elaborations (cf. Valsiner, 2017). While the process described here can be understood as *otherness* construction on a sameness–difference continuum (synchronicity), *identity* refers to constructions on a continuity and change continuum (temporal dimension), as we will show below. In addition, we would like to introduce the concept of *alterity*. While otherness refers to a recognizable other as different from me, alterity, in our understanding, refers to something that exceeds the self and its comprehensive categories:

> ... the dialogue between two places: the knowledgeable (as supposed by the subject who is constantly reconstructing [the] relationship with the other) and the unknowledgeable (the impossibility of full knowledge as lived and experienced by the subject in [the] relationship with the other).   (Simão, 2007, p. 20)

The *feeling* of continuity, which we consider essential for identity, can potentially be challenged by the experience that others have voices/positions different from the self, but also that different voices/positions exist within the same person – therefore individuals do not *have* an identity, but are actively and continuously engaged in their own self-construction (cf. Simão, 2010). They are (sometimes) able to find ways to resist and transform social determinations. These assumptions are in line with what has been suggested by so-called semiotic cultural constructivism (SCC) in psychology over the last two decades (cf. Simão, 2007, 2010, 2015), based on psychological ideas from Boesch (cf. 1991), Valsiner (cf. 1998, 2001, 2017), and Marková (2003, 2006, 2016), precursory contributions from Vygotsky (cf. 1927, 1934), James (cf. 1890, 1912), and Baldwin (cf. 1915), in dialogue with Gadamerian hermeneutics (cf. 1959), Bakhtinian dialogism (cf. 1934, 1979, 1986), and the phenomenology of Bergson (cf. 1938), Merleau-Ponty (cf. 1945, 1952, 1969), and Levinas (cf. 1980, 1993, 2004). For SCC, phenomenological first-person I–Other interactions that unfold and develop in the sociocultural space take on an essential role in the understanding of personal human developmental processes (Simão, 2010). Theoretical developments and ideas, including scientific concepts, are grounded on personal, actively lived processes that emerge in specific sociocultural contexts, depending, to a certain extent, on those very contexts.

Within the reflective framework of SCC, we focus on the construction and negotiation of meanings associated with identities emerging from exchanges between the phenomenological experience of a person with the others. For the Mapuche, on whom we will focus here, a central question has been, for example, whether *others* considered them to be *indigenous* or not. The consequences depended and still depend on the answers given, and have ranged from genocide in the past (cf. Bengoa & Caniguan, 2011) to eligibility for certain resources and support measures in the present (e.g., certifying one's own ancestry with documents of filiation and lineage at the request of the territorial planning authorities). Thus, power plays an important role in identity negotiations, the latter being understood here as a particular identity label, or membership in certain groups.

The term *indigenous identity* must be treated with care, however, because it "does not represent miraculously preserved pre-colonial traditions or even a special sort of marginalization. Rather, it reflects the convergence of existing identity categories with shifting global structures of development and governance" (Igoe, 2006, p. 399). Also of apparent importance are the strategies by which subgroups of the indigenous manage to present themselves as culturally distinct from others, in order to be successful in the struggle for economic and political liberalization. These examples touch on a topic that will not be discussed in detail here, and are only intended to illustrate the significance of power relations in questions of identity, such as: Who am I? Who am I allowed to be? (cf. Bamberg & Dege, Chapter 2 in this volume).

Focusing on the Mapuche weaver-women of Southern Chile as our example, we intend to show that identity labels associated with the category of being an indigenous woman are, indeed, all part of a dynamic web in which the individual negotiates relationships, positions, and perspectives pertaining to themselves, and positions and perspectives ascribed and offered/prescribed by others. All of this can only be understood when contextualized socioculturally as well as historically.

7.1 The Mapuche People of Southern Chile

The ethnographic study detailed here includes indigenous women weavers living in the Araucanía Region of Chile (see Figure 7.1).

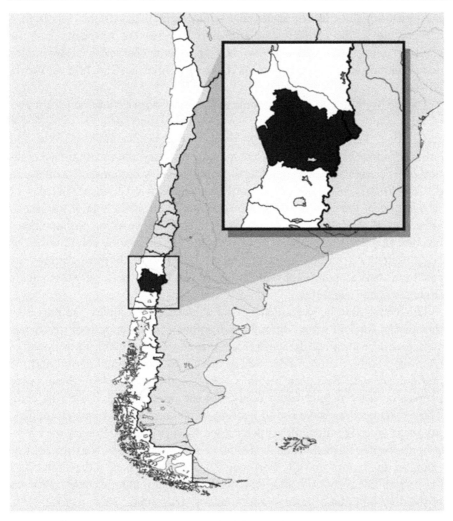

Figure 7.1 *Araucanía Region of Chile, South America (Wikimedia Commons, open source file)*

These women identify themselves as belonging to the Mapuche ethnic group. During this ethnographic study, one of the Mapuche participants clarified that in the Mapuzungun language,[2] *mapu* means earth and *che* means person, so a Mapuche is a person of the earth. The Mapuche people are the largest indigenous group in Chile, with a population of 1,745,147 according to the 2017 census (INE, 2017). After centuries of resistance against Spanish and Chilean forces, the Mapuche territories were occupied by the Chilean state at the end of the nineteenth century (Gerber, Carvacho, & González, 2016). Since the nineteenth century, there have been several attempts to take back

---

[2] One of the languages of the Mapuche people.

the territories that the Mapuche considered theirs. This conflict has been a cornerstone in the conflictive relationship between the Mapuche and the Chilean state, a relationship that has also been characterized by major discrimination on the part of nonindigenous Chileans (Radcliffe & Webb, 2016).

The history of the Mapuche people in Chile has been no different from that of most South American peoples, namely, a slow and tortuous struggle for recognition. This struggle has been marked by resistance against social and cultural genocide, and the fight to demarcate territory and secure the recognition of basic rights (cf. Bengoa & Caniguan, 2011). According to Fuentes and de Cea (2017), Chile is one of the world's most backward countries in terms of recognition of the rights of indigenous communities, being one of the last to adhere to ILO Convention No. 169 after eighteen years of parliamentary debate. This convention recognizes the right of indigenous communities to be consulted on matters affecting them. It does not, however, imply the constitutional recognition of indigenous peoples or further specify their rights (Fuentes & de Cea, 2017).

The relationship between identity and coloniality is complex and relates to the specific ways in which different indigenous peoples undertook resistance strategies. For instance, the various labels used to identify indigenous peoples from the South American lowlands date back to the colonial period and the first contact with European invaders, who sought to categorize these native peoples in order to gain better control of the population and seize its land. These classifications gave rise to a string of blunders and misunderstandings, perceived since the fifteenth century, when the Portuguese, French, and indigenous peoples clashed on the coastline of what we now know as Brazil. For example, the names that the Portuguese Jesuits called their indigenous allies "vary from one account to another to such an extent that little could be known of the division criteria of those communities" (Sztutman, 2005, p. 137).

The phenomenon of external designation is, in turn, met by the indigenous people with inevitable misunderstanding. This issue has been developed within mythical narratives about the first encounters with white people, such as the one transcribed below:

> The first time the white man saw an Indian, the latter was unclothed and was playing with a bat. ... The white man asked the Indian who he was and the latter, who did not understand Portuguese, replied in the language: I am killing [playing with] the bat. We call bats Kaxi. So the white man gave the name: "you and your tribe are the Kaxinawa (kaxi-nawa)." (Lindemberg Monte, 1984, cited in Lagrou, 2007, p. 182)

This mythical narration about an encounter between natives and colonizers emphasizes the perceptual information (white man and naked Indian), along with a misunderstanding. There is obviously a gap between the question that was asked ("Who are you?") and the response given in an effort to meet the other's expectations ("I am doing this"). The disjuncture in perspectives entails variations and noises in the semiotic makeup of the identity of each of them – the white man and the Indian – in a schema that is general, from an Amerindian perspective (cf. Viveiros de Castro, 2006), to all otherness relationships, not just those stemming from colonization. For a discussion on the notion of misunderstanding as a sign of differences in perspective, see Viveiros de Castro (2004) and Guimarães (2018).

7.1.1 The Mapuche Weaver-Women and Variations in the Symbols Depicted on Textiles as a Sign of Identity Transformation

Mapuche handcrafts have historically played a central role in cultural identity by depicting religious and economic aspects of these communities (cf. González & Mege, 2018; Mege, 1990, 1997). Among these handcrafts, textile creation has been pivotal for the community itself, for the textile weavers, and, most of all, for those who design and create textile patterns (González & Mege, 2018). According to Mege (1990), since the inception of historical records, Mapuche women have been in charge of textile production: They are the specialists. In other traditional Mapuche arts – jewelry, for example – men have participated in greater numbers. It is important to note that, historically – in ancient Rome, for example – weaving was a practice reserved for wealthy women who had free time from their domestic chores (Mege, 1987). Among the changes that have taken place in the Mapuche textile arts over the last two decades is the presence of different organizations in the IX region of Chile, dedicated to promoting this activity, in terms of both sales and instruction. Most of these organizations are not run by the native weavers, but by foreign (i.e., not indigenous) people, and regulated by the system known as Fair Price. The number of weavers has grown in the last decade thanks to the weaving workshops run by these organizations. This has led to a change in the progression of textile weaving, since in the past this Mapuche art was taught individually; only some women chosen by the elderly weavers could weave textiles in a given community. Instead of being passed down on an individual basis, from mother to daughter or from grandmother to granddaughter, the teaching of this practice has become a process that is imparted in group workshops. Currently, however, every Mapuche woman, irrespective of her economic standing and place in the social hierarchy, is usually dedicated to weaving. Additionally, strict commercial rules are imposed, promoting the use of natural colors and exact size measurements never before used in typical native textiles. Prior to accepting these rules, each weaver has to make a decision about where to circulate her work; for example, a typical Mapuche intense black is only achieved using industrial dye, and it became *traditional* a century and a half ago. Nevertheless, it is not acceptable for the Fair Price organizations. Moreover, the arrival of new (evangelical) churches, with new religious belief systems, also imposed new rules on textile creation: ancient symbols present in Mapuche iconography are now considered to be demonic portrayals and are thus prohibited from being woven.

The changes introduced by these Fair Price organizations and by the evangelical churches have played a central role how weaving is carried out by the indigenous women who took part in our ethnographic study, which was conducted over two years, simultaneously and with different Mapuche weaver-women. These new rules for textile creation, and the contexts in which these textiles are circulated, differ from the typical way in which things were made in the past. In addition, the social scenarios in which most of the Mapuche communities of Chile find themselves today have never been more culturally heterogeneous. A variety of externally imposed changes like these can be observed in many areas of the world – due to industrialization, for example. But the central question here is how these women build their identities as indigenous Mapuche weavers by reconciling processes of change imposed *from the outside* (by others) with the processes of constructing a sense of continuity associated with the Mapuche tradition. To answer this question, we will now analyze some examples taken from our ethnographic study, in which it is possible to perceive how meanings are constructed on the basis of the junction between what outsiders understand the Mapuche identity to be, or what they believe it should be, and how the women themselves understand what it means to be Mapuche.

One of the most important textiles for the Mapuche woman is the trariwe (see Figure 7.2).[3]

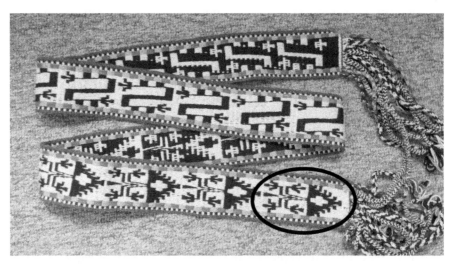

Figure 7.2 *A trariwe with two of the main Mapuche symbols: the treng treng-kai kai and the lukutue (the latter inside the circle)*

---

[3] The trariwe is a typical textile used like a girdle. For more details of this piece, see the works of Pedro Mege (1987, 1989).

Figure 7.3 *Two different versions of the lukutue (with kind permission of Al2, 2008, Wikimedia Commons, open source file)*

As a "semantic container of great amplitude" (Mege, 1987, p. 89), the trariwe is universally used to affirm the body of traditionally dressed women, being key to female identity in Mapuche culture. It is complex to construct, and "has a sign structure that surpasses any other textile within the Mapuche culture" (Mege, 1987, p. 89). Due to the influence of both the new commercial rules and the evangelical churches, its construction has been changing. On the religious side, change is experienced through the meanings that are transmitted. One of the symbols used is the above mentioned lukutue (see Figure 7.3; it is also depicted in the circle in Figure 2), a central figure in the Mapuche worldview and cosmology.

The lukutue can stand for, e.g., the incarnation of a superior being on earth or it can represent an asexual ritual character linked to the rogation ceremony of the Mapuche (*nguillatún*) that "links the members of the community, the community to the land and nature generally, and the living with their ancestors" (Ray, 2007, p. 151). These are, nevertheless, just two examples; the lukutue has multiple sacred meanings and the interpretations ranging from the anthropomorphic to the phytomorphic.

From the traditional Mapuche perspective, the meaning of the textile (e.g., the trariwe) is related to a number of other symbolic elements that are part of the Mapuche cosmology as experienced in daily life. In our ethnographic study, we were able to observe how the new perspectives arriving from the outside (represented by the Fair Price organizations and the evangelical churches) have reinterpreted those traditional elements.

Our decision to work with Mapuche weavers was driven by an interest in observing how, within groups with a strong cultural tradition, different processes of change (religious and commercial) would influence identity construction, both on an individual and a collective level. These characteristics were observed within Chile among members of the Mapuche indigenous communities, where the creation of textile art served as a propitious scenario

Table 7.1 *Characteristics of participants*

Participant (pseudonym)	Religion	Ethnic identity	Kind of weaver	Economic sustenance (in order)
Veronica	Christian (evangelical)	Mapuche	Traditional and commercial	(1) Textile (2) Agronomy (3) (Workshop dictation
Maria	Christian (evangelical)	Mapuche	Traditional and commercial	(1) Textile (2) Agronomy
Josefa	Mapuche[a]	Mapuche	Traditional and commercial	(1) Textile (2) Agronomy (3) Workshop dictation
Estela	Mapuche	Mapuche	Traditional and commercial	(1) Textile (2) Workshop dictation

[a]The Mapuche religion, or its worldview, has been described by various authors as cosmic, animist, and shamanic (see, e.g., Foerster, 1993).

for such study. Our ethnographic journey began by exploring case studies of various weavers from the cities of Valdivia, Futrono, Villarrica, and Mehuin (in the IX and X regions of Chile). For our ethnography, we chose four weavers from areas near the city of Temuco: Nueva Imperial, Almagro, Puerto Saavedra, and Vilcún (IX region). As inclusion criteria, weavers were required to recognize themselves as belonging to the Mapuche ethnic group and as part of a family with a history of producing traditional Mapuche fabrics. These women belong, or had belonged in the past, to organizations dedicated to the trade in textile art typical of their respective towns. The case studies in Nueva Imperial and Almagro were initiated after we collected the names of the textile creators whose work was exhibited in stores in the city of Temuco; then a search was performed in the places where these weavers lived. Data from weavers of Vilcún and Puerto Saavedra were obtained in conversations with people from the city who had heard these women identified as *master weavers*. The four participants in this study were Mapuche women aged between 45 and 65 (see Table 7.1). Furthermore, all names were replaced by pseudonyms in order to protect the weavers' anonymity.

Over the course of our two-year ethnographic study (2010–2012), we accompanied these four women as they carried out their daily routines, and analyzed the many ways in which each of them expressed and constructed their identity as Mapuche weaver-women. Without purporting to simplify the dynamic and fluid configuration of meanings that we observed for each woman, the most representative aspects of each case will be described below, such that it may help contextualize the analyses that follow.

Veronica learned to weave from her Mapuche grandmother, who raised her during childhood. But since then, she has traded her Mapuche beliefs for those of the evangelical church, in which she actively participates. Among Mapuche textile weavers, she is considered one of the best, recognized as a *maestra* (master). She knows the techniques of Mapuche weaving in depth, including its symbology and meanings. Yet she has stopped using Mapuche symbology in her weaving, because it is not allowed in her new religion.

Maria learned weaving when she was a child, from her grandmother and an aunt (both Mapuche). In her adolescence, she acquired, from elderly women, the main body of knowledge with respect to typical Mapuche weaving techniques and symbology. Eight years ago she left the Mapuche religion to become an evangelical Christian – an action that distanced her from her family of origin, because she was harshly confronted by her family for becoming evangelical.

Josefa learned weaving during her childhood with her grandmother and mother. She acknowledges having undergone the ritual to become a Mapuche weaver. Josefa identifies her textiles as "very traditional" and, at the same time, woven for commercial purposes. Josefa only weaves on old looms in the patio of her house, a space she shares with her granddaughter and parents. Even though she admits that she works for economic goals, her main objective is to maintain the traditions of the old weavers.

Estela was a member of several organizations and foundations devoted to the sale of textiles, and currently exports her own work to the United States and Europe. She learned the traditional techniques of Mapuche weaving from her maternal grandmother, and proudly tells us that she, too, had to complete the initiation ritual. Estela has been recognized by UNESCO for her traditional textiles.

Before focusing on the analysis if the four cases described here, we will, in the following section, present a series of theoretical proposals relevant to substantiating the view that identity is constructed in relation to others. Within these relationships, the self is confronted with interactions characterized by an imbalance of power that arises from negotiations between, in our cases, the Mapuche weaver-women and others in the role of alterities: tourists, churches, and Fair Price organizations. We also want to postulate connections between the individual and their sense of identity as it arises from relationships with different positions and voices representing these others, in a process that retains a sense of identity continuity despite the (sometimes extreme) changes that occur.

7.1.2 Sense of Continuity and Dialogicality in the Sense of Self

Following the ideas of Williams James (1890), we propose that the sense of identity is strongly related to the processes of the self. According to James, a sense of personal identity is not simply a cognitive synthesis, but includes the perception of an affective sense of sameness:

> The sense of personal identity is not, then, this mere synthetic form essential to all thought. It is the sense of a sameness perceived *by* thought and predicated of things *thought-about*. These things are a present self and a self of yesterday. The thought not only thinks them both, but thinks that they are identical. The psychologist, looking on and playing the critic, might prove the thought wrong, and show there was no real identity, – there might have been no yesterday, or, at any rate, no self of yesterday; or, if there were, the sameness predicated might not obtain, or might be predicated on insufficient grounds. In either case the personal identity would not exist as a *fact*; but it would exist as a *feeling* all the same; the consciousness of it by the thought would be there, and the psychologist would still have to analyze that.   (James, 1890, Chapter X)

The sense of *identity* thus represents the consciousness of personal sameness, and can be treated as both a subjective phenomenon and an objective deliberation. What is relevant in this case is that it emerges through a process carried out by the self (James, 1890). Taking advantage of one of the ancient senses of the term culture, we consider that, through handcrafts and textile activities, the self cultivates that sense of personal identity, and, at the same time, actively constructs the cultural scenarios that promote such cultivation (cf. Guimarães, 2020). Therefore, we need to deepen how these relationships between self and identity are established.

Since we are suggesting that this relationship between self and identity is not something that exists in isolation in each woman, but rather in relation to the positions assumed against *outside* identity demands (the others), we propose understanding such relationships as dialogical identity-building phenomena.

Accordingly, we consider it relevant to read our analysis from the standpoint of Dialogical Self Theory (DST; Hermans, 2001). Following the Bakhtinian *polyphonic* metaphor and James' division of the self into parts, Hermans (2001) conceptualized the self in terms of a dynamic multiplicity of various autonomous *I-positions*. The *I* owns the possibility of moving from one position to another, a movement that permits a variety of perspectives about the world to be obtained (Hermans, 2001, 2004). In contrast to the idea of an individual self in the sense of James (1890), the dialogical proposal assumes several I-positions that coexist within the same person. Hermans (2008) contrasts a notion of "multiplicity in unity" (p. 189) with the idea of a self as an indivisible unit, and this would coincide, as based on Bakhtin's ideas, with the notion of a multiplicity of voices. The unicity of self in this case, which does not deny a multiplicity, would arise due to the different positions to be assumed without losing the *continuity* of the *I*. Each I-position is endowed with a voice; thus the different positions of the self would relate dialogically to one another, giving an account of a polyphonic self (Hermans, 2001; Hermans, Konopka, Oosterwegel, & Zomer, 2017). One of the basic premises of DST is the understanding of the self as a society: "organized in such a way that other individuals and groups in the society at large are included as co-organizing parts and play contributing roles as positions in the mini-society of the self" (Hermans, Konopka, Oosterwegel, & Zomer, 2017, p. 510). Identity can then be understood just as James (1890) has suggested: as the feeling of sameness *despite* this multiplicity.

In the following section, we will return to the above-described four Mapuche weaver-women to show how different and heterogeneous perspectives and voices intertwine and connect, creating tension between them. These different configurations of perspectives and voices of the self-form an identity as a result of the negotiations in which the latter must engage against the demands of others (Fair Price organizations, churches and ministers, and tourists).

7.1.3 The Multiplicity of Positions in the Emergence of the Mapuche Weaver Identity

Due to the abovementioned changes in weaving and religious practices, contradicting I-positions, as well as the corresponding voices, emerge within the women; Veronica provides us with an example. On the one hand, she says that she feels great pride in being one of the few current weavers who know how to weave the lukutue (see Figures 2 and 3). On the other hand, she stopped weaving it, because the minister of the evangelical Christian church in Veronica's community, who believes that the lukutue is a devilish symbol, asked her to stop weaving it, since Veronica is a member of the church. She therefore adapted her weaving practices accordingly and points this out to the researcher: "This was the first thing I did [pointing to the lukutue on an old trariwe] and this [on a new one] is not the same as the other one. Notice that here's the [old version] and here's a [new] cross" (Veronica, 2011, fieldnote). Although this change was proposed by the minister of the church, Veronica describes the situation by recounting that, on the one hand, she feels somewhat frightened by the idea of the demonic connotations, and, on the other hand, it does not seem like changing the symbology, against the Mapuche symbological tradition, will be a problem for her:

> [I] do not want to get too involved in this piece of weaving, I teach it, but I see it as a common textile. A Mapuche monitor explained this to me: this [the symbol of lukutue] was like a winged bird that hides its head and is transformed in different ways. That's like witchcraft and I don't want to get involved in it. (Veronica, 2011, fieldnote)

Even though she does not agree with the traditional meaning of the Mapuche symbols, she still teaches others how to weave them in the ancient way (even though this is prohibited by the minister of the church). The tension emerges between the I-position of "I am a teacher who passes on traditional Mapuche weaving practices" and "I am a person who rejects this kind of religious-meaning system [that I depict in my textiles]."

When Veronica says, "That's like witchcraft and I don't want to get involved in it" (Veronica, 2011, fieldnote), her face and body betray a great fear of this sacrilegious meaning of the lukutue. It seems as if Veronica's evangelical voices are trying to silence the Mapuche voices, because she says that she has stopped weaving the lukutue out of fear, and now weaves symbols that contradict her convictions. This fear can be considered as an indicator of struggles creating tension (fear as consequence), because if the evangelical voices had triumphed, there would be no answer at all, only monological silence.

Veronica's case depicts her possible inner struggles quite vividly, but we also notice that the individual characteristics attributed to the symbol of the lukutue vary among individual Mapuche weavers. For example, Estela, one of the weavers who is most attached to the Mapuche worldview and does not accept the evangelical religion, tells us that "The lukutue is a drawing that only the Machi can use,[4] because it is sacred ... I could not use it because it makes me tense, I would not be able to walk peacefully, it stings, it makes me feel uncomfortable, angry" (Estela, 2012, fieldnote). While Veronica is proud of being able to weave the lukutue, but does not weave it, having been forbidden to do so by her church minister, Estela does not weave the lukutue either, but for totally different reasons. For both of them, not weaving it is a sign of respect for Mapuche symbols.

Thus, strengthening one's own Mapuche identity works in different ways for the participating women. While for Veronica, being highly skilled in traditional weaving techniques and being able to teach them to others are signs of being Mapuche, *not* weaving the lukutue is considered to be relevant to Estela's and Josefa's self-positionings as Mapuche. This is supported by the gestures and bodily expressions that underline their statements. When Josefa is asked, for example, to describe how the evangelical minister interprets the lukutue, she bursts out laughing and says: "It's just that these [people] know nothing about anything!" (Josefa, 2012, fieldnote), thus distancing herself from the "outsiders" who "know nothing." Veronica cannot use the same strategy to strengthen her Mapuche identity, and therefore needs to find other ways to negotiate her contradictory internal voices.

Reducing Tension through Symbol Alterations

Despite Veronica stating that she no longer weaves the lukutue, this turns out to be not totally accurate, as indicated by a closer look at her textile products: she would, in fact, weave it at times. This observation could be interpreted as the

---

[4] A Machi is a kind of shaman in Mapuche culture.

Figure 7.4a *A treng-treng symbol in a traditional trariwe (Pedro Mege's private collection) that does not show any leaves*

Figure 7.4b *Veronica's altered treng-treng symbol with leaves (white circle) and her altered lukutue with the added cross (black circle)*

evangelical voice winning over the Mapuche voice at times, while the Mapuche voices are not silenced completely. Veronica deliberately alters part of the lukutue, its head, by changing it into a cross (see the black circle in Figure 7.4b).

Secondly, this strategy of symbolic change is also carried out with another of the trariwe symbols: the treng-treng, which is visible in Figure 7.4a. Historically, this symbol represents serpents that embody the struggle of opposing forces in the Mapuche worldview. Since this symbol is also considered evil by the church minister, Veronica weaves a phytomorphic alteration of the treng-treng by adding vegetable leaves to the body of the snake (see the white circle in Figure 4b), which allows her to "argue that this is a flower" (Veronica, 2011, fieldnote).

Again, our data show that these tension-reducing techniques are only visible in – and necessary for – some of the women. Maria's Mapuche voice, for example, does not rely much on traditional symbols, since she does not know their meanings. Nobody had passed them on to her; she only learned the mechanics of how to make them and appreciates their aesthetic forms. Therefore, the weaving of symbols – both traditional and new ones – threatens neither her evangelical nor her Mapuche voices:

> depending on who is ordering it, because my mom likes pink for *nguillatún* . . . and this is achieved with dye . . . but [name of the foundation] does not accept these colors from me. The old lady who taught me the trariwe also had this color [pink] for *nguillatún* too, but for the foundation, these [pointing to natural yarn], if not, they are not sold . . .   (Maria, 2011, fieldnote)

Taking into account what has been analyzed so far, we can see different dynamics of different I-positions and the accordant voices among the four women of this study. In Veronica's case we observe a greater polyphony, in which traditional Mapuche voices and evangelical voices are both present. As for Josefa and Estela, the tensions within are less pronounced due to the fact that neither woman identifies with the evangelical church. In Veronica, we find a growing evangelical participation incorporating the voice of the pastor and the church and maintaining a struggle with the traditional Mapuche voices, which translates into an ambivalent position and creative solutions in the manufacture of textiles. However, as we will show below, these dynamics also vary within individuals when the perspective shifts from the technical to the commercial.

7.1.4 Sense of Continuity Despite Change and Innovations

> Each *ñimin* has meaning,[5] and it is a huge amount of work, and the price paid does not depict its worth. Look what happened to the people who make the *ñimin*, they make small ones ... but there they are selling themselves, so, in order to sell ... I don't sell myself! I innovate, I sell more flashy, more colorful products. (Estela, 2012, fieldnote)

In this short introductory quote, Estela describes a solution to another conflict of I-positions, namely, the I-position of "I as a Mapuche woman [who does not sell sacred textile art to strangers]" and the I-position of "I as a woman who needs to make money to support my community/family." Instead of selling traditional and sacred goods, she finds a creative solution by producing "innovative" textiles that she can sell without violating her values. However, another argument comes into play as well: "I am not paid for the *ñimin* ... because I have a great need to survive, so the traditional ones do not pay off, I work hard and I will not get paid the price that I ask for" (Estela, 2012, fieldnote). So, even if she *considered* selling them, she would not get the money that they are worth, which means that the argument in favor of selling "flashy products" is twofold. While for Estela the new products are the solution to an inner conflict, for Maria they are a potential source of it. As we have seen in the previous section, Maria has no objection to weaving with artificial colors for a traditional ceremony and, by contrast, using natural colors to be able to trade with the Fair Price organizations.

While certain colors are traditionally used in Mapuche textiles, these colors may not sell well in today's target market. As a consequence, organizations that buy products from the Mapuche in order to resell them demand that the Mapuche women no longer use certain traditional colors. Thus, an external commercial voice (i.e., the foundation not accepting certain colors) is

---

[5] *Ñimin*: Mapuche thread technique used to make the trariwe.

requesting something that contradicts weaving traditions. This creates a potential tension between the I-positions "I who want to preserve traditional weaving techniques and products" and "I who need to make money to support my family/community." Here, the discomfort does not stem from *selling* oneself by selling a traditional product, but from *betraying* oneself by producing products that are labeled traditional, but indeed are not.

While the tension in the above cases is not silenced at first, Veronica finds a way to turn something that is potentially conflict-inducing into a win–win situation: she earns more money by offering weaving workshops for the commercial circuit that the abovementioned organizations belong to as well. While this allows her to make a living, she also achieves something important to her personally: she does her part to ensure that the Mapuche traditions are not lost. The prospect that this could happen is a general fear for the community. However, Veronica must also adapt her expectations to the circumstances. While she is highly knowledgeable in the ancient ways of weaving, she teaches the workshops according to the rules of her (Fair Price organization) employer. Furthermore, although she is concerned with teaching and transmitting Mapuche symbols, she does so in a new version that is more in line with the evangelical vision promulgated by the minister of her church. While Veronica *justifies* her work for the organization by stressing that it also helps preserve the Mapuche tradition, contradictions can still be observed among the other women. Josefa, who has been identified as an *old master* at weaving, stresses on the one hand how strongly she rejects the new colors proposed by the incoming organizations. She says that the trariwe of her mother and grandmother used industrial dyes, and that she will continue to do the same, since "I learned it from them" (Josefa, 2012, fieldnote). On the other hand, she is one of the main instructors working for these organizations, and states, at other times, that she teaches according to the new rules because it "pays very well" (Josefa, 2012, fieldnote). Sometimes, it seems, voices that appear to be contradictory from the outside may not lead to immediate conflict as long as they coexist in one person but emerge at different times and on different occasions.

Toward the end of our ethnographic journey, in the face of these diverse ways of positioning oneself within the modern and traditional textile arts, Josefa was asked which of those textiles would still be Mapuche, given the changes they have undergone. She replied: "Well, all of them, since they have all been woven by Mapuche women." Therefore, their recognition as being Mapuche has more to do with the recognition by their creators that they belong to the Mapuche community than to the acknowledgment of, and attachment to, specific forms that are historically associated with Mapuche cultural identity; or, in particular, forms established from the standpoint of the foreigner, the colonizer, the churches, and the market, as regards what is supposedly the Mapuche identity, by transforming them into a commodity that is available for purchase and sale.

7.1.5 Discussing Identities on the Basis of Emerging Voices and Positions

We can identify and characterize three positions that are of potential importance for each of the cases presented in this chapter: the position of the traditional Mapuche weaver, the position of the (obedient) member of the evangelical church, and the position of women who need to make a living. Each position is reflected by corresponding voices that can coexist next to each other without (immediately) leading to conflict, or that can be in conflict with each other, leading to negative tension for which a solution must be found. This is possible when the women manage to find creative solutions, as shown above. In all cases, the individual voices are influenced by collectives. The traditional Mapuche position is confronted with the articulation and monitoring of those mandates received by an alleged tradition loaded with ancestral knowledge – in some of the above cases, personified by grandparents or the *machi*, for instance. The traditions are challenged by the second position, the evangelical one, which emerges from the religious mandate that demands alterations of traditional Mapuche symbols that apparently contradict the evangelical vision. As the representative of the evangelical community, the church minister enters the narratives of the women presented here.

The women try to counter the tension that potentially arises from the conflicting voices representing these two positions by suppressing or altering them. The third position is the one that leads to existential voices: "I need to make a living!" These voices come with a certain *need*, a need that can potentially be fulfilled by the commercial organizations that buy and resell Mapuche products. This external force is not a uniform position of power, but is represented by foreign trade companies, by Fair Price foundations, or even by members of the Mapuche community who commission garments for typical use and customs. With this in mind, each weaver must take a position based on who the recipient of the garment will be (Mapuche or foreign), how it will be used, and the domain within which the textile will be delivered (family, close group, or business). In the homes of these women, you can find time-honored and modern textiles, representing traditional voices and a means of trade, respectively. What the women of this study finally decide to do in order to fulfill the abovementioned existential need to make a living differs according to the strategy of dealing with the tensions described above. While some weavers focus on preserving traditions by participating in commercial marketing, others find it difficult to resolve the contradiction created by commercializing traditional products and selling them to people who neither know nor understand their value. Yet Estela manages not only to innovate products, but also to come up with an new I-position: she travels to the United States to fulfill export contracts, and attends courses on marketing and foreign trade – all of this without abandoning Mapuche rituals and customs. In Estela, we find a multiplicity of positions centered around Mapuche loom activity: *traditionalist*, *merchant*, *exporter*, and master. For Hermans (2008), a central feature of the Dialogic Self is the choice to opt for "innovation" (p. 192). Being able to take on new positions by, for example, combining existing ones and thereby obtaining new information allows for development and transformations triggered by direct exchanges with the social environment. Estela is the clearest example of these kinds of transformations, which – with respect to both Estela and the other weavers – occur in tandem with a sense of Mapuche authorship that enables a sense of continuity to be maintained in the midst of change.

Given this range of possibilities for multiple positions and the various voices that are articulated by them, it is worth noting that all these women, when asked how they would define themselves, identify as *Mapuche weavers*. This shows that positions and voices are maintained in parallel, but that labels like Mapuche weavers function in a totalitarian way. That is, homogenous identifications would tend to silence the dissenting and contrasting voices which, in many cases, coexist in parallel or within a conflictive relationship. However, this homogeneous identification enables a somewhat resistant stance to be held against an external position's questioning of identity.

7.2 Final Considerations and Open Questions

Mas você não gosta de ser Wari'?

Nós somos Wari' apenas porque vocês disseram. Antes não sabíamos.

But don't you like being Wari'?

We are Wari' just because you said so. We didn't know before.

This excerpt of dialogue between the anthropologist Aparecida Vilaça (2006) and an indigenous Amazonian person took place more than forty years after the first peaceful encounter between the latter's community and white people. She observes that when whites met these people in the 1960s, the Amazonians appeared to be a set of subgroups rather than a unified community. Government archives record the various names that were given to them, including the definition of a unit, now known as a Wari'. However, for the Wari', the organization of their community was conceived as something subject to constant transformation with respect to the relationship among subgroups. Each subgroup, having arisen within circumstantial historical contexts, was comprised of just a few families, and was identified through recognition by other allied subgroups, which assigned them a name that defined the subgroup unit.

In the case of the Wari', and in many other cases, the ethnonym that identifies a people comes from outside (from abroad). The external gaze cast by the outsider, in turn, does not enable a neutral designation to be constructed; instead, this is done in accordance with impressions or obvious characteristics that are observed, and with the various classification interests in play. Nevertheless, each indigenous community identifies itself using an expression that means *truly human beings* (cf. Lagrou, 2007; Lima, 1996, 1999; Viveiros de Castro, 1996, 2006), or simply *person of the earth*, as in the case of the Mapuche term. Also, from an Amerindian perspective, each being who holds subject status grasps their existence in a truly human manner. This means that the *subject* shares with the *other subjects* a subjective and an objective point of view, in a reality that they perceive as active constructive.

These propositions are accompanied, in Amerindian perspectivism, by a notion of human semiotic identity construction based on the fabrication of the body. The true human body is subjected to intentional fabrication processes: intervention in matter that is consolidated by the configuration of gestures and body shapes (cf. Viveiros de Castro, 1979). For the Kaxinawa, as an example, "ethnic identity and difference will be expressed in terms of how one lives and how one's body is modeled by others through conviviality and sharing with those one lives with or encounters on one's travels" (Lagrou, 2007, p. 533). The nature of this corporeality, which gives rise to the development of human identity, does not dispense with the relationship with the other, even if that other is nonhuman.

When the weaver Josefa indicates that all the textiles are Mapuche because they were woven by Mapuche women, she shifts the problem concerning the identity of the logic of the merchandise, which points to the production of objects on the basis of certain fixed characteristics that meet the criteria of the buyers. There is also a shift from an institutionalized religious logic, according to which writing and visual images, as well as other forms of expression, affect the environment in a supernatural way or constitute a representation of what is real. What is at stake, from the point of view of the evangelical church, seems to be the promotion of a lost memory that connects contemporary Mapuches to the values of their ancestors, through the alteration of the old graphics. From the standpoint of the Fair Price market, ancestral memory is presumed to be rekindled, but without taking into account a set of transformations that have often shaken the Mapuche communities since colonization. However, it also ignores the creative options of the communities which, in the face of new life scenarios, introduced new elements into the Mapuche world. The Mapuche identity is thus established by Josefa as being the historical memory of people's belonging to their communities, which also receive new members in the form of children whose bodies are constructed through coexistence with the carers closest to them right up to networks of relationships between the Mapuche communities and the various indigenous peoples.

As regards the importance of historical memory in shaping indigenous identities, the reflection of the shaman Ianomâmi Davi Kopenawa on the distinction between knowledge and wisdom is significant:

> The whites are ingenious; they have many machines and goods, but they lack wisdom. They no longer think about what their ancestors were when they

were created. In the first days, they were like us, but they lost all their old
words. Later, they crossed the waters and came in our direction. Then they
repeat what they discovered on this land. I only understood this when
I started to understand their language.   (Kopenawa, 1998, p. 21)

This reflection can be unfolded as follows. The characteristic ingenuity of the
white man has developed with the sophistication of technical and scientific
knowledge, which enables, among other things, Ianomâmis' lands to be
exploited using machines that extract the resources from the forest for the
production of goods. In the field of identity theories in psychology, this
ingenuity may enable the analysis of the infinite labels that people construct
to refer to themselves, including transience in the construction and usage of
these categories. However, Kopenawa (1998) juxtaposes this ingenuity, which
does not bring us close to the meaning of being indigenous as experienced by
the indigenous peoples themselves, with the notion of wisdom, which involves
recognition of, and reflection on, ancestry as a decisive component of the
actions and decision-making of a person in the present day. This is something
that Josefa appears to want to convey to us, by saying that an item is Mapuche
when it was made by a Mapuche. Being Mapuche cannot be defined by the
objective characteristics of such and such an object; rather, it arises from the
fact that it belongs to Mapuche life within various spheres of activity.

Social and community life are, in turn, experienced as a dynamic of
approaching and distancing among people and groups. We understand that
this process includes relations of alterity, which implies the appearance of new
elements. These new elements are expressed in the transformation of existing
bodies and in the emergence of substantial new bodies, stemming from social
relationships. For example, with the birth of a child, and in the formation of
parental relationships, one new element is understood as a social process that
points to the cultivation of people within families and communities. The
transformed textiles, for instance, also depict a creative process rendered
pertinent by the prevailing conditions of being and existing, giving continuity
to the life of the people within the communities: a dynamic unfolding of
traditions open to new encounters and world experiences. The serious problem
emerges when this opening-up gives rise to violence, such as that perpetrated
by the European invaders five centuries ago, and by the current local elite, on
the indigenous peoples and communities of these lands now called
South America.

Thus, in the encounter with the Mapuche weavers, we point out three
perspectives (see introductory paragraph for a definition of the term):

(1) the relationship of the Mapuche weavers to their peers, in which the
    recognition of belonging to the community ensures their identity as a
    person of the earth without further questioning (for instance, having been
    a son or daughter of, or having been raised by, someone recognized as
    being conceived within a local community);

(2) the relationship of the Mapuche weavers with the church, in which the variation of the graphics on the fabrics casts doubt, for an external observer, on whether or not the product is truly Mapuche (here, the identity of the Mapuche products might lead to the identity of the person as Mapuche being questioned, since in the church's view, the Mapuches must abandon their traditions and convert to evangelical Christianity); and

(3) the relationship of the Mapuche weavers with the Fair Price market, which seeks an objective similarity between the fabrics created by the Mapuches today and those appearing in historical documentation (here, the Mapuche identity is questioned, since it may not meet the stereotypical criteria that buyers expect).

Scenarios 2 and 3 described in the preceding paragraph do not show how identity is conceived by the Mapuches perspective, in accordance with trans-generational processes based on community coexistence – processes that include cultivating new bodies through the birth of children within local families. These self-perpetuating communities also undergo transformation to a greater or lesser extent, whether under the pressure of external circum-stances or of the heterogeneity and creativity inherent to all human societies. Each of these dialogues on the issue of identity coexists in the self of the Mapuche weaver. Our study therefore shows that the Mapuche weavers can position themselves within the dialogue on identity in at least three different ways, responding variously to specific interlocutors: changing the symbol for the evangelical minister; making fabrics in a few naturally dyed colors to please tourists, and artificially coloring the fabrics to please their communities. All these forms of self-positioning within the dialogue are pertinent as forms of resistance, and of ensuring the continuity of the Mapuche as people of the earth on an earth that is being transformed, requiring flexibility on the one hand and resistance strategies on the other.

We will now pose a new question that has arisen from the issues raised in this chapter: What interests are addressed by psychology's insistence on a notion of objectifiable cultural or ethnic personal identity? The interests of the Mapuche do not seem to be addressed here. In Brazil, where we are writing this chapter, we have a set of objective characteristics for determining who is indigenous and who is not, as something that caters to the interests of anti-indigenous social groups (cf. Viveiros de Castro, 2006). In the case of indigen-ous peoples, it is the duty of the State to promote public policies that remedy the violent actions perpetrated by the State itself in times gone by, guarantee-ing the indigenous communities' right to live in their territories, to be educated in their mother tongue, and to have access to health services that understand and respect the cultural specificity of those peoples. In other words, the idea of identity is used to exclude people who, on account of not possessing highly particular features of an objective identity, would not be able to access fundamental rights. Thus, all the pressure suffered by the indigenous peoples during colonization and in the current situation of coloniality is ignored as part of a process against which the peoples and communities have had to resist and adapt creatively, preserving, to a certain extent, the historical memory of their resistant stance toward the colonialist advances.

In order to include indigenous perspectives, the understanding of dialogical tensions surrounding the issue of identity needs to conceive of a multidimensionality of this tension: we have seen, in the case of the Mapuche weaver-women, that the issue of identity points to different objects depending on the indigenous person's interlocutor, and to different textiles that characterize various aspects of Mapuche identity. This issue also involves personal cultivation processes in which the interlocutor of the indigenous person is fellow indigenous person for whom the basic question is the process of semiotic construction of human identity, the fabrication of truly human beings who understand themselves to be part of the same ancestry. This is done through the specific care devised and practiced by each community, through their diversity and dynamic mutation, through the cultivation of people, through relations, and through their communities. Some of these notions and practices are maintained, others are transformed, as in any culture, and a fundamental claim of the present-day indigenous peoples is respect for their communities' ethnical self-affirmation processes:

> There is no future for the Amerindian peoples if they cannot maintain their habits and sustainable practices in their territories. These habits and practices should be the guidelines for the full exercise of the peoples' capacity to manage educational processes, promote healthcare and nourishment, organize their economy, create knowledge and make their own choices according to their intentions for the future generations.   (ABRASME, 2014)

Therefore, if "they cannot maintain their habits and sustainable practices in their territories," the options available to them so they may continue to be indigenous, Mapuche, or from any other community, will always be to adjust those practices, transforming them so as to continue living as human beings of the earth, and therefore keeping the memories of their ancestral community, linked to all the beings that strengthened the continuity of life.

We have also emphasized a possibility that the indigenous weavers articulate distinct cosmologies that configure cultural realities and their objects in multiple ways. They show that between distinct cultural traditions, there is not a direct confrontation of positions, but an affective – beautiful, intentional, rhythmic – interchange grounding multiple trajectories of dialogue, as the larger diversity of human cultural creation is grounded in traditional values that can coexist, without necessarily excluding each other. When looking at identity and the underlying processes in the self, we thus recommend never losing sight of the cultural embeddedness of these phenomena when conducting research in this field (cf. Guimarães, 2011; Simão, 2016). This work has discussed the idea of identity as a construction of meaning that seeks to articulate the demands of both the outsider and the indigenous person in conjunction with the meanings of tradition and ancestral culture. We thus seek to contribute toward delving deeper into a complex phenomenon that brings together a myriad of meanings that resist labels imposed from the outside. In this sense, the notion of identity in these Mapuche weaver-women gives an account of a dynamic notion emerging in the meanings relating to them, maintained as continuity through change. This notion reveals the density of nuance and the multitude of stances and perspectives in the experience of the weavers, articulating supposedly contrary dimensions such as the individual and the collective, present and past, resistance and change – dimensions that are continuously resolved in the experience of identity.

Finally, we have to ask the question whether we, as ethnographers, are imposing meaning from the outside. Overall, the intended interactional reciprocity between Amerindian peoples and non-Amerindian (Eurocentric) perspectives has been proven to be quite fragile (cf. Achatz & Guimarães, 2019; Guimarães, 2011, 2013, 2015, 2018, 2019, 2020; Jensen & Guimarães, 2018; Guimarães & Simão, 2017; Kawaguchi & Guimarães, 2019; Nigro & Guimarães, 2017). As researchers, we tend to draw conclusions in a totalitarian way: we try to depict the complexity of a phenomenon by integrating different data sources and existing empirical findings. This "integration" nevertheless remains an interpretation of scientists – and in our case, an interpretation made by two men about an ethnographic work on women that took place in a different time and space than that in which these men now find themselves.

From this perspective, we make use of discursive elaboration techniques to fill the unavoidable gaps provoked by the alterity of the other person. Understanding an indigenous person and their subjectivity implies apprehending how this *specific other* understands *the others* and *their cultures*. Since the indigenous person and the ethnographer are both agents constructing knowledge, the interactive process of data *construction* – and data publication – is always mediated and can be submitted to re-signification from both sides. This stresses the intersection between research and indigenous conceptions: both deal with the relational nature of identity and alterity constructions (cf. Guimarães, 2011).

Mutual understanding and co-authorship of how identities and alterities are constructed can only be achieved if the parties involved in the process, with their own cultivated *perspectives*, are open to transforming previous conceptions. Concepts such as self, voices, and positions run the risk of limiting meaning-making processes between the I and the other: if one commits oneself to these concepts as a theoretical framework, one may no longer be open to alternatives such as the indigenous connection between the affective body, land, and ancestry. These are connections that some of us might not focus on or be familiar with at all, but we should be open to them if we wish to ethically work *with* the *other*.

References

ABRASME [Associação Brasileira de Saúde Mental]. (2014). Carta de Manaus por uma saúde integral aos povos indígenas. 4° Congresso Brasileiro de Saúde Mental [Letter of Manaus for an integral health to the indigenous peoples. 4th Brazilian Congress of Mental Health]. Retrieved June 15, 2019, from www.congresso2014 .abrasme.org.br/informativo/view?ID_INFORMATIVO=127&impressao.

Achatz, R. W. & Guimarães, D. S. (2018). An invitation to travel in an interethnic arena: Listening carefully to Amerindian leaders' speeches. *Integrative Psychological and Behavioral Science, 52*(4), 595–613.

Bakhtin, M. M. (1934/2004). *The Dialogic Imagination.* Austin, TX: University of Texas Press.

Bakhtin, M. M. (1979/1992). *Estética da criação verbal* [Aesthetics of verbal creation]. São Paulo: Martins Fontes.

Bakhtin, M. M. (1986). *Speech Genres and Other Late Essays.* Austin, TX: University of Texas Press.

Baldwin, J. M. (1915). *Genetic Theory of Reality.* New York, NY: Knickerbocker Press. Retrieved April 26, 2021, from https://archive.org/details/ genetictheoryofr00baldrich.

Bamberg, M. & Andrews, M. (Eds.). (2004). *Considering Counternarratives: Narrating, Resisting, Making Sense.* Amsterdam: John Benjamins.

Bengoa, J. & Caniguan, N. (2011). Chile: los mapuches y el bicentenario [Chile: The Mapuche and the bicentennial]. *Cuadernos de Antropología Social, 34,* 7–28.

Bergson, H. (1938/2003). *La Pensée et le mouvant* [Thought and the moving]. Paris: PUF.

Boesch, E. E. (1991). *Symbolic Action Theory and Cultural Psychology.* Berlin: Springer.

Foerster, R. G. (1993). *Introducción a la religiosidad Mapuche* [Introduction to Mapuche religiosity, 2nd ed.]. Santiago de Chile: Editorial Universitaria.

Fuentes, C. & de Cea, M. (2017). Reconocimiento débil: derechos de pueblos indígenas en Chile [Weak recognition: Rights of indigenous peoples in Chile]. *Perfiles Latinoamericanos, 25*(49), 1–21, doi:10.18504/pl2549–003-2017.

Gadamer, H.-G. (1959/1985). *Truth and Method.* New York, NY: Lexington.

Gerber, M. M., Carvacho, H., & González, R. (2016). Development and validation of a scale of support for violence in the context of intergroup conflict (SVIC): The case of violence perpetrated by Mapuche people and the police in Chile. *International Journal of Intercultural Relations, 51,* 61–68, doi:10.1016/j. ijintrel.2016.01.004.

González, R. (2014). *Etnografía de los procesos psicológicos asociados a la construcción de identidades en tejedoras mapuche: entramados de comercio, religión y etnicidad.* [Ethnography of the psychological processes associated with the construction of identities in Mapuche women weavers: Networks of commerce, religion and ethnicity]. Santiago de Chile: Pontificia Universidad Católica de Chile.

Gonzalez, R. & Mege, P. (2018). Analysis of creative and identity processes among Mapuche women weavers in the Araucanía region. *Integrative Psychological and Behavioral Science, 52*(4), 614–629, doi:10.1007/s12124–018-9456-4.

Guimarães, D. S. (2010). Commentary: The complex construction of psychological identities in Palestine: Integrating narratives and life experiences. *Culture & Psychology*, *16*(4), 539–548.

Guimarães, D. S. (2011). Amerindian anthropology and cultural psychology: Crossing boundaries and meeting otherness' worlds. *Culture & Psychology*, *17*(2), 139–157, doi:10.1177/1354067X11398309.

Guimarães, D. S. (2013). Self and dialogical multiplication. *Interacções*, *9*, 214–242.

Guimarães, D. S. (2015). Temporality as reciprocity of activities: Articulating the cyclical and the irreversible in personal symbolic transformations. In L. M. Simão, D. S. Guimarães, & J. Valsiner (Eds.), *Temporality: Culture in the Flow of Human Experience* (pp. 331–358). Charlotte, NC: Information Age Publishing.

Guimarães, D. S. (2018). Affectivation: A cut across the semiotic hierarchy of feelings. In C. Cornejo, G. Marsico, & J. Valsiner (Eds.), *I Activate You to Affect Me*, Annals of Cultural Psychology (Vol. 3) (pp. 203–223). Charlotte, NC: Information Age Publishing.

Guimarães, D. S. (2019). Towards a cultural revision of psychological concepts. *Culture & Psychology*, *25*(2), 135–145.

Guimarães, D. S. (2020). *Dialogical Multiplication Principles for an Indigenous Psychology*. New York, NY: Springer.

Guimarães, D. S. & Simão, L. M. (2017). Mythological constrains to the construction of subjectified bodies. In M. Han (Ed.), *The Subjectified and Subjectifying Mind* (pp. 3–21). Charlotte, NC: Information Age Publication.

Hermans, H. J. M. (2001). The dialogical self: Toward a theory of personal and cultural positioning. *Culture & Psychology*, *7*(3), 243–281, doi:10.1177/1354067X0173001.

Hermans, H. J. M. (2004). Introduction: The dialogical self in a global and digital age. *Identity*, *4*(4), 297–320, doi:10.1207/s1532706xid0404_1.

Hermans, H. J. M. (2008). How to perform research on the basis of dialogical self theory? Introduction to the special issue. *Journal of Constructivist Psychology*, *21*, 185–199, doi:10.1080/10720530802070684.

Hermans, H. J. M., Konopka, A., Oosterwegel, A., & Zomer, P. (2017). Fields of tension in a boundary-crossing world: Towards a democratic organization of the self. *Integrative Psychological and Behavioral Science*, *51*(4), 505–535, doi:10.1007/s12124-016-9370-6.

Hugh-Jones, S. (2002). Nomes secretos e riqueza visível: nominação no noroeste amazônico [Secret names and visible wealth: Naming in the northwestern Amazon]. *Mana*, *8*(2), 45–68.

Igoe, J. (2006). Becoming indigenous peoples: Difference, inequality, and the globalization of East African identity politics. *African Affairs*, *105*(420), 399–420.

INE [Instituto Nacional de Estadísticas]. (2017). *Estadísticas sociales de los pueblos indígenas en Chile — Censo 2017: Informe de resultados* [Social statistics of indigenous peoples in Chile — 2017 Census: Results report]. Santiago de Chile: Instituto Nacional de Estadísticas.

James, W. (1890). *The Principles of Psychology. Vol I.* Retrieved April 26, 2021, from https://psychclassics.yorku.ca/James/Principles/.

James, W. (1912/1979). *Pragmatismo e outros textos* [Pragmatism and other texts]. São Paulo: Abril Cultural.

Jensen, M. & Guimarães, D. S. (2018). Expanding dialogical analysis across (sub-) cultural background. *Culture & Psychology*, *24*(4), 403–417.

Kawaguchi, D. R. & Guimarães, D. S. (2019). Is everybody human? The relationship between humanity and animality in Western and Amerindian myth narratives. *Culture & Psychology*, *25*(3), 375–396.

Kopenawa, D. (1998/2000). Descobrindo os brancos [Discovering white people]. In C. A. Ricardo (Ed.), *Povos indígenas no Brasil* [Indigenous people in Brazil] (pp. 20–23). São Paulo: Instituto Socioambiental.

Lagrou, E. (2007). *A fluidez da forma: arte, alteridade e agência em uma sociedade amazónica (Kaxinawa, Acre)* [The fluidity of form: Art, otherness and agency in an Amazonian society (Kaxinawa, Acre)]. Rio de Janeiro: Topbooks.

Levinas, E. (1980). *Totalidade e Infinito* [Totality and infinity]. Lisbon: Edições 70.

Levinas, E. (1993). *O Humanismo do outro homem* [The humanism of the other man]. Petrópolis: Vozes.

Levinas, E. (2004). *Entre nós: Ensaios sobre a alteridade* [Between us: Essays on alterity]. Petrópolis: Vozes.

Lima, T. S. (1996). O dois e seu múltiplo: reflexões sobre o perspectivismo em uma cosmologia Tupi [The two and their multiple: Reflections on perspectivism in a Tupi cosmology]. *Mana*, *2*(2), 21–47.

Lima, T. S. (1999). Para uma teoria etnográfica da distinção natureza e cultura na cosmologia Juruna [Towards an ethnographic theory of the distinction between nature and culture in Juruna cosmology]. *Revista Brasileira de Ciências Sociais*, *14*(40), 43–52.

Lima, T. S. (2005). *Um peixe olhou pra mim: o povo Yudjá e a perspectiva* [A fish looked at me: Yudjá people and the perspective]. São Paulo: UNESP.

Marková, I. (2003). Representations of the social: Bridging theoretical traditions. *Journal of Community Applied Social Psychology*, *13*, 413–416.

Marková, I. (2006). On the "inner alter" in dialogue. *International Journal for Dialogical Science*, *1*(1), 125–147.

Marková, I. (2016). *The Dialogical Mind: Common Sense and Ethics*. Cambridge: Cambridge University Press.

Mege, P. (1987). Los símbolos constrictores: una etnoestética de las fajas femeninas mapuches [The constricting symbols: An ethno-aesthetics of Mapuche feminine sashes]. *Boletín del Museo de Arte Precolombino*, *2*, 89–128.

Mege, P. (1989). Los símbolos envolventes. Una etnoestética de las mantas mapuches [The enveloping symbols: An ethno-aesthetics of Mapuche blankets]. *Boletín del Museo Chileno de Arte Precolombino*, *3*, 81–114.

Mege, P. (1990). *Arte textil Mapuche* [Mapuche textile art]. Santiago de Chile: Museo Chileno de Arte Precolombino.

Mege, P. (1997). *La imaginación Araucana* [The Araucanian imagination]. Santiago de Chile: Museo Chileno de Arte Precolombino.

Merleau-Ponty, M. (1945/1994). *Fenomenologia da Percepção* [Phenomenology of perception]. São Paulo: Martins Fontes.

Merleau-Ponty, M. (1960/2004). *O olho e o espírito* [The eye and the spirit]. São Paulo: Cosac Naify.

Merleau-Ponty, M. (1969/2002). *A prosa do mundo* [The prose of the world]. São Paulo: Cosac Naify.

Morais, B. M. (2017). *Do corpo ao pó: crônicas da territorialidade Kaiowá e Guarani nas adjacências da morte* [From body to dust: Chronicles of Kaiowá and Guarani territoriality on the threshold of death]. São Paulo: Elefante.

Nigro, K. F. & Guimarães, D. S. (2016). Obscuring cannibalism in civilization: Amerindian psychology in reading today's sociocultural phenomena. In J. Valsiner, G. Marsico, N. Chaudhary, T. Sato, & V. Dazzani (Eds.), *Psychology as the Science of Human Being. The Yokohama Manifesto* (pp. 245–263). Basel: Springer International Publishing.

Pfeifer, D. (2016). Charles Peirce, Josiah Royce's semiotic move, and communities of interpretation. In G. R. Owens & E. K. Katić (Eds.), *Semiotics. Yearbook of the Semiotic Society of America* (pp. 1–11). Charlottesville, VA: Philosophy Documentation Center.

Pierri, D. C. (2018). *O perecível e o imperecível: reflexões Guarani Mbya sobre a existência* [The perishable and imperishable: Mbya Guarani reflections on the existence]. São Paulo: Elefante.

Pissolato, E. (2007). *A duração da pessoa: Mobilidade, parentesco e Xamanismo Mbya (Guarani)* [The duration of the person: Mobility, kinship and Shamanism Mbya(Guarani)]. São Paulo: Editora UNESP.

Radcliffe, S. & Webb, A. (2016). Mapuche youth between exclusion and the future: Protest, civic society and participation in Chile. *Children's Geographies, 14*(1), 1–19, doi:10.1080/14733285.2014.964667.

Ray, L. (2007). *Language of the Land: The Mapuche in Argentina and Chile.* Copenhagen: IWGIA.

Silva, C. & Burgos, C. (2011). Tiempo mínimo-conocimiento suficiente: etnografía sociotécnica en psicología social [Minimum time-sufficient knowledge: Sociotechnical ethnography in social psychology]. *Psicoperspectivas, 10*(2), 87–108.

Simão, L. M. (2007). Why "otherness" in the research domain of semiotic-cultural psychology? In L. M. Simão & J. Valsiner (Eds.), *Otherness in Question: Labyriths of the Self* (pp. 11–35). Charlotte, NC: Information Age Publishing.

Simão, L. M. (2010). *Ensaios dialógicos: compartilhamento e diferença nas relações eu-outro* [Dialogical essays: Sharing and difference in self–other relationships]. São Paulo: Editora Hucitec.

Simão, L. M. (2015). The contemporary perspective of semiotic cultural constructivism: For an hermeneutical reflexivity in psychology. In G. Marsico, R. A. Ruggieri, & S. Salvatore (Eds.), *Reflexivity and Psychology* (pp. 65–85). Raleigh, NC: Information Age Publishing.

Simão, L. M. (2016). Culture as a moving symbolic border. *Integrative Psychological and Behavioral Science, 50*(1), 14–28, doi:10.1007/s12124–015-9322-6.

Sztutman, R. (2005). O profeta e o principal: Ação política ameríndia e seus personagens [The prophet and the principal: Amerindian political action and its characters]. Doctoral thesis, Faculdade de Filosofia Letras e Ciências Humanas, Universidade de São Paulo.

Valsiner, J. (1998). *The Guided Mind – A Sociogenetic Approach to Personality.* Cambridge, MA: Harvard University Press.

Valsiner, J. (2001). *Comparative Study of Human Cultural Development*. Madrid: Fundación Infancia y Aprendizaje.

Valsiner, J. (2017). *Between Self and Societies. Creating Psychology in a New Key.* Tallin: TLU Press.

Valsiner, J. (2019). *Culture & Psychology*: 25 constructive years. *Culture & Psychology*, *25*(4), 429–469.

Viveiros de Castro, E. B. (1979). A fabricação do corpo na sociedade Xinguana [The fabrication of the body in Xinguan society]. *Boletim do Museu Nacional, 32*, 2–19.

Vilaça, A. M. N. (2006). *Quem somos nós: os Wari' encontram os brancos* [Who we are: The Wari' find the whites]. Rio de Janeiro: EdUFRJ.

Viveiros de Castro, E. B. (1996). Os pronomes cosmológicos e o perspectivismo ameríndio [The cosmological pronouns and the Amerindian perspectivism]. *Mana, 2*(2), 115–144.

Viveiros de Castro, E. B. (2004). Perspectival anthropology and the method of controlled equivocation. *Tipití: Journal of the Society for the Anthropology of Lowland South America, 2*(1), 1–22.

Viveiros de Castro, E. B. (2006). *A inconstância da alma selvagem e outros ensaios de antropologia* [The inconstancy of the savage soul and other anthropological essays, 2nd ed.]. São Paulo: Cosac Naify.

Vygotsky, L. S. (1927/1991). El significado histórico de la crisis em psicología [The historical meaning of the crisis in psychology: A methodological investigation]. In L. S. Vygotsky, *Obras escogidas I: problemas teóricos y metodológicos de la Psicología* (pp. 257–407). Madrid: A. Machado.

Vygotsky, L. S. (1934/2001). *Obras escogidas (Tomo II): Pensamiento y lenguaje* [Thinking and language]. Madrid: Aprendizaje Visor.

8 Identity and Voices: A Language-Dialogical Take

Marie-Cécile Bertau

In the mid-1950s in the United States, the term *identity* became central to an increasing preoccupation around the "aching question" of "Who am I?" (Gleason, 1983, p. 912). In the 1960s, identity supplanted *self* and entered the social sciences and public discourse, significantly resonating in the context of the postwar interest in national character studies and the critique of mass society. Subsequently, the relationship between individual and society was considered as fundamentally problematic, which translated to a sharp contrast of individual and social built into the category of identity. This contrast was well suited to the "prevalent individualist ethos" and giving "particular salience ... to 'identity' concerns" (Brubaker & Cooper, 2000, p. 3). The intensified preoccupation with identity is thus specific to the postwar life forms in Western industrialized countries; in effect, identity can be seen as one of the belongings making up the equipment of the Western, individualist Me – "my identity" (James, 1890), or "our identity" (groups, nations). As such, identity is a central term to the vocabulary of individualism.

Markus and Kitayama (1991) formulated the normative imperative of many Western cultures for selves: to be independent of others. For the independent self-construal, "others are less centrally implicated in one's current self-definition or identity" (p. 246). Identity is a non-related sense of one's individuality that heightens the sense of (and the obligation to be) an agent as a (sole, autonomous) producer of one's actions. The term crystallizes the ideology of individualism: being a person in separation of others in a centrifugal movement that aggregates any agency into the person who grows into a "total agent." This movement toward an inside locus as the sole and true (*authentic*) origin of oneself is perfectly expressed by the term identity, meaning "sameness" (Latin *idem*). Being same to oneself in the form of "self-matching" is important in the normative imperative, summoning the independent self to be self-identical and repressing contradiction as morally unacceptable. Identity is the sign of the individual's essence that needs to be preserved from others and the outside, as "property" (Markus & Kitayama, 1991). With increasing criticism of methodological individualism in the social sciences since the 1980s, the conception of identity moved away from essentialism. In an effort "to avoid any reifying 'identity' by theorizing identities as multiple, fragmented, and fluid" (Brubaker & Cooper, 2000, p. 6), social science analysis reformulated a central tie of identity to individualism and moved toward a constructivist stance that is now prevalent. However, the term's academic treatment is heterogeneous with contrasting usages of identity. Some reject fundamental "sameness over time or across persons," whereas others preserve it and "continue to inform important strands of the literature on gender, race, ethnicity, and nationalism" (Brubaker & Cooper, 2000, p. 10). This striking ambivalence in the identity concept is reinforced toward reification by current identity politics where "identity" is considered an actual possession of vital importance.

Not questioning the fundamentally legitimate claims of marginalized, oppressed, or "invisibilized" persons and groups, this chapter aims at a non-individualistic account of identity that emphasizes the fundamental importance of social relations for identity, an experience granting the person with an articulable position in (and toward) the sociocultural and historical reality she lives. This account is a first element to depart from encapsulated identity-as-thing-in-possession and in reservation of others. It leads to contextualizing and "socializing" the "individualistic individual," thus making its other-relatedness manifest – a relatedness wherein identity is located as process. The second element to counter the term's individualistic framing is a take through language viewed as performative movement between individuals, relating them as much as distinguishing them from each other through a continuous movement of call and reply. This dialogic movement is carried forward into individual psychological processes. The link between inter-individual dialogues *with* others and intra-individual dialogues *without* actual others is the process of interiorization (Bertau & Karsten, 2018). The whole picture encompassed by the language-dialogical take hence explains the power of dialogic movements as origin and anchor to socio-psychological and individual-psychological processes – identity being as much a social as an individual psychological experience. The frameworks of dialogism (Linell, 2009) and cultural-historical theory (Yasnitsky, van der Veer, & Ferrari, 2014) are both used to construct this comprehensive notion of language.

Moving toward a notion of identity using a nonindividualistic and performative-dialogic approach indicates two challenges given by the term. The first challenge is the issue of entity versus process, which points to the larger conceptual frameworks of substance and process philosophy (Seibt, 2018). Substance philosophies have to explain movement in pre-given substances, while process philosophies need to explain permanence within given processes – the idea of sameness is at stake in both: How does an entity remain the same when moving over time and across contexts? And how can a process possibly create something that is recognizable as a "this-one"? The second challenge is the relationship between the social and the individual. For the ideology of individualism aligning to substance philosophy, the individual as entity stands facing the social and enters it with an extra step that makes both the gap and the opposition between individual and social sensible.

How can this type of oppositional relation be reconceived? The ideological category of identity plays a particular role here. This manifests in considering it a link between and integration of the social and the individual (e.g., Hammack, 2008): a kind of movement between the individual and the communal or social, yet – particularly in Erikson (1994) – still located in cores, thus displaying the "inherent ambiguity of identity" (Osbeck & Nersessian, 2017, p. 235).

I propose to further theorize the between-link and its ambiguity into an articulation of the social and the individual beyond their opposition and to propose a relational notion of identity. The nonindividualistic approach leads past the ego-logic of individualism by, firstly, including an other to the individual; and secondly, by including a third, namely public position to the dyad, a position given by language itself. Language is key to the relational notion of identity proposed and will be explained as a fundamentally dialogic phenomenon. A first important step is to emphasize that language is conventional, i.e., a common, communal, public means. It is through language activities that humans constantly transcend their unique individuality toward communality: I and You is always also some We (mostly more than one); I privately is always also You and some We. Identity will be located within that language-generated tension of self-other-communal. My central thesis is that identity is a process formed by calling voices of different types belonging to a common field of mediated activities.

In Section 8.1, I address dialogism framing language and self as dialogic. In Section 8.2, I explain the field of mediated activity where the identity process is situated, and I specify language with the term of the language spacetime and its types of voices in order to elaborate how identity works as fielded process. This is followed by an illustrative analysis in Section 8.3 and consolidated in Section 8.4. I conclude with a reprise of the two challenges in Section 8.5.

8.1 Dialogism

Dialogism is an epistemological framework significant at the beginning of the twentieth century in the works of scholars such as Bakhtin (1984), Vološinov (1986), and in the late work of Vygotsky (Bertau & Karsten, 2018). The Soviet scholars meet in a notion of consciousness as social and dialogical, originating in sociocultural verbal communication practices.

Dialogism stands in a sharp contrast to individualism (Linell, 2009). In individualism, others, sociality, cultural-historical contexts, and individuals' living bodies are treated as optional and additional aspects to the "essential individual"; in contrast, dialogism considers these add-ons as defining features of the individual who is viewed as a whole body-and-mind living being, immersed in a sociocultural and historical world of others and objects, where language plays a major role. Language is itself dialogic, since it is, first, a phenomenon that occurs and not an entity that is put to use: it is activity (Humboldt, 1999). Second, this activity is characterized by addressivity: any language act is addressed to other and/or to self. Therefore, language activity is experienced in space and time; it occurs as embodied meaningful verbal forms, which are shaped by being always turned toward some kind of addressee. The verbal forms (uttered words) are "caught" by the dialogic movement of call and reply (Bertau, 2013).

With Vološinov (1986), language is further specified as dialogic-public performance, since the activities constituting it (speaking, listening, replying, understanding) are anchored in a common, publicly practiced field of socio-culturally and historically specific human activities (see below). Language activities occur between situated, encultured, and embodied individuals, living in time and space and having a history; the activities are based in and in contact with a concrete field. For instance, when we act in a classroom as such a field, our specific forms and ways of talking, listening, replying, and under-standing are based in and in contact with the field "twentieth-century American classroom," where its spatio-temporal arrangement of things and people manifests certain socioculturally specific values.

Similarly, and inspired by Dialogical Self Theory (e.g., Hermans, 2001) the self is considered as dialogic in the sense that it is, first, related to an other by dialogical acts (call and reply), and second, that its structure is itself displaying dialogicality, since it originates in social dialogic relations to others. Importantly, it is by virtue of the dialogical acts as relational movement that mutually recognizable and co-related positions are gener-ated: self ↔ other. Such a self is a dynamic, manifold gestalt that allows for contradictions and differences in itself and toward others. In Bakhtin's (1984) and Vološinov's (1986) conceptualization of the individual and its consciousness as plural, polyphonic, and dialogically dynamic, a "self-match" is not only impossible, it would impede the individual's dynamics. Dialogism has a clear affinity to process philosophy, it dynamizes reified entities ("self," "identity," "language"). What needs thus to be explained are forms of persistence or structure within the dialogical movement's flow; that is, the sameness of an individual beyond a momentary emergence in a given relation.

For dialogism, language, self, and identity are interdependent dialogic phenomena on the basis of social relations. The individual cannot be its own source, but comes to be that specific individual via a detour leading through a socializing other, since self and other belong to a common language(d) com-munity, practicing common dialogic and public language activities (Bertau, 2008; Vygotsky, 1999). Through the other's voiced words, the other and the common-communal, publicly practiced, come to be inherent to self. So, otherness of a particular other and otherness of the communal both affect the self in qualitative distinct ways by language activity experienced in voiced words in speaking, listening, and thinking. As I will show in the next sections, identity comes to be a moment of being affected by otherness, a moment in the movement of call and reply between self-other-communal.

8.2 The Field of Mediated Activity

According to cultural-historical psychology, human beings are principally mediated to their reality. Their activity generates as well as uses different mediational means toward the environment and toward their own psychological processes: tools and signs. I propose to view mediated activity (working, celebrating, cooking, playing) as generating specific dynamic fields onto space and in time through meaningful formations and according to different socioculturally and historically specific activities. Generated by these formations, the fields are value-saturated as well as value-generating, where the values are established, repeated, negotiated, altered, and generally presented by activities involving natural objects and artifacts as well as signs of different types. As such, the fields can be described as spatio-temporal, dynamic semiotic arrangements.

Language plays a core role for fields of mediated activity. First, language is the privileged mediator in humans through which they construct, exchange, and understand a common reality (Gadamer, 1977). Second, an actual language activity constructs an own, new symbolic reality unto a given field of mediated activity, the unfolding language activity intertwines itself in a certain way with an established field of mediated activities. Importantly, these language activities do not simply index the field and its activities as a passive reflecting instrument, but rather confirm or contest it, and shape and reshape it in an autonomous way (however, they cannot exist without a field).

Fields of mediated activities need not to be actually languaged, as for instance in ritual dances, people crossing a street at a green light, paintings, or music; however, and this is my third point, it can be argued that the fields' dynamic semiotic arrangements are based in language granting us "all our knowledge of ourselves and ... all knowledge of the world" and thus "familiarity and acquaintance with the world itself and how it confronts us" (Gadamer, 1977, p. 62).

8.2.1 The Language Spacetime and Its Voices

The Language Spacetime

In order to account for the addressivity and sensible phenomenality of language while acknowledging its functioning as symbolic means, I introduced the "language spacetime" unfolding between speaking/listening individuals (e.g., Bertau, 2014). This links sensible forms-in-time with symbolic activity: the abstract language symbols (meaningful utterances) are understood by their grounding in actually shared, commonly structured space and time (where and how utterances are uttered and interlinked through time).

Each time language activity is performed, a specific space between partners is generated, which is situated in space and informed by the flow of time. Each spacetime is constructed and continuously altered by the ongoing language activities of the partners; these are positioned in relation to each other according to physical conditions (objects, location of activity) and with regard to their sociocultural positions (white teacher – African American students; Syrian immigrant – German of Syrian heritage). A spacetime consists of verbal forms interdependently emerging across time and entangled with gazes, bodily postures, mimics, gestures, and whole-body movements. A language spacetime is concretely experienced by languaging subjects.

Voices

In a language spacetime, the partners concretely touch and psychologically affect each other by their speaking. The psycho-physical double nature of the speaking voice is invoked to understand the way and quality of being touched and affected by the other's as well as by one's own speaking (Bertau, 2013). A speaking voice is a physical experience for both speaker (proprioceptive) and listener (perceptive). At the same time, a speaking voice is *speaking*: not producing noise but language forms that are symbolic, conventional means with psychological implications.

The voice's double-sidedness extends further, since a voice is always simultaneously socioculturally specific and individually unique with an origin and a history. It takes part in others' voices across time (Gratier & Bertau, 2012) and moves through different speakers and texts in different socio-historical-cultural fields. While a voice needs a material embodiment, it is not bound to a specific speaking body; rather, its power is to wander between speakers/listeners and to provide a felt contact to other and oneself that is continued intra-psychologically by applying the voiced word to oneself (Vygotsky, 1999).

Furthermore, as *speaking*, a voice amounts to more than this particular speaker: it is a voice attached to some form of communal language. Hence, each speaker speaks both as unique self-to-others *and* as representative of the communal called in by speaking (Bertau, 2014). Particular individual voices and communal, or collective, voices are the two principal types of voices speakers simultaneously enact; they can mark one type over the other by different verbal, paraverbal and nonverbal techniques. Using the term "cultural voice," almost synonymous with communal voice, O'Connor (1989) explains the effect of enacting such a voice: "Adopting a cultural voice involves assuming a dialogic orientation that is emotionally bound to the ideological principles and values of the cultural horizon" (p. 63).

So, communal voices are expressing the dominant discourse of a person's community as this community's stance toward reality and its normative imperative : a summons to its members leading them into activities of all sorts toward the norm's ideal (e.g., "Be yourself!", "Be authentic!"). The collective voice thus has a major organizing role for a person's identity process. Further, it enables the apprehension of a social dimension that "refers neither to interpersonal relationships, nor to abstract and de-contextualized social values and rules" (Grossen & Salazar Orvig, 2011, p. 498). Hence, this "transpersonal" voice is situated at a mid-level and grants access to an experience of the social beyond I, but also beyond You-and-Me without getting lost in the abstract social. Bamberg's (2004) level 3 positioning addresses a similar level: narrators "position themselves vis-à-vis cultural discourses and normative (social) positions" (p. 6). As Bamberg underscores, "such positioning is essential for claiming an identity that the others will work with and build on, because it is oriented toward culturally shared forms of continuity, including the potential for coherence" (p. 7). I understand this type of positioning as a reply to the imperative call coming from the collective voice.

A language spacetime that deploys concretely onto a field of mediated activity relates the partners in a specific way to each other, to themselves, and to their communicative topic. The verbal forms interdependently emerging through time shape these relations. Thus, language performances do not index positions, but generate and further shape these by their relating power within the (structural, lexical) possibilities of a given language. Dialogically related voices are the concrete embodiment, the experience of the positions generated, voices that call each other and invoke, reject, or silence other voices. The dialogical organization, or "orchestration" (Holland et al., 1998) of the different types of voices as voiced to the interlocutor(s) as well as to oneself creates these positions onto the given field of mediated activity and toward it. Voices are set into mutual dialogues and call-responses between different voices and types of voices give way to an *embodied and symbolic* experience of identity – both features are necessary, as Vološinov (1986) emphasizes: "there is no such thing as experience outside of embodiment of signs ... It is not experience that organizes expression, but the other way around – *expression organizes experiences*" (p. 85).

8.3 Identity as Fielded Process: An Illustration

I will now work microanalytically though a segment of a dialogic interaction publicly available as video (Bentgen, 2017)[1] to illustrate how

---

[1] I refer to the original video from the *New York Times Magazine*, available under the link given with the reference to Bentgen (2017). The edited and condensed transcription of the video provided by the *New York Times Magazine* is given under another link (see Baquet, 2017); for the transcription that I created and will address in the illustration below, I started with the *NYT Magazine*'s transcription. Subsequently, I will use "time stamps" to mark the time moment or phase on the video I am addressing. The time stamps I use follow the count given by the video,

identity is created and shaped through voices calling and addressing each other, making apparent the addressivity dynamics within a certain field.[2] Jay-Z, a famous African American rapper and successful businessman, was interviewed by Dean Baquet, the executive director of the *New York Times*, a well-known figure in US journalism. I start by describing the actual dynamic field as spatio-temporal semiotic arrangement wherein the language activity is deployed; beginning with the core phrase and its voices and proceeding from there, I then unfold the voice dynamics.

8.3.1 Field and Protagonists

The interview took place in the New York Times building, a high-rise in New York City. The site is a strictly ordered, light-gray space with elegant sofas, an armchair, a coffee table, sideboards with photographs, an oil painting on the wall, and precious objects (0:17).

Large windows show the height and topological context of the site. This artifactual arrangement displays symbolically the American sociocultural values of wealth and high social status, entangled with a club-like public-privacy, where men in high social positions have conversations. Social, gender, and economic power is displayed by the field that positions the actors and prompts them to position themselves. The field also shifts the interview genre to a conversation between peers, although a journalist and a person of public interest are meeting at the site of US journalism par excellence. However, the clearly assigned right to ask and duty to answer are respected by both partners throughout their interaction. The presentation of the interviewer in the field reinforces this reading. Baquet sits in the armchair in front of the windows between the two sofas. Waiting for Jay-Z (0:17), he browses through newspapers, a golden pen and a notebook next to him on the table (0:09).

The interview took place on September 29, 2017, after the release of Jay-Z's album *4:44* in June 2017. This album has been understood by critics as a reply to *Lemonade*, the previous album of Jay-Z's wife, the likewise wealthy icon of US music Beyoncé. The interview takes up – among other themes – the spouses' public dialogue via music albums, explaining why the interview took place at this time.

Jay-Z, born in Brooklyn, one of the most successful and wealthy rappers in the US, is in his late forties. Dean Baquet, born in New Orleans, is in his early sixties. He is the first black journalist to lead a top US newspaper, and he won the Pulitzer Prize for investigative reporting on corruption in Chicago; since

---

thus providing minutes and seconds (0:17 meaning at the time stamp of 0 minute and 17 seconds).

[2] My position in this analysis is shaped by being a white European female; having recently moved to a southern US state, I have had African American students tell me that they have heard "speak white" from their black peers – a community-internal stigmatization I knew from a female standpoint as a desolidarizing act among subordinates cementing power.

2014 he has been chief executive director of the *New York Times*. Baquet's person and the site grant the interview sobriety and trustworthiness; before the conversation unfolds, what will be said is thus positioned as authentic. This is intensified by the fact that both men are black and highly successful in the white man's world, meeting at this iconic place, both in their most successful moment, well-regarded, and comfortable in a context that is traditionally inhabited, *owned*, by white men – the field had a different agenda. Both men display a high level of professionalism, and they appear relaxed, friendly, and attentive to each other. The impression of overhearing an intimate conversation is reinforced by the camera led by the third professional participant: the eye of the stage, Nick Bentgen, a white, well-known cinematographer in his thirties. This eye directs the audience's witnessing from a sitting height, hence staying within intimacy.

The sophistication with which the given semiotic field is prepared for the actual conversation to unfold is an inherent part of the identity processes of both partners; they will have to start in this exact arrangement and position themselves toward it. Its most obvious element is the contrast between the prototypical American picture and its actual difference: everything is as usual, besides the fact that these two men are members of a community whose socio-economic and intellectual success is still not expected – a community determined through what is called "race." Indeed, right at the start of the interview, race is the first topic Baquet says he wants to talk about (0:50); it will lay the ground for Jay-Z's overarching goal of displaying himself as a transformed, responsible black man aiming to foster dialogue between the races. The interview has a total duration of 34:40, and the chosen segment occurs toward the end (26:50–27:42).

The reason for selecting this segment is that it contains a dialogue between collective voice and individual voice via "reported speech." This form of speech encloses an other's speech in the actual speaking; the actual and the alien voices are brought into a present dialogic contact. Typically, formulaic utterances ("pronoun/name was like" in English) introduce the shift to the alien voice; it is often marked by audible voice shifts (pitch, volume, accent) along with a different languaging. Research on reported speech (e.g., Tannen, 2007) systematically refers to Vološinov's (1986) consideration of the phenom-enon he defines as "the other's spoken word," as "speech within speech, utterance within utterance, and at the same time also *speech about speech, utterance about utterance*" (p. 115). Otherness via the other's words in one's own words is the sign of the pervasive dialogicality of language where no word is unvoiced and unpositioned (Bakhtin, 1984; Vološinov, 1986); this is rhet-orically used in instances of "speech within speech." Explaining the relation-ships between own and alien utterance, Vološinov demonstrates that the insertion of the alien voice always has a transformative effect on both voices. Therefore, Tannen (2007) calls reported speech "constructed dialogue." As this technique explicitly stages the dialogical contact between voices, I consider it an effective access to voice analysis.

Through the constructed dialogue at the core of the segment, Jay-Z enacts a conflictual dialogue with Baquet as witness. This documents the call-and-response dynamics between individual and collective voice and how the speaker navigates these to perform a fielded identity. Key to this enactment is the phrase "talking white," a topos in American culture, fueling ongoing debates on social and other media and thematized in movies, where protagonists code-switch to the Standard Accent ("white speaking") to enter the white-dominant world (e.g., the 2018 film *BlacKkKlansman*).

The phrase can be traced back to a poem written by Michèle Lalonde in 1974, where "speak white" means to speak English associated with British colonial imperialism; this extends to any "correct" (i.e., standard) declared language as instrument of white cultural imperialism subjugating proletarians and slaves of any ethnic background. As O'Connor (1989) notes, dominant groups "attempt to define their own cultural discourse as the legitimate public one . . ., as the official state language. [The] notion of 'cultural capital' can be described as the possession of those cultural voices endorsed by the powerful networks in a community" (p. 65). The phrase is used not only by colonialists toward colonized, but also within nondominant communities by members blaming each other for adopting the oppressor's language and thus affirming its power – this is currently strongly denounced in the US. The phrase in the segment thus has a tradition (Gergen, 2009): it encapsulates racism and (internalized) colonialism through an enacted cultural voice wandering through speakers.

Talking White, Transcript 1[3]

01 BAQUET: do you feel you have a DIfferent kind of obligation (.) to the people who listen to you than: if you were a white musician?

02 JAY-Z: yeah; = cause I have an ob=obligation

03   <u>going back to</u> the story of O.J.; <<voice more monodic and faster than surrounding>>

04   is to further conversation;

05 BAQUET: mhm'

06 JAY-Z: of an entire -

07   race of people.

---

[3] As said previously, the segment starts at 26:50 and lasts until 27:42. My transcription follows some of the minimal and basic transcript conventions of GAT2 (Couper-Kuhlen & Barth-Weingarten, 2011). On this basis, I assigned and numbered lines to which I will from now on refer. When referring to events *outside* this segment – such as the beginning of the interview, *not* transcribed – I will use the time stamp. The index ' means a rising of pitch to mid; a question mark indicates a rising to high; a semi-colon means a falling to mid; and a short dash indicates a level pitch movement. The sign = designates a fast continuation; the colon signifies lengthening; words in square brackets are simultaneously spoken; and (.) is a micropause. Non-verbal acts are given in (( )), and paraverbal events like laughing or chuckling, as well as notes on intonation and voice quality, are given in << >>. CAPITALS indicate stressed words or syllables.

08		not' me'

08   not' me'
09 BAQUET: mhm'
10 JAY-Z: ALL of us.
11   but (.) specifically me = since you're asking the question' is to (.) open up DIAlogue.
12 BAQUET: ((silent smooth nod))
13 JAY-Z: is OKAY: to think -
14   is OKAY to be smart -
15   =you know there was a time when people was like you're talkin' WHITE. <<fast monodic voice, last word with accentuated short falling>>
16 BAQUET: mhm'
17 JAY-Z: it's like (.) what does that even MEAN? <<short chuckle>>
18   I know I know wo:rds?
19 BAQUET: ((silent short nods))
20 JAY-Z: inTElligence is not a tribute to COlor.
21 BAQUET: mhm' ((marked slow nodding))
22 JAY-Z: and I'm sure you've heard it growing up many [times]=
23 BAQUET: [of course]
24 JAY-Z: = you're speaking [white'] or what? <<the word white is a reduced form of the one in line 15: shorter and less loud but same quality of intonation>>
25 BAQUET: [yeah;]
26   yeah;
27 JAY-Z: I'm speaking like I know wo:rds
28 BAQUET: yeah;
29 JAY-Z: and is okay' is fi::ne
30 BAQUET: mhm'
31 JAY-Z: You know so I have I have an obligation to (.) further the conversation in ALL ways

8.3.2 Performed Voices, Calls, and Replies

Lines 15–18 and Reprise 24–27

With line 1 Dean Baquet (DB) opens a new thematic episode in the interview, asking for a possible difference in the obligation of black and white artists to their audience. This question continues the overarching theme of race as introduced by DB as the first topic to talk about at the start of the interview at 0:47, which is not transcribed here. In answering the question, Jay-Z (JZ) constructs a digression spanning lines 13–30: this is the core addressed in the analysis. The instance of constructed dialogue in line 15 is introduced by applying the typical formula "people was like" immediately followed by what these people are saying: "you're talking white." The phrase is uttered again in line 24, this time in a reduced form (no introduction, reduced intonation of key word "white," and less loud). From line 22 mentioning JZ's experience growing up, "the people" can be presumed to be the black collective. This voice's enactment is followed in the initial form (l. 15) and in its reprise (l. 24) by a voice questioning back: "what does it even mean?" (l. 17), "or what?" followed by an answer proposal: "I know I know words?" (l. 18), "I'm speaking like I know words" (l. 27), respectively. Strikingly, as can be heard in the different intonations, this answer is transformed from a question to a statement in the reprise: the answer is now taken as affirmation of an identity positioning that is prohibited by "the people's" voice enunciating the phrase "you're talking white" as moral reproach (possible paraphrase: *Black people ought not to speak correct English, and if they do, they betray their community because they defect to the oppressor*).

I consider this shift as a performed identity development from a past ("there was a time," l. 15) to a present identity positioning using the given semiotic field and the language spacetimes formed appropriately to the club-like arrangement as evidence – yes, black men talk white and are smart and still responsible for their "people." The fieldedness of the identity shows the possible resolution of the dilemma created by the prohibiting voice for black people: talking white, one is still black, there is no betrayal. Neither the semiotic field, nor the white dominant, nor the black inferiorized community expects this identity positioning. Thus, the positioning derives its strong identificatory power from this exact fieldedness by putting into contact and dialogue: the field's here-and-now "whiteness" (Ahmed, 2007) with the black collective's reproachful-prohibitive voice, JZ's individual counter-voice, and DB as another successful black man enrolled by JZ as ally and supportively following the identification movements across the enacted dialogues. The identificatory power works toward JZ (the person he wants to present) and can flow over to his audience identifying with his development and dilemma resolution – as well-known, wealthy, successful, *and* speaking in this precise field, JZ is granted a privileged position of trustworthiness and rightness that can function as attractor for other members of the black community. Yet, this privileged position is *granted* – any mistake can lead to loss of this privilege.

Lines 20 and 22–23

The two dialogues (ll. 15–18 and 24–27) frame a stand-alone utterance (l. 20) as well as a short direct exchange between JZ and DB (ll. 22–23). Both events stand out in a particular way for themselves and in terms of their sequential positioning: both are intersected between the past and the present reply to the people's voice. I argue that they both serve the development from lines 15–18 to 24–27 by introducing supportive instances to this development. Forms and timing of both events are particular and in contrast to the environing utterances. Line 20, "intelligence is not a tribute to color" shows no pronoun, no addressee, and uses present tense and the genre form of a proposition – "x is (not) z:" – a language form used for unpositioned truth statements in Western cultures. This form declares the genuine, timeless truth; it comes from nobody in particular and speaks to everybody, without any consideration of differences. This impersonal voice can be said to address "all" (l. 10) as well as JZ's own self, echoing and indirectly supporting his counter-voice starting in line 17.

In stark contrast, the following move by JZ starts a short personal and direct exchange with DB (ll. 22–23). Pronoun use set a clear Me–You relationship, tied together by the past experience already mentioned (l. 15) but now personalized, focused on DB who is thus requested to share and co-position the development JZ is enacting (for co-positioning, see Bertau & Klee, 2016). In effect, DB aligns in a very marked way; as listener, he utters a word for the first time in the segment (l. 23), simultaneously with JZ's utterance end "times." This overt speaking (in contrast to closed-mouth continuers) occurs another time simultaneously between JZ's "white" and DB's "yeah" (ll. 24–25) and continues, now in alternation and thus flowing out, into lines 26–(27–)28. A close look into DB's listener activities shows that his engagement possibly starts at line 19, and then involves more body and overt sound activities up to the closing in line 30, which confirms the ending of the marked engagement (closed-mouth continuer, no word) and of the whole digression.

I consider lines 22–28 as a zone of heightened engagement where the partners come closely together, as shown by the form of their language activities at that moment. I see and hear here an instance of "being together in time" described for a mother–baby conversation building up as polyphonic narrative structure (Gratier & Bertau, 2012); the core of the narrative is enacted as a zone of heightened emotional engagement through speech/sound overlap. This zone is here the co-positioning of DB–JZ, both partners aligning to the same experience and rejecting it together (l. 24 "or what"). With this zone, the partners move together to the dissolution of the dilemma, and both co-enact a fielded identity able to disregard the prohibiting voice, affirming another black identity. Although short and not as elaborated as the example in Gratier and Bertau, the exchange with two moments of overlap and a marked voice–body engagement by the listener stands in clear contrast to surrounding forms of alternating turns.

Lines 13–14 and 29–30

Finally, the observation extends to the introduction of the first instance of constructed dialogue (ll. 15–18) in lines 13–14. JZ does not start the digression with the prohibiting voice, but introduces this voice by another one using the formula "it's okay to be X," which functions simultaneously as opening statement to elaborate the topic of who is allowed to speak "to an entire race of people" about race and racism; and also, I would argue, as reply to a silent critique saying that something is *not* okay (again, a possible paraphrase: *You cannot open up the dialogue; you are black, and using correct English for such a dialogue makes it exactly fake, because it's the oppressor's language – how can it ever enable a dialogue?*). So, JZ starts with a voice that is already a reply to the prohibiting voice, a support to his project of "opening dialogue of an entire race of people."

Similarly to the impersonal voice in line 20, this voice is not in a direct and overt dialogue with another voice enacted. However, it can be argued that there is addressivity present in the form; the utterance has been an instance of a colloquial formula, part of social language in the US for about twenty years. In general, it is a reply to a corrective critique of nonnormative appearance, act, or utterance of the form "it's not okay to be/do." The formula gives permission and calms and works by a power differential: an older friend, a parent, a teacher, or a therapist can utter these words out of a power position typically articulated through age, gender, race, or profession. Further, this voice is at some distance from the debate between the non-normative individual and the critiquing norm-voice of the collective, which deepens its power.

The formula is also reuttered in line 29 as closing result of the debate between the collective and the individual voice: "and is okay is fi::ne" – the elongation of the final syllable iconically presents the calming and the ending in harmony – it is fine for black people to talk white, to be smart, and to think. The permission given is also self-given: JZ legitimizes and affirms his right to speak the way he does and to conduct the dialogue about race. It can be assumed that this was the function of the digression JZ started in line 13: claiming and affirming the right to speak, against and for his own community.

So, the "it's okay"-voice acts as frame, holding the digression with the debate displayed as identity development. The heightened engagement (ll. 22–28) lies at the heart of the frame related to the Now of both protagonists. I view this sequential positioning as marking the importance of countering the collective voice of the black community within that community.

Overview of Voices in Call and Reply

Four voices are enacted by JZ and supported by DB; the special status of the collective voice is marked by using small caps in bold face (see Figure 8.1).

Voice A: the calming voice, permitting the transgression of the norm saying *Black people are not supposed to/cannot talk correct English*. Typically uttered from a benevolent power position to a lower power position.

Voice B: black collective voice, talking to all black people; statement "you are doing x" equals "you are betraying your community."

Voice C: individual voice, counter-voice, and reply to Voice B. JZ's former self, starting questioning the ideology of Voice B.

Voice D: impersonal voice of truth or reason. Speaks to all reasonable people; indirect support to Voice A and C. This is the "genuine truth," and it comes from nobody (in contrast to Voice B's truth sounding clearly positioned).

Voice B ↔ Voice C: two dialogues between the collective voice calling (B) and the individual voice replying (C) (ll. 15–18, 24–27).

Voice D: impersonal voice sequentially positioned within the dialogic exchange of B and C. Standing out within the segment by its form and timelessness; it is called in by JZ as support, and confirmed by DB.

Voice A → B and ALL and self from a distanced position, not involved in the dialogue between B and C: opening and closing (ll. 13–14, 29–30), addressing but no overt dialogue; addressivity: colloquial formula part of social language in the US; a reply to a corrective critique of nonnormative appearance, act, or utterance of the form "it's not okay to be/do."

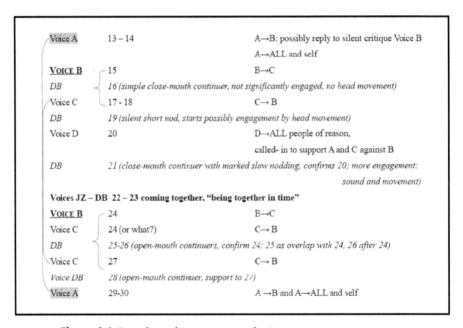

Figure 8.1 *Interdependent structure of voices*
*DB: Listener Dean Baquet, all other lines from speaker Jay-Z. **Bracket 13–30:** Frame built by Voice A. **Bracket 17–26:** Zone of heightened engagement between JZ and DB with common counter-positioning to Voice B. **Curly brackets 15–18 and 24–27:** Two dialogues between Voice B and Voice C, i.e., between collective and individual voice. Voices A–D are all enacted by JZ; he uses his own "now-voice" in 22 to address DB. In sum, JZ speaks with five voices, and DB follows, confirming each voice enactment and positional move across the different language spacetimes in their own time frames, including the timelessness of Voice D.*

8.4 Analytic Considerations

Starting with a description of the field as semiotic arrangement as presented through the camera and providing background information to the protagonists, I moved to a close observation of the topical phrase "talking white" and its enactment toward the process of fielded identity. This observation followed the lead of the phrase in its sequential and thematic context. This resulted in a topological-spiral reading circling through and linking same and different language acts that seems appropriate to the deployment of the language spacetime. This form of reading is based in the dialogical principle of utterances being interdependent, i.e., each utterance is related to previous utterances and anticipates possible future utterances (Jakubinskij, 1979). The sequential position of utterances thus matters for parts of its meaning (Linell, 2009), while other parts are generated over the whole conversation as intertextual process that might reach far back, even into one's own and others' previous conversations (which is especially the case for, even the function of, collective voices), creating the dialogic texture that characterizes language activity (Bakhtin, 1984; Vološinov, 1986). Further, utterances are acts seeking continuation and completion, specifically by the actual partner in order to be complete, i.e., to realize a meaning–form potential as co-creation gradually determined by the partners.

On that basis, I identified two dialogues starting with an instance of constructed speech that are framed and hold in spacetime and meaning by a power-positioned familiar voice giving permission to transgress a norm. Nested between the two dialogues is the voice of truth or reason, functioning like a stand-alone, a strong column without any perceptible actor and addressee, exactly because it is Truth. This is immediately followed by a zone of heightened engagement of the partners, who are thus pushed to the foreground.

Time flow is irreversible. The speakers thus progress in succession through their unfolding conversation. However, moving through the initial utterances and voices and their reprises (ll. 13–14~29–30 and 15–18~24–27) and adding literally outstanding moments (l. 20 and the exchange in ll. 22–28), they create a language spacetime with waves around a center (or two or three moving centers), a movement that works through the embodied, voiced language acts on the specific field. It iconically displays a development through negotiations that is narrated via language symbols.

Identifying voices follows the same lead and rests upon the dialogic reading. The case of constructed speech is clear; analysis continues from there by observing the languaging context and any differences in tone and wording, according to sequential positions and assuming interdependency of utterances. Voices A and D are thus more assumed than Voice B and C, but the formal and sequential characteristics of the deployed language spacetime are supportive of this interpretation. Important are the co-action movements, i.e., how the developed voices are supported, rejected, or developed by the listening partner. Identity is thus not only acted within and toward a given field, but also co-actively by languaging partners.

The clearest and strongest moment of a fielded identity process is certainly occurring in the dialogues between the collective and the individual voice displaying the normative power of the call of the collective, counteracted by the individual's replying voice through questions and statement affirming the nonnormativity of the chosen behavior as right. As said, this documents how speaker JZ navigates between these voices linked by call and reply, how he articulates and negotiates the call and develops his own reply – not least by adding outside voices, such as Voice A and Voice D, seeking confirmation from DB, and using the field. The result is a process occurring in space and time, through languaging co-actors, and anchored in the semiotic field of mediated activity: identity.

8.4.1 Identity: Being Called by Voices

The central thesis advanced here is that identity is a fielded process formed by calling voices of different types belonging to that field. This assumes an irreducible entanglement of subjects and their languaging. Subjects are considered as other-affected dialogical, polyphonic selves with individual and collective voices.

In accordance with Vygotsky (1999), the other's voiced word is taken to be primary in time and fact and viewed as a call to self. Being addressed-as-someone who can reply to the call is existentially needed and the base to become any "who." Since Spitz's (1945) observations of infants deprived of attention, attachment research shows this existential dimension of being-talked/communicated-to – i.e., being addressed, called by an other. Addressing is an act creating a focus, a direction toward an object made relevant and singled out *in relation to the actor*. Thus, it singles out the addressee *as addressee-to-the-caller*. Addressing is the movement creating a relation and therewith generating the partners as mutually related. I see the speaking voice as the basic form given to the address (see also Castarède & Konopczynski, 2005).

As a result, identity is a process occurring in a field of mediated activities generated and shaped by language activities deployed on that field. This leads to a call-and-reply dynamic of several crossing and blending voices. The following interrelated movements on three levels can be described, corresponding to different perspectives on identity.

First, from an outside, bystander perspective, identity occurs through the movements given with the basic relation of self-other-community. The subjects perform both individual and collective voices, resulting in calls of different moral-normative strength that can be brought into dialogues. Second, from the perspective of the interpersonal activities, identity happens through a movement coming from a You to a Me. This dyadic experience of "I as that-one-to-you" generates positionings with specific voices; through position and voice reversal in interiorization, "I as this-one-to-myself" is generated – a self-call is established, which can be acted upon in different ways. Importantly, the You utters an individual voice to Me-as-individual, and a collective voice to Me-as-individual or to Me-as-member of same/other collective. Accordingly, interiorized voicings will have different functions for the self. Third, on the grounds of interiorization, identity happens as a movement between I and Me. What happens at this level is particularly socioculturally and historically sensitive. Concerning individualistic societies and their cultures of self-autonomy, identity can be seen as element of a self in accordance with the normative imperative, or call. The firm ego of such a self will know about, reclaim, and seek identity to hold it as a precious possession.

The dyadic You–Me address movement (level 2) can only happen on the grounds of a language spacetime, experienced and performed by the subjects. Further, the I–Me address movement (level 3) can only happen on the grounds of and in renewed movements via the speaking You (unique and collective voice). Thus, identity is first of all a social call coming from others and the collective (level 1).

8.5 Challenges and Concluding

From the process philosophical and nonindividualistic stance here adopted, the first challenge is the issue of permanency creating sameness, or "identity." This can regard groups (sameness across individuals), or single individuals (sameness across time, situations, different others). The second challenge to the category of identity concerns the social and the individual. In substance philosophy, this is articulated in the way to link these phenomena, since entities are fundamentally separate. In the process view here chosen, the issue is how to *differentiate* entities from each other and render them discernible, i.e., how to not make the individual and the social replicas of each other and dissolve "identity" into an indistinguishable whole. Possibilities given throughout the chapter can be summarized as follows.

Sameness across groups presumes homogeneity between members of that group. Yet, for the cultural-historical and dialogical perspective adopted, homogeneity is a denial of plurality, of internal differences, and contradictions. Historically, homogeneity for Western types of modernity can be linked to the idea of a nation since the American and French Revolutions. Nation-building is significantly achieved through homogenizing state practices in educational, legal, military, and administrative institutions; a standard declared language is key to this achievement. Alternatively, heterogeneity that articulates in dialogical, sociocultural practices is the situation to understand a group's identity as incessant movement between several voices. Further, the argument can be made that comparability (Vygotsky, 1999) between members of a group sharing language and other reality-mediating practices is reached through sociogenesis – practicing being comparable to others is granting the group's identity as "same enough."

Sameness in a single individual across time, situations, and different others can also be conceived by sociogenesis that ties the individual to others' words and reality understandings. The other's word is affecting self, which is the moment of being comparable to this other. This links back to the self as polyphonic and thus heterogeneous constellation: otherness is crucial to this self who is in constant negotiations with others' voices in order to form. Hence, identity as matching with oneself is neither assumed nor necessary. Rather, the frictions given by inherent otherness are what prevent individuals from becoming asocial beings, disjointed from societal others. The individual is hence not self-made but comes to be that unique and socialized person via the other addressing that self within a common language(d) community. This is furthered by practices of recognizability. Being recognizable by others and oneself depends on being addressed-as by others, where the "as" is a manageable range of "as-whom"; I assume that human beings are able to manage a certain amount of voices to a certain number of others. Finally, having called the polyphonic self a gestalt, individual sameness can be theorized by the notion of gestalt consistency, first formulated by von Ehrenfels: as consistent gestalt, a melody is recognized as the same when transposed into another key (Schmicking, 2003). Per analogy, I view the self's gestalt experienced as a dynamic (transposable) consistency or permanence on the basis of socio-psychological perceptions of each other and oneself. Two movements hold this consistency: centrifugal forces toward multiplicity and disagreement, and centripetal forces driving the self's gestalt toward unity and agreement (Richardson, 2011). So, identity as process can be conceived as leading to provisional stages of stability that are open to further changes at different scales and velocities. In sum, identity in persons is not given or attained and then kept; rather, it is an interim, even fragile stage that needs to be constantly formed and lived through other's and one's communities address as-this-one.

Concerning the social and the individual, sociogenesis is again key. Understanding individual psychological processes through interiorized social practices, the difference between the social and the individual is at stake. As Vygotsky (1999) emphasized, interiorization is not a copying process but a unique, individual transformation appropriating the common. Uniqueness is given by the individual's unique body to certain others in certain socio-psychological, specific positions in time and space. The positioned voices leading the interiorization–exteriorization processes form unique, yet socially and culturally recognizable dialogical constellations. But the crucial element in the simultaneity of being unique and social lies in language and its specific strength to be objective (transindividual), yet flexible enough to subjectivity (individual). Incessant movements between uniqueness and commonality that are granted by language activity lead to discernible and "comparable" selves. Thus, it is language as conventional symbolic phenomenon that provides continuity across time and persons and interlinks social and individual.

References

Ahmed, S. (2007). A phenomenology of whiteness. *Feminist Theory*, *8*(2), 149–168.

Bakhtin, M. M. (1984). *Problems of Dostoevsky's Poetics*, translated and edited by C. Emerson. Minneapolis: University of Minnesota Press (originally published 1929).

Bamberg, M. (2004). Form and functions of "slut bashing" in male identity constructions in 15-year-olds. *Human Development*, *47*(6), 331–353.

Baquet, D, (2017). Highlights from Dean Baquet's interview with Jay-Z at the *New York Times* on September 29, 2017. Retrieved April 26, 2021, from www.nytimes.com/interactive/2017/11/29/t-magazine/jay-z-dean-baquet-interview.html.

Bentgen, N. (2017). Jay-Z and Dean Baquet, in conversation (11/29/2017). Retrieved April 26, 2021, from www.nytimes.com/video/t-magazine/100000005574909/jayz-interview.html.

Bertau, M.-C. (2008). Voice: A pathway as "social contact to oneself." *Integrative Psychological and Behavioral Science*, *42*(1), 92–113.

Bertau, M.-C. (2013). Voices of others unto the self, voices of others in the self. Polyphony as means and resource for constructing and reconstructing social reality. In A. Liégeois, J. Corveleyn, M. Riemslagh, & R. Burggraeve (Eds.), *"After You!" Dialogical Ethics and the Pastoral Counselling Process* (pp. 37–65). Leuven: Peeters.

Bertau, M.-C. (2014). Exploring language as the "in-between." *Theory & Psychology*, *24*(4), 524–541.

Bertau, M.-C. & Karsten, A. (2018). Reconsidering interiorization: Self moving across language spacetimes. *New Ideas in Psychology*, *49*, 7–17.

Bertau, M.-C. & Klee, M. (2016, September 7–9). Co-positioning in the self. Paper presented at the 9th International Conference on the Dialogical Self, Lublin, Poland.

Brubaker, R. & Cooper, F. (2000). Beyond "identity." *Theory and Society*, *29*(1), 1–47.

Castarède, M. F. & Konopczynski, G. (Eds.). (2005). *Au commencement était la voix*. Ramonville Saint-Agne: Érès.

Couper-Kuhlen, E. & Barth-Weingarten, D. (2011). A system for transcribing talk-in-interaction: GAT2. *Gesprächsforschung – Online-Zeitschrift zur verbalen Interaktion*, *12*, 1–51.

Erikson, E. H. (1994). *Identity: Youth and Crisis*. New York, NY: Norton (originally published 1968).

Gadamer, H.-G. (1977). Man and language. In H.-G. Gadamer, *Philosophical Hermeneutics*, translated and edited by D. E. Linge (pp. 59–68). Berkeley, CA: University of California Press (originally published 1966).

Gergen, K. J. (2009). Dialogue as collaborative action. *Journal für Psychologie*, *17*(2), 1–19.

Gleason, Ph. (1983). Identifying identity: A semantic history. *Journal of American History*, *69*(4), 910–931.

Gratier, M. & Bertau, M.-C. (2012). *Polyphony: A vivid source of self and symbol*. In M.-C. Bertau, M. M. Gonçalves, & P. T. F. Raggatt (Eds.), *Dialogic Formations. Investigations into the Origins and Development of the Dialogical Self* (pp. 85–119). Charlotte, NC: Information Age.

Grossen, M. & Salazar Orvig, A. (2011). Third parties' voices in a therapeutic interview. *Text & Talk*, *31*(1), 53–71.

Hammack, P. L. (2008). Narrative and the cultural psychology of identity. *Personality and Social Psychology Review*, *12*, 222–247.

Hermans, H. J. M. (2001). The dialogical self: Toward a theory of personal and cultural positioning. *Culture & Psychology*, *7*(3), 243–281.

Holland, D., Lachicotte, Jr. W., Skinner, D., & Cain, C. (1998). *Identity and Agency in Cultural Worlds*. Cambridge, MA: Harvard University Press.

Humboldt, W. von. (1999). *On Language. On the Diversity of Human Language Construction and Its Influence on the Mental Development of the Human Species*, edited by M. Lonsonsky, translated by P. Heath. Cambridge: Cambridge University Press (originally published 1830–1835).

Jakubinskij, L. P. (1979). On verbal dialogue, translated by J. E. Knox & L. Barna. *Dispositio*, *4*(11–12), 321–336 (originally published 1923).

James, W. (1890). *The Principles of Psychology, Vol. 1*. New York, NY: Henry Holt.

Linell, P. (2009). *Rethinking Language, Mind, and World Dialogically*. Charlotte, NC: Information Age.

Markus, H. R. & Kitayama, S. (1991). Culture and the self: Implications for cognition, emotion, and motivation. *Psychological Review*, *98*, 224–253.

O'Connor, T. (1989). Cultural voice and strategies for multicultural education. *Journal of Education*, *171*(2), 57–74.

Osbeck, L. M. & Nersessian, N. J. (2017). Epistemic identities in interdisciplinary science. *Perspectives on Science*, *25*(2), 226–260.

Richardson, F. C. (2011). A hermeneutic perspective on dialogical psychology. *Culture & Psychology*, *17*(4), 462–472.

Schmicking, D. (2003). *Hören und Klang*. [Hearing and sound] Würzburg: Königshausen & Neumann.

Seibt, J. (2018). Process philosophy. In E. N. Zalta (Ed.), *The Stanford Encyclopedia of Philosophy* [online]. Retrieved April 26, 2021, from https://plato.stanford.edu/archives/win2018/entries/process-philosophy/.

Spitz, R. (1945). Hospitalism: An inquiry into the genesis of psychiatric conditions in early childhood. *Psychoanalytic Study of the Child*, *1*, 53–74.

Tannen, D. (2007). *Talking Voices. Repetition, Dialogue, and Imagery in Conversational Discourse*. Cambridge: Cambridge University Press.

Vološinov, V. N. (1986). *Marxism and the Philosophy of Language*, edited and translated by L. Matejka & I. R. Titunik. Cambridge, MA: Harvard University Press (originally published 1929).

Vygotsky, L. S. (1999). Consciousness as a problem in the psychology of behavior. In N. Veresov (Ed.), *Undiscovered Vygotsky. Etudes on the Pre-history of Cultural-Historical Psychology* (pp. 256–281). Frankfurt am Main: Peter Lang (originally published 1925).

Yasnitsky, A., van der Veer, R., & Ferrari, M. (Eds.). (2014). *The Cambridge Handbook of Cultural-Historical Psychology*. Cambridge: Cambridge University Press.

9 Psychoanalytic Perspectives on Identity: From Ego to Life Narrative

Tilmann Habermas and Nina Kemper

Identity is not a current concept in psychoanalysis, despite the success Erikson's concept of psychosocial identity had outside psychoanalysis. Nevertheless, it owes psychoanalytic theory, and we suggest that later developments in psychoanalysis continue to potentially inform the concept of identity. We therefore take the approach to psychoanalytic perspectives on identity that Frosh (2012) did a decade ago, by providing a selective historical review of implicit contributions of psychoanalysis to the concept of identity. However, we discuss somewhat different authors, and our discussion does not stress an insurmountable impossibility of achieving identity, as did Frosh by reference to Lacan and Laplanche. Instead we will argue for a narrative and co-narrative conception of identity that acknowledges the interpersonal and social process character of identity based on a realist epistemological position.

This chapter outlines the development of the concept of identity in psychoanalysis in four steps, highlighting achievements and relative deficiencies for each:

(i) The concept of identity was initially only implicit in psychoanalytic theorizing, foremost in Freud's synthetic function of the ego and in Federn's cohesion of ego feeling.

(ii) Erikson (1946) introduced the concept of ego identity, also termed psychosocial identity, which served to extend a view of development driven by biological maturation and identifications to include sociocultural influences in adolescence and beyond. Based on sociological, cultural, and psychological theories, Erikson (1964, 1968) integrated a clinical view on the pre-reflective sense of self with a reflected self-image as it relates to central roles and values. Three aspects of ego identity are bipolar dimensions: individuality versus belonging to a group, synchronic consistency across situations versus situational flexibility, and diachronic self-continuity of still being an identical person across personal development and change. Erikson also stressed three other crucial aspects of identity, namely agency as the ability to initiate actions, give direction to one's life, and take on responsibility; feeling at home in one's body; and self-esteem. In addition, Erikson located the major development of identity in adolescence, linking it to the life story.

(iii) In the 1950s–1970s, more clinically oriented analysts elaborated theories of self-with-other. However, only Kernberg explicitly took up Erikson's concept of identity and integrated it with ego psychology and object relations theory.

(iv) Since the 1990s the idea of an integrated and more or less stable identity has been criticized for leaving out how others co-constitute identity and how it shifts from moment to moment. We discuss the radicalization of the epistemic stance by Ogden and Ferro, who undermine the classical importance of personal history and identity with more than a postmodern whiff.

Finally, we argue for a narrative conception of identity, bending back to Erikson's conception of identity as a life story that reaches beyond the couch, presenting an updated concept of narrative identity which is enriched by psychoanalytic developments of the past fifty years.

9.1 The Topic of Identity in Psychoanalysis before Its Conceptualization

The early years of psychoanalytic thinking prepared the introduction of the concept of identity in several ways. The basic insight of psychoanalysis is that we are *not* identical with whom we think we are, but that there is more to us than we are able to acknowledge. These non-identical, ego-dystonic parts of the person are excluded from awareness, but are nevertheless active in influencing actions, action tendencies (emotions), and random thoughts, perceptions, and feelings as well as symptoms. Freud (1894) built on Janet's (1889) concept of dissociation – introduced to describe a duplicity or multiplicity of states of consciousness that do not communicate among each other (dissociative state) – to introduce the concept of motivated defense. Psychological defense is directed against perceiving those wishes, emotions, and thoughts that are automatically appraised to be too much in conflict with how one sees and would like to see oneself. These unacknowledged strivings remain outside consciousness or appear only in dissociated states, but they continue to influence the person's experience and actions in a disguised form.

Thus, the main thrust of psychoanalysis is to undermine the self-assuredness of individuals who deem themselves to be identical with themselves. However, the term defense already indicates that individuals strive to defend themselves against their own strivings with which they cannot identify (they feel alien, ego-dystonic, have a not-me-quality) to maintain an image of themselves that is more or less integrated and in accord with their moral and ideal standards for themselves. Psychoanalysis is therefore not about personal non-identity of self-image and the actual person, but about the striving and struggling to achieve a semblance of an acceptable view of oneself that does not provoke negative feelings about oneself because of one's contradictoriness or one's shame or sinful aspects. Freud (1894) ascribed this struggle for unity and acceptability to what is experienced as "I" ("Ich" in German), which in the structural model (1923) he turned into a theoretical construct, translated into English as "ego." Its main function is to synthesize the strivings of the person, namely both biologically based needs, represented by the "id," and moral principles and ideals, represented by the "superego." Freud defined the ego by its function to synthesize, that is to create compatibility between different motives of the person so that the person can experience her- or himself as not too self-contradictory. This allows the individual to follow a consistent course of action and to entertain reliable relationships. As long as persons succeed in intentionally creating some degree of unity, the result is normally far from perfect, but individuals know about their internal contradictions. Only to the degree that the process of synthesizing relies on automatic defense mechanisms the aim of which is to hide contradictions from individuals – and some use of defense mechanisms is indispensable for anybody – is the result no longer intelligible and therefore undermines the aim of creating coherent individuals. Thus, the identity of self-image and the actual person in both cases remains an ideal that is never achieved, but striven for. The forces that work against the synthesizing of motives by the ego are, first, the varying conflicting tendencies and self-aspects that do not fit the desired self-image, and secondarily, the less-than-ideal means of automatically creating defensive compromises.

Freud (1917, 1923) added to the conflict between drives and norms another potential source of disunity, namely the results of processes of identification. He conceptualized three kinds of identification: an early primary identification with early caretakers, an identification with both parents to resolve the oedipal conflict, thereby establishing the superego, and identifications with those loved others who need to be given up as objects of desire. These processes lead to identifications as part of the individual's self, both in terms of values, ideals, and norms, and in terms of characteristics of the person that emulate aspects of the others one identifies with. These identifications stemming from various life phases may in turn be inconsistent with each other as well as with individuals' strivings and norms, and therefore also pose a challenge to the task of creating a somewhat united, self-identical person.

Thus, besides the formal aspect of what Erikson would later term identity as unity of the person, Freud also proposed a theory of how characteristics of individuals develop through selective identification with others. These identifications could form the superego when identifying with moral rules or striving to become like the other, or they could become part of the ego, that is, the person would actually take on characteristics of the other. Processes of identification contribute to individuals' sense of individuality and belonging. Freud (1921) discussed two cases of the absence of what he termed I or ego due to a lack of differentiation between oneself and others. He assumed that the cognitive differentiation of oneself and others emerged only in the course of the first year of life, a differentiation that helped to unite a set of disparate ego kernels to one single ego and to unite parts of others to integrated persons. A second case of lacking self–other differentiation may result from a specific mode of functioning of individuals in large hierarchical institutions like the military or the (Catholic) church in which they tend to identify with institutional or charismatic leaders whom they use as a substitute for their conscience and ideal self. This kind of hyper-identification with a live leader and the group erases individuality and individual conscience, a topic that has since been conceptualized in psychology as de-individuation (Reicher, Spears, & Postmes, 1995).

Besides Freud, Paul Federn made important contributions in the 1920s (published as a book in 1952) to a psychoanalytic conceptualization of what Erikson was to term identity. On the basis of observations of borderline and psychotic patients, he developed a terminology for describing disorders of the pre-reflective sense of self ("Ichgefühl," translated as "ego feeling") as it shows in states of estrangement like depersonalization and derealization as well as in hallucinations and thought disorder. Using the concepts of *ego-boundary* and *cathexis* of the ego, denoting the extension and the strength of subjectively felt me-ness of one's body and mental processes, he provided excellent clinical descriptions of subjective experiences of loss of ego-boundary and of a sense of aliveness of oneself and others. Federn termed them estrangement and disorders of the "I" – the immediate experience of being oneself is disordered. These ego-structural disorders were considered to be more severe than specific neurotic conflicts and symptoms. The problem of translating Freud's and Federn's term "I" as "ego" in English is that it often (Freud) or always (Federn) denoted a quality of pre-reflective experience which gets lost in the Latinism of "ego."

Thus, before Erikson (1946), psychoanalysis had not used identity as a concept, but had developed relevant ideas which Erikson could build on and integrate:

(a) a basic conflictedness resulting from the basic tension between id and superego as well as a partiality and distortedness of self-knowledge resulting from defensive processes motivated by the striving to synthesize and create unity of one's personality and view of oneself;

(b) the individual characteristics of personality and personal values and ideals as result of processes of identification;

(c) a giving-up of individual characteristics, agency, and values and ideals by taking over those of a leader and a group, accompanied by a pre-reflective experience of being part of a homogenous group; and

(d) a pre-reflective experience of oneself and others as alive and differentiated from each other indicating a basic unity and cohesion of oneself.

9.2 Erikson's Concept of Psychosocial Identity

Erikson (1946) introduced the concept of psychosocial or *ego identity* to psychoanalytic theory. It is the key concept of a multilayered, innovative developmental approach that operates at the interface of the intrapsychic and the interpersonal and social spheres of individuals.

Even though Erikson (1946) made some effort to couch the concept of identity in terms of the psychoanalytic ego psychology of his time, he was not overly interested in Freud's structural model. His primary interest was in the sense of identity, the subjective experience of continuous personal existence across space and time, and in the psychological and social conditions that either enable or endanger it: the feeling of having an identity is anchored in "two simultaneous observations: the perception of the self-sameness and continuity of one's existence in time and space and the perception of the fact that others recognize one's sameness and continuity" (1968, p. 50). This adds to Freud's and Federn's conceptions both diachronic identity, that is, the experience of continuity with oneself over time, and a psychosocial perspective that we can only know who we are and experience ourselves as being ourselves with all the six aspects of identity named at the beginning of the chapter if significant others acknowledge and confirm it.

Following and extending Federn, Erikson describes the subjective experience of Freud's ego that more or less successfully nonconsciously synthesizes strivings and, more importantly, identifications as a subjective sense of identity which is experienced as a background of well-being. This is accompanied by a sense of being securely rooted in one's own body, by confidence in being able to pursue one's path through life (agency), and certainty in being recognized by one's significant others and society (self-esteem).

Although Erikson (1959) sees the task of identity formation as specific for the period of adolescence, he also regards it as a continuing, lifelong developmental and interactive process. In late adolescence, "more lasting and more economical methods of maintenance and restoration are evolved and fortified" (p. 118). He locates the primordial origins of the sense of identity in the exchanges of toddlers with their early caregivers. This rudimentary sense of identity consolidates as soon as children learn to gain control over their bodily functions, while at the same time the environment recognizes their new abilities, so that they can develop a "realistic self-esteem" (Erikson, 1959, p. 22), which Erikson, in explicit opposition to Freud (1914), does not want to be understood as a cheap substitute for the infantile feeling of omnipotence, but as a "conviction that the ego is learning effective steps toward a tangible collective future, that it is developing into a defined ego within a social reality" (Erikson, 1959, p. 22). Children identify with their parents' gender roles and accept the different generational roles, but a little later also with their professional roles and their values and traditions.

In adolescence, individuals enter wider society and gain a certain autonomy from their parents, moving the task of developing an adult identity to center stage. The transition to adulthood requires taking on and committing to adult identities, such as gender, professional, and family identities, and identifying with corresponding values. Erikson conceived of a variety of possible developmental paths. He started with Bernfeld's (1923) observation of a prolonged adolescence in mostly bourgeois youths who engage in youth movements, elaborating this into a psychosocial moratorium of identity development provided by higher education. It provides youth with a safe space to try out a variety of identities. The moratorium, according to Erikson (1959), allows identifications acquired in childhood to be questioned and compared with other identities. At the end of the psychosocial moratorium, society expects individuals to commit to professional and family identities. Erikson termed the ideal outcome ego identity, in which the individual, partly deliberately, partly preconsciously, synthesizes selected, reconfirmed identifications from childhood with identities selected at the end of the moratorium. With the achievement of ego identity, the ego is prepared to cope with the psychosocial demands of adulthood – the experience of intimacy and sexuality within an intimate relationship and the exercise of a self-chosen professional activity. Ego identity is thus a highly individualized and more or less consciously chosen identity developed in the social context of the time, therefore allowing historical innovation. Erikson (1958, 1969) exemplified the achievement of ego identity and its role in historical change in writing the life stories of Gandhi and Luther.

During the time of role experimentation, individuals experience symptoms of role confusion or *identity diffusion*, namely a disintegration of the feeling of personal continuity and sameness. This transient inability of the ego to form an ego identity is overcome when a mature ego identity is formed. However, it may become chronic and pathological if identity crisis is not resolved. It is accompanied by a persistent feeling of shame, feelings of loneliness, the inability to draw satisfaction from any activity, and the loss of a sense of agency. Erikson (1959) added a third outcome of identity crisis to identity diffusion and ego identity, the flight into a negative identity, for example that of a delinquent. In this case, adolescents identify with what is socially considered as deviant. These adolescents are not able, for psychological and social reasons, to form an ego identity so that a complete identification with a deviant identity at least provides a firm sense of identity, albeit a negative one.

Finally, social circumstances and psychological factors may lead adolescents not to question their childhood identifications and to transition to adult roles without an identity crisis, following values they acquired in childhood. This seemingly least disturbed course of adolescence leads, in Erikson's conception, to a conventional identity (termed *foreclosure* by Marcia, 1993) which is less individualized and less historically innovative, because the person did not identify with elements of innovative youth cultures. Erikson (1959, p. 35f.)

illustrated this with a patient from the Midwest who was unconsciously attached to an image of womanhood that originated in her grandfather's world in the South. Her adherence to the historically outdated "prototype of the lady" (p. 35) did not fit into a society in which gender relations had become more egalitarian and premarital sexual experiences commonly accepted. Her sense of identity fell into a crisis when she was about to be engaged to a European and was equally attracted to and irritated by life in a cosmopolitan atmosphere. Thus, a conventional identity may offer less resilience against changing social circumstances because it is at least partially not consciously chosen.

Thus, Erikson conceptualizes different developmental trajectories leading to different outcomes: three kinds of identity are contrasted with a chronic state of identity diffusion. Although conventional, negative, and ego identity are accompanied by a subjective sense of identity, they differ in the degree of positive recognition received as well as in their individuality and probably also flexibility.

Compared to earlier psychoanalytic theorizing, for Erikson (1959) the ability to form a mature ego identity does not depend solely on early parent–child interactions and the individual psyche, but essentially on experiences of social interaction also beyond the family, on society and its institutions that provide opportunities to establish relationships of mutual recognition. Individuals need others with whom they can identify on a trial basis, and who in turn recognize them with their abilities and achievements, their individuality, their belonging to groups, and their personal continuity. For the development and maintenance of a sense of identity, therefore, not only stable internalized objects (resulting in basic trust; Erikson, 1959) and a certain ego maturity are necessary, but also a psychosocial moratorium provided by society in adolescence, social opportunities to try out identities and to be positively recognized. Even once ego identity is achieved, identity development remains a lifelong task to Erikson, requiring ongoing social opportunities of individual development and of being acknowledged in one's identity project.

Erikson thus transcended psychoanalytic theories of his day in two important ways. He conceived identity as psychosocial, operating at the interface of intrapsychic structure and sociocultural and historical context. Also, he conceived identity in a lifespan perspective, with a focus on adolescence, but integrating childhood developments as well as acknowledging that the task of maintaining and reconstructing identity continued to be a lifelong task. Thereby he highlighted the psychological importance of aspects of identity hitherto neglected by psychoanalysis, especially agency and diachronic identity over time. Although Erikson did provide examples of identity diffusion in his extensive clinical case descriptions, he did not integrate it in psychoanalytic or other nosologies of psychopathology. Also, despite using psychoanalytic concepts of unconscious conflicts between different identifications, he did not relate identity diffusion to defense mechanisms, nor did he spell out the clinical manifestations in the relationship to psychotherapists. This he left to later developments in psychoanalysis.

In the following two sections we review later developments in psychoanalytic theory by spelling out their implications for Erikson's concept of psychosocial identity. Except for Kernberg's work, these theories neither used the concept of identity nor referred to Erikson. However, by spelling out the implications of these theories we will demonstrate how they can be used to enrich Erikson's conception of identity.

9.3 Self in Relation to Others: Object Relations Theories

Parallel to and following Erikson's work on identity, Hungarian and British analysts revised Freud's individualistic psychology into a two-person psychology in which the individual could not be conceptualized without being in a relationship to another individual, in terms of both intrapsychic and social reality (e.g., Balint, 1935; Fairbairn, 1952). We highlight six important contributions from this tradition very broadly defined as *object relations theories*.

First, Klein (1935) took up Freud's dichotomy of partial versus integrated self and others as well as Federn's clinical dichotomy of disorders of the ego versus neurotic disorders, and related them to two different classes of defensive operations, termed positions. She related the experience of unintegrated self and others to the use of splitting the view of others and oneself into all-good and all-bad partial objects and to projecting and introjecting these parts so as to protect the individual from conflicts of ambivalence (paranoid-schizoid position). The use of projective-introjective mechanisms undermines self–other differentiation. It maximizes self-(and other-)consistency at any given point in time, but undermines consistency of oneself and other across situations and time. Only the ability to endure conflicts of ambivalence, simultaneously hating and caring for the other (and the self), enables individuals to engender an integrated view of oneself and others (depressive position). This is, according to Klein, the precondition for the ability to feel guilt, to take on responsibility, and to empathize with others and oneself. Thus, the main threat to identity integration here lies in splitting-based primitive defense mechanisms that lead to motivated gross splits.

Second, and more basically, Winnicott (1960a) argued that human beings in states of dependency such as infants and their caretakers, or patients and analysts, cannot be conceptualized as independent entities but need to be conceptualized in relation to the other. Fairbairn (1952) generalized the argument to any relationships and any wishes and defense mechanisms, which are always embedded in imagined and real relationships. This is in line with Erikson's conception of identity as a necessarily social phenomenon, extending it to the world of subjective phantasies.

Third, even the threat to knowing who one is posed by, as conceptualized by Freud, the conflict between biologically founded sexual urges and morality, as well as the dynamic unconscious resulting from defense against this conflict, was reinterpreted by Laplanche (1970) as rooted in social interaction. He surmised that the ego-dystonicity of sexual urges derived from their developmental origin: caretakers direct their sexual wishes at infants and thereby implant them as alien elements in infants' psyches. As a consequence, in this conception all elements to be integrated in identity are social in origin, either historically or at present.

Fourth, Winnicott (1960b) linked states of estrangement such as described by Federn (1952) to a defensive personality formation which he termed *false self*. He defined it as resulting from over-adapting to others' expectations and from the ensuing lack of access to what he termed *true self*. The latter basically represents individuals' spontaneous tendencies and motivational resources. Winnicott described the false self as a personality that is not as torn as someone functioning in the paranoid-schizoid position; rather it offers a consistent but inauthentic self which is cut off from the person's genuine emotions and wishes. Authenticity, according to Winnicott, developmentally requires having experienced holding relationships that accept and endure infants' impulses. Importantly, Winnicott (1971) related the ability to access one's urges and spontaneous tendencies to the ability to play, because play assimilates reality to subjects' tendencies and imaginations. Playing involves a flexible handling of the distinction between reality and fiction as well as of the differentiation between oneself and others, because spontaneous tendencies show in phantasy which in turn most easily materializes in playing with others. In playing, the contributions of oneself and other are not clearly distinguishable. Playing allows the transformation of spontaneous tendencies into creative acts, which in turn allows access to the true self. Thus, authenticity means feeling alive, being creative, and being able to engage in playful interactions with others and oneself, which Erikson had viewed as aspects of the subjective experience of an in integrated identity.

Fifth, Kernberg (1984) integrated Klein's dichotomy of defense mechanisms and the related partial versus integrated experience of others and oneself with Erikson's description of identity diffusion. Combined, splitting-based defense mechanisms and identity diffusion are the two distinctive characteristics of borderline personality organization. Splitting leads to identity diffusion, rendering the experience of oneself and others either contradictory over time, and therefore not allowing the construction of a continuous life story, or shallow and diffuse, comparable to the false self. In addition, splitting is defined in terms of contradictory pairs of relationship patterns (Caligor, Kernberg, Clarkin, & Yeomans, 2018) that characterize individuals' close relationships.

Sixth, Volkan (1981) applied the object relations approach and the mechanism of identification to things and groups. In complicated grief, people keep the deceased alive psychologically and materially by communicating with them through linking objects; thereby they cling to their own identity as someone-in-a-relationship to the deceased. Also, groups may define themselves by shared chosen collective historical traumas (like the Civil War for some Southerners in the US) from which they derive a sense of entitlement and legitimation for collective violence (Volkan, 1997). Volkan thus extends clinical concepts to describe mechanisms of stabilizing identity by denying change and to describe identification with a specific group identity.

To sum up, these selected trends in object relations theories fall short both of the wider social and cultural aspects of psychosocial identity (except for Volkan) as well as of Erikson's lifespan developmental perspective. Object relations theories support Erikson's conceptualization of identity as interpersonal in nature, extending it to the intrapsychic representation of identity as also always situated in relationships. Object relations theories enrich or add new aspects to the concept of identity, even if only Kernberg explicitly uses the concept of identity. They link identity formations not only to processes of identification and commitment, but also to the handling of conflicts via defense mechanisms, some of which (splitting) produce identity diffusion and identity foreclosure; the latter resembles in some respects the false self. Winnicott's work can be used to enrich Erikson's concept of the subjective experience of identity by underlining the significance of authenticity. Furthermore, Winnicott showed that exploration is not only important as adolescent identity exploration, but that playful and shared exploration, which is supported by the ability to establish a fictional space together, contributes to a sense of feeling alive and real – essential elements of the subjective sense of an integrated identity.

9.4 Epistemic Asceticism, or Identity as a Fleeting Momentary Co-Production

In the 1990s, psychoanalytic epistemological assumptions shifted drastically toward a more restricted stance. Although Kernberg (1984) had already focused clinical attention on the here and now of the patient–therapist interaction, thereby de-emphasizing the significance of biographical reconstruction, he still used the general ability to construct a somewhat coherent developmental life story as a diagnostic criterion for an integrated ego identity. In addition, he still contended that there was a clear difference between patient and professional therapist who could somewhat objectively judge the patient's identity integration.

More recent approaches have fundamentally undermined the concept of identity by maintaining that all that psychoanalysts can really know is what is going on in the here and now of the consulting room, and that their own subjectivity is inextricably involved in this knowledge. This trend materialized in concepts like the *analytic third* (Ogden, 1994) and the *bipersonal field* (Baranger & Baranger, 1961/1962; Ferro, 1992). They denote emotions and phantasies that evolve during a session due to unconscious contributions by both participants based on the expulsion of defended-against or non-symbolized urges which in turn influence the sensations, emotions, and thoughts of both participants. Ogden (1994) described how he tries to access this field of proto-emotions through letting his thoughts wander, termed *rêverie* by Bion (1962). His thoughts and sensations appear to be unrelated to what the patient is saying but may nevertheless indirectly hint at what is going on between the participants.

Ferro (1992) limited himself to picking up figures and motives from patients' narratives, adding new elements to patients' "storyworlds" and playing with them by joining patients in the activity of narrating. Both authors, Ogden and Ferro, considered the phantasies and narratives evolving in the session to be unconsciously co-produced by both patients and therapists. Ferro especially discounted the specific content of narratives, be they remote biographical memories, dreams, fictional stories, or recent experiences. What counted for Ogden and Ferro is that patients improve the ability to express symbolically present urges, wishes, and emotions through images and narratives without necessarily spelling them out.

The notion of identity appears to evaporate in these theories. Past and present life outside the consulting room seem to be reduced to narratives, and the sole referent of the narratives that counts for these authors is the present emotions and phantasies co-produced by patient and analyst. These approaches seem to have given up any claim to knowledge except for knowledge of the momentary emotion in the session. Although this need not be taken as a nihilistic postmodern stance, it is still a radically ascetic epistemological stance. However, the more forceful blow to the concept of personal identity was the contention that evolving emotions cannot be neatly attributed to either of the two participants. Therefore, they are informative about the couple, but not exclusively about one specific person and that person's identity. Implicitly, these authors broadened the concept of authenticity to include access not only to individual, but also to shared and co-authored sensations and tendencies.

On the other hand, these clinical theories did confirm and radicalize the interpersonal aspect of Erikson's conception of identity, namely that personal identity cannot be created by individuals alone, but that it needs others to attribute identities or to confirm or dispute identity claims. This aspect of identity had been left out by most other psychoanalysts. Despite Winnicott's (1960b) essentializing term "true self," he conceived authenticity not as a permanent state of knowing oneself, but as an ability to not only silently introspect but rather to play out desires and phantasies with others in an as-if mode. Radicalizing Winnicott, we understand both Ogden and Ferro to add to Erikson's conception of identity the role of shared phantasizing and storytelling as a method of accessing and forming the participants' unconscious, and thereby integrating it in a more authentic identity. These authors' writings imply that identity cannot be conceived of without a similarly open and receptive other.

Summarizing Sections 9.3 and 9.4 of this chapter, we suggest two major contributions by post-Erikson psychoanalytic writings to the concept of psychosocial identity. First, they specify authenticity as an essential aspect of psychosocial identity. To Erikson, signs of inauthenticity, such as not feeling alive, were part of identity diffusion and therefore an outcome of a failed adolescent struggle for identity. Even a conventional, foreclosed identity may be seen to lack authenticity, because the individual sticks to infantile identifications without critically evaluating them. Erikson seems to suggest that profound authenticity can only be gained through identity exploration by trying out experiences and roles in the moratorium, reserving authenticity to ego identity. We understand Ogden and Ferro to suggest that authenticity is not limited to accessing individual tendencies, but may include accessing shared, co-produced tendencies as part of the identity of that relationship, which in turn is part of both individual identities. This ability, in turn, may be related to the ability to engage in mutual relationships as rendered possible by the depressive position (Kernberg, 1984).

Second, post-Erikson psychoanalytic developments offer a microgenetic perspective on how splitting-based defense mechanisms undermine efforts to achieve synchronic and diachronic identity. They may operate even within the time frame of a clinical interview, rendering difficult consistency in the relationship to single others, not to speak of consistency across situations or across a lifetime (Kernberg, 1984). However, neither any of the psychoanalytic theories nor Erikson specify how a sense of self-continuity can be achieved despite biographical change.

Erikson's concept of psychosocial identity, in turn, goes beyond what may be known through the psychoanalytic method. Therefore, he could integrate the cultural and immediate social context of interactants with whom identity is negotiated in the concept of identity. This facilitates using the mechanism of identification with and committing to roles and values which is central for understanding identity from a developmental perspective, and for providing a sense of purpose and meaning in life. Finally, Erikson placed identity in a lifespan perspective, taking a biographical view on identity development. However, he stopped short of conceptualizing psychosocial identity as taking the form of a life story, or autobiography.

9.5 A Psychoanalytically Informed Conception of Narrative Identity: The Problem of Diachronic Identity and the Life Story

In the final section of this chapter we discuss how Erikson's concept of identity, enriched by later clinical psychoanalytic ideas, can be specified and complemented by the concept of the life story. It adds a decisive instrument for creating diachronic self-continuity and a sense of agency in an individualistic society. We present three conceptualizations of the life story as providing a medium for constructing and communicating identity, especially the aspects of individuality, agency, and self-continuity, which we qualify developmentally and culturally. Then we suggest four more specific ways in which life narratives deal with biographical ruptures, which we link to self-knowledge and authenticity. Finally, we discuss influences on the stability of the life story itself and what this says about the quality of identity integration.

9.5.1 Identity and the Life Story

Cohler (1982) explicated what had remained implicit in Erikson's writings, namely that the development of ego identity in adolescence uses the format of the life story. Its great advantage is that it may integrate multiple infantile and adolescent identifications in the form of a narrative.

Life narratives provide the best format to capture a person's individuality, both through recurrent themes that permeate the life as well as a developmental story that explains how individuals became who they are today (cf., Bruner, 1987; Freeman, 1984). Neurotic relationship patterns show as repetitive themes in life stories. In a more general sense, central and often highly individual self-definitions and values may be crystallized in self-defining memories of specific events (Singer et al., 2013). Similarly, psychological motives and themes such as power and intimacy may pervade the life story, depending on how important they are to individuals (McAdams, 1985). Thus, the thematic coloring of life stories reflects narrators' individuality.

Another aspect of life stories that is central to identity is the degree to which they support a sense of being an actor who is able to influence the course of events and the path that life takes. Together with commitments to relationships, roles, and values that give life a direction, agency is vital for a sense of purpose in life, because it enables individuals to move in the desired directions. Agency shows both in narrative content as well as in the linguistic forms that designate characters as intentional actors (Capps & Ochs, 1995; de Silveira & Habermas, 2011). Schafer (1983) interpreted the therapeutic action of psychoanalysis as turning life stories of victims into those of actors who as narrators retrospectively acknowledge their motives for acting, thereby taking on responsibility for their past. Thus, in successful psychotherapies a life that had apparently been determined by fate is retrospectively appropriated by acknowledging and appropriating the hitherto neurotically hidden motives. Agency as a general aspect of psychosocial identity regards the entire life and is therefore best explicated in life stories.

Besides reflecting pervasive themes and constructing agency, the life story also constructs developmental stories of paths taken by individual lives, structured more or less by plots. This offers narrators unique possibilities for creating diachronic self-continuity. Most cogently argued by Ricœur (1988, 1992), narratives normatively involve central characters, who are transformed by the course of an intentionally structured sequence of events and actions (plot). Only narrative, Ricœur argued, is able to establish a genuine sense of self-continuity across change, because the narrative transformations of the protagonist motivate and explain change and thereby create continuity of the protagonist-narrator. Ricœur termed this form of establishing diachronic self-continuity *narrative identity*.

One of us complemented this conception by suggesting that it is not only the protagonist's transformation by the plot which helps create self-continuity, because entire life narratives tend to be less well-structured by a unitary plot than smaller stories are. In addition, life narratives explicate how the protagonist is transformed by specific experiences (Habermas & Köber, 2015a). These explications are not per se narrative, that is, a sequence of actions or events, but rather *autobiographical arguments* (cf. Habermas & Bluck, 2000; Habermas, 2011). Self-continuity across change is supported specifically by autobiographical arguments that motivate personal change, most specifically if change in personality or insights is motivated by specific life experiences (Habermas & Paha, 2001; Pasupathi, Mansour, & Brubaker, 2007).

The life story is helpful especially in adolescence because it allows selected early identifications with parents to be combined with later identifications by linking them to experiences and integrating them into a story that justifies and motivates them. Adolescence is a crucial period for identity formation, because it is the time when an identity as child-of-my-parents needs to be transformed into an individual adult identity. Also, it is only in adolescence that the specific narrative format of the life story is acquired (Cohler, 1982; McAdams, 1985; Habermas & Bluck, 2000) as we demonstrated in the longitudinal MainLife Study (Köber, Schmiedek, & Habermas, 2015).

The life story is helpful especially in Western societies in which it is imperative to fashion an individual identity that goes beyond fixed roles. Taking up Bernfeld's (1923) observation of the class-specific prolongation of adolescence, Erikson (1959) had interpreted it as a moratorium, institutionalized by higher education. Ever since Erikson's writing, Western societies have experienced an extension of the system of higher education as well as some destandardization of the life course, rendering continuing identity work necessary across the adult lifespan. The life story offers the ideal format for this continuous work. Also, the life story is especially suited for a highly individualized identity, as can be seen in cultural differences in life narratives which are more coherent in a highly individualized society (Germany) compared to a society more based on family relations (Turkey) (Altunnar & Habermas, 2018).

9.5.2 Life Story Strategies to Create Self-Continuity across Biographical Ruptures and Self-Knowledge

Although in Western societies the life course has become more individualized and some change in identity is expected across adulthood, over the life course there are times of less and of more or even abrupt change. Abrupt change might be brought about by intended and planned events like marriage and changing job, but more often biographical ruptures (Bury, 1982) happen unintentionally through illness, incidents, or death. These changes lead to the attribution of a changed identity as a husband, a job-identity, or, for example, the identity of a cripple. How can diachronic identity be maintained while life circumstances, relationships, and the body change and with them the identities attributed by others? How are these changes reflected in the life story, and how can the life story help create diachronic identity across change? There are several ways to establish a sense of self-sameness over time if identity is stable, such as by vividly recalling the past or through the stability of intimate relationships and environment. However, when identity attributions change through biographical ruptures, these means do not suffice, because they rely on the absence of any change (Habermas & Köber, 2015a). When unintended change occurs in the self, we suggest four possible ways to react in terms of the life story. We exemplify them with the death of a spouse, referring to being part of a married couple as old identity and being a widow(er) as new identity.

First, the life story includes a new role (as a widowed person) and leaves it unconnected and unreconciled with an old role (as a spouse), leaving a biographical break in the life story. This might make it difficult for listeners to empathize with narrators and their development, and for narrators it may lead to a subjective sense of discontinuity. This is comparable to effects of dissociative mechanisms on diachronic identity, except that the disruption in the life story is not created by defense mechanisms but by an objective change in roles and therefore in the self.

Second, the narrator may exclude the change in role from the life story, denying it, pretending nothing had changed. This could show in simply leaving the death of the spouse out of the life story, as might happen in states of protracted grief (Volkan, 1981). Subjectively this may lead to a sense of self-stability – nothing has changed – but at the price of denying present reality. This makes it difficult to maintain a shared version of reality with others and to cope with everyday tasks.

Third, a subjective sense of self-stability may be created by including a new role in the life story and at the same time minimizing the biographical rupture by assimilating earlier parts of the life story to the new identity. This may happen either by selecting different events that fit better with the present identity, for instance by stressing professional and not family life, or by changing narratives of past events so that they fit better the present view of oneself, possibly by de-emphasizing the spouse's role in events (Conway & Pleydell, 2000). These assimilative tendencies are a robust finding in autobiographical memory studies (e.g., Ross, 1989). In contrast to the second strategy, this solution to the problem of creating self-continuity despite change in the self does not deny present identity and reality, but denies a past identity. Therefore, it probably comes at a lower cost, because it does not render dealing with reality more difficult and might create fewer frictions in the shared version of reality, because the past is more malleable than the present.

Fourth, contrasting old and new identities are part of the life story, but narrators do not just mention them like in the first strategy, but integrate them into a story. This means that the actions and events that led to the change in identity are causally and, more importantly, motivationally related to a change in identity. Thus, explaining the change (becoming a widowed person) by reference to events (death of a loved one and its causes) and by reference to their meaning (explaining why the change had had which effects on the narrator and how the narrator adapted) is a way to tell a story. This bridges the biographical rupture explicitly through the use of autobiographical arguments. We believe that their use allows narrators to keep both old and new identities as parts of the life story and to nevertheless keep up a subjective sense – not of self-*sameness* across time (because they have changed), but of self-*continuity*. This is supported by findings that people who acknowledge they changed do not assimilate their past to their present self (Ross, 1989), and that after a change in life circumstances the use of change-engendering autobiographical arguments in entire life narratives buffers its effect on the subjective sense of self-continuity (Habermas & Köber, 2015b).

The choice of any one of these strategies influences not only the subjective sense of identity over time, but also how well people know themselves. When it comes to *self-knowledge*, narrative theories and psychological theories of narratives tend to focus on narrative truth (Spence, 1984), that is, on the plausibility of narratives in terms of internal coherence and coherence with common sense. However, historical truth in terms of what really happened is similarly important when it comes to autobiographical memories in real life (Conway, Singer, & Tagini, 2004). And when identity changes, the choice of a strategy to depict the change in the life story most probably influences self-knowledge. The second strategy of denying change strongly distorts knowledge of oneself at present, whereas the third strategy of assimilating the past to the present distorts knowledge of oneself in the past, somewhat resembling the mechanism of repression.

The first and fourth strategies do not distort self-knowledge in terms of historical truth. However, they strongly differ in another kind of self-knowledge – knowing who one is. This kind of self-knowledge is provided by an integrated identity. It includes not only historical and present knowledge of one's social and bodily identity and consciously held values, but also – and this closes the circle to post-Erikson psychoanalysis – knowledge of one's spontaneous tendencies and reactions. The first strategy of simply leaving earlier and later identity unreconciled leaves narrators with a choice of contradictory selves which makes it difficult to know who they are and what their real sensibilities and values are. The fourth strategy, in contrast, synthesizes past and present selves, not directly rendering access to one's spontaneous reactions and emotions easier, but possibly rendering them more tolerable given that they can be understood better in light of the life story.

Mature ego identity is characterized by the use of the fourth strategy. It enables individuals to flexibly move to and fro between reality and phantasy, fact and fiction, because bridging change in identity requires the least distortion of reality and synthesizes past and present, empathizing with earlier identities that are different from the narrator's present identity. This secure use of the fictional mode allows access to one's motivational sources, one's spontaneous tendencies, as conceptualized by Winnicott, Ogden, and Ferro.

9.5.3 Stability of Lives and Life Stories

Life narratives differ in how they depict change and rupture in life. In addition, they may themselves be more or less stable. Recently McAdams (2019) suggested differentiating between a good and a bad form of life story stability and of life story change, which he termed stability versus stagnation and growth versus fluidity. Indeed, some stability is necessary, so that we can speak of someone as having a personality and not being a being who changes with every situation; at the same time, change is necessary, so that we can speak of someone as maturing and not stagnating (Habermas & Köber, 2015a). So ideal life narratives appear to be ones that evolve as life is being lived forward by adding recent developments and integrating them with the personal past.

However, there are two major reasons why also the older parts of life narratives which had already been in the past when a life had first been narrated may change when a life is told repeatedly. One reason may be that role-based or bodily identity has changed between two tellings of a life. This need not distort the past in the sense of the third strategy, but may consist in selecting different events as important for understanding who one has become (e.g., substituting the first meeting of the earlier partner with that of the present partner) or in telling the same events but interpreting them from a different angle (e.g., first meeting the husband as an act of rebellion against the family, later as an act of caring for a family; cf. Josselson, 2009; Habermas, 2019, ch. 10). A second major reason for changing old parts of life narratives in later retellings is that narrators may gain a different and possibly better understanding of themselves and their own past, for example by coping better with specific past events. This may in turn lead to selecting different events or to interpreting events differently by contextualizing them better and differently, although without changing the facts.

Above we added to the dichotomy of life story stability versus change the qualities of life narratives in terms of dealing with biographical change and rupture. They imply that to judge the functionality of a life narrative for diachronic identity, that is, for providing a sense of self-continuity as well as agency and individuality, the stability and change in the life lived needs to be taken into account. Lives with uncontrollable biographical ruptures will require more autobiographical reasoning and bridging in life narratives than more stable and predictable lives. Catastrophic experiences may even never be integrated into a life story (Langer, 1991). Stable lives allow a subjective sense of self-continuity with less autobiographical reasoning than lives with recent changes (Habermas & Köber, 2015a). The stability of lives may, in turn, be influenced by chance (accidents, illnesses), but also by how much leeway for agency is granted by social conditions in terms of class, gender, race, or ethnicity (cf. Fivush, Habermas, & Reese, 2019). In addition, identity diffusion due to the use of splitting-based defense mechanisms may not only make it difficult to construct a coherent life story, but also make it difficult to lead a life with somewhat stable relationships and a subjective direction. Finally, diachronic identity may be influenced less by the quality of the life story but by relationships in such cultures that define individuals by their family position and relations (Altunnar & Habermas, 2018).

9.6 Conclusion

We embedded Erikson's concept of identity in earlier and subsequent clinical psychoanalytic concepts and integrated it with the concept of the life story as narrative. Instead of summarizing, we highlight three results. First, the life story not only reflects and expresses past and present synchronous identities, but it is an essential instrument for constructing and maintaining identity. This is especially true for diachronic identity in the face of abrupt change as well as for agency, because narrating and acknowledging past agency is itself an agentic act by narrators, taking responsibility for the personal past and its narration.

However, the importance of the life story has been doubted because in everyday life it is never narrated as a whole. Rather small stories prevail, and narrators negotiate their identities by positioning themselves in the stories they tell and by how they tell them (Bamberg & Georgakopoulou, 2008; Giaxoglou & Georgakopoulou, Chapter 11 in this volume; Salgado & Cunha, Chapter 17 in this volume). Thus, second, narrating is not just a cognitive, but a communicative format, which is not the only, but a major medium in which identity is negotiated. And the life story, which is most fully realized in entire life narratives, structures also more partial narrating of specific experiences through the use of autobiographical arguments. Any bridging of biographical change presupposes the frame of a life story. Thus, narrating specifies the essentially social nature of identity, because in real life the act of narrating is always a more or less co-operative undertaking in which listeners co-construct stories and identities. The co-narrative nature of life narratives is most evident in the process of socialization when parents co-construct their adolescents' life stories, especially defining their early parts (Habermas, Negele, & Mayer, 2010), but also later on when we claim a right to co-narrate the life stories of those close to us (Thomsen & Pillemer, 2017). This also counts for psychoanalytic practice (Habermas, 2019, ch. 12), as developed by Winnicott, Ogden, and Ferro.

Finally, authenticity is an essential clinical aspect of life narrating, which we intuitively grasp in everyday life and clinical practice, but which has barely been studied systematically. We judge authenticity by the way a story is narrated non-verbally (cf. Norris & Matelau-Doherty, Chapter 14 in this volume) and possibly also by how much the narrating appears like an impromptu act and not merely the verbatim replication of a rehearsed story. Taking up Winnicott, Ogden, and Ferro, the authenticity of the telling will show not least in how playful the improvisation is and how well others can tune in to the story.

References

Altunnar, N. H. & Habermas, T. (2018). Life narratives are more other-centered, more negative, and less coherent in Turkey than in Germany: Comparing provincial-Turkish, metropolitan-Turkish, Turkish-German, and native German educated young adults. *Frontiers in Psychology, 9*, 2466, doi:10.3389/fpsyg.2018.02466.

Balint, M. (1935). Zur Kritik der Lehre von den prägenitalen Libidoorganisationen [Critical notes on the theory of pregenital organisations of the libido]. *Internationale Zeitschrift für Psychoanalyse, 21*, 525–543.

Bamberg, M. & Georgakopoulou, A. (2008). Small stories as a new perspective in narrative and identity analysis. *Text & Talk, 28*, 377–396.

Baranger, M. & Baranger, W. (1961/1962). La situación analítica como campo dinámico [The analytic situation as a dynamic field]. *Revista Uruguaya de Psicoanálisis, 4*, 3–54.

Bernfeld, S. (1923). Über eine typische Form der männlichen Pubertät [On a typical model of male puberty]. *Imago, 9*, 169–188.

Bion, W. R. (1962). *Learning from Experience.* New York, NY: Jason Aronson.

Bruner, J. (1987). Life as narrative. *Social Research, 54*, 11–32.

Bury, M. (1982). Chronic illness as biographical disruption. *Sociology of Health and Illness, 4*, 167–182.

Caligor, E., Kernberg, O. F., Clarkin, J. F., & Yeomans, F. E. (2018). *Psychodynamic Psychotherapy for Personality Pathology.* Washington, DC: American Psychiatric Association Publishing.

Capps, L. & Ochs, E. (1995). *Constructing Panic*. Cambridge, MA: Harvard University Press.

Cohler, B. J. (1982). Personal narrative and life course. *Life Span Development and Behavior, 4*, 205–241.

Conway, M. A. & Pleydell-Pearce, C. W. (2000). The construction of autobiographical memories in the self-memory system. *Psychological Review, 107*, 261–288.

Conway, M. A., Singer, J. A., & Tagini, A. (2004). The self and autobiographical memory: Correspondence and coherence. *Social Cognition, 22*, 491–529.

De Silveira, C. & Habermas, T. (2011). Narrative means to manage responsibility in life narratives across adolescence. *Journal of Genetic Psychology, 172*, 1–20.

Erikson, E. H. (1946). Ego development and historical change: Clinical notes. *Psychoanalytic Study of the Child, 2*, 359–396.

Erikson, E. H. (1958). *Young Man Luther: A Study in Psychoanalysis and History*. New York, NY: Norton.

Erikson, E. H. (1959). *Identity and the Life Cycle: Selected Papers*. New York, NY: International Universities Press.

Erikson, E. H. (1964). *Insight and Responsibility*. New York, NY: Norton.

Erikson, E. H. (1968). *Identity: Youth and Crisis*. New York, NY: Norton.

Erikson, E. H. (1969). *Gandhi's Truth*. New York, NY: Norton.

Fairbairn, W. R. D. (1952). *Psychoanalytic Studies of the Personality*. London: Routledge.

Federn, P. (1952). *Ego Psychology and the Psychoses*. New York, NY: Basic Books.

Ferro, A. (1992). *La tecnica nella psicoanalisi infantile. Il bambino e l'analista: Dalla relazione al campo emotive* [The bi-personal field: Experiences in child analysis]. Milan: Raffaello Cortina.

Fivush, R., Habermas, T., & Reese, E. (2019). Retelling lives: Narrative style and stability of highly emotional events over time. *Qualitative Psychology, 6*, 156–166.

Freeman, M. (1984). History, narrative, and life-span developmental knowledge. *Human Development, 27*, 1–19.

Freud, S. (1894). Die Abwehr-Neuropsychosen. [The neuro-psychoses of defence]. In S. Freud (1968), *Gesammelte Werke, 1* (pp. 57–74). Frankfurt am Main: Fischer.

Freud, S. (1914). Zur Einführung in den Narzissmus [On narcissism]. In S. Freud (1968), *Gesammelte Werke, 10* (pp. 137–170). Frankfurt am Main: Fischer.

Freud, S. (1917). Trauer und Melancholie [Mourning and melancholia]. In S. Freud (1968), *Gesammelte Werke, 10* (pp. 427–447). Frankfurt am Main: Fischer.

Freud, S. (1921). Massenpsychologie und Ich-analyse [Group psychology and the analysis of the ego]. In S. Freud (1968), *Gesammelte Werke, 13* (pp. 71–161). Frankfurt am Main: Fischer.

Freud, S. (1923). Das Ich und das Es [The ego and the id]. In S. Freud (1968), *Gesammelte Werke, 13* (pp. 235–290). Frankfurt am Main: Fischer.

Frosh, S. (2012). Identity after psychoanalysis. In A. Elliot (Ed.), *Routledge Handbook of Identity Studies* (pp. 71–88). London: Routledge.

Habermas, T. (2011). Autobiographical reasoning: Arguing and narrating from a biographical perspective. *New Directions in Child and Adolescent Development, 131*, 1–17.

Habermas, T. (2019). *Emotion and Narrative: Perspectives in Autobiographical Storytelling*. Cambridge: Cambridge University Press.

Habermas, T. & Bluck, S. (2000). Getting a life: The development of the life story in adolescence. *Psychological Bulletin, 126*, 748–769.

Habermas, T. & Köber, C. (2015a). Autobiographical reasoning is constitutive for narrative identity: The role of the life story for personal continuity. In K. C. McLean & M. Syed (Eds.), *The Oxford Handbook of Identity Development* (pp. 149–165). Oxford: Oxford University Press.

Habermas, T. & Köber, C. (2015b). Autobiographical reasoning in life narratives buffers the effect of biographical disruptions on the sense of self-continuity. *Memory, 23*, 564–574.

Habermas, T. & Paha, C. (2001). The development of coherence in adolescents' life narratives. *Narrative Inquiry, 11*, 35–54.

Habermas, T., Negele, A., & Mayer, F. (2010). "Honey, you're jumping about" – Mothers' scaffolding of their children's and adolescents' life narration. *Cognitive Development, 25*, 339–351.

Janet, P. (1889). *L'automatisme psychologique* [Psychological automatism]. Paris: Felix Alcan.

Josselson, R. (2009). The present of the past: Dialogues with memory over time. *Journal of Personality, 77*, 647–668.

Kernberg, O. F. (1984). *Severe Personality Disorders: Psychotherapeutic Strategies*. New Haven, CT: Yale University Press.

Klein, M. (1935). A contribution to the psychogenesis of manic-depressive states. *International Journal of Psycho-Analysis, 16*, 145–174.

Köber, C., Schmiedek, F., & Habermas, T. (2015). Characterizing lifespan development of three aspects of coherence in life narratives: A cohort-sequential study. *Developmental Psychology, 51*, 260–275.

Kohli, M. (2007). The institutionalization of the life course: Looking back to look ahead. *Research in Human Development, 4*, 253–271.

Langer, L. L. (1991). *Holocaust Testimonies. The Ruins of Memory*. New Haven, CT: Yale University Press.

Laplanche, J. (1970). *Vie et mort en psychanalyse* [Life and death in psychoanalysis]. Paris: Flammarion.

Marcia, J. E. (1993). The ego identity status approach to ego identity. In J. E. Marcia, A. S. Waterman, D. R. Matteson, S. L. Archer, & J. L. Orlofsky (Eds.), *Ego Identity: A Handbook for Psychosocial Research* (pp. 3–12). New York, NY: Springer.

McAdams, D. P. (1985). *Power, Intimacy, and the Life Story: Personological Inquiries into Identity*. New York, NY: Guilford Press.

McAdams, D. P. (2019). Continuity and growth in the life story – or is it stagnation and flux? *Qualitative Psychology, 6*, 206–214.

Ogden, T. H. (1994). The analytic third: Working with intersubjective clinical facts. *International Journal of Psychoanalysis, 75*, 3–19.

Pasupathi, M., Mansour, E., & Brubaker, J. R. (2007). Developing a life story: Constructing relations between self and experience in autobiographical narratives. *Human Development, 50*, 85–110.

Reicher, S. D., Spears, R., & Postmes, T. (1995). A social identity model of deindividuation phenomena. *European Review of Social Psychology, 6*, 161–198.

Ricœur, P. (1988). *Time and Narrative*. Chicago, IL: University of Chicago Press.

Ricœur, P. (1992). *Oneself as Another*. Chicago, IL: University of Chicago Press.

Ross, M. (1989). Relation of implicit theories to the construction of personal histories. *Psychological Review, 96*, 341–357.

Schafer, R. (1983). *The Analytic Attitude*. New York, NY: Routledge.

Singer, J. A., Blagov, P., Berry, M., & Oost, K. M. (2013). Self-defining memories, scripts, and the life story: Narrative identity in personality and psychotherapy. *Journal of Personality, 81*, 569–582.

Spence, D. P. (1984). *Narrative Truth and Historical Truth: Meaning and Interpretation in Psychoanalysis*. New York, NY: Norton.

Thomsen, D. K. & Pillemer, D. B. (2017). I know my story and I know your story: Developing a conceptual framework for vicarious life stories. *Journal of Personality, 85*, 464–480.

Volkan, V. D. (1981). *Linking Objects and Linking Phenomena*. New York, NY: International Universities Press.

Volkan, V. D. (1997). *Bloodlines: From Ethnic Pride to Ethnic Terrorism*. New York, NY: Basic Books.

Winnicott, D. W. (1960a). The theory of the parent–infant relationship. *International Journal of Psycho-Analysis, 41*, 585–595.

Winnicott, D. W. (1960b). Ego distortion in terms of true and false self. In D. W. Winnicott (1965), *The Maturational Processes and the Facilitating Environment* (pp. 140–152). London: Hogarth Press.

Winnicott, D. W. (1971). *Playing and Reality*. London: Routledge.

10 Erikson, the Identity Statuses, and Beyond

Jane Kroger and James E. Marcia

> The sense of ego identity, then, becomes more necessary (and more problematical) where a wide range of possible identities is envisaged. Identity, of course, is a term used in our day with faddish ease: I can, at this point, only indicate how very complicated the real article is . . .
>
> (Erikson, n.d., p. 115)

10.1 Erikson on Identity

Erikson's words above offer a prelude to what would become a central, overarching theme of both his personal and professional life – that of identity. Erikson has been considered by many as "identity's architect" (e.g. Friedman, 1999; Schlein, 2016). With his own identity struggles and feelings of "difference" in his family of origin, professional training, working environments, and his adopted American context more generally, Erikson was acutely attuned to this key problem of youth and the search for meaningful identity. As an artist and man of great breadth and depth of knowledge in fields well beyond psychoanalysis, Erikson was unconstrained by any single discipline in formulating his understandings of identity (Friedman, 1999).

For Erikson, identity was a psychosocial construct. Objectively, identity was observable when "a youngster 'becomes himself' . . . He suddenly seems to be 'at home in his body,' to 'know where he is going'" (Erikson, 1968a, p. 676). Subjectively, a "sense of ego identity is an accrued confidence that starts from the first moments of life – confidence that somehow in the midst of change, one has an inner sameness and continuity which others can recognize and which is so certain that it can be taken for granted" (Erikson, 1968b, p. 17). Identity, to Erikson (1968b), also involved the adoption of meaningful work, ideological values, and comfort in one's sexuality and form of sexual expression. Exploration and commitment processes were central to optimal identity formation, according to Erikson, in finding resolutions to these key psychosocial commitments. Erikson (1963) also pointed to the vital and reciprocal role that context played in both recognizing and being recognized by youth in their search for meaningful identity commitments.

Erikson's well-known depiction of the "identity vs. role confusion" task of adolescence involves explorations, experimentations, and, ideally, the eventual adoption of social roles and values that allow for the meaningful expression of one's biological givens and psychological needs, desires, and interests within a particular social context. Erikson (1963, 1968b) conceptualized all psychosocial tasks in terms of a dialectic, a struggle between positive and negative ends of a continuum; optimal identity development thus was a resolution on the *identity vs. role confusion* continuum located near the positive *identity achievement* pole. Themes of identity crisis and the *moratorium* phase, both vital processes or "turning points" prior to assuming identity commitments were illustrated by Erikson through the identity struggles of *Young Man Luther* (Erikson, 1958) and case studies appearing in *Identity: Youth and Crisis* (Erikson, 1968b).

Identity, latently a part of childhood psychosocial tasks, is never fully resolved by the end of adolescence, although identity's integrating foundations are ideally in place. Through his later writings, Erikson (1982; Erikson, Erikson, & Kivnick, 1986) showed how identity presides over adulthood, expressing itself in all later psychosocial tasks. Erikson's (1981) final publication began by moving beyond identity to a consideration of the essence of the "I" in human consciousness: "The *I*, after all, is the ground for the simple verbal assurance that each person is a center of awareness in a universe of communicable experience, a center so numinous that it amounts to a sense of being alive, and more, of being the vital condition of existence" (p. 323).

While he was never able to fully develop these ideas, Erikson's earlier writings laid broad foundations for subsequent explorations of identity in both research and clinical settings. A popular and enduring method of investigating identity processes during adolescence and adult life has come through an approach initiated by James Marcia that examined exploration and commitment variables in the identity formation process (e.g. Marcia, 1966, 1967; Marcia et al., 1993, 2011; Kroger & Marcia, 2011). Marcia describes the development of his identity status model in the following section.

10.2 The Meaning and Evolution of Marcia's Identity Construct

At a seminar in Germany, I (J. E. M.) was musing on my surprise that the identity statuses had endured well beyond the 20–25 years predicted by George Kelly to be the average lifespan of a psychological construct. A colleague suggested that this might be because of the statuses' "street cred" (acceptance based upon popularity). He had a point, but there are reasons why that street cred accrued. I think they are twofold: the carefulness of the initial identity research, and the subsequent linkage of the identity construct with concepts from other structural theories such as cognitive and moral development and object relations/attachment development. These two topics of careful initial research and established theoretical linkages will be the main foci of the next portion of this chapter.

All scientific research occurs within, and is influenced by, a social context. This is especially true for research in the social sciences, where the units under investigation are so mutable: i.e., persons, who are embedded in, and shaped by, the cultural conditions surrounding them. The context within which the identity status research began was the late 1960s in the United States. The adult society, having come through World War II, found itself confronted by their youth, who were objecting vociferously to the injustices wrought upon them by the Vietnam conflict. Vulnerable to being drafted to fight in a war they considered unjust and encapsulated in government lies, they took to the streets in protest. Moreover, they began to question a whole set of values that they felt had been hypocritically imposed upon them. It is no wonder that when the identity of the whole nation was being disrupted, Erikson's concept of the identity crisis became popular.

I became aware of Erikson's theory while on a clinical internship at Harvard Medical School, where my clinical supervisor was also a teaching assistant for Erikson. After we had mistakenly diagnosed as "schizophrenic" a late adolescent patient who then made a "miraculous" recovery after only six months in the hospital, my supervisor suggested that I read Erikson's description of "identity confusion." This led me to read all of Erikson's writings. He was a breath of fresh theoretical air compared with more turgid psychoanalytic authors. He wrote in vivid language that made psychoanalytic concepts directly relevant to my clinical work. When formulating my dissertation project, I decided that nothing could be more meaningful than trying to establish empirical validity for the most compelling of Erikson's theoretical ideas: identity development.

At Ohio State I had been well schooled in the use of "construct validity" as a means of determining the soundness of theoretical propositions. Although my first task was to formulate an operational definition of "identity," I could find nothing in Erikson's writings that approached this. Erikson was not supportive of empirical research of his theory, which he considered more "a way of looking at things" (Erikson, 1950, p. 339) than a formal theory. Identity formation was described, but not defined. It was buried in descriptive phrases such as "the [result of] the silent doings of ego synthesis." However, unobservable as identity seemed to be, it was possible to observe the results of identity formation that could be operationally defined in terms of commitments in the important life areas of occupation and ideology, domains noted by Erikson (attitudes and values concerning sexuality were added later to the interview). I reasoned that if a late adolescent (18–22 years) claimed such commitments, this could be taken as indicating the presence of a more complex underlying identity.

How were such commitments to be assessed? Erikson had arrived at his concepts via the lengthy, in-depth process of psychoanalysis, as well as literary and anthropological excursions. After considering and rejecting approaches such as the Rorschach test (Schafer, 1954), Kelly's Role Construct Repertory Test (Kelly, 1955) and fashioning a questionnaire, I decided upon a semi-structured interview as a method that would be consistent with Erikson's in-depth approach. It would give participants a chance to speak with their own voices about their identity-forming experiences, but such a measure would have to be objectively, reliably scoreable in order to be able to determine a relationship between the identity construct and other dependent variables.[1] Hence, a manual containing criteria and examples for scoring the newly developed interview was constructed.

Before developing the manual, though, I thought it would be important to talk with some young persons in depth to see if, in fact, the areas of occupation and ideology were important to them, as well as inquiring into their processes of identity formation. Interviewing a sample of twenty undergraduates, I found not only that the areas were important to them, but also that individuals differed in how they arrived at their commitments. Some just carried over into late adolescence what they had intended to do in childhood and what they had always believed, while others seemed to have undertaken a more or less fraught exploratory period. Also, I found some to be uncommitted and unconcerned about future occupational directions and current beliefs, while others were right in the middle of an exploratory period. These observations were the basis for the four identity statuses of foreclosure, identity achievement, identity diffusion, and moratorium (see Table 10.1).

I drew these identity status labels largely from Erikson's writings (Erikson, 1956, 1958, 1963). He spoke of persons who "foreclosed" on a "work identity" formed during the elementary school Industry period (aged approximately 8–12 years), which they then carried on, unexamined, through adolescence. Identity (achievement), itself, was Erikson's designation of the positive outcome of the fifth psychosocial stage occurring during late adolescence. Erikson called identity diffusion (later confusion) the negative outcome of this stage. "Moratorium" was seen by Erikson as a kind of societally granted "time-out" during which late adolescents were free to explore alternatives without having to accept adult responsibility. Although not especially literarily felicitous terms, these four designations did seem to encompass the identity formation alternatives I saw in my initial sample.

I then constructed a semi-structured interview protocol and a scoring manual to assess exploration and commitment in the areas of occupation and ideology (religious and political beliefs). I piloted both interview and

---

[1] This seemed especially desirable because I had become enamored of the scientific method and it seemed a meaningful challenge to see if such a complex concept could be studied thus. In addition, especially with the subsequent research, I had a "political" agenda: I wanted to get Erikson into introductory psychology textbooks. I did not think that would happen at that time unless empirical support was found.

Table 10.1 *Overview of identity statuses*

Identity Status	Exploration	Commitment
Identity achievement	+	+
Moratorium	current	vague
Foreclosure	−	+
Identity diffusion	−/+	−

scoring manual with a new sample of participants. For this pilot study, I used trained student interviewers. A trained scorer and I determined interscorer reliability. The interview and the scoring manual were then revised. At this point, I would like to share an observation that, to my knowledge, has never appeared in the literature. It concerns the experience of experimenters/interviewers and participants in these early identity status studies. Both the interviewers and many of the "subjects" commented upon how valuable the process was for them. The interviewers appreciated the opportunity to learn a valuable skill and to talk with participants about meaningful, personally relevant issues. The participants valued the chance to be treated as persons whose life decisions were of genuine interest. Many said that they liked the chance to think more deeply about themselves.[2]

One of the requirements for determining construct validity was the establishment of concurrent validity, correlating the new identity measure with an acceptable existing measure of identity (Cronbach & Meehl, 1955). Surveying the sparse literature existing at the time, I found no adequate measures of identity and only a few unreplicated questionnaire studies. Hence, I constructed a new alternative identity measure in order to demonstrate at least predictive, if not concurrent, validity with a more comprehensive measure of ego identity. As with the interview, I wanted a test that would give participants a chance to respond freely rather than simply endorsing my preconstructed statements. The format I chose was an incomplete sentences measure, using sentences that participants completed in their own words, such as the following:

I'm at my best when …
When I let myself go, I …
It seems I've always …
What happens to me depends …
To change my mind about my feelings toward religion…
As compared with four years ago, I …

---

[2] It is important to consider the historical context of this research and observation (1963–1964). "Qualitative" research was not much "in vogue" (cf. for example Truax's (1963) evaluation of Carl Rogers's humanistic approach to therapy using scales to assess empathetic understanding, the therapist's self-congruence and unconditional positive warmth), the scientific language reflected this by talking about the "experimenters" and "subjects" or "observers" and the "observed."

I intended this to be a comprehensive reflection of Erikson's overall identity construct, not just of the identity statuses. This gave me the opportunity to fashion scoring criteria that would include much of the rich content of Erikson's description of identity formation – content that had to be truncated in the interview measure in order to assess just the two variables of exploration and commitment. Two sample stems are: When I let myself go, I … (non-disastrous self-abandonment); It seems I've always … (self-initiative, continuity). It was necessary to establish interscorer reliability for this new measure as well; hence, another sample was collected and scoring reliability obtained.

Next came the quest for relevant dependent variables. I wanted two types, which could be called "near" and "far" according to their assumed theoretical proximity to the identity statuses' meanings. "Near" measures were those that had some face validity with respect to the descriptions of the statuses; "far" measures were ones that related to the statuses only through ego-psychoanalytic theory, the basis for Erikson's theory. As "near" (i.e., directly construct-relevant) measures, I chose questionnaires assessing authoritarianism (F scale; Adorno et al., 1950) to discriminate foreclosures, and questionnaires assessing anxiety (Taylor Manifest Anxiety Scale; Taylor, 1953) to discriminate moratoriums. As "far" measures, I constructed a "change in self-esteem" condition and a "concept attainment under stress" task. The "stress" condition in the latter measure consisted of overly reassuring statements given by the experimenter to the subject during task administration (e.g., "You're doing fine, don't worry"). In order to determine whether such statements were, in fact, stressful, another pilot study had to be undertaken; that made four pilot studies before the final study (or studies) was (were) run. Because these first two studies involved giving false information to participants, subjects had to be debriefed immediately after their participation; hence, the studies were run in two consecutive days in order to minimize possible subject communication. Both studies employed small groups of trained identity status interviewers and separate experimental measure administrators who were unaware of the identity status of their subjects, thus minimizing experimenter bias.

The results of these studies (Marcia, 1966, 1967) generally supported the construct validity of the identity statuses, laying the foundation for the next stages in the research. The first stage involved the expansion of the interview content and scoring manual to include women (the first two studies used only male participants because the writings of Erikson upon which this initial research was based concerned only men), as well as the accumulation of correlates of the statuses: in construct validity terms, the building of a "nomo-logical network." Students and I conducted these initial studies and were joined by a small group of researchers in other labs who became the nucleus of the Society for Research on Identity Formation. The next phase in which my students and I were involved saw mostly successful efforts at establishing relationships between the identity statuses and variables from relevant theories other than Erikson, namely, ego-psychoanalytic (Loevinger), cognitive developmental (Piaget), moral developmental (Kohlberg, Gilligan), and object-relational (Bowlby, Mahler).

One of the early criticisms of the identity statuses was that they did not "fully represent" Erikson's theory. To be sure, they did not. They were intended as a model to be used to test the validity of the identity formation process. While acknowledging that limitation, it should also be recalled that the statuses bore a strong relationship to the incomplete sentences measure whose scoring criteria contained many of Erikson's rich descriptions of identity formation. Most importantly, although initially *attenuating* Erikson's theory for the purpose of operationally defining identity, the subsequent volume of more than fifty years of research and hundreds of studies has now *enriched* that theory by establishing a vast array of concurrent, antecedent, and consequent relationships with other variables, as well as relationships with other structural theories. Without the initial operational definition furnished by the identity statuses' dual criteria of exploration and commitment processes, this result would not have occurred. That said, I do not think that the identity statuses constitute a *theory* in the formal sense. Rather, they are a model designed to test a central concept of Erikson's larger psychosocial developmental theory. Whether or not a model can *become* a theory is a question that must be left to philosophers of science.

10.2.1 What *Are* the Identity Statuses?

The identity statuses (see Table 10.1) were initially intended to delineate four ways in which any late adolescent/youth, aged about 18–22, might be resolving the issue of identity formation as it was described in the first paragraph of this chapter. These ages are approximate and would differ according to cultural context. For example, in current Western technological societies, the upper range might extend into the late twenties. In cultural contexts that do not allow for identity choice, the lower end of the age range might be at or immediately following puberty (for example, see Arnett, Zukauskiené, & Sugimura, 2014). Societies that prescribe occupational roles and religious/ political beliefs are commonly less tolerant of exploration and impose identities upon their youth, thus promoting foreclosed identities. Exploration-tolerant communities commonly yield both more identity achievements and more identity "casualties" – prolonged-to-permanent moratoriums and identity diffusions.

No Identity Status Is Necessarily Permanent

One may move out of an identity status in a normal developmental fashion (e.g., foreclosure to moratorium to achievement). One may also regress from achievement to moratorium, or even back to foreclosure or diffusion, due to pressing life events such as failing a crucial career-relevant college course or having to go to work due to financial concerns. In addition, as the individual moves through the psychosocial life cycle stages defined by Erikson (1982) succeeding Identity (Intimacy, Generativity, and Integrity), identity status would be expected to change, especially during the transition period, as the individual confronts each new crisis period in ego growth. In this way, each new adult stage affords the opportunity to "re-engage with" identity issues. For example, foreclosure parents at Generativity might find themselves confronted with a teenager making a nontraditional gender choice, thus challenging the adults' previous ideological beliefs and precipitating an identity "crisis" in the parents.

No Identity Status is Unmixed

While it is convenient to speak of a foreclosure or an identity achieved individual, in fact, any individual is an admixture of these statuses, usually with one status predominating. For example, one may be primarily identity achieved but with some remaining questions (moratorium), or a foreclosure with a moderate amount of diffusion. To my knowledge, there has been no research looking at differences among identity status patterns (e.g., A, M, F, D vs. A, F, D, M). This research could be undertaken if the interview were rated by giving different weightings to the relative saturation of different statuses rather than nominating only one predominant status, which is usually the case.

Identity Status Constructs Can Become Reified

Diagnostically, one speaks of obsessive-compulsives or borderlines; similarly, one speaks of foreclosures or moratoriums, often forgetting that these are descriptions only and not entities. At the most basic level, the identity statuses are labels that a researcher applies to their experience of another person. The problem with reified constructs is that they become closed; new information that might be disconfirming of the category can be overlooked in attempts to force-fit individuals into existing categories. The proliferation of identity status categories over the past thirty years, especially among sophisticated researchers, suggests that the tendency to reify has not been pernicious to the invention of new identity status constructs (e.g., "firm" vs. "developmental" foreclosures and ruminative moratoriums, Luyckx et al., 2008; Marcia et al., 1993).

10.2.2 The Identity Statuses: Associated Personality Variables, Antecedents, Consequences, and Patterns of Development

From early studies designed to validate and establish reliability of the identity statuses, well over 900 studies have now been undertaken to examine personality variables associated with Marcia's identity statuses, along with their familial antecedents, behavioral consequences, and developmental patterns of change over time. Studies utilizing Marcia's paradigm have now been undertaken in numerous countries as well as in different ethnic and subcultural contexts within North America. Both Marcia et al. (1993, 2011) and Schwartz et al. (2012) have recommended that content areas covered in identity status assessments should be adapted to suit cultural and other contextual conditions. It is only by focusing identity assessments around the psychosocial issues that are of greatest salience to an individual's identity that any meaningful understanding of one's underlying identity structure can be obtained. While a major review of identity status research is beyond the scope of this chapter, a few key findings for each of Marcia's identity statuses based on studies from over five decades of research are described below.

Identity achieved individuals are less reliant on the opinions of others in their decision-making processes, scoring consistently higher on "internal locus of control" measures than other identity statuses (from meta-analytic studies; Lillevoll, Kroger, & Martinussen, 2013a). They also perform well under stress and use deliberate planning and logical decision-making strategies compared to other identity statuses, although no significant differences in intelligence across the statuses have been found on a number of different intelligence measures (Boyes & Chandler, 1992; Marcia et al., 1993). Along with those evaluated as foreclosed, the identity achieved have demonstrated the highest levels of self-esteem compared with other statuses (from meta-analytic results; Ryeng, Kroger, & Martinussen, 2013a). Those evaluated as identity achieved are also most likely to be at post-conformist levels of ego development in Loevinger's (1976) scheme,[3] as well as post-conformist levels of moral reasoning (from meta-analytic studies; Jespersen, Kroger, & Martinussen, 2013a, 2013b). The identity achieved have evidenced more mature styles of intimacy as well as secure attachment patterns than other identity statuses (Beyers & Seiffge-Krenke, 2010; from meta-analytic studies, Årseth et al., 2009). Identity achieved adolescents and young adults come from families in which parents support their offspring's autonomy (Grotevant & Cooper, 1986). Generally, adolescents and young adults who are rated identity achieved have demonstrated more positive mental health outcomes (see Marcia et al., 1993 for a review).

Those rated as moratorium are in the process of making important identity-related decisions, tend to be anxious, sometimes depressed, changeable, and intense in their interpersonal relationships. Moratoriums have resembled identity achievements in their ability to perform complex cognitive operations, show higher levels of ego development and moral reasoning (from meta-analytic studies, Jespersen, Kroger, & Martinussen, 2013a, 2013b). They have

---

[3] Based on Erikson's and Sullivan's work, Loevinger (1976) proposed eight (nine) stages of ego in development, of which adulthood comprised six: conformist, conscientious-conformist, conscientious, individualistic, autonomous, and integrated. Like Erikson, she proposed that development must be seen as dynamic interaction between the inner self and the outer environment.

also tended to demonstrate greater openness to experience and an experimental orientation compared with other identity statuses (Stephen, Fraser, & Marcia, 1992; Tesch & Cameron, 1987), while at the same time showing greater degrees of skepticism than other status groupings (Boyes & Chandler, 1992). While able to express features of an intimate relationship, they often shy away from the commitment that genuine intimacy demands (Dyk & Adams, 1990; Josselson, 2017; Orlofsky, Marcia, & Lesser, 1973). Parents of moratorium adolescents have also stressed autonomy in their child-rearing practices (Frank, Pirsch, & Wright, 1990); attachment profiles of moratorium adolescents have been more mixed compared with the identity achieved (Årseth et al., 2009).

Adolescents and young adults rated as foreclosed have shown strong authoritarian attitudes relative to other identity status groupings (from meta-analytic studies; Ryeng, Kroger, & Martinussen, 2013b), often seeking approval from others and basing their actions on what others think. With their rigid, authoritarian values, foreclosures have also shown the lowest levels of anxiety relative to other statuses (Lillevoll et al., 2013a) and the lowest levels of openness to new experiences of all identity status groups (Stephen et al., 1992; Tesch & Cameron, 1987). Although foreclosures have utilized less complex cognitive styles than other statuses, meta-analyses have shown this status to be more mixed in terms of moral reasoning and ego development (Jespersen et al., 2013a, 2013b). In their intimate relationships, earlier studies have indicated foreclosure use of stereotypic or merger styles in intimate relationships (Dyk & Adams, 1990; Levitz-Jones & Orlofsky, 1985). More recent meta-analytic research, however, has found some interesting gender differences in close relationship patterns, suggesting that identity and intimacy may co-develop for some women (Årseth et al., 2009). Meta-analytic studies have also demonstrated foreclosures to be less secure in their attachment style than the identity achieved (Årseth et al., 2009). In terms of family relationships, foreclosure adolescents have shown overly close relationships with their parents, while parents, for their part, have promoted conformity and adherence to family values in their offspring (Frank et al., 1990).

Adolescents and young adults rated as identity diffuse have generally shown the most troubled patterns of behavior, relationships, and personality characteristics. Zuo and Crammond (2001) compared the most and least successful adults from Terman's long-term, longitudinal study of gifted individuals (Holahan & Sears, 1995) in terms of Marcia's identity statuses. Over half of all individuals designated as unsuccessful during adulthood were classed as identity diffusion, while only about 5 percent of successful individuals were so labeled. Meta-analytic studies have shown diffusions and moratoriums to have lower levels of self-esteem than foreclosure and achievement statuses (Ryeng et al., 2013a); diffusions have also had high levels of "external locus of control" and low levels of "internal locus of control" relative to other statuses (from meta-analytic studies; Lillevoll et al., 2013b). In terms of family relationships, diffusions have shown a lack of awareness of family issues (Gfellner & Bartoszuk, 2015) and have reported their parents to be distant and rejecting (Josselson, 2017). In general, diffusions have evidenced more risky or troubled behaviors as adolescents or young adults in comparison with the other identity statuses (Josselson, 2017).

Developmental patterns of identity status change have been examined primarily over the course of adolescence and young adulthood and have generally indicated progressive movements for those who do change (from meta-analytic studies, Kroger, Martinussen, & Marcia, 2010). Longitudinal meta-analytic studies have also shown, surprisingly, that only about one-third of individuals evidenced progressive change in identity development by the age of 22 (while about half remained stable). A meta-analysis of cross-sectional studies showed only about one-third of participants were rated as identity achieved by the age of age 22. About half of individuals were rated as identity achieved by the age of 30–36, however, and another 21 percent were rated as moratorium at this time. Foreclosure and diffusion statuses declined through mid-adolescence but fluctuated through late adolescence and young adulthood.

Subsequent longitudinal studies of identity status change over young to middle adulthood found either considerable stability or modest progression toward identity achievement (e.g. Carlsson, Wängkvist, & Frisén, 2015; Cramer, 2017; Fadjukoff, Kokko, & Pulkkinen, 2016; Josselson, 2017). Although such studies generally indicated progressive changes in identity status over time, the high rates of foreclosure and diffusion evaluations given to those entering young adulthood have led some to argue that Marcia's identity statuses fail to capture the identity formation process of adolescence. We believe, however, that a significant proportion of individuals simply remain in a foreclosed or diffusion position during young adult life, sometimes later evidencing identity progression, sometimes not.

10.2.3 Identity Exploration and Commitment Studies: Recent Developments From Marcia's Paradigm

Over the past decade, several research groups have drawn from the writings of Erikson and Marcia to focus more specifically on exploration and commitment processes in investigating adolescent identity formation experiences (e.g. Luyckx et al., 2006, 2008; Crocetti, Rubini, & Meeus, 2008). These research groups have developed paper-and-pencil questionnaire measures involving several different types of identity exploration and commitment scales. On the one hand, these instruments have been used to extract clusters, some of which resemble those of Marcia's identity status model; on the other hand, they have also been used to examine identity exploration and commitment processes independently.

Luyckx and his colleagues reasoned that the process of adolescent identity formation is based on reexamining one's identity-defining commitments over time.

They developed a 25-item paper-and-pencil measure presented in Likert-scale format, the Dimensions of Identity Development Scale (DIDS; Luyckx et al., 2006, 2008). Through this instrument, Luyckx and his co-workers differentiated three different forms of identity exploration (*exploration in breadth, exploration in depth,* and *ruminative exploration*) and two different forms of identity commitment (*commitment-making* and *identification with commitment*) for the domains of "education" and "future plans." *Exploration in breadth* refers to the degree to which individuals have considered a range of identity-defining commitments and is comparable to Marcia's concept of identity exploration. *Exploration in depth* assesses the extent to which existing identity commitments have been reexamined and refined with regard to an individual's own interests, needs, and values. *Ruminative exploration* refers to a kind of perpetual moratorium process in which an individual appears unable to make meaningful identity-defining choices and remains stuck in an ongoing process of identity exploration. *Commitment-making* refers to the degree to which individuals undertake meaningful identity-defining roles and values, similar to Marcia's commitment process, while the *Identification with commitment* scale refers to the degree to which individuals feel certain about or identify with the commitments that they have made.

With regard to the ruminative exploration process identified by Luyckx et al., (2008) and Luyckx and Robitschek (2014), several earlier studies had described this exploration pattern for some individuals (e.g. Hart, 1989; Mallory, 1988), though it was not empirically differentiated from other forms of exploration. Luyckx and colleagues also empirically differentiated the "classical" or troubled diffusion from a "carefree" diffusion. Luyckx, Klimstra, Schwartz, and Duriez (2013) showed that while troubled diffusions did attempt some unsystematic or haphazard exploration of identity issues over time, the carefree diffusions did not evidence any identity exploration at all.

Meeus, Crocetti, and their colleagues also examined several dimensions of identity exploration and commitment (Crocetti, Rubini, & Meeus, 2008). Their 13-item questionnaire for each of two domains (educational and friendship) is called the Utrecht Management of Commitments Scale (U-MICS). This instrument is comprised of three scales: Commitment, In-depth exploration, and Reconsideration of commitment. *Commitment* and *In-depth exploration* are comparable to the scales described in the Luyckx et al. (2008) study as well as commitment and exploration processes described by Marcia (1966; Marcia et al., 1993, 2011). The *Reconsideration of commitment* scale refers to abandoning of initial identity choices and undertaking evaluation of possible alternatives. Participants evaluate in a Likert format the degree to which each item reflects their current situation.

From their instrument, Crocetti et al. (2008) and Crocetti, Schwartz, Fermani, Klimstra, and Meeus (2012) derived four clusters that were given labels like those used by Marcia in defining his original identity statuses. A fifth cluster emerged that the investigators labeled "searching moratorium," characterized by those scoring high on all three scales (Commitment, In-depth exploration, and Reconsideration of commitment) in addition to the more traditional moratorium status. Those adolescents in these five identity statuses evidenced different levels of psychosocial adjustment over time (Meeus et al., 2012); the committed clusters (achievements and early closures) demonstrated generally positive psychosocial adjustments through adolescence, while the noncommitted statuses (moratorium and diffusion) showed higher levels of depression and delinquency over time. However, the searching moratoriums demonstrated a more adaptive trajectory, with lower levels of depression than those in the moratorium status.

Waterman (2015) has offered a thoughtful analysis, critique, and proposed remedies for, among other things, the assumed convergence between identity statuses based on cluster analyses of responses to both the DIDS and U-MICS and the original identity statuses assigned through Marcia's interview techniques. Waterman did find considerable differences between response patterns one might expect to see on both the DIDS and U-MICS and the identity statuses derived from Marcia's classic ones; in many instances it simply was not possible to identify a classic identity status from the DIDS or U-MICS, given the wording of paper-and-pencil questions on both of these latter instruments.

One particular problem is the inability of both the DIDS and U-MICS to assess identity explorations undertaken in the past; this information is vital in distinguishing the classic foreclosed and achieved identity statuses. While findings derived from the cluster analyses on both the DIDS and the U-MICS were generally highly replicable across studies using these two instruments, the identity status labels assigned to many clusters are conceptually inconsistent with those of Marcia's identity status paradigm. One of several conceptual problems Waterman identified, for example, is the identity status cluster labeled "searching moratorium" from the U-MICS; Waterman (2015) described this label as a paradoxical contradiction of terms. The "searching moratorium" cluster from the U-MICS is defined by those who score high on all commitment as well as exploration scales. Firstly, all moratoriums are searching for identity commitments. Furthermore, this pattern of searching while committed does not correspond with any identity status grouping from Marcia's identity status paradigm; such a group would most likely be labeled as "moratorium" in Marcia's rubric. Thus, considerable care is needed in attempting to make any direct comparisons and interpretations of findings between the identity statuses based on cluster analyses from the DIDS and the U-MICS with those from Marcia's classic identity status paradigm.

That being said, however, both the DIDS and the U-MICS have generated a range of findings concerning adolescent identity exploration and commitment processes. While a thorough review of findings is beyond the scope of this chapter, a few consistent findings are reported here. Negative associations between dimensions of identity commitment and depression and anxiety have been found on the DIDS, while positive associations between ruminative exploration and depression and anxiety have appeared (see Klimstra & van Doeselaar, 2017, for a review). In family relationships, parents with more committed identities have tended to have offspring evidencing stronger identity commitments and less ruminative exploration (Luyckx, Schwartz, & Klimstra, 2016), and older siblings were strong role models for younger siblings in the exploration of and commitment to identity-defining options (Wong et al., 2010).

Developmentally, studies using both the DIDS and U-MICS have assessed change in both identity status clusters as well as exploration and commitment variables primarily over the course of adolescence and young adulthood. From longitudinal studies in several different national contexts, diffusion and foreclosure status clusters have generally decreased or remained stable, as identity achievement status clusters have increased or remained stable from adolescence through young adulthood (e.g. in Belgium, Luyckx et al., 2013; Verschueren et al., 2017; in Japan, Hatano & Sugimura, 2017). Cross-sectionally in Trinidad, identity achievement was most prevalent in middle age compared to adolescence, emerging adulthood, and later adulthood as assessed by the U-MICS (Arneaud, Alea, & Espinet, 2016). Recent longitudinal findings from the DIDS have also pointed to links between structural changes in gray matter of the brain and identity exploration and commitment processes over time (Brecht et al., 2018).

When exploration and commitment variables have been assessed separately, Luyckx et al. (2008) found increases in commitment-making, exploration in breadth and depth across the college years. Luyckx et al. (2013) also found identity commitment processes to increase in a linear manner from age 14 to 30, while exploration in breadth and depth were highest for those in their early to mid-twenties. And while exploration in breadth and depth were strongly related to identity commitment processes in late adolescence and very early adulthood, these exploration processes were more strongly linked with ruminative exploration by the late twenties. Evidence of the slow development of identity achievement or identity commitments over time is similar to results from research utilizing Marcia's identity status paradigm.

10.2.4 Identity Exploration and Commitment Approaches: Gains and Losses

The DIDS and the U-MICS have enabled a number of positive developments in studies of those identity exploration and commitment processes that Erikson identified as being fundamental to the identity formation process of adolescence. The very nature of the paper-and-pencil formatting of these instruments has permitted a large number of individuals to be involved in identity-related investigations that has not been possible through the original interview methods devised by Marcia (1966, 1967; Marcia et al., 1993).

With the availability of larger sample sizes, it may also be possible to detect smaller effect sizes in relationships between identity exploration and commitment factors and dependent variables that smaller sample sizes obtained by interview would not enable one to do. The development of the DIDS and the U-MICS have also provided a more systematic examination of finite steps in identity decision-making processes and an appreciation of both the greater complexity and fluidity of how key identity-defining decisions are actually made. Furthermore, from an intervention perspective, these two instruments offer the potential for capturing incremental changes in exploration and commitment processes that may be helpful in structuring identity-related interventions for adolescents and young adults in need.

At the same time, however, use of the DIDS and U-MICS may have lost the ability to capture some aspects of identity that seem to lie at its very foundation. The individual's ability to identify those elements truly salient to his or her own identity, those identity-defining values and commitments that truly engage one with one's society and provide personal meaning as well as life directions and are simply not possible to identify and examine through use of these instruments; each measure addresses just two arenas of psychosocial functioning that may or may not be personally relevant to the individual in question. Furthermore, both instruments phrase items in the present tense only, so it is difficult to know what has led to one's current response and the basis for any potential identity commitment; thus, the ability accurately to discriminate traditional foreclosure from achievement statuses is not possible. Both paper-and-pencil instruments are also dependent upon a participant's interpretation of statements rather than evaluation by a highly trained interviewer, who has the ability to probe an individual's responses to statements. The advantages and disadvantages of each approach must be weighed carefully by researchers in considering how one might best address the identity-related questions at hand.

10.2.5 Clinical Implications of Marcia's Identity Status Approach

If one approaches intervention from the perspective of psychosocial development rather than mere symptom alleviation, the identity statuses and their defining criteria of exploration and commitment offer some therapeutic directions (see also Marcia & Josselson, 2012). In addition to the foundational resolution of Basic Trust in infancy, the period most relevant for identity is the initial separation-individuation period described by Mahler (1963), Bowlby (1988), and others. Optimal resolution of Basic Trust provides the individual with a secure sense of self as parental figures become internalized and no longer have to remain in proximity for the child to feel secure. The successful resolution of this period is heavily dependent upon how parents handle the child's growing sense of autonomy. The second individuation period during late adolescence is more under the control of individuals themselves. Parents provide a secure base from which to explore, and some communities furnish a time-out (a moratorium) from the assumption of adult responsibilities so that the late adolescent can "play around" with different career directions and beliefs, as well as offer viable areas for occupational and ideological commitments. The structure emerging from the initial separation-individuation period in early life is the self; the structure emerging from the second period in late adolescence is an identity. A secure sense of self is a necessary, but not a sufficient, condition for an achieved identity.

Parental and societal permission to explore as well as support for commitment to chosen alternatives are essential for optimal identity formation – identity achievement – in contexts that allow identity choices. A less than optimal foreclosure resolution in such contexts is produced by parental prescription of career paths and beliefs within an often supportive, but limited context that discourages exploration and questioning. The stage is set for diffusion by parental indifference or disparagement. The contrast in parenting styles here is between *too much* support within a narrow bandwidth of acceptance versus *too little* support and parental involvement. One may find relevant descriptions of these patterns of generativity in the work of Bradley (1997).

Identity achievements have successfully navigated the sometimes emotionally painful task of examining cherished childhood parental connections. While "leaving home" can be difficult for both youth and parent, the self-constructed emergent identity allows for a more equal and mutual relationship to be established with parents and others. Just as growing individual capabilities and social demands combine to make age 2–3 a crucial period for the formation of a self-structure, so individual capabilities (formal operational thought, developed sexuality, etc.) and the granting of a psychosocial moratorium make late adolescence a crucial period for the formation of an identity. Never again in the life cycle will such permission be given to explore. Because they have done their "identity work," all that identity achievements require of clinicians is information, encouragement, and a welcome into the adult world.

Not all moratoriums seek or need help. Those who do are usually in the midst of an identity crisis and present as anxious "crisis" cases. However, it is important to remember that this is a positive and developmentally meaningful crisis, not one to be prematurely abbreviated by medication or anxiety-reducing techniques. It is difficult for a clinician faced with a struggling young person not to try to intervene to "make things better." However, what the moratorium needs is support during an understandably difficult period, assurance that, however difficult this time is, it is developmentally important, and that it will likely end fairly shortly and positively when the work is done. Understandably, moratoriums will try to engage the therapist on one side or the other of their indecisive ambivalence in order to reduce the anxiety involved in choosing. If the clinician takes one side of the dialectic, this leaves the youth free to take the other side and to externalize what ought properly to be an internal struggle. What needs to be supported is not one of the alternatives, but the struggle itself. If we have the theoretical knowledge (and patience) to see this period not just as painful, but as positive and necessary on the way to an identity, then our clients/patients will, too.

Foreclosures usually appear for therapy only when some unavoidable external event has challenged their carefully guarded positions. A disequilibrating event for a foreclosure might be failure in a course necessary to their occupational goals, a serious injury interrupting an athletic career, or a romantic affair with the "wrong" person. Finding themselves so unexpectedly challenged, they may be confused, anxious, and/or depressed. Because they did not explore alternative identity directions during a moratorium period, they must now call into question previous positions that had been adopted unquestioningly. The problem facing clinicians with foreclosures is not just working with their unforeseen identity crisis, but modifying a cherished ego ideal. Foreclosures have learned how to be "good" people, but now that internal guide for self-esteem has been challenged. Not only do they fear being "bad," they may also fear being "nothing." The great temptation for the clinician is to merely attempt to retrench rather than to encourage a process of questioning and exploration in the client. The best therapeutic strategy is for the clinician to ally with those parts of the foreclosed client that are the most positive and to gently nudge the person into looking at some alternatives consistent with some part of their previously held values. To confront a foreclosed client directly is to risk either driving the person out of therapy or worse, to shatter their internal arbiter of self-worth, without allowing time for the development of an acceptable alternative. Even the most benign of foreclosed-upon values, e.g., "helping people," leaves the individual constricted and judgmental – constricted because they have not been able to conceive of alternatives (e.g., self-care) and judgmental because they must ward off the threat of acknowledging the validity of others' values (e.g., "oh, they're just selfish"). Working with a foreclosed late adolescent or young adult in crisis toward increased openness to unexamined parts of themselves will ultimately facilitate the development of an identity structure better able to not only withstand but also adapt positively to a multitude of contexts and future life circumstances.

Identity diffusions who are distressed (some are not; see Marcia, 1989) feel adrift, unconnected to others, internally empty, and ashamed of falling developmentally behind their peers. One may be a diffusion because of lack of early parental attention and investment, or because a foreclosed identity has been broken by life exigencies. In both cases, the demand on the therapist is to become the kind of parent that the diffusion lacked – attentive to the person's individuality, realistically supportive of abilities and efforts, and sometimes directive. In Kohut's (1977) terms, diffusions are both mirror- and ideal-hungry. They need the warming sun of (almost) unconditional approval as well as acceptance by a figure they can admire. Signing on to become a needed self-object for a diffusion is both lengthy and challenging. Even more than usual, the relationship with the therapist is paramount. This is not a situation well addressed by trenchant interpretations. Rather, an abundance of caring patience is required. Whereas the untreated foreclosure is often headed for a productive but narrowed life, the untreated diffusion is headed for a life of permanent drift – unless they can attach to a focused foreclosure or even to an achievement who has the patience to re-parent. Diffusions can become the raw material for the proliferation of cults and the cheering sections for dema-gogues. Lacking internal structure, they are especially vulnerable to the lure of external structures. The work in therapy is to build an internal structure, whether self, identity, or both.

10.3 Conclusions: Reflections on the Past and Future of Identity Study

This chapter has offered a brief review of Erikson's key identity concepts and processes through which Marcia developed his identity status model, including comments on what the identity statuses were and were not designed to do. A brief review of selected personality variables, antecedents, consequences, and developmental patterns of change over time for Marcia's original identity statuses was presented, prior to reviewing newer methods focusing on identity exploration and commitment processes in greater detail. A discussion of the strengths and limitations of these newer methods was presented, and the chapter has concluded with comments on implications for psychotherapeutic interventions that the identity statuses hold.

So what productive avenues lie ahead for identity research and practice? In terms of identity status/cluster work, a key issue is the development of future exploration and commitment measures that have the ability to determine past as well as present identity explorations and commitments as well as the (identi-ficatory) foundations upon which any such commitments are made. Much of the value of classic identity status research has been the ability to discriminate foreclosed from achievement positions, which, as Waterman (2015) has pointed out, is simply not possible through the paper-and-pencil identity measures reviewed here. Indeed, the late adolescent/young adult foreclosed has evidenced, through interview and alternative questionnaire methods, very different person-ality features, family antecedents, behavioral consequences, and developmental patterns of stability or change in relation to the other identity statuses. Additionally, such paper-and-pencil measures need to enable an individual to identify those psychosocial domains that are personally salient to his or her identity. And ideally, any such future paper-and-pencil measures would also supplement findings with a subgroup of individual narrative interviews to enable a deeper understanding of both impediments and supports to the identity formation process, both during adolescence and beyond.

Certainly many of Erikson's key identity concepts also remain to be explored: the role of the unconscious in identity development, integrative approaches to the relationship between psyche, soma, and society in the identity formation process across varied cross-cultural settings, an understanding of how identity continues to evolve and change through Erikson's psychosocial tasks of adult development at more frequent intervals than currently exist, and the nature of appropriate interventions for those struggling with identity issues well beyond the time of identity's normative crystallization during late adolescence. These are some of the questions that remain to be explored by new generations of identity researchers and practitioners.

References

Adorno, T. W., Frenkel-Brunswik, E., Levinson, D. J., & Sanford, R. N. (1950). *The Authoritarian Personality*. New York, NY: Harper & Brothers.

Arneaud, M. J., Alea, N., & Espinet, M. (2016). Identity development in Trinidad: Status differences by age, adulthood transitions, and culture. *Identity: An International Journal of Theory and Research, 16*, 59–71.

Arnett, J. J., Zukauskiené, R., & Sugimura, K. (2014). The new life stage of emerging adulthood at ages 18–29 years: Implications for mental health. *The Lancet Psychiatry, 1*, 569–576.

Årseth, A. K., Kroger, J., Martinussen, M., & Marcia, J. E. (2009). Meta-analytic studies of identity status and the relational issues of attachment and intimacy. *Identity: An International Journal of Theory and Research, 9*, 1–32.

Beyers, W., & Seiffge-Krenke, I. (2010). Does identity precede intimacy? Testing Erikson's theory on romantic development in emerging adults of the 21st century. *Journal of Adolescent Research, 25*, 387–415.

Bowlby, J. (1988). *A Secure Base: Parent–Child Attachment and Healthy Human Development*. New York, NY: Basic Books.

Boyes, M. C., & Chandler, M. (1992). Cognitive development, epistemic doubt, and identity formation in adolescence. *Journal of Youth and Adolescence, 21*, 277–304.

Bradley, C. (1997). Generativity – stagnation: Development of a status model. *Developmental Review, 17*, 262–290.

Brecht, A. I., Bos, M., Marieke, G. N., Nelemans, S. A., Peters, S., Vollebergh, W. A. M., ... Crone, E. A. (2018). Goal-directed correlates and neurological underpinnings of adolescent identity: A multimethod multisample longitudinal approach. *Child Development, 89*, 823–836.

Carlsson, J., Wängkvist, M., & Frisén, A. (2015). Identity development in the late twenties: A never ending story. *Developmental Psychology, 51*, 334–345.

Cramer, P. (2017). Identity change between late adolescence and adulthood. *Personality and Individual Differences, 104*, 538–543.

Crocetti, E., Rubini, M., & Meeus, W. (2008). Capturing the dynamics of identity formation in various ethnic groups. Development and validation of a three-dimensional model. *Journal of Adolescence, 31*(2), 207–222.

Crocetti, E., Schwartz, S. J., Fermani, A., Klimstra, T., & Meeus, W. (2012). A cross-national study of identity status in Dutch and Italian adolescents. *European Psychologist, 17*(3), 171–181.

Cronbach, L. J., & Meehl, P. E. (1955). Construct validity in psychological tests. *Psychological Bulletin, 52,* 281–302.

Dyk, P. H. & Adams, G. R. (1990). Identity and intimacy: An initial investigation of three theoretical models using cross-lag panel correlations. *Journal of Youth and Adolescence, 19,* 91–109.

Erikson, E. H. (n.d.). Life cycle and community. Unpublished manuscript, Item 95 M-2, Erikson Harvard Papers, MS Stor, Box 3 of 4.

Erikson, E. H. (1950). *Childhood and Society.* New York, NY: Norton.

Erikson, E. H. (1956). The problem of ego identity. *Journal of the American Psychoanalytic Association, 4,* 56–121.

Erikson, E. H. (1958). *Young Man Luther: A Study in Psychoanalysis and History.* New York, NY: Norton.

Erikson, E. H. (1963). *Childhood and Society, 2nd Ed.* New York, NY: Norton.

Erikson, E. H. (1968a). Memorandum for the conference on the draft. In S. Schlein (Ed.), *Erik Erikson: A Way of Looking at Things, Selected Papers from 1930–1980* (pp. 670–684). New York, NY: Norton.

Erikson, E. H. (1968b). *Identity: Youth and Crisis.* New York, NY: Norton.

Erikson, E. H. (1981). The Galilean sayings and the sense of "I." *The Yale Review, 70,* 321–362.

Erikson, E. H. (1982). *The Life Cycle Completed.* New York, NY: Norton.

Erikson, E. H., Erikson, J. M., & Kivnick, H. (1986). *Vital Involvement in Old Age.* New York, NY: Norton.

Fadjukoff, P., Pulkkinen, L., & Kokko, K. (2016). Identity formation: A longitudinal study from age 27 to 50. *Identity: An International Journal of Theory and Research, 16,* 8–23.

Frank, S. J., Pirsch, L. A., & Wright, V. C. (1990). Late adolescents' perceptions of their relationships with their parents: Relationships among de-idealization, autonomy, relatedness, and insecurity and implications for adolescent adjustment and ego identity status. *Journal of Youth and Adolescence, 19,* 571–588.

Friedman, L. J. (1999). *Identity's Architect: A Biography of Erik Erikson.* New York, NY: Scribner.

Gfellner, B. M. & Bartoszuk, K. (2015). Emerging adulthood in North America: Identity status and perceptions of adulthood among college students in Canada and the United States. *Emerging Adulthood, 3,* 368–372.

Grotevant, H. D. & Cooper, C. R. (1986). Individuation in family relationships: A perspective on individual differences in the development of identity and role-taking skill in adolescence. *Human Development, 29,* 82–100.

Hart, B. (1989). Longitudinal study of women's identity development. Doctoral dissertation, University of California, Berkeley.

Hatano, K. & Sugimura, K. (2017). Is adolescence a period of identity development for all youth? Insights from a longitudinal study of identity dynamics in Japan. *Developmental Psychology, 53,* 2113–2126.

Holahan, C. K. & Sears, R. R. (1995). *The Gifted Group in Later Maturity.* Stanford, CA: Stanford University Press.

Jespersen, K., Kroger, J., & Martinussen, M. (2013a). Identity status and ego development: A meta-analysis. *Identity: An International Journal of Theory and Research, 13,* 228–241.

Jespersen, K., Kroger, J., & Martinussen, M. (2013b). Identity status and moral reasoning: A meta-analysis. *Identity: An International Journal of Theory and Research, 13*, 266–280.

Josselson, R. (2017). *Paths to Fulfillment: Women's Search for Meaning and Identity.* New York, NY: Oxford University Press.

Kelly, G. A. (1955). *The Psychology of Personal Constructs, Vol. 1.* New York, NY: Norton.

Klimstra, T. A. & van Doeselaar, L. (2017). Identity formation in adolescence and young adulthood. In J. Specht (Ed.), *Personality Development across the Lifespan* (pp. 293–308). San Diego, CA: Elsevier Academic Press.

Kohut, H. (1977). *The Restoration of the Self.* New York, NY: International Universities Press.

Kroger, J. & Marcia, J. E. (2011). The identity statuses: Origins, meanings, and interpretations. In S. J. Schwartz, K. Luyckx, & V. Vignoles, (Eds.), *Handbook of Identity Theory and Research* (pp. 31–53). New York, NY: Springer.

Kroger, J., Martinussen, M., & Marcia, J. E. (2010). Identity status change during adolescence and young adulthood: A meta-analysis. *Journal of Adolescence, 33*, 683–698.

Levitz-Jones, E. M. & Orlofsky, J. L. (1985). Separation-individuation and intimacy capacity in college women. *Journal of Personality and Social Psychology, 49*, 156–169.

Lillevoll, K. R., Kroger, J., & Martinussen, M. (2013a). Identity status and anxiety: A meta-analysis. *Identity: An International Journal of Theory and Research, 13*, 214–227.

Lillevoll, K. R., Kroger, J., & Martinussen, M. (2013b). Identity status and locus of control: A meta-analysis. *Identity: An International Journal of Theory and Research, 13*, 253–265.

Loevinger, J. (1976). *Ego Development: Conceptions and Theories.* San Francisco, CA: Jossey-Bass.

Luyckx, K., Goossens, L., Soenens, B., & Beyers, W. (2006). Unpacking commitment and exploration: Preliminary validation of an integrative model of late adolescent identity formation. *Journal of Adolescence, 29*, 361–378.

Luyckx, K., Klimstra, T. A., Duriez, B., Van Petegem, S., & Beyers, W. (2013). Personal identity processes from adolescence through the late twenties: Age differences, functionality, and depressive symptoms. *Social Development, 22*, 701–721.

Luyckx, K., Klimstra, T. A., Schwartz, S. J., & Duriez, B. (2013). Personal identity in college and the work context: Developmental trajectories and psychosocial functioning. *European Journal of Personality, 27*, 222–237.

Luyckx, K. & Robitschek, C. (2014). Personal growth initiative and identity formation in adolescence through young adulthood: Mediating processes on the pathway to well-being. *Journal of Adolescence, 37*, 973–981.

Luyckx, K., Schwartz, S. J., Berzonsky, M. D., Soenens, B., Vansteenkiste, M., Smits, I., & Goossens, L. (2008). Capturing ruminative exploration: Extending the four-dimensional model of identity formation in late adolescence. *Journal of Research in Personality, 42*, 58–82.

Luyckx, K., Schwartz, S. J., Goossens, L, Soenens, B., & Beyers, W. (2008). Developmental typologies of identity formation and adjustment in female emerging adults: A latent class growth analysis approach. *Journal of Research on Adolescence, 18*, 595–619.

Luyckx, K., Schwartz, S. J., & Klimstra, T. A. (2016). Intergenerational associations linking identity styles and processes in adolescents and their parents. *European Journal of Developmental Psychology, 13*, 67–83.

Mahler, M. S. (1963). Thoughts about development and individuation. *Psychoanalytic Study of the Child, 18*, 307–324.

Mallory, M. (1988). Q-sort definition of ego identity status. *Journal of Youth and Adolescence, 18*, 399–412.

Marcia, J. E. (1966). Development and validation of ego identity status. *Journal of Personality and Social Psychology, 3*, 551–558.

Marcia, J. E. (1967). Ego identity status: relationship to change in self-esteem, "general maladjustment," and authoritarianism. *Journal of Personality, 35*, 118–133.

Marcia, J. E. (1989). Identity diffusion differentiated. In M. A. Luszcz & T. Nettlebeck (Eds.), *Psychological Development: Perspectives across the Life-span* (pp. 289–294). Amsterdam: Elsevier Science Publishers.

Marcia, J. E. & Josselson, R. E. (2012). Eriksonian personality research and its implications for psychotherapy. *Journal of Personality, 81*(6), 617–629.

Marcia, J. E., Waterman, A. S., Matteson, D. R., Archer, S. L., & Orlofsky, J. L. (1993, 2011). *Ego Identity: A Handbook for Psychosocial Research*. New York, NY: Springer.

Meeus, W. H., van de Schoot, R., Keijsers, L., & Branje, S. (2012). Identity statuses as developmental trajectories: A five-wave longitudinal study in early-to-middle and middle- to-late adolescence. *Journal of Youth and Adolescence, 41*, 1008–1021.

Orlofsky, J. L., Marcia, J. E., & Lesser, I. M. (1973). Ego identity status and the intimacy versus isolation crisis of young adulthood. *Journal of Personality and Social Psychology, 27*, 211–219.

Ryeng, M. S., Kroger, J., & Martinussen, M. (2013a). Identity status and self-esteem: A meta-analysis. *Identity: An International Journal of Theory and Research, 13*, 201–213.

Ryeng, M. S., Kroger, J., & Martinussen, M. (2013b). Identity status and authoritarianism: A meta-analysis. *Identity: An International Journal of Theory and Research, 13*, 242–252.

Schafer, R. (1954). *Psychoanalytic Interpretation in Rorschach Testing*. New York, NY: Pearson, Allyn, Bacon.

Schlein, S. (2016). *The Clinical Erik Erikson: A Psychoanalytic Method of Engagement and Activation*. London: Routledge.

Schwartz, S. J., Zamboanga, B. I., Meca, A., & Ritchie, R. A. (2012). Identity around the world: An overview. *New Directions in Child and Adolescent Development, 138*, 1–18.

Stephen, J., Fraser, E., & Marcia, J. E. (1992). Moratorium-achievement (Mama) cycles in lifespan identity development: Value orientations and reasoning system correlates. *Journal of Adolescence, 15*, 283–300.

Taylor, J. (1953). A personality scale of manifest anxiety. *Journal of Abnormal and Social Psychology*, *48*, 285–290.

Tesch, S. A. & Cameron, K. A. (1987). Openness to experience and development of adult identity. *Journal of Personality*, *55*, 615–630.

Truax, C. B. (1963). Effective ingredients in psychotherapy: An approach to unraveling the patient–therapist interaction. *Journal of Counseling Psychology*, *10*(3), 256–263.

Verschueren, M., Rassart, J., Claes, L., Moons, P., & Luyckx, K. (2017). Identity statuses throughout adolescence and emerging adulthood: A large-scale study into gender, age, and contextual differences. *Psychologica Belgica*, *57*, 32–42.

Waterman, A. S. (2015). What does it mean to engage in identity exploration and to hold identity commitments? A methodological critique of multidimensional measures for the study of identity processes. *Identity: An International Journal of Theory and Research*, *15*, 309–349.

Wong, T. M. L., Branje, S., VanderValk, I. E., Hawk, S. T., & Meeus, W. H. (2010). The role of siblings on identity development in adolescence and emerging adulthood. *Journal of Adolescence*, *33*, 673–682.

Zuo, L. & Crammond, B. (2001). An examination of Terman's gifted children from the theory of identity. *Gifted Child Quarterly*, *45*, 251–259.

PART III

Methodological Approaches

11 A Narrative Practice Approach to Identities: Small Stories and Positioning Analysis in Digital Contexts

Korina Giaxoglou and Alexandra Georgakopoulou

The power of stories for (per)forming identities is attested in the broader cultural turn to narrative as a tool – and a prerequisite, even – for answering the question "Who are you?" (Bamberg, 2012). In the context of largely confessional and therapeutic cultures (Illouz, 2008), storytelling is abundant in everyday and professional life, but also in the media and social media, where it is often equated with the presentation of an "authentic" self and experience. Celebrated as much as critiqued (see Atkinson, 2009), storytelling is by now recognized as a key site for the situated construction and negotiation of identities.

In this chapter, we outline the principles of approaching *narrative as practice* for the analysis of identity construction and negotiation. This mode of analysis attends to the different levels of *positioning* that storytellers take up in relation to the storyworld, their interactants, their self, and the world. As Bamberg (2012, pp. 104–105) suggests, a narrative practice approach to identity research addresses long-standing dilemmas in this line of work, namely dilemmas of:

(a) *constancy and change*: how one's sense of self balances moment by moment on a continuum of *no change at all* to *radical change*;
(b) *uniqueness and conformity*: how tellers negotiate the degree of their sameness to or difference from others; and
(c) *agency and construction*: how tellers navigate their sense of self as actor or undergoer on a continuum of *low* versus *high agency*.

In the first part of this chapter we summarize the key principles of a *practice approach to narrative* and outline the main elements of *small stories* and *positioning* for the study of identities. In the second part, we illustrate positioning as an empirical framework for examining how narrative as well as affective identities are emplotted and updated, reiterated and sedimented in digital contexts.

Throughout this chapter, the term "narrative" is used to refer to theoretical approaches, while the term "stories" and "storytelling" are used interchangeably to refer to aspects of story practice and performance.

11.1 Stories as/in Practice

The abundance of narrative and its importance in diverse domains of social life is matched by a diversity of approaches to its study over the years. An exhaustive summary of the intellectual *roots* and *routes* of narrative research is beyond the scope of this chapter, which takes as its starting point the *stories as/in practice approach* (for more detailed discussions of narrative turns, see De Fina & Georgakopoulou, 2012). This approach has emerged out of narrative "waves" variously enacting the narrative turn in the social sciences and the humanities and developing views of narrative as:

- a mode and way of knowing (Bruner, 1987);
- a cognitive-semiotic system used as a resource for problem-solving (Herman, 2017);
- an epistemology and method of inquiry (Riessman, 2008);
- a patterned text, which indexes sociolinguistic variation (Labov, 1972);
- an ethnopoetic way of speaking (Hymes, 1981) and performance (Bauman, 1986);
- a mode of communication and social interaction (Ochs & Capps, 2001)

Approaching stories as/in practice is grounded in the recognition that a particular type of stories, namely stories focused on the (re)telling of past events, had become the privileged object of analysis, leading to the neglect of interactional storytelling as a significant site of subjectivity and identity processes. Inspired (mainly) by insights from (qualitative) psychology, interactional sociolinguistics, and linguistic anthropology, the analysis of stories as/in practice called attention to the process of story-making as an interactionally achieved performance and a site of identity construction that can provide insights into "the messier business of living and telling" (Georgakopoulou, 2007, p. 154).

Also referred to as *small stories, storytelling in interaction*, or *storytelling practice research*, this line of research has by now emerged as an epistemology and a critical framework for narrative and identity analysis, challenging dominant idioms about the self and the life story. The small stories research paradigm challenges essentialist links between stories and identities and brings to the fore *counter-stories,* i.e., silenced, untold, devalued, and discarded stories in numerous institutional or research-regulated (e.g., interviews) contexts (see chapters in Bamberg & Andrews, 2004). The analysis of such story practices focuses on the communicative *how* of (counter-) stories and their association with more or less fleeting and resistant identities – as opposed to a focus on the biographical content and the *what* of stories (Phoenix & Sparkes, 2009, pp. 222–223). This requires attentiveness to identities as emergent and jointly drafted by participants (accepted, upheld, contested, negotiated, etc.) in contextualized moments of narrative contradictions and dilemmas.

According to Bamberg (2012, pp. 101–102), the key principles of a narrative practice perspective can be summed up as follows:

(1) Stories are parts of larger interactive activities.
(2) Analytic attention is paid not only to textual features, but also to story-performance features (based on recorded and transcribed spoken stories and, if possible, including visual display features, such as gestures, body posture, facial expression, and gaze).
(3) Stories are made up of references to an interconnected world of actors, places, and events, which is open to the analysis of the theme or the aboutness of the story.
(4) Stories are made up of components that follow particular culturally preferred principles of formation (*abstract, setting, problem, solution, coda*) commonly known as plot and which are also open to analytical scrutiny.
(5) Narratives are typically told for a purpose; these purposes are tied closely to the local context of the interactive setting.
(6) Storytellers reveal aspects of who they are; they engage in identity claims with regard to how they would like to come across as well as with regard to possible answers to the "who-am-I" question.

Stories as/in practices are studied through an ethnographic focus on speech events, which emerge out of specific *ways of telling*, *sites*, and *tellers* (Georgakopoulou, 2007, p. 22). This approach has proved to be an apt empirical framework for examining story-making practices and identities in digital contexts.

11.1.1 Sharing Stories as/in Practice Online

Stories shared on social media platforms, such as Facebook and Twitter, can take shape over a series of contributions often by multiple tellers in a single platform or across different platforms, drawing on a range of modalities (e.g., text, image, sound, and video) and prompting reactions from story recipients – both intended and unintended – in the form of likes, comments, and shares. Transportability and iterativity (with changes) emerge as distinctive characteristics of digital stories, echoing the way stories are shared among peers in face-to-face interaction (Georgakopoulou, 2007).

Stories online are not necessarily fixed to social media contexts, but rather move between the online and offline. For example, Georgakopoulou's (2014) ethnographic study of adolescents' (social) media engagements in school-based peer interactions has shown the prevalence of small stories about social media activities, including *breaking news stories* of very recent ("yesterday") and/or still happening ("just now") events that lead to further face-to-face storytelling activity relating to *updates* on the evolving events and/or *projections*, i.e., stories of events to take place in the near future (p. 230).

Three main analytical principles of stories in/as practice have proven to be of particular relevance to the study of digital storytelling:

(1) *Time and place* constitute key interactional resources in storytelling for signaling the teller's orientation to the (recent) past, the present moment, or the (near) future. In online stories, the most prevalent time and place configuration is the teller's "here and now" in *breaking news stories* (Georgakopoulou, 2007, p. 13; see also Georgakopoulou, 2015).

(2) Stories emerge as activities, which are *dialogic*, i.e., consisting of a multitude of tellers and orientations to the world, *variable* (and potentially *fragmented*), encompassing a variety of discourse activities and fleeting moments, and *transportable*, i.e., amenable to other contexts (Georgakopoulou, 2007, p. 86). All these are key aspects of storytelling activity online.

(3) Narrative identities are "invoked and traced both as roles and types of participation and as ways of telling and style" (Georgakopoulou, 2007, p. 152), which are closely tied to *emplotment* – the interpretive act of arranging events by forging meaningful connections between them from the narrator's present vantage point. Emplotment and narrative identities provide a point of entry into the examination of emergent storytelling online.

As mentioned above, the study of digital storytelling has affirmed the need to revisit the basic dimensions of narrativity, including *narrative temporality* and structure as closely tied with processes of *identities* and *positioning*. Based on Georgakopoulou's analysis of Facebook statuses and selfies posted by female adolescents (2016a) and the examination of circulation of Eurozone-related political events on YouTube (2016b), emplotment is defined flexibly as emergent in processes of (co-)authoring and distributing emblematic events in ways that create more or less meaningful connections among characters, events, actions, and interactions, assessments, and/or resolutions. This situated and dynamic understanding of emplotment calls for the use of heuristics, including for example, emblematic events, key actors, assessments of key actors, and participation roles that can reveal practices of *poly-storying*, i.e., the way different – and often conflicting – plots can be combined and made more widely available in association with specific positions for tellers and audiences (see Georgakopoulou & Giaxoglou, 2018). Furthermore, the production and performance of identities and stories online have been found to be associated with conventionalized ways of staging and authenticating experientiality with and for intimate publics, attesting to the specific ways in which intimacy, rapport, and sociality online are being reconfigured (Giaxoglou, 2021). The empirical framework of positioning analysis, presented in the next section, has proved an apt framework for addressing the complexities of such performances.

11.1.2 Levels of Positioning Analysis

The idea that others are variously placed or *positioned* in relation to ourselves in a way that keeps changing was already noted by Marcel Proust (2006) in Volume 2 of *Remembrance of Things Past*:

> Other people never cease to change places in relation to ourselves. In the imperceptible but eternal march of the world, we regard them [people] as motionless in a moment of vision, too short for us to perceive the motion that is sweeping them on. But we have only to select in our memory two pictures taken of them at different moments, close enough together however for them not to have altered in themselves – perceptibly, that is to say – and the difference between the two pictures is a measure of the displacement that they have undergone in relation to us. (Proust, 2006, p. 357)

The way that others are perceived to be changing by actively producing themselves in different and changing ways in the world became a prevalent object of study in social and cultural psychology and the concept of positioning – defined as "the discursive production of a diversity of selves" (Davies & Harré, 1990, p. 47). This concept became an integral part of systematic approaches to the study of selves and identities, foregrounding the importance of "rights" and "duties" in the organization and management of social action taken up as positions.

While initial theorizations of positioning assumed a straightforward and self-evident connection between identities and sets of beliefs and roles, more recent scholarship on positioning has shown the importance of local understandings and negotiations in the context of complex performances (see Bamberg & Georgakopoulou, 2008; De Fina, Schiffrin, & Bamberg, 2006; De Fina, 2013; Wortham, 2000). Identities are, thus, recognized as multilayered, dynamic, and often ambiguous, as social actors can project a number of different, sometimes conflicting positions and can have their positions interpreted by others differently than they had intended.

In addition to the acknowledgment of the emergent and dynamic nature of positioning acts, the careful analysis of empirical data has also foregrounded its ties to narrative practice. Narrative positioning has afforded analysts specific tools for investigating the interanimation of the here-and-now telling worlds with the narrated taleworlds uniquely involved in stories (Deppermann, 2015; Georgakopoulou, 2007). The stories' plots, the types of events and experience that they narrate, the ways in which they are interactionally managed during the telling, are all important in this respect. So are the intertextual links of the current story with other, previous and anticipated, stories.

In stories in/as practice research, positioning has become a powerful metaphor of identities as ways of locating oneself and others (Georgakopoulou, 2007, p. 124). The three levels summarized below have commonly served as heuristics for this line of analysis:

> *Positioning Level 1.* The level of the story or *taleworld*, i.e., the representation of characters through their description and evaluation in event sequences. At this level the analyst asks, "How are the characters positioned to one another within the reported events?"
>
> *Positioning Level 2.* The level of interaction or *storyrealm*, i.e., the interactional uses and rhetorical functions that aspects of the story construction are used for. At this level the analyst asks, "How does the speaker position him/herself to the audience?" and "How does the speaker address the question 'Who are you?'"
>
> *Positioning Level 3.* The level of the self, i.e., the establishment of a sense of self. At this level the analyst asks, "How do narrators position themselves to themselves?", "How do tellers address the question 'Who am I?'" and "What kinds of alignment or disalignment with related dominant discourses or master narratives about related social and moral identities do these acts of positioning index?" (see Bamberg & Georgakopoulou, 2008; De Fina, 2013).

Positioning at these three levels captures aspects of representation, action, and performance, as well as biographical dimensions of identities. It also makes it possible to link tellers' identity claims to broader sociocultural discourses and norms. These refer to socially based group conventions, which guide how people enact specific identities and how they assess their own and others' behavior, as, for example, in the case of tellers assessing their own or others' behavior as "right" or "wrong" in alignment with societal moral norms. Such links can be pinpointed by the analyst through ethnographic work that pays attention to common assumptions and themes that appear in related stories and broader Discourses that can be said to have an impact on (re)presentations of experience and the self in specific contexts, for example in research interview contexts (see De Fina, 2013). In this line of research, "the actual unit of analysis is the practice, not the story" (Bamberg, 2012, p. 107).

The study of the third level of positioning has raised discussions around the nature of identity as stable and continuous or as changing and fluid. Georgakopoulou (2013) has pointed out that positioning is an iterative process, which involves repeated constructions of social roles and identity formations that often become associated to certain contexts, activities, and types of stories. To analyze positioning, then, access is needed to multiple kinds of data and sites, for example across online and offline contexts, so that the analyst can answer the question of "why this type of story and this type of positioning here and now."

Ethnographically informed refinements to positioning analysis have also invited a more systematic reflection of the researcher's role in participants' identity projections, especially in the case of the analysis of interviews, pointing to the need to also focus on the researcher and her positioning in the data collection and elicitation process. In the case of the use of interview methods for the study of identity, for example, this involves a reflexive approach to the researcher's motivation, questions, and methods and a careful consideration of ways of intervening in, interrupting, or supporting the interaction (De Fina, 2013). In cases that involve ethnographic observations of identity performance, the researcher is invited to bring in the analysis relevant aspects of their own roles and relationships with participants as part of a form of auto-phenomenology (Georgakopoulou, 2016a).

11.1.3 Positioning Cues

The analysis of positioning is based on *iterativity*, i.e., the identification of recurrent language and narrative choices used by tellers, also known as *positioning cues* (Wortham, 2000; Georgakopoulou, 2013). The reiteration of cues in social interactions and their association with recognizable social positions explains how such forms accumulate social meanings and become indexes. In this respect, positioning cues are also types of entextualization markers, i.e., linguistic cues that point to the local context but also to invoked contexts, past and future, that can reveal processes of narrative and identity sedimentation (Giaxoglou, 2019). According to Wortham (2001, pp. 70–75) there are five main types of cues: (i) *reference*, i.e., personal pronoun choice, and *predication*, i.e., phrase and sentence construction choices that contribute to the description of actions, characters, and links between them (e.g., compare the phrases "the Lord" to "the Lord of the Rings"); (ii) verbs of saying (e.g., answer, exclaim, whisper, demand), also known as *metapragmatic verbs*; (iii) *quoted speech*; (iv) *evaluative indexicals*, which encompass a broad range of signs that can be used to characterize and evaluate characters and participants (e.g., "little boy"); and (v) *epistemic modalization*, i.e., the way tellers calibrate their epistemic status in storytelling practice, claiming, for example, a God's-eye view or the status of a mere participant.

Lucius-Hoene and Deppermann (2000) have also suggested different kinds of temporal and interactive sources of positioning. The analysis of small stories of mourning on a Facebook memorial wall has shown the centrality of time, space, and person referencing as interactional positioning resources for signaling the sharer's distance from or proximity to the death event, the dead, and the grieving self (Giaxoglou, 2015). More recently, Bamberg (2020) has pointed to visual cues as an integral part of narrative performance features serving as positioning cues, such as gaze, head movement, and breath intake, and the coordination between them.

In positioning analysis, the para/linguistic cues described above are not taken as a priori categories but rather as heuristics that can be drawn as required by the researcher's specific questions and data to reveal the updating, reiteration, and sedimentation of narrative identities and social positions as ways of telling and as types of participation. As we argue in the remainder of this chapter, positioning analysis has proved a productive and flexible framework not only for the study of identity in digital contexts, but also for the analysis of affect performances.

11.1.4 Affective Positioning

Despite the growing recognition of affect as an integral part of embodied communication (Busch, 2020), aspects of emotional stance-taking have been only marginally attended to in empirical studies of identity positioning so far. For example, Bamberg's analysis of an interview in the *Boston Globe* with a person called Clark Rockefeller draws attention to the interviewer's questions-prompts for the interviewee's self-disclosure, e.g., *Does that trouble you?* and *Does that worry you? What do you feel about that?* as revealing of an empathic concern for the interviewee at one level (Bamberg, 2012, p. 112). Such prompts can be linked to the interviewer's alignment with social discourses about self-disclosures as being central in social actors' emotional state and well-being, indexing modern folk theories of narrative identity, which draw on the "therapeutic" master narrative (see Illouz, 2008). The "therapeutic" master narrative indexes a social and cultural shift in modern capitalist economies to an ethos of self-realization and growth with a central concern about well-being and emotional rights. Given the instrumental bearing of these shifts to the forms of modern identities and the increasing pervasiveness of affect in domains of social life, narrative approaches to identity need to attend more systematically to the affective dimensions of tellers' identity positioning.

As Busch (2020) notes, the study of affect – i.e., the specific performances of emotion and their effects – requires the study of visible discursive practices through which emotions are produced and taken up within specific constraints. In digital contexts, in particular, additional constraints involve platform-specific sociotechnological affordances and limitations, which bear on the selection, styling, and dissemination or amplification of shared affect. The study of affect should, thus, not be restricted to the level of emotion labels (e.g., "love," "sadness," "anger") or explicit expressions of feeling states (e.g., "I feel sad"), but, instead, it should be examined as an integral part of storytelling interaction and as an embodied practice, i.e., a practice that comes out of bodies and is interpreted in the context of lived, embodied experiences of audiences (Heavey, 2015).

The concept of positioning can be calibrated so as to address dimensions of affect performance, in what can be termed *affective positioning*. Affective positioning can be analyzed empirically at the three levels posited for the study of identity positioning, namely the taleworld, the storyrealm, and the teller, with a focus on how tellers emplot degrees of affective proximity to or distance from the storyworld, their audiences, and their own emotional self (see Giaxoglou, 2021). In digital contexts of sharing, social actors are not only faced with the identity dilemmas of *constancy and change, uniqueness and conformity (sameness and difference)*, and *agency and construction* (Bamberg, 2012), but they also have to navigate dilemmas which relate to the production and authentication of experientiality, that is, the investment of an experiential telling with credibility and genuineness. These dilemmas include, for example, the negotiation of the degree of *uniqueness and representativeness of the shared personal experience*, the call for *audience identification or distancing*, and the sharer's *display of emotional control or loss of control* on recounted situations in line with existing templates for storying the self and sharing emotion in different social media platforms.

In summary, the analysis of affective positioning attends to the three levels posited for identity positioning with a special focus on affective dimensions in each level:

Positioning Level 1. The level of the story or taleworld; at this level, the analysis examines how events and characters are described and evaluated as falling into particular types of affective events (e.g., "tragic," "fun") and characters (e.g., "suffering," "strong," "vulnerable").

Positioning Level 2. The level of interaction or storyrealm; at this level, the focus is on the affective stances communicated through different (para) linguistic and visual cues and the kinds of relationships established through these with story recipients as intimate, proximal or distant. The analyst also considers the particular kinds of reactions, for example "support," "empathy," or "solidarity," which are fostered through these relationships.

Positioning Level 3. The level of the self, i.e., the communication and establishment of a sense of an emotional self through the projection of particular types of affective states, e.g., as "sad," "happy," more or less "in control" of a situation. These inflect and are inflected by broader sociocultural and social-mediatized norms of emotional displays.

The study of death-writing of the moment, which extends modes of life-writing of the moment as a prevalent mode of narrating everyday life, prompted by social media affordances of sharing in the here and now, is a rich site for the study of stories as practices associated with specific kinds of affective positionings. As we will show below in an extract from a vlog about living with – and despite – illness, the analysis of such practices can shed light on digitally afforded practices of mediatized story, identity, and affect performance and participation.

11.1.5 Affective Positioning in Death-Writing of the Moment

Sharing significant life moments with and for networked audiences involves the selection and entextualization of significant moments as small stories through which actions, thoughts, and feelings can circulate widely (John, 2017; Androutsopoulos, 2014; Georgakopoulou, 2015). Importantly, sharing online also involves acts of positioning, through which sharers locate themselves socially as participants in the context of specific types of digital interaction and affectively, (re)producing relationships to each other as well as to their own self. Part of the analysis of a vlog of a young adult documenting her life with – and despite cancer – until her passing will serve to illustrate, even if summatively, key aspects of the connections between storying and affective positioning in online performances.

The vlog is publicly available on YouTube and documents Charlotte Eades' experience with cancer from June 2014 until her passing in February 2016.[1] The vlog counts 112 videos posted by Charlotte herself and three additional updates posted by her mother on behalf of her updating viewers on the vlogger's last days and, ultimately, her passing. After her death, Charlotte's mother, Alex Eades, and her brother Miles, alongside Charlotte's cat, Nala, have taken over the vlog, having broadcast, at the time of writing, a total of 100 videos.

The analysis of story-making in the vlog from its launch to the vlogger's passing has pointed to three parts in the vlogger's overall emplotment of her illness, which are revealing of the changing stances to her illness, her audience, and her own self and emotions. The first part of the vlog includes videos that deal with everyday aspects of living with the diagnosis as a "teenager with a twist" and make up the majority of the videos (63 percent), while the second part of the vlog, which deals with the aftermath of the diagnosis about the growth of the tumor includes fewer videos (29 percent). The shorter part of the vlog covers the last period of her illness (8 percent), where cancer treatment results in a visible transformation in her appearance and ability to walk and talk.

Transitions to each of these three parts can be said to be signaled by three videos, respectively which set the tone for the vlogger's selections of content and tone of the videos, namely (i) *When Things Aren't Going to Plan* (October 27, 2014), which focuses on the vlogger's identity dilemmas of being a teenager with cancer, (ii) *Bad News* (September 9, 2015), where the vlogger announces the news of the tumor's growth and shares her reactions and feelings about it,

---

[1] "Welcome to my channel," Charlotte Eades YouTube channel. Retrieved February 28, 2021, from www.youtube.com/watch?v=4ShO2QZ98Ro.

and (iii) *Fed Up* (December 28, 2015), a short video about the vlogger's deterioration of health and the related difficulties.

Viewers of the vlog watch the vlogger's identity and affective positioning change across these three different parts associated with different types of storying the vlogger's everyday experience of cancer. Content selections for the videos shift from a focus on general, relatable aspects of the teenage experience, which are not "normal," to more personal, visible, and raw aspects of the experience of being (terminally) ill. The vlogger is seen to shift from affective positions of being in control, reflecting on how to best get on with her everyday life (*When Things Aren't Going to Plan*), to positions between losing and (re) claiming control (*Bad News*) and, ultimately, to being irrevocably transformed and alienated from herself (*Fed Up*) (for a full analysis, see Giaxoglou, 2021).

The remainder of this section illustrates how the vlogger engages in affective positioning practices in the context of her visual story-making, focusing on a selected extract from the video *When Things Aren't Going to Plan* (October 27, 2014).

Level 1: Affective Positioning vis-à-vis Cancer

In Extract 1, reproduced below, the vlogger plots her personal experience with cancer in the form of a retrospective account (1.21 "recently"), where she reflects on the impact that cancer has been having on her everyday life with an orientation to the present moment ("I *have* cancer," 1.26; "I *can't drive* for two years," 1.28; "it's extremely difficult to get a job," 1. 31; "I *don't really get* to socialize," 1. 34).

Extract 1: *When Things Aren't Going to Plan* (27 October 2014)[2] [lines 20–34]

20 I for some reason
21 I've been having a few problems recently
22 with dealing with things
23 and feeling normal
24 Umm I will quickly go through this:
25 the first reason why I don't feel normal
26 is because I have cancer
27 the second reason being
28 I can't drive for two years
29 because I had a seizure last year
30 the third reason being
31 it's extremely difficult to get a job
32 which I'm sure a lot of you can relate to
33 and the third reason being
34 that I don't really get to socialize that much.

---

[2] In this transcript, numbering reflects the position of this extract in the longer transcript of the full video from which it is taken. Lines have been segmented ethnopoetically (Hymes, 1981) so as to maintain a sense of rhythm and oral patterning: verbal phrases, adverbials, discourse markers, and short pauses have been used as cues marking a new line or *idea unit* (Gee, 1999).

This retrospective account is a small story that can be described as a recount, in that it is organized as a report-like listing of the everyday difficulties in the life of a teenager with cancer, featuring little explicit evaluation and echoing the story genres of blogging on illness analyzed by Page (2011). Evaluation is limited to assessments of the practical and social consequences of cancer, which is viewed as a disruption to "normal" life (l. 25), to everyday life activities, such as driving (l. 28), and to plans for the future, such as getting a job (l. 31). The emplotment of cancer as a major disruption in the teenager's everyday life and plans points to the way the vlogger is constructing her affective positioning at the first level – the level of the taleworld – where she is seen to take a relative distance from her illness in an attempt to reaffirm her identity as a teenager.

Level 2: Affective Positioning vis-à-vis the Viewing Audience

At the second level – the level of the viewing audience – the vlogger's recount of difficulties is framed as an experience that can resonate with viewers ("which I'm sure a lot of you can relate to," 2.32). Here, the vlogger is constructing her unique experience as more broadly representative of human experience in moments of crisis. This explicit orientation to her viewers as having a personal interest in what she's talking about is inscribed in her discursive attempt to construct an affective positioning of proximity – and even intimacy – to them. This type of affective positioning in proximity to a personal public is central to this vlogger's video-storying practice. It is also carefully managed throughout the vlog based on a set of linguistic, discursive, and visual cues. These cues will be discussed by considering a multimodal transcription of two further extracts from the video *When Things Aren't Going to Plan*, namely its opening and closing (see Extract 2).

Extract 2: When Things Aren't Going to Plan (27 October 2014)

Time	Line	Verbal	Nonverbal
00:00	0	n/a	

Getting the camera on

Extract 2: (*cont.*)

Time	Line	Verbal	Nonverbal
00:03	1	Hi everybody	
	2	I am with a (.) really sudden video	
	3	which I decided to film	
	4	in the space of about 10 minutes	
	5	(.)	
	6	I'm not wearing any makeup	
	7	uhm I've just come out of the	
	8	bath	
	9	it's a Sunday evening	
	10	but while I was in the bath	
	11	I had a thought	
	12	and I really wanted	
		to share it with everybody	
		and get the message out there	
		[. . .]	
05:13	133	[. . .]	
05:41	134	anyway	
	135	I will film another video soon	
	136	I'm sorry for the crappy quality	
	137	you may have realized from the	
	138	viewfinder	
	139	But please just remember to stay	
	140	true to yourself	
	141	and sometimes you can be your	
	142	own worst enemy	
	143	but you all can do it	
	144	and please just share this video	
	145	remember to speak to someone	
		don't ever hold things in	
		thank you for watching	

The opening and closing parts in this video, which are typical of videos in the vlog, are used as *meta-communicative devices*, connecting this video to the ongoing series of videos that self-document the moments the vlogger selects as potentially interesting for her audience. These devices are drawn upon by the vlogger as authenticating strategies for affirming the spontaneity of content creation on the vlog ("really sudden video," 2.2), creating a sense of "natural-ness" and "realness" ("I'm not wearing any make up," 2.5). These verbal authenticating strategies are supplemented by nonverbal choices, for example the choice of shooting the video in the intimate space of her bedroom and her bodily proximity to the camera. These combined strategies construct her affective positioning at the second level, helping the vlogger to negotiate aspects of privacy and publicness and forging an intimate relationship with her viewers, who are thus constructed as "a personal public" (Androutsopoulos, 2015, p. 74).

The second level of affective positioning is further marked visually through shifts in head-positions: the vlogger's head shifts from the viewer's right-hand side, during the camera setup and preparation for launching into (Extract 2, line 0) or moving out of (Extract 2, line 145) broadcasting mode, to the viewer's left-hand side, which seems to be the base mode for the vlogger's entering into the self-broadcasting mode of performance.

Uses of addressivity, for example the choice of using the pronoun "you" ("but please just remember," 2.137), are central in the vlogger's affective positioning of intimacy to her viewers. The closing, in particular, where the vlogger fashions her experience into a small story directly addressed to her viewers (2.133–145), opens up a space for her followers to share in her struggles and potentially, also, intimate their own stories of difficult situations in the comments space ("don't ever hold things in," 2.144). This mode of affective positioning is thus intricately linked to the vlogger's identity positioning to her viewers as an "inspirational" teenager, who transforms her personal experience of suffering into an experience that can unite others facing similar difficulties and create a (YouTube) compassionate community.

Level 3: Affective Positioning vis-à-vis the Self

Lastly, at the third level of positioning the vlogger affectively positions herself as strong, positive, and largely in control of what's happening, even "when things aren't going to plan," creating thus a relative distance from her emotional self and the experience of cancer. The emphasis of the vlogger's self-presentation is on the "frontstage" (Goffman, 1956) as part of efforts to create and maintain a sense of control over the illness experience in line with norms of avoiding oversharing of emotion online and norms for presenting the self online.

And yet, subtle nuances of the vlogger's affective positioning to herself surface in the paralinguistic features of the videos. In the video under focus, aspects of the "backstage" of the vlogger's affective positioning are given in the part immediately following the opening, which brackets the main part of the sharing and brings attention to the affective "I." A selection of these features is annotated in the multimodal transcript below (Extract 3; see Appendix for Transcript Key).

Extract 3: When Things Aren't Going to Plan (27 October 2014)

Time	Line	Verbal	Nonverbal
00:42	1	-h I (.) <	

Time	Line	Verbal	Nonverbal
00:43	2	for some reason: > (.)	

Time	Line	Verbal
	3	>I've been having<
00:46	4	a few-h (.) problems. (.)
	5	recently .
	6	with (.)
	7	dealing with things and (.)
00:52	8	feeling: (.) normal. (.)
	9	Uhm ((slightly moves back))
00:55	10	I will quickly go through this

The section opens with the utterance of "I" (3.1),[3] which is marked paralinguistically by multiple features: it is fronted by an audible in-breath, and its sound is elongated over one second and followed by a short pause and a shift of the vlogger's head and gaze to the left. The overlaying of multiple paralinguistic cues in the utterance of a single sound places emphasis on the affective "I" through the production of a cumulative emotional effect. This is continued in the utterance of the phrase "for some reason," pronounced with an elongated final consonant "-n" at a pace slower than her earlier quick pace, while her head returns to the neutral position (right-hand side), which marks her being "out of" broadcasting mode. The phrase "problems recently" (l. 2) is uttered in a low pitch and a low fall, audibly marking the weight of these issues for the teller. The vlogger moves her head and body slightly closer to the camera, when she utters "dealing with things" (l. 7) and utters each of the words in the phrase "and feeling [normal]" (l. 8) almost separately, adding emphasis to what she says. The move to the next part of the video is signaled by the discourse marker "uhm" (l. 9), accompanied by a slight move of her head backward, taking some distance from the camera, and a change of "affective gear" to the quick-paced summary of the reasons that cumulatively create "problems" for her. The accumulation of paralinguistic features at this section mark it as part of "affective" sharing or embodied affective positioning, calling attention to affect as an emotionally invested performance which is to be empathically witnessed.

11.2 Summary and Conclusion

In summary, in this vlog affective positioning was examined in relation to emplotment in the following three interrelated levels:

Level 1. Evaluations of the illness thematized as the main topic or focus of the story or other focalized moments and events through which the vlogger balances the uniqueness versus the broader representativeness of her experience;

Level 2. The vlogger's interpersonal orientation to her viewers, shaped by modulations of proximity to her viewers and calling viewers' identification with the portrayals of her experience as a source of inspiration and motivation;

---

[3] Note that lines in the multimodal transcript start from 1 for ease of cross-reference in the text; they do not represent the place of this snippet in the transcript.

Level 3. The vlogger's positioning vis-à-vis her projected affective self, privileging the projection of emotional control through the vlogger's explicit orientation to her viewing audience and norms of sharing emotion online, despite the leaks of emotion in acts of unintended embodied positioning. At this level, there is further scope for connecting the choice of the vlogger's presentation of emotional self to generic plot types of illness narratives (Frank, 1997) and master therapeutic discourses, as well as social media affordances and constraints for positioning.

The discussion of this example draws attention to practices of affective positioning in storytelling as acts of modulating proximity to or distance from the illness, the viewing audiences, and the emotional self as an integral part of identity performance and the staging of authenticity. It also highlights the importance of examining para/linguistic and embodied resources as cues of affect and identities in storytelling activities alongside the affordances and constraints of specific digital platforms.

To conclude, our discussion calls for the need to embed in the analysis of small stories and positioning – which so far has mainly focused on the study of face-to-face encounters – aspects of the way stories have been changing in the digital era. For example, the increasing use of stories as *designed activities* on social media requires a combined attention to the communicative "how," "what," and "who" with sociotechnical aspects of stories. In response to these "new" dilemmas and tensions for storytellers/ sharers and their recipients, there is scope for considering aspects of *pre-positioning* in stories, especially in relation to Level 3 of positioning analysis, which links the production of situated identities in local storytelling contexts to broader social categorizations and roles. This recalibration of positioning analysis, which lies beyond the scope of this chapter, can provide a critical lens on how technical and metrics considerations pre-position tellers vis-à-vis audiences and vice versa, and what feedback loops this subsequently generates among storytelling tools, affordances, and actual practices (Georgakopoulou, Iversen, & Stage, 2020). Our chapter has foregrounded the continued relevance of positioning analysis for the study of identities in digital contexts and the need to keep updating it in response to changes in story- and identity-making practices.

References

Androutsopoulos, J. (2014). Moments of sharing: Entextualization and linguistic repertoires in social networking. *Journal of Pragmatics* (Special issue: The pragmatics of textual participation in the social media), *73*, 4–18.

Androutsopoulos, J. (2015). Negotiating authenticities in mediatized times. *Discourse, Context & Media, 8*, 74–77.

Atkinson, P. (2009). Illness narratives revisited: The failure of narrative reductionism. *Sociological Research Online, 14*(5), 196–205.

Bamberg, M. (2012). Narrative practice and identity navigation. In J. Holstein & J. Gubrium (Eds.), *Varieties of Narrative Analysis* (pp. 99–125). London: Sage.

Bamberg, M. (2020). Narrative analysis: An integrative approach – Small stories and narrative practices. In M. Järvinen & N. Mik-Meyer (Eds.), *Qualitative Analysis – Eight Traditions* (pp. 243–265). London: Sage.

Bamberg, M. & Andrews, M. (Eds.). (2004). *Considering Counternarratives: Narrating, Resisting, Making Sense*. Amsterdam: John Benjamins.

Bamberg, M. & Georgakopoulou, A. (2008). Small stories as a new perspective in narrative and identity analysis. *Text & Talk, 28*, 377–396.

Bauman, R. (1986). *Story, Performance, and Event: Contextual Studies of Oral Narrative*. Cambridge: Cambridge University Press.

Bruner, J. (1987). *Actual Kinds, Possible Worlds*. The Jerusalem–Harvard Lectures. Cambridge, MA: Harvard University Press.

Busch, B. (2020). Discourse, emotions, and embodiment. In A. De Fina & A. Georgakopoulou (Eds.), *The Cambridge Handbook of Discourse Studies* (pp. 327–249). Cambridge: Cambridge University Press.

Davies, B. & Harré, R. (1990). Positioning: The discursive production of selves. *Journal for the Theory of Social Behaviour, 20*(1), 43–63.

De Fina, A. (2013). Positioning level 3: Connecting local identity displays to macro social processes. *Narrative Inquiry, 23*(1), 40–61.

De Fina, A. & Georgakopoulou, A. (2008). Introduction: Narrative analysis in the shift from texts to practices. *Text & Talk, 28*(3), 275–281.

De Fina, A. & Georgakopoulou, A. (2012). *Analyzing Narrative. Discourse and Sociolinguistic Perspectives*. Cambridge: Cambridge University Press.

De Fina, A., Schiffrin, D., & Bamberg, M. (Eds.) (2006). *Discourse and Identity*. Cambridge: Cambridge University Press.

Deppermann, A. (2015). Positioning. In A. De Fina & A. Georgakopoulou (Eds.), *The Handbook of Narrative Analysis* (pp. 369–387). Hoboken, NJ: Wiley-Blackwell.

Frank, A. W. (1997). *The Wounded Storyteller: Body, Illness, and Ethics*. Chicago, IL: University of Chicago Press.

Gee, J. P. (1999). *An Introduction to Discourse Analysis Theory and Method*. London: Routledge

Georgakopoulou, A. (2007). *Small Stories, Interaction and Identities*. Amsterdam: John Benjamins.

Georgakopoulou, A. (2013). Building iterativity into positioning analysis: A practice-based approach to small stories and self. *Narrative Inquiry, 23* (1), 89–110.

Georgakopoulou, A. (2014). "Girlpower or girl (in) trouble?" Identities and discourses in the (new) media engagements of adolescents' school-based interaction. In *Mediatization and Sociolinguistic Change* (pp. 217–244). Berlin: Mouton de Gruyter.

Georgakopoulou, A. (2015). Small stories research: *Methods – analysis – outreach*. In A. De Fina & A. Georgakopoulou (Eds.), *The Handbook of Narrative Analysis* (pp. 178–193). Hoboken, NJ: Wiley-Blackwell.

Georgakopoulou, A. (2016a). From narrating the self to posting self(ies): A small stories approach to selfies. *Open Linguistics, 2*(1), 300–317.

Georgakopoulou, A. (2016b). Friendly comments: Interactional displays of alignment on Facebook and YouTube. In S. Leppänen, S. Kytölä, & E. Westinen (Eds.), *Discourse and Identification: Diversity and Heterogeneity in Social Media Practices* (pp. 178–207). Abingdon: Routledge.

Georgakopoulou, A. & Giaxoglou, K. (2018). Emplotment in the social mediatization of the economy: The poly-storying of economist Yanis Varoufakis. *Language@Internet, 16*, article 6.

Georgakopoulou, A., Iversen, S., & Stage, C. (2020). *Quantified Stories: A Narrative Analysis of Metrics and Algorithms on Social Media*. London: Palgrave.

Giaxoglou, K. (2015). "Everywhere I go, you're going with me": Time and space deixis as affective positioning resources in shared moments of digital mourning. *Discourse, Context & Media, 9*, 55–63.

Giaxoglou, K. (2019). Trajectories of treasured texts: Laments as narratives. In E. Falconi & K. Graber (Eds.), *Storytelling as Narrative Practice: Ethnographic Approaches to the Tales We Tell* (pp. 136–162). Boston, MA: Brill.

Giaxoglou, K. (2021). *A Narrative Approach to Social Media Mourning: Small Stories and Affective Positioning*. London: Routledge.

Goffman, E. (1956). *The Presentation of Self in Everyday Life*. New York, NY: Doubleday.

Heavey, E. (2015). Narrative bodies, embodied narratives. In A. De Fina & A. Georgakopoulou (Eds.), *The Handbook of Narrative Analysis* (pp. 429–446). Cambridge: Cambridge University Press.

Herman, D. (2017). *Storytelling and the Sciences of Mind*. Cambridge, MA: MIT Press.

Hymes, D. (1981). *"In Vain I Tried to Tell You": Essays in Native American Ethnopoetics*. Lincoln, NE: University of Nebraska Press.

Illouz, E. (2008). *Saving the Modern Soul: Therapy, Emotions, and the Culture of Self-Help*. Berkeley, CA: University of California Press.

Jefferson, G. (2004). Glossary of transcript symbols with an introduction. In G. H. Lerner (Ed.), *Conversation Analysis: Studies from the First Generation* (pp. 13–31). Amsterdam: John Benjamins.

John, N. (2017). *The Age of Sharing*. Cambridge: Polity Press.

Labov, W. (1972). *Language in the Inner City*. Philadelphia, PA: University of Pennsylvania Press.

Lucius-Hoene, G. & Deppermann, A. (2000). Narrative identity empiricized: A dialogical and positioning approach to autobiographical research interviews. *Narrative Inquiry*, *10*(1), 199–222.

Ochs, E. (1979). Planned and unplanned discourse. In T. Givón (Ed.), *Discourse and Syntax* (pp. 51–80). New York, NY: Academic Press.

Ochs, E. & Capps, L. (2001). *Living Narrative: Creating Lives in Everyday Storytelling*. Cambridge, MA: Harvard University Press.

Page, R. (2011). Blogging on the body: Gender and narrative. In R. Page & B. Thomas (Eds.), *New Narratives: Stories and Storytelling in the Digital Age* (pp. 220–238). Lincoln, NE: University of Nebraska Press.

Phoenix, C. & Sparkes, A. C. (2009). Being Fred: Big stories, small stories and the accomplishment of a positive ageing identity. *Qualitative Research*, *9*(2), 219–236.

Proust, M. (2006). *Remembrance of Things Past, Vol. 2*, translated by S. Moncrieff. London: Penguin.

Riessman, C. K. (2008). *Narrative Methods for the Human Sciences*. Thousand Oaks, CA: Sage.

Wortham, S. (2000). Interactional positioning and narrative self-construction. *Narrative Inquiry*, *10*(1), 157–184.

Wortham, S. (2001). *Narratives in Action: A Strategy for Research and Analysis*. New York, NY: Teachers College Press.

Appendix

Transcript Key

(.)	pause length placed before utterance
.	low fall
?	high rise
!	exclamatory utterance
CAPITAL LETTERS	increased volume
____	emphasis
:::	lengthened syllable
-h	audible in-breath
h	audible out-breath
↑	upward eye-gaze
↓	downward eye-gaze
⇒	right-directed eye-gaze
●	centered and focused gaze
}	eyes frown

(( ))	gestures
>	head tilted to the right
<	head tilted to the left
[...]	omitted text

Adapted from Ochs, 1979 and Jefferson, 2004

12 Conversation Analysis and Ethnomethodology: Identity at Stake in a Kinship Carers' Support Group

Julie Wilkes and Susan A. Speer

This chapter introduces an ethnomethodological and conversation analytic approach to identity, illustrated by reference to findings from a study that investigates how kinship carers construct and manage parental identities. First, we provide a brief overview of the ethnomethodological background of conversation analysis (CA) and the development of CA's approach to identity, with specific reference to studies of family identities. Second, we introduce "kinship care," where close relatives take over the parental role from parents who are unable to care for children, and explain how identity has featured in kinship care studies. Third, we explain how these studies have traditionally theorized identity, and contrast this with CA's approach, including our methodology and how we define our unit of analysis. Fourth, we provide examples of analysis of interaction recorded in carers' support group meetings which demonstrate the advantages CA can bring to the study of identity. We end by considering the implications of a CA approach for understanding how people negotiate and manage identity interactionally, the limitations of this approach, and directions for future studies.

12.1 Conversation Analysis: Its Ethnomethodological Background

As a student of Parsons in the 1950s, Garfinkel became dissatisfied with the prevailing sociological framework of "systems theory" (Parsons, 1937) in which social order is seen as a process by which members of society internalize dominant ideas and values "top-down," and become "simply the passive bearers of sociological and psychological attributes" (Heritage, 1984, p. 2). Garfinkel's critique focused instead on members' *practices* (including how they talk) as a "bottom-up" basis for understanding the production and reproduction of social life (see Lynch, 1997; Maynard & Clayman, 2003). This critical approach is known as ethnomethodology: the study of people's (*ethno*) methods (*methodology*) of shared sense-making as displayed in everyday social interaction (Garfinkel, 1967). The kind of sense-making envisaged is not based on people agreeing with each other; but without shared *methods* for under-standing, "coordinated and meaningful actions, regardless of whether they involve cooperation or conflict, are impossible" (Heritage, 2001, p. 2).

Ethnomethodological researchers adopt an "anti-cognitivist" view of analysis, which means their research is not set up to discover people's thoughts or ideas in order to collect or interpret them (Antaki & Widdicombe, 1998, p. 1). Instead, they look for the regular methods people use when handling everyday encounters. Ethnomethodologists have produced wide-ranging programs of enquiry in arenas such as science, law, medicine, and the arts (Atkinson, 1988), using a range of methods of data collection including ethnography, experiments, and observation (see ten Have, 2004). The systematic study of conversation (CA) only began with Sacks's work in the 1960s (Silverman, 1998), since which time the investigative approaches of CA and ethnomethodology have developed in parallel (Maynard, 2013).

CA's ethnomethodological principles include *indexicality*; that is, how the meaning of words and phrases varies according to the context and the manner in which they are spoken, rather than being fixed or predefined (see Heritage, 1984, 1987). The importance of this for research design is that interaction must be analyzed in situ, and not removed from its context (Sacks, 1984). Another principle is *relevance*; that is, how people hear and respond in ways that they see as appropriate to a particular context, from which we can tell how *they* are defining the context they are in (Silverman, 1998). CA began when Harvey Sacks, Emmanuel Schegloff, and Gail Jefferson undertook the task of identifying systematic ways of examining talk "as an object in its own right" (Schegloff, 1992, p. xviii; for introductions to CA, see Pomerantz & Fehr, 2011; Sidnell, 2013; Sidnell & Stivers, 2013).

12.2 The Development of CA's Approach to Identity

Traditional social science views identity as a way of explaining the relationships between society and its members (see Giddens, 1993), and so uses identity as a means for classifying individuals into social groups according to particular membership criteria (such as common lifestyles or cultural practices). At the level of the individual, standard cognitive and symbolic interactionist approaches in psychology attempt to explain identity in terms of individuals' active "internalization" of social structures, treating identity as if located inside people "as a product of minds, cognition, the psyche or socialization practices" (Benwell & Stokoe, 2006, p. 9). These principles give rise to research designs that treat research participants "as informants about what identities they have" (Antaki & Widdicombe, 1998, p. 1). By contrast, CA treats identity as the moment-by-moment emergence of recognizable social categorizations (both implicit and explicit) which are made relevant in the course of social interaction. For example, identity is made relevant when people "cast" themselves or others as members of a social category, often implicitly, for example, in the way they use recognizable references in descriptions, such as talking about your child, without referring to yourself as a "parent" (see Antaki & Widdicombe, 1998, p. 3). Within CA, identities are not treated as essentialist, or stable across contexts, or determined in advance (i.e., by social constructs, groups, and structures, or through internalized "traits" or "cognitions"). Rather, identity is treated as the particular attribute or aspect of social being that is constructed and made consequential to an interaction (Francis & Hester, 2004). CA shows how reference to activities, such as "taking children to school," can be used to bring about particular attributions of commonly associated membership of a category or social group, such as "parent" (Antaki & Widdicombe, 1998; Benwell & Stokoe, 2006). Various conversational practices make category-bound characteristics relevant in talk (see Benwell & Stokoe, 2006, chapter 2), including using specific category terms (e.g., "daughter"); shifting in the course of a conversation between different operative identities, say, from "grandmother" to "carer" or "I" to "people" (Sacks, 1992, Vol. 2, p. 327; Schegloff, 1988; Speer, 2012); or addressing someone according to affordances of status or knowledge that reflect their relationship to you (e.g., teacher–student). Looking at the ways people do "identity work," that is, how they construct and use identity ascriptions as resources in interaction, allows us to investigate how people formulate identity and orient toward the norms and constraints of culture and circumstance, affording a richer and more active sense of the way aspects of identity and context are mobilized in interaction (Robles, DiDomenico, & Raclaw, 2018; Robles & Parks, 2019; Speer, 2019).

12.3 CA Studies of Identity and Family Identities

CA studies have shown how identities are constructed, reproduced, and challenged in interactions in which issues relating to an identity category are foregrounded, including gender (Speer, 2005; Widdicombe, 1995), ethnicity (Whitehead, 2019; Widdicombe, 2015), and age (Coupland, Coupland, & Giles, 1989; Llewellyn, 2015). They have also shown how identity is made relevant in specific social contexts, such as in youth subgroups (Widdicombe & Wooffitt, 1995), internet chatrooms (Giles, 2016), and in media interaction (Clayman, 2010; Pomerantz, 1989). CA has addressed how particular participant roles are constituted in institutional exchanges (Drew & Heritage, 1992), such as in education (Gardner, 2013), healthcare (Buttny, 1996; Gill & Roberts, 2013), advice (Butler, Danby, & Emmison, 2009; Peräkylä, 2013), in legal settings (Komter, 2013), in sales environments (Stokoe, Sikveland, & Humă, 2017), and in the way people establish their identities online (Giles et al., 2015). Studies have shown how identity is co-constructed in the use of categorization and person reference (i.e., what people call themselves and others) (Enfield & Stivers, 2007; Sacks, 1979), how they answer the phone (Drew, 2002), handle praise (Pillet-Shore, 2015; Speer, 2012), and self-deprecate (Speer, 2019). Identity construction is also observed as an outcome of describing or evaluating activities such as gun ownership (McKinlay & Dunnett, 1998) or the use of social media (Robles et al., 2018).

A significant group of CA identity studies have used Sacks's notion of *membership categorization analysis* (MCA) to account for the way people commonsensically attach particular activities, rights and obligations to particular identities (Schegloff, 2007). Whereas CA's focus spans interactions that bring about a wide range of social actions, from greetings to disagreements, MCA uses insights from CA to understand how people do categorial identity work, including in institutional settings such as media and public organizations (Fitzgerald & Housley, 2015). MCA shares with CA a "micro" focus on turns of talk and their sequencing, and on how speakers make connections between identity categories and actions (Sacks, 1972). The classic example from Sacks's work is the line he told from a story: "The baby cried. The mommy picked it up," in which we automatically hear that "mommy" as the mommy of that baby. This works, Sacks explains, because the "device" of "family" operates as a context in which two categories ("baby" and "mommy") are paired together in a commonsense way. So we hear identity categories as linked to particular activities, and vice versa, together with conventional expectations, which make exceptions noticeable. He pointed out that membership categories are "inference-rich," operating as very potent mechanisms for expectations, justifications, explanations, and other interpersonal social business (Sacks, 1992).

CA studies of parental identities enacted in institutional contexts (e.g., education, health, and mediation settings) show how parental identity is made relevant in the way people talk knowledgeably or responsibly about their children (Adelswärd & Nilholm, 2000; Pillet-Shore, 2015, 2016; Stokoe & Edwards, 2015). Studies of family roles shed light on how reference to actions and activities normatively associated with, for instance, the socialization of children, provides a frame of reference to judge behavior (Butler & Fitzgerald, 2010; Nguyen & Nguyen, 2017), enabling inferences regarding parents' moral character if they fail to achieve the "correct" standard. Membership categorization analysts make the case that all categorial talk is moral in character, as it inevitably judges correctness of fit with category attributes, in terms of how members should behave (Jayyusi, 1984; Sterponi, 2003).

By the same token, CA studies of real family interactions show how family identities are actively invoked in everyday settings such as mealtimes and social occasions, principally through:

- issuing role-oriented directives (e.g., "No, put that down") in family inter-actions (Butler & Fitzgerald, 2010; Butler & Wilkinson, 2013; Craven & Potter, 2010; Goodwin & Cekaite, 2013) and showing who is entitled to direct who to do what (Stevanovic & Peräkylä, 2012; Stevanovic, 2013);

- delivering assessments (e.g., "Wow! Good Laura!"); admonishments (Potter & Hepburn, 2020) and moral alignments (e.g., "Don't you have to take a shower?") (Fasulo, Loyd, & Padiglione, 2007, pp. 16–20); and aligning with children's own assessments (Keel, 2016, chapter 5) as part of doing socialization;
- displays of appropriate knowledge and rights, such as those that norma- tively belong to a grandparent role (such as familiarity with your grand- children's characters) (Kitzinger, 2005; Raymond & Heritage, 2006).

In this chapter, we provide an example from research into the way kinship carers manage their identity in their discussions in peer support group meetings. Kinship care provides a useful example because role- and generation-specific expectations (regarding standard relational pairings of mother–daughter and grandmother–grandchild, with associated role attributes, obligations, and responsibilities) are rendered ambiguous in this family arrangement.

12.4 Kinship Care and the Question of Identity

Kinship care is an arrangement where family members (typically grandparents or siblings) take on full parenting responsibilities because a child's birth parent is unable to look after the child, typically through parental neglect, alcohol or substance misuse, mental ill-health, or domestic violence (Selwyn & Nandy, 2014). When kinship carers "step in" to give a permanent home to a relative's child, they are simultaneously stepping away from off-the-peg traditional family roles and stage-of-life expectations (Backhouse & Graham, 2012). Identity features in kinship care studies principally in terms of the benefits to children of continuing connections with their family of origin (Vis et al., 2016; Winokur, Holtan, & Batchelder, 2018), and is treated cognitively, as a coherent, stable, inner sense of worth and capacity, developed in relationships (Erikson, 1968), and as "flow(ing) from family history and culture" (Wilson & Chipungu, 1996, p. 387).

In studies of kinship carers' own identity issues (Backhouse & Graham, 2012; Hunt, 2018; Nixon, Elliott, & Henderson, 2019), identity appears as a dynamic phenomenon (Burke, 1980; Stryker, 1968), in which individuals are seen as having simultaneous multiple roles (mother, carer, wife, grandparent), in which they struggle to balance the demands of "salience" (what is relevant here) against their "commitments" (their responsibilities and attachments to aspects of themselves) (see Burke & Reitzes, 1981; Burke, 1991). Studies of carers' experiences conclude that role strains, role conflicts (Backhouse & Graham, 2012), and thwarted stage-of-life expectations (LeFebvre & Rasner, 2017) are inherent in kinship care, and invariably recommend changes in social policy and practice to help support carers experiencing these prob- lems (Hunt, 2018). In common with the majority of studies of family identities, kinship care studies decontextualize participants' utterances in order to search for prevalent themes and patterns (Hillman & Anderson, 2019; Sampson & Hertlein, 2015) and the interactive process of identity construction is not shown. By contrast, CA offers a way to investigate how people are constructing, orienting to, and making sense of identity for themselves, without interposing researcher-led categories and codifications.

12.5 CA's "Method" and Unit of Analysis

CA uses sequences of real interaction that have been carefully transcribed as the primary source of data (Mondada, 2013). Not all CA studies focus on the same aspects of interaction. Some focus on the use of lexical terms or discourse markers, e.g., "well" (Heritage, 2015) and "oh" (Heritage, 2018); some on sequential stages such as phone call openings (Schegloff, 1968) or initial greetings (Mondada, 2018); some on actions or activities, such as explanations (Antaki, 1988), compliments (Pillet-Shore, 2015), questions (Hayano, 2013), and flirting (Speer, 2017); and some on broader social projects or contextual frames, for example, "troubles-telling" (Jefferson, 2015) or courtroom interaction (Komter, 2013).

As evidence of the regular organization of interaction, CA's unit of analysis can therefore be a single episode, analyzed as an example of a more general social action, such as a claim to "ownership" of a grandchild (Raymond & Heritage, 2006); or a set of instances derived from a larger data set, on which the case for the significance of the phenomenon is based, such as how answers to polar questions are normally given (Enfield et al., 2019).

Detailed transcription is core to CA, and a set of conventions is commonly used in transcription of video- and audio-recordings which are specifically designed to retain significant features of talk in its temporal sequence, including, for example, speaker overlaps (shown in square [ ] brackets); the location and timing of pauses and gaps (timed -1.0); spoken emphasis (under<u>lined</u>); volume (in CAPitals); elongated words (yes::); in- and out- breaths (-.hh; hhh!), and laughter particles (see Jefferson, 2004; see also transcripts below), all of which help the analyst to track relevant aspects of the delivery of the exchange. Wherever possible, current CA practice requires video-recording as a basis for analyzing co-present interactions (Mondada, 2013, 2016). Video records are important when participants are co-present in order to grasp nonverbal cues such as head nods and gestures (Heath, 2011), which, together with transcripts, form the data set. This data set can then be trawled for regularities and patterns of interaction, identified as the phenomena of interest, for example, how a troubles-telling sequence is typically constructed (Jefferson, 2015). CA research publications also sometimes include photographs or drawings, so that the analytic argument refers directly to evidence representing the original context (Goodwin & Cekaite, 2018; De Stefani & Mondada, 2014).

The validity of CA analysis is typically supported by repeated review of groups of data extracts containing potential examples of the phenomenon proposed and selected by the analyst, examined alongside previous CA research findings (Peräkylä, 2011). One method for establishing validity is the "next turn proof procedure" (Schegloff, Jefferson, & Sacks, 1974, p. 729), by which analysts can show how the recipients of an utterance treated what just happened, and use this as evidence in their analytic claims. The CA literature provides a wide resource bank of findings to draw on, and analysis is often assisted in sessions of teams or groups of trained researchers convened for the purpose of sharing and analyzing data ("data sessions"), supported by international online databases and researcher networks. Findings of CA studies will always include transcripts of data in support of argument for the phenomenon identified (Parry & Land, 2013; Peräkylä, 2011). The presentation of data extracts in the text is important in order that readers can follow, and also debate the analytic argument presented (Sidnell, 2013).

12.6 Identity at Stake in a Kinship Care Support Group: Establishing Identity in Third-Party Complaints

Our illustration of the CA approach demonstrates how kinship carers handle matters of family identity in a support group environment. Data are drawn from ten carer support group meetings that took place at local venues in England in 2016–2017. Extract 1 is part of a group discussion about the typical problems that arise for carers in the context of the cared-for child's school. It shows how, in formulating a very brief complaint, a carer deals with a number of issues relevant to her identity.

Extract 1: Video SF1 03:12

1	Sam:	Your kids have grown up and it's like you've gone
2		back again, you gotta deal with t'parents in
3		playground and stuff,
4	Val:	I know.
5	Sam:	And er you t- you tek your daughter that comes to
6		here, >'Is she the mother.'<. And it's like, 'No, she's
7		the auntie'.

Here Sam, a support group member, is complaining about having to "deal with" the presence of other "parents" at the school gates (line 2), where she has gone with her daughter, also a user of the family center where the support group meets (lines 5–6), to pick up the child Sam now cares for. This short example shows how, in a reported question of only four words: "Is she the mother" (line 6), a significant amount of identity work is transacted.

First, the reported question is *recipient-designed* (Schegloff et al., 1974) in that it shows an orientation to the category membership and circumstances of the people being talked about. The composition of the question possibly refers to three parties: the addressee (Sam); 'the mother' (of the child Sam is there to collect), and 'she' - the person with Sam, who may or may not be 'the mother'. It indicates that a third party was present (who was not addressed), that is, the "daughter that comes to here" (lines 5–6), who is mistaken for "the mother," and so must fit the expected characteristics of that role (young, female) at the school gate. The reported question "Is she the mother" is delivered in a brisk tone, without hedging or any other concession to delicacy or entitlement (see Curl & Drew, 2008), and hence is built as rather peremptory. In the directness of its formulation, we hear how the reported question addresses the recipient (Sam) as someone familiar to the speaker, and, noticeably, as someone who is fully expected to be able to answer it. Sam is apparently known at the school gate, in an authoritative role, but is clearly *not* "the mother" herself. The reported question is also designed to indicate the speaker's lack of acquaintance with *both* of Sam's daughters, "the daughter that comes to here" and, more importantly, with "the mother" (they do not know what she looks like): in the context of the playground, this is socially significant. We noted earlier that categories, particularly parental categories, are associated with normative standards of performance. Nonappearance (and nonrecognition) of a child's mother in activities such as collecting children from school, normatively associated with the "mother" or "parent" membership category, is one such instance.

Sam has already announced in lines 2–3 that this query is an instance of stuff she has "gotta deal with," indicating it is burdensome to her. This is part of her categorially appropriate "territory of feelings, knowledge and ownership" (Raymond & Heritage, 2006, p. 701). She constructs this territory by her use of *person reference*. Even the simplest references to persons perform social business (Enfield, 2013; Lerner & Kitzinger, 2007; Sacks & Schegloff, 1979). Sam has performed significant identity work in her preface to her complaint, by cueing her recipients to co-align with her experience: "*Your* kids have grown up" (line 1); "it's like *you*'ve gone back again" (lines 1–2). Sam's repeated use of the generic hybrid person referent *you* (Lerner & Kitzinger, 2007) in addressing the group in lines 1–5, offers a candidate generic experience for the group in terms of "someone in *(y)(our)* position."

Sam's use of the referent "*your kids*" (line 1) indexes her identity as a mother, but not as any mother: she is a mother of "grown-up" children: an older, child-free mother. She describes her second-time carer role, "you've *gone back again*," and her announcement "you *gotta deal with*" is "trouble-implicative" (Jefferson, 2015, p. 35), alerting the group (line 2) that she has to contend with encounters with the other parents at the school gate "and stuff." Sam's brief three-line preface therefore provides a "knowing" stance from which recipients can view the encounter she is reporting next. Val's response in line 4 ("I know") confirms mutuality (Stivers, 2008), affiliating with Sam's description of issues with the "time-disordered" identity (Hirshorn, 1998) of kinship carers.

The reported question "Is she the mother" contains an additional inference: that Sam may have brought "the mother" of the child along with her to the school gates. This refers to a mother who is not known, but is known *about* (Enfield, 2013, p. 449). To bring a birth parent that has lost parental responsibility of a child to collect that child is an accountable matter. So the reported question is formulated as also indicating that something is known to be amiss in the child's family circumstances. Sam reports her own "dealing with" the question, briskly returning the same form of words (lines 6–7), "No, she's the auntie," attending to the potential for criticism, and declining its potentially negative inference. In this reported correction, Sam is portraying herself as having brought an "innocent" family member to the school gate, rather than "the mother" who has lost responsibility for the child. That this reply is to be heard as a rebuttal is evident from its quick delivery in the reported sequence of turns. Sam has effectively defended her actions: her choice of companion is not reproachable, and so her identity as protective parent is established.

If we were to treat only the propositional content of this account as material for interpretative analysis, as in standard kinship studies, we would be likely to gloss the reported question "Is she the mother?" as evidence of a lack of awareness or ignorance about the family structure. The person referent "she" (line 6) could be seen as, as Schegloff (2007) puts it, "referring *simpliciter*" (p. 436) – simply referring, in this case, to the daughter, standing next to Sam at the school gate. So the analytic theme would be one of public ignorance and confusion about kinship care. It may report that kinship carers find handling queries burdensome, and advocate greater "awareness." This may be a perfectly valid approach. However, it would say nothing about how, in reporting the way they deal with such challenges, kinship carers adopt stances that co-constitute their identities.

But in a CA analysis, taking into account the trouble-premonitor "have to deal with" (Jefferson, 2015) at the start of the complaint sequence (lines 1–3), together with the categorizations in the reported question and answer, and the questioner's "knowing" epistemic stance, we propose a more nuanced reading: the way persons are referenced in the question addressed to Sam demonstrates the questioner's prior knowledge, that the child's mother is not routinely at the gates, and that the recipient of the question is regarded as the accountable adult. The carer's reported response manages the implications of the choice she has made about who she has brought with her, and thus establishes her membership of the "good parent" category, which is the identity issue on which her complaint turns (Wilkes & Speer, 2021a; 2021b).

The reader will see how, from even a brief data extract, CA offers tools for an empirical analysis of the construction and management of identity grounded in participants' own actions. Using the same analytic tools, we will look at a longer stretch of group interaction, again formulated as a complaint, in terms of formulations of fault and displays of indignation, which concerns the transgression(s) of a third party (Drew, 1998). Rita, a carer, is complaining to the support group about her daughter, who is the birth parent of the granddaughter that Rita is caring for. Her daughter, according to Rita, has just announced that she wants the child back:

Extract 2: SA2 0:18:50

1	Rita:	My daughter wants:: the granddaughter back now, she
2		even wants ter move house .hh so she's like near
3		back to where we live hh (1.0) so she can see her
4		more, an (.) y'know (1.0) take her to school an all
5		the rest of it, cos I do all the school runs an all
6		o' that hh erm, (1.0) but when she was livin' with
7		my- my daughter, hh she wasn't takin' her to school.
8		(2.0)
9	Pat:	Hmm.
10	Sal:	Mm. ((nods))
11	Rita:	Sh - she y'know she was lettin' her stop up till
12		one o'clock two o'clock in the mornin' watchin' all
13		these horror movies, which are still havin' (.) an
14		impact on her now.
15		(1.2)
16	Rita:	Y'know, havin' er nightmares and things, and hh
17		bein' scared of the dark and all of this because of
18		these horrible movies hh. she was allowed to watch,
19		(1.2) when she was smaller (1.0) a-and hh not
20		getting (.) up hh in the mornin (1.0) and not going
21		to school, hh or going to school very late, (.) an
22		things like that y'know.
23		(1.0)
24	Rita:	So I've had to (.) try try an turn- turn that round
25		(1.0) to a bedtime routine and (.) hh regular
26		school, (2.0) an' things like that, hh but (.)
27		she's insistin' she wants ter (.) hh move house
28		(1.0) thh tk an' be sorta (.) living nearer (.) to
29		where we are.
30		(3.0)
31	Jan:	So she can come an' as- [as
32	Rita:	[So she can see (1.0) th
33		granddaughter more an' (.) do (.) a little bit more
34		on the school runs an' things.
35		(2.0)
36	Rita:	Is this a good idea (.) or not. [hhh
37	Pat:	[I would hate my
38		son to live near me. HHHH. ((laughs))

39	Rita:	I know my granddaughter said she <u>does</u> <u>miss</u> her a-
40		a- mam.
41		(1.0)
42	Rita:	Y'know. hh
43		(.)
44	Rita:	She <u>misses</u> her (.) very <u>much</u> and emmm (3.0) tkk
45		you're sorta stuck between the devil an the deep
46		blue sea.
47		(.)
48	Rita:	I- it's (1.0) [what's-
49	Jill:	[What's [ap-
50	Rita:	[What's best [for the child
51	Lin:	[It's where do
52		you start something, it's where it's hard to go
53		back.
54	Jill:	It's emotional <u>black</u>- it's emotional <u>blackmail</u>.
55	Rita:	It is.
56		(1.0)
57	Rita:	I know it is yes:: it's emotional blackmail.
58	Jill:	She can't behave like an adult an look after
59		herself.
60	Rita:	Yeah but can I stop my daughter (2.0) moving house.
61		(2.0)
62	Jill:	Probably not, but who's to say that's [that's er
63	Rita:	[If that's
64		her- if that's her <u>wishes</u>.
65	Jill:	But she could do that she could do it for a few
66		weeks just to prove hersel' then and go back to the
67		way she was before an then start askin' for
68		overnights and stuff an' then- (1.0)
69	Rita:	Yeah.
70	Jill:	End up <u>not</u> takin' her to school an' then- so you're
71		the one <u>that's</u> em-
72	Rita:	Exactly so this is what the problem was in the very
73		beginning, plus her behavior.

Rita's use of "my," "the," and "we" in lines 1–3 in her preface to her complaint set out the generational identities of the family members involved, in terms of *who they are* to each other. "*My* daughter" is wanting "*the* granddaughter" back, and is proposing, for starters, to move nearer to where "*we*" (Rita, her partner, and the child) live. These referents set out the geography of relationships. Note how the choice of definite article for "*the* granddaughter" (rather than naming her, or calling her "my granddaughter") places the child in a neutral position, somewhere between "my daughter" and "us." The significance of her daughter's recent proposals to change the family's current positioning is developed further in the sequence.

As in our first example, expectations of standards of performance of parental attributes regarding school are evident. Rita pitches a description of her own remedial efforts, "I do all the school runs an all o' that hhh" (lines 5–6) against a description of her daughter's activities (lines 7–13): "she wasn't takin' her to school" and "she was lettin' her stop up till one o'clock two o'clock in the mornin' watchin' all these horror movies," clearly built as neglectful, with damaging results for the child in terms of lost schooling and nightmares (lines 16–21). Taking a child to school and observance of proper bedtimes and of suitable viewing material are normatively attributed to the "good parent" category, and, as in all category attribution, become accountable if not done, or not done to the right standard (Jayyusi, 1984). These activities, provided as a backdrop against which recipients can evaluate her daughter's expressed wishes, are described as impacting not only in the past, but continuing into the present (lines 13–14): "still havin' (.) an impact on her now." Rita claims she has established proper bedtime routines and regular school (lines 24–26), thereby attributing a positive parental identity to herself, in contrast to that of her daughter.

A support group participant, Jan, seeks to confirm the daughter's reasons for the proposed house move (line 31). Rita's answer, "so she can see the granddaughter more" and "do a little bit more on the school runs" (lines 32–34), is hearable as a careful, faithful representation of what the birth mother is saying to her (as opposed to Rita's own gloss that launched her complaint at line 1: that she "wants:: the granddaughter back now"). Then, after a gap during which no-one responds (line 35), Rita throws a question out to the group: "Is this a good idea. (.) Or not" (line 36). We can observe in Rita's question an important aspect of the management of identity in terms of how a speaker's motives may be assessed and attributed: that is, the way in which self-interest is managed in interaction (Edwards & Potter, 2005). Motives or intentions are "built inferentially out of descriptions of actions and events ... and they attend reflexively to the speaker's stake or investment in producing those descriptions" (Edwards & Potter, 2005, p. 246). Because someone's expression of their own wishes can undermine the validity of the case they are presenting, speakers find various ways of downplaying their personal stance or interest (Edwards & Potter, 1992). Rita's question is built to appear unbiased in its dilemmatic formulation.

Pat's answer (lines 37–38) orients to the "territory of feelings" (Raymond & Heritage, 2006, p. 701) associated with kinship carer identities, by offering a position statement (often issued in situations of controversy; see Billig, 2001, p. 214) as a candidate reaction: "I would hate my son to live near me." Rita nevertheless pursues her display of even-handedness, balancing her report of the granddaughter's missing her mother "very much" (line 44) with the formal consideration in line 50 "what's best for the child" (i.e., an "official" judgment). She frames the situation as a quandary "stuck between the devil and the deep blue sea" (lines 45–46): this is moral identity work (Danby &

Emmison, 2014; Sterponi, 2003) in which Rita displays the selflessness required of the carer role, holding her daughter accountable for falling short of the right parental standards, while balancing this risk against the child's wishes. The complaint began with a highly resonant description of the mother's actions as neglectful, to which the group refers back as they advise caution, denouncing the mother's actions as "emotional blackmail" (line 54), with which Rita readily agrees (line 57) once she has safely countered the risk of appearing self-interested or unreasonable. As in Extract 1 above, Rita has effectively dealt with any potentially negative inferences about her judgment, and thus validated her identity as "good parent" (Wilkes & Speer, 2021a).

Again, if the propositional content of this exchange were taken out of context and scanned for evidence of identity issues for kinship carers, it would possibly be interpreted in terms of an individual cognitive phenomenon, such as a moral dilemma (Kohlberg, 1981), and coded, as happens in kinship studies, as an example of "role strain" (Denby, 2012; Denby et al., 2015; Young & Kahana, 1989): Rita's utterances could be viewed as an example of a grandparent having difficulty balancing her role as mother (to her daughter) and carer (to her granddaughter). Rita's two-sided description and the posing of her question could be viewed as a manifestation of an internal conflict, standing in need of resolution, or help, and there may be a recommendation that family mediation services should be made more available. There may even be questions raised about Rita's capacity to put the interests of the child first, because of her conflicted parental loyalties. By treating Rita's utterances as pieces of information about her internal state that can be mapped onto ready-classified cognitive phenomena, researchers would fail to notice the important interactional business going on in her account. CA, however, provides an alternative, more active reading grounded in Rita's actions in their sequential context. Her powerful assessment of her daughter's behavior as unparental, coupled with careful management of her own "stake" in her account, attending to what is expected of kinship carers, can be understood as performing strategic parental identity work, delivering the affirmation of judgment she seeks, and strengthening the group's mutual positioning as co-producers of knowing, resilient, kinship carer identities.

12.7 Discussion

We have shown how CA offers an investigative approach to identity studies based on ethnomethodological principles, focuses on the mundane and the everyday, and places the active management of identity by participants *on their own terms* at the heart of the investigation (Raymond, 2019). An examination of how kinship carers construct and manage their identities has both local interactional, and potentially wider, social implications. CA provides a means for identifying matters at stake in identity construction across a wide variety of contexts, including casual talk, family life, service encounters, and educational, professional, and institutional settings. By studying identity as an aspect of social life at the level of talk-in-interaction, members can be seen making (and managing) their own connections with identity categories and associated characteristics (Fitzgerald & Housley, 2015). We have also demonstrated the use of socially shared and recognizable pairings and groupings of identities or "devices" (Sacks, 1992), in terms of aspects of the "family" device and its associated norms; and how the role demands of an institutional frame on parents (i.e., school) are reproduced in talk. How participants make these connections relevant is, with the right analytic tools and observational stance, made clearly visible at the surface of the talk, in a way that both orients to a general category, such as parent, but in a way that serves the interactional business of each specific encounter.

Conversation analysts necessarily share participants' basic interpretative cultural resources in order to observe how participants are making identity relevant (Hutchby & Wooffitt, 2008). However, analysts are not using their observations to explain how recognizable "attitudes" or "behaviors" arise per se (Potter & Edwards, 2012). The goal of analysis is to show how identity is constructed in the interactional functions and consequences of such constructions (Wooffitt, 1990). Observations about how identities are "worked up" by speakers serve to illuminate the kinds of social obligations, rights, and responsibilities that are being associated with them (Benwell & Stokoe, 2016; Humǎ, 2015; Speer, 2012). CA's microlevel analysis supports its primary interest in social action, rather than either the linguistic components of talk or whatever social representations might be reflected in it (Atkinson & Heritage, 1984). A line-by-line engagement with data is the beginning, not the end-point of analysis. In making the organization of talk visible, CA findings frequently challenge common assumptions about how language works – for example, that it simply transmits, rather than constructs, information about identity (Stokoe, 2018).

CA reveals a level of social organization that is overlooked in studies that rely on structural or cognitive identity theory to explain participants' behavior (Hogg, 2018; Williams, 2000), or approaches in which utterances are viewed as fragments of wider "discourses" or as positionings in social "narratives" concerning identity (Andreouli, 2010; McGhee, Moreh, & Vlachantoni, 2019). Participants in CA studies are not viewed as "cultural dupes" (Garfinkel, 1967) of either macro- or micro- level structures or patterns, including of identity categories themselves: instead, participants are shown to be creative language users, capable of subverting rules and patterns (Edwards, 1997, p. 96) and of making trouble for normative category assumptions, for example by actively reshaping what membership of an age or sexuality category entails (King, 2016).

The CA approach to participants' constructions of, and orientations toward, identity, has been criticized for inattention to the ubiquity of broader structural phenomena such as gender or race, and for ignoring the operation of power, culture, and identity politics (Hollway, 1989; Speer & Stokoe, 2011, Stokoe, Hepburn, & Antaki, 2012; Weatherall, 2000; Wetherell, 1998). CA's approach to identity does present a challenge to studies that treat the casting of identities in descriptions of self and others as a reflection either of internal cognitive states or of deterministic social forces, where the relations between broader "macro"-level structures and people's identities are treated as given (Hogg, 2018; Oakes, Haslam, & Turner, 1994). However, it is not the case that CA ignores "relations of power" (Fairclough, 1995, p. 23); rather, CA neither *assumes nor denies* these relations, but instead raises issues concerning "the nature of claims that can legitimately be made" without detailed analysis of interaction (Hutchby & Wooffitt, 2008, p. 217). CA studies show how language practices can re-establish social associations between particular identities and norms (such as the way a discussion about whether or not "Barbies are for girls" is organized; see Raymond, 2019). Studies of the robust nature of reasoning and explaining practices about identities may offer useful insights into ways in which "macro" social phenomena operate, and what alternative ways of organizing talk might have to offer (Heritage, 1988; Raymond, 2019; Speer, 2005).

Current trends and future directions for the investigation of identity include "applied" CA, particularly in health settings where we can learn much about the "real-world" impact of communication practices on roles and relationships (Antaki, 2011, Sametband & Strong, 2018; Stokoe, 2018; Tseliou, 2018). There is growing interest in how the unique affordances of online mediated social interaction feature in the construction and negotiation of identity (Hutchby, 2013; Lamerichs & Stommel, 2018; Meredith & Richardson, 2019). In sum, the analytical tools developed within CA offer the means to discover novel insights into the many ways participants deal with questions of identity as they confront the increasing complexity of contemporary life and the challenges this poses. Insights from CA are preeminently based in participants' own orientations, unclouded by predefined agendas, and arguably allow us to "see" and get closer to what identity means in practice.

References

Adelswärd, V. & Nilholm, C. (2000). Who is Cindy? Aspects of identity work in a teacher–parent-pupil talk at a special school. *Text – Interdisciplinary Journal for the Study of Discourse, 20*(4), 545–568.

Andreouli, E. (2010). Identity, positioning and self–other relations. *Papers on Social Representations, 19*(1), 14.1–14.13.

Antaki, C. (1988). *Analysing Everyday Explanation: A Casebook of Methods.* London: Sage.

Antaki, C. (Ed.). (2011). *Applied Conversation Analysis: Intervention and Change in Institutional Talk*. London: Springer.

Antaki, C. & Widdicombe, S. (Eds.). (1998). *Identities in Talk*. London: Sage.

Atkinson, J. M. & Heritage, J. (Eds.). (1984). *Structures of Social Action*. Cambridge: Cambridge University Press.

Atkinson, P. (1988). Ethnomethodology: A critical review. *Annual Review of Sociology*, *14*(1), 441–465.

Backhouse, J. & Graham, A. (2012). Grandparents raising grandchildren: Negotiating the complexities of role identity conflict. *Child & Family Social Work*, *17*(3), 306–315.

Benwell, B. & Stokoe, E. (2006). *Discourse and Identity*. Edinburgh: Edinburgh University Press.

Benwell, B. & Stokoe, E. (2016). Ethnomethodological and conversation analytic approaches to identity. In S. Preece (Ed.), *The Routledge Handbook of Language and Identity* (pp. 92–108). London: Routledge.

Billig, M. (2001). Discursive, rhetorical and ideological messages. In M. Wetherell, S. Taylor, & S. J. Yates (Eds.), *Discourse Theory and Practice: A Reader* (pp. 201–221). London: Open University.

Burke, P. J. (1980). The self: Measurement requirements from an interactive perspective. *Social Psychology Quarterly*, *43*, 18–29.

Burke, P. J. (1991). Identity processes and social stress. *American Psychological Review*, *56*, 836–849.

Burke, P. J. & Reitzes, D. C. (1981). The link between identity and role performance. *Social Psychology Quarterly*, *44*(2), 83–92.

Butler, C. W., Danby, S., Emmison, M., & Thorpe, K. (2009). Managing medical advice seeking in calls to Child Health Line. *Sociology of Health & Illness*, *31*(6), 817–834.

Butler, C. W. & Fitzgerald, R. (2010). Membership-in-action: Operative identities in a family meal. *Journal of Pragmatics*, *42*(9), 2462–2474.

Butler, C. W. & Wilkinson, R. (2013). Mobilising recipiency: Child participation and 'rights to speak' in multi-party family interaction. *Journal of Pragmatics*, *50*(1), 37–51.

Buttny, R. (1996). Clients' and therapist's joint construction of the clients' problems. *Research on Language and Social Interaction*, *29*(2), 125–153.

Clayman, S. E. (2010). Address terms in the service of other actions: The case of news interview talk. *Discourse & Communication*, *4*(2), 161–183.

Coupland, N., Coupland, J., & Giles, H. (1989). Telling age in later life: Identity and face implications. *Text – Interdisciplinary Journal for the Study of Discourse*, *9*(2), 129–152.

Craven, A. & Potter, J. (2010). Directives: Entitlement and contingency in action. *Discourse Studies*, *12*(4), 419–442.

Curl, T. S. & Drew, P. (2008). Contingency and action: A comparison of two forms of requesting. *Research on Language and Social Interaction*, *41*(2), 129–153.

Danby, S. J. & Emmison, M. (2014). Kids, counselors and troubles-telling: Morality-in-action in talk on an Australian children's helpline. *Journal of Applied Linguistics and Professional Practice*, *9*(2), 263–285.

De Stefani, E. & Mondada, L. (2014). Reorganizing mobile formations: When "guided" participants initiate reorientations in guided tours. *Space and Culture*, *17*(2), 157–175.

Denby, R. W. (2012). Parental incarceration and kinship care: Caregiver experiences, child well-being, and permanency intentions. *Social Work in Public Health*, *27*(1–2), 104–128.

Denby, R. W., Brinson, J. A., Cross, C. L., & Bowmer, A. (2015). Culture and coping: Kinship caregivers' experiences with stress and strain and the relationship to child well-being. *Child and Adolescent Social Work Journal*, *32*(5), 465–479.

Drew, P. (1998). Complaints about transgressions and misconduct. *Research on Language & Social Interaction*, *31*(3–4), 295–325.

Drew, P. (2002). Out of context: An intersection between domestic life and the workplace, as contexts for (business) talk. *Language & Communication*, *22*(4), 477–494.

Drew, P. & Heritage, J. (1992). *Talk at Work: Interaction in Institutional Settings*. Cambridge: Cambridge University Press.

Edwards, D. (1997). *Discourse and Cognition*. London: Sage.

Edwards, D. & Potter, J. (1992). *Discursive Psychology, Vol. 8*. London: Sage.

Edwards, D. & Potter, J. (2005). Discursive psychology, mental states and descriptions. In H. Te Molder & J. Potter (Eds.), *Conversation and Cognition* (pp. 241–259). Cambridge: Cambridge University Press.

Enfield, N. J. (2013). Reference in conversation. In J. Sidnell, & T. Stivers (Eds.), *The Handbook of Conversation Analysis* (pp. 433–454). Malden, MA: Wiley-Blackwell.

Enfield, N. J. & Stivers, T. (Eds.). (2007). *Person Reference in Interaction: Linguistic, Cultural and Social Perspectives, Vol. 7*. Cambridge: Cambridge University Press.

Enfield, N. J., Stivers, T., Brown, P., Englert, C., Harjunpää, K., Hayashi, M., & Raymond, C. W. (2019). Polar answers. *Journal of Linguistics*, *55*(2), 277–304.

Erikson, E. H. (1968). *Identity: Youth and Crisis*. New York, NY: Norton.

Fairclough, N. (1995). *Critical Discourse Analysis*. London: Longman.

Fasulo, A., Loyd, H., & Padiglione, V. (2007). Children's socialization into cleaning practices: A cross-cultural perspective. *Discourse & Society*, *18*(1), 11–33.

Fitzgerald, R. & Housley, W. (Eds.). (2015). *Advances in Membership Categorisation Analysis*. London: Sage.

Francis, D. & Hester, S. (2004). *An Invitation to Ethnomethodology: Language, Society and Interaction*. London: Sage.

Gardner, R. (2013). Conversation analysis in the classroom. In J. Sidnell & T. Stivers (Eds.), *The Handbook of Conversation Analysis* (pp. 433–454). Malden, MA: Wiley-Blackwell.

Garfinkel, E. (1967). *Studies in Ethnomethodology*, Englewood Cliffs, NJ: Prentice Hall.

Giddens, A. (1993). *Sociology, 2nd Ed*. London: Polity Press.

Giles, D. (2016). Observing real-world groups in the virtual field: The analysis of online discussion. *British Journal of Social Psychology*, *55*(3), 484–498.

Giles, D., Stommel, W., Paulus, T., Lester, J., & Reed, D. (2015). Microanalysis of online data: The methodological development of "digital CA." *Discourse, Context & Media*, *7*, 45–51.

Gill, V. T. & Roberts, F. (2013). Conversation analysis in medicine. In J. Sidnell & T. Stivers (Eds.), *The Handbook of Conversation Analysis* (pp. 433–454). Malden, MA: Wiley-Blackwell.

Goodwin, M. H. & Cekaite, A. (2013). Calibration in directive/response sequences in family interaction. *Journal of Pragmatics, 46*(1), 122–138.

Goodwin, M. H. & Cekaite, A. (2018). *Embodied Family Choreography: Practices of Control, Care, and Mundane Creativity*. London: Routledge.

Hayano, K. (2013). Question design in conversation. In J. Sidnell & T. Stivers (Eds.), *The Handbook of Conversation Analysis* (pp. 395–414). Malden, MA: Wiley-Blackwell.

Heath, C. (2011). Embodied action: Video and the analysis of social interaction. In D. Silverman (Ed.), *Qualitative Research* (pp. 266–282). London: Sage.

Heritage, J. (1984). *Garfinkel and Ethnomethodology*. Cambridge: Polity Press.

Heritage, J. (1987). Ethnomethodology. In A. Giddens (Ed.), *Social Theory Today* (pp. 224–272). Stanford, CA: Stanford University Press.

Heritage, J. (1988). Explanations as accounts: A conversation analytic perspective. In C. Antaki (Ed.), *Understanding Everyday Explanation: A Casebook of Methods* (pp. 127–144). Beverly Hills, CA: Sage.

Heritage, J. (2001). Goffman, Garfinkel and conversation analysis. In M. Wetherell, S. Taylor & S. J. Yates (Eds.), *Discourse Theory and Practice: A Reader* (pp. 47–56). London: Sage.

Heritage, J. (2015). Well-prefaced turns in English conversation: A conversation analytic perspective. *Journal of Pragmatics, 88*, 88–104.

Heritage, J. (2018). Turn-initial particles in English: The cases of oh and well. In J. Heritage & M. L. Sorjonen (Eds.), *Between Turn and Sequence: Turn-Initial Particles across Languages* (pp. 155–192). Amsterdam: John Benjamins.

Hillman, J. L. & Anderson, C. M. (2019). It's a battle and a blessing: The experience and needs of custodial grandparents of children with autism spectrum disorder. *Journal of Autism and Developmental Disorders, 49*(1), 260–269.

Hirshorn, B. A. (1998). Grandparents as caregivers. In T. Sinovac (Ed.), *Handbook on Grandparenthood* (pp. 200–214). Westport, CT: Greenwood Press.

Hollway, W. (1989). *Subjectivity and Method in Psychology: Gender, Meaning and Science*. London: Sage.

Hogg, M. A. (2018). *Social Identity Theory*. Stanford, CA: Stanford University Press.

Humă, B. (2015). Enhancing the authenticity of assessments through grounding in first impressions. *British Journal of Social Psychology, 54*(3), 405–424.

Hunt, J. (2018). Grandparents as substitute parents in the UK. *Contemporary Social Science, 13*(2), 175–186.

Hutchby, I. (2013). *Conversation and Technology: From the Telephone to the Internet*. London: John Wiley.

Hutchby, I. & Wooffitt, R. (2008). *Conversation Analysis: Principles, Practices and Applications, 2nd Ed*. Cambridge: Polity Press.

Jayyusi, L. (1984). *Categorization and the Moral Order*. Boston, MA: Routledge & Kegan Paul.

Jefferson, G. (2004). Glossary of transcript symbols with an introduction. *Pragmatics and Beyond New Series, 125*, 13–34.

Jefferson, G. (2015). *Talking about Troubles in Conversation*. New York, NY: Oxford University Press.

Keel, S. (2016). *Socialization: Parent–Child Interaction in Everyday Life*. London: Routledge.

King, A. (2016). Queer categories: Queer (y) ing the identification 'older lesbian, gay and/or bisexual (LGB) adults' and its implications for organizational research, policy and practice. *Gender, Work & Organization, 23*(1), 7–18.

Kitzinger, C. (2005). Heteronormativity in action: Reproducing the heterosexual nuclear family in after-hours medical calls. *Social Problems, 52*(4), 477–498.

Kohlberg, L. (1981). *Essays on Moral Development: The Psychology of Moral Development, Vol. 2*. San Francisco, CA: Harper & Row.

Komter, M. (2013). Conversation analysis in the courtroom. In J. Sidnell & T. Stivers (Eds.), *The Handbook of Conversation Analysis* (pp. 612–629). Malden, MA: Wiley-Blackwell.

Lamerichs, J. & Stommel, W. (2018). Online talk about mental health. In J. F. Nussbaum (Ed.), *Oxford Research Encyclopedia of Communication*, doi:10.1093/acrefore/9780190228613.013.273.

LeFebvre, L. E. & Rasner, R. D. (2017). Adaptations to traditional familial roles: Examining the challenges of grandmothers' counterlife transitions. *Journal of Intergenerational Relationships, 15*(2), 104–124.

Lerner, G. H. & Kitzinger, C. (2007). Extraction and aggregation in the repair of individual and collective self-reference. *Discourse Studies, 9*(4), 526–557.

Llewellyn, N. (2015). "He probably thought we were students": Age norms and the exercise of visual judgement in service work. *Organization Studies, 36*(2), 153–173.

Lynch, M. (1997). *Scientific Practice and Ordinary Action: Ethnomethodology and Social Studies of Science*. Cambridge: Cambridge University Press.

Maynard, D. (2013). Everyone and no one to turn to: Intellectual roots and contexts for conversation analysis. In J. Sidnell & T. Stivers (Eds.), *The Handbook of Conversation Analysis* (pp. 11–31). Malden, MA: Wiley-Blackwell.

Maynard, D. & Clayman, S. (2003). Ethnomethodology and conversation analysis. In C. Albas, P. Adler, D. Albas, D. Altheide, & E. Clarke (Eds.), *Handbook of Symbolic Interactionism* (pp. 173–202). Lanham, MD: Rowman.

McGhee, D., Moreh, C., & Vlachantoni, A. (2019). Stakeholder identities in Britain's neoliberal ethical community: Polish narratives of earned citizenship in the context of the UK's EU referendum. *British Journal of Sociology, 70*(4), 1104–1127.

McKinlay, A. & Dunnett, A. (1998). How gun-owners accomplish being deadly average. In C. Antaki & S. Widdicombe (Eds.), *Identities in Talk* (pp. 34–51). London: Sage.

Meredith, J. & Richardson, E. (2019). The use of the political categories of Brexiter and Remainer in online comments about the EU referendum. *Journal of Community and Applied Social Psychology, 29*, 43–55.

Mondada, L. (2013). The conversation analytic approach to data collection. In J. Sidnell & T. Stivers (Eds.), *The Handbook of Conversation Analysis* (pp. 32–56). Malden, MA: Wiley-Blackwell.

Mondada, L. (2016). Challenges of multimodality: Language and the body in social interaction. *Journal of Sociolinguistics*, *20*(3), 336–366.

Mondada, L. (2018). Greetings as a device to find out and establish the language of service encounters in multilingual settings. *Journal of Pragmatics*, *126*, 10–28.

Nixon, C., Elliott, L., & Henderson, M. (2019). Providing sex and relationships education for looked-after children: A qualitative exploration of how personal and institutional factors promote or limit the experience of role ambiguity, conflict and overload among caregivers. *British Medical Journal Open*, *9*(4), e025075.

Nguyen, H. T. & Nguyen, M. T. T. (2017). "Am I a good boy?": Explicit membership categorization in parent–child interaction. *Journal of Pragmatics*, *121*, 25–39.

Oakes, P. J., Haslam, S. A., & Turner, J. C. (1994). *Stereotyping and Social Reality*. London: Blackwell.

Parry, R. H. & Land, V. (2013). Systematically reviewing and synthesizing evidence from conversation analytic and related discursive research to inform healthcare communication practice and policy: An illustrated guide. *BMC Medical Research Methodology*, *13*(1), 69–82.

Parsons, T. (1937). *The Structure of Social Action*. New York, NY: McGraw-Hill.

Peräkylä, A. (2011). Validity in research on naturally occurring social interaction. In: D. Silverman (Ed.), *Qualitative Research, 3rd Ed.* (pp. 264–382). London: Sage.

Peräkylä, A. (2013). CA in psychotherapy. In J. Sidnell & T. Stivers (Eds.), *The Handbook of Conversation Analysis* (pp. 551–574). Malden, MA: Wiley-Blackwell.

Pillet-Shore, D. (2015). Being a "good parent" in parent–teacher conferences. *Journal of Communication*, *65*(2), 373–395.

Pillet-Shore, D. (2016). Criticizing another's child: How teachers evaluate students during parent–teacher conferences. *Language in Society*, *45*(1), 33–58.

Pomerantz, A. (1989). Introduction to the section (The Dan Rather/George Bush episode on CBS News). *Research on Language and Social Interaction*, *22*(1), 213–326.

Pomerantz, A. & Fehr, B. J. (2011). Conversation analysis: An approach to the analysis of social interaction. In T. A. Van Dijk (Ed.), *Discourse Studies: A Multidisciplinary Introduction* (pp. 165–190). London: Sage.

Potter, J. & Edwards, D. (2012). Conversation analysis and psychology. In *The Handbook of Conversation Analysis* (pp. 701–725). London: John Wiley.

Potter, J. & Hepburn, A. (2020). Shaming interrogatives: Admonishments, the social psychology of emotion, and discursive practices of behaviour modification in family mealtimes. *British Journal of Social Psychology*, *59*(2), 347–364.

Raymond, C. W. (2019). Category accounts: Identity and normativity in sequences of action. *Language in Society*, *48*(4), 585–606.

Raymond, G. & Heritage, J. (2006). The epistemics of social relations: Owning grandchildren. *Language in Society*, *35*(5), 677–705.

Robles, J. S., DiDomenico, S., & Raclaw, J. (2018). Doing being an ordinary technology and social media user. *Language & Communication*, *60*, 150–167.

Robles, J. S. & Parks, E. S. (2019). Complaints about technology as a resource for identity-work. *Language in Society*, *48*(2), 209–231.

Sacks, H. (1972). On the analysability of stories by children. In D. Hymes & J. J. Gumperz (Eds.), *Directions in Sociolinguistics: The Ethnography of Communication* (pp. 35–39). New York, NY: Holt, Rinehart and Winston.

Sacks, H. (1979). Hotrodder: A revolutionary category. In G. Psathas (Ed.), *Everyday Language: Studies in Ethnomethodology* (pp. 7–12). New York, NY: Irvington Publishers.

Sacks, H. (1984). Notes on methodology. In J. M. Atkinson & J. Heritage (Eds.), *Structures of Social Action: Studies in Conversation Analysis* (pp. 21–27). Cambridge: Cambridge University Press.

Sacks, H. (1992). *Lectures on Conversation*, 2 vols. (Fall 1964–Spring 1972). Oxford: Blackwell.

Sacks, H. & Schegloff, E. A. (1979). Two preferences in the organization of reference to persons in conversation and their interaction. In G. Psathas (Ed.), *Everyday Language: Studies in Ethnomethodology* (pp. 15–21). New York, NY: Irvington Publishers.

Sametband, I. & Strong, T. (2018). Immigrant family members negotiating preferred cultural identities in family therapy conversations: A discursive analysis. *Journal of Family Therapy*, *40*(2), 201–223.

Sampson, D. & Hertlein, K. (2015). The experience of grandparents raising grandchildren. *Grandfamilies: The Contemporary Journal of Research, Practice and Policy*, *2*(1), article 4.

Schegloff, E. A. (1968). Sequencing in conversational openings. *American Anthropologist*, *70*(6), 1075–1095.

Schegloff, E. A. (1988). From interview to confrontation: Observations of the Bush/Rather encounter. *Research on Language and Social Interaction*, *22*(89), 215–240.

Schegloff, E. A. (1992). Introduction. In G. Jefferson (Ed.), *Harvey Sacks, Lectures on Conversation (Fall 1964–Spring 1968), Vol. 1* (pp. ix–xii). Oxford: Blackwell.

Schegloff, E. A. (1996). Some practices for referring to persons in talk-in-interaction: A partial sketch of a systematics. In B. Fox (Ed.), *Studies in Anaphora* (pp. 437–485). Amsterdam: John Benjamins.

Schegloff, E. A. (2007). A tutorial on membership categorization. *Journal of Pragmatics*, *39*, 462–482.

Schegloff, E. A., Jefferson, G., & Sacks, H. (1974). A simplest systematics for the organization of turn-taking for conversation. *Language*, *50*(4), 696–735.

Schegloff, E. A. & Sacks, H. (1973). Opening up closings. *Semiotica*, *8*(4), 289–327.

Selwyn, J. & Nandy, S. (2014). Kinship care in the UK: Using census data to estimate the extent of formal and informal care by relatives. *Child & Family Social Work*, *19*(1), 44–54.

Sidnell, J. (2013). Basic conversation analytic methods. In J. Sidnell & T. Stivers (Eds.), *The Handbook of Conversation Analysis* (pp. 77–99). Chichester: Wiley-Blackwell.

Sidnell, J. & Stivers, T. (2013). Introduction. In J. Sidnell & T. Stivers (Eds.), *The Handbook of Conversation Analysis* (pp. 1–8). Chichester: Wiley-Blackwell.

Silverman, D. (1998). *Harvey Sacks: Social Science and Conversation Analysis*. Cambridge: Polity Press.

Speer, S. A. (2005). *Gender Talk: Feminism, Discourse and Conversation Analysis*. London: Routledge.

Speer, S. A. (2012). The interactional organization of self-praise: Epistemics, prefer- ence organization, and implications for identity research. *Social Psychology Quarterly*, *75*(1), 52–79.

Speer, S. A. (2017). Flirting: A designedly ambiguous action? *Research on Language and Social Interaction*, *50*(2), 128–150.

Speer, S. A. (2019). Reconsidering self-deprecation as a communication practice. *British Journal of Social Psychology*, *58*(4), 806–828.

Speer, S. A. & Stokoe, E. (Eds.). (2011). *Conversation and Gender*. Cambridge: Cambridge University Press.

Sterponi, L. A. (2003). Account episodes in family discourse: The making of morality in everyday interaction. *Discourse Studies*, *5*(1), 79–100.

Stevanovic, M. (2013). Deontic rights in interaction: A conversation analytic study on authority and cooperation. Doctoral thesis, University of Helsinki.

Stevanovic, M. & Peräkylä, A. (2012). Deontic authority in interaction: The right to announce, propose, and decide. *Research on Language and Social Interaction*, *45*, 297–321.

Stivers, T. (2008). Stance, alignment, and affiliation during storytelling: When nodding is a token of affiliation. *Research on Language and Social Interaction*, *41*, 31–57.

Stokoe, E. (2018). *Talk: The Science of Conversation*. London: Robinson.

Stokoe, E. & Edwards, D. (2015). Mundane morality: Gender, categories and com- plaints in familial neighbour disputes. *Journal of Applied Linguistics and Professional Practice*, *9*(2), 165–192.

Stokoe, E., Hepburn, A., & Antaki, C. (2012). Beware the "Loughborough school" of social psychology? Interaction and the politics of intervention. *British Journal of Social Psychology*, *51*(3), 486–496.

Stokoe, E., Sikveland, R. O., & Humă, B. (2017). Entering the customer's domestic domain: Categorial systematics and the identification of "parties to a sale." *Journal of Pragmatics*, *118*, 64–80.

Stryker, S. (1968). Identity salience and role performance. *Journal of Marriage and the Family*, *30*, 558–564.

ten Have, P. (2004). *Understanding Qualitative Research and Ethnomethodology*. London: Sage.

Tracy, K. (2002). *Everyday Talk: Building and Reflecting Identities*. New York, NY: Guilford Press.

Tseliou, E. (2018). Conversation analysis, discourse analysis and psychotherapy research: Overview and methodological potential. In O. Smoliak & T. Strong (Eds.), *Therapy as Discourse: Practice and Research* (pp. 163–186). Cham: Palgrave Macmillan.

Vis, S. A., Handegård, B. H., Holtan, A., Fossum, S., & Thørnblad, R. (2016). Social functioning and mental health among children who have been living in kinship and non-kinship foster care: Results from an 8-year follow-up with a Norwegian sample. *Child & Family Social Work*, *21*(4), 557–567.

Weatherall, A. (2000). Gender relevance in talk-in-interaction and discourse. *Discourse & Society*, *11*(2), 286–288.

Wetherell, M. (1998). Positioning and interpretative repertoires: Conversation analysis and post-structuralism in dialogue. *Discourse & Society*, *9*(3), 387–412.

Whitehead, K. A. (2019). Using ethnomethodology and conversation analysis to study social categories: The case of racial categories in South African radio talk. In S. Laher, A. Fynn, & S. Kramer (Eds.), *Transforming Research Methods in the Social Sciences: Case Studies from South Africa* (pp. 251–264). Johannesburg: Wits University Press.

Widdicombe, S. (1995). Identity, politics and talk: A case for the mundane and the everyday. In S. Wilkinson & C. Kitzinger (Eds.), *Feminism and Discourse: Psychological Perspectives, Vol. 9* (pp. 106–127). London: Sage.

Widdicombe, S. (2015). "Just like the fact that I'm Syrian like you are Scottish": Ascribing interviewer identities as a resource in cross-cultural interaction. *British Journal of Social Psychology, 54*(2), 255–272.

Widdicombe, S. (2017). The delicate business of identity. *Discourse Studies, 19*(4), 460–478.

Widdicombe, S. & Wooffitt, R. (1995). *The Language of Youth Subcultures: Social Identity in Action.* Hemel Hempstead: Harvester Wheatsheaf.

Williams, R. (2000). *Making Identity Matter: Identity, Society and Social Interaction.* Durham: Sociology Press.

Wilkes, J., & Speer, S. A. (2021a). Reporting Microaggressions: Kinship Carers' Complaints about Identity Slights. *Journal of Language and Social Psychology, 40*(3), 303–327.

Wilkes, J., & Speer, S. A. (2021b). 'Child's time': Kinship carers' use of time reference to construct parental identities. *Journal of Pragmatics, 175,* 14–26.

Wilson, D. B. & Chipungu, S. S. (1996). Introduction: Special issue on kinship care. *Child Welfare, 75*(5), 387–395.

Winokur, M. A., Holtan, A., & Batchelder, K. E. (2018). Systematic review of kinship care effects on safety, permanency, and well-being outcomes. *Research on Social Work Practice, 28*(1), 19–32.

Wooffitt, R. (1990). On the analysis of interaction: An introduction to conversation analysis. In P. Luff, N Gilbert & D. Frohlich (Eds.), *Computers and Conversation* (pp. 7–38). London: Academic Press.

Young, R. F. & Kahana, E. (1989). Specifying caregiver outcomes: Gender and relationship aspects of caregiving strain. *The Gerontologist, 29*(5), 660–666.

13 Foucauldian-Informed Discourse Analysis

Sarah Riley, Martine Robson, and Adrienne Evans

Foucauldian-informed discourse analysis (also known as poststructuralist discourse analysis) identifies what ideas people use to make sense of themselves; how these ideas come to be "thinkable" at that moment; and the consequences for what someone can say, think, feel, or do when thinking with these ideas. This approach to studying identity developed from the ideas of Michel Foucault, a poststructuralist philosopher and historian of ideas who lived from 1926 to 1984 and whose work continues to inform analysis of identity issues today.

Foucault revisioned the way we think about language, power, and truth, arguing that ideas of power as repressive – the coercive, forcing you to do something kind of power – misses an understanding of power as a producing force that produces ideas about people and how the world works. He argued that our ideas about people are different in different socio-historical periods, making the ideas that we think of as "truths" more a set of socially accepted ideas about the world within a particular cultural moment. Such ideas circulate between people, and people use them to think, shaping their innermost thoughts and feelings. From this standpoint, how we understand ourselves is produced through socially shared forms of sense-making. Such sense-making is often tied to institutional power.

Foucault's ideas changed over his career and have subsequently been developed in many ways. In this chapter, we outline his concepts most relevant for identity researchers, describing how this work was taken up in Britain and the analytics from this work that we consider particularly valuable for contemporary identity research. We finish with an example of a study on which we performed a Foucauldian-informed discourse analysis.

13.1 Key Foucauldian Ideas for Identity Researchers

Foucault's body of work is exceptional, covering a range of topics including sexuality, crime, and madness, and offering an extraordinary number of concepts that continue to inform research today. A cross-cutting theme in this work is the relationship between power and how people think about themselves.

In much of psychology, there is the assumption that the self is coherent and stable enough that, with the right scientific tools and rigor, researchers can identify its real nature. This assumes that the focus of identity research is the individual, conceptualized as an independent entity, albeit one that develops as they interact with others in society. In contrast, Foucault radically "decenters" the subject, directing analytical attention to the wider cultural sensemaking in which a person operates, because people are understood as being constituted through language and discourse.

Discourse is defined as practices which systematically form the object of which we speak (Foucault, 1978). Discourse "governs the way that a topic can be meaningfully talked about ... how ideas are put into practice and used to regulate the conduct of others" (Hall, 2001, p. 72). Since discourses shape how people can understand an issue, they have the power to constitute subjects, producing recognizable identities and delineating their boundaries. For example, some people feel guilty about not exercising, Foucauldian researchers would see these feelings as enabled by our contemporary ideas about health and lifestyle choices and not because we "naturally" feel guilty about exercise; and they would also look at the role of medical, psychological, and economic institutions in producing and circulating these ideas.

At different socio-historic periods, certain discourses take on the status of truth. These "regimes of truth" (Foucault, 1988, p. 18) naturalize particular ways of understanding an issue. For example, in contemporary consumerist societies, there is a recognizable discourse of health as an individual responsibility managed through lifestyle choices. Foucault's approach was to compare the discursive regimes of different historical periods, and explore how a concept was understood differently at different times, for example, how madness might be understood as related to spirituality, a rejection of rationality, or as a mental illness (1988). Foucault's method developed from an "archaeological" approach, which focused on identifying different concepts people had for thinking about an issue at different historical moments, into a "genealogical" analysis, which also explored how these ideas developed. Foucault's genealogy involved taking an historical perspective to explore the antecedents to contemporary ideas, examining the historical continuities and ruptures that enable contemporary understandings of that issue, highlighting the need to explore how ideas coalesce at particular times to produce particular understandings of people. For example, in his work on sexuality, Foucault explored how homosexuality shifted from a practice (understood as something men *did* in ancient Greece) to an identity (something men *were* in modern times) (Foucault, 1984a). Much of his analysis focused on institutions, including medicine, psychiatry, education, and law, as these were understood as having particular power to define people.

In *The Subject and Power*, Foucault defined the exercise of power as the "way in which certain actions modify others" (1982, p. 788), in this, Foucault was talking about productive, rather than coercive, power. Elsewhere,

Foucault describes this power as "conduire des conduites" (1994, p. 237), roughly translated as managing the conduct of conduct. Managing the conduct of conduct works through people's psychology, by eliciting in them desires to act in a certain way. For example, subtitling the UK's National Health Service website "Your health, your choices" interpellates British citizens to understand that their health is an outcome of their individual choices, and to choose to work on themselves toward better health. This also points to identities as a site where power is exercised, and also to thinking about identities in complex ways. For example, Foucault suggests the paradox that power works through freedom, since to modify the actions of others requires those being modified to feel like it is their choice.

Understanding that freedom is part of power is important for identity researchers, because freedom and individual choice are often evoked to manage people. For example, genital cosmetic surgery is advertised to women as an empowered personal choice (Braun, 2009). In this example, we might see how Foucault conceptualized power as productive, in that it produces an understanding of an issue through discourse. This productive aspect of power works because people do not feel like power is wielded against them. Instead people are interpellated, incited to understand themselves through discourses that seem to offer important or positive ways to make sense of themselves, such as being "clean" or "tidy" as in the genital cosmetic surgery example. As Foucault stated: "What makes power hold good, what makes it accepted, is simply the fact it doesn't only weigh on us as a force that says no, but that it traverses and produces things, it induces pleasure, forms knowledge, produces discourse" (1980, p. 119).

Because people use discourses to think, our ideas about ourselves – who we are, what it means to be a good person or live a good life – are constituted through discourse. Being constituted through a discourse is *disciplinary* power, understood through the metaphor of Bentham's panopticon, a prison where the central tower held a guard who potentially could, at any time, be viewing one of the prisoners, themselves separated and illuminated in backlit cells built in a circle around the guard tower. Prisoners, never sure if they are being viewed or not, come to regulate their own behavior, as if the guard was looking – "interiorizing to the point that he is his [sic] own overseer, each individual thus exercising this surveillance over, and against himself. A superb formula: power exercised continuously and for what turns out to be a minimal cost" (Foucault, 1980, p. 155). Conceptualizing power as productive and disciplinary directs analysts to consider practices of self-regulation produced through discourses (Bartky, 1997). Power is also diffused, with discourses circulating across various people and institutions rather than coming from a central source. Analysts thus consider the actors and mediums through which discourses circulate, including institutional and individual claims to expertise that legitimate particular discourses.

Foucault is criticized for being part of a negative tradition, however, his later work (e.g., Foucault, 1978, 1984a, 1988) suggested a theoretical move from a docile subject who was spoken through discourses to a self who could "actively fashion their own identities" (McNay, 1992, p. 3). For example, Foucault's concept of technologies of the self, described practices that people employ on themselves,

> which permit individuals to effect by their own means, or with the help of others, a certain number of operations on their own bodies and souls, thoughts, conduct, and way of being, so as to transform themselves in order to attain a certain state of happiness, purity, wisdom, perfection or immortality. (Foucault, 1988, p. 18)

It is important to note too that across both his earlier and later work, Foucault theorized resistance, arguing that discourses produced their own counter-discourses "Where there is power, there is resistance … consequently, this resistance is never in a position of exteriority in relation to power" (1982, p. 794). For example, feminist body image researchers are critical of the thin ideal, but can only be critical of the thin ideal because it is a culturally available discourse for them to push back against. Thus, although in any given socio-historical period there will be powerful discourses, these operate within a nexus of other discourses, discourses that might support each other, work in parallel, or offer alternatives that challenge accepted ideas. This opens up the possibility for people to exercise agency, but within the nexus of discourses available to them.

The concepts we have outlined above of discourse, power (productive, diffuse, disciplinary), and technologies of self offer some key analytics for the identity researcher. For example, in *Postfeminism and Health* we used a Foucauldian-informed analysis to look at body mass index (BMI), a proxy measure for health produced by dividing a person's height by their weight (Riley, Evans, & Robson, 2018). We analyzed BMI as produced through a medical discourse, and as a form of productive power, since through BMI people see themselves in particular ways in relation to their weight, for example, as "normal" or "healthy." BMI is a ubiquitous measure – if you've registered with a doctor in the last ten years, chances are your BMI was taken. The ubiquitous aspect of BMI makes it diffuse, since it is not just at the doctor's surgery that you might be exposed to the logic of BMI, but on commercial and government websites related to health and weight loss, health and lifestyle magazines, government policy documents, perhaps everyday conversations with friends and family. BMI is also disciplinary, because many of us understand our health or monitor our health through it. We might, for example, feel happy if our BMI is in the "healthy weight" category.

Foucauldian ideas of genealogical analysis also directed us to consider how ideas linking weight and health developed, exploring how BMI moved from being a population-level measure to one used to regulate individuals within a wider discourse of health as a lifestyle choice. We were also able to explore weight loss surgeries as a form of technology of the self, performed with the help of experts, to transform the person, and often motivated by articulated desires to be normal. Our BMI example shows how Foucauldian concepts offer us a framework for thinking about how culture gets "inside," shaping our thoughts and feelings and producing our sense of self and identity. But despite these observations, very few would classify Foucault as an "identity theorist."

Foucauldian-informed scholars reject the term "identity" because of its connotations of a relatively fixed sense of self, located in the individual. Rather than focus on the individual as the source of themselves Foucauldian analysis focuses on discourses and how they produce particular subjects, since it is through discourse that a person comes to understand themselves (including, for example, that they are an individual who should have autonomous identities). This theorizing "decentered" the subject.

In decentering the subject, and arguing that people understand themselves through multiple discourses available to them, Foucault understood the self as fluid, partial, and contradictory. This is because people are conceptualized as dynamically moving through different discourses in the course of their everyday sense-making, discourses which have their own historical antecedents, continuities, and ruptures, and which may only be partially formed or conscious.

This a far cry from an understanding of identity implied in other psychological models of a more or less fixed sense of who one is, produced within the psyche of relatively stable individuals who undergo experiences that shape their identity, but who are in essence independent entities who interact with society. Thus, while we might use the term "identity" as a communication tool when disseminating our research, for example in public dissemination, it is not the term we use in specialist academic writing, preferring instead the term "subjectivity," a preference reflected in early engagement with Foucauldian work in British psychology, including the seminal text *Changing the Subject* (Henriques et al., 1984).

13.2 Changing the Subject

Foucauldian-informed discourse analysis developed in the UK as part of a radical challenge to British psychology by discourse analysts arguing that if language actively constructs reality, then the "job" of psychology is to explore what "truths" are constructed in language, and their consequences for how people can understand themselves or others.

Key texts developing Foucauldian-informed discourse analysis in UK psychology included *Social Being: A Theory for Social Psychology* (Harré, 1980); *Changing the Subject* (Henriques et al., 1984), *Beyond Attitudes and Behaviour* (Potter & Wetherell, 1987) and the same authors' subsequent work *Mapping the Language of Racism* (Wetherell & Potter, 1992); *Arguing and*

Thinking and *Ideological Dilemmas* (Billig, 1987; Billig et al., 1988), and a range of work by Ian Parker and colleagues, including *Discourse Dynamics* (Burman & Parker, 1993; Parker, 1992). This body of work considered what a decentered subject might mean for psychology, arguing for a discourse analysis focused on studying language in situ to identify the discourses people draw on to make sense of themselves.

Early British discourse analysis drew on various elements and interpretations of Foucault's work, as well as other bodies of work on language and social interaction. Informed by Austin's speech act theory, Foucauldian understandings of discourse and power, and semiotics, Potter and Wetherell (1987), for example, suggested the analytics of construction, variation, and function. In this work, construction focused on what reality was produced in talk, variation cued analysts to look for the different ways that an issue was constructed, and function considered the consequences for using one construction rather than another at a particular moment.

Other researchers emphasized contradiction over function. For example, with their framework of "ideological dilemmas," Billig and colleagues (Billig, 1987; Billig et al., 1988) argued that within any culture there are multiple and contradictory ideas circulating, associated with various relationships of power, value, and interest. Thus, when people try to make sense of their world to themselves or others, their arguing and thinking reflects these contradictions. Parker (1992) also emphasized contradiction, relating his argument more closely with Foucault and the institutional production of discourse. Subsequently, Hook (2007) also critiqued British discourse analysis as failing to properly engage with elements of Foucault's work around power, while Arribas-Ayllon and Walkerdine (2008) critiqued it for not engaging more with genealogy. Others connected Foucauldian ideas with feminism and Lacanian psychoanalytic concepts (e.g., Malson, 1998; Walkerdine, Lucey, & Melody, 2001). Additional influences on Foucauldian-informed discourse analysis came from a cross-fertilization of ideas between poststructuralism, postmodernism, feminism, critical Black scholarship, Marxism, the sociology of scientific knowledge, conversation analysis, and ethnomethodology.

Over time, psychological discourse analysis developed into some forms with very clear delineations, while other forms had more permeable boundaries (see Wiggins, 2017 for a typology). To understand what informed the development of contemporary forms of Foucauldian-informed discourse analysis we outline five areas of scholarship below: discursive psychology, subject positions, norms and governmentality, agency, and feminism.

Drawing more from conversation analysis than Foucault, discursive psychology analyses how people talk in situ and the rhetorical strategies used to produce particular outcomes, for example, to support particular identity claims (Wiggins, 2017). The influence of discursive psychology is evident in some forms of Foucauldian-informed discourse analysis that include analytics from discursive psychology (e.g., Riley, 2002; Riley, Thompson, & Griffin, 2010; Wetherell, 2007; Willig, 2001).

A different development comes from Davies and Harré (1990), whose concept of subject positions developed Foucault's thinking about subjectivity, to describe the types of persons, roles, or locations an individual may inhabit or connect with that are produced within a discourse. Subject positions have associated ways of speaking and acting, and can be long-term or fleeting, as people shift between occupying different positions related to different parts of their lives and the discourses to which they are exposed. For example, in their analysis of British men's dancing, where fluid hip movements were understood as feminine, Owen and Riley (2019) described dancing with "stiff hips" as allowing men to inhabit subject positions associated with traditional masculinities.

Davies' work on normalization and subjectivity is also important for contemporary Foucauldian-informed discourse analysts. Normalization comes from Foucault's (1984b, 2003) argument that administrative, clinical, and governmental distinctions between normal and abnormal led to people desiring to be "normal." Davies further ties this into psychology by arguing that if people think with discourse, then to reject a discourse (and associated subject positions) is, in effect, to lose an aspect of oneself, since they do not "exist" outside of discourse. The outcome is a "passionate attachment" (Davies, 2013, p. 24) to these norms, a longing to fulfill them, creating powerful emotions such as fear, anger, anxiety, or disgust "toward the one (which might include oneself) who transgresses the norms and thereby risks destabilizing them" (Davies, 2013, p. 24). Her work points to the importance of looking at norms and their affective capacities within a Foucauldian-informed discourse analysis.

Normalization is a core component in governmentality, the process by which governments create desire in people to "choose appropriately." Foucault's concept of governmentality was significantly developed in sociology by Rose (e.g., 1999), who describes how normalization renders people "knowable" in particular ways and allows them to be evaluated and then managed in relation to how much they conform or deviate against particular standards. Using our BMI discussion above as an example, the "healthy" weight category creates a form of sense-making by which we understand ourselves as healthy or not, and by which we are evaluated by our doctors. These standards are created by and distributed through semi-autonomous actors, what Foucault called "dispositive," that include institutions, bodies of knowledge, disciplines, organizations, and other agents. This understanding of governmentality relates to ideas of power as productive *and* diffuse, and directs researchers to consider the range of mediums through which discourses circulate, including traditional and social media (see for example Lupton, 2017 for discussion of norms developed through digital media).

Aligned with work on governmentality is research on neoliberalism, an economic theory of market forces driving late-capitalist economic policies that is also understood as producing a range of identity-related discourses on citizenship and health (e.g., Gill, 2007; Evans & Riley, 2014; Riley, Evans & Robson, 2018; Walkerdine, 2002; Wetherell, 2009).

Work on neoliberalism also linked to debates about agency, which were particularly strong in feminist research on gendered identities (e.g., Duits & van Zoonen, 2011; Evans, Riley, & Shankar, 2010; Gill, 2007). One way to navigate arguments around agency is to consider that people have the possibility to exercise agency but only within the nexus of discourses available to them. This approach directs the analyst to explore how people might differently engage with discourses, for example taking them up in uncritical or enthusiastic ways, reappropriating, revising, or resisting them. See for example, Riley, Thompson, and Griffin's (2010) analysis of how drug users used discourses of citizenship to justify their drug use. Such a framing of agency also allows us to explore power in technologies of self, where people work on themselves to produce themselves in a particular desired subject position, but where these desires often align with pervasive discourses.

As well as debates on agency, Feminist scholarship also raises concerns on how Foucault (a gay man) focused on sexuality and men's experiences rather than gender and women's experiences; how his theorizing undermined notions of collective action based on fixed identity characteristics (e.g., of being a woman); and that in drawing on Foucault and other poststructuralist philosophers, feminists drew on the ideas of old, white, European, dead men (e.g., McNay, 1992; Ramazanoglu, 1993). Acknowledging these concerns, Macleod and Durrheim (2002) argue however, that there are many shared interests:

> including a focus on sexuality as a key area of political struggle; an expansion of the political to include social domination; a critique of biological determinism, humanism, and the search for a scientific "truth"; a critical stance concerning human sciences insofar as they have participated in modern forms of domination; an analysis of the politics of personal relations and everyday life; a critique of the rational subject. (2002, pp. 42–43)

Further, feminist Foucauldian-informed work has been significantly developed by critical Black feminist scholarship. For example, the concept of intersectionality draws analytic attention to the way racialized, classed, gendered, and other social positionalities intersect to produce particular understandings or experiences of power and privilege (for an overview, see Collins & Bilge, 2016). For discourse analytics, this highlights that people will be constituted differently by their multiple positionalities.

Above, we have outlined some key Foucauldian concepts, and discussed how they were taken up by psychologists developing discourse analysis in the UK both as a theoretical perspective and as a method. One outcome of this diverse body of work is that there is no set procedure for Foucauldian-informed discourse analysis, nor a set of confirmed analytics to use. How we tend to start is with participants' sense-making on an issue that seems culturally or psychologically important and which has no clear answer. We then look at how people talk about that issue (or otherwise represent the issue in text or image), and we ask what version of reality is being produced and what discourses enable this sense-making, including both "commonsense" everyday discourses and those more obviously connected to institutions. These questions involve a consideration of contemporary discursive conditions of possibility, that is, what enables these ideas to be thinkable now and might also lead to a genealogical analysis.

We also consider the rhetorical technicalities of the talk. For example, does this talk repeat the main point to emphasize it? Attention to the rhetorical elements allows us to see how the discourse is used and made to sound plausible in that particular social interaction. Considering what discourses used and how they are mobilized helps to address questions about the consequences of talking in this way for what people can say, think, feel, or do. These questions relate to subject positions and subjectivity, and might involve further exploration of the data to explicitly identify particular subject positions in the talk.

We also consider how the discourses we see in the talk might be related to governmentality and the management of conduct through psychology and desires to be normal or meet culturally valued ideals. And we look for forms of resistance in discourses that offer new, more affirming forms of sense-making. Always though, with the recognition that the consequences of discourse are unpredictable and complex, so Foucauldian-informed discourse analysis is not the search for "good" and "bad" discourses, but the exploration of what a discourse makes possible (and by implication what possibilities are limited).

13.3 Worked Example

Our worked example comes from a study on how couples in long-term relationships navigate lifestyle advice after one of them has a diagnosis of coronary heart disease (CHD) (Robson, 2016). Cardiovascular disease, including CHD, is a leading cause of death (World Health Organization, 2019), and lifestyle changes are shown to improve mortality rates. But people find it difficult to make changes to their diet, exercise, smoking, and drinking, difficulties rarely recognized in contemporary health promotion, which, based on socio-cognitive models designed to enhance self-efficacy, articulate a message that lifestyle change is a simple, rational process undertaken by autonomous individuals (Robson & Riley, 2019). This individualization also ignores how lifestyle behaviors take place in the context of social relationships. Research on health practices of people in long-term intimate relationships often focus on interpersonal factors such as relationship quality, and their communication and attachment styles (Robles et al., 2014), but from a Foucauldian perspective, we suggest that it is important to contextualize couple's sense-making in relation to pervasive social norms and discourses, including those around health and love. A discourse analysis of couples' sense-making around engaging with lifestyle advice in the context of CHD, would, we argued, shed light on why so few people appear able to engage in sustained lifestyle change.

13.3.1 Planning, Access, and Ethics

The decision was made to undertake an interview project. In contrast to discursive psychology, Foucauldian-informed discourse analysis sees value in interviews as a method, because the interview context itself is considered a social situation in which societal discourses are articulated. Moreover, if we consider the prominence of the interview – a mode of communicating ideas that has led others to define society as an "interview society" (Atkinson & Silverman, 1997) – then an interview is no less "natural" than any other way to present ideas. For Foucauldian-informed discourse analysis, since the aim is to analyze discourse, what is most important is that the interview provides access to discourses that a participant uses when making sense of an issue. The theory is that if discourses are circulating in public enough to structure thought, then they will be articulated in an interview, while recognizing that not all discourses the participant has access to might be articulated and that the analysis needs to study talk as produced in situ – for example, in response to a particular question asked by a particular researcher.

The interviews were conducted as part of a longitudinal design, conducted once a month for three months following a participant's diagnosis with CHD. The longitudinal design enabled an in-depth exploration of how participants talked about and negotiated lifestyle advice based on research questions that, in line with Foucauldian-informed discourse analysis, asked about how life-style advice was constructed by these participants and the consequences for what they might say, think, feel, or do. The interviews were conducted with couples, since couples' stories and perspectives, as well as their interactions with each other during the interview, would afford insights into the complexity that might arise when intimate partners negotiate multiple discourses, health norms, and romantic relationships (note that the participants were given the option of being interviewed alone).

The counseling service Relate provided for guidance on interviewing. Planning also involved liaison with various stakeholders, including a hospital, specialist medical staff related to an NHS cardiac rehabilitation program, and NHS ethics committees, since recruitment occurred on an NHS site. The researchers undertook NHS good clinical practice training to prepare for research in healthcare settings. Project-specific ethical issues included being sensitive to the wider discourses of morality and health that might stigmatize participants talking about their engagement (or not) with lifestyle advice. To help address this, unstructured interviews were used so participants could talk about their experiences, priorities, and concerns more on their own terms and avoid distress from talking about topics that they did not wish to discuss; and to increase the possibility of unexpected findings, such as lifestyle change not being salient in their management of their illness and recovery. Interviewing couples raises ethical issues of mutual consent, protecting both partners' right to withdraw, the potential to cause or expose conflict and tensions between partners, and partners being anxious about what is disclosed if their partner chooses to do an individual interview (see Robson, 2016 for further discussion on these ethical issues).

13.3.2 Data Collection Processes

Thirty-seven interviews were held with twenty-two people in a long-term cohabiting relationship (relationship length ranging from 15 to 50 years). Nine couples were interviewed together, and four men with CHD chose to be interviewed alone. Most were interviewed three times; two couples did fewer interviews and one couple did four interviews (at their request).

All participants identified as heterosexual, with an age range spanning from their fifties to eighties, and a mean age of 63 years; all but three were of white British descent, mapping the population ethnicity of the rural Wales area of recruitment. Interviewing couples and individuals after the major life event of a diagnosis with CHD evoked powerful and emotional narratives. The interviewer was experienced in empathic listening, and sought to be as free from intrusion as possible, allowing silences to form, but using gentle prompts to signal interest and allow exploration of feelings and experiences by participants. The interviews lasted between 30 and 90 minutes and were audio-recorded using good-quality recording devices. For more discussion on interview process, see for example, King, Horrocks, and Brooks (2018) and Magnusson and Mareck (2015).

In line with our institutional interpretation of the General Data Protection Regulation (GDPR), the recordings were encrypted, stored on password-protected computers, kept separate from participant information, and deleted after transcription. Audio-recordings were anonymized as they were transcribed, at which point they were not subject to GDPR. Anonymization included giving participants pseudonyms, while other names, places, professions, or potentially identifying details were changed or omitted. Transcription involved a simplified version of the Jeffersonian transcription notation (Jefferson, 2004), to give a good sense of how the participants spoke, but without the detail required for discursive psychology. This might include standard punctuation marks (comma, full stop, question mark, respectively representing a notable shift in speech indicative of a grammatical comma; downward intonation as if at the end of a sentence; and stronger, "questioning" intonation, irrespective of grammar); up and down arrows to show intonation contours; underlining for emphasis; square brackets for other relevant information (e.g., [laughs]); round brackets with dots indicating a pause timed to the second, for example, (.) for less than one second. There are others, too, including for speed of speech, loud/softness, drawing out of sounds, and showing reported speech (e.g., then he said "what are you eating"). Choices on how much notation is based on what analytics are used, readability, and communicating a good sense of the talk.

13.3.3 Analysis

Foucauldian-informed discourse analysis, as with other qualitative methods of analysis, requires familiarization, involving listening to the recordings and reading and rereading the transcripts. We often make notes as we progress through this stage, highlighting issues, key themes, or ways of talking about those themes. We use this familiarization phase to develop an understanding of content and tone. Transcribing helps with familiarization too.

The next step is what we think of as "breaking into the data." We often start with a form of thematic analysis, using the left-hand side of a transcript's margin to write short, often one- or two-word descriptions of the main topic being discussed, such as *health*. We highlight when our original topic of interest is discussed – in this case, "lifestyle advice" – but we stay open to noticing new topics; for example, participants talked about healthy eating in terms of "fairness," which we had not expected. As we go through this early coding process, we often find we are using different words for a similar issue (e.g., *fairness, equality, sharing*); noticing this, we go back to recode those extracts with one overarching descriptor.[1] Aligning with Foucault's (1984a) notion of "problematization," we also highlight talk that is explicitly labeled as a problem by participants or which demonstrates rhetorical trouble through emphasis, repetition, disclaimers orienting to dispreferred identities (e.g., "I'm not a racist, but …"), emotional tone,[2] or other ways of showing troubling (e.g., nervous-sounding laughter, changing topic, stopping mid-topic, or making a lot of "um" and "er" sounds).

The above techniques are ways to identify issues or themes in the talk, and may point to where discourses are "rubbing up" against each other. We then deepen our analysis by asking the question "What is being constructed in this talk?" and using the right-hand side margin for more detailed commentary. For example, in the left-hand side margin, we had coded as "food" participant-Joe's talk about not bringing chocolate into the house because his

---

[1] This is an example of the iterative process of qualitative methods, where, informed by new insights, researchers might return to early "steps" in the process. And we note, therefore, that any linear approach to Foucauldian-informed discourse analyses that we offer is by default a simplification and offered for clarity of reading.

[2] In affective discourse analysis, this becomes a central focus; see for example, McConville et al. (2019).

partner Julie was struggling with weight gain.[3] In the right margin, we developed our analysis, drawing on Foucault's definition of discourse as constructing an object, by asking "How is 'food' being constructed?" We answered this question in two different ways: that this talk constructed "health as a joint endeavor between partners" and "food as risk." Here we see a shift in our analysis from "food" as a theme (topic being discussed) to describing two discourses.

As we go through our data, particular constructions become prevalent or seem to shed light on our research question. We focus on these, collating the extracts that reference a topic (e.g., food), allowing us to produce, for example, a discourse analysis of the different ways that food was constructed in the talk (e.g., as risk, as pleasure, as a sign of love). This process aligns with the construction and function analytics of Potter and Wetherell (1987) and offers a structured way to produce a Foucauldian-informed discourse analysis focusing on how an object is constructed in discourse. But there are other ways. In this example, the data, research question, and our interests led us to focus further on "health as a joint endeavor" and whether this discourse was supported or challenged by other forms of sense-making in the talk.

Once we have decided what discourse(s) to focus on, we collate all the extracts coded under one discourse (e.g., health as a joint endeavor), and examine each extract in terms of how participants rhetorically produce their accounts, considering again *what* is being constructed, so we can develop our thinking further,[4] but also *how* it is said, paying attention to the exact words and phrases. We do this to explore the interactional aspect of talk, for example, in the way emphasis might draw attention to its importance; the way a participant might seek agreement from the interviewer with the phrase "isn't it?"; or how not finishing a sentence might introduce an unsaid or unsayable issue (see Riley & Wiggins, 2019; Wiggins, 2017 for discussion on rhetorical strategies).

We also look for subject positions. This means that as well as asking about *what* is said and *how* it is said, we also think about *who* is being talked about, asking if there are any people or types of people implied in the text and, if so, what they can do (or not do), and what norms are implied in these construc-tions. These questions also apply to how people position their own subjectivity in the text. For example, Joe explains not bringing chocolate into the house because "we've both got to work together." We consider that his talk

---

[3] The extract read: she'll eat what I'm having you see and she loves chocolate and she loves crisps and just like anyone else, but because of the way I I just keep buying it [laughs] so so really that that's when we've both got to work together really I've got to do it buy it and keep it in the car or stop it altogether really.

[4] Again, this might be a point at which we cycle back to earlier stages of analysis, but with a new perspective on how we might think about the data. This should never be considered a failure, but rather the process the researcher needed to undergo to get to this moment.

constructs not only health as a joint endeavor, but a subject position of himself as a "supportive partner" in a collaborative couple.

In our application of Foucauldian-informed discourse analysis, we are interested in asking "What are the consequences for what people can say, think, feel or do from this subject position?" In Joe's statement, for example, we see the idea that partners should eat healthily together. So, if Joe and Julie do not eat healthily, Joe is in danger of devaluing his relationship with Julie. This helped us develop the idea that participants problematized their "unhealthy" eating in terms of a relationship-identity threat and helped us consider what discourses may be underpinning the talk (e.g., partners support each other) and what is being avoided (e.g., criticizing their partner).

Considering subject positions also means paying attention to talk of any work people do on themselves. For example, participant-Henry's talk about his exercise classes as allowing him to "get a bit of a sweat on so it's obviously doing some good" points to participating in the class as a technology of self, enabling him to take up a subject position of a "good patient" defined in terms of engaging in exercise aligned with lifestyle advice after CHD.

At this stage in our analysis, we have an understanding of the ways our object of study (engaging with lifestyle advice) might be constructed (e.g., health as a joint endeavor, food as risk), and the kinds of subject positions described (e.g., "supporting partner," "good patient") and implications for what they can say and do (e.g., supportive partners do not criticize their loved one, good patients go to exercise classes). We might also look for any affect or emotion in the talk to explore consequences for how people might feel (e.g., "bad" patients/partners might feel guilty). We then shift analysis out of the text to consider what wider discourses give this talk its rationality, asking *why* they would say this in terms of available commonsense notions that are often linked to economic or political public discourse or to institutions such as medicine, psychology, education, or government.

For example, we have already seen the relationship norm of being supportive and uncritical of one's partner in Joe's talk about Julie. He does it several times, such as when he explains that Julie eats chocolate because she loves it "just like anyone else." This talk constructs Julie's chocolate eating as normative, rather than, for example, her lacking will power or being to blame for her weight gain. Willpower, blame, and responsibility – missing in Joe's talk of Julie – are, however, key tropes of a prevalent discourse of health citizenship, known in the literature as *healthism*. Healthism constructs health as a risk managed by good citizens through appropriate eating and exercise and is itself enabled by neoliberalism (Crawford, 1980, 2006; Riley, Evans, & Robson, 2018). In Joe's talk of Julie, we thus see an absence of a discourse (healthism), which directs us to consider why he might not use it here (e.g., it would lay blame on Julie, which suggests a norm of not criticizing his partner). We also know Joe could use this discourse, because he does elsewhere. For example, we see it structuring his talk when he describes Julie's weight gain as "my fault," talk that ties his partner's health to a sense of blame and responsibility, but his rather than hers.

Across the dataset we saw a similar pattern where participants made sense of themselves and their partners through healthism, but to monitor, manage, or question one's partner in line with healthism was to contravene norms of relationships that included unconditional acceptance. Our participants thus had to negotiate two competing norms, critically monitoring their partner's health behaviors in line with healthism *and* not critiquing or controlling such behavior in line with relationship norms. In the larger study, we were able to argue how healthism is a form of governmentality, structuring participants' sense-making of themselves and their partners in ways that often produced anxiety, guilt, and shame, rather than a sense of self-efficacy in their ability to apply lifestyle advice.

We also considered the dispositif circulating healthism discourses. This includes government policy, healthcare providers, and the resources they used (e.g., NHS websites), magazines, and news reports about "lifestyle" diseases. This led to genealogical considerations of healthism, allowing us to explore how these ideas developed out of an assemblage of consumerism and neoliberal economic and government policies that enabled health to become a site of identity formation. Yet, it was in paying close attention to the talk – for example, noticing and answering questions like "Why is blame relevant here?" – that we were able to develop this conceptual analysis of the wider discourses structuring our participants' negotiation of lifestyle change advice.

We also employed a deviant case analysis, looking for alternatives to healthism in our data. For example, Lewis described how he and his partner had increased their exercise. He described buying walking boots together, taking a packed lunch, and cycling back on a beautiful day as romantic, fun, and bringing a "real closeness" between him and his partner. In this talk of exercise, the relationship had primacy and the prescribed lifestyle change became constructed through pleasurable embodied experiences and joyful emotions of interpersonal connections "a real sense of fun … laughing and enjoying life." This suggested a more affirmative alternative to healthism and was a sharp contrast to individually participating in a spin class, which he described as "torturous."

Deviant case analyses often help identify alternative discourses, and are also a validation practice. Other actions that evidence quality include demonstrating participant orientation to the issue, coherence in argument as well as between argument and data presented, transparency of practice, and making a case that the analysis uses Foucauldian analytics appropriately with reference to relevant literature. Other quality criteria orient around being fruitful or generative, meaning that the analysis helps answer an existing question in new, insightful ways, or generates new ways of thinking about it (Potter & Wetherell, 1987).

Writing up a Foucauldian-informed discourse analysis often involves a brief overview of all the discourses to be discussed, signposting the main arguments, for example, that participants had to negotiate contradictory discourses which constructed good relationships as ones where health is managed as a joint endeavor and ones where partners are not critical of each other. Each discourse would then be discussed in turn, in a section that summarized and illustrated the discourse, with extracts acting as exemplars, and analyzed in depth using the analytics described above and summarized as *what*, *how*, *who*, and *why* questions. Extracts are usually chosen on the basis that they are clear articulations of the discourse, offer something interesting in the analysis (e.g., several subject positions articulated), or have some other value to the research (e.g., a story that enabled further understanding of the discourse), while being mindful of not just picking the most colorful or sensational extracts.

13.4 Conclusion

For Foucault, power is in discourse, producing understandings that people use to make sense of themselves. This makes Foucauldian-informed discourse analysis an important method for identity researchers, particularly when identity is central to the way neoliberal capitalist societies manage the conduct of conduct, as Foucault wrote prophetically: "Never, I think, in the history of human societies ... has there been such a tricky combination in the same political structures of individualization techniques and of totalization procedures" (1982, p. 782). What this points to is the need for identity researchers to consider power in a nuanced way, to explore the way people make sense of themselves through the discourses available to them, ones that might appear common sense or benevolent (e.g., that we are free to manage our health and can make easy lifestyle changes) but when examined turn out to require people to negotiate difficult demands. Identifying these contradictions points to the utility of Foucauldian-informed discourse analysis, in terms of understanding the limits to how people may make sense of themselves, and, through these, directions for more affirmative alternatives.

Any one method has limitations too, and for Foucauldian-informed discourse analysis this includes a relatively limited engagement with materiality, embodiment, and affect, which is why we sometimes combine Foucauldian analytics with concepts from other poststructuralists, such as Deleuze (e.g., Riley, Evans, & Robson, 2018), or with psychoanalytic ideas (e.g., Evans & Riley, 2014; Walkerdine, Lucey, & Melody, 2001). Psychoanalytic ideas may also offer us directions for why, in a world of multiple discourses, some seem to "stick" more than others (Hook, 2007). Understanding this "stickiness" is a particularly fruitful area for future discourse analysts.

References and Further Reading

Arribas-Ayllon, M. & Walkerdine, V. (2008). Foucauldian discourse analysis. In C. Willig & W. Stainton-Rogers (Eds.), *The Sage Handbook of Qualitative Research in Psychology* (pp. 91–108). London: Sage.

Atkinson, P. & Silverman, D. (1997). Kundera's immortality: The interview society and the invention of the self. *Qualitative Inquiry*, *3*, 304–325.

Bartky, S. L. (1997). Foucault, femininity and the modernization of patriarchal power. In K. Conboy, N. Medina, & S. Stanbury (Eds.), *Writing on the Body: Female Embodiment and Feminist Theory* (pp. 129–154). New York, NY: Columbia University Press.

Billig, M. (1987). *Arguing and Thinking: A Rhetorical Approach to Social Psychology*. Cambridge: Cambridge University Press.

Billig, M., Condor, S., Gane, M., Middleton, D., & Radley, A. (1988). *Ideological Dilemmas: A Social Psychology of Everyday Thinking*. London: Sage.

Braun, V. (2009). "The women are doing it for themselves": The rhetoric of choice and agency around female genital "cosmetic surgery." *Australian Feminist Studies*, *4*(60), 233–249.

Burkitt, I. (2008). *Social Selves: Theories of Self and Identity*, 2nd Ed. London: Sage.

Burman, E. & Parker, I. (Eds.). (1993). *Discourse Analytic Research: Repertoires and Readings of Texts in Action*. London: Routledge.

Collins, P. H. & Bilge, S. (2016). *Intersectionality*. Cambridge: Polity Press.

Crawford, R. (1980). Healthism and the medicalization of everyday life. *International Journal of Health Services*, *10*(3), 365–388.

Crawford, R. (2006). Health as a meaningful social practice. *Sociology of Health and Illness*, *10*(4), 301–320.

Davies, B. (2013). Normalization and emotions. In K. G. Nygren & S. Fahlgren (Eds.), *Mobilizing Gender Research: Challenges and Strategies*. Sundsvall: Mid Sweden University.

Davies, B. & Harré, R. (1990). Positioning: The discursive production of selves. *Journal of Theory of Social Behaviour*, *20*(1), 43–63.

Duits, L. & Zoonen, L. V. (2011). Coming to terms with sexualization. *European Journal of Cultural Studies*, *14*(5), 491–506.

Evans, A. & Riley, S. (2014). *Technologies of Sexiness: Sex, Identity and Consumption*. Oxford: University Press.

Evans, A., Riley, S., & Shankar, A. (2010). Technologies of sexiness: Theorizing women's engagement in the sexualization of culture. *Feminism & Psychology*, *20*(1), 114–131.

Foucault, M. (1978). *The History of Sexuality*. New York, NY: Pantheon Books.

Foucault, M. (1980). *Power/Knowledge: Selected Interviews and Other Writings, 1972–1977*. New York, NY: Pantheon.

Foucault, M. (1982). The subject and power. *Critical Inquiry*, *8*(4), 777–795.

Foucault, M. (1984a). *The History of Sexuality. Vol 2: The Use of Pleasure*. London: Penguin.

Foucault, M. (1984b). Polemics, politics, and problematizations. In P. Rabinow (Ed.), *The Foucault Reader: An Introduction to Foucault's Thought* (pp. 381–390). London: Penguin Books.

Foucault, M. (1988). Technologies of the self. In L. Martin, H. Gutman, & P. Hutton (Eds.), *Technologies of the Self: A Seminar with Michel Foucault* (pp. 16–49). Amherst, MA: University of Massachusetts Press.

Foucault, M. (1994). *Dits et écrits IV*. Paris: Gallimard.

Foucault, M. (2003). *Abnormal: Lectures at the College de France 1974–1975*. London: Verso.

Gill, R. (2007). Critical respect: The difficulties and dilemmas of agency and 'choice' for feminism: A reply to Duits and van Zoonen. *European Journal of Women's Studies*, *14*(1), 69–80.

Gough, B. (Ed.). (2017). *The Palgrave Handbook of Critical Social Psychology*. Basingstoke: Palgrave Macmillan.

Hall, S. (2001). Foucault: Power, knowledge and discourse. In M. Wetherell, S. Taylor, & S. J. Yates (Eds.), *Discourse Theory and Practice: A Reader* (pp. 72–81). Thousand Oaks, CA: Sage.

Harré, R. (1980). *Social Being*. Oxford: Blackwell.

Henriques, J., Hollway, W., Urwin, C., Venn, C., & Walkerdine, V. (1984). *Changing the Subject: Psychology, Social Regulation and Subjectivity*. London: Methuen.

Hook, D. (2007). *Foucault, Psychology and the Analytics of Power*. Basingstoke: Palgrave Macmillan.

Jefferson, G. (2004). Glossary of transcript symbols with an introduction. In G. Lerner (Ed.), *Conversation Analysis: Studies from the First Generation* (pp. 13–31). Amsterdam: John Benjamins.

King, N., Horrocks, C., & Brooks, J. (2018). *Interviews in Qualitative Research*, 2nd Ed. London: Sage.

Lupton, D. (2017). *Digital Health: Critical and Cross-Disciplinary Perspectives*. Abingdon: Routledge.

Macleod, C. & Durrheim, K. (2002). Foucauldian feminism: The implications of governmentality. *Journal for the Theory of Social Behaviour*, *32*(1), 41–60.

Magnusson, E. & Mareck, J. (2015). *Doing Interview-Based Qualitative Research. A Learner's Guide*. Cambridge: Cambridge University Press.

Malson, H. (1988). *The Thin Woman*. London: Routledge.

McConville, A., Wetherell, M., McCreanor, T., Borell, B., & Moewaka Barnes, H. (2019). "Pissed off and confused"/"grateful and (re)moved": Affect, privilege and national commemoration in Aotearoa New Zealand. *Political Psychology*. Online first, doi:10.1111/pops.12610.

McNay, L. (1992). *Foucault and Feminism: Power, Gender and the Self*. Cambridge: Polity Press.

Owen, C. & Riley, S. (2019). A poststructuralist-informed inclusive masculinity theory (PS-IMT): Developing IMT to account for complexities in masculinities, using learning to dance Latin and ballroom as an example, *Journal of Gender Studies*, *29*(5), 533–546, doi:10.1080/09589236.2019.1675498.

Parker, I. (1992). *Discourse Dynamics: Critical Analysis for Social and Individual Psychology*. London: Routledge.

Potter, J. & Wetherell, M. (1987). *Discourse Analysis: Beyond Attitudes and Behaviour*. London: Sage.

Ramazanoglu, C. (Ed.). (1993). *Up against Foucault: Explorations of Some of the Tensions between Foucault and Feminism*. London: Routledge.

Riley, S. (2002). Constructions of equality and discrimination in professional men's talk. *British Journal of Social Psychology*, *41*, 443–461.

Riley, S., Evans, R., & Robson, M. (2018). *Postfeminism and Health*. London: Routledge.

Riley, S., Thompson, J., & Griffin, C. (2010). Turn on, tune in, but don't drop out: The impact of neo-liberalism on magic mushroom users (in)ability to imagine collectivist social worlds. *International Journal of Drug Policy*, *21*, 445–451.

Riley, S. & Wiggins, S. (2018). Discourse analysis. In C. Sullivan & M. Forrester, (Eds.), *Doing Qualitative Research in Psychology: A Practical Guide* (pp. 233–256). London: Sage. Youtube video www.youtube.com/watch?v= iYKuTHdFMPw.

Robles, T., Slatcher, R., Trombello, J., & McGinn, M. (2014). Marital quality and health: A meta-analytic review. *Psychological Bulletin*, *140*(1), 140–187.

Robson, M. (2016). Couples' management of lifestyle change in health and after heart disease: A Foucauldian–Deleuzian approach. Doctoral thesis, Aberystwyth University.

Robson, M. & Riley, S. (2019). A Deleuzian rethinking of time in healthy lifestyle advice and change. *Social and Personality Psychology Compass*, *13*(4), e12448, doi:10.1111/spc3.12448.

Rose, N. (1999). *Governing the Soul: The Shaping of the Private Self*. London: Free Association Books.

Walkerdine, V. (2002). *Challenging Subjects: Critical Psychology for a New Millennium*. Basingstoke: Palgrave Macmillan.

Walkerdine, V., Lucey, H., & Melody, J. (2001). *Growing Up Girl*. New York, NY: New York University Press.

West, S. (2015–). Philosophize This! Podcast, available at http://philosophizethis.org/.

Wetherell, M. (2007). A step too far: Discursive psychology, linguistic ethnography and questions of identity. *Journal of Sociolinguistics*, *11*(5), 661–681, doi:10.1111/j.1467-9841.2007.00345.x.

Wetherell, M. (2009). *Identity in the 21st Century: New Trends in Changing Times*. Basingstoke: Palgrave Macmillan.

Wetherell, M. & Potter, J. (1992). *Mapping the Language of Racism*. New York, NY: Columbia University Press.

World Health Organization. (2019). World health statistics 2019: Monitoring health for the SDGs, sustainable development goals. Geneva: WHO, retrieved May 02, 2021 from https://apps.who.int/iris/handle/10665/324835.

Wiggins, S. (2017). *Discursive Psychology: Theory, Method and Applications*. London: Sage.

Willig, C. (2001). *Introducing Qualitative Research in Psychology: Adventures in Theory and Method*. Milton Keynes: Open University Press.

14 A Methodology to Examine Identity: Multimodal (Inter)action Analysis

Tui Matelau-Doherty and Sigrid Norris

This chapter discusses and showcases aspects of the theoretical/methodological framework multimodal (inter)action analysis developed and used for the analysis of identity in everyday life (Norris, 2002, 2011). In this analytical framework, the notion of the psychological unit of an individual is connected to the sociological notion of identity being produced by and through society and connected to the discursive notion of identity as being produced in and through language and interaction. While the framework connects the analysis of identity from psychology, sociology, and linguistics, it goes beyond each of these areas of research as it moves beyond the individual as unit of identity; moves beyond society as the enforcer of identity; moves beyond language as the predominant way to produce identity; and moves beyond interaction between individuals as the basis for identity. The analytical framework is quite vast, and therefore we limit our chapter to an introduction of its history and the discussion of particular notions, such as identity elements, the social actor, mediated action, vertical identity production, the site of engagement, practices, and larger societal discourses.[1] After a theoretical introduction, the chapter progresses to an example of a Māori creative artist navigating their identity in everyday life, highlighting how these introduced concepts are used and what kind of findings can be gained from using them.

Māori are the indigenous people of New Zealand. Due to their colonized history, Māori identity production is complex. Pre-colonization, Māori lived in tribal and familial groups on ancestral land, and identity was constructed through fulfilling obligations to the tribe and family (Houkamau, 2010, p. 182).

Today, contemporary research into Māori identity reveals four different categories: traditional, marginalized, fluid, and hybrid Māori identities. The traditional, essentialist view, which is taken to present the more authentic Māori identity, consists of cultural markers such as the ability to speak Māori, and engage with and practice traditional cultural values and norms

---

[1] Not discussed here is framework's psychological dimension of attention levels and simultaneous identity element production (Norris, 2011, 2020).

(Brougham & Haar, 2013; Houkamau & Sibley, 2015; McIntosh, 2005; Moeke-Maxwell, 2005, 2008; Paringatai, 2014). For Māori who construct themselves in terms of a marginalized Māori identity, their experience of being Māori is shaped by material disadvantage (Borrell, 2005). Emerging fluid identities are perceived as more positive and inclusive, as they combine new ideas about culture, language, tradition, and the present social environment (McIntosh, 2005; Moeke-Maxwell, 2005, 2008). Finally, hybrid identities allow for the construction of ethnic identities that draw on more than one ethnic heritage (Webber, 2006). Moeke-Maxwell (2008) argues for further exploration of fluid and hybrid Māori identities, as identity continuum arguments that position authentic Māori on the one side and inauthentic Māori on the other do not allow for the valid construction of alternative Māori identity.

14.1 Multimodal (Inter)action Analysis: Background

Multimodal (inter)action analysis (MIA) is a methodology with strong theoretical foundations (Scollon, 1998, 2001; Wertsch, 1998; Norris, 2019) that is applicable for the analysis of actions and interactions that people take in the world. All actions and interactions are viewed as identity-telling (Scollon, 1997; Norris, 2011). With origins in sociocultural psychology (Wertsch, 1998) and sociology (Goffman, 1959, 1963, 1974, 1981), interactional sociolinguistics and discourse analysis (Gumperz, 1982; Tannen, 1984; Schifrin, 1987; Hamilton, 1998), and the early work in social semiotics (Kress & Van Leeuwen, 1996, 2001; Van Leeuwen, 1999), multimodal (inter)action analysis was developed in the first instance to gain insight into everyday identity production (Norris, 2002). Sociocultural psychology moves the study of identity away from the individualistic point of view, and sociology places the study of identity within society, whereas sociolinguistics and discourse analysis places identity as being co-constructed through talk in interaction, whereby the term interaction always incorporates at least two individuals speaking to one another. In the early work of social semiotics, identity is viewed as being presented in layout of magazine images, for example in a picture of a child's bedroom (Kress & Van Leeuwen, 2001). However, when aiming to research identity in everyday life, Norris (2002) found that identity of the participants in her study neither produced their identity only as individuals, nor only through the social, nor only or even predominantly through talk, nor was their identity only or predominantly present in the layout of their houses. While the participants certainly did produce aspects of their identity as individuals, through the social and cultural, in and through talk, and they certainly did display aspects of their identity within their homes, Norris found that identity production in everyday life was much more complex.

Goffman's work (1959, 1963, 1974, 1981) originally was highly influential upon Norris's developing theoretical framework. However, the notion of society forcing and enforcing identity production upon the person also appeared to be only an aspect of a person's identity produced in everyday life. Norris was facing several issues as she proceeded with her empirical work, in which she video- and audio-recorded everyday moments in the lives of her participants, in which she spoke with them, interviewed them, and interacted together with them in their families, extended families, and networks over the course of a year, read the books they read, watched the movies they watched, ate the food they ate, and listened to the music that they listened to. The first methodological issue that she faced was that there was no way of working with such diverse data sets as the one that she was collecting. Then, there was no transcription system that would allow her to depict the multi-modal actions and interactions, and no analytical framework available that allowed for the analysis of the multiplicity and the layering of everyday identity production.

Traditional identity research has interesting things to say about identity. However, most of it investigates identity as emerging from an individual, being contained within the individual, which, nevertheless emerged from social interaction (Mead, 1974). The self, selfhood, and the sense of self were important concepts within this train of thought. However, what Norris began to argue was that there was much that emerged from without rather than from within, bringing her back to Goffman and sociology, where, however, the intricacies of the person's agency were overlooked, bringing her back once again to traditional identity researchers. As she proceeded with her empirical work, she found that others who interacted with the participants forced aspects of identity upon them, but at the same time the participants actively produced their identities and were continuously negotiating their identity in their everyday lives. Moreover, Norris found that identity was often multiple, based upon and enacted through the actions that participants produced. Scollon (1997) had already argued that every action is identity-telling, but Norris (2011) found that often her participants engaged in more than one action at a time, producing several identities simultaneously. In order to make sense of these various identities, she came to call them "identity elements." Norris (2011) shows that in her study, a participant could produce a mother identity element at the very same time as she (a caterer by profession) produced her catering identity element. While the mother identity element was something quite strong and stable, the caterer identity element was an identity element that could (and eventually did) disappear. By viewing identity as being made up of elements that can come into being, stay over a long duration, change, or even disappear at some point, the notion of *identity elements* can be used to show how identity is produced and how it changes over time. Identity elements are produced by social actors (Norris, 2011). Social actors, as proposed by Wertsch and Scollon, are people. This term alludes to the fact that people act or do things in the world and that they are not acting as pure individuals, but rather as social beings. Even when one social actor acts (does something) alone, they act as social (and cultural) beings. The social is thus a part of the person, and a person is never thought of as individual without the social. When speaking of actions, the notion needed to be clarified, and Norris borrowed the concept of mediated actions from cultural/social psychology (Wertsch, 1998; Scollon, 1998, 2001).

Mediated actions are defined as a *social actor acting with or thought mediational means/cultural tools*, where the terms mediational means and cultural tools can be used interchangeably. A mediational means is what makes the action possible, and each mediational means is also a cultural tool, since in this framework all actions are socially and culturally embedded (Scollon, 1998, 2001). As an example, when a person picks up a cup of coffee to drink, this action is produced by the social actor (the person) with/through the social actor's hand/arm and the cup of coffee (the mediational means). This action in turn produces the social actor's identity element of a coffee drinker.

While a coffee drinker, a caterer, and a mother identity element are certainly of different kinds, all of them feature in importance in a social actor's everyday life. Through the concept of identity element we can showcase (or make evident) an aspect of a person's identity, and can, for example, trace it along through time and see how it may change in everyday life. The concept of *mediated action*, defined as a social actor acting with/through cultural tools, allows us to see how actions and interactions in everyday life are produced, shaped, and changed through the use of different mediational means, for example, thereby concretely demonstrating how identity elements are produced, shaped, and changed.

Identity elements are thus produced through mediated actions in everyday lives. But identity elements cannot only be produced simultaneously as in the mother and caterer identity element discussed above. Rather, identity elements are also layered vertically, because they contribute to various layers of discourse from the central (the concrete mediated action being produced by a social actor) to the intermediary (the concrete mediated action being produced by a social actor in connection with their social networks) and the outer layer of discourse (the concrete mediated action produced by the social actor in connection with concrete institutions and society that the social actor is a part of) (Norris, 2011, 2020). What this means is that one and the same mediated action contributes to (1) the central layer of discourse, and produces an immediate identity element; (2) the intermediary layer of discourse, and produces a continues identity element; and (3) the outer layers of discourse, and produces a general identity element.

As long as the three vertical layers overlap, they are usually invisible. This means that a mediated action that a social actor produces in real time creates an immediate identity element. For example, the mediated action of a

mother doing homework with her child creates her immediate mother identity element. This same mediated action also produces her continuous
mother identity element, as it is customary in her network(s) to do homework with children. Simultaneously, this action produces her general mother
identity element, as it is customary for parents whose children attend the
school that her child attends, and in the society that they live in, to do
homework with a child.

As long as the three layers overlap, the social actor producing the mediated
action and thereby producing their identity element has a sense of well-being.
In contrast, when one or more of the vertical layers do not overlap, the
discrepancy not only becomes visible, but in fact may result in a feeling of
distress. Norris (2002, 2011) found that the discrepancy between the layers of
discourse/identity can lead to a feeling of inadequacy, aggression, and even
depression, but can also lead to a change in identity and likely to a range of
other reactions. Layers of discourse afford agency to a varying degree, so that
the most agency that a social actor has is usually found in the central layer of
discourse, where the social actor produces the mediated action and the immediate identity element. Here, the mediated action (such as doing homework
with a child) is largely agentive in that it can be produced when and how the
social actor deems correct. In the intermediary layer of discourse, made up of
the networks that the social actor is a part of, however, agency is often less
strong. Here, mediated actions (such as doing homework with a child) and the
resulting identity element are often enforced by the networks (so that a mother
who usually helps her child with homework in the afternoon before dinner is
reprimanded when she is seen chatting with a friend at a café instead). At the
outer layers of discourse, mediated actions (such as doing homework with a
child) are even more strongly enforced, producing an (often) largely non-
agentive identity element (so that a mother who is not helping her child with
homework may be told at a parent–teacher conference that she is expected to
do so, whereby the institution "school" enforces the production of a specific
mother identity element).

A social actor who agentively performs the concrete mediated action (in our
example, doing homework with her child), as deemed correct by the networks
that they belong to and by the institutions that they are a part of, has a strong
feeling of belonging and self-worth and is unaware of the various layers of
discourse. In contrast, a social actor who does not perform actions deemed
correct by the intermediary and/or the outer layers of discourse is aware of
that discrepancy and on some level as not fitting in, and may feel psychologically stressed and unwell. But the matching of the three layers is only one
possibility of many. Quite frequently, there are various outer layer discourses
that impact a person's actions. In a case study, Norris (2011) found that
during a divorce, a woman was impacted by two different outer layer legal
discourses, which did not match either her intermediary layer discourses
(which concretely linked to her networks and produced her continuous

identity elements) or the central layer of discourses (her largely agentively produced concrete mediated actions that produced her immediate identity element). The participant, unable to reconcile these two outer layers of identity, went into psychotherapy when the forces of the legal discourses became too overwhelming. The general divorcee identity elements for were thus highly confusing and conflicting (p. 185).

But it is certainly not only these three layers of discourse that impact identity in everyday life, since they are only the concrete connections that a social actor has with their concrete networks and concrete institutions. When analyzing identity, we also need to consider the practices and larger societal discourses that are impacting social actors in their everyday identity production. For this, we use the site of engagement as analytical tool, which is defined by Scollon (1998, 2001) as a window opened up by practices and discourses to make concrete actions possible. This *window* is utilized in multimodal (inter) action analysis (Norris, 2014), helping to connect the concrete mediated actions with their concrete vertical layers (and the resulting identity elements) with practices and discourses that are present in society in an ephemeral manner. Practices, according to Scollon (1998), are mediated actions with a history; and discourses (of the larger ephemeral kind), according to Norris (2019), are practices with an institutional or ideological dimension. Practices and (large) discourses are thus theorized in a coherent manner with the mediated action, building a larger aspect of what and how actions that social actors engage in are impacted by larger dimensions within society.

Practices are those mediated actions with a history that we learn throughout life. Going back to the example of the mother helping her child with homework, we can surmise that she herself has learned how to do homework with a child through the actions of her own mother or father. Whether she now produces her concrete actions in ways similar or dissimilar to the ways her own parents produced them is something that may come out in her way of speaking about doing homework when conversing with her friends, her partner, or the researcher. But no matter how she relates to this learned practice, she does produce her own concrete mediated actions in relation to the practice. At the same time, she produces her own concrete mediated actions of helping her child with homework in relation to larger societal discourses. One such discourse may be that children who have a parent helping them with homework are more successful in school. Although only one practice and one large discourse that may impact her concrete mediated actions and her immediate mother identity element are described here, there are of course always many more.

Just as concrete layers of discourse and the concretely linked identity elements produced impact a person's well-being, so do the ephemeral practices and societal discourses that shape and largely enforce particular ways of producing identity elements in a society. In our illustration below, we demonstrate the layering of agentive, less agentive, and enforced identity production.

As mentioned above, we always begin our analysis by examining the mediated actions that participants take, as it is these mediated actions that produce the participants' identity elements in their everyday lives. In order to showcase an analysis, we begin by analyzing an interview.

14.2 An Illustration

This example is taken from a larger ethnographically informed study of six Māori and Pacific artists in New Zealand. The study entailed observations, video data of the participants' art productions, and video recorded interviews. Here, we exemplify our methodology by use of excerpts from one of our participants. First, we examine an excerpt from her interview, where she reflects on emigrating to New Zealand and the tensions she experienced between the outer and intermediary layers of discourse that shaped her general and continuous Māori identity elements. Second, we analyze an excerpt from her art practice, in which she highlights a connection between the central layers of discourse that shape both her dance identity element and her Māori identity element. We begin by working through a relatively large multimodal interview excerpt that runs over three pages (Figure 14.1). Then, in our text, we zoom into particular instances of this transcript, showing the particular images again in order to facilitate detailed readings of the multimodal complexity.

14.2.1 Conflict Between Continuous and General Identity Elements

In Figure 14.1, a dancer and choreographer who was born in Australia and then moved to New Zealand describes the layers of discourse that have shaped her Māori identity element. She identifies as Māori and Pakeha, being a third-generation Australian whose great-grandparents moved to Australia from New Zealand. Her Māori ancestry comes from her great-grandmother, who left behind her tribal relationships when she moved to Australia.

When our participant lived in Australia, she was involved with aboriginal community groups campaigning against industrial activity that threatened local ecological systems. She became frustrated with the limited communication channels within traditional activism and started dancing. At this point, she moved to New Zealand to study dance and has been involved as a choreographer and dancer in many productions that have an environmental focus. Moving to New Zealand also gave her the opportunity to learn about her Māori ancestry and to learn about the Māori culture.

Figure 14.1 depicts a transcribed excerpt from an interview in which the participant discussed the construction of her creative identity element. In the transcribed mediated action (Figure 14.2), she describes her first perception of Māori when she moved to New Zealand. Her gesture changes from an open-palm gesture to a beat gesture in which she taps her thigh with her index finger.

Figure 14.1 *Conflict between the general Māori identity element and the continuous Māori identity element*

Figure 14.1 (*cont.*)

Figure 14.1 (*cont.*)

Figure 14.2 *Opening of a new mediated action*

The change in gesture here indicates the beginning of the mediated action as well as emphasizing the timing of her experience, "cause when I first got here." She uses volume to also emphasize the word "first."

She continues by saying, "I did have a moment where I went." She then speaks at a quieter volume as she describes her reaction to the intermediary and outer layers of discourse relating to Māori. "I don't know if I want to be Māori." Her voice returns to her normal volume as she says, "because, man these buggers." By referring to Māori as "these buggers," as seen in Figure 14.3, she indicates that she did not identify with the group.

Figure 14.3 *Open facial expression and closed posture demonstrating ambivalence*

She continues "I don't like the way they behave." In Figure 14.4, the participant shrugs her shoulders (circled in yellow with the movement indicated by the arrows), reinforcing her spoken language: "I don't relate to how they behave."

Figure 14.4 *Shoulder shrugs reinforcing response to the outer layers of discourse*

As she says "I don't relate," her facial expression indicates the negative emotions that she was feeling. Figure 14.5 shows her gesturing to her head as she begins to list the values that she does relate to: "ahm I relate to the values, I relate to the values my nan taught me."

Figure 14.5 *Gesture highlighting values enforced through intermediary layers of discourse*

Now, the participant explains that her nan (grandmother) taught her values *about being human* and about family, "that your family is your center and you'll always have their backs." Figure 14.6 shows her repeatedly using spoken language and beat gestures to highlight the values she learned from her grandmother, at the same time highlighting that she did not perceive these values within the Māori community when she first arrived in New Zealand. She continues to describe the values she learned from her grandmother, "and that loyalty to family and respect for one another."

Figure 14.6 *Gesture and spoken language highlighting values enforced through intermediary layers of discourse*

Figure 14.7 *Shift in gesture to indicate the shift from discussing the intermediary layers of discourse to the general layers of discourse*

Her gesture changes, as shown in Figure 14.7, when she begins to list what she did perceive of Māori in New Zealand.

Figure 14.8 *Open-palm gesture signifying the ongoing discussion of the general layers of discourse*

Her palm opens from a closed fist with her fingers pointed toward the side. She maintains this gesture as she repeats that she saw "violence" and expands "and disrespect and horrible behavior" (Figure 14.8). She continues to maintain the gesture as she describes how these outer layers of discourse shaped her general Māori identity element: "and I thought, wow, is this what it means to be Māori?"

Within this transcript, we can see the tension between the outer layers of discourse that have shaped our participant's general Māori identity element and the intermediary layers of discourse that have shaped her continuous Māori identity element. The general Māori identity element that she perceived when she first arrived in New Zealand was a marginalized/colonized Māori identity element. This Māori identity is constructed as having low rates of educational achievement and employment, and high rates of crime and health issues. The behaviors that the participant lists – "violence and disrespect and horrible behavior" – fit within the marginalized/colonized Māori identity construct. She does not specifically state where she perceived these behaviors, and her open-palm gesture (Figure 14.8) indicates that this impression was derived from anywhere, pointing to discourses that she perceives as general layers of discourse.

This perceived general marginalized/colonized Māori identity element did not overlap with the continuous Māori identity element that had been constructed by the participant's grandmother. Her use of repetition when she says, "and that your family is your center" and "that loyalty to family and respect for each other," combined with beat gestures, highlights that importance of family within her continuous Māori identity element.

The incongruence between the continuous Māori identity element that had been constructed by her grandmother and the general marginalized/colonized Māori identity element led her to distance herself from her Māori identity element when she first immigrated to New Zealand. This is shown by her spoken language and prosody, as seen in Figure 14.9 when she says, "I did have a moment where I went, I don't know if I want to be Māori."

Figure 14.9 *Change in prosody revealing response to general layers of discourse*

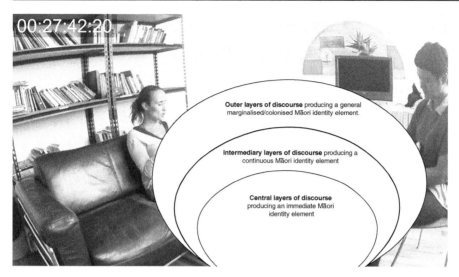

Figure 14.10 *Vertical layers of discourse producing Māori identity elements*

Figure 14.10 portrays the way in which these concrete layers of discourse come together. A marginalized/colonized identity is enforced through the outer layers of discourse. In contrast, the continuous Māori identity that the participant constructs is significantly shaped by her Māori grandmother's teachings on the importance of family. Within the site of engagement, the participant's negotiation of the outer layers of discourse and intermediary layers of discourse produce her immediate Māori identity element.

14.2.2 Bringing in Meso Practices and Macro Discourses to Make Sense of the Micro Actions

When utilizing the site of engagement as our analytic tool, we can go beyond the concrete levels of discourse/identity and examine how practices (mediated actions with a history) and discourses (mediated actions with a history with an institutional or ideological dimension) have an impact on the participant's identity production (Figure 14.11).

Within this site of engagement, racism discourse and marginalization practices that can shape identity construction for Māori become more visible. In New Zealand, the historical framework in which the racism discourse is situated is colonization. The colonial project stemmed from the foundation that one race was superior to another, and this assumption contributes to contemporary racism discourse. The site of engagement has its emphasis on micro actions produced with/through/in response to practices and larger societal discourses. This analytical tool allows us to connect the micro, the meso, and the macro levels. As the participant was born in Australia, she had not experienced or perceived the racism discourse in connection to Māori prior to

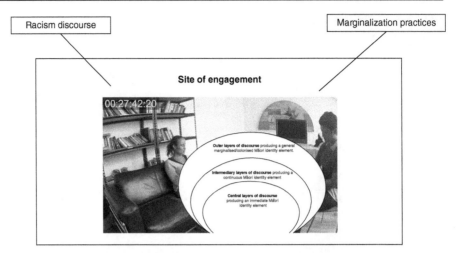

Figure 14.11 *Intersection of wider discourses, practices, and vertical identity production within a site of engagement*

her arrival in New Zealand. When she first arrived, she was thus more likely to see Māori through the racism discourse lens that constructs a marginalized/colonized Māori identity element through marginalization practices.

Our participant's use of the present and past tense at different times during her recollection of arriving in New Zealand (Figure 14.1) indicates that she did not appropriate the marginalized/colonized Māori identity being enforced by outer layers of discourse. She uses the present tense when she describes her response to the outer layers, "I don't like the way they behave, I don't relate to how they behave," which shows her first response when she came to New Zealand. Her use of the past tense shows that these perceptions and actions are not current, as the longer she stayed in New Zealand, the more her perception of Māori shifted *beyond* the original marginalized identity element that was constructed through racism discourse.

14.2.3 Production of a Fluid Identity Element

In this section, we show an interaction in which the participant's immediate fluid Māori identity element is visible. Within the transcribed mediated action, she is meeting with a Māori audio technician to explore the possibility of working together on a creative project. Earlier within the site of engagement, she had experimented with audio technology. While the participant and the technician spoke about possible project ideas, she asked him if he was interested in working in a *kaupapa Māori* context (translated as a Māori value approach). He explained that he was still learning about Māori culture.

The transcript begins with our participant responding to the technician's comment about *filling in the blanks*. She responds by relating her experience of learning *Māoritanga* (translated as Māori practices and beliefs). When the

Figure 14.12 *Participant listening to the technician*

Figure 14.13 *Spoken language, gesture, and layout indicating the significance of dance to central layers of discourse*

technician says, "I'm filling in the blanks as I'm going," our participant maintains eye contact with him (Figure 14.12).

The participant begins the mediated action with a single-handed gesture and utterance, "yeah." She then looks away while saying, "well totally, and I mean that's, part of dance has been, a journey of learning" (Figure 14.13).

The participant performs a single-handed, palm-down gesture with her fingertips as she says "learning." She continues the gesture as she says, "you know," and then adds a beat as she lists *Māoritanga*. She continues with "and you know an understanding of these things" (Figure 14.14).

Here the participant performs a similar single-handed gesture as in Figure 14.12, which, however, becomes a deictic gesture pointing at the technician when she says, "so I'm like." She then performs a two-handed gesture as she says, "like you, I'm still gathering and learning." She looks at the technician, and as she lowers her left hand, she pauses it at table height before saying "growing." As the participant says, "ahm" and looks away, her chin resting in her right hand, this indicates the shift to the next mediated action.

In the transcript, the participant performs the action of relating her experience of learning *Māoritanga* through the use of gesture, spoken language, gaze, and layout (the dance studio). For example, she performs a two-handed gesture indicating her sweeping things toward herself while saying, "like you I'm still gathering." Then her gesture changes to a static two-handed pose as if she were holding something (Figure 14.14).

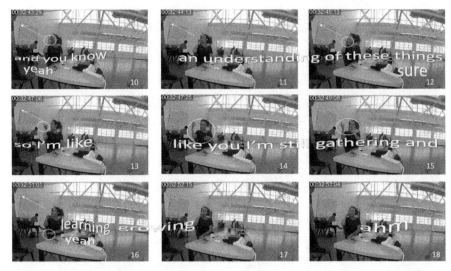

Figure 14.14 *The participant comparing her journey to the interlocutor's*

This combination of gesture and spoken language produces her immediate fluid Māori identity element as one where she is discovering what it means to be Māori. This in turn produces her immediate creative identity element, as she returned to New Zealand in order to study contemporary dance and choreography and at the same time learn more about her Māori ancestry. Therefore, through her dance and choreography, the participant produces and constructs her fluid Māori identity element alongside her creative identity element.

14.2.4 Bringing in Meso Practices and Macro Discourses to Make Sense of the Micro Actions

When we utilize the site of engagement as our analytical tool, we can see how the participant's identity differs from the one explicated above (Figure 14.15).

Within the site of engagement, both our participant's and the audio technician's actions intersect with wider colonial discourses as they are constructing themselves as both on a journey of learning their *Māoritanga* (translated as Māori practices and beliefs).

During colonization, the main economic resource that was exploited by the British was Māori land. Māori land was bought, stolen, acquired through legislation, and confiscated. The loss of land removed the economic base for many Māori and forced them to move into the cities in search of employment. The disconnection from tribal lands has led to the loss of whakapapa (genealogical) knowledge and connections for some Māori. Within this site of engagement, we see both our participant and the interlocutor express though spoken language, gesture, gaze, and layout that they are attempting to reconnect with their Māori heritage.

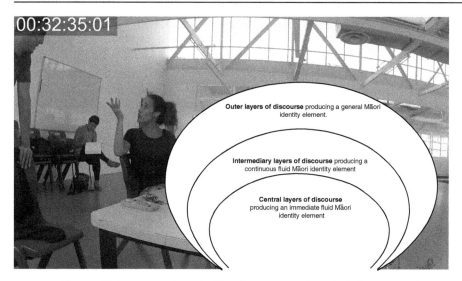

Figure 14.15 *Intersection of wider discourses and vertical identity production within a site of engagement*

14.3 Conclusion

As we tried to demonstrate in the above analysis, for our participant, the colonial discourse intersects with her ethnic identity as she searches for her lost tribal connections. Figures 14.11 and 14.15 depict two sites of engagement where the participant produces multiple identity elements. By focusing on the production of her Māori identity element, the layers of discourse that shape her general, continuous, and immediate Māori identity elements can be delineated and, by doing so, the discrepancy between certain layers becomes visible. Within the site of engagement depicted in Figure 14.11, the wider racism discourse and marginalization practices construct a general Māori identity element for her that conflicts with the continuous Māori identity element shaped by her interactions with her grandmother. The participant's use of language, gesture, and volume shows that this conflict caused her distress, as she did not want to appropriate the marginalized/colonized Māori identity element being enforced on her by the outer layers of discourse, the wider racism discourse, and wider marginalization practices. This shows that just as concrete layers of discourse and the concretely linked identity elements produced impact a person's well-being, so do the ephemeral practices and societal discourses that shape and largely enforce particular ways of producing identity elements in a society.

In contrast, Figure 14.15 depicts an overlap of identity elements as the participant produces both a fluid Māori continuous identity element and a fluid immediate Māori identity element. Her use of gesture, spoken language, gaze, and layout indicate that she is content being on a journey of learning

Māoritanga. Although her actions, and the interlocutor's actions, intersect with the wider colonial discourse, the participant produces agency as she gathers, learns, and grows in her knowledge of *Māoritanga*. Furthermore, her journey of learning produces an immediate fluid Māori identity, which contributes central, intermediary, and outer layers of discourse that positively shape the ethnic identity construction of other Māori. By producing a fluid Māori identity, she combats layers of discourse that construct marginalized/colonized Māori identity and creates space for nontraditional Māori identities. Furthermore, through her creative work, the participant contributes outer layers of discourse that shape the identity construction of other Māori.

Thus, creatives may be particularly well equipped to deal with identity discrepancies such as the ones shown in Figure 14.3. However, not all social actors fare well when identity discrepancies emerge. Rather, as demonstrated in Norris (2011), identity discrepancies between or among micro levels of discourse and/or meso and/or macro levels may result in forms of depression and mental ill-health. It is particularly this aspect of identity production that warrants closer inspection and requires further research.

References

Borrell, L. N. (2005). Racial identity among Hispanics: Implications for health and well-being. *American Journal of Public Health*, *95*(3), 379–381.

Brougham, D. & Haar, J. M. (2013). Collectivism, cultural identity and employee mental health: A study of New Zealand Māori. *Social Indicators Research*, *114*, 1143–1160. doi:10.1007/s11205-012-0196-6.

Goffman, E. (1959). *The Presentation of the Self in Everyday Life*. New York, NY: Doubleday.

Goffman, E. (1963). *Behaviour in Public Places*. New York, NY: Free Press of Glencoe.

Goffman, E. (1974). *Frame Analysis*. New York, NY: Harper and Row.

Goffman, E. (1981). *Forms of Talk*. Philadelphia, PA: University of Pennsylvania Press.

Gumperz, J. (1982). *Discourse Strategies*. Cambridge: Cambridge University Press.

Hamilton, H. E. (1998). Reported speech and survivor identity in on-line bone marrow transplantation narratives. *Journal of Sociolinguistics*, *2*(1), 53–67.

Hoogvelt, A. (1997). *Globalization and the Postcolonial World: The New Political Economy of Development*. Baltimore, MD: Johns Hopkins University Press.

Houkamau, C. (2010). Identity construction and reconstruction: The role of socio-historical contexts in shaping Māori women's identity. *Social Identities*, *16*(2), 179–196.

Houkamau, C. & Sibley, M. (2015). The revised multidimensional model of Māori identity and cultural engagement (MMM-ICE2). *Social Indicators Research*, *122*(1), 279–296. doi:10.1007/s11205-014-0686-7.

Kress, G. & Van Leeuwen, T. (1996). *Reading Images: The Grammar of Visual Design*. New York, NY: Routledge.

Kress, G. & Van Leeuwen, T. (2001). *Multimodal Discourse: The Modes and Media of Contemporary Communication*. London: Edward Arnold.

McIntosh, T. (2005). Māori identities: Fixed, fluid, forced. In J. H. Liu., T. McCreanor., T. McIntosh, & T. Teaiwa (Eds.), *New Zealand Identities, Departures and Destinations* (pp. 38–51). Wellington: Victoria University Press.

Mead, G. H. (1974). *Mind, Self and Society, from the Standpoint of a Social Behaviorist*, ed. by C. W. Morris. Chicago, IL: University of Chicago Press.

Moeke-Maxwell, T. (2005). Bi/multiracial Māori women's hybridity in Aotearoa/New Zealand. *Discourse: Studies in the Cultural Politics of Education, 26*(4), 497–510.

Moeke-Maxwell, T. (2008). Creating place from conflicted space: Bi/multi-racial Māori women's inclusion within New Zealand mental health services. In K. E. Iyall Smith & P. Leavy (Eds.), *Hybrid Identities: Theoretical and Empirical Examinations* (pp. 198–225). Retrieved May 02, 2021 from http://ebookcentral.proquest.com/lib/unitec/detail.action?docID=467684.

Norris, S. (2002). A theoretical framework for multimodal discourse analysis presented via the analysis of identity construction of two women living in Germany. Doctoral dissertation, Georgetown University, Washington, DC.

Norris, S. (2011). *Identity in (Inter)action: Introducing Multimodal (Inter)action Analysis*. Berlin and Boston: Mouton.

Norris, S. (2014). The impact of literacy based schooling on learning a creative practice: Modal configurations, practices and discourses. *Multimodal Communication, 3*(2), 181–195.

Norris, S. (2019). *Systematically Working with Multimodal Data: Research Methods in Multimodal Discourse Analysis*. Hoboken, NJ: Wiley-Blackwell.

Norris, S. (2020). *Multimodal Theory and Methodology: For the Analysis of (Inter)action and Identity*. London: Routledge.

Pack, S., Tuffin, K., & Lyons, A. (2016). Accounts of blatant racism against Māori in Aotearoa New Zealand. *Sites: A Journal of Social Anthropology and Cultural Studies, 13*(2), 85–110. Retrieved May 02, 2021 from https://sites.otago.ac.nz/Sites/article/view/326.

Paringatai, K. (2014). Māori identity development outside of tribal environments. *Aotearoa New Zealand Social Work, 26*(1), 47–54, doi:10.11157/anzswj-vol26iss1id54.

Schifrin, D. (1987). *Discourse Markers*. Cambridge: Cambridge University Press.

Scollon, R. (1997). Handbills, tissues, and condoms: A site of engagement for the construction of identity in public discourse. *Journal of Sociolinguistics, 1*(1), 39–61.

Scollon, R. (1998). *Mediated Discourse as Social Interaction*. London: Longman.

Scollon, R. (2001). *Mediated Discourse: The Nexus of Practice*. London: Routledge.

Tannen, D. (1984). *Conversational Style: Analyzing Talk among Friends*. Norwood: Ablex.

Van Leeuwen, T. (1999). *Speech, Music and Sound*. London: Macmillan.

Webber, M. (2006). Explorations of identity for people of mixed Māori/Pakeha descent: Hybridity in New Zealand. *International Journal of Diversity, 6*(2), 7–13.

Wertsch, J. (1998). *Mind as Action*. New York, NY: Oxford University Press.

15 Autoethnography

Keith Berry

This chapter examines the contributions associated with using autoethnography to study identity. I begin by describing the theoretical and philosophical perspectives that inform how I orient to identity research. I then define autoethnography and describe its history and three cultural conditions that shaped its development. I continue by detailing the commitments and practices that guide autoethnographers in "doing autoethnography." I next convey four reasons for why autoethnography matters in the study of identity. I conclude by reflecting on the outlook for using autoethnography for future identity research.

15.1 Orienting to the Study of Identity

I am a teacher and researcher in the field of Communication. My work primarily explores relational communication, or the ways in which conversation partners use linguistic (verbal) and embodied (nonverbal) messages to co-constitute, or jointly make and remake, meaning within the social interaction and relationships that comprise our ongoing, mundane, and everyday lives (Wilmot, 1995; Wood, 2000). A relational orientation assumes that communication is a mode of symbolic interaction (Blumer, 1986) in which interdependent persons come to understand ourselves, each other, and our participation within lived experience, generally. In these ways, relational communication is a dynamic and complex process of mutual influence shaped by diverse perspectives, interactional styles, and meanings.

Identity is a common focus in relational communication research. I take the concept to mean self-understanding and the constitution of subjectivity (Schrag, 2003). Put more simply, identity is who conversation partners understand ourselves, and others, to be. A relational approach to studying identity focuses on how identity influences the ways partners communicate, or do not communicate (i.e., what, how, and why partners interact, and the meanings of interactions), and, in turn, the ways in which partners co-constitute identities within the process of interacting and sustaining relationships (i.e., how communication forms identities) (Wilmot, 1995; Wood, 2000; Gergen, 2009). Thus, while genetics and biology certainly influence relating and being, a relational approach primarily focuses on identity as an inherently social process that is ongoing and fluid, and not static or fixed. Indeed, identity is subject to be as dynamic and complex as the lived experience in which it matters, and comes to be.

Three additional factors inform this orientation to identity. First, identity is comprised not of a singular self, but a multiplicity of selves, or ways of performing and understanding ourselves, which coexist and impact relational communication (Gergen, 1991, 2009; Schrag, 1997, 2003). Identity is a multi-dimensional phenomenon. Thus, examining identity relationally necessarily entails considering identit*ies*.

Second, identities are culturally distinctive (Carbaugh, 1996; Wilmot, 1995; Wood, 2000). Culture is "a socially constructed and historically transmitted pattern of symbols, meanings, premises, and rules" constitutive of, and illus-trated within, communication (Philipsen, 1992, p. 9). Rather than being an issue merely of one's biology or genetics, or something to which one claims member-ship, culture is a discursive accomplishment, or resource, which informs, and is informed by, the ways partners relate within situated contexts of communi-cation (Carbaugh, 1996). This perspective assumes that communication and culture are intrinsically related social phenomena that result in an understand-ing of who partners are, or are not, in terms of any number of dimensions that pertain to identity (e.g., ability status, class, ethnicity, political affiliation, race, sex/gender, sexual orientation) (Carbaugh, 1996; Philipsen, 1992).

Third, a closer inspection of the communicative co-constitution of identities would suggest that who people are, or become, is often not only a matter of identity formation but identity *negotiation* (see Allen, 2011; Bardhan & Orbe, 2012; Berry, 2007; Durham, 2014; Goffman, 1963; Jackson, 2002). To charac-terize identity as something conversation partners "negotiate" assumes that the making and remaking of identities is a contested process, which is informed, and sometimes governed, by social constraints (e.g., power). In this sense, partners negotiate who we are with and for others, which, in turn, entails the experience of "gains" and "losses" concerning who we may or may not understand ourselves to be. Overall, this standpoint serves as a way for researchers to uncover and interrogate the taken-for-granted assumptions and expectations that shape normative conceptualizations of identities, and to reimagine more inclusive ways of relating and being, and conducting research on identity.

I also orient to identity research by drawing on hermeneutic phenomenology. This philosophical worldview entails the descriptive and contingent examin-ation of people's "lifeworld" (i.e., everyday reality), and, more specifically, the ways in which we discern human understanding (inter)subjectively, or from the unique vantage point of our lived experience with others (Husserl, 1970/1954; Langsdorf, 1994; Schrag, 2003). Phenomenologically speaking, there are no two identical ways of interpreting any one given phenomenon. Thus, the issues that shape lived experience, including identity issues, are subject to multiple inter-pretations. In addition, phenomenology focuses primarily on concrete and particularized instances of social practices and their meanings, and aims to enact more circumspect, or "rounded," examinations. Not all autoethnographers know or use phenomenology, and I might not always explicitly invoke the worldview in writing. Nevertheless, phenomenology guides all of my research.

15.2 Autoethnography: A Personal and Cultural Story

Autoethnography is a qualitative and interpretive approach to research and writing in which researchers systematically draw on the unique vantage point of our lived experience to describe, interpret, and sometimes critique issues concerning cultural lives and identities. More specifically, Ellis and Bochner (2000) define autoethnography as:

> an autobiographical genre of writing and research that displays multiple layers of consciousness, connecting the personal to the cultural. Back and forth, autoethnographers gaze, first, through an ethnographic wide-angle lens, focusing outward on social and cultural aspects of their personal experience; then, they look inward, exposing a vulnerable self that is moved by and may move through, refract, and resist cultural interpretations. As they zoom backward and forward, inward and outward, distinctions between the personal and cultural become blurred, sometimes beyond recognition.   (p. 739)

Scholars engage with this (inter)subjective process to call into question the status quo, using inquiry to trouble and reimagine "canonical ways of doing research and representing others and to treat research as a political, socially-just, and socially-conscious act" (Ellis, Adams, & Bochner, 2011). Autoethnographers' personal stories dwell at the heart of the research, and identities commonly serve as primary focal points in these stories. The stories are often untold accounts that "mainstream" social scientific research has overlooked or ignored. Thus, autoethnography enables scholars to acknowledge, explore, and advocate a multiplicity of stories (and beings) that exist, are valuable, and merit inclusion and care.

Autoethnography is known for its diversity in concept and form (Ellis & Bochner, 2000). Conceptually, autoethnographies tend to focus on cultural issues that entail hardship. They show people relating in the process of addressing powerful cultural topics and issues, including, but not limited to ableism (Scott, 2018), classism (Boylorn, 2013; Dunn, 2018), "coming out" as gay (Adams, 2011), death, grief, and loss (Ellis, 2018; Paxton, 2018), LGBTQ cultures and identities (Berry, Gillotti, & Adams, 2020) and queer people of color (LeMaster, 2014), marriage (Faulkner, 2016), normative motherhood (Faulkner, 2012, 2014), racism (Calafell, 2016), transphobia (Nordmarken, 2014), and meta-methodological issues that condition the enactment of research and writing that uses autoethnography (Berry, 2021; Berry & Warren, 2009; Ellis, 2009). In terms of form, scholars often represent autoethnographies by using a heightened attention to creativity and experimentation. Bochner and Adams (2020) write:

> Usually written in the first-person voice, autoethnographic texts take a variety of forms – short stories, poetry, fiction, novels, documentaries, photographic essays, personal essays, journals, fragmented and layered writing, and social science prose. In these texts, concrete action, dialogue, emotion, embodiment, spirituality, and self-consciousness are featured in relational, family, institutional, and community stories affected by history, social structure, and culture, which themselves are revealed through action, feeling, thought, and language.   (p. 715)

Taken together, the commitment to openness in concept and form provides scholars with an especially inclusive, complex, and generative mode of inquiry.

The aims and scope of autoethnography enable scholars to operate with an unapologetic engagement of personhood; orienting to the "bias" of subjectivities not as a deterrent to, but a resource for enacting meaningful research and writing (Ellis, 2004). Consequently, autoethnography does not pursue the ideal of objectivity, nor does it address issues of validity and reliability. Instead, autoethnographers aim to write stories that evoke a sense of verisimilitude, or "a feeling that the experience described is lifelike, believable, and possible, a feeling that what has been represented could be true" (Ellis, Adams, & Bochner, 2011). In these ways, as I describe more fully below, autoethnography creates the conditions for scholars to draw on, and work through, issues pertinent to our unique lived experience, and, to convey them in ways that others might be able to identify *their* stories in *ours* (Berry & Patti, 2015; Ellis, Adams, & Bochner, 2011; Holman Jones, Adams, & Ellis, 2013).

15.3 History and Development of Autoethnography

The history of autoethnography traces back to the 1970s, when researchers began to invoke the term to consider the relevance of the self and subjectivity to research (Goldschmidt, 1977; Hayano, 1979; Heider, 1975). In the 1980s, more scholars in a number of fields, such as Communication and Sociology, worked in ways that demonstrated and advocated the benefits of research that entailed personal narrative, subjectivity, and reflexivity (see Denzin, 1989; Van Maanen, 1988). In this decade scholars wrote themselves "into" their research and addressed issues concerning this practice, effectively troubling the normative research ideal of objectivity, and speaking to the ways in which researchers' subjectivities influence this work (Ellis & Adams, 2014). The presence and use of autoethnography increased significantly during the 1990s when more scholars began to use personal narratives in/as research (Ellis & Adams, 2014; Brockmeier & Harré, 1997). For instance, scholars explored the vitality of writing as a "vulnerable observer" (Behar, 1996), engaging in "sociological introspection" (Ellis, 1991), and writing as a "method of inquiry" (Richardson, 1994). In addition, Arthur Bochner and Carolyn Ellis established the Ethnographic Alternatives book series; manuscripts published in the series demonstrated various uses of personal stories and autoethnography in research.[1] Overall, the 1990s was a significant and exciting decade for the method which "helped carve out a special place for emotional and personal scholarship, and the term 'autoethnography' soon became the descriptor of choice" (Ellis & Adams, 2014, p. 256).

The engagement of autoethnography as an academic space that welcomes personal, emotional, and reflexive accounts of cultural experiences and identities exploded in the new millennium. Ellis and Bochner (2000) detailed the benefits and challenges inherent to using autoethnography and personal narrative.[2] Additionally, in 2005 Norman Denzin created the International Center for Qualitative Inquiry and the International Congress of Qualitative Inquiry (ICQI), an organization and annual conference that provides a venue for research that uses autoethnography and other creative and experimental approaches. Also, in 2013 scholars saw the publication of the first edition of the *Handbook of Autoethnography* (Holman Jones, Adams, & Ellis, 2013).

Today, at the beginning of the third decade of the new millennium, autoethnography is comprised of a burgeoning interdisciplinary and international community of scholars who represent a diverse number of disciplines (e.g., anthropology, business, communication, criminology, education, music, nursing, psychology, political science, sociology) and different parts of the world (e.g., Australia, Canada, England, Germany, Mexico, Poland, Scotland, the United States, South Africa) (Adams & Herrmann, 2020; Turner et al., 2018; Ellis, Adams, & Bochner, 2011; Holman Jones, Adams, & Ellis, 2013). The ICQI continues to meet annually, and the International Association for Autoethnography and Narrative Inquiry was recently formed and will hold an annual conference for scholars to share autoethnographic research. Also, Adams and Herrmann (2020) recently founded the *Journal of Autoethnography* to serve as the first academic journal dedicated exclusively to autoethnography.[3]

***

Adams, Holman Jones, and Ellis (2015) describe three historical issues that led to the development of autoethnography. These issues relate to cultural

---

[1] The series continues today under the name Writing Lives: Ethnographic Autoethnographic Narratives, edited by Arthur Bochner, Carolyn Ellis, and Tony Adams (Routledge).

[2] Ellis and Bochner (2000) is one of the major milestones in the history of autoethnography in terms of how it beautifully introduces scholars to the method. At the time of writing the current chapter, Google Scholar shows that scholars have cited this handbook chapter 6,694 times. Also, scholars have cited Ellis, Adams, and Bochner (2011), the follow-up chapter to Ellis and Bochner (2000), 4,803 times.

[3] See Ellis and Adams (2014), Holman Jones, Adams, and Ellis (2013), and Adams, Holman Jones, and Ellis (2015) for a more detailed history of the method.

conditions occurring around the time when autoethnography first began to develop. Although they are interrelated, I address each issue individually.

Part of the advent of autoethnography relates to an evolution in scholars' ways of orienting to and conducting research. The "crisis of representation" shined a light on and questioned normative research commitments and practices, including the pursuit of "universal Truths" and the ideal of "objectivity"; the prevalence of fixed and certain positions on people's experiences and identities; the prejudice against and discounting of the use of affect and emotion in research; the disregard for the ways researchers' identities shape inquiry processes; the privileging of generalized over "local" forms of knowledge; the exclusion of narrative ways of knowing; and the intrusive, objectifying, and colonialist assumptions and practices that inform "traditional" ethnographic research (Adams, Holman Jones, & Ellis, 2015; Ellis & Adams, 2014). Autoethnography invited researchers to tell and learn from a different kind of story about culture and cultural beings, emphasizing and legitimizing particularized or local forms of knowledge; contingent and uncertain accounts of lived experience; uses of affect and emotion in research; the influence and benefits of researchers' identities in research processes; and the use of personal stories as resources for understanding others and ourselves (Adams, Holman Jones, & Ellis, 2015; Ellis & Adams, 2014).

Ethical issues concerning ethnographic research, including issues of power and representation, also led to the development of autoethnography (Adams, Holman Jones, & Ellis, 2015). Often also known as "realist" ethnography (VanMaanen, 1988), ethnography commonly entailed extensive fieldwork in a cultural context, and conducting interviews with cultural members. In this way, ethnographers served as cultural auditors, "outsiders" who worked in the field to audit, report on, and eventually write up a meaningful story on cultural life. Although some ethnographers accounted for personal issues in relationship to the culture they studied, often in the form of "confessional tales" (VanMaanen, 1988), ethnography was supposed to be about studying "others." Realist ethnography has produced vital work that conveys fascinating cultural accounts. Yet, ethical questions remained with respect to the nuances of the research including: What is the relationship between ethnographers and the persons being studied? How do ethnographers affect people's lives, and to whose benefit and at whose expense? After all, when ethnographers speak *about* a cultural group, we are effectively speaking *for* the group (Alcoff, 1991). In what ways can ethnography benefit by valorizing "insider" information, such as the perspective for which autoethnography provides, and in ways that do not protect against, but directly engage with and confront ethnographers' biases?

Autoethnography developed also as a response to increased societal issues concerning identities. The 1960s and 1970s in the United States are known historically for significant civil rights issues and movements – e.g., Black Power, second-wave feminism, the Stonewall Riots, Vietnam, to name just a few – and related protests and social unrest (Adams, Holman Jones, & Ellis, 2015; Holman Jones,

Ellis, & Adams, 2013). These issues led to the emergence of identity politics, which uncovered the ways identities, and problems related to one's difference, inform, and sometimes govern, people's everyday lives and research. Identity politics stressed that people's identities were important, and scholars should not take them lightly. As I explore below, autoethnography invited researchers to position identities, and issues pertaining to cultural identities, at the center of inquiry.

15.4 Doing Autoethnography

Scholars design their autoethnographic research projects in a variety of ways. For instance, some autoethnographers draw on the language (e.g., "unit of analysis," "data") and format (e.g., literature review, research questions, findings) of social scientific inquiry, because the approach is often more accessible and understandable across disciplines (Adams, Holman Jones, & Ellis 2015). Yet, others use language and format in ways that distinguish themselves from established conventions. For instance, most autoethnographers do not use the term "unit of analysis" and few use the term "data." In addition, some autoethnographers ask formal and explicit research questions, while others ask more implicit or less formal questions (Adams, Holman Jones, & Ellis, 2015). Thus, project design is yet another aspect that further illustrates the commitment to openness in autoethnography (Ellis & Bochner, 2000).

Although there is no one, singular way to design and enact autoethnography, scholars do tend to draw on common ways of orienting to, and practicing, the research (Adams, Holman Jones, & Ellis, 2015). The following section provides an overview of the commitments and practices that scholars often incorporate in their inquiry. Experiences from the research process that led to the publication of *Bullied: Tales of Torment, Identity, and Youth* (hereafter *Bullied*) (Berry, 2016) are included to illustrate the main ideas.

Bullied uses autoethnography to examine the societal problem of youth bullying from a relational communication and identity perspective. The symbolically negotiated interactions, relationships, and identities produced within bullying experiences serve as its particular focus. The basis for the book is a research study conducted in conjunction with the students who were enrolled in two sections of a past interpersonal communication course at my university.[4] The stories students wrote for their final course projects, and my own

---

[4] The Institutional Review Board (IRB) at University of South Florida (USF) approved this study (Pro00014179). All of the names listed in the book and the current chapter are pseudonyms, chosen by each of the women. I solicited participation for this study after I formally submitted grades for the course. USF's IRB does not consider autoethnography "human subjects research," largely because the research does not seek generalizable findings; thus, research that uses the method is typically exempted from needing institutional approval. However, the study that led to the publication of *Bullied* required IRB approval because I was utilizing former students' stories.

stories, served as the primary focus of the investigation. These research questions guided the inquiry: "In what ways is bullying a mode of relational communication?" and "In what ways do youth co-constitute identities within the communication and relationships comprising bullying?"

There are four central dimensions to *Bullied*. First, the project as a whole is an autoethnographic account that tells the story of my teaching the class and mentoring students in learning about bullying, interpersonal communication, and autoethnographic storytelling. The story begins on the first day of class and ends on the last day of the semester. Second, the book conveys and examines five autoethnographic stories of bullying written by students, all of whom are women (Iman, Jessi, Jezebel, Lauren, and Ena). Each chapter includes one of the woman's stories written for class and my analysis of her story (see below). Third, joining the women's stories are five "reflexive interludes," smaller autoethnographic stories that explore the bullying I experienced during my youth. One interlude appears in between each of the main chapters. Fourth, each interlude ends with a "methodological dilemma" which investigates practical issues that relate to using autoethnography to study issues of violence, such as bullying, as learned in the process of completing the study and writing my book. The dilemmas demonstrate a number of issues including those related to my uncertainty about ways of mitigating the emotional and psychological risks students took in writing and sharing their stories.

Enacting or "doing" autoethnography typically entails a wide array of commitments and practices. First, *doing autoethnography entails autobiography and ethnography* (Ellis, Bochner, & Adams 2011; see also Bochner & Ellis, 2016). As a mode of *autobiography*, scholars reflect on and write about cultural experiences from the past, drawing on memories (Bochner, 2014) of life-shaping events to demonstrate the ways those experiences influence a particular way of living and being. The method also involves writing about/ through epiphanies, the moments of lived experience that had a significant impact on writers' lives. Working retroactively in these ways immerses auto-ethnographers in a complex investigation of subjectivity that seeks to render experiences and identities meaningful (Bochner, 2000).

As a mode of *ethnography*, autoethnographers study the ways in which people create, use, and interpret culture and cultural identities (Ellis, Bochner, & Adams, 2011). This orientation also immerses scholars in a "field" to observe and document cultural life as it is being lived. Autoethnographers also sometimes conduct ethnographic interviews, to learn more about the meaningfulness of the observed phenomena. In these ways, using autobiography and ethnography provides autoethnographers with a space in which to move "inward" and "outward," thus, creating a "blurred" portrait of the personal and cultural (Ellis & Bochner, 2000, p. 739).

The research process that led to *Bullied* involved both of these research practices. For instance, I encouraged students to engage in informal conversations with family members, friends, or others who might offer them memories and insights about the bullying. My own writing process also entailed this relational practice. These interactions aimed to enrich our perspectives. In addition, the choice itself to convey and explore the women's stories in *Bullied*, and not limit the project to only *my* stories, served as a way to create a more expansive and richer understanding of bullying, its impact, and the scope of the problem.

Second, *doing autoethnography entails choices in type of representation and different approaches to theory and analysis.* There is a range of forms scholars use in autoethnography (see Bochner & Ellis, 2016; Ellis, Adams, & Bochner, 2011). Autoethnographies often take the form of *personal narratives* in which scholars focus on creating stories that show us living through a series of episodes or scenes comprising a cultural issue. They also can take the form of *layered accounts*, which entail scholars integrating moments or aspects of their lived experience with other materials, such as statistics and ideas from extant literature. In this case, each layer offers a distinct idea concerning the focus of the account. *Co-constructed narratives* emphasize relational experiences and struggles and are written relationally, or jointly, by two autoethnographers. This approach entails the consideration of multiple vantage points taken by writers in response to a shared experience or cultural issue. There are additional approaches to representation used in autoethnography, including some that combine one or more of the above styles, and some that involve photography, poetry, and other aural/visual artifacts.[5]

Scholars approach analysis in autoethnographies in various ways (Ellis, 2004; Ellis, Adams, & Bochner, 2011). Some autoethnographers forgo formal analysis, in favor of simply telling a good story, out of a concern that analysis will interrupt readers or audience members as they move through the account.[6] Other scholars include analysis, but set the analytical sections apart from the story itself, for the same reason mentioned above. Similarly, scholars often engage with theory and theorizing with autoethnographies (Adams, Holman Jones, & Ellis, 2015), a choice that is accomplished in a variety of ways. For instance, some autoethnographies embed a theoretical insight at the specific moment of a story to which the idea relates. Others include theory and theorizing in a separate analytical section. Yet others chose not to explicitly incorporate theory at all in autoethnographies.

The stories in *Bullied* take the form of personal narratives. Each narrative includes several "episodes" or scenes from the storyteller's lived experience with bullying. All students who participated in the study had the opportunity to revise their stories prior to submitting them for inclusion in the book. None

---

[5] See Ellis (2004), Ellis, Adams, and Bochner (2011), and Bochner and Ellis (2016) for additional approaches and examples.

[6] Hereafter, for ease in prose, I use "readers" to refer to both the persons who read printed scholarship and those who serve as audience members to staged performances.

of them chose to revise. In addition, each chapter includes my analysis of the given story rooted in issues concerning relational communication, identity, and bullying. The analyses primarily focused on the ways in which the women's stories demonstrated identity negotiation regarding issues of stigma (Goffman, 1963) and related passing and covering practices (Yoshino, 2007). Once polished full drafts of the chapters were completed, I met and had lunch with each woman individually. At these meetings, each woman reviewed her chapter, had the chance to express concerns and offer corrections, and, if desired, withdraw from the research process. Concerns were limited to one woman (Jessi) feeling that I had overcharacterized an aspect of her identity in the analysis of her story. Jessi and I worked together to correct that moment to match her understanding. No one withdrew from the project.[7]

For the reasons mentioned above, the women's stories, and my reflexive interludes, do not use theory or theorizing. Also, there is a format break in between the women's stories and my analysis of their accounts. Their accounts told such powerful stories, so I did not wish to take away from them by incorporating analysis. My analyses of their stories draw on theory.

Third, *doing autoethnography is personal and entails vulnerability*. Most scholars practice reflexivity, or work introspectively to reflect and draw on one's lived experience with respect to the cultural issue being explored (Berry & Clair, 2011; Bochner & Ellis, 2016; Ellis, 2004; Goodall, 2000). This practice entails taking seriously the (inter)subjective nature of research and lived experience, more generally. In turn, autoethnographers commonly reflect on, document, and investigate intimate aspects of our identities and fraught cultural issues of hardship, which renders the work personal. Similarly, the method also requires vulnerability, a readiness to open oneself to processing intimate, complex, and often difficult experiences and, in doing so, subject oneself to the gaze and potential evaluation of others. It also entails working to be open to our own reactions (e.g., self-criticism, sadness, uncertainty).

Iman is a Black American woman whose story in *Bullied* centers on mental illness, race, and bullying. She wrote about being diagnosed with severe depression at a young age, and being bullied at school for, according to the peers who bullied her, trying to "act White," and at home for "not being Black enough" in the eyes of some family members. Seeing no relief in the near future, Iman became suicidal.

> There were nights when I'd be in my room, lying on my bed, and in a constant battle with myself on why my life was worth living. No one accepted me. No

---

[7] The students spent the entire semester writing their stories. Their instructions were to write a personal story that talks about and shows the bullying they experienced in their youth, whether that be as the person who bullied others, was bullied by others, and/or witnessed bullying; make sure the story they tell relates to relational communication and identity; and try to use specific and vivid detail. One student did not feel she had a bullying story to tell; she received an alternative final project assignment. See Berry (2016) for an extensive discussion of the teaching philosophy and other aspects of the research protocol.

> one liked me, and because of that, I didn't like myself. Even if people around me were smiling, they still would make a negative comment about my not fitting in, or not being good enough. The negative energy I endured over the years that made me hate myself. I was never good enough for anything, or anyone, so my life didn't seem to me to be of much value. There were several nights when I cried myself to sleep with thoughts of committing suicide. I cried because I knew I shouldn't want to take my life, yet the thoughts constantly running through my mind told me suicide was the only option. I could not identify my purpose for living. Was I here for others' comical relief?   (Berry, 2016, p. 32)

Iman's prose and overall story speak to the candid prose and intimate details revealed in many autoethnographies, and the need to write vulnerably when using this approach. Granted, not all autoethnographies write about issues as extreme as suicidal ideation; but, most, if not all, are personal and vulnerable. There is no one set formula for use in determining *if* a writer should share an intimate detail, and just how intimate one writes. Also, autoethnographers need to feel safe in telling our stories (Ellis, 2004).

Fourth, *doing autoethnography is relational.* Autoethnography commonly shines a light on interpersonal issues that shape people's lives (Bochner & Ellis, 2016; Ellis, 2004). Scholars write stories that display the interconnected nature of beings and bodies, the mutual influence people have on one another, and the complications that arise in trying to live a meaningful life.

In *Bullied*, Jezebel conveys her story of being bullied by "Cruella" over the course of three consecutive days in the school lunchroom, a social space Jezebel dreaded. Her story highlights the relational insights that comprise stories, in this case in regards to the challenges of coping within bullying. At the center of the story is her best friend, Rose.

> "Rose!" There Rose was, stumbling around like a lost puppy, someone I identified with. I instinctively waved her over in a reeling sort of motion with my hands; I needed her help. I could feel the dark fog, the grimacing stares around me clear away as I realized I was not alone. With a bright smile that almost creased all the way to her eyebrows, her shoes turned into pogo sticks as she gleefully bounced over to me and joined me in the line. Safe, I was finally safe. I could breathe a sigh of relief as the loneliness and worry evaporated away from me.   (Berry, 2016, p. 75)

Rose routinely helped to keep Jezebel calm and collected. Jezebel relied on her. However, one day Rose did not defend her, inaction that devastated Jezebel.

> She was a first-hand witness, and she made no effort to actively ease the situation. It was almost as if she was trying to embody a stranger, a bystander, someone who isn't expected to step in. Her own fear stifled her from being a hero to a close friend. In that moment she was a cold stranger to me.   (Berry, 2016, p. 80)

Jezebel felt betrayed and alone. At the end of her story, she surmised that Rose may have wanted to be there to support her, but did not think she could defend both herself and Jezebel at the same time. She forgave Rose, and the two remained best friends. The relationships that comprise autoethnographers' lives are commonplace in autoethnographies (Ellis, 2004), and the focus varies based on the type of relationship (e.g., friendship, romantic, family), the quality of the bond (e.g., intimate, loving, distant), and the impact of the relationship on characters' lives and identities (e.g., affirming, disconfirming).

Fifth, *doing autoethnography entails ethical considerations.* Autoethnography engages with the vital issue of ethics in at least two main ways. On one level, autoethnographers routinely ask questions and make decisions and adjustments to research protocols that concern the goal of "doing no harm" to others, including the people who participate in one's research. Yet, because it is a personal story-based approach to research and writing, autoethnographers often also have questions to ask about relational ethics (Ellis, 2007). What are the risks associated in this work for the people portrayed in a story? How *are* autoethnographers portraying others? How does the story make them appear? What personal details are autoethnographers free to tell? How will a story, or a particular story moment, impact the relationship portrayed? The stakes are significant in autoethnographies, and there are no easy answers to ethical questions. Still, autoethnographers must ask them persistently.

On another level, the relational nature of autoethnography creates opportunities for autoethnographers to reflect on, and incorporate into writing, issues concerning the ethical treatment of others in everyday lives. For instance, Jessi's story in *Bullied* detailed the ways her friends bullied her, and how she bullied them in return. Most of this aggression entailed cyberbullying. She writes:

> It was just so easy to say horrible words online without consequences. None of us ever had the guts to say anything to each other in person. We threatened each other physically online, but none of us said those same words to each other at school. Online you forget there is a person on the other side. You don't see their emotions, or their physical reactions. It's easy to forget your humanity, and to decipher right from wrong, especially when you are young and still learning, especially when you aren't face to face to see the impact of your choices.   (Berry, 2016, p. 55)

Jessi's account demonstrates how the method invites scholars to pause and begin to reflect on the choices people make relationally, and the meanings of those choices in terms of the well-being of others and ourselves.

Sixth, *doing autoethnography entails descriptive and evocative writing.* Scholars enact the practice of "thick description" (Geertz, 1973), a heightened attention to detail, to represent cultural life. This often also involves writing that "shows" the cultural issues being lived, to create an engaging account that invites others to feel as if they are there "with" the writer in the lived experience being conveyed (Ellis & Bochner, 2000; Ellis, Adams, & Bochner, 2011; Holman Jones, Adams & Ellis, 2013; Adams, Holman Jones, & Ellis, 2015).

Similarly, autoethnographic stories often entail evocative writing, or prose that is highly sensorial and uses vivid detail and emotion to compel readers to think and feel "with" the story and its author/s (Bochner & Ellis, 2016; Ellis, 2004). Good autoethnographic writing moves readers.

Several passages in *Bullied* show this practice in action. For instance, although Iman, thankfully, did not end her life, she did secretly resort to the self-harming process of "cutting" to find relief. She conveys the first night of cutting herself in vivid detail:

> I looked all over the house for the right blade, and I knew right where to look: my dad works on houses, and so he had all sorts of blades and construction tools. While looking for his tools I stumbled across a very sharp paper opener, or maybe it was an envelope opener – I'm not sure the correct terminology for the device. The blade was sharp, and so after that night, the opener became my tool of relief. My stomach was the spot on my body where I chose to cut. I wanted an area where no one could see any marks, unless I showed them.   (Berry, 2016, p. 32)

Also, Lauren's story uses evocative detail to convey the bullying she endured, which often targeted the blonde highlights she had in her hair. To the peers who bullied her, she was the abject "highlight girl." Their bullying was so harmful to Lauren that she decided to remove the highlights in her hair.

> I remember that day vividly. Sitting in the stylist's chair, I closed my eyes as she put the chemicals in my hair. My scalp burned, but I told myself the sting was nothing compared to the ways I would feel once my hurt was gone. Once she was done, the stylist let me look in the mirror, and the person I saw staring back at me was overwhelmingly soothing to me. I felt like a different person ... As I ran my hands through it, I got a little choked up. I assured my mom I was happy with how it turned out. Yet, I knew the true reason for my happiness: I was a new girl. I was untouchable.   (Berry, 2016, p. 106)

Iman's and Lauren's stories create the conditions for powerful reactions. Personally, I am "by" Iman's side as she looks for her "tool of relief," but I want to talk her out of cutting herself, out of sadness and worry for her. Also, I can feel Lauren's burning scalp as I read her description, but just wish she did not have to change her appearance to alleviate the bullying. These samples show the ways autoethnographers use specific and vivid language to engage readers, to help us understand the lived experience enacted, and what it feels like and means to be human.

Seventh, *doing autoethnography highlights and responds to cultural norms.* As mentioned above, autoethnographies often serve as a response to canonical stories or normative conceptualizations of cultural life, in ways that create a space in which to convey the stories and validate the storytellers who have been left out of, or ignored, in mainstream research. In doing so, this work uncovers and investigates myriad social problems.

Ena conveys her story about horrible acts of sexual assault and rape that she experienced in her childhood and youth, which she contends were modes of bullying. She wrote:

> To think we do not live in a culture of violence, a culture of rape, and a culture of blaming the victim is to perpetuate something so problematic it causes young people to live through unacceptable harm.   (Berry, 2016, p. 131)

> Sexual assault is often excluded in conversations about bullying, and that's a problem. I've brought it up to people, and almost every time they say I am being "dramatic," and that assault is on a completely different plane. But sexual assault *is* bullying because of the intense power it gives the bully, and the embarrassment it leads victims to feel. Victims of sexual bullying, like me, feel guilt and shame. Our feelings are not present in "typical" bullying stories. It would help to expand our thinking on bullying!   (Berry, 2016, p. 131)

> My story makes me feel the "fault" for this problem is bigger than any one of us. We all did this. Our culture says we need to "lighten up," "get over it," "grow thicker skin," and that "it gets better." Twitter and Facebook are overrun with the most heinous jokes about rape, or statements suggesting there's nothing wrong with bullying, or that bullying isn't an issue. Parts of our culture even suggest that victims "asked for it," or that we had as much of a role in the violence as perpetrators. Well, now I understand that as a young person I never allowed bullying and abuse, I just *endured* and *survived* it.   (Berry, 2016, p. 132)

Ena's account is, to me, as important as it is disturbing. She resists ambiguity by choosing the precise words to describe and critique the normative behavior related to the violence she "endured" and "survived." Her account speaks to the ways in which autoethnography offers scholars a path on which to respond to violence and social injustice, more generally. Not all autoethnographies examine cultural issues that are so grave, nor do all autoethnographers engage in explicit critique and calls for action or social reform. However, autoethnographies do usually draw attention and respond to cultural norms in ways that challenge people to think more deeply and inclusively about cultural life.

Eighth, *doing autoethnography entails evaluation.* The open nature of autoethnography might tempt some scholars to assume that "anything goes" in terms of enacting autoethnography, and that the personal nature of stories, accounts of hardship no less, makes critiquing autoethnographers' stories feel insensitive, and maybe even wrong. Granted, these factors do in fact sometimes make responding to and critiquing autoethnographies a tenuous process (Berry, 2006); but there are established criteria for the evaluation of autoethnography.

For instance, Richardson (2000) asks whether the autoethnographies she is reviewing make a "substantial contribution . . . to our understanding of social-life" (p. 254) and expects them to do so. Bochner (2000) looks for "abundant, concrete detail . . . structurally complex narratives . . . that express a tale of two selves; a believable journey from who I was to who I am, a life course reimagined or transformed by crisis" (pp. 270–271). Ellis (2000) asks what she has learned from the story: "Is there anything 'new' here or a new way to view or twist the familiar?" (p. 275). She also looks at plot and the development of characters and scenes, and ethical considerations concerning both the authors and the persons portrayed in stories (Ellis, 2007). To be sure, there are "good" and "bad" autoethnographies. These and other factors help autoethnographers assess quality, and in ways that align with established autoethnographic commitments and practices.[8]

15.5 Why Autoethnography Matters

There are at least four main reasons why autoethnography matters in the study of identity. I describe each of these next, and then conclude this chapter with a brief outlook for future research that uses the method to study identity.

15.5.1 Autoethnography/Identities as Intertwined

Autoethnography matters because the method and identities are irrevocably intertwined. Given that identities dwell at the foreground of the research, researchers are able to examine this focus in sustained and thorough ways, and consider the positive and negative ways in which people's participation in relational and cultural life impacts who we understand ourselves to be. In fact, it is difficult to think of a way in which autoethnography would exist or survive without a concern and priority for identities.

The ways autoethnographers engage with identities adds further credence to the usefulness of the method. On one level, autoethnography invites scholars to engage with a confounding but vital existential issue – the relationship between selves and others. Autoethnographies show people moving through life, relating with others, and working to reconcile experiences together that are, at once, difficult and joyous, and perilous and promising. On another level, the detailed telling of *intimate* and *inclusive* stories matters. Ellis and Adams (2014) write, "[i]f our goal is to do *social* science research, to study people, then we should include as much of the person as possible, and not relegate parts of our lives and our selves to the periphery" (p. 258, emphasis in the original). Indeed, it is vital to get up close and personal when attempting to learn how people live, who people are, and how people affect each other. Autoethnographies assist by putting meat on the bones, so to speak, to this learning process.

---

[8] See Richardson (2000), Bochner (2000), and Ellis (2000) for additional criteria.

15.5.2 Cultural Issues (on Identities)

Autoethnography's emphasis on difficult cultural issues is another reason why the method matters. As described above, scholars take up challenging and, at times, some of the most awful issues related to identities. The method provides a much-needed platform for inquiry that aims to better understand these issues and to stress their importance, in ways that try to make life better.

The communicative nature of the method and its aim to write stories that will resonate with the experience of people who read them create the conditions for responses to this work that matter. For instance, some readers might identify with the problem being conveyed and explored in an autoethnography. Here the research makes possible a sense of connection and understanding. It provides them with a story on which they might be able hook their own story and not feel alone. At the same time, others might have little or no connection to the identity issues being investigated. Autoethnography provides these readers with a pedagogical possibility that matters, as it creates an opportunity to learn about identities different than one's own, and cultural issues of difference that call for critique and reform (Boylorn & Orbe, 2014).

15.5.3 Uneasiness with Identities

Autoethnography matters because it helps to uncover a fundamental uneasiness that some scholars feel when it comes to talking about identities. This dis-ease shows itself in the concerns that some scholars assign to autoethnography, and is curious and worthy of reflection.

Scholars might feel uneasy because they are unaware of the aims and scope of autoethnography and the writing practices it entails. For instance, they might not yet know that effective autoethnography is never only about autoethnographers (Berry & Patti, 2015; Bochner & Ellis, 2016; Ellis, 2004). In addition, scholars may be uncomfortable with the practice of writing so personally and intimately, and as a function of research, leading them to label stories as being "self-indulgent" and "not real research." These worries, at least in part, signal the sort of political position that shows lasting signs of the pursuit of objectivity and Truth that still governs inquiry, by having a stranglehold on how people orient to, understand, represent, and practice identities and research. Additionally, some may be uneasy because of the canonical cultural story that suggests that talking about oneself generally is necessarily self-centered and conceited. Also, some scholars may be uncomfortable because of the ways in which an *autoethnographic* engagement of identities disrupts and destabilizes what they believe to be true about personhood. For instance, an autoethnography that explores racism or homophobia might challenge their racist or homophobic beliefs. Yet, some scholars may be comfortable with practicing reflexivity in ethnography, but not in the more intimate ways in which the practice often happens in autoethnography. Similarly, some scholars may be uneasy because engaging with stories of hardship is difficult and sometimes frightening work. Sometimes it is easier for me, too, to take a pass on the labor of engaging with vulnerable identities, experiences, and stories. Overall, I suspect many of these possibilities create the conditions for the possibility of uneasiness, which further speaks to the contested (and fascinating) task of engaging identities in identity research.

15.5.4 Autoethnography for Autoethnographers

Autoethnography matters because of the potential impact the research process has on autoethnographers. First, the inclusion of untold stories and silenced storytellers functions as a way to affirm the scholars' identities and experiences. In this way, the method "says" *you and your stories are welcome, legitimate, and valuable*. Autoethnography matters because it assumes all people's identities matter and merit consideration and respect.

The importance of the method for autoethnographers also extends beyond the potential for affirmation. By focusing on lived struggles, scholars are able to work through personal issues in ways that are potentially therapeutic (Adams, Holman Jones, & Ellis, 2015; Holman Jones, Ellis, & Adams, 2013). In this sense, the method immerses scholars in a process of confronting current and/or past problems, asking pointed questions, and trying to come to terms with what happened and what it meant. Also, and similarly, autoethnography creates the conditions for a transformation of subjectivity for autoethnographers (Berry, 2016, 2013; Ellis, 2004; Pelias, 2019). Working through memories, dialoguing with loved ones, exploring cultural artifacts, interacting with interviewees: the process of participating in these practices allows opportunities for scholars to come to understand ourselves, for good and bad, in novel ways.

15.6 Outlook on Autoethnographic Research

The outlook for autoethnography in terms of future research on identity is promising. First, the aims and scope of the method, along with its flourishing community, position autoethnography as a leading approach in the study of applied research on social problems (Berry & Patti, 2015; Bochner & Adams, 2020). As I described above, autoethnographers are poised to investigate complex problems of lived experience, including relational issues and the social interactions and relationships that make them possible, to convey first-person accounts that show with depth and breadth the ways issues occur and their influence on people's lives.

Second, there is room and need for more scholars to examine the same identity issues, the same conceptual focus of research, as they are experienced over time. This practice, or working in "revision" (Ellis, 2009), provides an interesting way to identify and reflect on changes that show over time, and the meaningfulness of such shifts in terms of identity.

Third, the criteria discussed by Richardson (2000), Ellis (2000), and Bochner (2000) have served autoethnographic research well for over twenty years. More recently, Pelias (2013) explores the poetic and performative qualities that make for effective autoethnography. Looking ahead, it is important to ask ourselves about the extent to which these criteria are still important, and to consider what, if any, adjustments are needed.

Finally, autoethnographers are well positioned to help in leading scholars whose mission includes confronting, examining, and seeking to diminish issues of discrimination, bigotry (e.g., Black Lives Matter, homophobia, transphobia, xenophobia), and social injustice, in general. The method's stories create the conditions for accounts that investigate the impact such violence has on vulnerable people. They give us just reason to act, and now.

Let us make good use of these stories, identities, and autoethnographies, and in mindful ways that help scholars to better understand and respond to identities, and lives, more generally.

References

Adams, T. E. (2011). *Narrating the Closet: An Autoethnography of Same-Sex Attraction*. Thousand Oaks, CA: Left Coast Press.

Adams, T. E. & Herrmann, F. A. (2020). Expanding our autoethnographic future. *Journal of Autoethnography*, *1*, 1–8, doi:10.1525/joae.2020.1.1.1.

Adams, T. E., Holman Jones, S., & Ellis, C. (2015). *Autoethnography*. New York, NY: Oxford University Press.

Alcoff, L. (1991). The problem of speaking for others. *Cultural Critique*, *20*, 5–32, doi:10.2307/1354221.

Allen, B. J. (2011). *Difference Matters: Communicating Social Identity*, *2nd Ed*. Long Grove, IL: Waveland Press.

Bardhan, N. & Orbe, M. (Eds.). (2012). *Identity Research in Intercultural Communication: Reflections and Future Directions*. Lanham, MD: Lexington Books.

Behar, R. (1996). *The Vulnerable Observer*. Boston, MA: Beacon Press.

Berry, K. (2006). Implicated audience member seeks understanding: Reexamining the "gift" of autoethnography. *International Journal of Qualitative Methods*, *15*, 1–12, doi:10.1177/160940690600500309.

Berry, K. (2007). Embracing the catastrophe: Gay body seeks acceptance. *Qualitative Inquiry*, *13*, 259–281, doi:10.1177/1077800406294934.

Berry, K. (2013). Spinning autoethnographic reflexivity, cultural critique, and negotiating selves. In S. Holman Jones, T. E. Adams, & C. Ellis (Eds.), *The Handbook of Autoethnography* (pp. 209–227). New York, NY: Routledge.

Berry, K. (2016). *Bullied: Tales of Torment, Identity, and Youth*. New York, NY: Routledge.

Berry, K. (2022). Meditations on the story I cannot write: Autoethnography, reflexivity, and the possibilities of maybe. In T. E. Adams, S. Holman Jones, & C. Ellis (Eds.), *The Handbook of Autoethnography, 2nd Ed.* (pp. 29–40). New York, NY: Routledge.

Berry, K. & Clair, R. P. (Eds.). (2011). Special Issue: The call of ethnographic reflexivity: Narrating the self's presence in ethnography. *Cultural Studies ↔ Critical Methodologies, 11*, 95–209, doi:10.1177/1532708611401339.

Berry, K., Gillotti, C. M., & Adams, T. E. (2020). *Living Sexuality: Stories of LGBTQ Relationships, Identities, and Desires*. Rotterdam:Brill/Sense.

Berry, K. & Patti, C. J. (2015). Lost in narration: Applying autoethnography. *Journal of Applied Communication Research, 43*, 263–268, doi:10.1080/00909882.2015.1019548.

Berry, K. & Warren, J. T. (2009). Cultural studies and the politics of representation: Experience/subjectivity/research. *Cultural Studies ↔ Critical Methodologies, 9*, 597–607, doi:10.1177/1532708609337894.

Blumer, H. (1986). *Symbolic Interactionism: Perspective and Method*. Berkeley, CA: University of California Press.

Bochner, A. P. (2000). Criteria against ourselves. *Qualitative Inquiry, 6*, 266–272.

Bochner, A. P. (2014). *Coming to Narrative: A Personal History of Paradigm Change in the Human Sciences*. Walnut Creek, CA: Left Coast Press.

Bochner, A. P. & Adams, T. (2020). Autoethnography as applied communication research method. In H. D. O'Hair & M. J. O'Hair (Eds.), *The Handbook of Applied Communication Research, Vol. 2* (pp. 709–729). Hoboken, NJ: John Wiley & Sons.

Bochner, A. P. & Ellis, C. (2016). *Evocative Autoethnography: Writing Lives and Telling Stories*. New York, NY: Routledge.

Boylorn, R. M. (2013). *Sweetwater: Black Women and Narratives of Resistance*. New York, NY: Peter Lang.

Boylorn, R. M. & Orbe, M. P. (Eds.). (2014). *Critical Autoethnography: Intersecting Cultural Identities in Everyday Life*. Walnut Creek, CA: Left Coast Press.

Brockmeier, J. & Harré, R. (1997). Narrative: Problems and promises of an alternative paradigm. In D. A. Carbaugh & J. Brockmeier (Eds.), *Narrative and Identity: Studies in Autobiography, Self, and Culture* (pp. 39–58). Amsterdam: John Benjamins Publishing.

Calafell, B. M. (2016). *Monstrosity, Race, and Performance in Contemporary Culture*. New York, NY: Peter Lang.

Carbaugh, D. (1996). *Situating Selves: The Communication of Social Identities in American Scenes*. Albany, NY: State University of New York Press.

Denzin, N. K. (1989). *Interpretive Biography*. Newbury Park, CA: Sage.

Dunn, T. R. (2018). *Talking White Trash: Mediated Representations and Lived Experiences of White Working-Class People*. New York, NY: Routledge.

Durham, A. (2014). *Hip Hop Feminism: Performances in Communication and Culture*. New York, NY: Peter Lang.

Ellis, C. (1991). Sociological introspection and emotional experience. *Symbolic Interaction, 14*, 23–50, doi:10.1525/si.1991.14.1.23.

Ellis, C. (2000). Creating criteria: An ethnographic short story. *Qualitative Inquiry*, *6*, 273–277, doi:10.1177/107780040000600210.

Ellis, C. (2004). *The Ethnographic I: A Methodological Novel about Autoethnography.* Walnut Creek, CA: AltaMira Press.

Ellis, C. (2007). Telling secrets, revealing lives: Relational ethics in research with intimate others. *Qualitative inquiry*, *13*, 3–29, doi:10.1177/1077800406294947.

Ellis, C. (2009). *Revision: Autoethnographic Reflections on Life and Work*. Walnut Creek, CA: Left Coast Press.

Ellis, C. (2018). *Final Negotiations: A Story of Love, Loss, and Chronic Illness.* Philadelphia, PA: Temple University Press.

Ellis, C. & Adams, T. E. (2014). The purposes, practices, and principles of autoethnographic research. In P. Leavy (Ed.), *The Oxford Handbook of Qualitative Research* (pp. 254–276). Oxford: Oxford University Press.

Ellis, C., Adams, T. E., & Bochner, A. P. (2011). Autoethnography: An overview. *Forum Qualitative Sozialforschung/Forum: Qualitative Social Research*, *12*, http://nbn-resolving.de/urn:nbn:de:0114-fqs1101108.

Ellis, C. & Bochner, A. P. (2000). Autoethnography, personal narrative, reflexivity: Researcher as subject. In N. Denzin & Y. S. Lincoln (Eds.), *The Handbook of Qualitative Research, 2nd Ed.* (pp. 733–768). Thousand Oaks, CA: Sage.

Faulkner, S. (2012). That baby will cost you. An intended ambivalent pregnancy. *Qualitative Inquiry*, *18*, 333–340, doi:10.1177/1077800411431564.

Faulkner, S. (2014). Bad mom (my) litany: Spanking cultural myths of middle-class motherhood. *Cultural Studies ↔ Critical Methodologies*, *14*, 138–146, doi:10.1177/1532708613512270.

Faulkner, S. (2016). TEN (The promise of arts-based, ethnographic, and narrative research in critical family communication research and praxis). *Journal of Family Communication*, *16*, 9–15, doi:10.1080/15267431.2015.1111218.

Gergen, K. (1991). *The Saturated Self: Dilemmas of Identity in Contemporary Life*. New York, NY: Basic Books.

Gergen, K. (2009). *Relational Being: Beyond Self and Community*. New York, NY: Oxford.

Geertz, C. L. (1973). *The Interpretation of Cultures: Selected Essays*. New York, NY: Basic Books.

Goffman, E. (1963). *Stigma: Notes on the Management of Spoiled Identity*. Englewood Cliffs, NJ: Prentice Hall.

Goldschmidt, W. (1977). Anthropology and the coming crisis: An autoethnographic appraisal. *American Anthropologist*, *79*, 293–308.

Goodall, H. L., Jr. (2000). *Writing the New Ethnography*. Lanham, MA: AltaMira.

Hayano, D. M. (1979). Auto-ethnography: Paradigms, problems, and prospects. *Human Organization*, *38*, 99–104.

Heider, K. (1975). What do people do? Dani-autoethnography. *Journal of Anthropological Research*, *31*, 3–17, doi:10.1086/jar.31.1.3629504.

Holman Jones, S., Adams, T. E., & Ellis, C. (Eds.). (2013). *The Handbook of Autoethnography*. New York, NY: Routledge.

Husserl, E. (1970/1954). *The Crisis of European Sciences and Transcendental Phenomenology*, translated by D. Carr. Evanston, IL: Northwestern University Press.

Jackson II, R. L. (2002). Introduction: Theorizing and analyzing the nexus between cultural and gendered identities and the body. *Communication Quarterly*, *50*, 242–250, doi:10.1080/01463370209385662.

Langsdorf, L. (1994). Why phenomenology in communication research? *Human Studies*, *17*, 1–8, doi:10.1007/BF01322763.

LeMaster, B. (2014). Telling multiracial tales: An autoethnography of coming out home. *Qualitative Inquiry*, *20*, 51–60, doi:10.1177/1077800413508532.

Nordmarken, S. (2014). Becoming ever more monstrous: Feeling transgender in-betweenness. *Qualitative Inquiry*, *20*, 37–50, doi:10.1177/1077800413508531.

Paxton, B. (2018). *At Home with Grief: Continued Bonds with the Deceased*. New York, NY: Routledge.

Pelias, R. J. (2013). Writing autoethnography: The personal, poetic, and performative as compositional strategies. In S. Holman Jones, T. E. Adams, & C. Ellis (Eds.), *The Handbook of Autoethnography* (pp. 384–405). New York, NY: Routledge.

Pelias, R. J. (2019). *The Creative Qualitative Researcher: Writing That Makes Readers Want to Read*. New York, NY: Routledge.

Philipsen, G. (1992). *Speaking Culturally. Explorations in Social Communication*. Albany, NY: State University of New York Press.

Richardson, L. (1994). Writing: A method of inquiry. In N. K. Denzin & Y. S. Lincoln (Eds.), *Handbook of Qualitative Research* (pp. 516–529). Thousand Oaks, CA: Sage.

Richardson, L. (2000). Evaluating ethnography. *Qualitative Inquiry*, *6*, 253–255, doi:10.1177/107780040000600207.

Schrag, C. O. (1997). *The Self after Postmodernity*. New Haven, CT: Yale University Press.

Schrag, C. O. (2003). *Communicative Praxis and the Space of Subjectivity*. West Lafayette, IN: Purdue University Press.

Scott, J. A. (2018). *Embodied Performance as Applied Research Art and Pedagogy*. London: Palgrave MacMillan.

Scott, J. W. (1991). The evidence of experience. *Critical Inquiry*, *17*, 773–797, doi:10.1086/448612.

Turner, L., Short, N. P., Grant, A., & Adams, T. E. (Eds.). (2018). *International Perspectives on Autoethnographic Research and Practice*. New York, NY: Routledge.

VanMaanen, J. (1988). *Tales of the Field: On Writing Ethnography*. Chicago, IL: University of Chicago Press.

Yoshino, K. (2007). *Covering: The Hidden Assault on Our Civil Rights*. New York, NY: Random House.

Wilmot, W. W. (1995). *Relational Communication*. New York, NY: McGraw-Hill.

Wood, J. T. (2000). *Relational Communication: Continuity and Change in Personal Relationships, 2nd Ed*. Belmont, CA: Wadsworth.

16 A Sociocultural Approach to Identity through Diary Studies

Tania Zittoun and Alex Gillespie

Diary data are particularly useful for obtaining insight into the dynamic nature of identity. Using a sociocultural approach, we conceptualize how diaries can be used to study identity dynamics at two levels: first, one can look within each diary entry to study how the author externalizes and reacts to their own thoughts; second, one can compare across diary entries to study how the author changes over time in interaction with their environment. At both levels, diaries provide rich, content-full data, that bring into focus meaning and specifically the role of meaning in identity dynamics.

We begin by introducing a sociocultural approach to identity which distinguishes identity dynamics at the level of the stream of thought (microgenesis) and at the level of the individual lifecourse (ontogenesis). We argue that diary data is particularly well suited to studying both change processes. After providing a three-step methodological procedure for making these dynamics visible within diary data, we present excerpts from a diary case study to illustrate the approach.

16.1 A Sociocultural Approach to Identity

A sociocultural approach to identity focuses on change (Penuel & Wertsch, 1995). It aims to understand how individuals change through time, how they develop as they move between different contexts and encounter new social groups (Zittoun & Gillespie, 2016b). It also aims to understand more micro-changes, such as how an individual's identity might shift during a single interaction, as new aspects of their identity are foregrounded or come into tension with the immediate situation (Gillespie, 2005; Valsiner, 2002). The underlying process is *semiotic mediation*, that is, how meanings, coming from the environment, other people, or the individual's own subjectivity, mediate ongoing thought and action (Valsiner, 2001). Each act of semiotic mediation leads to new thoughts or actions, which in turn become the basis for another round of semiotic mediation. The meanings at time 1 produce outcomes that become new meanings at time 2 which in turn are reacted to and become new meanings for time 3, and so on.

A sociocultural approach to identity draws upon the ideas of both Vygotsky and Mead (Holland & Lachicotte, 2007). Vygotsky (1978) proposed the concept of semiotic mediation, that is, how signs, finding their origin in culture and carrying meanings, mediate thought and action. From the early American pragmatists James (1893) and Mead (1934) we get the concept of the reflexive and inherently dynamic self. These come together into a dynamic model of identity as "duplex":

> Whatever I may be thinking of, I am always at the same time more or less aware of *myself*, of my *personal* existence. At the same time it is *I* who am aware; so that the total self of me, being as it were duplex, partly known and partly knower, partly object and partly subject, must have two aspects discriminated in it of which for shortness we may call one the Me and the other the *I*. (James, 1893, p. 176)

It is this fracture at the heart of the self, between the "I" and the "me" that provides the core dynamic at the center of identity. The "I" is the original action or thought at time 1, which can be observed by self as a "me" (i.e., the actor having acted can see their own action as an object in the world) at time 2. The reaction to the "me" is itself a new "I," which in turn can become reflected upon (i.e., become a "me" that is reacted to at time 3), and so on. This action–reaction dynamic operates at a very micro level, moment by moment, as it mediates the emergence of new thoughts and actions. But the decisions made within this micro level can have long-standing consequences for the overall development of the person in her lifecourse.

More recently, this idea that the self, or identity, is internally fractured has been developed by research on the dialogical nature of the self (Hermans & Gieser, 2012; Marková, 2016; Valsiner, 1999). In this line of thinking the duplex self of James becomes a multiplicity, and the self a bundle of impulses, or voices, which interact with each other to produce internal dialogical dynamics; these move the development of the self forward. A dialogical approach invites us to identify these many voices in people's flow of consciousness or externalization, for example, as they talk about themselves in the past or future, or refer to real or imagined others, positioning themselves relatively to other situations, social discourses, etc. (Grossen & Salazar Orvig, 2011). Our approach to identity is thus based on this dialogical understanding: it is the semiotic movement between or across these voices which constitutes an identity-in-the-making.

The sociocultural dynamics of identity occur at two levels. Microgenesis operates at the level of seconds and minutes. It refers to the moment-by-moment, thought-by-thought, or turn-by-turn interactions in which semiotic elements clash, react, and emerge (Gillespie & Zittoun, 2010). For example, this could be changes occurring within the course of a conversation or within a single stream of thought as one idea, or semiotic element, interacts with another to produce a third. Ontogenesis operates at the level of days, months, and years. It refers to the lifecourse, and how an individual changes over time. For example, this could be how an individual's values, beliefs, hopes, and dreams change over time, perhaps as they move between contexts and encounter new social groups. Both microgenesis and ontogenesis always occur within a social context, and the term sociogenesis refers to the changes that are occurring at the level of the social context (Valsiner, 1994). Of course, sociogenesis shapes identities, and people can transform the social world; yet for the purpose of the present chapter we will mainly be focusing on the microgenesis and ontogenesis of identity.

16.2 Diaries: A Technology of Identity

Diaries have been advocated as a source of data for longitudinal research that starts and ends with the rich particularities of an individual life (Allport, 1942; Bolger, Davis, & Rafaeli, 2003). While we are fully in agreement that diaries provide rich data on identity, we argue that their value for identity research goes deeper: diaries do not merely reflect identity dynamics, they are part of these. Diaries are a technology of the self, a sociocultural tool for mediating one's relationship to oneself and thus participating in, or constituting, the dynamics of identity.

In the Ancient Greek and Roman periods, aspirants who strove to "know themselves" would write letters to mentors which would include close self-examination, and commitments on how to improve the self in the future (Foucault, 1998). During the Christian Era in Europe, these examinations of the self were directed inwards, first through confession, and then through diary writing to oneself (Heehs, 2013). The fact that diaries are usually not meant for anyone else betrays their peculiar role in identity: they are instances of people writing to themselves. Even when they are addressed to a real or imaginary other (a distant person, an imaginary friend, or posterity, Lejeune, 1998, 2000), they stimulate self-reflexive moments. Authors externalize their thoughts, see their own thoughts on the page, and then react to those thoughts such that higher levels of reflection on their own lifecourse become possible. Reacting to the thought, they may not only reorient their reflection upon themselves, but also bring them to real changes in their lives. In James's terminology, they enable the author to reflect back on themselves as a "me" and thus facilitate the dialogue between the "I" and the "me." In dialogical terms, diaries enable the diversity of inner voices to be expressed, and met by the diarist, to be put in dialogue. Diaries can thus provide data on both the microgenesis and ontogenesis of identity.

Microgenesis can be studied in diaries by looking within individual entries. If the author has written the entry fluidly, in one sitting, then it can be read as a reflection of the author's stream of thought at the given point in time. Methods for capturing the contentful stream of thought have been difficult to develop, and no method is without limitations (Gillespie & Zittoun, 2010). Fluidly written diary entries arguably capture a portion of the individual's self-dialogue, where one can see how a line of thought develops, including moments of hesitation, contradiction, or even outright disagreement (for example, by crossing out previously written text). Thus moment by moment, and word by word, one can study how ideas emerge, how beliefs, ideas about significant others, and one's own self-concept mediate the emergence of new ideas. In diaries, authors don't only refer to their own beliefs, but they spend much time talking about the beliefs of others and positioning themselves vis-à-vis those beliefs (Gillespie, Cornish, Aveling, & Zittoun, 2008). This enables one to study the "other-within-self" and particularly the role of significant others in the micro-dynamics of identity (Marková, 2003).

Ontogenesis can be studied in diaries by comparing entries across time. As the overall timespan of the diary increases, so it increasingly enables the researcher to study lifecourse changes in the author's identity, such as their priorities, aspirations, and plans. Diaries can be used to reveal both objective changes in the authors circumstance (i.e., moving geographic location, encountering new people, and interacting with new symbolic resources) and also the author's subjective interaction with these new elements (Zittoun & Gillespie, 2015). Accordingly, diaries can be used to plot the objective and subjective elements of a lifecourse, thus providing insights on the role of the broader social environment in identity transformations. Of course, it is very difficult to distinguish how much observed ontogenetic transformations are due to the technology of the diary itself – but it is possible that the reflectivity brought about by self-writing may have participated in identity development. Where such an interpretation seems reasonable, then, the diary can reveal both the mechanism and the outcome of identity dynamics.

Any diary analysis should always include a broader analysis of the social context of the author. All diaries are written in a context which shapes what is written and how it is written (May, 2018). Contexts are evolving, because societies and social environments are changing. Many events that people face, and which shapes their identity, are due to broader social transformations; each such context will shape the dynamics of the diary in terms of what is noticed, what is recorded, how it is responded to, what lessons are taken from it, and how the diary is integrated as a tool within into the author's identity dynamics. Diaries can also be analyzed to provide a window on changing social contexts. Although not everyone occupies nodal points in history, many people changing their identities through time do constitute social transformations (Zittoun, Aveling, Gillespie, & Cornish, 2012). However, we will not explore this further here as our focus is identity, not history.

16.2.1 Diary Analysis Methodology

If diaries are externalizations of people's thoughts and experiences over time, and also contribute to their development, how can we analyze ontogenetic and microgenetic transformations within a specific context? We propose an analysis in three stages.

A. Chronology

First, we need a way to render visible identity transformations over time. For this, we need to identify the chronological time of the person's trajectory against the background of social history. Having time markers allows comparison of identity dynamic through time. Diaries, which are per definition written over a period of time and with some regularity, follow historical time in the chronology of their entries. This is to be distinguished from subjective time expressed by the text, which is not a pinpoint in time, but a relative positioning in some duration (Bergson, 1910). Subjective time is also referred to as duration; it is imagination that brings both past and future into the present (Zittoun & Gillespie, 2016b). Hence, to construct chronology, we propose two steps.

The first step is to identify the historical time organizing the writer's experience; for this the analysist can identify and reconstruct events met by a person (Riessman, 2008). Diaries usually indicate dates. Some dates correspond to events which are socially and historically relevant; some others are culturally salient (Christmas, birthdays, etc.), and some are personally significant (e.g., one's first day of work). These temporal anchors are extremely useful, both to have a contextual point of reference to analyze ontogenesis, and second, to identify reflexive assessments of ontogenesis. That is to say, people's diaries often include reflexive assessments of their own development, as the diary helps to make their own ontogenesis an object of contemplation. This often occurs in diary entries at the start of a new year, with diarists reflecting on the year past ("an uneventful year" or "I could never have imagined") and making commitments for the year to come (such as New Year's resolutions and commitments to guiding principles) which provide insight into how the diarist is trying to steer themselves through chronological time.

The second step is to analyze subjective time, that is, events that people experience as ruptures and that catalyze identity work. The indicators of ruptures in subjective time include people's explicit indications of an event disturbing the flow of time (e.g., "today was a big day"). But the disruption can also be marked by changes in rhythm and lengths of entries within a diary (e.g., a period with an excessive number of diary entries). Even more subtly, the genre and structure of writing usually varies when the person experiences an important rupture in their subjective life or identity transformations: diary entries may be longer, focusing on and returning to specific issue; the text can be confused and knotted, or even self-contradictory; the handwriting can change as the tempo of writing changes, words can be deleted or added, and the diarist may introduce implicit or explicit code to mark personally meaningful events. Each diarist writes differently: but within a diary, these indicators provide a methodological route to locate identity development, in socio-historical time (Zittoun & Gillespie, 2012).

B. Microgenesis

But what is it that changes through time? Because it is difficult to analyze exhaustively a whole diary, we recommend focusing on sequences identified through the chronological analysis.

Identity transformations are actually negotiated at the microgenetic scale, and this is where a second series of analytic indicators can be identified. All such indicators should correspond to the analysts' theory of identity. In what follows, we identify six such indicators that correspond to a sociocultural approach to identity. Specifically, we conceptualize that identity emerges as a semiotic process establishing a dialogical dynamic that can be analyzed along six dimensions.

First, identity is relational, and it emerges through dialogues with significant others (Mead, 1934; Marková, 2003, 2016). These others are people on whom the self depends, and who shape how the self understands oneself. Diaries reveal these "others within the self" – the voices of significant others as they reverberate and echo around the subjectivity of the diarist (Gillespie et al., 2008). In diaries, people report what they think about others, what others told them, and what they think these others think about them. Diarists may also have imagined interactions, for example, imagining how a lover might react to a marriage proposal or the discovery of a betrayal. Of course, the imagined others within are not strictly the same as the actual, significant others existing outside the subjectivity of the diarist; yet, arguably, it is these others within which become the psychological reality of significant others – these are inner alters (Marková, 2006). Detecting the others within is usually fairly straightforward, using verbal markers such as "I," "he/she," and names of others. They can be simple ("She told me X") or complex and reflexive ("I told her X and she responded Y in an attempt to make me feel Z").

Second, the relational aspects of identity are also often connected to experiences of group dynamics; diarists position themselves as members of groups, against other groups, or feel they can or cannot do certain actions as members of specific communities. This is often marked by indications of "we/they," or of belonging ("as X, I"), or of boundary marking (Dahinden & Zittoun, 2013; Gillespie et al., 2008; Gillespie, Kadianaki, & O'Sullivan-Lago, 2012). Of course, these two first dimensions are often connected, as it can be that groups or belonging are manifested through a specific significant person (e.g., "my mother tells me that as a decent woman I cannot do A").

Third, sense-making and identity dynamics are primarily expressed through the connection of present experiences, with past and future ones; this is due to identity demanding self-continuity through change (Erikson, 1959). Time work, that is the integration of the present into the duration of past and future, becomes visible through attending to the tenses of verbs. The tense of verbs indicates the positioning of the identity in the subjective experience of time. Temporal dynamic can take simple forms ("I did A," "I will do B") or complex, looping ones ("I will not do C which, in the past, I thought I would do in the future"). It can also be useful to identify whether the diarist is focusing on the past, present, or future, and how the mood and tone of, for example, the present compares to their subjective experience of the past. Such analyses can reveal how the developing identity understands itself in time and orients to the future.

Fourth, identity is constituted by moves between what is real or plausible for self in a specific context, or what is nonreal or implausible. People engage in identity work when they think about what is, but also what could be or what could have happened; in diaries, they write about hope, dreams, regrets; they explore possible lives, they express fantasies, the play with memoires, they make plans (Abbey & Valsiner, 2004; Josephs, 1998; Phillips, 2013; Zittoun & Valsiner, 2016). Hence, an important part of the analysis is to identify these traces of the work of imagination, as it may substantially guide the person's actual, present, and future conduct (Zittoun, 2014; Zittoun & Gillespie, 2016a, 2016b).

Fifth, identity is materially and symbolically mediated and distributed: people experience who they are through places where they feel at home, through objects and belonging they value, through films and songs that they feel move them or represent them (that is, symbolic resources), or social discourses they resonate with (James, 1890; Winnicott, 1990; Zittoun, 2006). Identity dynamics in diaries can thus be identified through mentions of any of these elements that become associated to self, and especially through what people write about these things and resources: resonating with a fictional character, experiencing a diminution of the self through losing a preferred object, or feeling reinforced by a social discourse (Zittoun, Cornish, Gillespie, & Aveling, 2008; Zittoun & Gillespie, 2013). In order to analyze how the diarist engages with and uses these discourses, objects, and resources, it can be useful to track references and uses both over diary entries and within diary entries, as this can reveal the shifting supports for and constructions of identity.

Sixth, from a sociocultural perspective, an important aspect of psychological development is progressive distanciation from (affective, embodied) experience through semiotic elaboration (Valsiner, 2013, 2015; Zavereshneva & van der Veer, 2018). It may entail differentiation, integration, and generalization of experiences (Gillespie & Zittoun, 2013; Werner & Kaplan, 1963), as well as transfer or experience and progressive abstraction or schematization (Zittoun & Gillespie, 2015; Zittoun et al., 2013). This work of progressive elaboration is often made explicit through textual markers of distancing or modulation: "I think that X," "I always feel Y," Semiotic distanciation can also be observed when the same topic, or semantic field, is repeatedly

Table 16.1 *Three-step analysis of identity dynamics in a diary*

A. Chronology. Across diary entries: analyze the chronology of events and events or periods that have subjective significance.

B. Microgenesis. Within selected diary entries: analyze the microgenesis of identity:
   1. Who is part of inner dialogues?
   2. What communities or groups are present?
   3. How is past connected to present, present to futures?
   4. How do possibilities and impossibilities emerge?
   5. What semiotic and symbolic resources are used?
   6. Is psychological distancing emerging?

C. Ontogenesis. Compare responses to questions B at two or more moments in time A in order to understand how the identity has changed and, perhaps, the role of microgenetic moments in that change.

addressed but with changing vocabulary. For example, if very emotionally laden descriptions are replaced by more analytical ones, the writer starts to establish correspondences across experiences; when the diarist replaces a depiction of specific events with more general terms, then this indicates that he or she is beginning to step outside of their experiences, to turn the "I" into a "me," and thus take another step in identity development.

C. Ontogenesis

Once the chronologic (A) and microgenetic (B) analyses have been concluded, we recommend examining how the latter change over time: identity dynamics come to the fore, when different microgenetic transformations (on one or more of these five aspects, or others) can be compared across time. Specific moments in time can be chosen for more detailed analysis according to different rationale (same theme addressed, temporal criteria, etc.); this is how we can speak of ontogenetic identity transformations.

16.2.2 Illustrative Diary Analysis

We will now illustrate the outline method for analyzing identity in diary data with examples drawn from our previously published analysis of the diary of a young English woman during World War II (Gillespie et al., 2008; Zittoun, 2008; Zittoun et al., 2012, 2008; Zittoun & Gillespie, 2015). The diary, from a woman we called "June," comprises about a quarter of a million words, beginning in 1939 when she was 18 and ending in 1945 with the end of the war. The diary was collected as part of the Mass-Observation archive (Sheridan, 2000). Mass-Observation, established in 1937 (and used to monitor morale during the war), invited people to keep daily diaries about their lives and their communities and to respond to regular surveys so as to contribute to a "people's anthropology," with the aim of documenting the experience of everyday life; these diaries have thus been addressed to a specific audience (Bloome, Sheridan, & Street, 1993). Several hundred ordinary people across Britain volunteered, and Mass-Observation has archived these diaries and survey responses. The diaries are kept in the library at the University of Sussex, where they are available for free to interested researchers.

One added benefit of using diaries to study identity is that the data are often publicly available. This enables subsequent researchers to reanalyze the data, which opens interpretations to more rigorous critique and debate. Analyzing identity in publicly available diaries is thus highly consonant with recent movements toward open science (Bartling & Friesike, 2014). Researchers working on the same data can promote theoretical integration, prevent fragmentation, and spur theoretical innovation (Cornish, Zittoun, & Gillespie, 2007; Zittoun, Gillespie, & Cornish, 2009). Our analysis will focus on the publicly available diary 5324, accessible in the Mass-Observation archive.

A. Chronology

Our analysis will follow June for six years, as she moves through three chronological transitions. In terms of historical time, first, at the beginning of the war, June is 18 years old, and she lives with her elder sister and mother in Norfolk. Norfolk is on the East coast of England, and near the sea, that is, on the first line of German air raids. The family runs a garage which sells petrol and other goods. Second, as the war progresses, June leaves home. Between 1941 and 1943, as part of the home front and women's participation in the war effort, she works on a number of farms as a gardener, getting exposure to new people and ideas and boyfriends. Third, between 1944 and 1945, due to a health condition, June ends the war living in a hostel and working in a shop. During this final stage of her diary, the end of the war is imminent, and her focus is on what she should do with her life. Hence, these three transitions correspond to June's ontogenetic development. However, to identify this development, we need to focus on a more subjective experience of time. Thus we chose excerpts of each of these three periods which pertain to a single theme: June's reflection on what it is to be a woman, and her relationship to men. We now can start a microgenetic analysis of each excerpt, after locating them in chronological time.

B. Microgenesis at Three Periods

The first excerpts from June's diary are written while she is living at home, in 1940. They come in a series of entries in which June reports her everyday life, but also discussions following the government's call urging women to join the home front. During this period, June's writing is intense and very dialogical, as she reports the many people with whom she discussed her possible activities on the home front: to become a nurse, a teacher, or a land girl?

Excerpt 1

[1940] <u>Sun March 16th</u>. This evening Mother went clean off the deep end over the business & we had the biggest row ever. I am not surprised by the new order as the press has said it would come & I thought the 20's would be first, but *Mother has persisted that women were different from men & could not be conscripted. She seems to dread me going although in a way* **I do not mind. The war is pretty dull here. I should not join the services if it had not been for this because of the stigma of man-chasing attatched** [sic] **to it if one volunteered, & because usually the sort of girl that goes in is what I consider rather brainless,** *& also Mother would not have let me if I had wanted to. (I never did.* **It did not occur to me.)**

[Tuesday 2nd April 1940] *One [code name for a man] invited me to go for a walk with him this evening,* **but I refused because (a) I don't go for walks with anyone unless I knew then well & (b) I thought he was married & too old. (over 35)**

In these two diary entries, we first see the others with whom June is in dialogue: her mother, and a man, "One," who invited her for a walk. The inner dialogue following real-world dialogue that took place is for instance visible when June writes: "mother would not have let me even if I wanted to. (I never did)." Here, the writing reproduces a dialogue that has or could have taken place. Second, June makes a clear group boundary between women that appear as "man-chasing" and "brainless," as probably described by her mother, and other women, to whom she, together with her mother, belong. It is that by verbally declaring allegiance to such "we" (decent women) that she states that she does not "go for walks with anyone unless I know them well." Third, in terms of temporality, June is here moving on a short time duration: she speaks about what happened today, and near-term decisions, such as whether to go for the walk "this evening." Fourth, in terms of exploring plausible or more imaginary options, we see that June enters in a complex hypothetical reasoning: even if she had wanted to join the forces, her mother would not have let her do so. In other words, she may have played with the imagination of joining the forces as a possible future; but this was excluded by her mother, who made it nonplausible, a taboo, in the name of a set of moral rules governing their group. Comparably, it is likely that June imagined how it would be to go out with the man who invited her; but this imagination was cut short by a moral imperative and a more personal, affective reason: she imagined he was married and found him too old. Regarding the fifth dimension, there are not so many mentions of symbolic resources or personal material objects: however, there is mention of the press, and June engages in dialogue with it, as well as more clichéd images or social representations of the "brainless" women. Sixth, June is here still depicting quite concrete events, yet evaluating them in terms of more general values (moral norms). Also, there seems to be a brief "I"-to-"me" self-reflection in her asserting "I never did" and "It did not occur to me," where, arguably, she is beginning to question herself and her motives.

Eventually, because of the "stigma of the man-chasing" girls in the armed forces, June choses to become a land girl, which is seen as a more wholesome occupation. In October 1941, June writes about her work as a land girl, her learning of the trade, her growing expertise in the fields. She also starts to mention how she and her friends are popular with soldiers and men in the dancehalls. In terms of identity change, there are indications of a triple transformation. First, June's knowledge and expertise grows as she is transformed into a farmer. This is evident in her use of technical vocabulary and her pride in being a land girl. Second, her body is transformed in appearance, through the physical field work. Third, there is an emerging identity change in how June relates to men, which we will analyze in more detail.

By mid-1942 many diary entries pertain to the young men that June meets when going for walks or at dances. In these entries, June narrates her encounters with men; she walks with them, speaks with them about various topics – and also quickly evaluates them, in terms of being "rather charming" or "dull." One June 13th, she mentions a milkman with whom she has a date: "I took good care he walked one side of the field & I the other & I insist it will remain so." Here, she still seems to keep to the principles of decency learned at home. However, over the next days, more encounters with men occur, and her actions ("I") challenge her own identity ("me") as a woman. The following two excerpts reveal the intense inner dialogue and the many voices and resources on which June draws as she reflects on her changing identity:

Excerpt 2

[1942] <u>Tues June 17th</u>. Working all day. Last 2 days a heat wave & too hot to move. Trying to keep in shady part of garden. I am sunburnt tonight. **I am also almost in love! Or is it in love with love?** *Ye Gods, what fools men do make of themselves!* [large 's' in red pencil over text] I went out with my French Canadian soldier again tonight. He is sweet. **What it is to be young & foolish! It certainly is good for morale in wartime to be made love to! I am not quite sure if I am happy about it or not. It is pleasant. It is fun.** He is nice & a gentle-man. **I would not go out with him if I did not feel safe & trust him. He is lonely & so am I. We are both [far] from home & friends. How silly life is!** *I am meeting him Thursday. I am not quite sure whether I promised to go back to Canada with him or not!! I will be his friend anyway.* **I blame the war for this!**

[1942] <u>Sat June 28th</u>. I thoroughly enjoyed it [a local dance]. My airman of last night was there & persisted in making a date for Sun night. I did not have to dance with him half the time as all his pals asked me to annoy him & he had to catch 10.15 train. After he had gone I had a good change round & in last dance made another date for Tues night with another airman from a different aerodrome. We were cycling home & 2 boys caught us up & cycled with us. We had danced with them during the evening. They also were trying to make a date. **I thought by this time in any case I was going to get in a hell of a mess so left**

them without any promises. *I shall keep the 2 dates as they seem both nice fellows providing my soldier doesn't turn up on either of these nights!* **I don't know what is becoming of me.** *I wouldn't have dreampt [sic] of doing this sort of thing at home. I wouldn't have been allowed to for one thing.* **I don't know if the land is demoralising me. I sometimes think so! Or else the war.** *I know I should not have done it before the war.* **Oh well I shan't be young for ever & my looks won't last, so now or never.**

Analyzing these two excerpts from 1942 in terms of our six dimensions, we can first see the many others present in these entries: her "French Canadian"; two airmen from two airdromes; and the two boys. Second, she creates small communities of fate – she and her French Canadian, "we," are both very lonely; they share the same values ("We are both [far] from home & friends"). There is also a more diffuse sense of being part of a very specific war-youth generation, when she writes, "What it is to be young & foolish! It certainly is good for morale in wartime to be made love to." Note that this interjection, which interrupts the flow of writing, suggests that a different voice has entered her writing; it seems to be the voice of the "doxa" or the general common sense – as if she could imagine adults judging her. We will come back to this, as this voice is expressed through the use of specific semiotic resources.

Third, in terms of temporality, June moves between the close present ("working all day"; "Trying to keep in shady part of garden") and the close past and future ("went out again with my French Canadian tonight" and "I am meeting him Thursday"). This also opens immediately a future which is uncertain; for example, her fear that double dating could lead to trouble: "in any case I was going to get in a hell of a mess." This is followed by a more distant reflection on the past: "I wouldn't have dreampt [sic] of doing this sort of thing at home."

Fourth, June's new experiences create both possibilities and problems, "I don't know what is becoming of me," which is contraposed to what she would have done home "I wouldn't have been allowed to for one thing." Here, June expresses her trouble by imagining the woman she is becoming (given her actions); drawing on her past, she can evaluate that this greatly differs from what, in the past, she (and her home community) imagined she would become. Her emerging identity seems to resemble the "man-chasing women" she used to reject in conformity with her home community. Hence, her possible new future is judged implausible on the moral grounds of the past ("I know I should not have done it before the war"). We will come back to this: a tension starts to emerge, whereby June has to oppose her real experience and the futures it leads to, with the past expectations she used to have. This is not just a moral dilemma; it is an identity conflict.

The fifth dimension invites us to consider the symbolic and semiotic resources present in the diarist's writing. In this sequence, there are many interjections that could be traces, or echoes (Aveling, Gillespie, & Cornish, 2015), of commonsense sayings, perhaps from magazines or films. In the first entries, these are joyful: "I am also almost in love! Or is it in love with love?"; "What it is to be young & foolish!"; and "How silly life is!" These common-sense expressions, or their adaptation, seem to have an expressive function. They give a joyful and excited tone, which contrasts on a macro scale with the context of World War II and, more personally, with the second excerpt, where June seeks an explanation of her conduct in the "demoralizing war." The tension is temporarily silenced by the semiotic resource, in this case a narrative trope: "I shan't be young forever."

The sixth, and last, dimension of analysis concerns psychological distancia-tion. In the June 17th entry, June is very concrete (e.g., "I am sunburnt tonight"), and also gives way to her excitement about her recent experiences. She seems to be trying to name and qualify her feelings: "I am not quite sure if I am happy about it or not. It is pleasant. It is fun. He is nice & a gentle-man. ... [I] feel safe & trust him." This emerging understanding of herself is what, in Excerpt 3, enables her to evaluate him as potentially appropriate. In the June 28th entry, June moves from factual descriptions ("We had danced with them during the evening. They also were trying to make a date") to taking a reflective stance: "I thought by this time in any case I was going to get in a hell of a mess so left them without any promises." However, that sentence of "reasons" is immediately followed by one expressing a quite different position: "I shall keep the 2 dates as they seem both nice fellows providing my soldier doesn't turn up on either of these nights!" It is probably while writing, as an "I," that June took another perspective on her utterance, as a "me," and realized how crudely she expressed her desire to be with at least one of these men, so that the immediate next sentence expressed a radical distan-ciation: "I don't know what is becoming of me." This interruption breaks her narration with a new voice. As mentioned, this distance taken then enables her to make the rapid move between what her mother and community would have promoted, her past imagination of herself, their related values, and the clash with her present situation. She tries to solve this moral dilemma by trying to interpret it from a wider distance, in the context of her current life situation, or on the ground of sociogenetic events: Is it because of the countryside? Is it because of the war? ("I don't know if the land is demoralizing me. I sometimes think so! Or else the war. I know I should not have done it before the war.") Interestingly, her current dilemma (to enjoy going out with men or remain a "decent" woman) is thus being rephrased in more general values – to live according to the land and, even more, the war values. This tension is resolved by what can be seen as another jump into a different register of meaning. Personal desire and common sense meet in the following thought that tempor-arily silences her dilemma: "Oh well I shan't be young for ever & my looks won't last, so now or never." The tension is thus resolved by a creative synthesis, a semiotic shortcut (Valsiner, 2015), something that cuts from the social situation to the reality of her body and identity in the context of the opportunities offered by the war.

The final two excerpts we analyze are from the last pages of the diary, in 1944, as the end of the war approaches. June is now living and working in a hostel, and she is reflecting on her future. She has been considering whether to go back to her home community, or to follow one young man, D, with whom she started a long-standing relationship to become his wife on his farm. She writes repeatedly about this decision; although settling down would be a decent choice in the eyes of her home community, she questions whether she really loves D and whether that is the life she wants.

Excerpt 3

[1944] <u>Sat May 26th</u>. B [sister] has gone home this weekend to take some of her things. *Mother has written today begging her to come home as soon as possible.* **This last month I have not known what to do to decide my future. I am constantly changing my mind.** *Some days I want to marry D* [boyfriend] *as soon as he can afford it, the next I think he is not the right one for me. Then comes the uncertainty of if I reject him shall I ever replace him by anyone as true.* **Then I think single life is all I want, the next day I feel crazy for love & sex.** *Sometimes I decide to leave here & go to Devon to him as he wishes, then I want to stay here. Then I want to go home. Home with its many attractions will be another two hundred miles from D and it will annoy D immensley* [sic] *if I go. I like my present job & will have a difficulty in getting one with so many benefits. When B goes it will be less attractive here and I shall be lonely. I think then I shall not mind leaving, but feel I could do with two months rest before going to another job. This will annoy* [. . .] *D who thinks I can go to him straight away from here.* Lately my nerves have been very bad and if they do not improve after B goes I intend to see the doctor. The slightest thing makes me jump lately. I feel a bundle of nerves.

[1944] <u>Sun June 10th</u>. [. . .] **I am rather unsure if I want to marry D at all now. I am not in love with him any longer.** *Is a loveless marriage hell? He is still as keen as ever on me.* That's why I feel so mean and cannot tell him.

In the diary entry for 26th May, we can again see the many significant others in her life: her sister B on a visit, her mother, who wants her to go back home, and D, who wants her to marry him. The most intense dialogue is between what she wants and what she thinks D thinks. In terms of the second analytic dimension, community, nothing is mentioned in terms of "we." It is interesting to note that this time June speaks only for herself. The third analytic dimension enables us to see that after a description of recent events, the sister's visit, June's writing goes back in the past – she has been undecided for the past month – and especially the future about which she has been uncertain, and then goes back in the present (she is constantly "changing her mind"). She then examines the future suggested by D, who wants her to live with him on his farm, but also the fact that she will have difficulty finding a job as good as she has. She then considers an alternative future where she stays in her job for a few more months; but the place will be less nice when her sister leaves. These possible futures are thus in tension and, regarding the fourth analytic dimension, all equally plausible: "Some days I want to marry D as soon as he can afford it, the next I think he is not the right one for me. Then comes the uncertainty of if I reject him shall I ever replace him by anyone as true." What would happen if she rejects him? Will she find someone else? And if she goes home, would D be annoyed? If she stays for two months, will he be annoyed? Regarding the fifth dimension, no resources are clearly mentioned. This, again, may suggest how much this issue is a personal one, for which no resources are available. Thus, in terms of the sixth dimension, June is on her own in trying to find a way to distance herself from this endless merry-go-round of alternatives. Rather than distancing into general ideas, June examines her embodied state, her emotions, and creates distance by naming them. This appears at two moments. First, when evoking these tensions, she tries to name the desires that underpin them: "Then I think single life is all I want, the next day I feel crazy for love & sex." Second, later in the text, she expresses the tension as it is embodied, in a somatic way: she has become "a bundle of nerves," where "the slightest thing makes me jump," an illness that eventually leads to her visiting a doctor.

The tension is gone in the diary entry for June 10th. She has been visiting D on his farm and observing him work. She writes factually, without emotion or enthusiasm. She again examines her feelings, and acknowledges that she is not in love with D anymore, uses a semiotic resource ("is a loveless marriage hell?"), and imagines the difficulty of telling him this. Indeed, in the further diary entries, D makes few appearances: June having decided not to marry him, chooses to stay on her own.

C. Ontogenesis

The third stage of the proposed analysis is to connect the microgenetic analyses (B) with the chronology (A) in order to understand how the diarist's identity has changed, and developed, over time. To facilitate this comparison it is useful to examine how the elements analyzed along our six dimensions (in Table 16.1) evolve.

First, from a developmental, attachment, lifecourse or dialogical perspective, self is fundamentally defined by and through the others with which he or she relates (Ainsworth, Blehar, Waters, & Wall, 2015; Elder & Giele, 2009; Marková, 2003). This is shown in our analysis of three sequences in the first two dimensions. Initially, in 1940, June is a young woman dialoguing with her mother, and is part of a "we," decent women, against "they," morally questionable women. In 1942, after leaving home, June is in dialogue with a plurality of men, and "we" are people experiencing solitude at war. Finally, in 1944, the mother is back, as well as the sister, and one man, D; here, no community is invoked. Through this simple evolution, we already see June's identity going through changes: the war brings her into new relationships and communities, which bring her to question the values of her family and home community, in turn, leading her to find her own voice at the end of the war (Gillespie et al., 2008).

Next, we can consider the analytic dimensions of time, plausibility, resources, and psychological distanciation together. This is in effect what we have done through the "loop model," which enables the analyst to conceptualize the movement of imagination (Zittoun & Gillespie, 2016b). That model visualizes three dimensions as coordinates of a three-dimensional space: time (from past to future), distanciation (from concrete to general and abstract), and plausibility (from real or accepted in a given social context, to implausible). The movement of imagination, here visible through the writing, thus moves along these dimensions, as a loop, coming back to the present; we can also represent the resources or the voices of others as what feeds this loop and, at times, invalidates it.

In Figure 16.1, representing 1940, June explores, from the present, possible futures; some are quickly invalidated, due to the social representation of "that kind of woman."

In 1942, confronted with her experience of multiple dating, she is rather confused, as her actions would not have been allowed at home (Figure 16.2). Using a semiotic resource such as "being young only once," she manages to accept her actions: she has not become a "man-chasing" woman; she is now, sensibly and pragmatically, enjoying her youth and body.

In 1944, June imagines her possible futures (Figure 16.3). One resembles her past, and June rejects it: she has changed, she enjoys her work. One is highly plausible as socially accepted and resembling her past, possible future, marrying D; yet she would lose her job and draws on the romantic resource of "loveless marriage is hell" to reject it. In the third, she may go on living alone, resting, working, and loving at her own pace. Although there is no social acknowledgment of this choice, or no symbolic resource for it, June will go for it, as it corresponds to her "gut feeling" – here she draws on her embodied experience.

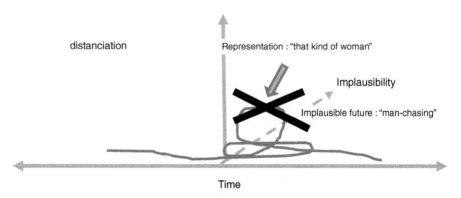

Figure 16.1 *June in 1940 and the implausible future of man-chasing*

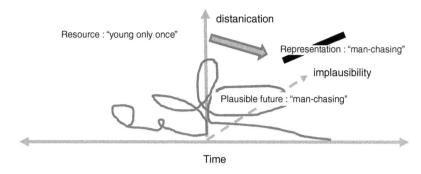

Figure 16.2 *June in 1942, land girl*

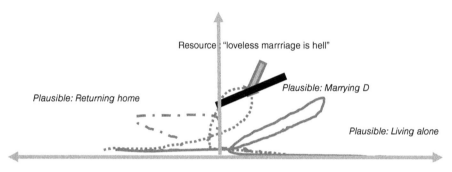

Figure 16.3 *June in 1944, an independent woman*

From such analysis, then, we see identity development in the sense that the dynamics of identity move. In 1940, she is supported by the discourses and values of her home community, leading to choices to avoid social judgment. In 1942, outside her home community, she makes decisions based on the feeling of being young and in love and bound to a man by a shared fate, yet nourished by a variety of available social discourses and semiotic resources. In 1944, she elaborates personal sense and decisions based on her own intimate feelings and experience, regardless of what her various communities or others may think. Thus, across these three time points in a young woman's life, we can see the progressive dynamics of identity integration and definition, toward more autonomy (Erikson, 1959; Zittoun & Gillespie, 2015).

16.3 Conclusion

We have proposed a three-step method and six dimensions to analyze identity dynamics in diaries, on the basis of our dialogical and semiotic theoretical understanding of identity. A different theoretical approach would likely lead to new steps or other analytic dimensions. One of the advantages of public diaries is that they can form empirical touchstones against which multiple theories can be compared and debated (Cornish et al., 2007). We have proposed June's diary as one such public resource (Zittoun & Gillespie, 2015), where dialogue and debate, grounded in the specifics of the diary, can spur theoretical integration and development.

Whichever theoretical approach one adopts, diaries are a valuable source of data about identity because they simultaneously document ontogenetic change, across diary entries, and microgenetic externalizations of thought, within diary entries. Diaries can reveal not only the actuality of identity change, but also the mechanism of identity change: as the writer reads and responds to herself, she uses the diary to reflexively build an identity and make decisions to guide herself along her own lifecourse trajectory. Thus, at their core, diaries are an externalization of the "I" and "me" dynamics which are constitutive of identity.

References

Abbey, E. & Valsiner, J. (2004). Emergence of meanings through ambivalence. *Forum Qualitative Sozialforschung/Forum: Qualitative Social Research, 6*(1), article 23.

Ainsworth, M. D. S., Blehar, M. C., Waters, E., & Wall, S. N. (2015). *Patterns of Attachment: A Psychological Study of the Strange Situation*. New York, NY: Psychology Press.

Allport, G. W. (1942). *The Use of Personal Documents in Psychological Science: Prepared for the Committee on Appraisal of Research*. New York, NY: Social Science Research Council.

Aveling, E.-L., Gillespie, A., & Cornish, F. (2015). A qualitative method for analysing multivoicedness. *Qualitative Research, 15*(6), 670–687, doi:10.1177/1468794114557991.

Bartling, S. & Friesike, S. (2014). *Opening Science: The Evolving Guide on How the Internet is Changing Research, Collaboration and Scholarly Publishing*. Cham: Springer.

Bergson, H. (1910). *Time and Free Will: Essays on the Immediate Data of Consciousness*, trans. by F. L. Pogson. London: G. Allen.

Bloome, D., Sheridan, D., & Street, B. (1993). Reading Mass-Observation writing: Theoretical and methodological issues in researching the mass-observation archive (The Mass-Observation Occasional Papers Series No. 1).

Bolger, N., Davis, A., & Rafaeli, E. (2003). Diary methods: Capturing life as it is lived. *Annual Review of Psychology, 54*(1), 579–616, doi:10.1146/annurev.psych.54.101601.145030.

Cornish, F., Zittoun, T., & Gillespie, A. (2007). A cultural psychological reflection on collaborative research. Conference essay: ESF Exploratory Workshop on Collaborative Case Studies for a European Cultural Psychology. *Forum Qualitative Sozialforschung/Forum: Qualitative Social Research, 8*(3), article 21.

Dahinden, J. & Zittoun, T. (2013). Religion in meaning making and boundary work: Theoretical explorations. *Integrative Psychological and Behavioral Science*, *47* (2), 185–206, doi:10.1007/s12124–013-9233-3.

Elder, G. H. J. & Giele, J. Z. (Eds.). (2009). *The Craft of Life Course Research*. New York, NY: Guilford Press.

Erikson, E. H. (1959). *Identity and the Life Cycle. Selected Papers*. Retrieved May 5, 2021, from www.archive.org/details/identityandtheli011578mbp.

Foucault, M. (1998). Technologies of the self. In L. Martin, H. Gutman, & P. Hutton (Eds.), *Technologies of the Self: A Seminar with Michel Foucault* (pp. 16–49). Amherst, MA: University of Massachusetts Press.

Gillespie, A. (2005). Malcolm X and his autobiography: Identity development and self-narration. *Culture & Psychology*, *11*(1), 77–88.

Gillespie, A., Cornish, F., Aveling, E.-L., & Zittoun, T. (2008). Living with war: Community resources, self-dialogues and psychological adaptation to World War II. *Journal of Community Psychology*, *36*(1), 35–52.

Gillespie, A., Kadianaki, I., & O'Sullivan-Lago, R. (2012). Encountering alterity: Geographic and semantic movements. In J. Valsiner (Ed.), *Oxford Handbook of Culture and Psychology* (pp. 695–719). Oxford: Oxford University Press.

Gillespie, A. & Zittoun, T. (2010). Studying the movement of thought. In A. Toomela & J. Valsiner (Eds.), *Methodological Thinking in Psychology: 60 Years Gone Astray?* (pp. 69–88). Charlotte, NC: Information Age.

Gillespie, A. & Zittoun, T. (2013). Meaning making in motion: Bodies and minds moving through institutional and semiotic structures. *Culture & Psychology*, *19*(4), 518–532, doi:10.1177/1354067X13500325.

Grossen, M. & Salazar Orvig, A. (2011). Dialogism and dialogicality in the study of the self. *Culture & Psychology*, *17*(4), 491–509, doi:10.1177/ 1354067X11418541.

Heehs, P. (2013). *Writing the Self: Diaries, Memoirs, and the History of the Self*. New York, NY: Bloomsbury.

Hermans, H. J. & Gieser, T. (Eds.). (2012). *Handbook of Dialogical Self Theory*. Cambridge: Cambridge University Press.

Holland, D. & Lachicotte, W. (2007). Vygotsky, Mead, and the new sociocultural studies of identity. In H. Daniels, M. Cole, & J. V. Wertsch (Eds.), *The Cambridge Companion to Vygotsky* (pp. 101–135), doi:10.1017/ CCOL0521831040.005.

James, W. (1890). *The Principles of Psychology*. New York, NY: Dover.

James, W. (1893). *Psychology*. Harvard, MA: Henry Holt.

Josephs, I. E. (1998). Constructing one's self in the city of the silent: Dialogue, symbols, and the role of "as-if" in self-development. *Human Development*, *41*(3), 180–195.

Lejeune, P. (1998). *Pour l'autobiographie. Chroniques*. Paris: Seuil.

Lejeune, P. (2000). *"Cher écran ..." Journal personnel, ordinateur, internet*. Paris: Seuil.

Marková, I. (2003). *Dialogicality and Social Representations: The Dynamics of Mind*. Cambridge: Cambridge University Press.

Marková, I. (2006). On the "inner alter" in dialogue. *International Journal for Dialogical Science*, *1*(1), 125–147.

Marková, I. (2016). *The Dialogical Mind: Common Sense and Ethics*. Cambridge: Cambridge University Press.

May, V. (2018). Belonging across the lifetime: Time and self in Mass Observation accounts. *British Journal of Sociology*, *69*(2), 306–322, doi:10.1111/1468-4446.12276.

Mead, G. H. (1934). *Mind, Self and Society, from the Standpoint of a Social Behaviorist*, ed. by C. W. Morris. Chicago, IL: University of Chicago Press.

Penuel, W. R. & Wertsch, J. V. (1995). Vygotsky and identity formation: A sociocultural approach. *Educational Psychologist*, *30*(2), 83–92, doi:10.1207/s15326985ep3002_5.

Phillips, A. (2013). *Missing Out: In Praise of the Unlived Life*. London: Penguin Books.

Riessman, C. K. (2008). *Narrative Methods for the Human Sciences*. Thousand Oaks, CA: Sage.

Sheridan, D. (2000). Reviewing Mass-Observation: The archive and its researchers thirty years on. *Forum Qualitative Sozialforschung/Forum: Qualitative Social Research*, *1*(3). Retrieved May 5, 2021, from www.qualitative-research.net/index.php/fqs/article/view/1043.

Valsiner, J. (1994). Bidirectional cultural transmission and constructive sociogenesis. In W. de Graaf & R. Maier (Eds.), *Sociogenesis Reexamined* (pp. 47–70), doi:10.1007/978-1-4612-2654-3_4.

Valsiner, J. (1999). I create you to control me: A glimpse into basic processes of semiotic mediation. *Human Development*, *42*(1), 26–30, doi:10.1159/000022606.

Valsiner, J. (2001). Process structure of semiotic mediation in human development. *Human Development*, *44*(2–3), 84–97, doi:10.1159/000057048.

Valsiner, J. (2002). Forms of dialogical relations and semiotic autoregulation within the self. *Theory & Psychology*, *12*(2), 251–265, doi:10.1177/0959354302012002633.

Valsiner, J. (2013). Creating sign hierarchies: Social representation in its dynamic context. *Papers on Social Representations*, *22*, 16.1–16.32.

Valsiner, J. (2015). The place for synthesis Vygotsky's analysis of affective generalization. *History of the Human Sciences*, *28*(2), 93–102, doi:10.1177/0952695114559530.

Vygotsky, L. S. (1978). *Mind in Society. The Development of Higher Psychological Processes*, edited by M. Cole, V. John-Steiner, S. Scribner, & E. Souberman. Cambridge, MA: Harvard University Press.

Werner, H. & Kaplan, B. (1963). *Symbol Formation. An Organismic-Developmental Approach to Language and the Expression of Thought*. New York, NY: John Wiley.

Winnicott, D. W. (1990). *Home Is Where We Start From: Essays by a Psychoanalyst*. New York, NY: Norton.

Zavereshneva, E. & van der Veer, R. (2018). *Vygotsky's Notebooks. A Selection*. Singapore: Springer.

Zittoun, T. (2006). *Transitions. Development through Symbolic Resources*. Greenwich, CT: Information Age.

Zittoun, T. (2008). Sign the gap: dialogical self in disrupted times. *Studia Psychologica*, *6*(8), 73–89.

Zittoun, T. (2014). Three dimensions of dialogical movement. *New Ideas in Psychology*, *32*, 99–106, doi:10.1016/j.newideapsych.2013.05.006.

Zittoun, T., Aveling, E.-L., Gillespie, A., & Cornish, F. (2012). People in transitions in worlds in transition: Ambivalence in the transition to womanhood during World War II. In A. C. Bastos, K. Uriko, & J. Valsiner (Eds.), *Cultural Dynamics of Women's Lives* (pp. 59–78). Charlotte, NC: Information Age.

Zittoun, T., Cornish, F., Gillespie, A., & Aveling, E.-L. (2008). Using social knowledge: A case study of a diarist's meaning making during World War II. In W. Wagner, T. Sugiman, & K. Gergen (Eds.), *Meaning in Action: Constructions, Narratives and Representations* (pp. 163–179). New York, NY: Springer.

Zittoun, T. & Gillespie, A. (2012). Using diaries and self-writings as data in psychological research. In E. Abbey & S. E. Surgan (Eds.), *Emerging Methods in Psychology* (pp. 1–26). New Brunswick, NJ: Transaction Publishers.

Zittoun, T. & Gillespie, A. (2013). Symbolic resources. In K. D. Keith (Ed.), *The Encyclopedia of Cross-Cultural Psychology*. Chichester: Wiley, doi:10.1002/9781118339893.wbeccp527.

Zittoun, T. & Gillespie, A. (2015). Integrating experiences: Body and mind moving between contexts. In B. Wagoner, N. Chaudhary, & P. Hviid (Eds.), *Integrating Experiences: Body and Mind Moving between Contexts* (pp. 3–49). Charlotte, NC: Information Age.

Zittoun, T. & Gillespie, A. (2016a). Imagination: Creating alternatives in everyday life. In V. P. Glăveanu (Ed.), *The Palgrave Handbook of Creativity and Culture Research* (pp. 225–242). London: Palgrave.

Zittoun, T. & Gillespie, A. (2016b). *Imagination in Human and Cultural Development*. London: Routledge.

Zittoun, T., Gillespie, A., & Cornish, F. (2009). Fragmentation or differentiation: Questioning the crisis in psychology. *Integrative Psychological and Behavioral Science*, *43*(2), 104–115, doi:10.1007/s12124-008-9083-6.

Zittoun, T. & Valsiner, J. (2016). Imagining the past and remembering the future: how the unreal defines the real. In T. Sato, N. Mori, & J. Valsiner (Eds.), *Making of the Future: The Trajectory Equifinality Approach in Cultural Psychology*, (pp. 3–19). Charlotte, NC: Information Age.

Zittoun, T., Valsiner, J., Vedeler, D., Salgado, J., Gonçalves, M., & Ferring, D. (2013). *Human Development in the Lifecourse. Melodies of Living*. Cambridge: Cambridge University Press.

17 Positioning Microanalysis: A Method For the Study of Dynamics in the Dialogical Self and Identity

João Salgado and Carla Cunha

This chapter will present Positioning Microanalysis as a methodological proposal to study identity according to a dialogical framework, namely through the lens of the Dialogical Self Theory (Hermans, 1996, 2001a, 2001b, 2003), inspired by Bakhtinian dialogism (Bakhtin, 1981; Salgado & Clegg, 2011). Our focus is mainly on the self, but as we will explain, identity here is considered as highly dependent on selfhood processes, at least from the point of view of a dialogical approach.

The notion of identity has been subjected to different interpretations in psychology and in common sense. Nevertheless, and regardless of that diversity, it is usually considered that a sense of identity is vital for living "a good life." The Delphic advice to "know thyself" still stands in our contemporary life, and by knowing who you are, you come to know your identity. At a general outlook, identity entails assuming a set of values, interests, vocations, and pursuits that remain among the variations of daily life, while building an overarching self-narrative uniting the trajectory throughout life (McAdams, 2020). By doing that, a sense of identity is achieved. However, this also happens moment by moment and, ever since John Locke (1689/1975) created the riddle of identity ("How can a person be considered the same in two distinct moments in time?"), the answer relies heavily on self-reflective processes. This means that a sense of identity is created through a constant observation and relation with oneself, along the ongoing relation with the world. Thus, it is our conviction that a theory about the self, such as the dialogical self theory (in which Positioning Microanalysis is rooted), is beneficial to the understanding of identity.

In this chapter, we will initially provide an overview of the dialogical approach, emphasizing its contributions to understanding and studying human identity, change, and development. We will highlight several characteristics of the dialogical self – usually conceived as multiple, multifaceted, and multivoiced – while also drawing attention to some challenging theoretical and empirical questions in this domain, especially as a specific perspective to conceive and study identity. Then, we will elaborate upon the Positioning Microanalysis method, which we have developed, emphasizing how it can be applied to study identity and change processes and, through the study of segments of a first session of psychotherapy, illustrate its analytic steps and potential findings.

17.1 The Dialogical Self and the Notion of Position

The Dialogical Self Theory, proposed by Hermans and colleagues (see Hermans, 1996, 2001a, 2001b, 2003; Hermans & Kempen, 1993), has been an alternative and engaging perspective for the study of self and identity within social sciences (see Hermans & Gieser, 2011; Konopka, Hermans, & Gonçalves, 2019; Wijsen & Hermans, 2020). It has led to prolific applications in the fields of counseling, clinical psychology, and psychotherapy (e.g., Hermans & Dimaggio, 2004; Konopka, Hermans, & Gonçalves, 2019; Neimeyer, 2006), developmental psychology and education (e.g., Bertau, 2004; Meijers & Hermans, 2018), social and cultural psychology (e.g., Hermans & Hermans-Konopka, 2010; Marsico & Valsiner, 2018), and political sciences (e.g., Hermans, 2018; Wijsen & Hermans, 2020).

Together, these authors share the idea of the dialogical self as "a dynamic multiplicity of relatively autonomous I positions ... The I has the possibility to move, as in a space, from one position to the other in accordance with changes in situation and time" (as proposed by Hermans, Kempen, & van Loon, 1992, p. 28). Therefore, the dialogical self is conceived as a tensional multiplicity of positions in the self (or I-positions), each expressing different perspectives (sometimes metaphorically addressed as *voices* in the self), as they relate to distinct experiences (in time or place), specific existential points of view, or multiple social roles occupied by a person (Holquist, 1990). This notion of I-position allows surpassing a self-enclosed, solipsistic notion of the mind by making use of the Bakhtinian *law of placement* (Holquist, 1990): Everything that a human agent says or does is placed within a certain social and historical context (a specific *chronotope*, a notion created by Bakhtin; see Raggatt, 2010). This also implies a spatial metaphor: Every human act is performed according to the social background and surroundings of the person, while it is also directed at someone or something else. We will later further elaborate this notion, but for now we will illustrate what we mean by *position* with an example.

Imagine a man expressing to his father how angry he still feels and how he deeply regrets feeling neglected by him in a specific period of their relationship. At this moment, his position can be termed as "regretful" (given the physiological state, specific emotions the person is aware of, and an understanding of the meaning of that experience), since the agent (the "I") assumes this feeling toward a specific interlocutor (his father) about an object (their past relationship). At the same time, this position is intermediated by some inner audiences that modulate his expressions (for example, some inner voice may be saying something like "Don't shout at your father!"). Thus, a position implies a relationship with social others and the material world. That happens even when positions emerge without the presence of someone else. Imagine this same man expressing the same experience about the situation, but in a written form in his private diary. The position may be termed in a similar way (regretful), since the agent is expressing the same feeling regarding the same object, but in this case there is no real interlocutor. However, from a dialogical point of view, there is a virtual other addressed by the written words – which may be his father, if he is addressing him in some form of direct speech (as if talking to or writing a letter to him), someone who may listen and understand his pain, someone opposing his expression, and so on. Thus, every position implies an addressee, which makes it always socially rooted. Therefore, we prefer to use the term position, instead of Hermans' wording (*I-position*), just to highlight the contextuality and addressivity of the self: the I emerges always within a social background and addressing specific audiences, and the sense of self is based on this socialized process (Bento, Cunha, & Salgado, 2012; Cunha & Salgado, 2017).

At the same time, the self is always in a *process of positioning*, which accompanies the flow of irreversible time and experience (Simão, Guimarães, & Valsiner, 2015; Valsiner, 2002). Consequently, the self is always on the move from one moment to the next, in a process of repositioning, and a chain of successive positions unfolds over time. As Hermans et al. (1992, p. 28) observed: "The I fluctuates among different and even opposed positions." Within this multiplicity, several positions can enter into a dialogue, opposing each other, succeeding each other as distinct and independent voices in a conversation, and creating an intense, internal dialogical space, that fades the frontiers between the self and society (Cunha & Salgado, 2017).

In addition, the dialogical self brings tension, alterity, and otherness into the core of the self (Bento, Cunha, & Salgado, 2012). This perspective conceives the self as "a society of the mind" (Hermans, 2001a, p. 147). This is a radically different perspective from the classic antinomies which contrast the I vs. Other, the Individual vs. Society/Culture, conceiving the self as rooted precisely in a sociocultural milieu from which one may struggle to become independent or distant, yet is forever embedded into (Bertau, 2004; Cunha & Salgado, 2017; Salgado & Hermans, 2005). When we are expressing a position, even when we are alone, there is always a virtual other, as well as other inner audiences (Bento, Cunha, & Salgado, 2012; Salgado & Cunha, 2018). A dialogical stance configures an approach to human psychological phenomena in an attempt to integrate three levels simultaneously in a coherent way: the experiential (i.e., what I perceive and feel in the flow of experiencing), the socio-relational (i.e., how I and others relate to my experiences), and the semiotic-linguistic elements of the human mind (i.e., how I make sense of them and give them meaning) (see Bento, Cunha, & Salgado, 2012; Salgado & Cunha, 2018).

Hence, different self-positions may oppose each other, enter into conflict and disagree, ignore or silence each other, becoming dominating, oppressive, or dismissive (Hermans, Kempen, & van Loon, 1992; Valsiner, 2002). Such tensions bring forth an interplay of centripetal (attraction) and centrifugal (distancing) forces that mediate the flow between self-positions.

17.1.1 The Triadic Structure of a Dialogical Position

The notion of position stands out as a main element for several dialogical proposals (Hermans, 2001a; Leiman, 2011; Salgado & Valsiner, 2010). Thus, we claim that at each and every moment a human agent is in relation with the world, and this relation is framed according to social and semiotic tools that are brought to the moment by the person, and also by the social contexts at stake (Cunha & Salgado, 2017; Salgado & Cunha, 2018).

The notion of position, in the way we have been developing it (Salgado & Valsiner, 2010; Salgado & Cunha, 2018), entails combining the phenomenological experience of being-in-the-world with the dialogical framework we adopted. Following this view, at every moment, human experience entails a position. This rule may have some exceptions, such as states of altered self-awareness (e.g., during some phases of sleep), but it applies to the majority of the moments of our psychological awake life. Thus, position and experience are coexistent – every position is a response to a lived phenomenological experience (Holquist, 1990). If I am sitting on the bank of a river, observing attentively its flow and sound, that river is my focal object of awareness in the present moment. I have a phenomenological experience, but this also entails a response to that experience – it entails a position. The river becomes the center of my phenomenological field, mainly constituted by the river and the feelings it brings to me. This goes along with an inner feeling of serenity and thoughts around it ("how relaxing this is"). This situation also inherently convokes some virtual other who is able to hear and understand this position. I also have some other inner audiences that modulate the present moment: past experiences and relationships that shape or modulate my present position. All these co-relative elements (the agent, the object, the addressees) are constitutive elements of the position at that moment – that can be termed as something like "I relaxing while observing the flow of the river" or just simply "relaxed."

Thus, we may attribute a triadic structure to any position. It entails (1) an agent, who purposeful responds within a specific situation (2) to a present or virtual addressee (3) about specific objects. We have discussed this structure in more detail elsewhere (Salgado & Cunha, 2018; Salgado & Valsiner, 2010). In those elaborations, we claim that signs of varied degrees of abstraction mediate this triadic relation. As a dialogical or socialized relationship, this triangle implies some form of articulation with real or virtual others, and that is achieved with semiotic means. A sign is something that stands for something else, that substitutes the material object with some abstract form, and this varies between more rudimentary forms (or proto-signs), such as sensations or feelings, to words and complex verbal linguistic systems (Valsiner, 2007).

As we previously said, a position is always on the move, it is constantly changing from moment to moment. For example, while sitting on a river bank, thoughts may come to the foreground (e.g., a memory from childhood), some other objects that remain in the periphery of that field (e.g., the sunlight reflected in the trees), or even some inner reaction to this situation ("you should do this more often"). New positions are constantly emerging, in a process of constant repositioning.

17.1.2 Looking at Identity through the Lens of the Dialogical Self

The notion of self and identity are overlapping and dependent. The APA online dictionary (American Psychological Association, 2018), for instance, defines identity as "an individual's sense of self defined by (a) a set of physical, psychological, and interpersonal characteristics that is not wholly shared with any other person and (b) a range of affiliations (e.g., ethnicity) and social roles. Identity involves a sense of continuity . . ." In other words, identity is rooted in the sense of self. At the same time, it is closely related to what makes a particular person unique and singular, but also associated, as argued centuries ago by Locke (1689/1975), with how a person remains the same in two temporally different moments.

Following that stance, in this work we assume identity as a sense of continuity across time, but also as a mark of distinctiveness. It involves self-reflective processes: the knowledge and feeling of who I am across time (sameness), and how I am different and unique (difference). As a matter of self-reflexivity, identity becomes dependent on selfhood processes. Following a dialogical approach, we will assume that each emerging position of the self is always embodied and entails a dialogical relationship with inner audiences that constrain, observe, and respond to the position at stake. Within this view, self-reflection and self-awareness always involve a tensional and dialogical relationship with oneself, from which a sense of continuity is achieved – in other words, a sense of identity. On the other hand, since this process is inherently dialogical and socialized, it is also rooted in worldly manifestations – every position is a response to a social and material world, and it involves life preferences and goals that may acquire some stability across time (Bento, Cunha, & Salgado, 2012).

Given that alterity, tension and otherness are crucial features of the dialogical self and, at first glance, the contrast and divergence between positions can look like a disorganized cacophony (Hermans, Kempen, & van Loon, 1992). Yet, how the person deals with this inner (and outer) multiplicity that continually unfolds throughout life is a crucial aspect for the construction of identity, the maintenance of temporal stability. Also, it is from this tension and contrast that there may be room for self-innovation and personal change.

Thus, in the domain of the dialogical self theory we face two major challenges: to explain how novelty emerges, but also how stability is maintained. We would affirm that stability, which is more commonly associated with identity, has to do with this second part of the problem – the organization of coherence and continuity across time. However, stability and change are part of the same generic process of self-organization. For example, in some sense a person who keeps being attracted to new challenges and novelties will have this feature as part of their own stability and identity, which characterizes them.

From a dialogical point of view, both stability and change need to be understood within the process of a dialogical interplay between different positions. And since the multifaceted and narrative nature of identity is recognized, identity needs to be understood as the product of dialogue between several positions (Cunha, 2007). We should add that stability and change need to take into consideration the time frame of observation. The previous examples in this chapter have referred to very quick changes, in a moment-to-moment observation of positions. We can claim that these are microanalytic observations; as Leiman (2011) has argued, we were observing the basic unit of analysis of a dialogical perspective, namely, a position. Nevertheless, other time frames are possible and important. Following the general terminology coming from Vygotskian tradition and developed by Valsiner (e.g., 2007), the emergence of positions can be observed according to three distinct frames: microgenetic, mesogenetic, and macrogenetic. Thus, we can frame the observation of positions in different ways – from seconds to lifetime periods. In terms of dynamics, we expect the person to be microgenetically very unstable, with high fluctuation between positions, but macrogenetically the tendency will be to observe a low level of fluctuation.

According to these different ways to frame our observations, we propose here a distinction between micropositions, mesopositions, and macropositions. A macroposition will be a general, but observable, position of the person, typically composed by different mesopositions, and a mesoposition will be a generic aggregation of micropositions. For example, if a person assumes a position of being "sad" regarding the results of the Parliament election, and then discriminates this as being "disappointed," and later on affirms being "really frustrated," these three positions could be understood as micropositions, but also as parts of the same sort of mesoposition, which could be labeled as "I as frustrated with these elections." At a higher hierarchical level, and governing this mesoposition, we can have a global general position, for example, "I as a Labour Party supporter." Theoretically, this implies an assumption: that different levels of positions cohere somehow in their content and contribute to the same sort of global stance and action toward a segment of the world; at the same time, some positions can have hierarchical power over others, governing or influencing them. For example, positions connected with strong values tend to be very generalized and, at the same time, very influential in terms of self and identity.

Methodologically this implies the crafting of research tools that enable the study of how identity is achieved throughout time, based on the interplay between different positions, while considering specific different levels of observation and generalization.

17.2 Positioning Microanalysis: A Methodological Proposal to Study the Dynamics of the Dialogical Self and Identity

Different methods have been developed to study the dialogical self. In our view, the most well-known ones are the Self-Confrontation Method, developed by Hermans and Hermans-Jansen (1995), and the Personal Position Repertoire, developed by Hermans (2001a), which we have reviewed elsewhere, highlighting their potentialities and constraints (Cunha, Salgado, & Gonçalves, 2012; Salgado, Cunha, & Bento, 2013). Yet, one of the main problems of the field has been the lack of empirical methods dedicated to the study of selfhood dynamics as they unfold throughout time.

More specifically, we felt the need for the development of a method (a) to capture the natural dynamics of positioning in the self, for the purpose of understanding microanalytically the ongoing flow of positions in time; (b) to allow for a naturalistic observation of life events or research material, such as clinical sessions or open interviews; and (c) which could be a methodological proposal that would not rely completely on the participant's explicit self-reflexivity (i.e., not departing from an initial, explicit recognition by the person of their own relevant positions, as the previous methods usually do). This would allow us to characterize the dynamics of the self in movement and enable other possibilities, such as capturing positions not recognized by the person, as a means to study change, development, and self-organization. Through this process, we could get access to the most important positions that constitute the matrix of that person's identity, i.e., their sense of personal coherence, distinctiveness, and uniqueness.

As a result of this ambition, we have developed the Positioning Microanalysis method (Salgado, Cunha, & Bento, 2013), a methodological proposal based on a dialogical approach, which aims the systematic tracing by trained observers of the dialogical dynamics of positions as they unfold over time. This proposal had various phases of development (for a review, see Cunha et al., 2012). The method was originally developed by Cunha (2007, under the name Dialogical-Discursive Microgenetic Analysis) to study the self-organization processes of positioning during interviews exploring participants' personal problems. This work laid the ground for the contribution of Salgado, Cunha, and Bento (2013) establishing the basic aims and conceptual tools of the method. Thus, Salgado, Cunha, and Bento (2013) developed and refined this method into its current form, making it more systematic and flexible, renaming it Positioning Microanalysis (henceforth PM), and making it applicable in the field of psychotherapy process research, through the study of psychotherapy transcripts and videos aimed at exploring change processes. The studies on psychotherapy were originally devoted to individual sessions (e.g., Salgado & Cunha, 2012), but more recently it has been applied to couples therapy (Cunha, Figueiredo, & Salgado, 2020). Nevertheless, we consider it can be applied to other kinds of research material, such as interviews, focus groups, or potentially any other verbatim data.

The main unit of analysis of PM is the emergent position, which is characterized by a basic triadic relation (I–Other–Object). This method, on a first level of analysis, depicts the microgenetic movements of positions from moment to moment, but it also allows for meso and macro levels of analysis, by describing stable sequences or cycles of positions. Thus, it makes it possible to study selfhood dynamics of stability and change, with that identity, in a given historical moment of the person regarding specific themes or relevant objects. This method will now be detailed, step by step, and illustrated by its application to the initial session of a psychotherapy case.

17.2.1 Phases of Analysis

There are five different phases in PM:

(1) Preliminary work;
(2) Division of verbatim data into units of analysis (unitizing);
(3) Aggregation of units into themes;
(4) Labeling of positions;
(5) Interpretative developmental analysis.

Along with the characterization of each of these steps, we will use illustrative segments of a clinical case, with the pseudonym of "Lisa."

Lisa was clinically depressed when she participated in a randomized clinical trial (York I study; Greenberg & Watson, 1998). She received sixteen sessions of emotion-focused therapy following her diagnosis of major depression, and the final outcome of psychotherapy was considered successful, with full recovery from symptoms. This is a well-known case in the psychotherapy literature, and it has been the object of analysis of different research teams in several previous publications (see Angus, Goldman, & Mergenthaler, 2008). Likewise, we were granted access to the transcripts of all the sessions. Here, we will use PM to describe and understand the sequences of positions around the main clinical problems that this client brought to therapy.

17.2.2 Phase 1: Preliminary Work

There is some work to be done before starting the analysis itself. First, the object, dataset, and purpose of the study need to be defined. The method per se does not define the specific research questions to be addressed, even if it constrains the potential findings. Thus, these decisions must be made previously. For example, we may frame the study around the positioning processes that maintain stability and identity across time. Once the research questions are decided upon, researchers need to be familiarized with the theory and be trained in the procedures. Then, they need to read the transcripts and, whenever possible, hear the session recordings or watch the session videos.

Research Questions and Data Selection

The research problems can be varied, and they will guide the process of selecting data that will be necessary to run the analysis. Since PM can be highly time-consuming, it is advisable to focus on specific questions and then select specific extracts to avoid analysis of material that will in the end be irrelevant to addressing the research questions. The selection of data can be determined in varied ways. For example, after determining that the main goal is to describe the sequence of positions emerging while talking about the main clinical issue in a first session of therapy, a senior researcher and a clinician can individually read the transcripts, and decide in a joint meeting what is the major clinical issue and which are the relevant passages to be analyzed subsequently.

Training

Researchers start by reading the PM manual we have developed, explaining the basic conceptual tools and methodological procedures (Salgado et al., 2013). After that, they usually perform practical exercises with workbooks, each devoted to a specific phase of analysis: unitizing, identification of themes, characterization and labeling of self-positions, as well as interpretative final work. After concluding each workbook, a group discussion takes place, in which researchers receive feedback about their results. Whenever needed, additional exercises may be introduced to increase the effectiveness of the training. After effective training is completed, researchers start focusing on the material under analysis (e.g., selecting relevant excerpts and dividing them into units).

Illustration of Phase 1: Exploring and Understanding Sequences of Positions around Clinical Problems in the Case of Lisa

As stated previously, the client Lisa was suffering from major depression and all the illustrations will be based on an analysis of the first session of this psychotherapy case. We approached this case with the goal of studying the global process of change in this client (Salgado et al., 2011). The project had several parts, and the initial part was concerned with the dialogical understanding of Lisa's main clinical problems, with a special interest in the following question: How was stability around these problems achieved and maintained in terms of positioning dynamics? In this illustration we will use segments of that initial part of the project.

   This specific aim set the criteria for selecting relevant passages of session 1. Then, since we (the authors) are simultaneously researchers and clinicians, we discussed and selected passages that are relevant to addressing the following question: What are the main clinical problems presented by Lisa in the first session? After reaching an agreement through discussion, the relevant passages were later analyzed involving other researchers (involved specifically as raters). In the current study, the researchers were two Master's students who were trained by two senior researchers in all the procedures until they acquired the necessary skills to independently analyze and perform their tasks autonomously. The two senior researchers acted as trainers in that training period, and later audited the process of analysis.

17.2.3 Phase 2: Dividing the Transcript into Response Units (Unitizing)

This step involves dividing the verbatim transcripts into small units of analysis. Each unit is considered in this method as an observed microposition. In order to detect these units of analysis, we adopted Hill's (2009) procedures for unitizing transcripts. These are based on the notion of "response unit" (Cunha et al., 2012, p. 540), which is defined as an independent unit of meaning. Thus, researchers need to read the transcript and divide it into independent units of meaning, each of them expressing a different perspective.

   We recommend using at least two researchers (raters) to perform this task autonomously to allow the possibility of calculating inter-rater agreement (see Hill, 2009, for further details). A degree of 90 percent agreement is recommended in this phase. Remaining disagreements can be resolved through consensus after discussion. An auditor guides and reviews the whole process.

Illustration of Phase 2

The selected passages were given to the two trained researchers and then Lisa's transcripts (turn-takings) were divided into response units (unitizing audited by a senior researcher). To illustrate how response units are distinguished, take the following small passage, in which the therapist is asking Lisa about the negative feelings that she tries to avoid and ignore. A slash indicates the division of a response unit:

THERAPIST: mm-hm. mm-hm, so it's like even if you try to ignore them they just, they're there
LISA: /they're always there, yeah/
THERAPIST: uh-huh
LISA: /the sadness/ and um I guess resentment still there/

THERAPIST: resentment towards?
LISA: /um - oh it would be my family (Therapist: uh-huh)/ and my
              husband/

The therapist initially is just mirroring what Lisa previously said (that she tries to suppress negative feelings without success). After that, five units are present, each of them expressing a specific perspective:

(1) "they're always there, yeah," i.e., the feelings do not go away, they are there, in spite of her attempts to suppress them;
(2) "the sadness," i.e., she feels sad;
(3) "and um I guess resentment still there," i.e., she feels resentful;
(4) "um - oh it would be my family," i.e., she feels resentful toward her family (later on in the session, we will understand that this is related to her upbringing, so she is referring to her father and mother);
(5) "and my husband," i.e., she resents her husband.

In this phase, we are not yet labeling positions, even though these very small units are the basic building blocks that will allow positions to be found. Thus, each unit will constitute a microposition, according to this method, since they express a specific attitude perspective or attitude toward an object.

17.2.4 Phase 3: Aggregating Units into Thematic Objects

This phase consists in detecting the object that is at stake in every response unit, and, after that, aggregating those objects into themes. We define a theme as a generic domain or macrostructure (Stinson et al., 1994) around which segments of a conversation revolve around. A theme can be something like "my marriage" or "my upbringing." The procedure is based on answering the following questions:

(1) What is the referential object of this response unit?
(2) Is this referential object similar to another one expressed in other response units?

The first question identifies the object; the second concerns the aggregation in larger thematic units.

Illustration of Phase 3

We will use again the previous excerpt. Regarding the first question (What is the referential unit in this response unit?), we see that Lisa was describing her negative feelings, in all the first three responses to her therapist. In the first one, they are referred to generally ("they're always there, yeah"); in the second, she identifies sadness; and in the third, she identifies resentment. So, we may distinguish three objects: negative feelings, sadness, and resentment.

Nevertheless, they all refer to a global topic: "my negative feelings." Thus, we can group them under this same, more generic theme. Notice that in the following two response units, guided by the therapist's question ("resentment towards?"), the object becomes the recipient of this resentment, which are her family of origin (response 4) and her husband (response 5). They can both be grouped as a more generic theme, such as "my family."

The two researchers performed this phase. The global procedures that we will describe are similar to the next phases. They started by autonomously reading and identifying the referential object of each response unit, and then they discussed their findings. This discussion is always aimed at reaching a consensus regarding each unit and the themes found. After reaching consensus, the researchers' results were discussed with the auditor, until a final consensus was reached.

17.2.5 Phase 4: Characterization and Labeling of Positions

This phase consists in analyzing each response unit in two steps. First, we need to identify the I and the Others involved in each response unit. This implies the following distinctions:

- The agent: Who is speaking? The most frequent situation is when agent and the speaking person coincide. Nevertheless, there are exceptions. If a person is voicing someone else's perspective (e.g., "and then he said to me: *you are wrong!*"), the agent is this other person (who utters the expression appearing in italics). It can also happen that situations in which the person voices a collective standpoint (e.g., a representative of a panel of assessment saying "we all appreciated your work very much"), in which all the agents need to be accounted for (in this example, the panel).
- The addressee: To whom is the agent speaking? The addressee is the focal person or group addressed in the unit. We are aiming here to disclose the symbolic addressee, and not the real interlocutor (in our case, Lisa's therapist). It coincides with the recipient disclosed in the content of the message. For example, by saying "I love her," this person is addressing the loved one. Thus, it does not coincide with the interlocutor. The addressee can be vague, and in some situations it will be impossible to code (e.g., "What a beautiful river this is"; here it will not be possible to code this parameter, given that we may not know to whom the agent is speaking).
- Inner audiences: Who are all the others involved in this response unit? When specifying these others, we have two more frequent situations: the interlocutors, whenever they are not the addressee; and other people referred in the discourse. Imagine a man saying to the therapist: "My parents are quite homophobic, so I was very, very anxious on my first date with a man." The final response ("I was very anxious on my first date") includes the person whom I was dating as the addressee, but his parents are still there as inner

audiences. It should be noted that in several situations, it is impossible to determine these audiences. Yet, there is a final remark. The person themself is always working as an inner audience, since all the responses are open to self-reflection; however, since this self-referential act is a constant, we consider that there is no need to code the self as an inner audience.

As a second step of this phase, and based on the previous steps (finding the "what," "who," and "to whom" of all response units), researchers need to label each unit as a whole. This label will identify a specific microposition. The rule is to find a label that stays as close as possible to the phenomenological content of the response. So, if a person says, "I felt awkward," the label can be "I as awkward."

We have developed a set of specific guidelines to help in this process (see Salgado et al., 2013, for a more detailed account), and we will briefly describe the most important here:

- As said before, the rule is to stick with a label that captures the global perspective or attitude toward the referential object.
- When synonyms are used (e.g., frightened and scared), the same label should be applied to these different units.
- If the same unit contains different internal states, this unit needs to be divided into different positions (e.g., "It's sad and scary" should be labeled as "I as sad" and "I as scared").
- When the person who speaks does not coincide with the speaker, we name these positions as "counterpositions" to distinguish them from all other regular positions. These counterpositions may be relevant for the analysis of inner dialogical dynamics.
- Throughout the sequence of labeling, researchers go through a process of systematic comparison, similar to content analysis (Fassinger, 2005), in which some labels are aggregated in wider categorizations. This implies going back and forth relabeling previously assigned labels.

Illustration of Phase 4

We will illustrate this phase with the same passage. However, right now we will analyze the turn-taking that took place just before, which starts as follows:

THERAPIST: you're saying that the merry go round speaks something of your depression

LISA: /yeah, feelings are um well they recur,/ they haven't gone away,/, they're just more suppressed than all of them

THERAPIST: mm-hm. mm-hm, so it's like even if you try to ignore them they just, they're there [and then the conversation follows with the previous extract]

In this sequence the main parameters remain the same: the object is her negative feelings, the agent is Lisa, the addressee is the therapist, and it is not possible to code any inner audiences. The next step consisted in labeling these positions. Initially, these were coded as "I as having recurrent feelings," "I as having feelings that do not go away," and "I as suppressing feelings." At the beginning, these labels tend to be extensive and quite close to the original words. However, even before this passage, Lisa had already defined her state as depressive (also confirmed by her inclusion in this trial), and it became clear that all these micropositions were part of her description of her depressive state. So, these micropositions were then grouped under a mesoposition called "I as depressed." Thus, this more general position termed "I as depressed" could be described micronanalytically as a loop between "I as feeling bad" (which can be subdivided into feeling sad, resentful, and angry, among others), leading to "I as suppressing bad feelings," leading again to "I as feeling bad," and so on. This kind of sequencing is already part of the next phase, but while doing this relabeling, these sequences are frequently already becoming clear to the researchers, and they should bookmark them for future steps of the analysis.

17.2.6 Phase 5: Finding Patterns of Positioning through Interpretative Analysis

The global result of the previous phase is a very detailed micronanalytic description of positions emerging moment by moment. This new phase aims to build a more generic description by detailing more generalized sequences of positions. In other words, this phase creates a macrolevel description of the positioning process, in articulation with the more microlevel and mesolevel descriptions obtained in the previous phase.

After concluding the labeling of positions, researchers can now observe repetitive sequences and sudden changes in those patterns. Thus, for example, we may witness a regular and repetitive movement between positions such as *p1: I as afraid – p2: I as avoidant – p3: I as frustrated*. We may also witness variations in this sequences (e.g., *p1 – p1 – p3*); oscillations in this pattern through the emergence of new positions (e.g., *p1: I as afraid – p4: I as courageous – p2: I as avoidant*). These observations can be used to draw a diagram of these sequences or cycles of positioning. At the same, they can be used to compare the change in these sequences or cycles throughout time. For example, if *p1 – p2 – p3* was the initial problematic pattern in therapy, later on, in a good outcome case, we may find a different pattern, such as *p2: I as courageous – p3: I as not afraid anymore – p4: I as free*. At this stage of the analysis, we can only describe the changes in positions, and thereby we cannot explain how changes happened. Nevertheless, we can then dive again into the data in order to look for moments in which novelties occurred, and look in detail into what happened before, informed by a microgenetic and interpretive perspective (Valsiner, 2007).

Although statistical analysis can be used for detecting sequences, we have been using only this more interpretive mode of analysis, which involves the careful reading of the transcripts and labeling of positions with special attention to repetitions. We have developed the following guidelines for this (Salgado & Cunha, 2012; Salgado, Cunha & Bento, 2013):

(1) *Highly frequent positions.* A very frequent position is a recurrent one, and therefore it must be involved in some form of regular pattern. This can be a good starting point for detecting sequences, and then going on to observe the preceding and proceeding positions.

(2) *Themes and their regularity.* More frequent themes are more likely to involve regularities. Moreover, positions are usually organized around some specific thematic objects.

(3) *Adjacent occurrences, sudden shifts, and semantic justifications.* These devices can help in the process of detecting and specifying the sequence. If we see that position 2 follows position 1, p2 is *adjacent* to p1. If this happens regularly, then we have a good trace of a possible pattern. Sudden shifts of position and/or theme are also important, because they can highlight the presence of a pattern (e.g., if *p1: I as afraid* leads frequently to *p2: I as hard worker*, this may indicate not only a pattern, but also sudden changes in the referential object, which may be relevant). Shifts toward the opposite positions (e.g., *I as courageous* leading to *I as afraid*) can also be frequent and important to look at in detail. We also need to consider explicit descriptions by the person. For example, a passage like "since I am always thinking pessimistically, I am always anxious" suggests explicitly a small sequence that should be taken into account.

(4) *Disappearance of positions and emergence of new ones: Variations and alternative patterns.* Whenever a new position emerges, this can be taken as an index of potential variations and change on the usual sequences. The same is true whenever one position disappears or becomes less frequent in a certain sequence.

These guidelines can be used, but this phase of work is largely "discovery-oriented." The sequences are described, and whenever a particular sequence repeats itself or is considered important for some particular reason (e.g., the client has a strong emotional reaction), the researchers produce a description of this pattern. This acts as a working hypothesis that needs to be refined through successive corrections. The same applies to variations to those patterns. This process ends only when the researchers have achieved a satisfactory description of patterns and their variations. We have been calling these patterns *cycles of positions*, and they can be represented in a narrative format and/or through a diagram displaying the most relevant positions and their sequencing.

The combination of these three last phases produces a multilayered description of the emerging positions, from microgenetic descriptions of positions, to the intermediate level in which some patterns and regularities are abstracted, to the proposal of the main cycles of positions. These cycles necessarily have stability throughout time and are directly involved in the creation of an identity. When applied to human change processes, in psychotherapy or in other contexts, this method can also be used as a tool for the detection of modifications in those patterns.

Illustration of Phase 5: Finding Patterns of Positioning through Interpretative Analysis

We will now flesh out this last phase by describing some of the more central parts of the analysis conducted around Lisa's definition of her own clinical problems. We will not give a full description of the analysis, since our goal is to illustrate this final step.

As we have seen previously, Lisa associated her state of depression with feelings of resentment toward her parents and her husband. After disclosing this feeling of resentment, the session continues as follows (in square brackets we will add the positions as they were identified):

THERAPIST: uh-huh, you can feel that (Lisa: um); like right now is that what's kind of, what's present

LISA: /yes, yeah it's present, /it's clear (sniff)/ it's there *[I as resented] – [I as resented] – [I as resented]*

THERAPIST: uh huh

LISA: /not that I um, well I-I don't want to hate them/ *[I as forgiving]*

THERAPIST: yeah, so there's another part of you that doesn't want to feel really strong hatred

LISA: /that's right, yeah/ *[I as forgiving]*

THERAPIST: and yet you do have resentment

LISA: /yes I do, yeah - - / but I-I'm willing to forgive/ *[I as forgiving]*

THERAPIST: uh-huh, do you feel sad when you say that

LISA: /um, to forgive?/ [I as asking for a clarification]

THERAPIST: yes

LISA: /um yes, yeah I - - - -/well I-I under, I think I understand and you know, why it happened/ *[I as sad] – [I as forgiving]*

THERAPIST: uh-huh, your parents or your husband as well

LISA: /yeah, my parents and my husband/ *[I as forgiving]*

THERAPIST: it's like you can almost step into their shoes and see (/Lisa: yeah/); how it is that they were like that (/Lisa: that's right/); and why they did what they did towards you *[I as forgiving] – [I as forgiving]*

Lisa: /yeah, it-it's more of um, I understand it/ but then, you know, the anger and the resentment is still there/ *[I as forgiving] - [I as resented]*

In this excerpt, we witness the development of an interplay between two main and somewhat contradictory positions: I as resented and I as forgiving. Actually, I as forgiving is a mesoposition composed by some other

Main cycle

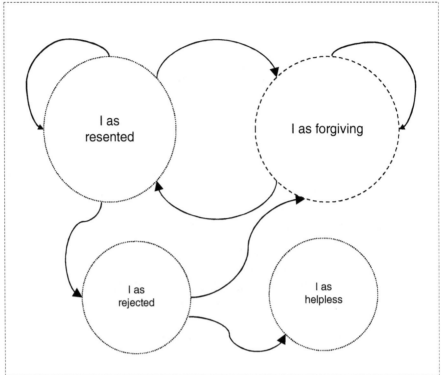

Figure 17.1 *The main cycle of positioning around which Lisa's clinical problems revolved*

micropositions such as I as understanding (e.g., "well I-I under, I think I understand and you know, why it happened") and I as avoiding hatred feelings (e.g., "well I-I don't want to hate them"). This can be illustrated through a diagram (see Figure 17.1). These positions, besides some self-referential own feeding (e.g., "I as resented" feeding on itself three times, on the first turn-taking), they also feed each other, even if they are quite opposite. So, they maintain a sort of dynamic and, also, a tensional stability between the positions of resentment and forgiving and understanding. This cycle is repeated several times across the session.

A few moments later, after disclosing that her husband has a serious gambling problem and how that makes her feel rejected [I as rejected becomes the prevalent position in that phase], we observe another relevant sequence:

THERAPIST: so it-it's like the feeling of being kind of locked in
LISA: /yeah, /more as uh, isolated/ *[I as locked in] – [I as isolated]*
THERAPIST: uh-huh
LISA: /you know I can't do anything about it, it's happening but I/
            [I as helpless]

THERAPIST: so you start almost feeling helpless
LISA: /that's right,/ I'm um, I'm helpless about it, /I can't do anything/
               [I as helpless] – [I as helpless] – [I as helpless]

Thus, we witness a gradual differentiation of the resented position into a more specific complaint about feeling rejected, which later feeds into this feeling of helplessness. Then, two turn-takings later we observe this:

THERAPIST: because you still end up feeling hurt inside
LISA: /yeah, the feelings are-are very much there/ even though
               I understand (laugh) the disease and the character in him/ *[I as
               rejected] – [I as forgiving]*

Thus, the position "I as rejected" makes room for the position of "I as forgiving," maintaining this cycle in a dynamic stability. This cycle is not only described several times in the session, but also portrayed as something happening frequently in her daily life. We may say that this is part of her identity, at the moment, even though she is now making a strong effort to find a way out of this situation. In this analysis, we have left out some other elements that also feed this dynamic stability (such as her fear of neglecting her kids or her values), but the main cycle of positioning that we obtained is the one depicted above.

17.3 Conclusion

PM aims to be a useful tool for studying the dynamics of the dialogical self and, therefore, we argued here that it is also a useful method for studying identity, in its dynamics of stability and change. Based on a dialogical approach, PM studies the moment-by-moment change of the self in its process of positioning and analyzes each position in a microanalytic way. The several phases of the PM method were described and illustrated throughout this chapter: the preliminary work, before the actual analysis (phase 1); the unitizing of research data, such as session transcripts or interviews (phase 2); the aggregation of the segments of research data into thematic objects, or themes (phase 3); the actual pragmatics of characterizing and labeling positions of the self, which includes the analysis of the agent, addressee, and inner audiences (phase 4); and, finally, arriving at a depiction of patterns between positions, through an interpretive analysis of the dynamics between positions (phase 5).

Through this systematic and detailed tracing and analysis of positions, PM also allows a focus on different, increasing levels of generalizability in the self. It departs from micropositions to arrive at meso and macro levels of description of the dialogical self. In other words, it allows us to find regularities, and redundancies, between positions, and to characterize recursiveness in the self in terms of sequences, patterns, and cycles between positions, which can also be interpreted as a hierarchical ordering of positions within the self, on our view. This represents, for us, a systematic way to access one of the most important aspects of our identity, which is the sense of self or sameness, as a product of the self-organization and regulation of multiplicity within the dialogical self. Given that this is a phenomenologically based method, it provides a tool to grasp and characterize, more directly, what we may later recognize as identity in the making, rooted in the ever-changing flow of experiences (at the microgenetic level), and capturing the process of organization of this flow of experiencing and meaning-making (at the mesogenetic and macrogenetic levels) which constructs us as an individual, with characteristic, unique and singular features.

In addition, using the PM as a method that can be replicated several times with the same person, such as when we apply it to psychotherapy sessions, allows to notice changes (i) through the emergence of new positions and (ii) through modifications in the patterns and cycles between positions. Although PM's potential to capture and describe personal change has not yet been applied outside the realm of psychotherapy, we believe the method is applicable to and could be useful in other types of longitudinal studies. Thus, we believe that PM could be a starting point for other forms of dynamic analysis of self and identity through time, namely studies that focus on an analysis of personal change or identity shifts during life transitions, such as marriage, widowhood, the transition to motherhood/fatherhood, the adjustment to chronic illness, a new profession, or migration, among other topics.

In itself, the PM method does not explain how one person remains the same across different moments of life, or how change and stability are made compatible. Nevertheless, by remaining close to the lived phenomena of psychic life, it allows us to describe how the person creates sameness and change, by studying the positions of the self as they naturally unfold; and the final description matches different levels of generalization within the self and identity. Therefore, it becomes a very distinct alternative to other well-known dialogical methods (reviewed by Cunha, Salgado, & Gonçalves, 2012).

References

Angus, L., Goldman, R., & Mergenthaler, E. (2008). Introduction. One case, multiple measures: An intensive case-analytic approach to understanding client change processes in evidence-based emotion-focused therapy of depression. *Psychotherapy Research*, 6, 629–633, doi:10.1080/10503300802430673.

American Psychological Association (APA). (2018). Identity. In *APA Online Dictionary of Psychology*. Retrieved May 05, 2021, from https://dictionary.apa.org/identity.

Bakhtin, M. M. (1981). *The Dialogic Imagination: Four Essays by M. M. Bakhtin*, translated by C. Emerson & M. Holquist. Austin, TX: University of Texas Press.

Bento, T., Cunha, C., & Salgado, J. (2012). Dialogical theory of selfhood. In J. Valsiner (Ed.), *The Oxford Handbook of Culture and Psychology* (pp. 421–438). Oxford: Oxford University Press.

Bertau, M. C. (Ed.). (2004). *Aspects of the Dialogical Self*. Berlin: Lehmanns Media.

Cunha, C. A. C. (2007). Processos dialógicos de mudança: Um estudo microgenético [Dialogical change processes: A microgenetic study]. Master's thesis, University of Minho, Braga.

Cunha, C., Figueiredo, C., & Salgado, J. (2020). "Let's dance:" A dialogical proposal for analyzing interactions and positions in couples therapy. *Journal of Constructivist Psychology*, *34*(2), 1–20, doi:10.1080/10720537.2020.1717149.

Cunha, C., Gonçalves, M. M., Hill, C. E., Sousa, I., Mendes, I., Ribeiro, A. P., Angus, L. & Greenberg, L. S. (2012). Therapist interventions and client innovative moments in emotion-focused therapy for depression. *Psychotherapy*, *49*, 536–548, doi:10.1037/a0028259.

Cunha, C. & Salgado, J. (2017). Social frames and the dialogical self: A dynamic account of subjectivity within a subjectified world. In M. Han & C. Cunha (Eds.), *The Subjectified and Subjectifying Mind* (pp. 69–84). Charlotte, NC: Information Age.

Cunha, C., Salgado, J., & Gonçalves, M. M. (2012). The dialogical self in movement: Reflecting on methodological tools for the study of the dynamics of change and stability in the self. In E. Abbey & S. Surgan (Eds.), *Emerging Methods in Psychology* (pp. 65–100). New Brunswick, NJ: Transaction.

Fassinger, R. (2005). Paradigms, praxis, problems, and promise: Grounded theory in counseling psychology research. *Journal of Counseling Psychology*, *52*, 156–166.

Greenberg, L. S. & Watson, J. (1998). Experiential therapy of depression: Differential effects of client-centered relationship conditions and process experiential interventions. *Psychotherapy Research*, *8*, 210–224, doi:10.1080/10503309812331332317.

Hermans, H. J. M. (1996). Voicing the self: From information processing to dialogical interchange. *Psychological Bulletin*, *119*(1), 31–50.

Hermans, H. J. M. (2001a). The construction of a personal position repertoire: Method and practice. *Culture & Psychology*, *7*(3), 323–366.

Hermans, H. J. M. (2001b). The dialogical self: Toward a theory of personal and cultural positioning. *Culture & Psychology*, *7*(3), 243–281.

Hermans, H. J. M. (2003). The construction and reconstruction of a dialogical self. *Journal of Constructivist Psychology*, *16*, 89–130.

Hermans, H. J. M. (2018). *Society in the Self: A Theory of Identity in Democracy*. Oxford: Oxford University Press.

Hermans, H. J. M. & Dimaggio, G. (Eds.). (2004). *The Dialogical Self in Psychotherapy*. Hove: Bruner-Routledge.

Hermans, H. J. M. & Gieser, T. (Eds.). (2011). *Handbook of Dialogical Self Theory*. Cambridge: Cambridge University Press.

Hermans, H. J. M. & Hermans-Jansen, E. (1995). *Self-Narratives*. New York, NY: Guilford.

Hermans, H. J. M. & Hermans-Konopka, A. (2010). *Dialogical Self Theory: Positioning and Counter-Positioning in a Globalizing Society*. Cambridge: Cambridge University Press.

Hermans, H. J. M. & Kempen, H. (1993). *The Dialogical Self: Meaning as Movement*. San Diego, CA: Academic Press.

Hermans, H. J. M., Kempen, H., & van Loon, R. (1992). The dialogical self: Beyond individualism and rationalism. *American Psychologist, 47*, 23–33.

Hill, C. (2009). *Helping Skills: Facilitating Exploration, Insight, and Action*. New York, NY: American Psychological Association.

Holquist, M. (1990). *Dialogism: Bakhtin and His World*. London: Routledge.

Konopka, A., Hermans, H. J., & Gonçalves, M. M. (Eds.). (2019). *Handbook of Dialogical Self Theory and Psychotherapy: Bridging Psychotherapeutic and Cultural Traditions*. New York, NY: Routledge.

Leiman, M. (2011). Mikhail Bakhtin's contribution to psychotherapy research. *Culture & Psychology, 17*, 441–461.

Locke, J. (1689/1975). *An Essay Concerning Human Understanding*. Oxford: Oxford University Press.

McAdams, D. P. (2020). Self and identity. In R. Biswas-Diener & E. Diener (Eds.), *Noba Textbook Series: Psychology*. Champaign, IL: DEF. Retrieved May 5, 2021, from http://noba.to/3gsuardw.

Marsico, G. & Valsiner, J. (2018). *Beyond the Mind: Cultural Dynamics of the Psyche*. Charlotte, NC: Information Age.

Meijers, F. & Hermans, H. J. M. (2018). Dialogical self theory in education: An introduction. In F. Meijers & H. J. M. Hermans, (Eds.), *The Dialogical Self Theory in Education* (pp. 1–17). Cham, Switzerland: Springer Nature.

Neimeyer, R. A. (2006). Narrating the dialogical self: Toward an expanded toolbox for the counselling psychologist. *Counselling Psychology Quarterly, 19*, 105–120.

Raggatt, P. T. (2010). The dialogical self and thirdness: A semiotic approach to positioning using dialogical triads. *Theory & Psychology, 20*(3), 400–419.

Salgado, J. & Clegg, J. W. (2011). Dialogism and the psyche: Bakhtin and contemporary psychology. *Culture & Psychology, 17*(4), 421–440.

Salgado, J. & Cunha, C. (2012). Positioning microanalysis: The development of a dialogical-based method for idiographic psychology. In S. Salvatore, A. Gennaro, & J. Valsiner (Eds.), *Making Sense: Generating Uniqueness. Yearbook of Idiographic Science, Vol. 4* (pp. 221–244). Charlotte, NC: Information Age.

Salgado, J. & Cunha, C. (2018). The human experience: A dialogical account of self and feelings. In A. Rosa & J. Valsiner (Eds.), *The Cambridge Handbook of Sociocultural Psychology* (pp. 503–517). Cambridge: Cambridge University Press.

Salgado, J., Cunha, C., & Bento, T. (2013). Positioning micronalysis: Studying the self through the exploration of dialogical processes. *Integrative Psychological and Behavioral Science, 47*, 325–353.

Salgado, J., Lourenço, P., Barbosa, E., Santos, A., Greenberg, L.S., & Angus, L. (2011). A study of the change process through the analysis of the positioning dynamics in an EFT good outcome case. Paper presented at the 42nd Society for Psychotherapy Research (SPR) International Annual Meeting, Bern, Switzerland.

Salgado, J. & Hermans, H. J. M. (2005). The return of subjectivity: From a multiplicity of selves to the dialogical self. *E-Journal of Applied Psychology, 1*, 1–13.

Salgado, J. & Valsiner, J. (2010). Dialogism and the eternal movement within communication. In C. B. Grant (Ed.), *Beyond Universal Pragmatics: Studies in the Philosophy of Communication* (pp. 101–121). New York, NY: Peter Lang.

Simão, L. M., Guimarães, D. S., & Valsiner, J. (Eds.). (2015). *Temporality: Culture in the Flow of Human Experience*. Charlotte, NC: Information Age.

Stinson, C., Milbrath, C., Reidbord, S. & Bucci, W. (1994). Thematic segmentation of psychotherapy transcripts for convergent analyses. *Psychotherapy: Theory, Research, Practice, Training, 31*, 36–48.

Valsiner, J. (2002). Forms of dialogical relations and semiotic autoregulation within the self. *Theory & Psychology, 12*(2), 251–265.

Valsiner, J. (2007). *Culture in Minds and Societies: Foundations of Cultural Psychology*. New Delhi: Sage.

Wijsen, F. & Hermans, H. J. (2020). Editors' introduction: Radicalization and deradicalization from the perspective of dialogical self theory. *Journal of Constructivist Psychology, 33*, 231–234, doi:10.1080/10720537.2019.1677534.

18 Synthesized or Confused Field? A Critical Analysis of the State-of-the-Art in Identity Status Research Methods

Oana Negru-Subtirica and Theo Klimstra

18.1 Identity Statuses: Inception and Beyond

The dynamic of personal identity has been a central concern of identity discourse since Erikson's (1968) seminal work. He viewed identity as "the awareness of the fact that there is self-sameness and continuity to the ego's synthesizing methods, the style of one's individuality" (p. 50). This definition frames identity as an interplay between a strong allegiance to one's uniqueness and an adaptation of this uniqueness across time and contexts. This interplay then constructs the "style of one's individuality," encompassing both an enduring commitment to who one is and an accommodation of this commitment to changing situations. So, identity seems to emerge from knowing who you are, but also integrating new information into this core structure of the self over time.

This co-occurrence of stability and change in constructing one's identity was further explored and refined in the work of Marcia (1966) on identity statuses. On the basis of extensive clinical work, Marcia proposed four identity statuses, as "modes of reacting to the late adolescent identity crisis" (1966, p. 551). These statuses were based on the processes of commitment and exploration. Identity commitment was defined as personal investment in goals, convictions, and ideals. Identity exploration was viewed as an indicator of personal destabilization with the adolescent being engaged in investigating possible alternatives in different life domains. The identity statuses are: achievement (i.e., strong commitments as a result of exploration), foreclosure (i.e., strong commitment without past exploration), moratorium (i.e., current/ exploration without a present commitment), and diffusion (i.e., lack of commitment with no current or past/exploration). These identity statuses were initially derived using interviews (e.g., the Identity Status Interview), focusing on topics of career, family, and religion. Structured interviews could capture the co-occurrence of stability/commitment and exploration in identity formation, as they relied on the individual's description of life events and personal reflections. Drawing on the person's recollection of events, these accounts captured past and present subjective and objective experiences and the co-occurrence or temporal sequence of commitment and exploration (see Kroger and Marcia, Chapter 10 in this volume).

Thus, the identity status interview provided descriptive data on individual's identity status, tapping into personal experiences and life events. That is why this technique is still used (for a recent illustration, see e.g., Carlsson, Wängqvist, & Frisén, 2016). However, the coding process and the between-person comparison on different identity dimensions based on interview material can be difficult and time-consuming. To increase efficiency and make large-sample research on identity formation more attainable, questionnaires were developed starting in the 1980s (e.g., Grotevant & Adams, 1984).

However, these questionnaires did not solve another problem in identity status research: that is, the statuses provide a static snapshot of identity development and tell us little about the identity formation process, which is why a more dynamic approach was needed (e.g., Grotevant, 1987). To fulfill the need for a more dynamic approach, two major models have been developed: the three-factor identity model (Crocetti et al., 2008) and the dual-cycle identity model (Luyckx et al., 2006, 2008). The three-factor model differentiates the structural dimensions: commitment, in-depth exploration, and reconsideration of commitment. Identity is viewed as an interplay of an identity formation cycle that confirms commitments and reconsiders commitments that are no longer satisfactory and an identity maintenance cycle, with commitments that are strengthened by in-depth exploration (Crocetti, 2017). The dual-cycle model is organized around the formation (i.e., exploration in breadth leads to commitment-making) and evaluation (i.e., exploration in depth leads to identification of commitments) of commitments. A fifth process, ruminative exploration, indicates a maladaptive form of appraising alternatives, marked by self-doubt and negative self-talk (Luyckx et al., 2008). Next, we will detail current approaches to investigating identity statuses through the questionnaire measures based upon these two-cycle approaches.

18.2 Person-Centered Questionnaire Approaches to Deriving Identity Statuses

In this section, we focus on how status clusters can be delineated through a person-centered approach (e.g., cluster analysis, LCAs/LPAs). Person-centered approaches focus on the individual as unit of analysis, assuming the uniqueness of each person, and target how structures and processes are organized within an individual (Von Eye, Bogat, & Rhodes, 2006).

These approaches can depict how multiple variables are configured within persons as opposed to depicting differences on one variable between persons.

For this purpose, identity statuses as indicated by questionnaire data are derived. We detail the theoretical rationale for deriving identity statuses using such approaches and focus on how these approaches integrate classic identity status research (e.g., Marcia, 1966) with more novel identity process research (e.g., Crocetti, 2017; Luyckx et al., 2008; see also Kroger and Marcia, Chapter 10 in this volume). We also critically discuss the differences in the way that statuses are derived with interviews compared to questionnaires (Waterman, 2015). From a theoretical standpoint, we analyze the complexity of "classic" identity statuses (i.e., achievement, moratorium, foreclosure, diffusion) and more novel identity statuses (e.g., moratorium versus searching moratorium; carefree diffusion versus troubled diffusion). We conclude this section by highlighting how a person-centered approach for deriving identity status clusters can advance identity status research.

With the advent of identity process models that consist of more than two dimensions, the organization of identity processes within the individual remained an important research endeavor, but a more data-driven approach to classification was pursued. Person-centered quantitative approaches have been useful tools in this endeavor. Specifically, two particular types of analysis have frequently been used: cluster analysis and LCAs/LPAs.

18.2.1 Identity Process Models

Identity process models focus on depicting the dynamic of identity formation through different types and sequences of exploration and commitment (Crocetti & Meeus, 2015). Process models test the assumption that "commitments are formed and revised in an iterative process of choosing commitments, evaluating, and questioning them" (p. 103). One of their advantages is that they "have been shown to possess the unique possibility of generating identity status trajectories without using any preset classification criteria" (Meeus, 2011, p. 89). Previous work on deriving identity statuses mainly relied on preset coding systems based on multiple dimensions (e.g., Adams, 1999) or on median splits to distinguish high versus low levels of commitment and exploration (Meeus et al., 1999). Identity process models approached the dynamic of identity formation through variable-centered and person-centered approaches. Variable-centered approaches focus on variables as units of analyses, such as change and stability in in-depth exploration, or correlations between in-depth exploration and depressive symptoms. Thus, a variable-centered approach considers one identity dimension at a time and is not focused on whether commitment and reconsideration levels matter when examining the link between in-depth explorations and depressive symptoms. Also, rare patterns of levels across multiple identity dimensions in small groups of individuals that do not align with the general pattern of correlations at the sample level are overlooked in a variable-centered approach. In sum, variable-centered approaches focus on (co)variance of variables at the sample level and are not suited for drawing conclusions about individuals. Instead, this chapter will analyze only person-centered quantitative approaches to help describe how structures and processes are organized within individuals.

Cluster analysis is a statistical approach to classifying people into groups named clusters, depending on their degree of similarity defined on specific properties of the group (Kaufman & Rousseeuw, 1990). In identity research, the most frequently used form of cluster analysis involves a two-step procedure, combining a hierarchical cluster analysis using Ward's method and squared Euclidean distances, followed by an iterative nonhierarchical k-means cluster procedure (Gore, 2000; Luyckx et al., 2008). However, cluster analysis has some disadvantages that related techniques known as LCAs/LPAs do not have.

LCAs use categorical variables, while LPAs use continuous variables in depicting groups within a sample, but like cluster analysis both techniques are aimed at classifying individuals in groups based on their similarity or dissimilarity to other individuals in the sample (Masyn, 2013). Both LCAs and LPAs use the raw scores for the variables of interest and include the entire sample in creating classes/profiles. To our knowledge, few published studies depicted identity statuses from identity processes using LPA (for exceptions, see Meens et al., 2018; Meeus et al., 2010).

More generally, the attractiveness of a person-centered approach for depicting identity statuses resides in the possibility of investigating how identity processes are simultaneously structured within groups of individuals at a certain time point. This is achieved by constructing a profile based on each individual's standing on different variables of interest (Gore, 2000; Rupp, 2013). In our case, these variables are identity processes, and the profiles are based on each person's scores on these identity processes. These individual profiles are first generated from the individual's scores on identity processes. Then, they are grouped in types or clusters of profiles that explain a certain percentage of the variance in the study sample. Individual profiles can then be organized in different (but finite) numbers of groups, based on different criteria (e.g., previous empirical work on the topic, theoretical background, parsimony). Thus, unlike in qualitative approaches, "person-centered" in these quantitative approaches does not refer to a detailed description of a single individual as the end-product of the analysis, but rather to the individual being the unit of analysis.

Both cluster analysis and LCAs/LPAs offer the possibility of exploring the grouping of individual profiles from a study sample in different numbers of groups that could all have different sizes. In other words, prototypes are created and hence cluster analyses as LCAs/LPAs specifically are typological approaches within the broader family of person-centered approaches. We now analyze how these approaches integrate classic identity status research (e.g., Marcia, 1966) with more novel identity process research (e.g., Crocetti, 2017; Luyckx et al., 2008; see Meeus, 2011 for a review).

18.2.2 Integrating Identity Status Research with Identity Process Research

Identity statuses are at the core of identity research since the taxonomy proposed by Marcia offers an empirical operationalization of the identity versus role confusion developmental task proposed by Erikson (1968). The four statuses (i.e., achievement, foreclosure, moratorium, diffusion) are important for understanding both identity structures at a given time point and identity change across time (Kroger, Martinussen, & Marcia, 2010). As identity formation is a main developmental task during adolescence and young adulthood, detailed descriptions of identity statuses can help in order to make sense of self-formation – understood as changes in status or changes in, e.g., commitment and exploration – in these developmental time frames. This necessity was signaled by more recent meta-analyses and reviews of identity formation, with Kroger and colleagues' meta-analysis including categorical and continuous assessments of identity status and Meeus's (2011) review focusing primarily on continuous longitudinal assessments.

Categorical assessments are conducted mainly with structured interviews (e.g. the Identity Status Interview, Marcia, 1966, 1993), and they assign participants to one identity status based on patterns of exploration and commitment depicted from personal descriptions. Continuous assessments use questionnaires and they can derive levels of commitment and exploration (e.g., Ego Identity Process Questionnaire – EIPQ; Balistreri, Busch-Rossnagel, & Geisinger, 1995), which can allow for the organization of identity statuses based on these levels. Such status clusters thus represent individual differences in common patterns of quantitative levels of exploration and commitment within a specific study sample (e.g., Zimmermann, Mantzouranis, & Biermann, 2010).

Categorical assessments draw on the personal experience of each participant, dwelling on past and present exploration of and commitment to identity alternatives. Their main merit resides in offering a voice to each individual and highlighting the uniqueness of identity pursuits through interview excerpts. Although the interview-based status comes with thorough scoring manuals to objectify classification, this classification is still based on very different life events that are relevant for identity pursuits. That is, two people who are classified in an achieved status may have very different subjective accounts of what brought them to this state. This is an asset, as the classification draws on the personal, idiosyncratic experiences of each individual, and it values the subjective perceptions and interpretations of these events. At the same time, it is a limitation, as it reduces the comparability of participants. In addition, the extracted profiles are not based on seemingly objective quantitative data and do not reflect a sample-specific clustering based on individuals' quantitative score patterns. Instead, the profiles that are derived are typically based on theory, although they could also be based on unanticipated common themes that a researcher observes in a particular sample.

Continuous assessments using identity processes instruments (e.g., the Dimensions of Identity Development Scale for the dual-cycle model; Luyckx et al., 2006, 2008; the Utrecht Management of Identity Commitments Scales for the three-factor model; Crocetti et al., 2008) depict levels of identity processes that co-occur for the same person at a given time point. In this manner, an identity status can be inferred at the person-level from identity processes through cluster analysis. Because the exact same information is available from different individuals (i.e., the same items have been administered across the sample and the same response options were available to these different individuals), those individuals can be directly compared on the same metric.

Both types of assessments try to address the question of how much commitment and exploration are enough (i.e., intensity of identity pursuits) for an adolescent (for instance) to be classified as having an achieved identity. For categorical assessments, information is first elicited by interviewing individuals in a guided manner. Next, the complex information provided is used to gain a deeper understanding of the process of identity formation for that specific person (Marcia & Archer, 1993). The intensity of identity commitment and exploration is not quantified in a seemingly exact number, but researchers decide on whether the level is high, medium, or low using detailed protocols. In high-quality qualitative research, such protocols are used only after elaborate observer training to assure that identity status assignment is transparent and criterion-based. As previously detailed, continuous assessments in identity process models depict identity statuses based on seemingly exact scores (e.g., 3.38 instead of high, medium, or low) for an individual on all processes. This approach may appear to be more objective than identity status interview protocols, but it should be noted that a difference of, for example, 0.20 on a five-point scale may not be meaningful. Moreover, questionnaire items can be understood in different ways by different individuals (e.g., Diriwächter, Valsiner, & Sauck, 2005). Hence, between-person comparisons based on the same items are by no means error free, and there is no reason to regard the quantitative questionnaire-based approach as superior to an interview-based approach, or vice versa.

Yet, identity profiles that are inferred through cluster analysis or LCAs/LPAs are data-driven, despite the limitations of these data. The profiles are based on the sample scores and on the types and similarity of individual profiles within the sample, which are then grouped in a parsimonious number of profiles (Gore, 2000; Rupp, 2013). They are labeled "identity statuses" after the researcher analyzes the intensity of each process within a cluster and matches the derived profile to the theoretical characteristics of identity statuses. So, in a manner of speaking, though there are hypotheses based on theory and previous empirical studies, researchers do not know what clusters they will "get." In cluster analysis and LCAs/LPAs, decisions on whether levels of dimensions within clusters are high, medium, or low are typically decided upon by examining their distance from the sample mean, often using z-scores. However, much like with explorative factor analyses, the labeling is based on eyeballing without clear rules-of-thumb. This leads to differences in z-scores of status clusters with the same name across different studies (Carlsson, 2015).

Waterman (2015) proposed an ad hoc classification of identity process levels in cluster-analytic studies to solve this problem. For instance, the process of identification with commitment can have a very low (e.g., a least a standard deviation below the mean), moderately low (e.g., half a standard deviation below the mean), medium (e.g., around the mean), moderately high (e.g., half a standard deviation above the mean), or very high (e.g., at least a standard deviation above the mean) level. In addition, he proposed guidelines for what pattern of dimensional scores a particular status cluster should be characterized by. For example, a ruminative moratorium should be characterized by high exploration in breadth, high to intermediate exploration in depth, a negative emotional tone (e.g., high ruminative exploration), and low levels on commitment dimensions. Using such guidelines, the identity statuses derived through cluster-analytic studies may become more comparable across studies.

However, there still are problems with comparing z-scores across samples, as these scores are centered on the sample means. Achieved individuals are those who would score high on the commitment dimensions and exploration in breadth and depth, and low on ruminative exploration compared to the sample mean. The mean scores on the identity dimensions can be very different in different samples. For example, a study comparing eating disorder patients to a control group showed that the differences between the two groups were large, with Cohen's ds >1 for the commitment dimensions and ruminative exploration (Verschueren et al., 2017). This indicates that the differences in the means of the two samples were larger than one pooled standard deviation. Verschueren et al. (2017) accounted for this by running cluster analysis in a combined sample and then examining the distribution of the controls and patients across the clusters, but when comparing cluster solutions across different studies, a similar situation would have made the achieved individuals in one study have an undifferentiated profile in another study. Thus, it is of crucial importance to keep in mind that identity status clusters do not represent an individual's state of identity formation in an absolute sense, but relative to the rest of the particular samples one employs. If this caveat is kept in mind, comparisons of identity clusters across studies can still be useful.

Beyond persisting problems with comparing the similarly labeled clusters across samples, applying cluster analysis to new process-based models of identity formation that come with more than two dimensions has led to the identification of status clusters different from the "classic" ones. It is

Table 18.1 *Identity profiles mirroring variations of identity statuses depicted through cluster analysis using identity process models*

Identity profile	Level of identity process
Searching moratorium (Crocetti et al., 2008; Crocetti et al., 2012)	Medium high levels of commitment processes, high levels of exploration processes
Early closure (Meeus et al., 2010)	Medium high to high levels of commitment processes, low levels of exploration processes
Carefree diffusion (Luyckx et al., 2008) Diffused/troubled diffusion (Luyckx et al., 2008; Skhirtladze et al., 2016)	Medium low to low scores on all identity processes Very low commitment, intermediate exploration in depth and exploration in breadth, and high to very high ruminative exploration
Undifferentiated (Zimmermann et al., 2015)	Scores close to the sample mean on all identity processes

important to specify that most cluster-analytic work on identity is cross-sectional and references one identity domain and one time point. Table 18.1 presents new identity profiles that were found in such studies.

These "new" status clusters nuance the "classic" status clusters in that they depict variations in, for instance, diffusion, depending on the level of ruminative exploration. The fact that Luyckx's and colleagues' (2008) model differentiated among three exploration processes (i.e., in breadth, in depth, and ruminative) allowed the depiction of a carefree and a troubled diffusion cluster. This differentiation was replicated in multiple cross-sectional studies from different cultures (e.g., Italy, Sestito et al., 2015; Georgia, Skhirtladze et al., 2016; France and Switzerland, Zimmermann et al., 2015). From a theoretical standpoint, it brought some proof to Marcia's (2006) claim that even though identity diffusion is the status associated with the severest forms of psychopathology, there are "playful" variations of it. These variations are characterized by a careless attitude (e.g., "I don't know where I want to go with my life, I have no interest in finding out where I should go, and I just live in the moment") and can be accompanied by relatively few problems and a seeming capability to adapt to rapid changes in society.

Another new status that was initially found and labeled by Crocetti and colleagues (2008) is searching moratorium. This status is differentiated from the classic moratorium by a moderately high level of commitment that accompanies the high(er) levels in exploration processes, as these people "are seeking to revise commitments that have already been enacted, and they are able to do so from the base provided by their current commitments" (Crocetti et al., 2012, p. 734). So, beside exploration without commitments (i.e., moratorium), people may also engage in exploration based on existing commitments (i.e., searching moratorium). This explanation challenges the classic theoretical assumptions regarding identity statuses, as one of the core tenets of moratorium is the lack of commitments (for an in-depth analysis, see Waterman, 2015). This status also emerged across studies and cultures, in studies employing both Luyckx's and colleagues' (2008) and Crocetti and colleagues' (2008) process models (e.g., Turkish youth, Morsünbül et al., 2016; Georgian university students, Skhirtladze et al., 2016).

One possible explanation for searching moratorium that Waterman (2015) advances is that new/young generations may have to be more open to new opportunities and have to explore them even if they have current commitments. However, there are also issues with this status cluster. A minor issue is that a moratorium already implies that individuals are searching, making the "searching moratorium" label seem tautological. Other than that, the well-above-average scores on all three dimensions, including commitment and reconsideration, which tend to be negatively correlated (Crocetti et al., 2015), may also indicate that this status at least partly captures an acquiescent response bias. On the other hand, the searching moratorium status has been shown to have a distinctive set of correlates and therefore seems well-validated. Still, the question remains whether these youth are further exploring current commitments, in line with Crocetti and colleagues' (2012) explanation, or whether they are actually exploring new/different alternatives while holding (some level of) current commitments. To clarify this, in-depth interviews with youth in searching moratorium would be very useful, as they would detail subjective experiences and decision-making processes.

Summing up, we need more granularity when looking at the structure of the searching moratorium status, and we also need to see how these processes are grouped within a person. The dynamic of identity formation has changed since the seminal work of Marcia (1966, 1993) due to changes in socio-economic conditions, globalization, technological advancement, life role characteristics, and transitions. In the twenty-first century, youth who attend university studies tend to explore more, faster, and for longer periods of time (Arnett, 2014). This makes extensive exploration between the ages of 20 and 30 more normative. Hence, identity statuses also need to be reconsidered, and one of the main merits of research focusing on identity profiles derived through cluster analysis is that it showed that there is more nuance and complexity to these statuses than previously thought.

18.3 Cluster Analysis and Latent Class/Profile Analysis (LCA/LPA) in Deriving Identity Statuses

In this section, we use concrete examples for cluster analysis from a study by Negru-Subtirica et al. (2017). To compare cluster analysis with LCA/LPA, we apply LCA/LPA to this same dataset. We explain how identity status clusters were derived using participants' scores on identity processes and detail the steps involved in each procedure, variations of each procedure, advantages, and limitations.

18.3.1 Cluster Analysis

For the cluster analysis, we focus on a step-by-step description of how we depicted identity statuses in a sample of Romanian emerging adults. We present and discuss, for the same dataset, two different cluster solutions: a five-cluster and a six-cluster solution. Additionally, we detail requirements, general concerns regarding person-centered approaches, and specific concerns for each technique.

Negru-Subtirica and colleagues (2017) investigated identity profiles through cluster analysis in a sample of Romanian emerging adults attending theological schools (N = 326, M_{age} = 19.82 years, SD_{age} = 4.37, age range 18–29; 65.3 percent males; 34.7 percent females), using the dual-cycle model of identity (Luyckx et al., 2008). The Romanian version of the Dimensions of Identity Development Scale (DIDS, Luyckx et al., 2008; Negru-Subtirica et al., 2016) was used to investigate identity processes in the domain of future plans. The DIDS has twenty-five items, divided equally into five subscales, which are detailed in Table 18.2.

The cluster analysis procedure was conducted in SPSS. As preliminary actions, the researchers checked for outliers in the sample's scores and standardized the scores within the total sample. In cluster analysis, outliers can influence the number and content of generated profiles, possibly reducing the reliability of the generated cluster solutions and violating the assumptions that need to be met before a data-analytical technique should be applied (Almeida et al., 2007). The most common procedure for outlier detection in identity process research is the Mahalanobis distance measure, which indicates where a participant's score is placed compared to the center of the multidimensional distribution (Kim, 2000; Penny, 1996). For this study sample, which was quite homogenous (i.e., participants attending the same type of niche schools, namely theological schools), the researchers did not detect any outliers, so the analyses were conducted on the entire sample. In some applications of cluster analysis all participants from the sample are included in the data analyses, whereas researchers do not report on whether or not outliers have been removed (e.g., Schwartz et al., 2011). This can be problematic, especially if the outliers are participants with obvious random response patterns (e.g., consistently filling out a "5" one a one-to-five scale regardless of whether the items are positively or negatively worded).

The next preliminary action for cluster analysis is the standardization of scores within the total sample. Standardization is a requirement for cluster analysis (Rupp, 2013), and while multiple techniques exist in the literature, the one commonly used in identity process literature is the transformation of raw scores into z-scores. Z-scores have a mean of zero and a standard deviation of one.

Table 18.2 *Sample items for the Dimensions of Identity Development Scale (DIDS)*

Sample item	Sample item
Commitment-making	"I have decided on the direction I want to follow in my life."
Identification with commitment	"I sense that the direction I want to take in my life will really suit me."
Exploration in breadth	"I regularly think over a number of different plans for the future."
Exploration in depth	"I regularly talk with other people about the plans for the future I have made for myself."
Ruminative exploration	"It is hard for me to stop thinking about the direction I want to follow in my life."

Source: Luyckx et al., 2008

When raw scores of different variables are transformed into this metric, they can be more easily compared. These standardized scores then become input variables for subsequent analyses.

After the preliminary actions are conducted, the cluster analysis procedure can be implemented. For cluster analysis on identity processes in the study we discuss, a two-step procedure was employed (Gore, 2000). First, hierarchical cluster analyses were conducted using Ward's method and squared Euclidean distances (Steinley & Brusco, 2007) on the s-scores for the identity processes. In this step, the researchers specified the number of clusters to be retained (e.g., four, five, or six clusters). This procedure ensured the generation of the starting values or cluster centers for the second step. At this point, researchers also checked how much variance was explained in each identity process through the cluster solution they were currently investigating, using the value of the adjusted R^2. The five-cluster solution explained "66% of the variance in commitment-making, 56% of the variance in identification with commitment, 60% of the variance in exploration in breadth, 51% of the variance of exploration in depth, and 62% of the variance in ruminative exploration" (Negru-Subtirica et al., 2017, p. 117). A rule of thumb is that at least 50 percent should be explained for each dimension in the cluster solution (Milligan & Cooper, 1985). Second, the initial cluster centers were used as nonrandom starting points in an iterative nonhierarchical k-means clustering procedure. This procedure created the final classification, based on the number of clusters determined a priori in step one. The advantage of the k-means procedure is that it allows individuals to be reassigned to a different cluster, based on the initial cluster centers' values. Hence, this two-step procedure refines and adjusts the initial cluster solution (Gore, 2000).

Figure 18.1 presents the five identity profiles depicted through this two-step procedure in the study of Negru-Subtirica and colleagues (2017). The distance between the cluster means and the total sample standardized mean, expressed in standard deviations, can be interpreted as an effect size (Scholte et al., 2005). By employing Cohen's (1988) conventional criteria for effect sizes, 0.2,

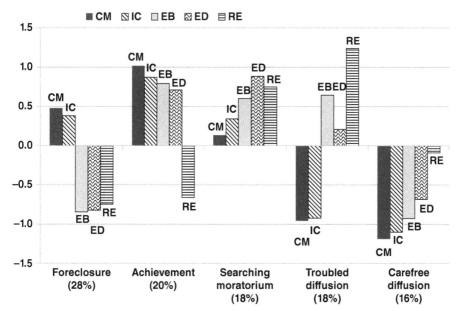

Figure 18.1 *Z-scores of identity processes for the five-clusters solution*
CM = Commitment-making, IC = Identification with commitment, EB = Exploration in breadth, ED = Exploration in depth, RE = Ruminative exploration
Source: Negru-Subtirica et al., 2017, p. 117

0.5, and 0.8 standard deviations were interpreted as small, moderate, and large effects.

The final five-cluster solution was retained according to (a) theoretical predictions, (b) parsimony of the cluster solution, and (c) explanatory power (Luyckx et al., 2008; Zimmermann et al., 2015). Using these three criteria, the five-cluster solution was compared to the six-cluster solution. The authors also tested a six-cluster solution, as in several previous studies using clustering with the dual-cycle identity model (Luyckx et al., 2008), six identity profiles were found. The six identity profiles are presented in Figure 18.2.

This solution explained (adjusted R^2) 64 percent of the variance in commitment-making, 60 percent of the variance in identification with commitment, 64 percent of the variance in exploration in breadth, 62 percent of the variance of exploration in depth, and 65 percent of the variance in ruminative exploration. The clusters were labeled foreclosure (high levels in commitment processes, low levels in exploration processes), foreclosure "light" (medium high levels in commitment processes, medium low levels in exploration processes), achievement (high levels in commitment processes, exploration in breadth and in depth, and low level of ruminative exploration), searching moratorium (medium high levels in commitment processes and high levels in all exploration processes), troubled diffusion (low levels in commitment processes, high levels in exploration in breadth and ruminative

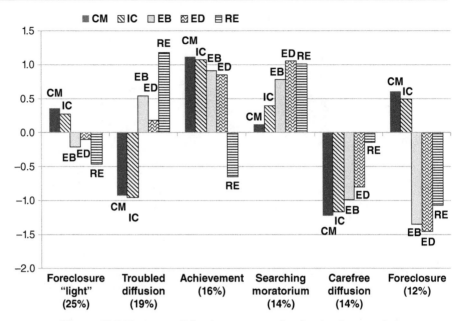

Figure 18.2 *Z-scores of identity processes for the six-cluster solution*
CM = Commitment-making, IC = Identification with commitment, EB = Exploration in breadth, ED = Exploration in depth, RE = Ruminative exploration
Analysis on the dataset employed in Negru-Subtirica et al., 2017, p. 117. This analysis presents previously unpublished results.

exploration, medium level of exploration in depth), and carefree diffusion (low levels on all identity processes). The explanatory power of the six-cluster solution was superior to that of the five-cluster solution for all identity dimensions. Nevertheless, from theoretical and solution parsimony perspectives, the clusters labeled foreclosure and foreclosure "light" could not be clearly theoretically differentiated and were somewhat similar in terms of levels of identity processes. As we illustrate below, this example shows the delicate balance between theoretical assumptions and statistical consideration when conducting cluster analysis.

First, identity profiles can only be interpreted considering existing theories and empirical advancements on identity statuses, as their generating process is data-driven rather than theory-driven. Decisions regarding the selection of a cluster solution and the labeling of depicted clusters require a theoretical choice on what each identity status entails. For instance, Waterman (2015) discusses foreclosure as a status of firm commitments that were assumed without past exploration in breadth, mostly due to external identifications (e.g., parents, peers). Nevertheless, these commitments are explored in depth in the present which further fuels and strengthens them. So, an identity profile of a foreclosed person would also entail current exploration in depth.

Nevertheless, when we look at the foreclosure profile in the Negru-Subtirica and colleagues' (2017) study in Figure 18.1, we see that in this sample it has low levels in all exploration processes, including exploration in depth. So, we have commitments without exploration in depth, which raises the question of how these commitments are maintained. As the authors explain:

> [this foreclosure profile] proved to be a double-edged sword. Many theology students seemed to have embraced their current life goals without further exploration, a choice that can be linked to the somewhat foreclosed cultural context, in which religion is an omnipresent axiom, a given (i.e., Christian Orthodox baptism is conducted shortly after birth), directly related to an institution perceived as trustworthy and powerful (i.e., the Orthodox church). Therefore, the Foreclosed profile proved to be somewhat adaptive in this cultural context, in that it was linked to higher levels of cognitive religiosity, but to lower levels of subjective and behavioural religiosity. These findings may indicate that Foreclosed theology students embraced the teaching of their religion (i.e., higher levels of cognitive religiosity), but they explored these teachings to a lesser degree (i.e., lower levels of subjective and behavioural religiosity). Hence, in line with previous study, a Foreclosed profile had a positive, but also a negative dimension . . .
> (Negru-Subtirica et al., 2017, p. 121)

This suggests that strong identity commitments with limited exploration may be partially adaptive when we analyze them in a specific context (e.g., the Romanian religious education context, which prepares male youth for becoming priests and females for missionary work) and in relation to variables that are personally relevant and important for particular groups of participants (e.g., religiosity, which is a core life domain for theology students). By immersing identity clusters in a specific life context that is relevant for specific people, researchers may better grasp their multiple, (mal)adaptive roles.

Second, identity clusters derived through cluster analysis are dependent on the number of clusters that are chosen in the first step of the above-described procedure. Though the procedure proposed by Gore (2000) combines hierarchical and nonhierarchical clustering, researchers still have to specify an initial number of clusters. When different cluster solutions are then tested to derive the most parsimonious solution, the levels of dimensions for some clusters may also change, as in the example from the study of Negru-Subtirica and colleagues (2017). When conducting cluster analyses, the "best" solution is chosen based on existing theory, solution parsimony, and explanatory power, but to date there are no statistical tests that compare cluster solutions. In this respect, LCAs/LPAs would provide more insight into deriving and comparing identity classes/profiles.

18.3.2 Latent Class Analysis/Latent Profile Analysis (LCA/LPA)

LCAs/LPAs have several advantages over cluster analyses. First, simulations (e.g., Magidson & Vermunt, 2002) have shown that LCAs/LPAs outperform cluster analyses in correctly classifying individuals. Additional advantages are that unlike cluster analyses, LCAs/LPAs come with fit criteria and classification inaccuracy can be accounted for. This raises the question of why LCAs/LPAs are not more often favored over cluster analyses. One reason could be related to sample size. Experts on LCA/LPA often refrain from providing guidelines, as these depend too much on "model complexity; the number, nature, and separation of the 'true' classes in the population; and the properties of the latent class indicators themselves" (Masyn, 2013, p. 607). In some cases, LCA/LPA might work with very small samples (n = 30), but in other cases very large samples with thousands of subjects are needed (Lubke, 2010). However, an often informally communicated rule of thumb is a sample size >300. Although several recent studies had smaller samples than that, others that likely had a sufficiently large sample also did not employ LCAs/LPAs (e.g., n = 9,034; Schwartz et al., 2011). Therefore, the fact that few studies on identity formation have used LCAs/LPAs may also be related to a lack of familiarity with the approach. Other reasons for not using LCAs/LPAs include a tendency to follow previous research and stick to what seem to be the "accepted" procedure within the field and a focus on replication by exactly following the plan of analysis of previous studies.

By explaining LCAs/LPAs and their added benefits in more detail, we hope that these techniques will be used more often in future studies. We use the sample from the Negru-Subtirica et al. (2017) study to illustrate how LCA/LPA can be performed in a cross-sectional design, using Mplus. Next, we will point to additional advantages that further increase the benefits of LCAs/LPAs over cluster analyses. Finally, we will briefly point to an add-on and a longitudinal extension of LCA/LPA previously used by Meeus et al. (2010) that we believe is interesting for all researchers with large longitudinal datasets.

Performing LCAs/LPAs can be explained in three steps (Bakk, Tekle, & Vermunt, 2013). In Step 1, the number of classes is determined by balancing an optimal representation of the data and a match with theory. Models with a varying number of classes are estimated and compared. After determining the optimal number of classes, one can advance to Step 2 in the three-step approach: obtaining predictions about the likelihood of each individual belonging to each of the classes. This information on individual-level classification accuracy can be saved in displayed in a data file and is also used to estimate the entropy. The entropy captures classification accuracy of the solution across the entire sample. There are different calculation methods for the entropy, but for the calculation method used in Mplus (Muthén & Muthén, 2017), values >0.70 are often listed as good (Reinecke, 2006). In a regular three-step approach, Step 3 would be to relate the clusters that were obtained in the two previous steps to outcome variables.

In order to exemplify Step 1 and Step 2 from this procedure, we conducted an LPA in Mplus 8.2 (Muthén & Muthén, 2017), using the sample from the Negru-Subtirica and colleagues (2017) study (N = 326, M_{age} = 19.82 years, SD_{age} = 4.37, age range 18–29; 65.3 percent males; 34.7 percent females) that we also used to illustrate cluster analysis. We aimed at capturing different identity classes based on the pattern of participants' scores on the five identity processes (i.e., commitment-making, identification with commitment, exploration in breadth, exploration in depth, and ruminative exploration). The LPA was specified in Mplus using the default commands for this procedure, with the model specification part of the Input detailed below for the six-class solution (CO_M, ID_CO, EX_B, EX_D, and RU_EX refer to identity dimensions):

```
Classes = c (6);
ANALYSIS:
TYPE IS MIXTURE;
starts = 100 10;
Model:
%overall%
CO_M ID_CO EX_B EX_D RU_EX;
```

To determine the optimal number of identity classes of the statistical model (i.e., Step 1), we considered three criteria: (1) the Bayesian information criterion (BIC), which indicates the relative model fit; (2) the entropy, which indicates classification accuracy; and (3) the meaningfulness of several solutions. First, a solution with k classes should have a BIC that is at least ten points smaller than the BIC of a model with k−1 classes in order to be considered substantially better (Kass & Raftery, 1995). Second, an entropy with values of 0.70 or higher indicates accurate classification (Reinecke, 2006). Third, the most parsimonious solution is chosen as the final one (Muthén & Muthén, 2000). As a fourth criterion, the parametric bootstrapped likelihood ratio (BLRT) test (Asparouhov & Muthén, 2012) can be used, which directly indicates whether a solution with k classes significantly outperforms a model with k−1 classes. The BLRT test can be obtained in the Mplus output using the TECH14 command. As one of the criteria to determine the optimal number of classes is the entropy, which summarizes whether or not individuals clearly belong to one class, this procedure also includes Step 2 of the broader three-step approach to LCA/LPA.

Based on these criteria, the results of the LPA on the Negru-Subtirica et al. (2017) dataset indicated that a six-class solution (BIC = 3726.121; entropy = 0.819) was better than a three-class solution (BIC = 3887.014; entropy = 0.763), a four-class solution (BIC = 3789.912; entropy = 0.816), and a five-class solution (BIC = 3755.160; entropy = 0.835). The BLRT test had a p value lower than 0.001, indicating that the six-class solution is better than a five-class solution. Thus, we chose the six-class solution as the final one. This solution included classes labeled achievement (24.84 percent of participants), troubled diffusion (22.1 percent), undifferentiated (21.47 percent of participants), foreclosure (15.34 percent), searching moratorium (10.73 percent), and carefree diffusion (5.52 percent). Figure 18.3 presents the classes for the six-profile solution.

Participants in the achievement class had high levels in all commitment and exploration processes and low levels of ruminative exploration. Those

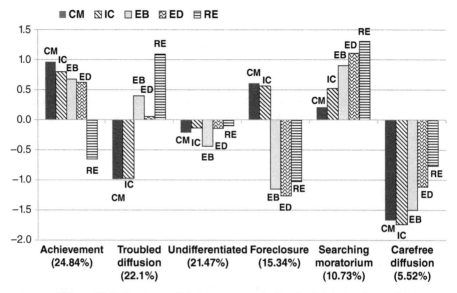

Figure 18.3 *Z-scores of identity processes for the LPA six-class solution*
CM = Commitment-making, IC = Identification with commitment, EB = Exploration
in breadth, ED = Exploration in depth, RE = Ruminative exploration
Analysis on the dataset employed in Negru-Subtirica et al., 2017, p. 117. This LPA
concerns previously unpublished results.

assigned to the troubled diffusion class displayed low levels on both commitment dimensions, medium levels of exploration in breadth and in depth, and
high levels of ruminative exploration. Participants in the undifferentiated class
had scores close to the mean on all identity processes. Participants in the
foreclosed class displayed high levels of commitment-making and identification with commitment and low levels on all exploration dimensions.
Relatively high levels on both commitment dimensions and very high levels
on all exploration dimensions characterized those in the searching moratorium class. Finally, participants assigned to the carefree diffusion class were
characterized by low levels on all identity dimensions.

A comparison of the six-cluster solution of the cluster analysis and the six-
class of the LPA indicated that the convergence between the two methods
was much better than would be expected by chance, χ^2 (25, 326) = 905.704,
$p < 0.001$. Table 18.3 presents the results of the crosstabulation, specifying the
convergence between the classification in the cluster analysis and the LPA.
The undifferentiated and foreclosure "light" statuses are unique to the cluster
and respectively the LPA solution. Nevertheless, these two statuses are still
compatible. Taking this into consideration, 73.6 percent of all cases are
classified in the same status across the two methods. However, the degree of
convergence differs by status, and it also depends on whether the LPA solution
or the cluster analysis is used as the reference. Thus, despite the partial

Table 18.3 *Convergence between the classification based on cluster analysis and the classification based on latent profile analysis (LPA)*

Cluster analysis class	LPA class					
	Carefree diffusion	Foreclosure	Troubled diffusion	Undifferentiated	Searching moratorium	Achievement
Carefree diffusion	18	0	11	18	0	0
Foreclosure	0	38	0	1	0	0
Troubled diffusion	0	0	58	3	1	0
Foreclosure "light"	0	12	0	43	0	26
Searching moratorium	0	0	4	5	33	5
Achievement	0	0	0	0	1	50

Note: Numbers in the cells represent the number of cases classified in a combination of classes derived from the cluster analysis and LPA. For example, 11 cases who were classified in Carefree diffusion in the cluster analysis, were classified in Troubled diffusion in the LPA solution. Likewise, five of the cases who were classified as Undifferentiated in the LPA were classified in Searching moratorium in the cluster analysis.

405

similarity in results, our illustration should not be interpreted as evidence for cluster analyses being similarly suitable as LPAs. Furthermore, we specified the LPA using the Mplus defaults, whereas there are numerous alternative ways of specifying LPAs. Finally, when looking at these results, one must also keep in mind that the LCA/LPA has the advantage of accompanying statistical tests that allow for the comparison of different class solutions (e.g., the BLRT).

The issue that still needs to be carefully addressed is how researchers label each identity cluster/class. In the six-class solution of the LPA, a new class emerged that did not exist in the five-cluster, six-cluster, or five-class solution: an undifferentiated class (21.47 percent of participants) with negative albeit close to the mean values of all identity processes (results are available from the first author). Due to this shape, we chose this label. Still, when we also look at the carefree diffusion class, the sign of the values for each identity process (i.e., negative, below the mean) is similar to the undifferentiated class, so an alternative name for this class could be carefree diffusion "light."

Typically, a categorical cluster membership variable is used as a predictor in these analyses, but this procedure does not account for the fact that the classification of individuals into identity status clusters is imperfect. To account for this, a bias-adjusted approach was developed and is now recommended. As previously mentioned, this bias-adjusted procedure employs information from the two previous steps to estimate the associations of class membership with outcome variables. Of particular importance is a correction for classification error in Step 3 of the three-step approach: estimating the association with outcome variables (Bakk, Tekle, & Vermunt, 2013).

The classification error estimates are obtained in Step 2 of the three-step approach and correcting for these alleviates concerns regarding individual differences within the same status cluster (e.g., not all "achieved" individuals are identical) and of some individuals having characteristics that are typical for two or more clusters (e.g., individuals that fall in between "achievement" and "foreclosure"). Software packages such as Latent Gold (Vermunt & Magidson, 2013) and Mplus (Muthén & Muthén, 2017) allow for such corrections. The way these procedures work is that when an individual fits better in a cluster, they have a higher weight in determining the association of that cluster with an outcome variable, whereas those who fit less well into a certain cluster have a lower weight. Research using a typological approach to examine associations between parent–adolescent relationships and a set of outcome variables (Hadiwijaya et al., 2015) found that the predictive power of clusters increased substantially when these corrections were used.

LCAs/LPAs can also be relatively easily adapted for longitudinal research purposes. A first adaptation is Latent Profile Transition Analysis (LPTAs; note that Latent Class Transition Analysis is also possible), which was used in a study by Meeus et al. (2010). To use LTPA, LPAs at several consecutive measurement occasions have to be conducted. Next, the researcher needs to examine whether similar clusters can be found at these different measurement occasions (i.e., establish invariance). If this is the case, an LPA including data from all measurement occasions can be estimated to ensure comparability of classes across measurement occasions. Next, transitions between clusters can be examined. Using this approach, Meeus et al. (2010) showed that stability in identity status was common, but that, if change occurred, it was usually change toward high-commitment statuses (i.e., achievement and early closure/closure). Alternatively, one can also extract latent clusters by considering both levels and changes in processes using growth mixture modeling (Muthén & Muthén, 2000) or latent class growth analysis (LCGA; Nagin, 1999). Using LCGA (which technically should be referred to as LPGA given the continuous variables that were used, but the use of LPGA as an abbreviation is uncommon in this context), Luyckx et al. (2013) reproduced many of the commonly identified identity status clusters (with the exception of the undifferentiated cluster) as developmental trajectories.

Summing up, cluster analyses and LCAs/LPAs are important and useful procedures to examine identity status clusters. Specifically, these are data-driven procedures that allow for the identification of patterns of scores on a set of identity dimensions that are commonly displayed by individuals in a particular sample. Thus, these procedures provide a useful compromise for researchers who like to work with samples that are too large for individual-level descriptions, but still want to make the individual the unit of analysis. Although the use of cluster analyses is appropriate for smaller samples, LCAs/LPAs are more appropriate for larger samples and appear to be underused in research on identity formation. With this description of cluster analyses and LCAs/LPAs, we hope to stimulate better usage of both types of analyses and more usage of LCAs/LPAs given the advantages they come with.

18.4 The Future Is Wide Open: Directions for Future Studies

In this section, we present limitations of this approach and detail directions for future research. We ground this discussion on the results of recent studies that depicted identity statuses through cluster-analytic procedures in different cultural contexts (e.g., Georgia, Switzerland, France, Romania, Belgium, and Italy) in order to analyze differences and points of convergence. In addition to issues we raised before, such as the comparability of the "same" identity status across studies, we focus on the temporal dimension of identity exploration and commitment processes and the relevance of identity processes.

Cluster-analytic studies using cross-sectional designs cannot depict the *temporal sequence or order of different identity processes*. They rely on questionnaire data that reference one identity domain and one time point (i.e., the present for the three-factor identity model, Crocetti et al., 2008; the future for the dual-cycle model, Luyckx et al., 2008). Hence, these studies cannot distinguish if, for instance, for foreclosed individuals, a low level of in-depth exploration in the present is due to intense exploration in the past that ended when these people assumed strong commitments (Waterman, 2015). The fact that most cluster-analytic studies depicted identity profiles of foreclosure that had low or around-the-mean levels of exploration in depth could indicate that indeed, for foreclosure, firm commitments do not entail concomitant exploration of these commitments. This could be tentatively linked to coping mechanisms that foreclosed people may use in order to maintain commitments that are based on external identifications. This could, for instance, be illustrated with the aforementioned example of students attending theological schools in the study of Negru-Subtirica and colleagues (2017).

In order to tackle this limitation, one direction, suggested also by Waterman (2015), would be that future studies integrate items tapping into past identity work for a specific domain (e.g., work, school, religion) for commitment and exploration processes. This could help the creation of a past–present combination of identity profiles that capture perceived changes in the amount of identity work for each process. Unfortunately, evaluations of the past will likely be "tainted" by how identity information is processed in the present. In order to avoid quantifications of the past in the present, another direction would be to propose longitudinal designs that apply latent transition analysis to investigate how people move (or not) from one identity profile to another across time (Meeus et al., 2010).

Identity domains differ in their *level of significance for a person*, meaning that they can be more or less central for their self-construction (Cobb et al., 2019). By choosing a person-centered approach to identity profiles, researchers need to also integrate this aspect into the generation of these profiles. To date, most research employing cluster analysis has preselected identity domains to be appraised based on the types of developmental tasks that are salient for people in a certain age group. For instance, for adolescents and emerging adults, education and vocation/career are the two core identity domains that tend to be appraised. The assumption that an identity domain that reflects an age-graded developmental task (e.g., to finish school) is central for all people who are active in this domain can easily be challenged. In order to approach this issue, we need to first test which identity status clusters emerge when study participants can choose the identity domain that they will appraise, on criteria pertaining to how central it is in their lives in the present. Assessments of identity domain centrality need to be multidimensional and to include perceived importance and alignment to personal values, as well as cognitive, behavioral, and emotional involvement in identity work. Among the assessments that can be used are sentence-completion tasks (e.g., the Twenty Statements Test; Kuhn & McPartland, 1954) and quantitative identity centrality assessments that focus on appraisals of an identity domain's importance for a person's self-concept (e.g., importance of one's racial/ethnic group;

Cobb et al., 2019). Nevertheless, the latter would need to be adapted to tap into the personal identity domains. Applying such techniques would allow a better grasp on whether one's identity status in a particular domain is likely relevant to this individual's functioning. We are unaware of studies on identity statuses that explicitly appraise identity domain centrality.

To conclude, there are important innovations in identity status research. The implementation of new multidimensional process models of identity formation led to the identification of more nuanced versions of identity statuses. Now that advanced techniques to identify statuses, such as LCA/ LPA, have become more widely available, opportunities to examine identity statuses and their correlates in a more robust and reliable manner arose. More than fifty years after the first publication on the topic (Marcia, 1966), identity status research has lost none of its relevance and keeps on innovating.

References

Adams, G. (1999). *The Objective Measure of Ego Identity Status: A Manual on Theory and Test Construction.* Guelph, ON: Department of Family Relations and Applied Nutrition, University of Guelph.

Almeida, J. A. S., Barbosa, L. M. S., Pais, A. A. C. C., & Formosinho, S. J. (2007). Improving hierarchical cluster analysis: A new method with outlier detection and automatic clustering. *Chemometrics and Intelligent Laboratory Systems, 87,* 208–217.

Arnett. J. (2014). *Emerging Adulthood. The Winding Road from the Late Teens through the Twenties.* New York, NY: Oxford University Press.

Asparouhov, T. & Muthén, B. (2012). Using Mplus TECH11 and TECH14 to test the number of latent classes. Mplus Web notes: no. 14. Retrieved May 05, 2021, from www.statmodel.com/examples/webnotes/webnote14.pdf.

Bakk, Z., Tekle, F. B., & Vermunt, J. K. (2013). Estimating the association between latent class membership and external variables using bias-adjusted three-step approaches. *Sociological Methodology, 43,* 273–311.

Balistreri, E., Busch-Rossnagel, N. A., & Geisinger, K. F. (1995). Development and preliminary validation of the Ego Identity Process Questionnaire. *Journal of Adolescence, 18,* 179–192.

Carlsson, J. (2015). Evolving identities: Contents and processes of identity development among people in their late twenties. Doctoral Dissertation, University of Gothenburg.

Carlsson, J., Wängqvist, M., & Frisén, A. (2016). Life on hold: Staying in identity diffusion in the late twenties. *Journal of Adolescence, 47,* 220–229.

Cobb, C. L., Meca, A., Branscombe, N. R., Schwartz, S. J., Xie, D., Zea, M. C., ... & Sanders, G. L. (2019). Perceived discrimination and well-being among unauthorized Hispanic immigrants: The moderating role of ethnic/racial group identity centrality. *Cultural Diversity and Ethnic Minority Psychology, 25,* 280–287.

Cohen, J. (1988). *Statistical Power Analysis for the Behavioral Sciences, 2nd Ed.* Hillsdale, NJ: Erlbaum.

Crocetti, E. (2017). Identity formation in adolescence: The dynamic of forming and consolidating identity commitments. *Child Development Perspectives, 11*(2), 145–150.

Crocetti E., Cieciuch, J., Gao, C-H, Klimstra, T., Lin, C.-L., Matos, P. M, Morsünbül, Ü., Negru, O., Sugimura, K., Zimmermann, G., & Meeus· W. (2015). National and gender measurement invariance of the Utrecht Management of Identity Commitments Scale (U-MICS): A ten-nation study with university students. *Assessment, 22*, 753–768.

Crocetti, E. & Meeus, W. (2015). The identity statuses: Strengths of a person-centered approach. In K. C. McLean, & M. Syed (Eds.), *The Oxford Handbook of Identity Development* (pp. 97–114). New York, NY: Oxford University Press.

Crocetti, E., Rubini, M., Luyckx, K., & Meeus, W. (2008). Identity formation in early and middle adolescents from various ethnic groups: From three dimensions to five statuses. *Journal of Youth and Adolescence, 37*, 983–996.

Crocetti, E., Scrignaro, M., Sica, L. S., & Magrin, M. E. (2012). Correlates of identity configurations: Three studies with adolescent and emerging adult cohorts. *Journal of Youth and Adolescence, 41*, 732–748.

Diriwächter, R., Valsiner, J., & Sauck, C. (2005). Microgenesis in making sense of oneself: Constructive recycling of personality inventory items. *Forum: Qualitative Social Research, 6*, article 11.

Erikson, E. H. (1968). *Identity: Youth and Crisis*. New York, NY: Norton.

Gore, P. A., Jr. (2000). Cluster analysis. In H. E. A. Tinsley, & S. D. Brown (Eds.), *Handbook of Applied Multivariate Statistics and Mathematical Modeling* (pp. 297–321). San Diego, CA: Academic Press.

Grotevant, H. D. (1987). Toward a process model of identity formation. *Journal of Adolescent Research, 2*(3), 203–222.

Grotevant, H. D. & Adams, G. R. (1984). Development of an objective measure to assess ego identity in adolescence: Validation and replication. *Journal of Youth and Adolescence, 13*, 419–438.

Hadiwijaya, H., Klimstra, T. A., Vermunt, J. K., Branje, S., & Meeus, W. (2015). Parent–adolescent relationships: An adjusted person-centered approach. *European Journal of Developmental Psychology, 12*, 728–739.

Kass, R. E. & Raftery, A. E. (1995). Bayes factors. *Journal of the American Statistical Association, 90*, 773–795.

Kaufman, L. & Rousseeuw, P. J. (1990). *Finding Groups in Data: An Introduction to Cluster Analysis*. New York, NY: John Wiley.

Kim, M. G. (2000). Multivariate outliers and decompositions of Mahalanobis distance. *Communications in Statistics: Theory and Methods, 29*, 1511–1526.

Kroger, J., Martinussen, M., & Marcia, J. E. (2010). Identity status change during adolescence and young adulthood: A meta-analysis. *Journal of Adolescence, 33*, 683–698.

Kuhn, M. & McPartland, T. S. (1954). An empirical investigation of self-attitudes. *American Sociological Review, 19*, 68–76.

Lubke, G. H. (2010). Latent variable mixture modeling. In G. R. Hancock & R. O. Mueller (Eds.), *The Reviewer's Guide to Quantitative Methods in the Social Sciences* (pp. 209–220). New York, NY: Routledge.

Luyckx, K., Goossens, L., Soenens, B., & Beyers, W. (2006). Unpacking commitment and exploration: Preliminary validation of an integrative model of adolescent identity formation. *Journal of Adolescence, 29*, 361–378.

Luyckx, K., Klimstra, T. A., Schwartz, S. J., & Duriez, B. (2013). Personal identity in college and the work context: Developmental trajectories and psychosocial functioning. *European Journal of Personality, 27*, 222–237.

Luyckx, K., Schwartz, S. J., Berzonsky, M. D., Soenens, B., Vansteenkiste, M., Smits, I., & Goossens, L. (2008). Capturing ruminative exploration: Extending the four-dimensional model of identity formation in late adolescence. *Journal of Research in Personality, 42*, 58–82.

Magidson, J. & Vermunt, J. (2002). Latent class models for clustering: A comparison with k-means. *Canadian Journal of Marketing Research, 20*, 36–43.

Marcia, J. E. (1966). Development and validation of ego-identity status. *Journal of Personality and Social Psychology, 3*, 551–558.

Marcia, J. E. (1993). The ego identity status approach to ego identity. In J. E. Marcia, A. S. Waterman, D. R. Matteson, S. L. Archer, & J. L. Orlofsky (Eds.), *Ego Identity: A Handbook for Psychosocial Research* (pp. 3–21). New York, NY: Springer-Verlag.

Marcia, J. E. (2006). Ego identity and personality disorders. *Journal of Personality Disorders, 20*, 577–596.

Marcia, J. E. & Archer, S. L. (1993). Identity status in late adolescents: Scoring criteria. In J. E. Marcia, A. S. Waterman, D. R. Matteson, S. L. Archer, & J. L. Orlofsky (Eds.), *Ego Identity: A Handbook for Psychosocial Research* (pp. 205–240). New York, NY: Springer-Verlag.

Masyn, K. E. (2013). Latent class analysis and finite mixture modeling. In T. D. Little (Ed.), *The Oxford Handbook of Quantitative Methods in Psychology: Vol. 2: Statistical Analysis* (pp. 551–611). Oxford: Oxford University Press.

Meens, E. E. M., Bakx, A. W. E. A., Klimstra, T. A., & Denissen, J. J. A. (2018). The association of identity and motivation with students' achievement in higher education. *Learning and Individual Differences, 64*, 54–70.

Meeus, W. (2011). The study of adolescent identity formation 2000–2010: A review of longitudinal research. *Journal of Research on Adolescence, 21*(1), 75–94.

Meeus, W., Iedema, J., Helsen, M., & Vollebergh, W. (1999). Patterns of adolescent identity development: Review of literature and longitudinal analysis. *Developmental Review, 19*, 419–461.

Meeus, W., Van De Schoot, R., Keijsers, L., Schwartz, S. J., & Branje, S. (2010). On the progression and stability of adolescent identity formation: A five-wave longitudinal study in early-to-middle and middle-to-late adolescence. *Child Development, 81*, 1565–1581.

Milligan, G. W. & Cooper, M. C. (1985). An examination of procedures for determining the number of clusters in a data set. *Psychometrika, 50*, 159–179.

Morsünbül, Ü., Crocetti, E., Cok, F., & Meeus, W. (2016). Identity statuses and psychosocial functioning in Turkish youth: A person-centered approach. *Journal of Adolescence, 47*, 145–155.

Muthén, B. O. & Muthén, L. K. (2000). Integrating person-centered and variable-centered analyses: Growth mixture modeling with latent trajectory classes. *Alcoholism: Clinical and Experimental Research, 24*, 882–891.

Muthén, L. K. & Muthén, B. O. (2017). *Mplus User's Guide, 8th Ed*. Los Angeles, CA: Muthén & Muthén.

Nagin, D. S. (1999). Analyzing developmental trajectories: A semi-parametric group-based approach. *Psychological Methods, 4*, 139–157.

Negru-Subtirica, O., Pop, E. I., & Crocetti, E. (2018). Good omens? The intricate relations between educational and vocational identity in adolescence. *European Journal of Developmental Psychology, 15*, 83–98.

Negru-Subtirica, O., Pop, E. I., Luyckx, K., Dezutter, J., & Steger, M. F. (2016). The meaningful identity: A longitudinal look at the interplay between identity and meaning in life in adolescence. *Developmental Psychology, 52*, 1926–1936.

Negru-Subtirica, O., Tiganasu, A., Dezutter, J., & Luyckx, K. (2017). A cultural take on the links between religiosity, identity, and meaning in life in religious emerging adults. *British Journal of Developmental Psychology, 35*, 106–126.

Penny, K. I. (1996). Appropriate critical values when testing for a single multivariate outlier by using the Mahalanobis distance. *Applied Statistics: Journal of the Royal Statistical Society Series C, 45*, 73–81.

Reinecke, J. (2006). Longitudinal analysis of adolescent's deviant and delinquent behavior. *Methodology, 2*, 100–112.

Rupp, A. A. (2013). Clustering and classification. In T. D. Little (Ed.), *The Oxford Handbook of Quantitative Methods in Psychology: Vol. 2: Statistical Analysis* (pp. 517–550). Oxford: Oxford University Press.

Scholte, R. H. J., van Lieshout, C. F. M., de Wit, C. A. M., & van Aken, M. A. G. (2005). Adolescent personality types and subtypes and their psychosocial adjustment. *Merrill-Palmer Quarterly, 51*, 258–286.

Schwartz, S. J., Beyers, W., Luyckx, K., Soenens, B., Zamboanga, B. L., Forthun, L. F., ... & Whitbourne, S. K. (2011). Examining the light and dark sides of emerging adults' identity: A study of identity status differences in positive and negative psychosocial functioning. *Journal of Youth and Adolescence, 40*, 839–859.

Sestito, L. A., Sica, L. S., Ragozini, G., Porfeli, E., Weisblat, G., & Di Palma, T. (2015). Vocational and overall identity: A person-centered approach in Italian university students. *Journal of Vocational Behavior, 91*, 157–169.

Skhirtladze, N., Javakhishvili, N., Schwartz, S. J., Beyers, W., & Luyckx, K. (2016). Identity processes and statuses in post-Soviet Georgia: Exploration processes operate differently. *Journal of Adolescence, 47*, 197–209.

Steinley, D. & Brusco, M. J. (2007). Initializing K-means batch clustering: A critical evaluation of several techniques. *Journal of Classification, 24*, 99–121.

Vermunt, J. K. & Magidson, J. (2013). *Latent GOLD 5.0 Upgrade Manual*. Belmont, MA: Statistical Innovations.

Verschueren, M., Luyckx, K., Kaufman, E. A., Vansteenkiste, M., Moons, ... & Claes, L. (2017). Identity processes and statuses in patients with and without eating disorders. *European Eating Disorders Review, 25*, 26–35.

Von Eye, A., Bogat, G. A., & Rhodes, J. E. (2006). Variable-oriented and person-oriented perspectives of analysis: The example of alcohol consumption in adolescence. *Journal of Adolescence, 29*, 981–1004.

Waterman, A. S. (2015). What does it mean to engage in identity exploration and to hold identity commitments? A methodological critique of multidimensional measures for the study of identity processes. *Identity: An International Journal of Theory and Research, 15*, 309–349.

Zimmermann, G., Lannegrand-Willems, L., Safont-Mottay, C., & Cannard, C. (2015). Testing new identity models and processes in French-speaking adolescents and emerging adults students. *Journal of Youth and Adolescence, 44*, 127–141.

Zimmermann, G., Mantzouranis, G., & Biermann, E. (2010). Ego identity in adolescence: Preliminary validation of a French short-form of the EIPQ. *Revue Européenne de Psychologie Appliquée/European Review of Applied Psychology, 60*, 173–180.

19 Criminals' Narrative Identity

Donna Youngs, David Rowlands, and David Canter

In this chapter we discuss systematic procedures that explore criminals' identities as embedded in their personal narratives. The approach is influenced by McAdams's (1993) Narrative Identity Theory (NIT), which proposes that dominant cultural themes shape identities and are expressed in narrative forms. Thus, formulas for self-storying experience are limited. Narrative studies adopting NIT in personality (Bauer & McAdams, 2004), criminology (Stone, 2016), psychotherapy (Adler et al., 2015), psychiatry (Holms, Thomsen, & Bliksted, 2018), and addiction (Rowlands, Youngs, & Canter, 2019) have quantified identity-shaping themes in respondents' stories, illustrating the use of agency and communion for determining individual differences that map onto motives and behaviors. This chapter reports on our adaptation of McAdams' Narrative Identity (NI) approach for the study of criminal identity and identity differences among criminal populations.

Firstly, we discuss design and utilization of the Narrative Roles Questionnaire (NRQ). The NRQ assesses how well role statements describe offenders' experiences during crime commission, allowing quantitative exploration of criminal identity at the episodic level of the criminal act. Our studies revealed four criminal identities: professional, revenger, victim, and hero (Youngs & Canter, 2012). Practical relevance of the narrative roles' framework is supported by associations we found with specific crime types (Ioannou et al., 2015), while the identities themselves provide insights important in guiding interventions.

Though our methodology is innovative, this perspective is not presented as an entirely new way of conceptualizing criminal actions, rather as a framework that integrates many existing psychological approaches and concerns relating to criminal identity and activity. In particular, the narratives suggest ways in which specific emotions, cognitions, and interpersonal aspects, that have been implicated in criminality by diverse authorities (Bandura, 1990; Katz, 1988; Sykes & Matza, 1957), may combine. Interestingly, the core distinctions identified in these different criminological domains do appear to map onto the four preliminary narrative forms (Youngs & Canter, 2012). These narrative themes articulate the quality of the agency that activates various psychological components of offending. In so doing, they offer an approach to explaining what Presser (2009) referred to as the "here and now" of crime that criminological thinking usually lacks. We suggest offense narratives are also the basis for understanding the "how" of offending: explorations that move beyond general issues of "why," or broad causal factors, on to considerations of the meaning of the specific unfolding actions for the protagonist that reinforces the underlying identity facilitating criminal behavior.

Beyond offender roles, criminal identity can be understood within the context of an offender's life narrative. Life narratives are constructs used to make sense of experiences and facilitate action. Benefits of studying offenders' life narratives are indicated by the way changes to self-storying can facilitate rehabilitation and prosocial behavior. Maruna's (2001) study illustrated how generating redemption narratives supported desistance, while Ward's (2010) Good Lives approach frames rehabilitation in terms of rewritten stories. However, the starting point for such approaches lies with understanding the destructive narratives that underpin criminal behavior (Canter, 1994). Recognizing this, and building on our narrative roles' studies, we began exploring offenders' narratives at the broader scale of life trajectory.

The Life as a Film (LAAF) procedure was designed as a subtler, less threatening lifestorying task, more suitable for engaging marginalized populations (Canter & Youngs, 2015). In tandem with its design, we developed a thematic content analysis framework, drawing on NI theories and psychological concepts identified as pertinent to individual agency in relation to criminal action. As with the NRQ, our studies revealed suitability in the LAAF, criminals producing psychologically richer accounts than they did when responding to typical life narrative prompts (e.g., McAdams, 1993). The power of the procedure was illustrated in uncovering criminal constructs that had remained hidden through decades of prior forensic research (Youngs, Canter, & Carthy, 2016).

19.1 Bridging the Gap between Social Science and Jurisprudence

There is a trend in social science explanations of criminality to reduce concerns with offenders' intentionality. The emphasis, typically, is on aspects of individuals and the social circumstances that are inherently out of their control: their genetics, biology, personality, upbringing, and culture. This is at variance with the legal emphasis on *mens rea* and the conscious decision to knowingly break the law. The emerging psychological considerations of criminals' personal narratives, including the ways in which their experience of offending influences their actions, provides a much-needed bridge between the law and an understanding of the accounts criminals give of themselves. This extension comes in positioning the criminal as an agent in the construction of their narratives and therefore their criminal identity (Toch, 1993). The idea recognizes that while certainly influenced by external forces, narrative accounts (episodic or life) are constructs of interpretation rather than factual records (Singer, 2004). In this understanding a degree of choice is afforded (Fleetwood, 2016), allowing not only a sense of personal responsibility for one's identity and actions, but facility for reinterpretation with the emergence of new identities and different behaviors (McAdams & McLean, 2013). This theorization is supported by studies illustrating narratives of ex-offenders rewritten in facility of prosocial identities (Maruna, 2001; Stone, 2016). Such attributions of choice, or personal agency, are important for stimulating change (Adler, 2012; McConnell, 2016).

19.2 Narrative Identity

A person's storied understanding of themselves – the narrative accounts they give of their actions and lives – provides a valuable lens through which to articulate identity and its role in behavior. This follows Bruner's (1987) account of how personal narratives contribute to an individual's experience of reality, providing coherence, continuity, and scripts for behavior. McAdams (2015) is perhaps the most prolific proponent of the approach, proposing that identity arises from a meaningful interpretation of past events to orientate individuals toward a purposeful future. Accordingly, McAdams and associates argue that identity is best understood through the collection and analysis of people's personal narratives.

Adopting this methodology, studies demonstrate that personal identity can be fruitfully seen as shaped around the prevailing twin strivings of agency and communion, where agency is concerned with power and achievement and communion with love and intimacy (McAdams, 1993, 2015; McAdams et al., 1996). The combination of the extremes of these two dimensions gives rise to four narrative forms: high agency and high communion, high agency and low communion, low agency and high communion, and low agency and low communion. Interestingly, it is possible to relate these narratives to the idea that there are four basic plots throughout the literary tradition. These are described in detail in Frye's (1957) seminal book. He calls these plots Tragedy, Romance, Adventure, and Irony.

19.2.1 Narrative Roles as the Essence of Criminal Identity

When considering criminal identity, the story told of crime episodes is of special interest. These can be encapsulated in the role the offender considers themselves to have played during the commission of a crime. To explore such roles, we drew upon an extensive psychological and criminological literature, developing the idea that the roles admitted by an offender when describing a crime are useful proxies for their broader narrative identity (Youngs & Canter, 2012). This concept of the "role" extends previous thinking on cognitively focused scripts of actions and reactions in violent scenarios (Huesmann, 1988).

The declaration of which role a person remembers to have been salient when committing a crime raises the possibility of the roles being shaped as a form of reasoning and justification. They are also likely to be influenced by the context of eliciting the roles, as all storytelling is understood and shaped by the intended audience. The influence of rationalizations and context always need to be borne in mind when interpreting the results of studies using this approach. Our research takes these processes into consideration by presenting respondents with a number of possible roles and asking them how much each one described the experience they remembered (Youngs & Canter, 2012). This reduces the generation of any specific role as the obvious dominant one. It also allows for a more subtle analysis of the themes that bring together different role selections for any individual.

19.2.2 The Narrative Roles Questionnaire (NRQ)

Following Presser (2009), it is argued that a particular crime narrative has the following components: (1) the offender's interpretation of the event and their actions within that event, (2) an identity in the interpersonal crime event, and (3) related emotional and other experiential qualities of the event for the offender.

In order to develop a standard procedure to explore these components, we held open-ended pilot interviews with thirty offenders. The imprisoned offenders had been convicted of offenses covering the full range from burglary to murder. During interviews they were asked to describe their feelings and experiences when committing a recent offense. Each interview was transcribed verbatim and content-analyzed. This consisted of deriving categories from the transcripts and establishing clear definitions for each category. The reliability of the assignment of material to categories was checked by having more than one person use the defined categories, establishing that the same material was assigned to the same categories by different people. The three components were used to guide the derivation of categories. We then grouped the categories into themes and a representative verbatim statement from the interviews selected to capture each theme.

The resulting set of thirty-three statements captures typical sets of words that might be used by an offender. They describe key descriptions of their experience of the event (e.g., It was the only thing to do; I was doing it because I had to; I found I couldn't help myself; I was doing a job), the offender's self-awareness/identity (e.g., I was a victim; I was like a professional; I was in control; It was a manly thing to do) and emotional state during the offense (e.g., It was fun; It was like I wasn't part of it; I just wanted to get it over with). These statements comprised the first version of the NRQ.

Narrative Roles SSA

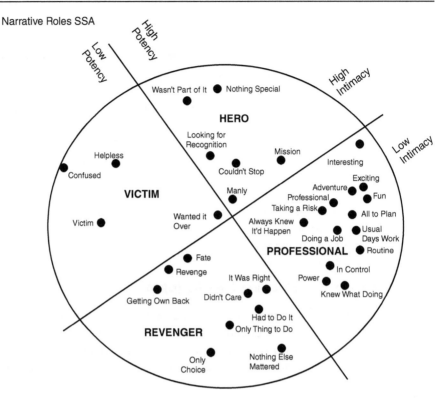

Figure 19.1 *SSA-I Results for seventy-one offenders' responses to the Roles Questionnaire (Youngs & Canter, 2012)*

The statements were used in the study of offenders' roles during crimes by asking them to consider a crime they had committed and describe the activity in detail (Youngs & Canter, 2012). They were then asked to complete a questionnaire listing the thirty-three role statements in order to indicate, on a five-point Likert scale, the extent to which they agreed/disagreed that each role statement described their experience. Responses were related to a given criminal context, enabling the qualities of agency and communion underpinning the action in that event.

19.2.3 Different Offense Narrative Roles

To identify the underlying themes inherent within the thirty-three different roles possible during offending, we collected responses from seventy-one offenders (Youngs & Canter, 2012). Multivariate analysis was then conducted on the responses, identifying the structure presented in Figure 19.1. This analysis represents the relative degree of co-occurrence of any pair of roles as a relative distance in a two-dimensional space. So, for example, roles that co-occur often, such as "being on a mission" and "looking for recognition," are closer in the configuration than "I was confused" and "it all went to plan," which were never selected by the same person, and are far apart.

The resulting configuration of the thirty-three role statements is open to interpretation that reflects the two facets of agency and communion (McAdams, 1993). Agency is reflected in the distinction between narratives of power and potency, such as being a professional or seeking revenge. This contrasts with those accounts in which the individual is a weak victim pushed by fate. Communion is illustrated by the contrasts in intimacy between those experiences that are ego-involved in the process, such as "getting one's own back," rather than taking a risk that kept the experience independent of the person. Combining these dichotomies generates the four narrative roles:

- The Professional (Adventure narrative) role is one of calm, competency and mastery of the environment.
- The Revenger (Tragedy) role is one of distress and blame.
- The Victim (Irony) role is one of disconnectedness and despair.
- The Hero (Quest) role is one of hubris, of taking on and overcoming challenges.

Items capturing each of these thematic roles are given in Table 19.1. The items comprising the four roles are related to the three components of narratives proposed by Presser (2009), namely identity, cognitive distortions, and affective components, reflecting the distinctions presented in Table 19.2.

Table 19.1 *Indicative statements that define themes of narrative roles taken from the Narrative Roles Questionnaire*

Narrative role	Indicative statement
Professional	"I was like a professional." "For me, it was like a usual day's work." "I was doing a job." "It was routine."
Hero	"I was looking for recognition." "I couldn't stop myself." "It was like I wasn't part of it." "It was a manly thing to do."
Victim	"I was a victim." "I was helpless." "I was confused about what was happening." "I just wanted to get it over with."
Revenger	"I was trying to get revenge." "I didn't care what would happen." "It was my only choice." "I had to do it."

Source: Youngs & Canter, 2012

Table 19.2 *Narrative integration of affective, cognitive, and offense-specific identity components of offending*

Narrative role	Offense identity	Cognitive distortion	Emotional state
Quest narrative: Hero role	Strong; Others significant	Present own alternative evaluations of actions; Refocus impact in terms of offender's own objectives	Calm; Displeasurable
Tragedy narrative: Revenger role	Weak; Others not significant	Responsibility attributed to others; Minimize impact	Aroused; Neutral
Adventure narrative: Professional role	Strong; Others not significant	Present own alternative evaluations of actions; Minimize impact	Calm; Neutral
Irony narrative: Victim role	Weak; Others significant	Responsibility attributed to others; Refocus impact in terms of offender's own objectives	Aroused; Displeasurable

19.2.4 Summary of the Four Narrative Roles

Connecting cognitive, affective, and narrative perspectives on criminality, our findings propose that four dominant themes emerge as underlying roles that characterize the narrative identity of offenders.

In the Revengeful Mission role, the offenders, who see themselves as strong and powerful, are seeking a specific impact on (an)other person(s). This is often part of a Romantic Quest narrative, underpinned by high levels of the two fundamental psychological dimensions of potency (agency) and intimacy (communion). This role is further revealed in distorted cognitions about the ends or consequences of their actions, while accepting responsibility for the means. The adoption of this role is associated with a calm, nonaroused, but negative emotional state.

In the Tragic Hero role, the respondent regards the offense as an inevitable, justified response, one which the offender is powerless to avoid. The commission of the crime is entirely about the enactment of the offender's Tragedy – the victim is irrelevant. Underpinned by a low potency and intimacy identity, this role is further revealed in cognitive attributions of the responsibility to others as well as the dismissal of the harm done. Adoption of this role is associated with an aroused but not entirely negative emotional state.

The Professional role is one in which the crime is an opportunity to demonstrate strength and expertise as part of an unfolding adventure. The focus is on the mastery of the environment in pursuit of the gains the protagonist seeks rather than the victim or target. The role features high levels of potency but low levels of criminal intimacy. The hallmark cognitive distortions are produced by a combination of ignoring the victim but owning responsibility for actions, while reinterpreting the end consequences in one's own terms. The emotional state that facilitates the adoption of this role during the commission of the crime is one of calm neutrality.

When acting out the Victim role, offenders regard their actions as the consequence of their powerlessness at the hands of others, as part of a generalized Irony narrative. Within this role, responsibility is attributed to others and the offender is in an aroused, negative emotional state. The crime is interpreted by the offender as happening as a result of a confused helplessness and feelings of alienation from others.

The focus of our methodology on direct descriptions of an offender's experience of events does not require overt justification that would be susceptible to social desirability biases, or conscious positioning across items. Such techniques, rather than an overt life story interview, may be particularly useful in narrative research, as they do not require the individual to make explicit the underlying themes within their narrative or to provide a coherent "life story" account. Indeed, the roles' technique may help reduce the "rewriting" of narratives and reveal the presence of narrative themes of which the individual may not be fully aware. In studies of criminals' experience, where those themes may be less socially acceptable, or where respondents may be less articulate, such techniques have proven particularly powerful. The NRQ provides a more objective account of the themes dominant in a criminal's actions, describing the role being played while carrying out a specific crime, than a qualitative analysis of the motifs that emerge from a free-flowing account, though such qualitative material can enhance theory and enrich understanding, as our research shows (Youngs & Canter, 2012).

This narrative perspective offers a framework for integrating a broad psychological literature on criminal identity, combining emotional, cognitive, and interpersonal aspects implicated by previous studies (Bandura, 1990; Katz, 1988; Sykes & Matza, 1957). The roles suggest a specific relationship between the cognitive, affective, and identity concepts that have previously been studied in isolation (Youngs & Canter, 2012). They indicate, for example, that through the Hero role, a tendency to distort cognitive interpretations of crime by focusing on one's own objectives and presenting one's own evaluation of events, rather than attempting to minimize the harm, will tend to co-occur in criminal activity underpinned by a negative, nonaroused emotional state, during which the offender will have a strong sense of self-awareness and where the others involved are insignificant. Many other refutable hypotheses can be derived from the narratives of criminal actions.

The specific nature of narrative themes carries direct intervention implications. For example, an intervention focus in respect of a Victim role may be the rewriting of past disappointments, while for the Revenger issues of anger management may be more pertinent. Furthermore, the articulation of "the problem" (the offense) in a narrative form opens up the possibility of treatment in the form of direct counternarratives, in much the same way that Ward's Good Lives model focuses on developing positive general life stories.

In preliminary explorations of this approach with clinical interventions, it has been found fruitful to use the NRQ as a starting point for discussions. This allows consideration of the many forms of psychological processes that are inherent in the narrative themes of given crimes. However, framing the therapeutic intervention within the narrative perspective is less threatening and invasive for offenders than a direct confrontation over thought patterns and beliefs. It also allows the therapist to embed the intervention in the cultural storylines with which the offender is familiar.

One particularly interesting possibility is that distinct narrative roles may relate to different diagnostic categories. Intriguingly, research in its early stages (Spruin et al., 2014) has indicated that psychiatric patients are able to complete the NRQ and produce meaningful answers. Studies with a population of mentally disordered offenders (MDOs) reveals the applicability of the narrative identity framework, demonstrating that while MDOs may not have the capacity to understand their actions in the eyes of the legal system, they did show an ability to process their criminal actions and identify with a narrative role during the commission of their crime, implying that interventions at the level of narrative identity may be fruitful for rehabilitation.

By developing a systematic research instrument that uses groupings of roles as summaries of narrative identity, it has been possible to provide more precise definitions as well as reliable measurements that capture material given in much fuller open-ended interviews. This paves the way for broader applications of the methodology for identifying themes inherent to different types of role-taking. The nature of the identity revealed within these narrative roles has also been clarified through careful consideration of the complex mixture of psychological processes captured by the NRQ. Youngs and Canter (2012) show that the four narrative themes map readily onto the two axes of Potency and Intimacy that McAdams (1985) argues underpin narrative identity. There is, thus, an interesting research question as to the ways in which the four narrative themes operate in relation to larger-scale life narratives.

19.3 Life Narrative and Identity

Numerous studies explore the importance of how offenders see their lives in supporting their criminality (Adams et al., 2005; Baumeister, Bushman, & Campbell, 2000; Baumeister, Smart, & Boden, 1996; Bushman & Baumeister, 1998; Zechmeister & Romero, 2002). For example, Baumeister, Smart, and Boden (1996) argued that violence was associated with favorable self-appraisals, combined with some form of ego threat, while Adams et al. (2005) related criminality to a diffuse-avoidance identity processing style, characterized by uncertainty, procrastination, and a tendency toward an external locus of control. In contrast to cognitive and individualistic processes, criminal identity is considered an interpersonal rather than an intrapersonal dimension. One argument is that identity is socially constructed through the roles that people play in the society (or groups) to which they belong (Hogg, Terry, & White, 1995). A lack of strong attachments to others may lead to a variety of psychological and behavioral problems. Baumeister and Leary (1995) discuss the importance of strong and stable relationships in reducing the likelihood of criminality. Relatedly, in an examination of personal construct systems, Miller and Treacher (1981) demonstrate that delinquents identified more readily with fictional characters, showing a preference for the masculine and popular heroes who were likely to use direct action to solve their problems. The researchers concluded that delinquents were less able to identify with the adults closest to them due to poor social anchorage, with recourse to self-identity via fictional characters through projective processes.

Again, the literature calls for an integrated perspective, appreciating the experiential contexts from which criminal identities evolve. Life narratives propose to offer such a vantage point, though disruptive interpersonal and biographical factors informing construction of offenders' narratives should be heeded.

19.3.1 The Life as a Film (LAAF) Approach to Criminal Narratives

Studying criminal identity through broader life narrative provides a perspective on the meaning of crime within the context of an unfolding personal story (Canter, 1994; Maruna, 2001; Sandberg, 2009; Ward, 2012; Youngs & Canter, 2012). Complementing the episodic focus of the NRQ, a standard procedure for exploring how offenders see their own overall life trajectory was developed, building on life narrative accounts that McAdams (1993) explored in his "Life as a Book" procedure. His method was developed with effective individuals leading constructive lives and relies on a fluency and an understanding of themselves and their lives that are rare in an offending population. These intensive procedures also orient to concrete accounts of life events and episodes rather than an overarching perspective that emphasizes identity and the dynamics of an unfolding story.

Our initial explorations with convicted people revealed a poor understanding of their life as a book (Canter & Youngs, 2015). Often, their conceptualizations of their life showed limited coherence, either because their life had been so dysfunctional or because of limited cognitive abilities and/or education. The generally low literacy of people in prison (Greenberg, Dunleavy, & Kutner, 2007) also greatly limits their ability to articulate accounts of themselves with reference to literary models.

Beyond the practical challenges that require a direct, engaging process with potentially reluctant participants, there are also the conceptual, psychological demands of finding a mechanism that allows offenders to generate content/material that reveals the dynamic processes of an unfolding story; not any plausible story, but one that elucidates the ways in which their narratives indicate perspectives on their past and aspirations, or beliefs, about their future. This is a requirement for a procedure that indicates naturally unfolding events that lead forward in time.

The life as book approach (McAdams, 1993) tends to generate a historical, "autobiography"-style account, structured by social milestones (e.g., leaving school, getting married) rather than by significant events that are intrinsic to a personal perspective on their life story. These challenges to obtaining offender life narratives when taken together with benefits of exploring such narratives as indicated by Toch (1993), Agnew (2006), Maruna (2001), Presser (2009, 2010) as well as Youngs and Canter (2012) indicate there would be value in a methodology that complements earlier procedures, developing a shorter, less threatening, yet engaging process to which convicted men and women would respond readily.

With this objective, we developed a procedure based on a modification of the techniques used by McAdams (1993, 2001) for the derivation of constructive life stories. This is the LAAF (Life as a Film) procedure (Canter & Youngs, 2015). Unlike the Life as a Book or other life story interviews, the film framework elicits a future orientation. It requires some sort of conclusion or outcome rather than only emphasizing what has happened in the past. This assists in exploring the respondents' understanding of what their life trajectory might be, which contributes further to indicating their self-identity.

It is also possible to derive essential components that are present for any film, giving a rich source of psychological insights. This includes aspects of the dominant characters, inevitably including a representation of the self. It reveals interpersonal interactions, changes over time, and of course some kind of plot, with a beginning and an ending. There are also structural issues that relate directly to the developing narrative model we put forward (Canter & Youngs, 2012), which are revealed by asking the respondent what sort of film (genre) is being described.

19.3.2 The LAAF Procedure

The general LAAF technique used to elicit narrative-relevant content is presented below. A short version (Section A) of the procedure using an open-ended prompt and four key prompts can be used alone. When time and sample characteristics allow, a longer version with a range of additional prompts can be used in addition (Sections A and B).

Instructions for an LAAF Elicitation Interview

Section A
If your life were to be made into a film, what type of film would it be?
Basic prompts
What would happen?
Who would the main characters be?

What would the main events that might happen in the film be?
How do you think it might end?

Section B
The main scene of the film
What happens in the most exciting scene in the film?
Where is it?
What is going on?
Who else is there? What are they doing?
How are you acting?
How do you feel?

How the film opens
When does the film start?
What is going on?
What are you like then?
Now tell us in as much detail as you can what happens between this opening scene and the main scene!

You in the film
What sort of person are you?
Who do you have good feelings about and why?
Who do you have bad feelings about and why?
What do other people think about you?
What mistakes do you make?
How do you change during the film?

Content Analysis Framework

The LAAF responses are subjected to an interpretation procedure to derive a detailed understanding of the substantive content. The content is assessed in terms of four classes of issue:

(1) Psychological complexity
(2) Remit: Implicit psychological content
(3) Explicit processes used to organize content
(4) Nature of agency vis-à-vis others and the world.

This content analysis framework was developed from first principles in combination with existing narrative psychology theories and frameworks and a range of psychological concepts identified in Investigative Psychology studies as pertinent to the nature of an individual's agency in relation to criminal action.

Psychological Complexity

The categories assigned to this class of issue provide a basis for interpreting the accounts in terms of the richness of the narrative generated. This is considered on a substantive basis (e.g., number of distinct people; number of distinct psychological ideas) and a formal basis (e.g., account length/number of words, presence of contingent type sequences). It represents an internal validation of the LAAF approach by demonstrating the extent to which respondents are putting thought into their storylines and incorporating their experiences and contacts with others.

The Remit: Implicit Psychological Content

This category allows the researcher to review the narrative based on what each person describes as their LAAF. Given the open-ended nature of the procedure, one level of interpretation should consider the way in which the individual understands the LAAF task in terms of what to talk about. For example, the focal content of the narrative is expressed through different scenes and events and the way in which that content is cast. The implicit content of the narrative may be cast in different formats, such as the generic presentation of the LAAF, which is expressed through the individual's likening of their life to a specific genre of film. In a similar vein, the resolution of the narrative will also vary between each narrator. Hankiss (1981) provides a typology of the resolution of a narrative which is differentiated according to movement between good past vs. bad past and good present vs. bad. He describes this movement as four narrative forms: "dynastic" (good past, good present), "antithetical" (bad past, good present), "compensatory" (good past, bad present), and "self-absolutory" (bad past, bad present). In the LAAF procedure the resolution focuses on the ending only (happy vs. sad) and what the individual seeks to achieve through the task. This is coded by the researcher using Sandberg's (2009) work on the implicit messages in accounts of deviant activities.

The Explicit Processes

This section of the content dictionary organizes the LAAF narrative in terms of the psychologically active components. These are the psychological processes of the narrative content that are structured to produce substantive connections and movement between the components which produce the storyline. A range of psychological structuring processes that have been identified by McAdams (1993) in general narrative psychology, as well as the offense-specific narrative roles identified by Canter and Youngs (2009; 2012) and Youngs and Canter (2012), are assessed.

Nature of Agency

This category assesses variations in the descriptions of how the individual's identity deals with the world. Here, the LAAF framework draws on Bandura's (1986) work on psychological incentives to highlight core motivations for the actions that are described in the LAAF narratives, for example, how the individual views the world will include an element of locus of control. In the LAAF content framework this is assessed by descriptions of avoidant or confrontational behaviors in the narrative. One argument is that people are limited by their moral obligations and therefore create coping strategies when internal conflicts arise. Bandura (1990) argues that moral disengagement allows a person to avoid self-condemnation when standards have been violated.

Following the LAAF protocol, we conducted a study of sixty incarcerated offenders and ninety-one nonoffenders (Youngs et al., 2016). In terms of psychological complexity, offenders appeared to embrace the task more carefully and thoroughly than did nonoffenders, typically generating more events with more people and a clearer structure and roles for characters than nonoffenders. This gave more psychological richness to their accounts, supporting arguments put forward in our earlier study that the LAAF is especially suitable for such respondents (Canter & Youngs, 2015). This increases confidence that the components of offenders' responses are of significance and the dominant aspects of value in understanding the processes underlying their criminal activity.

In terms of implicit psychological content, the dominant emphasis of offenders' LAAF responses was criminality, often expressed in dramatic terms as a crime or tragedy film. This shows a marked tendency for offenders to focus on criminality and related imprisonment as central to their identity in their life as a film.

A third prevalent theme distinguishing offenders from nonoffenders was a preoccupation with the materialistic. Offenders' stories were notably more concerned with material success as the focal content of their life stories, and offenders' actions were markedly more motivated by material/financial gain than those of the nonoffenders.

The identification of key differences with many similarities across the offender and nonoffender samples supports the validity of the LAAF approach. Although they had a generally lower level of educational attainment than nonoffenders, the offenders were still able to construct detailed and psychologically rich narratives about their lives. The respondents saw the LAAF as an opportunity to talk about themselves, their identities, and their aspirations. In no case did they invent a total fantasy that did not relate to their actual life experiences. The LAAF thus generated the psychological essence of an individual's narrative by characterizing their life in an active, plot-driven, character-focused, dramatic format, highlighting features less immediately obvious in static, standard psychological processes.

Taken together, the themes that characterize offenders' narratives show criminality couched in negative terms that focus on material concerns. Yet despite this focus, relations with others are important but typically problematic and described in terms of wrong done and loss. This implies an unresolved identity dissonance between the need for rewarding engagement with others, yet an emphasis on material gains. The unresolved dissonance is further implied in the declarations of potency, happy endings, and self-mastery within an overriding negative presentation of their lives.

This identity dissonance emerges through use of the LAAF procedure because of its emphasis on free-flowing accounts, structured by the offenders themselves. The complex interplay of concepts that produce the characteristics of dissonance has been difficult to identify using other procedures. Research on a number of psychological constructs, from self-esteem (Baumeister, Smart, & Boden, 1996; Bushman & Baumeister, 1998; Trzesniewski et al., 2006) to empathy-deficit (Covell & Scalora, 2002; Jolliffe & Farrington, 2007), has not established the particular components that differentiate those involved in crime from those who are not.

Dealing directly with unresolved dissonance has considerable rehabilitative potential. Dissonance can lead to both commitment and resistance to change through cognitive, dispositional and environmental influences (Draycott, 2007, 2012). For interventions to be successful, a commitment to change by the individual is necessary. The unresolved dissonance identified in the LAAF accounts of the offenders demonstrates aspects of the narrative that may challenge the individual's commitment to change. In an earlier study, we identified the importance of a more refined understanding of the substantive nature of offenders' narratives in developing the opportunity to use more narrative ideas in treatment, suggesting that "framing the therapeutic intervention within the narrative perspective is less threatening and invasive for offenders than a direct confrontation over thought patterns" (Youngs & Canter, 2012, p. 272).

Offenders' narratives revealed through the LAAF do not explain how or why offenders desist from crime, but rather reflect the psychological aspects of their experiences that are relevant to desistance. This can contribute to rehabilitative practices. The discrepant themes revealed in the unresolved dissonance, such as criminal identity and materialistic focus with problematic relationships, are issues to address during therapeutic interventions. Ward's Good Lives approach (e.g., Ward, 2010) points to the value of helping offenders to reconstruct their personal narratives. Therefore, identifying what areas of the narrative need to be recast is important to making the changes which interventions aim to achieve. What the LAAF offers is a method of self-reflection that allows offenders to organize their life story into a meaningful narrative, a similar cognitive process to the developmental ideas of the reflective function (Fonagy & Target, 1997; Fonagy, 2004). The reflective function is a method of self-organization, which Ansbro (2008) argues mirrors the reflective aspects of the narrative approach and is a useful tool when working with offenders.

Narrative approaches are gaining currency within psychiatric and social science discussions of human behavior (Canter, 2012; Lewis, 2014). The Good

Lives approach (e.g., Ward, 2010) has highlighted the potential of helping offenders to develop constructive Good Life narratives. The above research suggests some components of the destructive narrative identity that need to be recast, such as the materialistic focus and emphasis on criminality and its dramatic qualities. It offers positive features specific to offenders for rehabilitative efforts to focus on, such as the highly potent self-identities. But most centrally, it implies a systemic reconstruction of narratives that address the inconsistencies at the heart of the unresolved dissonance in offenders' life stories. The LAAF approach may be a useful tool in deriving the essential psychological details of the individual's life narratives and assessing progress in the reconstructive process. Importantly, it does seem to be a technique with which offenders and nonoffenders alike can engage.

19.4 Conclusions and Developments

Together the LAAF and NRQ give a dynamic, unfolding perspective on criminal identity. It is not regarded as a static characteristic of a person but is expected to change in the light of the individual's interpretation of the experience of criminality. This allows for interventions with offenders by helping them to reassess who they are and reconstruct their personal narrative. Recent studies are showing the real potential of the practical significance of this approach. For example, studies by Rowlands, Youngs, and Canter (2018, 2019, 2020) have used the LAAF to demonstrate that the transformation from a low agency/communion substance-using identity toward a high agency/communion recovery identity parallels the movement away from drug addiction, indicating that these themes are focal to personal growth and positive change processes. This research demonstrates the power of our methods for articulating and differentiating identities and a prospect for interventions that explore the way individuals see their life story unfolding and how that can be reconstructed. Building on well-established NI methods, adapted for marginalized groups, our approach meets challenges for studying narrative identity in criminals, offering guidelines for more systematic enquiry. As such, it is likely that the NRQ and LAAF can be extended to consider other marginalized identities and role-taking more broadly.

References

Adams, G. R., Munro, B., Munro, G., Doherty-Poirer, M., & Edwards, J. (2005). Identity processing styles and Canadian adolescents' self-reported delinquency. *Identity*, 5, 57–65.

Adler, J. M. (2012). Living into the story: Agency and coherence in a longitudinal study of narrative identity development and mental health over the course of psychotherapy. *Journal of Personality and Social Psychology*, *102*(20), 367–389.

Adler, J. M., Turner, A. F., Brookshier, K. M., Monahan, C., Walder-Biesanz, I., Harmeling, L., et al. (2015). Variations in narrative identity is associated with trajectories of mental health over several years. *Journal of Personality and Social Psychology*, *108*(3), 476–496.

Agnew, R. (2006). Storylines as neglected causes of crime. *Journal of Research in Crime and Delinquency*, *43*, 119–147, doi:10.1177/0022427805280052.

Ansbro, M. (2008). Using attachment theory with offenders. *Probation Journal*, *55*(3), 231–244, doi:10.1177/0264550508092812.

Bandura, A. (1986). *Social Foundation of Thought and Action: A Social Cognitive Theory*. Englewood Cliffs, NJ: Prentice Hall.

Bandura, A. (1990). Mechanisms of moral disengagement. In A. Reich (Ed.), *Origins of Terrorism: Psychologies, Ideologies, Theologies, States of mind* (pp. 161–191). New York, NY: Cambridge University Press.

Bauer, J. J. & McAdams, D. P. (2004). Personal growth in adults' stories of life transitions, *Journal of Personality*, *72*(3), 573–602.

Baumeister, R. F., Bushman, B. J., & Campbell, W. K. (2000). Self-esteem, narcissism, and aggression: Does violence result from low self-esteem or from threatened egotism? *Current Directions in Psychological Science*, *9*(1), 26–29, doi:10.1111/1467- 8721.00053.

Baumeister, R. J. & Leary, M. R. (1995). The need to belong: Desire for interpersonal attachments as a fundamental human motivation. *Psychological Bulletin*, *117* (3), 497–529.

Baumeister, R., Smart, L., & Boden, J. (1996). Relation of threatened egotism to violence and aggression: The dark side of high self-esteem. *Psychological Review*, *103*, 5–33. doi:10.1037/0033-295X.103.1.5.

Becker, H. S. (1963). *Outsiders: Studies in the Sociology of Deviance*. New York, NY: Free Press.

Bushman, B. & Baumeister, R. (1998). Threatened egotism, narcissism, self-esteem, and direct displaced aggression: Does self-love or self-hate lead to violence? *Journal of Personality and Social Psychology*, *75*, 219–229.

Brookman, F., Copes, H., & Hochstetler, A. (2011). Street codes as formula stories: How inmates recount violence. *Journal of Contemporary Ethnography*, *40*(4), 397–424, doi:10.1177/0891241611408307.

Bruner, J. (1987). Life as narrative. *Social Research*, *54*, 11–32.

Canter, D. V. (1994). *Criminal Shadows: Inside the Mind of the Serial Killer*. London: Harper Collins Publishers.

Canter, D. V. (2008). In the kingdom of the blind. In D.V. Canter & R. Zukauskiene (Eds.), *Psychology and Law: Bridging the Gap* (pp. 1–22). Aldershot: Ashgate.

Canter, D. V. (2012). Challenging neuroscience and evolutionary explanation of social and psychological processes. *Contemporary Social Science: Journal of the Academy of Social Sciences*, *7*(2), 95–115, doi:10.1080/21582041.2012.702527.

Canter, D. V. & Heritage, R. (1990). A multivariate model of sexual offence behavior: Developments in "offender profiling." *Journal of Forensic Psychiatry*, *1*, 185–212.

Canter, D. V. & Youngs, D. E. (2009). *Investigative Psychology: Offender Profiling and the Analysis of Criminal Action*. Chichester: John Wiley & Sons.

Canter, D. V. & Youngs, D. E. (2012). Sexual and violent offender' victim role assignment: A general model of offending style. *Journal of Forensic Psychiatry & Psychology, 23*(3), 297–326, doi:10.1080/14789949.2012.690102.

Canter, D. V. & Youngs, D. E. (2015). The LAAF procedure for exploring offenders' narratives. *The Howard Journal of Criminal Justice, 54*(3), 219–236.

Covell, C. N. & Scalora, M. J. (2002). Empathic deficits in sexual offenders: An integration of affective, social, and cognitive constructs. *Aggression and Violent Behaviour, 7*(3), 251–270, doi.org/10.1016/S1359–1789(01)00046.

Dancer, L. J. & Woods, S. A. (2006). Higher-order factor structures and intercorrelations of the 16PF5 and FIRO-B. *International Journal of Selection and Assessment, 14*(4), 385–391.

Draycott, S. (2007). Hunting the shark: The concept of motivation. *Issues in Forensic Psychology, 7*, 26–33.

Draycott, S. (2012). Dissonance, resistance and commitment: A pilot analysis of moderate meditation relationships. *Criminal Behaviour and Mental Health, 22*, 181–190, doi:10.1002/cbm.1830.

Fleetwood, J. (2016). Narrative habitus: Thinking through structure/agency in the narratives of offenders. *Crime, Media, Culture, 12*(2), 173–192, doi:10.1177/1741659016653643.

Fonagy, P. (2004). The developmental roots of violence in the failure of mentalization. In F. Pfafflin & G. Adshead (Eds.), *A Matter of Security: The Application of Attachment Theory to Forensic Psychiatry and Psychotherapy* (pp. 13–56). London: Jessica Kingsley.

Fonagy, P.,& Target, M. (1997). Attachment and reflective function: Their role in self-organisation. *Development and Psychopathology, 9*, 679–700.

Frye, N. (1957). *Anatomy of Criticism: Four Essays*. Princeton, NJ: Princeton University Press.

Greenberg, E., Dunleavy, E., & Kutner, M. (2007). Literacy behind bars: Results from the 2003 National Assessment of Adult Literacy Prison Survey. NCES 2007-473, National Center for Education. Statistics, http://nces.ed.gov/help/orderinfo.asp.

Hankiss, A. (1981). On the mythological rearranging of one's life history. In D. Bertaux (Ed.), *Biography and Society: The Life History Approach in the Social Sciences* (pp. 203–209). Beverly Hills, CA: Sage.

Heimer, K. & Matsueda, R. L. (1994). Role-taking, role commitment, and delinquency: A theory of differential social control. *American Sociological Review, 59*(3), 365–390.

Hermans, H. J. M. (1996). Voicing the self: From information processing to dialogical interchange. *Psychological Bulletin, 119*(1), 31–50, doi:10.1037/0033-2909.119.1.31.

Hogg, M. A., Terry, D. J., & White, K. M. (1995). A tale of two theories: A critical comparison of identity theory with social identity theory. *Social Psychology Quarterly, 58*(4), 255–269.

Holms, T., Thomsen, D. K., & Bliksted, V. (2018). Themes of unfulfilled agency and communion in life stories of patients with schizophrenia. *Psychiatry Research, 269*, 772–778.

Horgan, J. G. (2009). *Walking Away from Terrorism: Accounts of Disengagement from Radical and Extremist Movements*. London: Routledge.

Huesmann, L. R. (1988). An information processing model for the development of aggression. *Aggressive Behavior, 14*(1), 13–24, doi:10.1002/1098-2337(1988) 14:1<13::AID-AB2480140104>3.0.CO;2-J.

Ioannou, M., Canter, D. V., Youngs, D. E., & Synott, J. (2015). Offender crime narratives across different types of crimes. *Journal of Forensic Psychology Practice, 15*(5), 383–400.

Jolliffe, D. & Farrington, D.P. (2007). Examining the relationship between low empathy and self-reported offending. *Legal and Criminological Psychology, 12*(2), 265–286, doi:10.1348/135532506X147413.

Katz, J. (1988). *Seductions of Crime: Moral and Sensual Attractions in Doing Evil*. New York, NY: Basic Books.

Leary, T. (1957). *Interpersonal Diagnosis of Personality: A Functional Theory and Methodology for Personality Evaluation*. Oxford: Ronald Press.

Lemert, E. M. (1951). *Social Pathology: A Systematic Approach to the Theory of Sociopathic Behavior*. New York, NY: McGraw-Hill.

Lewis, B. (2014). Taking a narrative turn in psychiatry. *The Lancet, 383*(9911), 22–23, doi:10.1016/S0140-6736(13)62722-1.

McAdams, D. P. (1985). *Power, Intimacy and the Life Story: Personological Inquiries into Identity*. New York, NY: Guilford Press.

McAdams, D. P. (1993). *The Stories We Live By: Personal Myths and the Making of the Self*. New York, NY: Guilford Press.

McAdams, D. P. (2001). The psychology of life stories. *Review of General Psychology, 5*, 100–122.

McAdams, D. P. (2006). *The Redemptive Self: Stories Americans Live By*. New York, NY: Oxford University Press.

McAdams, D. P. (2015). *The Art and Science of Personality Development*. New York, NY: Guilford Publications.

McAdams, D. P., Diamond, A., St. Aubin, E., & Mansfield, E. (1996). Stories of commitment: The psychosocial construction of generative lives. *Journal of Personality and Social Psychology, 72*(3), 678–694, doi:10.1037/0022-3514.72.3.678.

McAdams, D. P., Hoffman, B. J., Day, R., & Mansfield, E. D. (1996). Themes of agency and communion in significant autobiographical scenes. *Journal of Personality, 64*(2), 339–377, doi:10.1111/j.1467-6494.1996.tb00514.x.

McAdams, D. P. & McLean, K. C. (2013). Narrative identity. *Current Directions in Psychological Science, 22*, 233–238.

McAuley, J. (1994). *The Politics of Identity: A Loyalist Community in Belfast*. Aldershot: Avebury.

McConnell, D. (2016). Narrative self-constitution and recovery from addiction. *American Philosophy, 53*(3), 307–322.

Mahoney, J. M. & Stasson, M. F. (2005). Interpersonal and personality dimensions of behaviour: FIRO-B and the Big Five. *North American Journal of Psychology, 7*(2), 205–215.

Maruna, S. (2001). *Making Good: How Ex-convicts Reform and Rebuild Their Lives*. Washington, DC: American Psychological Association.

Maruna, S., Immarigeon, R., & LeBel, T. P. (2004). Ex-offender re-integration: Theory and practice. In S. Maruna & R. Immarigeon (Eds.), *After Crime and Punishment: Pathways to Ex-offender Reintegration* (pp. 1–25). Cullompton: Willan.

Maruna, S. & Mann, R. E. (2006). A fundamental attribution error? Rethinking cognitive distortions. *Legal and Criminological Psychology*, *11*(2), 155–177, doi:10.1348/135532506X114608.

Massoglia, M. & Uggen, C. (2010). Settling down and aging out: Toward an interactionist theory of desistance and the transition to adulthood. *American Journal of Sociology*, *116*(2), 543–582, doi:10.1086/653835.

Mead, G. H. (1914/1982). Class Lectures in social psychology. In D. L. Miller (Ed.), *The Individual and the Social Self. Unpublished works of George Herbert Mead* (pp. 27–105). Chicago, IL: University of Chicago.

Miller, K. & Treacher, A. (1981). Delinquency: A personal construct theory approach. In H. Bonarius, R. Holland & S. Rosenberg (Eds.), *Personal Construct Psychology: Recent Advances in Theory and Practice* (pp. 241–249). London: Macmillan Publishing.

Presser, L. (2009). The narratives of offenders. *Theoretical Criminology*, *13*, 177–200, doi:0.1177/1362480609102878.

Presser, L. (2010). Collecting and analysing the stories of offenders. *Journal of Criminal Justice Education*, *21*(4), 431–446.

Rowlands, D., Youngs, D. E., & Canter, D. V. (2018). Exploring an agency-communion model of identity transformation in recovery from substance misuse. *Journal of Substance Use*, *24*, 265–272. doi:10.1080/14659891.2018.155273.

Rowlands, D., Youngs, D. E., & Canter, D. V. (2019). Themes of agency and communion and rehabilitation from substance misuse. *Drug and Alcohol Dependence*, *205*(1), 107611, doi:10.1016/j.drugalcdep.2019.107611.

Rowlands, D., Youngs, D. E., & Canter, D. V. (2020). Victory or defeat: Narratives of recovery and chronic substance misuse revealed through the "Life as a Film." *Journal of Substance Use*, *25*(2), 163–172, doi:10.1080/14659891.2019.1672816.

Russell, J. A. (1997). How shall an emotion be called? In R. Plutchik & H. R. Conte (Eds.), *Circumplex Models of Personality and Emotions* (pp. 221–244). Washington, DC: American Psychological Association.

Sandberg, S. (2009). A narrative search for respect. *Deviant Behaviour*, *30*(6), 487–510, doi:10.1080/01639620802296394.

Schutz, W. (1992). Beyond Firo-B: Three new theory-derived measures – Element B: Behavior, Element F: Feelings, *Element S: Self. Psychological Reports*, *70*(3), 915–937, doi:10.2466/pr0.1992.70.3.915.

Singer, J. A. (2004). Narrative identity and meaning making across the adult lifespan: An introduction. *Journal of Personality*, *72*(3), 437–459, doi:10.1111/j.0022-3506.2004.00268.

Spruin, E., Canter, D. V., Young, D. V., & Coulsten, B. (2014). Criminal narratives of mentally disordered offenders: An exploratory study. *Journal of Forensic Psychology Practice*, *14*, 438–455, doi:10.1080/15228932.2014.965987.

Stone, R. (2016). Desistance and identity repair: Redemption narratives as resistance to stigma. *British Journal of Criminology*, *56*(5), 956–975.

Sykes, G. M. & Matza, D. (1957). Techniques of neutralization: A theory of delinquency. *American Sociological Review*, *22*(6), 664–670.

Tannenbaum, F. (1938). *Crime and Community*. New York, NY: Columbia University.

Toch, T. (1993). Good violence and bad violence: Self-presentations of aggressors through accounts and war stories. In R. B. Felson & J. T. Tedeschi (Eds.), *Aggression and Violence: Social Interactionist Perspectives* (pp. 193–206). Washington, DC: American Psychological Association.

Trzesniewski, K. H., Donnellan, B. M., Moffitt, T. E., Robins, R. W., Poulton, R., & Caspi, A. (2006). Low self-esteem during adolescence predicts poor health, criminal behaviour, and limited economic prospects during adulthood. *Developmental Psychology*, *42*(2), 381–390, doi:10.1037/0012-1649.42.2.381.

Ward, T. (2000). Sexual offenders' cognitive distortions as implicit theories. *Aggression and Violent Behavior*, *5*(5), 491–507, doi:10.1016/S1359–1789(98)00036-6.

Ward, T. (2010). The good lives model of offender rehabilitation: Basic assumptions, etiological commitments, and practice implications. In F. McNeill, P. Raynor & C. Trotter (Eds.), *Offender Supervision: New Directions in Theory, Research and Practice* (pp. 41–64). Devon: Willan.

Ward, T. (2012). Commentary: Narrative identity and forensic psychology: A commentary on Youngs and Canter. *Legal and Criminological Psychology*, *17*(2), 250–261, doi:10.1111/j.2044-8333.2011.02028.

Youngs, D. E. & Canter, D. V. (2012). Offenders crime narratives as revealed by the Narrative Roles Questionnaire. *International Journal of Offender Therapy and Comparative Criminology*, *57*(3), 1–23, doi:10.1177/0306624X11434577.

Youngs, D. E., Canter, D. V., & Carthy, N. (2016). The offender's narrative: Unresolved dissonance in "Life as a Film" (LAAF) responses. *Legal and Criminological Psychology*, *21*(2), 251–265.

Zechmeister, J. S. & Romero, C. (2002). Victim and offender accounts of interpersonal conflict: Autobiographical narratives of forgiveness and unforgiveness. *Journal of Personality and Social Psychology*, *82*, 675–686, doi:10.1037/0022-3514.82.4.675.

20 Experimentation within the Social Identity Approach: History, Highlights, and Hurdles

Lucas B. Mazur

> [I]f philosophers keep neglecting the technological dimension of science, experimentation will continue to be seen as a mere data provider for the evaluation of theories. If they start taking the science–technology relationship seriously, however, doing experiments can be studied as a topic in its own right, which poses ... many interesting and important philosophical questions.
>
> (Radder, 2003a, p. 8)

At the start of the twentieth century, one of the main arguments in support of the establishment of psychology and sociology as independent disciplines was the claim that they were empirical sciences (Valsiner, 2012). In this way, advocates of these newly emerging disciplines would try to separate them from their parent discipline, philosophy. At that time, the terms *empirical* and *experimental* were used almost interchangeably by psychologists, and thus much of the early "experimental" research would generally not be thought of as such today (Danziger, 2000, 1992). As both theories and methods change, it is worth pausing from time to time to take stock of the degree to which the latter meaningfully translate the postulates of the former into empirical practices. Are the methodological assumptions of the theories we use best expressed in our choice of methods, and conversely, do the methods we use accurately encapsulate our theoretical positions and in what ways do they shape theory? The methodological link between theory and method is not ontologically neutral, as it fundamentally shapes the way we understand the object of study (Danziger, 1988; Valsiner, 2017). The current chapter attempts to explore these links in the realm of identity research, and we will explore these issues on the basis of the methodological assumptions underlying experimental research within the Social Identity Approach (SIA).

The SIA constitutes a rich example of the bidirectional influence between theory and method within experimental approaches to the study of identity. Despite the broad and rich philosophical foundations of the SIA, foundations that point in a wide range of possible research directions (even in disciplines beyond psychology, Abrams & Hogg, 2010), psychologists working explicitly within this tradition tend to focus on empirical, quantitative experiments.

For this reason, the SIA provides a particularly insightful example of the "what, why, and how" of an experimental approach within identity research; we can examine what SIA researchers are trying to study, why they are taking that particular methodological approach, and how they go about doing so by means of particular methods. What is more, we can also explore the consequences of these decisions for SIA theory. It will be argued that this particular constellation of theoretical assumptions and practical methods has produced an insightful, and yet simultaneously limited and at times problematic, understanding of identity. What is more, the choice to use experimental methods has also led to the establishment and entrenchment of methodological biases of which researchers often seem to be unaware, but which nevertheless considerably influence the study of identity within the social identity tradition. Thus, while drawing attention to important, and hereunto underappreciated aspects of identity, research within the Social Identity Approach also generally fails to appreciate other features of identity. Some of these blind spots arise from the theoretical assumptions of social identity theory itself, but the majority of them are the product of the experimental methods most widely used in research within the social identity tradition over the last several decades. It will be argued that much of the criticism aimed at the Social Identity Approach is in fact addressed to the experimental methods used in SIA research, not to SIA theory itself.

In the spirit of honest and open reflection that this chapter is attempting to encourage, it is perhaps useful at the start to set realistic expectations regarding methodology, and especially regarding the links between theory and empirical methods. All empirical methods are impoverishments of theory, just as all theory is an impoverishment of an infinitely more complex reality (Radder, 2003b). With this in mind, we ought not to expect a perfect fit between methods and theory, as something is always lost in translation (e.g., between construct, conceptualization, and operationalization). This is nicely captured in the following reflections on the work of Floyd Allport, someone who is often held up as an early proponent of the experimental shift in psychology:

> Floyd Allport's program defined social psychology in terms of experimentation and controlled inquiry, in opposition to armchair theorizing. He held that research should take place in a laboratory setting, but, if necessary, in the field. Though the claim of being scientific was central to Allport's program for social psychology, his *Social Psychology* is nonetheless noteworthy for his armchair theorizing and lack of scientific research.   (Parkovnick, 2000, pp. 429–430)

Like all people, psychologists are not always consistent in what they say and do, and they can often quite simply change their minds, even about their basic philosophical positions (Samelson, 2000). Hence, for many reasons – both logical and practical – it would be grossly unrealistic to expect a one-to-one relationship between theory, methodology, and method, especially across time or among a large group of researchers as constitutes any school of thought. That being said, an awareness of the different but interrelated natures of theory, methodology, and methods can help shed light on many a perennial argument in psychology. However, before we can reflect on whether or not experimental methods accurately reflect SIA theory, it is first important to review just what both SIA theory and experimental methods are all about.

In the section to follow we will briefly review the foundational assumptions of the SIA, and readers unfamiliar with the SIA will be provided with a brief overview and genealogy of this approach. We will then examine the development and nature of what has become the dominant understanding of experimentation within the Social Identity Approach. More particularly, as an example of this methodological choice we will look at the Ingroup Projection Model (Mummendey & Wenzel, 1999; Wenzel, Mummendey, & Waldzus, 2007). This example speaks to similar experimental trends within the psychological study of identity more broadly, and within the experimental study of identity in the social sciences more broadly yet. We will then look at how the theoretical and methodological assumptions of the Social Identity Approach became in practice largely wedded to that particular understanding of experimentation, and then how that combination has led to several, often implicit, assumptions about identity and identity research.

20.1 The Social Identity Approach

What is known as the Social Identity Approach (SIA) arose out of Henri Tajfel and John Turner's Social Identity Theory (SIT) and Turner's subsequently developed Self-Categorization Theory (SCT) (Tajfel & Turner, 1986). The SIA has been succinctly summarized at length elsewhere (e.g., Hogg, 2006, 2012; Reicher, Spears, & Haslam, 2010; Sindic & Condor, 2014; Spears, 2011), and so will only be briefly reviewed here. The understanding of identity within the SIA is both social and cognitive, and it is fundamentally rooted in the social-psychological mechanisms of categorization (Hammack, 2015). Tajfel and Turner (1986, p. 16) identified social identity as "those aspects of an individual's self-image that derive from the social categories to which he perceives himself as belonging." Thus, the SIA posits that social identity entails not just nominal group membership or even simple awareness of group membership. Rather, it asserts that the group becomes an "identity" in as far as it is taken into the psychological sense of self, involving the engagement of various psychological processes: "the external designations of ... groups as such have very little, if any, correspondence with the development and existence of internal (i.e., psychological) criteria for membership" (Tajfel, 1982, pp. 491–492). One might thus say that within the SIA an "identity" is a meaningful "category" that has been attached to the psychological sense of self (including the perception of the self-ness of others).

Within the SIA, when identifying with a collective, people engage in several important social-psychological processes, such as evaluating the group (e.g., its status) on the basis of intergroup comparisons (e.g., its status being determined in relation to other groups). In effect, Tajfel applied Individual-Level Balance Theory (as developed by the likes of Fritz Heider, Gustaw Ichheiser, and Leon Festinger)[1] to collective identities (Tajfel, 1972; Turner, 1975). In doing so, Tajfel asserted that, when thinking of identity, we can do so on either an individual or collective level, and importantly, that collective-level identities cannot be reduced to the psychology of the individual (Tajfel & Turner, 1979), as was arguably claimed by Floyd Allport in his earlier, if not later, writings (Samelson, 2000). Some have taken this even further, claiming that "our sense of self derives from the groups and categories we belong to, and in many ways individuality may 'merely' be the unique combination of distinct groups and categories that define who we are" (Hogg, 2012, p. 502). Within the SIA, all identity – even individual identity – is generally understood to be inherently social in nature.

We can identify several key theoretical elements of the SIA (for more thorough reviews, see Hogg, 2012; Hogg & Williams, 2000; Reicher, Spears, & Haslam, 2010; Spears, 2011). For example, the SIA assumes that collective identities are characterized by depersonalization, wherein people do not lose their sense of self but rather understand the self through the lens of the collective identity; when thinking on the level of collective identity, the collective identity is stressed above that of individual group members. As a result, intergroup differences stand out above and beyond intragroup differences. In order for such collective identities to emerge they must be salient in the given situation, which is to say that they must be seen as useful. That utility is determined by means of their normative or comparative "fit," that is, by the degree to which they are frequently used in the given context and the degree to which the categories are useful for making meaningful intergroup comparisons. This utility is also determined by the extent to which such comparisons strengthen optimal distinctiveness and enhance positive collective-level self-esteem. If such self-enhancement is not possible, all things being equal, the SIA assumes that a negative state will emerge and that people will take steps to alter this state.

Thus, recognizing the plasticity and motivated reactivity of identity within the ever-shifting social environment (from which identity cannot actually meaningfully be separated), the SIA represents a dynamic, context-sensitive, and nonreductionist understanding of identity (Hogg & Williams, 2000; Tajfel,

---

[1] Broadly speaking, balance theory refers to an understanding of perception and motivation, which posits that people tend to seek perceived consistency – or balance – between simultaneously entertained cognitions and/or behaviors. Perhaps the most well-known balance theory is "cognitive dissonance."

Fraser, & Jaspars, 1984). This understanding of identity has immediate implications for countless areas of interest to social psychologists. For example, the SIA largely rejects understandings of intergroup animosity and prejudice based primarily on assumptions of individual irrationality (e.g., "individual frustration"; Dollard et al., 1939) or individual personality features (e.g., "authoritarianism"; Adorno et al., 1950). Instead, the SIA asserts that "stereotypes" and even "prejudice" are largely the (often undesirable) outcome of otherwise normal social psychological mechanisms underlying identity.

Research within the SIA has grown over the last several decades, leading the SIA to become one of the most significant and widely used theoretical approaches within social psychology (Hogg, 2012; Reicher, Spears, & Haslam, 2010). The reach of the SIA has even extended beyond social psychology into such disciplines as organizational management and leadership studies (Haslam, 2004), expanding so considerably that some have claimed that within social psychology a "discussion of social identity is therefore inevitably a discussion of social identity theory" (Hogg, 2012, p. 503).

20.2 The Ingroup Projection Model as an Example of Identity Research in the SIA Tradition

As an example of experimental identity research within the Social Identity Approach we can examine the Ingroup Projection Model (IMP; Mummendey & Wenzel, 1999; Wenzel, Mummendey, & Waldzus, 2008). The IPM can be thought of as an attempt to quantify the theoretical building blocks of the SIA. In brief, the IPM is built upon quantitative comparisons, via Likert-scale-like ratings, of three identity categories; i.e., the ingroup, an outgroup, and a "superordinate category" to which both groups belong (hence both the ingroup and the outgroup are referred to as "subordinate categories"). In the spirit of the SIA, the IPM asserts that intergroup comparison is only possible when one posits the existence of a metric that is shared between the two (Turner & Reynolds, 2010). Within the IPM, such a metric is found in the form of a third category (in the language of the IPM: the "superordinate category") that is applicable to both identities (or rather, within which both conceptually fit). The tripartite nature of this interactive model can be thought of as similar to the social philosophy of numbers developed by Georg Simmel, whereby the dyad and the triad, in dynamic mutual interaction, constitute the foundations of the social, including identities (Simmel, 1950). The two subordinate categories can only be meaningfully compared by means of the third, linking category, while the superordinate category is only a superordinate category in the presence of the dyad. For example, a comparison of *teachers* with *administrators* feels meaningless if not absurd without the presence of an additional superordinate category allowing for a meaningful, shared metric. However, were we to compare them as two groups within a school or college, the comparison is possible (e.g., Which department is more in line with institutional goals? Which set of workers is more representative of the institution as a whole?).

In order to calculate the measurement of what is called (relative) ingroup projection, participants are asked to rate the degree to which a set of characteristics describes the subordinate ingroup to which they belong, the subordinate outgroup to which they do not belong, and the superordinate groups to which both subordinate groups belong. Ratings of their applicability to the various groups in question are made on Likert-like scales, for example from 1 (not at all) to 5 (very much). To provide a more concrete example, Wenzel, Mummendey, Weber, and Waldzus (2003) conceptualized *Poles* and *Germans* as two subordinate categories within the superordinate category of *European*. In this particular example, Poles and Germans rated both groups, as well as Europeans, on a series of traits, such as "family-oriented," "lazy," and "well-organized." Ingroup projection is understood as a higher degree of trait rating similarity between the ingroup and the superordinate group relative to that between the outgroup and the superordinate category. One is said to "project" ingroup traits to the extent that the superordinate category is rated more similarly to the ingroup than to the outgroup. For example, if the subordinate ingroup is understood to be highly "hardworking" but not very "fun-loving," and the outgroup is said to be low on the trait "hardworking" and high on the trait of "fun-loving," ingroup projection would imply that the superordinate category is also high on the trait of "hardworking" and low on the trait of "fun-loving." On the basis of these measurements we can conclude that the superordinate category is understood by the rater to be more similar to the ingroup than to the outgroup. It is important to highlight that, as seen in this example, the IPM is sensitive to both high and low ratings, understanding projection to be a greater degree of rating similarity between the ingroup and the superordinate group *relative* to that between the outgroup and the superordinate group. Rather than examining only "positive" similarities (i.e., traits that are applicable to the groups in question), the IPM involves the calculation of the absolute distance between ratings. A high degree of projection could therefore be seen in the case of low ratings on the given traits, that is, as long as both the ingroup and the superordinate category are rated low on those traits and more similarly to each other relative to the ratings between the superordinate category and the outgroup. The following formula is often used to calculate a single score of relative ingroup projection (with T referring to the given trait as assessed for the superordinate category, the outgroup, and the ingroup):

$$\sqrt{\sum(T(\text{SUPER})_i - T(\text{OUT})_i)^2} - \sqrt{\sum(T(\text{SUPER})_i - T(\text{IN})_i)^2}$$

In line with the philosophy of the SIA, the nature of ingroup projection is understood to change in response to which outgroup is in question, hence the model is to a degree inherently context-sensitive. For example, Wenzel et al. (2003) reported that while high projection scores among Germans involved relatively high ratings of "fun-loving" for both Germans and Europeans when the comparative outgroup was the English (who are understood in Germany to be stereotypically lower on that trait than Germans), that trait became less important for Europeans when the comparison group was Italians (who are seen in Germany as stereotypically higher on that trait than Germans). In that case, "hardworking" became more important for high projectors, thereby allowing them to rate both Germans and Europeans high on that trait, and Italians low on it. Similarly, they also rated both Germans and Europeans lower on "fun-loving" and Italians higher "fun-loving." These context-sensitive shifts in trait ratings happen in a manner that asserts the ingroup's prototypicality in the superordinate category relative to the outgroup.

In line with the SIA more broadly, there are also understood to be several factors determining which groups are compared with each other and along which shared metric they will be compared, such as relative fit and accessibility (Turner & Reynolds, 2010). It should also be mentioned that there are different approaches to calculating scores of ingroup projection and discussions regarding exactly how to interpret the measure (see Ullrich, 2009). What is more, ingroup projection is expected to appear under the condition that both the superordinate category and the superordinate category are valued parts of one's identity (Sindic & Reicher, 2008). Similarly, the IPM does not preclude the possibility that the outgroup image is simply more strongly associated with the superordinate category than the ingroup, thereby rendering high projection scores (in absolute terms) unrealistic.

Importantly, the IPM posits that the tendency toward relative ingroup projection correlates with ingroup favoritism. For example, if "European" is taken as the superordinate category and various European nations as the relevant subordinate identities, on the basis of the IPM we might expect that higher projection scores would be predictive of greater levels of ingroup favoritism regarding the distribution of European Union funds, greater favoritism for the politics of one's own nation, a greater preference for the traditions of one's own nation over those of the subordinate outgroup, etc. Like earlier research on the Minimal Group Paradigm,[2] the IPM closely links the meaningfulness (and the very notion) of collective identities with both intergroup comparison and tendencies toward ingroup favoritism. More recently, additional caveats have been added to the list of conditions necessary for the appearance of this constellation of identity-based intergroup dynamics, such as perceiving the outgroup as posing an identity-related threat (e.g., Rosa & Waldzus, 2012).

---

[2] The Minimal Group Paradigm involves the random assignment of participants into arbitrary groups, often within artificial experimental settings. It has been found that such groups can be sufficient to elicit various forms of ingroup favoritism (Tajfel et al., 1971; Turner, 1978).

20.3 Reflecting on the Foundations: Experimentation in Psychological Research

In order to understand the use of experimental methods within the Social Identity Approach, it is important to reflect on what we have come to understand experimentation to mean within psychological research. The meaning and use of the term "experiment" has significantly changed and narrowed over the last century. While Wilhelm Wundt thought of himself as an "experimental" psychologist, and he is generally considered the founder of psychology as an experimental field (Hogg & Williams, 2000), his *Völkerpsychologie* would not be categorized as experimental by most standards of today (Danziger, 1990, 1992). Attesting to the looser use of the term "experiment" at that time, the various utopian communities widely discussed in that era were considered "social experiments," and even early textbooks on "experimental social psychology," such as that by Murphy and Murphy (1931), would not be considered experimental today in that they do not contain many of the elements currently associated with experimentation discussed below (materiality, short term, replicability, and reproducibility, etc.). In the first half of the twentieth century and before, much of what was called "experimental" would today be thought of as "empirical" (but not experimental). The frequent use of the term experimental in this way at that time is not without significance, as it was in that era that social scientists, primarily psychologists and sociologists, were attempting to establish their fields as independent disciplines. Convincing themselves and others that the uniquely empirical approach of psychology and sociology separated those fields from philosophy was a key element of their argument (Valsiner, 2012). Thus, psychologists attempted to direct the field toward the empiricist understanding of the physical sciences (for whom empirical data was important), and away from the generally rationalist position of philosophy (for which gathering empirical data was not necessary).

An important shift in how psychologists understood the notion of experimentation is seen in the work of Kurt Lewin (1943). Lewin's thinking was considerably influenced by Gestalt psychology, something that is reflected in his interest in the holistic nature of the person in their environment (Lana, 1969). He found support for his interest in "fields" and "vectors" in the philosophy of science of Ernst Cassirer (1910/1923). Rather than isolating variables for study, Cassirer, and subsequently Lewin, argued that the main focus of the scientific study of psychological life should be on systems and the individual therein (Lana, 1969; MacMartin & Winston, 2000). It is for this reason that Lewin was interested in broad phenomena such as attitudes (Lana, 1969). Lewin believed that experiments could not be repeated in exactly the same way, as both the surrounding system and the individual or group therein were constantly changing, and because they were both influenced by the work of the researcher (hence he supported what he called "systemic replication"; Lana, 1969). This put him at odds with the ahistorical approach of behaviorism.

The immediate challenge for any empirical research on holistic systems is the simple fact that all such research is inherently unable to grasp the whole of the system in question; life is simply too complex. Therefore, the likes of Cassirer and Lewin needed to somehow justify their ability to empirically study systematic holism, and they did so by developing a particular under-standing of the "purity" of their empirical ("experimental") research (for an interesting discussion of the use of the notion of "purity" in how psychologists write about experiments, see MacMartin & Winston, 2000). Cassirer (1910/1923, p. 254) argued that "the experiment never concerns the real case, as it lies before us here and now in all the wealth of its particular determinations, but the experiment rather concerns an ideal case, which we substitute for it." The particulars illuminated in experimental research were understood to gain holistic purchase when combined with theory. It is for this reason that Lewin (1943) supported the assertion that "there is nothing as practical as a good theory"; psychology was to combine empirical data with meaningful theory so as to explore the systematic nature of psychological life. Lewin believed that experiments gained their validity not from their ability to capture causal relations, but in as far as they illustrate broader laws, which themselves become intelligible on the basis of "good theory" (MacMartin & Winston, 2000). In this sense, Lewin would generally fall on the side of Aristotelian thinking, and not on the side of Cartesian-Humean thought, wherein the former examines the structure of psychological processes and the latter studies cause-and-effect relationships between isolated elements of our psychological lives (Toomela, 2010).

Lewin's endorsement of the "pure case" – the link between empirical data and theory – would inspire others to justify the use of empirical data by means of some version of "purity" (MacMartin & Winston, 2000). However, in the decades that followed, just how psychologists understood the idea of purity would shift away from the systemic, Gestalt-like understanding of Lewin and Cassirer so as to embrace the notions of variable isolation and variable control as endorsed by the likes of Leon Festinger: "In most laboratory experiments such a situation would certainly *never* be encountered in real life. In the laboratory, however, we can find out exactly how a certain variable affects behavior or attitudes under special, or 'pure,' conditions" (Festinger, 1958, as cited in MacMartin & Winston 2000, p. 360, italics original). Thus, within this new understanding of the experiment, Cassirer's and Lewin's understanding of the purity of the experiment was replaced by the idea of "empirical purity," whereby single variables could be isolated and manipulated within controlled conditions. These variables would not only be thought of as isolated, but as conceptually measurable on linear scales, and the complexity of psychological phenomena would be reflected in the multiplication and interaction of unidir-ectional variables (Danziger, 2000, 1988). By the 1960s, the notion of the structural model was widely replaced by the "conceptual variable" (Aronson & Carlsmith, 1968; Danziger, 2000). Similar to the singular variable, participants in psychological research came to be understood as interchangeable units whose value came from their membership in the conceptual population around about which aggregate statistical analyses could be run. Concrete social identities were no longer allowed to be idiosyncratic within psychological research, but were conceptually determined on the basis of assumed statistical populations, within which the variables of interest are assumed to be "normally distributed" (Danziger, 2000, 1988; Michell, 2004).

Thus, following World War II, the notion of experimentation in psychology largely rejected the Gestalt-like features of experimentation advocated by Cassirer and Lewin, while it retained the sense of experimental purity, albeit in an altered form. The experiment became fundamentally linked with the form in which it largely remains today, i.e., as involving such elements as the isolation of independent and dependent variables, the control of extraneous variables, the manipulation of the independent variable, and the prediction of the dependent variable (Abelson, Frey, & Gregg, 2012; Danziger, 1997; Winston, 1990). This conceptualization of experimentation did not become but one understanding of experimentation among others – it became *the* understanding of experimentation, and is widely believed to be the *only* way to determine causation (Danziger, 2000, 1988; Stam, Radtke, & Lubek, 2000; Winston & Blais, 1996).

While the shift to this understanding of causation began in roughly the 1930s in the United States, it did not come to dominate textbook definitions in social psychology until several decades later (Toomela, 2007). The reasons for this turn are often believed to be "science envy" relative to the physical sciences, such as physics and chemistry. Interestingly, in the textbooks of these fields at the same time there is rarely if ever an explicit definition of an experiment given (Winston & Blais, 1996), nor of such constructs as independent and dependent variables (Winston, 1990; Winston & Blais, 1996). Danziger (2000) has argued that it was not physics and chemistry that served as the model for the definition of experimentation taken (implicitly) into social psychology, but rather, those produced by such fields as agriculture, education, and engineering. These fields were appealing trendsetters because of their undeniable practical value. The foundations of this practical bend in psychology, especially in American psychology, might reasonably be traced back further to earlier practices, such as Hugo Münsterberg's support of the Pragmatism of William James and Charles Sanders Peirce, and his rejection of Wilhelm Wundt's structuralism as being exact, but useless ("Ja, das ist exakt, aber das ist nichts nützlich" [sic]; cited in Landy, 1992, p. 788).

These developments led to the establishment of several key features of the psychological experiment as widely understood today (including work on the IPM discussed above). These features of the contemporary experiment illustrate how its epistemological assumptions are not neutral and that the practices it entails developed historically within a wider social context.

(1) *Materiality*. This is the general assumption that psychological phenomena can be captured by means of particular tools within experimental research (e.g., something visual outside the mind). This is arguably related to the broader notion of "science-as-technology" (Radder, 2003b). In its current form, this usually implies measurement along Likert, or Likert-like, scales (Michell, 2004).

(2) *Short term*. Experiments tend to focus on effects that can be seen quickly (within the time of the experiment), and that are spread out neither across time nor space. This is what Danziger (2000) calls the quality of being "local."

(3) *Demotic*. The results have to be "common," which is to say that they cannot be idiosyncratic lest they be unintelligible to others (or to the scientists studying them). This is a direct rejection of the focus on the "ideal" ("pure") nature of the experimental case, which assumes the idiosyncratic nature of individual cases, as seen in the thinking of Lewin (MacMartin & Winston, 2000).

(4) *Reproducibility of experiments and replicability of outcomes*. Experiments are believed to be reproducible and the results are expected to be replicable. In this sense, the modern experiment is generally nomothetic, and modern experimenters often even reject echoes of an ideographic nature in their own work (as can be seen in such practices as removing outliers) (Wagoner, 2017).

(5) *Decomposable*. This is the belief that complex psychological phenomena can be broken down into separate elements (variables) that can be studied independently of other variables and independently of the wider context (Danziger, 2000).

(6) *Fungibility*. The presumed fungibility of research participants is nicely illustrated by the common call for random assignment of participants to conditions. Researchers do not study "real" groups wherein people actually know each other or interact with each other, but rather they study "statistically constituted groups" comprised of strangers (Michell, 2004; Valsiner, 2017).

(7) *Proximal causation*. Within the contemporary experiment, the anticipated effect is expected to follow shortly after the cause, thereby making the cause identifiable. This also includes the assumption that the objects of experimental research do not occur randomly (Lana, 1969).

(8) *Prediction*. Experimentation contains the assumption of predictive power (despite the actually weak predictive power of experimental psychology; Smedslund, 2016). Stated in the reverse, the causes of psychological phenomena are believed to be discoverable and predictive of the same phenomena in the future (Lana, 1969).

(9) *Plasticity*. This is the assumption that variables can be manipulated by the researcher. Within identity research, this often presumes the malleability and naturally lability of identities (Oakes, 2002; Oyserman, Elmore, & Smith, 2012).

This particular understanding of experimentation has come to dominate textbook definitions of the psychological experiment and the majority of "mainstream" psychological experiments (Toomela, 2007). These features can be seen in research within the SIA, and more particularly within that on the IPM. However, this is certainly not the only way experiments are understood by psychologists. For example, Valsiner (2017, p. 69) defines an experiment as "a version of extrospective methods – an observation with specific performance tasks superimposed upon the participant and recording of the action sequences, while keeping the interview part of extrospection to the minimum," a definition that allows for ideographic research of idiosyncratic subjects. Other psychologists not only reject the now-dominant definition of experimentation, but they challenge the degree to which psychology can even be an empirical science in the first place (Smedslund, 2016; cf. Mazur & Watzlawik, 2016). The assertion of dominance by a particular understanding of experimentation can also speak to its (at least implicitly) contested nature (Winston & Blais, 1996, p. 609). That this understanding of experimentation was not *the* understanding held by everyone is nicely illustrated by the following statement made my Raymond Cattell (1990, as cited in Winston & Blais, 1996, p. 611):

> In my first visit to the United States in 1937 … I was surprised to note a course labelled as "experimental psychology." Was not all psychology experimental? … An experiment is an analysis of carefully observed data, controlled or uncontrolled … I once submitted a multivariate experimental article to the *Journal of Experimental Psychology* when Arthur Melton was editor and had it returned with "This is not an experiment."

Regardless of how interesting other conceptualizations of experimentation might be, the understanding discussed above has come to dominate psychology, including research conducted within the SIA (discussed above). However, the use of the experiment is not the only way SIA researchers work, nor need it be. We will now examine how this particular combination of theory and experimental methods within the SIA has shaped how identity is understood within this school of thought.

20.4 The Social Identity Approach and Experimental Research: Strange Bedfellows?

> It is vastly important to realize how much experimental thinking is controlled by experimental method and by experimental instrumentation and how hard it is, once methods and instruments have become accepted and established, to break away from their use.   (Bartlett, 1958, as cited in Wagoner, 2017, p. 40)

> In experiments we actively interfere with the material world. In one way or another, experimentation involves the material realization of an experimental process (the object[s] of study, the apparatus, and their interaction). The question, then, is this: What are the implications of this action and production character of scientific experimentation or philosophical debates on ontological, epistemological, and methodological issues about science? (Radder, 2003a, p. 4)

The SIA constitutes a theoretically broad and rich understanding of psychological life. Given its breadth, some understand it to approximate a "grand theory" in social psychology (Spears, 2011). At the same time, and for similar reasons, others criticize the SIA as being in effect unfalsifiable (Hogg & Williams, 2000). Interestingly, criticism of the SIA often arises not from issues related to theory, but from issues related to the experimental methods frequently employed in SIA research. For example, Jackson and Sherriff (2013) argue that SIA research has been largely limited by the methods researchers tend to employ. Similarly, Huddy (2001) is critical of many of the conclusions that are easily and often drawn from experimental research in the SIA (e.g., arguing that the "variables" in the Minimal Group Paradigm experiments are too simple, and that the assignment of participants to arbitrary groups is too artificial). It is important to underscore the fact that these are primarily methods-based critiques. However, SIA researchers often respond to such criticisms with theory-based arguments. For example, in responding to Huddy (2001), Oakes's (2002) riposte is largely based on the broader and more complex nature of SIA theory (e.g., that the psychological mechanisms underlying the Minimal Group Paradigm speak to more complicated and richer elements of SIA theory). Both claims may in fact be justified, but because they are speaking different languages – one related to the experimental methods and the other related to theory – they are each unable to satisfy the other. It is for this reason that the same arguments on both sides perennially appear in professional conversations, at conferences, and in the literature (e.g., Jackson & Sherriff, 2013). In as far as psychologists want experimental research to transcend the particular form and context of their creation and, from the other direction, in as far as psychologists believe theory to be open to empirical study, theory and method need to be made, at least temporarily, mutually intelligible by means of thoughtful reflection on their methodological assumptions. As illustrated in the quotations at the start of this section, one ought therefore to reflect on the use of experimental methods within the SIA, on what their effects are both with regard to the vision of identity that has resulted, and on the identity-related research practices of SIA researchers.

In order to better understand the use of experimental methods in the study of identity within the SIA, it is particularly useful to examine what are undoubtedly the most well-known studies in the SIA tradition, namely, those on the Minimal Group Paradigm (MGP; Tajfel et al., 1971; Turner, 1978). Within research on the MGP, participants are randomly assigned to one of two groups, and the degree of group-based discrimination is subsequently assessed. Tajfel and colleagues found that in such situations participants tend to favor the ingroup relative to the outgroup. Thus, the MGP asserts that assignment to a group is usually enough to evoke many of the group-based biases associated with group membership (e.g., ingroup favoritism, perceptions of ingroup homogeneity and intergroup difference). It is perhaps ironic that this paradigm should have arisen out of a school of thought that asserts the importance of the given social context for the study of identity – as the MGP in effect says that we can empirically study the social psychology of collective identities in the laboratory and in ways abstracted from "real" meaningful contexts. Important for our current discussion, the MGP nicely illustrates how supporters and critics of the SIA often speak different languages; one of experimental methods and one of SIA theory, as seen in the debate between Huddy (2001) and Oakes (2002) mentioned above. While supporters of SIA research often point to the breadth and depth of theory, criticism is frequently pointed at the limitations of experimental methods, which in effect leaves the debate, and particular contentious issues, perennially open. While early research in the SIA tradition was intended to champion a nonreductionist approach to social psychology (Hogg & Williams, 2000; Tajfel, Fraser, & Jaspars, 1984), the experimental methods SIA researchers employee suggest precisely the reductionist elements of the modern experiment discussed above. Thus, in the work of the SIA's "founding fathers," Tajfel and Turner, we see research with one foot on the ground of holistic system thinking and the other on that of the contemporary understanding of experimentation. In other words, the theoretical assumptions at the heart of the SIA retain the holism of earlier research (e.g., Lewin), while their empirical expressions in experimentation are significantly narrower in scope.[3]

A helpful example of the tension often found between theory and experimental method is seen in what are generally thought of as the independent and dependent variables within experimental research on the MGP. In as far as research on the MGP is understood to be an experiment – in the contemporary sense of the term discussed above – it is not surprising that people understand the random assignment of participants to groups as the independent variable, and the degree of subsequent ingroup-favoring discrimination to be the

---

[3] Similar tensions between broader theoretically derived methodological positions and experimental methods are seen in much of the seminal research in social psychology, such as Asch's (1951) work on conformity and Bartlett's (1932) work on memory. While these researchers were interested in broader, systemic understandings of psychological life – something that was reflected in *parts* of the way they approached data collection (e.g., post-experimental qualitative interviews, the belief in the idiosyncratic nature of subjects and experimental settings) – many subsequent researchers would see in them advocates of the contemporary experiment. Interestingly, Floyd Allport – who is often thought of as one of the earliest champions of controlled experimentation in social psychology – was himself pulled by both side of this more recent version of the classic dispute over methods, the *Methodenstreit* (Samelson, 2000).

dependent variable. This interpretation is widespread, and it lies at the heart of Huddy's (2001) criticism of the paradigm and of the SIA more broadly ("groups were designated by nothing other than a common label," p. 132). Speaking to how this interpretation has spread, we find the following explanation of the minimal paradigm in Aronson's (2012) popular textbook: "In this procedure ... complete strangers are divided into groups *using the most trivial, inconsequential criteria imaginable*" (p. 144, italics added). Speaking to this paradoxical combination of experimental methods and the SIA's (nonreductionist) methodology Hornsey (2008, p. 205) wrote:

> Given social identity theory's credentials as a theory with a strong focus on how the social context affects intergroup relations, it seems paradoxical that the ideas were framed by an experimental paradigm in which context was stripped away altogether: the "minimal group paradigm"... participants were allocated to groups on the basis of meaningless and arbitrary criteria.

When defending the MGP and the SIA more broadly against such attacks, Oakes (2002) argues that within SIA *theory*, random assignment to groups is not understood to be sufficient for ingroup favoritism. Carrying this over to this particular experimental work, she points to Turner's conclusion that "identification with these categories [by the subjects] needs to be firmly made. The latter seems to be a necessary condition for the influence of the former [i.e., categorization]" (Turner, 1978, as cited in Oakes, 2002, p. 811). Taking a category meaningfully into the self, by definition, makes that category no longer truly "arbitrary" for the participants (even if they may be so for the experimenters). Tajfel (1978) appreciated this element of identity, as he understood identity to possess both evaluative and cognitive characteristics. If the kind of group categorization seen in this research necessarily requires such a richer, more holistic psychological identification with the categories involved, we might then reasonably ask what such identification actually entails. As a wide body of psychological and philosophical literature indicates, it is reasonable to assume that that which is understood to constitute "me" – either individually or socially – will often be understood to be entitative, consistent, prioritized, and positive (Wetherell, 2010). In other words, making a category part of one's (psychological) identity can be thought of as, by itself, including these elements (Spears et al., 2009). Interestingly, in SIA research, these elements often appear to be the dependent variables of experimental research – those variables independent of and influenced by processes of categorization – as seen in the classic example of ingroup favoritism. In as far as they are treated as such, Huddy's (2001) reservations about the validity of random assignment to arbitrary groups seems to be founded. However, in as far as we give priority to Turner's broader interpretation, Oakes's (2002) claim of a richer understanding of psychological life seems justified, and importantly, this position in effect removes the clear distinction between independent variable and dependent variable as required by our contemporary understanding of the experiment. In other words, if we treat research on the minimal group paradigm as an experiment, we can expect people to look for independent variable(s), dependent variable(s), and the manipulation of the independent variable(s). However, if we do not interpret this research through the prism of such an experimental paradigm, we are free to interpret it in a more holistic, systemic manner.

In addition to the artificial separation of independent and dependent variables, there are several other implicit assumptions frequently made within SIA research on the basis of claims to experimentalism (as the concept is generally understood today). Given the space limitations of the given chapter we are only able to touch briefly on several of them here.

Cause-and-effect relationships. Researchers working within the SIA tradition frequently make claims of causal relationships between otherwise independent variables. As in the case of the definitional separation of independent and dependent variables discussed above, the possibility of simultaneity is ostensibly removed and replaced by linear, causal chains between separate variables. The predictive power supposedly gleaned from such relationships has a unique appeal to researchers and the wider public alike, and has been identified as one of the reasons for the unique popularity of experimental methods in psychological research in general (Oyserman, Elmore, & Smith, 2012; Smedslund, 2016).

The additive fallacy. When the predictive power of experiments fails or exceptions are found, additional "rules" are added. If identification with the group is not enough to evoke ingroup favoritism, something else must be added to explain the failed causal relationship (such as different kinds of ingroup identification, like the distinction between "identification" and "glorification"). If the drive for positive self-regard does not necessarily lead to competitive intergroup comparison, another rule explaining this failed connection needs to be added (e.g., the comparison has to been threatening). Such an explosion of rules for rules for rule underlies much of the SIA research we have seen in the past several decades. Similar processes are found in other areas of social psychological research, and speak to the deeply atomistic positivism of contemporary social psychology (for a discussion of the additive fallacy in relation to the psychological study of power, see Mazur, 2015). This tendency arises in large degree from claims to experimentation, and it would not necessarily appear in more holistic or systemic approaches to identity research within the Social Identity Approach.

Implicit essentialism. Related to the issues above, within SIA research (if not theory; Reicher & Hopkins, 2001), it often looks as though researchers posit the existence of groups prior the psychological identification therewith (Reicher, Spears, & Haslam, 2010). For example, we read that "group identity is likely to emerge among members of a high-status group because membership positively distinguishes group members from outsiders" (Huddy, 2001, p. 134). This reading of the SIA would certainly fit if group identification is understood as a variable independent of psychological processes of group identification. However, Oakes (2002) is right to claim that such a reading does not match the theoretical spirit of the SIA which, in fact, rejects such a "static conception" of a group whereby groups stand "side by side, almost like herring packed in a box, coming to life to 'perceive' each other whenever prodded into doing so" (Tajfel, 1982, p. 485). Within the SIA, identity is something that is *done*, not something that simply *is*. Identity is a verb, not a noun; part of "the identity *process* rather than fixed aspects of cognitive structure or personality" (Oakes, 2002, p. 817, italics original). These theoretical assertions aside, within the framework of contemporary experimentation, the ostensibly independent nature of variables suggests a degree of existence apart from the holistic system. What is more, essentialism is particularly appealing, and seems to fit widely held lay understandings of identity (Oyserman, Elmore, & Smith, 2012). Allport (1954, p. 174) wrote that identities are "nouns that cut slices" through our environment, and Verkuyten (2005, p. 47) stated that an "ontological definition is not about a gradual difference in terms of more or less of something, but about an absolute difference in the sense of being or not being. Social identities are expressed in the language of nouns." The claim to experimentation strengthens these assumptions (e.g., by requiring clearly distinguishable and independent variables), assumptions that are arguably not in line with the initial thinking of Tajfel and Turner.

Ahistoricity of objects and tools. To the extent that SIA research is thought to be experimental, it will be understood to concern itself with causal relations that can be observed in short time intervals. While the "introduction" and "general discussion" sections of research articles may contain references to history (where broader issues of theory can also be discussed), the "methods" and "results" sections will be ahistorical, in that both the initial manipulation and subsequent reaction need to be captured in the short period within which the experiment was run. This not only largely blinds researchers to the longer historical development of particular identities and the psychological mechanisms underlying identity, but it also overshadows the development of identities over time more broadly (Burkitt, 2011). For example, the features of experimental research discussed above seem to be particularly well suited to our modern understanding of identities as being multiple, fragmented, often conflictual or at least competitive, and often involving choice (e.g., Taylor, 1989; Baumeister, 1986; Bamberg & Dege, Chapter 2 in this volume). It seems less well suited to the integrated, complementary, and largely ascribed identities described over a century ago by the likes of Max Weber, Gustaw Ichheiser, and Émile Durkheim. According to Danziger (2000, p. 345) "the model of social life presupposed by the most popular procedures of the social psychological laboratory seem[s] to approximate an anomic state in which isolated individuals without historical ties drift from one brief encounter to another." For similar reasons, SIA research may also in many ways be surprisingly culture-specific. For example, the presumed drives toward the reduction of uncertainty and toward a relative positive image may be important in some cultures but not others (Yuki, 2003), and such research often overlooks the historicity of social identities in general (e.g., historical shifts in who identifies in the US as Native American; Nagel, 1995). Thus, the "purity" of the controlled experiment comes – by definition and design – at a price.

Evaluation via comparison. The contemporary experiment requires some form of comparison, either across experimental conditions or between experimental and control conditions. If such explicit comparisons are not given, there is often an implicit ex post facto assumption of a steady state prior to the administration of the manipulation (Lana, 1969). Establishing such a "base state" or "neutral state" was actually the initial goal in Tajfel's minimal group studies and in Milgram's (1963) well-known obedience studies. The focus on competitive (intergroup) comparisons has also at least partially contributed to the decline of intragroup research (Wittenbaum & Moreland, 2008), something that may be encouraged in some, but not other, research contexts (e.g., as intragroup comparisons have been reported to be more important than intergroup comparisons in some communities; Yuki, 2003). The assumption that evaluations can only be made on the basis of comparisons fits well with (or has perhaps even fueled) a wider intellectual climate in which (relative) abnormality, illness, and even conflict are deemed more interesting (as they are necessarily determined via comparison) than "invisible" normality, health, or "hidden harmony" (which need not require comparison) (Mazur, 2015; Mazur & Sztuka, 2021).

Thus, while SIA theory would seem to support a broad understanding of identity on a theoretical level, that broad conceptualization is necessarily narrowed to the extent that it is expressed by means of the contemporary experiment. Such tension between experimental methods and theoretical positions within SIA research on identity is nicely illustrated in the example of the IPM discussed above. In as far as it is understood to be "just" a correlational model, the IPM does not contain those additional elements that historically came to separate the contemporary experiment from empirical research (i.e., independent variables, dependent variables, the manipulation of the independent variables, and causal relations between variables). However, the IPM can be, and often is, studied via experimental methods (e.g., by manipulating group assignment or comparison group). In other words, in as far as work on the IPM does not constitute an experiment, it can be understood as a systemic model that is generally in line with Gestalt-like, systemic thinking. Seen through this lens (as a correlational model), the IPM posits no clear distinction between independent and dependent variables, as ingroup projection is expected to *correlate with*, not necessarily *cause*, ingroup favoritism. The two might just as easily be thought of as simultaneously occurring elements of the larger psychological mechanisms underlying identity. Within such a nonexperimental understanding, the IPM avoids the additive fallacy in as far as new knowledge is rooted in theory (in the Lewinian spirit), rather than nomothetic, aggregate empirical data and presumed causal links between independent variables. Implicit essentialism is avoided to the extent that all of the identity categories and characteristics involved are mutually interdependent, and collectively determining of the characteristics that become salient (they are not "fixed" and "out there" in the world before they take on psychological significance). The IPM avoids removing identities and their evaluations from the broader historical context to the extent that participants are able themselves to identify and define the identities and identity features in question, and due to the fact that the analysis is not limited to the short time window of an experiment. In that regard, the features identified in the IPM can be thought of as similar to the influence of history and culture within Bartlett's serial reproduction task. While nonexperimental research on the IPM need not contain these first five "experiment friendly" assumptions, it does assume that evaluations are made on the basis of comparison. This assumption lies at the core of the SIA, and will appear in any work within that tradition (and it will be strengthened within experimental work) (Spears, 2011). Thus, we can see that some, but not all, of the assumptions discussed above arise primarily from the use of experimental methods, and not necessarily from SIA theory. Once these distinctions are more clearly understood, we can reflect on the degree to which experimentation, relative to SIA theory, is desirable or undesirable, helpful or distracting, enlightening or misleading.

20.5 Conclusions

"If . . . human reactions had been built up to meet a series of unchanging environments, emphatic insistence upon rigidity of [experimental] conditions would be justifiable. Obviously, they are not so built" (Bartlett, 1930, as cited in Wagoner, 2017, p. 40). This quotation nicely captures Frederic Bartlett's skepticism toward the demands of experimental methods (as here discussed) when it comes to the study of human psychology. A similar tension between reductionist experimental methods and nonreductionist theory can be found in the seminal work on identity of Tajfel and Turner, and subsequently in those who would work in what has come to be known as the Social Identity Approach (SIA). It has been argued in the current chapter that in as far as the study of identity within the SIA is understood to be experimental it will be constrained in the various ways discussed above – for better and/or for worse. It is therefore incumbent upon psychologists working within the SIA tradition to reflect on the degree to which experimental methods are true to the methodological assumptions of SIA theory, and if those methods are able to help us address the questions we are asking as psychologists.

Identity researchers have long been aware of how easy it is to artificially limit the nature of their subject, either explicitly or implicitly. For example, the utility of a priori identity categories, such as those that appear on national surveys, has been long debated (Bowker & Star, 1999). The same issues lie at the heart of many criticisms of the Minimal Group Paradigm (e.g., Huddy, 2001), criticisms which are not entirely satisfied by pointing to richer, more complex theory (e.g., Oakes, 2002). The methods we use in themselves contain methodological assumptions, and those assumptions may or may not be in line with the methodologies we would produce on the basis of theory alone. All six of the experimental-based methodological assumptions discussed above (the artificial separation of independent and dependent variables, cause-and-effect relationships, the additive fallacy, implicit essentialism, the ahistoricity of objects and tools, and evaluation via comparison) appear when contemporary experimental methods are used in SIA research, and the fact that such methods are not summarily rejected by SIA researchers for that reason attests to the fact that they *at least appear to* fit SIA theory to some degree in the eyes of SIA researchers. To be clear, however, not all research within the SIA is experimental (e.g., Jackson & Sherriff, 2013). It also needs be mentioned that there are other schools of thought outside the SIA wherein researchers can and do categorically reject the experimental methods described above (e.g., various versions of cultural psychology, social constructionism, narrative psychology, discursive analysis, psychoanalytical psychologies).

To be clear, this chapter ought not to be understood as a rejection of experimental methods. Rather, it is an attempt to point to some of the ways in which the use of experimental methods within the SIA influence the ways we understand identity, primarily by constraining the scope of inquiry in various important ways. Such constraints are, after all, built into the scientific method itself:

> This is the paradox of imagination in science, that it has for its aim the impoverishment of imagination. By that outrageous phrase, I mean that the highest flight of scientific imagination is to weed out the proliferation of new ideas. In science, the grand view is a miserly view, and a rich model of the universe is one which is as poor as possible in hypotheses.
> (Bronowski, 1964, p. 46)

At the same time, the scientific method is also by design both eternally open to further development and encouraging of what Ernst Mach (1883, as cited in Rheinberger, 2007, p. 8) called "toleration of an incomplete conception of the world and the preference for it rather than an apparently perfect, but inadequate conception." In this spirit, many have called for greater tolerance of uncertainty in our attempts to understand the world, including identity (e.g., Bancroft, 2014). Therefore, in methods and theory, we can simultaneously strive for greater conceptual clarity and remain skeptical of our ability to ever complete the picture. Within identity research in the SIA tradition, the artificiality of the experimental method is both a strength and a weakness. Keeping this in mind will allow researchers to examine the degree to which criticisms of those methods are in fact criticisms of SIA theory. It has been argued in this chapter that the majority of such criticisms do not in fact speak to SIA theory: "The very richness of the theory is also a source of danger. Particular postulates can be drawn from the overall framework and developed in ways that ignore or even contradict its foundational premises" (Reicher, Spears, & Haslam, 2010, p. 45). The lessons discussed in this chapter are therefore also important for the growth of theory. Within the proliferation of data gathering that has come to color a large portion of social psychological publications (Valsiner, 2017), greater clarity about methodological assumptions will allow for deeper reflection on what the data might mean for theory. In this vein, we can see that the current "replication crisis" in social psychology can only be partially addressed by more replication itself, and it cannot be more fully addressed without careful thought given to the methodological assumptions underlying our research, especially the methodological links between method and theory. A more open discussion of the methodological assumptions of method and theory within experimental research on identity (and empirical identity research more broadly) would therefore allow for constructive discussions about the limitations and strengths of both method and theory and of potential matches and mismatches between them.

References

Abelson, R. P., Frey, K. P., & Gregg, A. P. (2012). *Experiments with People. Revelations from Social Psychology, 2nd Ed*. New York, NY: Psychology Press.

Abrams, D. & Hogg, M. A. (2010). Social identity and self-categorization. In J. F. Dovidio, M. Hewstone, P. Glick, & V. M. Esses (Eds.), *The Sage Handbook of Prejudice, Stereotyping and Discrimination* (pp. 179–193). London: Sage.

Adorno, T. W., Frenkel-Brunswik, E., Levinson, D. J., & Sanford, R. N. (1950). *The Authoritarian Personality*. New York, NY: Harper & Brothers.

Allport, G. W. (1954). *The Nature of Prejudice*. Reading, MA: Addison-Wesley.

Aronson, E. (2012). *The Social Animal, 11th Ed*. New York, NY: Worth.

Aronson, E. & Carlsmith, J. M. (1968). Experimentation in social psychology. In G. Lindzey & E. Aronson (Eds.), *Handbook of Social Psychology, 2nd Ed., Vol. 2* (pp. 1–79). Reading, MA: Addison-Wesley.

Asch, S. E. (1951). Effects of group pressure on the modification and distortion of judgments. In H. Guetzkow (Ed.), *Groups, Leadership and Men* (pp. 177–190). Pittsburgh, PA: Carnegie Press.

Bancroft, J. (2014). *Tolerance of Uncertainty*. Bloomington, IN: Author House.

Bartlett, F. C. (1932). *Remembering: A Study in Experimental and Social Psychology*. Cambridge: Cambridge University Press.

Baumeister, R. F. (1986). *Identity: Cultural Change and the Struggle for Self*. New York, NY: Oxford University Press.

Bowker, G. C. & Star, S. L. (1999). *Sorting Things Out: Classification and Its Consequences*. Cambridge, MA: MIT Press.

Bronowski, J. (1964). *The Identity of Man*. Garden City, NY: American Museum Science Books.

Burkitt, I. (2011). Identity construction in sociohistorical context. In S. J. Schwartz, K. Luyckx, & V. L. Vignoles (Eds.), *Handbook of Identity Theory and Research* (pp. 267–283). New York, NY: Springer.

Cassirer, E. (1910/1923). *Substanzbegriff und Funktionsbegriff: Untersuchungen über die Grundfragen der Erkenntniskritik*. Berlin: Bruno Cassirer. Trans. by W. C. Swabey & M. C. Swabey as *Substance and Function*. Chicago, IL: Open Court.

Danziger, K. (1988). On theory and method in psychology. In W. J. Baker, L. P. Mos, H. V. Rappard, & H. J. Stam (Eds.), *Recent Trends in Theoretical Psychology* (pp. 87–94). New York, NY: Springer-Verlag.

Danziger, K. (1990). *Constructing the Subject: Historical Origins of Psychological Research*. Cambridge: Cambridge University Press.

Danziger, K. (1992). The project of an experimental social psychology: Historical perspectives. *Science in Context, 5*, 309–328.

Danziger, K. (1997). *Naming the Mind: How Psychology Found Its Language*. London: Sage.

Danziger, K. (2000). Making social psychology experimental: A conceptual history, 1920–1970. *Journal of the History of the Behavioral Sciences, 36*(4), 329–347.

Dollard, J., Miller, N. E., Doob, L. W., Mowrer, O. H., & Sears, R. R. (1939). *Frustration and Aggression*. New Haven, CT: Yale University Press.

Hammack, P. L. (2015). Theoretical foundations of identity. In K. C. McLean & M. Syed (Eds.), *The Oxford Handbook of Identity Development* (pp. 11–32). Oxford: Oxford University Press.

Haslam, S. A. (2004). *Psychology in Organisations: The Social Identity Approach, 2nd Ed*. London: Sage.

Hogg, M. A. (2006). Social identity theory. In P. J. Burke (Ed.), *Contemporary Social Psychological Theories* (pp. 111–136). Stanford, CA: Stanford University Press.

Hogg, M. A. (2012). Social identity and the psychology of groups. In M. R. Leary & J. P. Tangney (Eds.), *Handbook of Self and Identity, 2nd Ed*. (pp. 502–520). New York, NY: Guilford Press.

Hogg, M. A. & Williams, K. D. (2000). From I to we: Social identity and the collective self. *Group Dynamics: Theory, Research, and Practice, 4*, 81–97.

Hornsey, M. J. (2008). Social identity theory and self-categorization theory: A historical review, *Social and Personality Psychology Compass, 2*(1), 204–22.

Huddy, L. (2001). From social to political identity: A critical examination of social identity theory. *Political Psychology, 22*(1), 127–155.

Jackson, C. & Sherriff, N. (2013). A qualitative approach to intergroup relations: Exploring the applicability of the social identity approach to "messy" school contexts. *Qualitative Research in Psychology, 10*, 259–273.

Lana, R. E. (1969). *Assumptions of Social Psychology*. New York, NY: Appleton-Century-Crofts.

Landy, F. J. (1992). Hugo Münsterberg: Victim or visionary? *Journal of Applied Psychology*, *77*(6), 787–802.

Lewin, K. (1943). Psychology and the process of group living. *Journal of Social Psychology*, *17*(1), 113–131.

MacMartin, C. & Winston, A. S. (2000). The rhetoric of experimental social psychology, 1930–1960: From caution to enthusiasm. *Journal of the History of the Behavioral Sciences*, *36*(4), 349–364.

Mazur, L. B. (2015). Defining power in social psychology. *Orbis Idearum*, *2*(1), 101–114.

Mazur, L. B. & Sztuka, M. (2021). Hidden harmony. Converging interests in the development of prison reform. *Theoretical Criminology*, *25*(1), 149–168.

Mazur, L. B. & Watzlawik, M. (2016). Debates about the scientific status of psychology: Looking at the bright side. *Integrative Psychological and Behavioral Science*, *50*(4), 555–567.

Michell, J. (2004). *Measurement in Psychology: Critical History of a Methodological Concept*. Cambridge: Cambridge University Press.

Milgram, S. (1963). Behavioral study of obedience. *Journal of Abnormal and Social Psychology*, *67*(4), 371–378.

Mummendey, A. & Wenzel, M. (1999). Social discrimination and tolerance in intergroup relations: Reactions to intergroup difference. *Personality and Social Psychology Review*, *3*, 158–174.

Murphy, G., & Murphy, L. B. (1931). *Experimental Social Psychology*. New York, NY: Harper.

Nagel, J. (1995). American Indian ethnic renewal: Politics and the resurgence of identity. *American Sociological Review*, *60*, 947–965.

Oakes, P. (2002). Psychological groups and political psychology: A response to Huddy's "Critical examination of social identity theory." *Political Psychology*, *23*(4), 809–824.

Oyserman, D., Elmore, K., & Smith, G. (2012). Self, self-concept, and identity. In M. R. Leary & J. P. Tangney (Eds.), *Handbook of Self and Identity, 2nd Ed.* (pp. 69–104). New York, NY: Guilford Press.

Parkovnick, S. (2000). Contextualizing Floyd Allport's *Social Psychology*. *Journal of the History of the Behavioral Sciences*, *36*(4), 429–441.

Radder, H. (2003a). Toward a more developed philosophy of scientific experimentation. In H. Radder (Ed.), *The Philosophy of Scientific Experimentation* (pp. 1–18). Pittsburgh, PA: University of Pittsburgh Press.

Radder, H. (2003b). Technology and theory in experimental science. In H. Radder (Ed.), *The Philosophy of Scientific Experimentation* (pp. 152–173). Pittsburgh, PA: University of Pittsburgh Press.

Reicher, S. & Hopkins, N. (2001). Psychology and the end of history: A critique and a proposal for the psychology of social categorisation. *Political Psychology*, *22*, 383–407.

Reicher, S., Spears, R., & Haslam, S. H. (2010). The social identity approach in social psychology. In M. Wetherell & C. T. Mohanty (Eds.), *Sage Handbook of Identities* (pp. 45–62). Los Angeles, CA: Sage.

Rheinberger, H.-J. (2007). *On Historicizing Epistemology: An Essay*, translated by D. Fernbach. Stanford, CA: Stanford University Press.

Rosa, M. & Waldzus, S. (2012). Efficiency and defense motivated ingroup projection: Sources of prototypicality in intergroup relations. *Journal of Experimental Social Psychology*, *48*, 669–681.

Sindic, D. & Condor, S. (2014). Social identity theory and self-categorization theory. T. Capelos, C. Kinvall, P Nesbitt-Larkin & H. Dekker (Eds.), *The Palgrave Handbook of Global Political Psychology* (pp. 39–54). Basingstoke: Palgrave.

Sindic, D. & Reicher, S. D. (2008). The instrumental use of group prototypicality judgments. *Journal of Experimental Social Psychology*, *44*, 1425–1435.

Samelson, F. (2000). Whig and anti-Whig histories – and other curiosities of social psychology. *Journal of the History of the Behavioral Sciences*, *36*(4), 499–506.

Simmel, G. (1950). *The Sociology of Georg Simmel*, translated and edited by K. H. Wolff. New York, NY: Free Press.

Smedslund, J. (2016). Why psychology cannot be an empirical science. *Integrative Psychological and Behavioral Science*, *50*(2), 185–195.

Spears, R. (2011). Group identities: The social identity perspective. In S. J. Schwartz, K. Luyckx, & V. L. Vignoles (Eds.), *Handbook of Identity Theory and Research* (pp. 201–224). New York, NY: Springer.

Spears, R., Jetten, J., Scheepers, D., & Cihangir, S. (2009). Creative distinctiveness. Explaining in-group bias in minimal groups. In S. Otten, K. Sassenberg, & T. Kessler (Eds.), *Intergroup Relations. The Role of Motivation and Emotion* (pp. 23–40). New York, NY: Psychology Press.

Stam, H. J., Radtke, H. L., & Lubek, I. (2000). Strains in experimental social psychology: A textual analysis of the development of experimentation in social psychology. *Journal of the History of the Behavioral Sciences*, *36*(4), 365–382.

Tajfel, H. (1972). Some developments in European social psychology. *European Journal of Social Psychology*, *2*(3), 307–321. (Ed.) (1978). *Differentiation between Social Groups: Studies in the Social Psychology of Intergroup Relations*. London: Academic Press.

Tajfel, H. (Ed.). (1982). *Social Identity and Intergroup Relations*. Cambridge: Cambridge University Press.

Tajfel, H., Billig, M. G., Bundy, R. P., & Flament, C. (1971). Social categorization and intergroup behavior. *European Journal of Social Psychology*, *1*, 149–178.

Tajfel, H., Fraser, C., & Jaspars, J. M. F. (Eds.). (1984). *The Social Dimension: Volume 1: European Developments in Social Psychology*. Cambridge: Cambridge University Press.

Tajfel, H. & Turner, J. (1979). An integrative theory of intergroup conflict. In W. G. Austin & S. Worchel (Eds.), *The Social Psychology of Intergroup Relations* (pp. 33–48). Monterey, CA: Brooks & Cole.

Tajfel, H. & Turner, J. (1986). The social identity theory of intergroup behavior. In S. Worchel & W. G. Austin (Eds.), *Psychology of Intergroup Relations* (pp. 7–24). Chicago, IL: Hall Publishers.

Taylor, C. (1989). *Sources of the Self: The Making of the Modern Identity*. Cambridge, MA: Harvard University Press.

Toomela, A. (2007). History of methodology in psychology: Starting point, not the goal. *Integrative Psychological and Behavioral Science*, *41*, 75–82.

Toomela, A. (2010). Quantitative methods in psychology: Inevitable and useless. *Frontiers in Quantitative Psychology and Measurement*, *1*(29), 1–14.

Turner, J. C. (1975). Social comparison and social identity: Some prospects for inter-group behaviour. *European Journal of Social Psychology*, *5*(1), 1–34.

Turner, J. C. (1978). Social categorization and social discrimination in the minimal group paradigm. In H. Tajfel (Ed.), *Differentiation between Social Groups: Studies in the Social Psychology of Intergroup Relations* (pp. 235–250). London: Academic Press.

Turner, J. C. & Reynolds, K. J. (2010). The story of social identity. In T. Postmes & N. Branscombe (Eds.), *Rediscovering Social Identity: Core Sources* (pp. 13–32). New York, NY: Psychology Press.

Ullrich, J. (2009). Reconsidering the "relative" in relative ingroup prototypicality. *European Journal of Social Psychology*, *39*(2), 299–310.

Valsiner, J. (2012). *A Guided Science: History of Psychology in the Mirror of Its Making*. Piscataway, NJ: Transaction.

Valsiner, J. (2017). *From Methodology to Methods in Human Psychology*. Cham: Springer.

Verkuyten, M. (2005). *The Social Psychology of Ethnic Identity*. New York, NY: Psychology Press.

Wagoner, B. (2017). *The Constructive Mind: Bartlett's Psychology in Reconstruction*. Cambridge: Cambridge University Press.

Waldzus, S. & Mummendey, A. (2004). Inclusion in a superordinate category, ingroup prototypicality, and attitudes towards outgroups. *Journal of Experimental Social Psychology*, *40*, 466–477.

Wenzel, M., Mummendey, A., & Waldzus, S. (2008). Superordinate identities and intergroup conflict: The ingroup projection model. *European Review of Social Psychology*, *18*(1), 331–372.

Wenzel, M., Mummendey, A., Weber, U., & Waldzus, S. (2003). The ingroup as *pars pro toto*: Projection from the ingroup onto the inclusive category as a precursor to social discrimination. *Personality and Social Psychology Bulletin*, *29*(4), 461–473.

Wetherell, M. (2010). The field of identity studies. In M. Wetherell & C. T. Mohanty (Eds.), *Sage Handbook of Identities* (pp. 3–26). Los Angeles, CA: Sage.

Winston, A. S. (1990). Robert Sessions Woodworth and the "Columbia Bible": How the psychological experiment was redefined. *American Journal of Psychology*, *103*, 391–401.

Winston, A. S. & Blais, D. J. (1996). What counts as an experiment? A transdisciplinary analysis of textbooks, 1930-1970. *American Journal of Psychology*, *109*, 599–616.

Wittenbaum, G. M. & Moreland, R. L. (2008). Small-group research in social psychology: Topics and trends over time. *Social and Personality Psychology Compass*, *2*(1), 187–203.

Yuki, M. (2003). Intergroup comparison versus intragroup relationships: A cross-cultural examination of social identity theory in North American and East Asian cultural contexts. *Social Psychology Quarterly*, *66*, 166–183.

PART IV

Current Domains

21 Critical Perspectives in Clinical Psychology: Autistic Identities

Alessandra Fasulo

When Australian comedian Hannah Gadsby wrote her first stand-up show, *Nanette* (2018), about her experience as a gay woman, she had also been recently diagnosed with autism, but decided against mentioning it. She went on to discuss her autism only in her second show, *Douglas*, written two years later. Gadsby thought the stigma around autism might have undermined the rest of her story and she needed time to process her diagnosis (Thomas, 2020). Conversely, UK playwriter Rhiannon Lloyd-Williams wrote her first theater piece, *The Duck* (2016), right after her diagnosis. After five years, she reflects:

> I couldn't write it now. Being autistic was something new to me, it was a beacon, it stood out as my most relevant label because I was still processing the information I'd been given. Being autistic is still an important part of who I am [but] ... somewhere along the way that label slipped in alongside all my other ones; it sits comfortably alongside "mother" and "Welsh." (Lloyd-Williams, 2020)

Both Gadsby and Lloyd-Williams were diagnosed with autism in their twenties but, in entering the public arena for the first time (as good an identity claim as ever there was one), one felt that being autistic was less urgent and defining than being gay, whereas for the other autism took precedence and oriented her self-understanding, as the metaphor of the beacon reveals. Both Gadsby's second show *Douglas* and Lloyd-Williams's *Duck*, however, have in common the drive to explain autism to their audiences, and, to use Gadsby's words "create points of accessibility"; they also emphasize that people in the autistic spectrum are not necessarily similar to one another.

The story of those two women is a good introduction for how identity and autism are going to be interpreted in this chapter. Autism is a powerful label, and when a person gets diagnosed, they – and their closest circle – can feel all the weight of already-established notions and expectations. Autism, however, neither determines the personality, skills, preferences, and life choices of the individuals with the condition, nor does it have to be foregrounded in all social

I wish to thank Philip Adrian Hunt, a long-standing collaborator in autism research who has opened up this field for me; the editors, especially Carolin Demuth and Michael Bamberg, for the fine-comb revision, and Steven Kapp, autism scholar, advocate of neurodiversity, and colleague in Portsmouth, for enriching both my reading list and my general perspective on autism.

transactions. Furthermore, every new person living with autism is adding to the general understanding of what autism is, altering, for them and everyone else with the condition, the very atmosphere that the identity breathes.

Definitions of autism that are produced in different arenas of the public sphere – science, media, individuals with and without autism – are always intersecting, but here will be treated separately for analytical and theoretical purposes. Thus, after a critique of the notion of identity within the social sciences, and a brief history of autism, this chapter will discuss autistic identity under three separate strands: as collective identity, as identification, and as self-understanding.

21.1 Identity: Limits and Alternatives of a Concept

The term identity has recently gone under scrutiny in the social sciences because of a mismatch between the meaning of the word – the semantics of which incorporates "sameness" – and the processes it is currently used to describe, i.e., the dynamics of multiple and contextually variable identifications (Bendle, 2002; Block, 2006; Brubaker & Cooper, 2000; see Fasulo & Piazza, 2015 for a review). Brubaker and Cooper (2000) argue that is not clear why something so fleeting and mutable should also be so important for social actors. Others criticize constructivist approaches to identity because, while stressing identity's multiplicity and situated nature, often do not challenge the reality and internal homogeneity of the social categories the identities refer to – for example, gender, ethnicity, or indeed a condition like autism – thereby reinstating the essentialist view that they were trying to get rid of in the first place (Caniglia, 2013).

Brubaker and Cooper (2000) distinguish three different types of phenomena that, they argue, are conflated under the term identity in current socio-psychological research. The first is collective identity, or groupness, and refers distinctly to the feeling of being associated with others under a particular label. Collective identities can be more salient when groups act together in public performances or to achieve social change, but the sense of belonging can also remain entirely in the symbolic sphere. The second type, identification, looks at the semiotic processes – discourse, narratives, imagery – that fabricate identity by generating shared meaning around labels and social categories. Finally, there is the dimension of self-understanding, which concern the ways in which labels or social categories become part of individual subjectivities.

Autism is a label for a medical and psychiatric condition, but it is also a cultural phenomenon, a flag for political activism and a type of subjectivity. Given this complexity, it is all the more relevant to distinguish between the different threads delineated above. Definitions and understandings, and therefore criteria for assigning people to the autistic spectrum disorder (ASD), are interdependent and in constant motion (Silberman, 2017). Furthermore, to use McGrath's term, (2017) there can be "cultural disorders" in portraying both the condition and the people who are diagnosed with it, with substantial consequences for autistic people and the society at large, because such understandings will affect how we can create environments in which people with autism can thrive.

This chapter will illustrate identity in autism following the tripartite organization explained above, after a brief history of how autism came about in psychiatry and its current medical definitions.

21.2 Autism: The Makers

Autism was not named as a distinct condition until the 1940s; around that time, psychiatrists Hans Asperger (1940) in Austria and Leo Kanner (1943) in the United States gave the same name to a syndrome they had observed in children (Frith, 1991). Apart from some differences that will be explained later, both scientists described the condition as characterized by social and affective isolation, inflexible and repetitive patterns of behavior, restricted interests, and communication impairments.

There is evidence of more connections between the two scholars than previously thought;[1] however, the almost simultaneous identification of the syndrome has been interpreted in relation to cultural changes preceding the discovery. Autism is diagnosed on an entirely behavioral basis, and therefore medical and societal culture in general are the background against which autism-related behaviors will stand out as pathological (Belmonte, 2008).[2] A factor possibly partaking in the creation of autism is the diffusion of modernism, the literary and aesthetic sensibility that swept across most of the Western world in the first decades of the twenty-first century.[3] Modernist fiction presented socially isolated characters, who doubt that they share the same reality as their contemporaries, have trouble communicating, and are constantly in pursuit of their own identity (McDonagh, 2008). "Modernism," McDonagh argues (2008, p. 111), "articulated the complexities of the modern identity, and in so doing enabled physicians

---

[1] Silberman (2017) reported that a close collaborator of Asperger in Vienna was later hired as assisstant in Kanner's lab in the US.

[2] Barazzetti et al. (2017), analyzing the archive of an Italian psychiatric hospital, argue that until the end of the nineteenth century, "idiocy" was probably the diagnosis most autistic children would get; this would result in institutionalization that in turn prevented any developmental adjustment through participation in social life. McDonagh (2008) further argues that psychiatrists had fine differentiations about types of idiocy and their causes, so the lack of a category for autism was not due to absence of close examination of children and adults with this diagnosis, but to cultural reasons.

[3] Examples of such new literary characters are the protagonists of the books of Samuel Beckett, Robert Musil, James Joyce, and Virginia Woolf, as well as Melville's iconic *Bartleby, the Scrivener*. As reported in the opening lines of McDonagh's chapter, changes in the idea of personhood and self driven by modernism were apparent even for people living at the time.

to perceive that new form of being, the autistic person, defined by an extreme aloneness, apparent egoism, and an idiosyncratic use of language." Further factors that might have heightened the visibility of autism are the growth of importance of psychological sciences and mass schooling, the convergent effects of which was an increased attention and control over children's performances, as well as production of a "discursive field" for it (Davies, 2015, p. 202).

Between Kanner and Asperger, it was Kanner's work which had initially the strongest influence on medical understandings of autism, because Asperger's publication remained buried under the ashes of the Nazi regime for several decades. Kanner was an Austrian psychiatrist who had studied in Germany, but had moved to the United States in the 1930s. There he established his lab and enjoyed a very fortunate career. Despite some accurate descriptions that remain in use for autism diagnosis to date (Kanner 1943), his contribution is controversial. He divulged the theory that autism was caused by parental rearing practices and especially by the "refrigerator mother," even disregarding evidence against these claims among his own patients; he also restricted the diagnosis to those children who appeared profoundly disconnected from their social environment, and either did not speak at all or used language in noncommunicative ways. Not surprisingly, the syndrome was reputed to be very rare, as only about 0.5% of children present the full symptom configuration Kanner had insisted on.

Asperger's work was rediscovered at the end of the 1970s by Lorna Wing,[4] an English psychiatrist with an autistic daughter. Unlike Kanner, Asperger believed in the efficacy of interventions and worked with his collaborators to develop educational strategies for autistic children (Asperger, 1940/1991). His diagnostic criteria allowed more variation in terms of children's linguistic abilities and social behavior, and included the possible presence of other strengths, sometimes at exceptional levels. Wing, on the basis of Asperger's paper and her own observations, became convinced that heterogeneity was an intrinsic characteristic of this condition, and coined the term "autistic spectrum" to refer to such variability. However, because autism was by this time known as a very frightening disorder, Wing thought that parents might find it easier to come forward if a different diagnostic label were used for children with less evident manifestations (Silberman, 2017). "Asperger syndrome" was thus born, and was later included, alongside Kanner's autism, in the fourth edition of *Diagnostic and Statistical Manual of Mental Disorders* (APA, 1994).

The new label, which protected people from the worst images associated with autism, favored the development of the "Aspie" identity, a nickname and a profile that came to identify a group of people, mostly male, with odd behaviors and poor social abilities, but above average skills in some specific

---

[4] A further delay was caused by publishers' resistance to printing Asperger's work because he had served under the Nazi regime. Eventually, Uta Frith managed to add a translation of Asperger's original paper in her 1991 edited volume.

area of interest. Autism and Asperger were reunified under the same diagnostic category in 2013 with the fifth edition of the *Diagnostic and Statistical Manual of Mental Disorders* (DSM 5), because the distinction introduced by Wing did not prove diagnostically useful in the long run. In the twenty years that had passed, medical and societal views on autism had changed substantially, so, although not without some shaking within the community, the label of autism now offered an identity that was not exclusively in negative terms. It is also worth noting that, for the first time, autistic people contributed to the revision of the *Manual* for the autism entry (Kapp, 2020).

While the diagnostic criteria in the most widely used classifications nowadays (like the DSM 5, or the ICD-11)[5] are still centered on social impairments and restricted interests, research has been recently focusing more on the peculiarities of the sensorial system (Markram & Markram, 2010) and the neurological characteristics at the basis of the difficulty in initiating behaviors (Muratori & Maestro, 2007; Trevarthen & Delafield-Butt, 2013). Such new perspectives have led to the hypothesis that social and communicative difficulties may not be intrinsic characteristics of the condition (like the autistic withdrawal), but cascade consequences of other impairments preventing developmental learning.[6]

Researchers agree on general characterizations of autism that are often also appropriated by autistic people as an aid for making sense of what they struggle with. These are a predominance of local over global coherence, e.g., attention and memory for details but difficulties with narrative and synthetic discourse, and impairments in executive functioning, which is involved in forming and executing plans (Frith, 2003). The shift from a psychological to a neurological etiology,[7] besides clearing the parental role as regards the insurgence of the condition, also changed the understanding of autism from a developmental disorder to a permanent disability, and with it the emphasis from intervention as cure to forms of lifelong support instead.

We now turn to consider issues of identity in autism according to the three areas outlined in the first part of the chapter.

21.2.1 Autism as Collective Identity, or "Groupness"

The component of identity that we can call "collective," or refer to as the "groupness" aspect of identity, includes both commonality and connectedness.

---

[5] The International Classification of Diseases 11th Revision is the diagnostic manual developed by the World Health Organization.

[6] For example, according to the Theory of the Intense World (Markram & Markram, 2010) the heightened intensity with which an individual experiences the social environment is the cause of withdrawal and anxiety, not a lack of motivation for social contact and relations.

[7] To date, research has not been able to confirm specific genetic factors or neurological anomalies related to autism, because existing results are compatible with different hypotheses (Belmonte, 2008).

Commonality captures the sharing of some common attributes, whereby a certain number of individuals can be labeled in the same way; connectedness indicates that those individuals are part of a network defined by such label gathering (Brubaker & Cooper, 2000, p. 20). Whether or not people are actively taking part in common enterprises or social gatherings, the network is there as a possibility.

The history of the development of an autistic collective identity begins with the initiative of parents of autistic individuals. Parents started to meet, and to get to know each other, at conferences organized by medical or charitable institutions; soon enough, frustrated by the dismissal of their experiences and the lingering suspicions around bad parenting, they formed independent associations and online discussion spaces (Silberman, 2017). These new arenas, free of the control of the medical establishment, started then to see the participation of autistic people themselves; this in turn led to the creation of new spaces entirely managed by people in the spectrum, facilitated by the diffusion of the Internet. The first Internet community entirely self-managed by autistic people was *Independent Living (InLv)*, founded in 1996 (Dekker, 2020).

These new spaces were instrumental in producing discourses subverting not only the idea of autism as a disastrous condition but also as a development disorder that would disappear with the right treatment. One of the first figures to acquire prominence in the emergent autistic communities was Jim Sinclair. His conference presentation and autistic manifesto "Don't mourn for us" (1993) challenged the discourse of grieving parents for children lost to autism and built the pillars of the autistic collective identity that would develop in the following years. A key point that Sinclair insisted on was that autism is constitutive of the person, not something added to, or corroding, their personality:

> Autism is a way of being. It is *pervasive*; it colours every experience, every sensation, perception, thought, emotion, and encounter, every aspect of existence. It is not possible to separate the autism from the person – and if it were possible, the person you'd have left would not be the same person you started with.   (Sinclair, 1993, p. 5)

The point Sinclair raises in the quote consequential because it means that autism is not attached to a person as something to be hidden or to get rid of, but something that people can be open about and recognize for what it contributes to one's way of being. A second key point of Sinclair's paper countered the idea that autistic people lack interest in social relations. Sinclair in fact turns the claim on its head, and denounces the failure of nonautistic people to notice the efforts in their direction made by those with autism:

> Autism is not an impenetrable wall ... Yes, that takes more work than relating to a nonautistic person. But it *can* be done – unless nonautistic people are far more limited than we are in their capacity to relate. Each of us who

> does learn to talk to you, each of us who manages to function at all in your society, each of us who manages to reach out and make a connection with you … We spend our entire lives doing this. And then you tell us that we can't relate.   (Sinclair, 1993, p. 12)

This point also has important implications in terms of the autistic collective identity. First, it proposes and makes salient an "us," a population of individuals engaged in the same endeavor of getting by in a world not designed for them, and a "you," the rest of society, who systematically misunderstand them. Second, it undermines one of the most otherizing descriptions of autism, that of people who lack the basic feature of humanness, which is sociality. Third, it opens the space for a sociality internal to the group itself, which will continue to flourish in the years to come.

Sinclair's activism, it is argued, laid the foundation for the *neurodiversity* movement (Pripas-Kapit, 2020), which is perhaps the most influential incarnation of autistic advocacy at present. The first use of "neurodiversity" is credited to Judy Singer, an InLv member who drew on the group's discussion in her academic work; the term was later popularized by the American journalist Harvey Blume (1998). The concept of neurodiversity is inclusive of all variations in the wiring of human brains. Its basic assumption is that variability is the norm and people who have different neurological assets will contribute to society and humanity in general according to their particular capacities and specialties. Singer was inspired by the notion of diversity in ecosystems, i.e., as a factor promoting health, with adaptive value for the species (Singer, 2019). In its principles and objectives, the concept is similar to that of Universal Design (Preiser & Smith, 2011), arguing in favor of shifting the focus from the disabled person and their specific problems to how the material and social infrastructure of society can accommodate as many people as possible.

As such, the term neurodiversity indicates an indisputable fact, i.e., that every person is neurologically different, and some argue that for this reason it is ultimately meaningless (Valtellina, 2018). Moreover, the neurobiological emphasis of the word can sound reductionist and exclude considerations of culture and politics in the creation of diversity. However, the movement going under this name has a propulsive force, and is also reaching beyond the specific condition of the people who started it to join forces with other "neurodivergent" groups (e.g., people with ADHD, dyslexia, or even progressive degenerative brain conditions) (Kapp, 2020). Advocating for the value of diversity is not an abstract proposition, but implies taking on the fight for guaranteeing full participation, autonomy, and the support that can enable those goals. The inclusive value of the neurodiversity movement is also demonstrating a sort of moral leap forward: in the first decades of their existence as a group, the autistic community used the term "neurotypical" to denote the strange habits and attitudes of nonautistic people. The term had a clear critical slant and resulted in the creation of a binary opposition. The concept of neurodiversity instead erases such barriers and invites to apply a compassionate and inclusive outlook to variation in cognitive strengths and weaknesses, including, as Robinson (2019, p. 3) puts it, everyone who may "see themselves as both gifted and disabled."

The neurodiversity movement is not a single group or organization and has no leader. It is a banner that can be endorsed by politically active groups, and a label that can make autistic people and their family members feel proud and empowered. The collection of accounts in Kapp's (2020) edited book testifies to the great variety of paths and forms of activism of people who recognize themselves in the movement.

The autistic community is vocal, active, and diverse, and the debate about new term introduced in the field, is always vibrant, sometimes heated; it is therefore not surprising that the same is happening with "neurodiversity" and "neurodivergent." However, the arc of autistic identity is remarkable; autistic people and their families took the condition away from its understanding as a developmental disorder – a children's problem in which the protagonists were talked about by others and infantilized – and made it into a frontline movement that speaks out for all kinds of diversity and disability. It is also an educational story about identity: A distinctive element or attribute shared in a group can generate a sense of belonging and separateness, and fuel collective action; however the dynamic that is generated can sometimes take a group to trespass its own identity boundaries, extending the benefits of its action to a larger group.

21.2.2 Autism Identifications

> I'm not geek chic. And I'm not the Rain Man. I'm not the astrophysicist or the train spotter. I'm not without speech. But sometimes I like to sign. I am an artist, not an engineer. My special interest is people, not machines. Is it any wonder that growing up it never occurred to me to consider that I might be a duck?   (Lloyd-Williams, 2016)

We reconstructed in the previous section how autism has become the name for a collective, a category in the name of which people can carry out concerted action. In this section we will discuss the streams of discourse and actions that contribute to socially shared images of autism and reflect the way ASD-diagnosed individuals interpret their relation with the condition.

As Brubaker and Cooper (2000, p. 14) note, speaking of identification (rather than identity) "invites us to specify the agents that do the identifying. And it does not presuppose that such identifying (even by powerful agents, such as the state) will necessarily result in the internal sameness." The agents can thus be impersonal, anonymous discourses or public narratives with the power to shape social encounters. Processes of identification can include the intellectual as well as the emotional relation to a label or category, and the term has the advantage of making space for ambivalence or apprehensions that are not fully articulated (see also Cameron & Kulick, 2003 and Kulick, 2005).

Early Autistic Narratives

Two clusters of ideas shaped the public understanding of autism, one was derived by Kanner and subsequent medical interpretations, it defined the autistic person as unmotivated to engage in social relations and incapable of experiencing affective relationships,[8] to the point of psychopathy (Kapp, 2020); the second was the discourse of "cure" that permeated the medical and research culture for most of the twentieth century (exemplified by charities with names like Cure Autism Now). Beside spreading rumors of alternative remedies based on diet or danger of vaccines, this discourse also informed the first autobiographies of autistic people, such as Temple Grandin (Grandin & Scariano, 1986) and Donna Williams (Williams, 1992/2009). These autobiographies were written when Grandin and Williams were adults, the first with a successful career as a mechanical engineer for livestock equipment, the second making a living as an artist. Both works are remarkable and offer insights into the sensory, emotional, and intellectual experience of growing up with autism; according to many voices in the autistic community, though, they were aligned with the "cure" agenda, feeding into parental hopes for the autism to go away from their children and endorsing organizations financing cure research rather than lifelong support. The two narratives, that of isolation and that of cure, are in fact holding each other up, since if the first is true, then autistic people who appear to be in touch with the external world beyond their restricted sphere of interest must have somehow "emerged." The prevalence of such narratives, and their support from the most powerful organizations at the time, meant that voices trying to tell a different story were marginalized.[9] Today, the autistic community rejects the idea of cure as getting rid of autism, favoring types of childhood interventions that facilitate intersubjectivity and social interaction by approaching the child on its own terms (Milton, 2014a).

There is an aspect of the cure narrative that has more to do with the discourse genre itself, i.e., the difficulty of structuring a narrative in which the initial problematic circumstances do not change into a more positive outcome for at least one of the characters (Osteen, 2008). As explained above in the 1980s the fact that Grandin and Williams were able to tell their stories was synonymous with having been cured, even though, reading their autobiographies with a contemporary sensibility, an intertwined counternarrative is revealed, that of "creativity emerging from within autism" (Osteen, 2013, p. 274) rather than despite of it; both authors in fact describe how autism bestowed on them a different way of perceiving and reasoning which had been instrumental to their personal and professional development.

---

[8] Even Oliver Sacks's (1995) sympathetic account of Temple Grandin's story ends with words that hint at Grandin probably being incapable of loving her mother.

[9] Sinclair was ostracized for speaking against these views; he could not find a permanent job, despite being qualified and at work in counselling, and was not granted the same visibility as Grandin and Williams, despite growing public interest in autism (Pripas-Kapit, 2020).

Some of the initial stories by parents also adopted the narrative of transformation, only it is the parent's own journey that is depicted. Osteen points out how the autistic person becomes here a "prosthesis" for the main character to develop. However, there are stories told by family members that embrace the narrative with no resolution, offering instead sketches of the life shared with the person with autism, like the father's account in *Running with Walker* (Hughes, 2003) or the brother and sister's mix of text and drawings *The Ride Together* (Karasik & Karasik, 2003). These types of stories, which might be called "care narratives,"[10] ultimately show how full acceptance is the only way, but do not hide the challenges and the uneven path that families go through; perhaps it is telling that both the books cited as examples of this approach have in their title an image of "moving with," a sense of "going along" with the person with autism rather than trying to steer them away from the condition.

As McGrath (2017), an autistic author, also notes, the narrative gestalt does not always come natural to autism; in a way, a coherent and compact story line would betray the nature of the autistic intelligence. Osteen (2013) gives many examples of literary or filmic strategies that reflect a different organization of content the nerratives are made up of different intersecting perspectives and micronarratives are used for illuminating particular experiences, rather than presenting a single story line with a definite ending. Autobiographical narratives from autistic people also show ways of telling personal stories without a resolution, realizing narrative tension and literary value in depicting the vicissitudes of their different subjectivity. Many of those accounts are explicitly *about* autism, displaying the commitment of autistic people to explaining themselves and attacking the most resistant prejudices. Exemplary in this regard is thirteen-year-old Naoki Higashida's *The Reason I Jump* (2007/2013), organized in question/answer short chapters in which he explains types of behavior that puzzle nonautistic people. Frequently, as time goes on, what had been an undercurrent in Grandin's and Williams's stories became central in later autobiographies, i.e., how autism shapes a person's assets and abilities. Dawn Prince-Hughes's *Songs of the Gorilla Nations* (2004) is subtitled "My Journey through Autism," but it is also a startling depiction of her friendship with gorillas in Woodland Park Zoo in Seattle, her discovery of intersubjectivity through that relationship, and how the sensitivity that allowed that bond to form shaped her future career and life (she will become an anthropologist). In the more recent *Diary of a Young Naturalist* by Dara McAnulty (2020), autism is not foregrounded per se but becomes apparent through the interaction between the young man and the natural and social world. The diary format short-circuits the problem of a progressive narrative, and the reader, sharing the day-to-day life of McAnulty's family of five (all

---

[10] The author wishes to thank Michael Bamberg for the suggestion.

autistic except the father), gradually comes to inhabit their sensibility and worldview.

Poetry is a medium well suited for conveying the particular relationship to the external world that a different sensoriality allows (cf. for example Limburg, 2017), and also for capturing the way language can impose images and connections over ordinary meaning (a much-cited poem in this respect is "The Tune on Your Mind," by acclaimed Australian poet Les Murray).

Fictional Autism

Fiction is also an important source of general knowledge and imagery about autism. The enormously influential film *Rain Man* (1988) was for many years the only representation the general public could attach the label autism to (Silberman, 2017). The film has many merits, not only artistic but also in generating awareness and acceptance of autism; still, it represents someone with savant abilities who can only survive in an institution. In the first two decades of the twenty-first century, there has been an exponential increase in novels, TV series, and films with autistic protagonists who have jobs, relationships (albeit complicated), and who can use their skills profitably (e.g., *The Syndicate*, *The Bridge*, and *The Curious Incident of the Dog in The Night-Time*). Such exposure has increased awareness and acceptance of the condition, and has even helped people who grew up without a diagnosis to recognize the source of their difficulties. Several critics have noted, however, that these products also consolidated new type of autistic narrative and trope, that of the genial eccentric figure with skills in the area of science and technology (Osteen, 2008; McGrath, 2017). The fact that often in such fictions the autism of the character remains implicit (sometimes appearing only in the paratext advertising them) can further obfuscate the life experience of people in the spectrum for the general public. More specifically, McGrath (2017, pp. 176–177) sees the problem in the fact that this choice "severely restricts the possibilities of how a narrative or script might critically acknowledge this condition as an experience, an impairment, a disability, a diagnosis, and a social label," which "undermine[s] the reality that autistic adults may need to talk about this subjectivity and identity," and "evade[s] addressing the condition as a disability, because the health and lifestyles of these characters are seldom significantly impaired by autistic tendencies." Writing from an autistic standpoint, McGrath evaluates positively fiction, such as that of Morrall (2008) or Wolitzer (2013), that represent autistic subjectivities in a credible way, for example showing how autistic traits – with less drive toward conformity or inflexible thinking patterns in some areas – may give rise to diversity more than sameness among the population of people with autism. Finally, McGrath notes the absence in fiction of the pivotal moment of diagnosis, despite its cataclysmic effect on a person's sense of self and public identity, as illustrated in the last section of this chapter.

Cultural Playfields

Like many groups with a minoritarian collective identity, autistic communities around the world also share preferences, mythologies, and iconic cultural expressions that are syntonic to their experience. To mention just a few examples, Schwarz (2008) explains how films can support processes of autistic identification; McGrath (2017) shows how E. M. Forster's novel *Howards End*, The Who's 1969 album *Tommy*, and the Michael Andrews/Gary Jules song "Mad World" may resonate with autistic members of the audience, even if they are not about autism. There are cultural worlds related to fandom and the related practice of cosplay – wearing costumes of favorite fiction characters – in which many people with autism meet, play, and produce their own literature. The latter practice, called fan fiction, consist in creating new episodes and side narratives based on fantasy literature or animation. In the liminal space of fantasy worlds, themes that are key to a person's self-discovery can be elaborated, such as social difficulties, sexuality, and autism itself (for a personal account, see Poe, 2019; for an ethnographic study on role-playing games in autism, see Fein, 2015).

Deconstructing and Reconstructing Scientific Narratives

The relationship of the autistic community with the descriptions produced by scientific research is complex. On the one hand, science can offer explanations for the discontinuity between the experience of people with autism and that of others, and a vocabulary to go with those. For example, people with autism often refer to their troubles in terms of lack of theory of mind or executive functioning. On the other hand, for decades autism has been framed in experimental research almost exclusively in terms of deficits. Headline-grabbing descriptions evoking "zero empathy" (Baron-Cohen, 2011), lack of imagination (Craig & Baron-Cohen, 1999), and a weak sense of self (Lombardo & Baron-Cohen, 2010) make it harder to build a public persona around being autistic. Many descriptions plainly do not match what can be easily observed in the achievements of autistic people; famously Sinclair (1992, p. 1) starts his "Bridging the Gaps" paper by recalling that "In May of 1989 I drove 1200 miles to attend the tenth annual TEACCH conference, where I learned that autistic people can't drive." Experimental comparison between people – most often children or youth – with autism and with typical development perpetuate understandings in terms of haves and have-nots rather than exploring genuine diversity and solutions devised via alternative routes. Another consequence of the diagnostic descriptions that for a long time were considered the ultimate science on autism was to cover up rather than expand the knowledge about autistic realities: the unempathic, uncaring, unimaginative profile that captured media attention made the autism of many people – caring parents, artists, women – invisible, and their claims distrusted.

Networks such as Critical Autism, whose members are autistic and non-autistic scholars and practitioners, promote awareness of the limitations of deficit-only accounts and try to offer complementary information, while also highlighting the sociocultural forces shaping dominant versions of autism (Woods et al., 2018; Kapp, 2020). Central to such networks is the identification of research practices that produce descriptions of autism that more faithfully represent the heterogeneity and the lived experience of autistic people (Milton 2013, 2014b). If research has been until recently conducted mostly with a third-person perspective, i.e., with the autistic participants as experimental subjects, first-person and second-person perspectives are promoted in these circles. First-person research goes from autoethnographic accounts, on academic (Yergeau, 2013) or non-academic platforms,[11] to phenomenological research that uses those accounts to understand the nature of self-processes and embodied experience (Fletcher-Watson et al., 2019; Boldsen, 2018). Second-person research can look at the mutual influences during social interaction between autistic and nonautistic people (Fasulo & Fiore, 2007; Sterponi, de Kirby, & Shankey, 2015; Sterponi & Fasulo, 2010), or carry out participatory research that builds research expertise in autistic participants, in order to arrive at findings as a merging of perspectives (Fletcher-Watson et al., 2019). Descriptions of autism produced with such approaches are, among other things, more syntonic with the experience of people in the spectrum, while making identifying as autistic less socially threatening.

Autistic Vocabularies

The autistic community participates in shaping the language autism is spoken by. This is done by creating new terms and formulas, or through "appropriative practices" (Blommaert & Rampton, 2011, p. 29) that reclaim, with a twisted meaning, expressions that were born out of different groups and agendas.

Person-first language (i.e., "people with autism") was one of the first practices spoken against with regard to autism, as it implies the representation of autism as disease, something attached to the person but not constitutively part of it (Sinclair, 1999; Pripas-Kapit, 2020).

The terminology of "high-functioning" and "low-functioning" autistic people, which was used sometimes in parallel, sometimes in overlap, with the nomenclature "Asperger" and "classic autism," essentially referred to oral language proficiency, and has been deemed an arbitrary and damaging classification (Kapp, 2020). Firstly, it poses limits to what a person can achieve, with many autistic biographies showing that borders are continually trespassed by people diagnosed in childhood as low-functioning; secondly, it

---

[11] Examples of nonacademic accounts are the pieces on the Flash Blog *This Is Autism* (http://thisisautismflashblog.blogspot.com), as well as the blog by the cited playwriter Lloyd-Williams, *Autism and Expectations: Demystifying Autism* (autisrhi.com).

perpetuates the focus on oral linguistic abilities that has led to the systematic underestimation of autistic people's level of literacy, which is typically higher in reading and writing than in speech; finally, coexisting low- and high-functioning areas are the norm in autistic individuals, as well as uneven performances in the same area under different circumstances.[12] A growing section of the scientific community now accepts heterogeneity and constant developmental changes as one of autism's defining characteristics (López, 2015).

A powerful metaphor and associated vocabulary that have long informed reciprocal attitudes between autistic and nonautistic people is that of the "alien" (Hacking, 2009a). The word was used in Hans Asperger's original publication, and the image was popularized by Oliver Sacks's catchy title *An Anthropologist on Mars* (about the story of Temple Grandin). The image of the alien has often been adopted by autistic people themselves to render their failure to comprehend the way nonautistic people behave. Initially, the metaphor lingered in the coinage, within autistic circles, of the term "neurotypical" and the in-jokes around "otherizing" descriptions of nonautistic behavior:

> We had a bit of fun with it; tongue-in-cheek terms like "neurotypical syndrome" and "social dependency disorder" were thrown around ... As we were so used to being misunderstood, patronized, and pathologized, it was a relief to have the shoe on the other foot.   (Dekker, 2020, p. 45)

The use of the term "neurotypical" had the effect of denaturalizing normative social behavior and constituting an outgroup that strengthened the bonds within the autistic group. However, as autistic advocacy developed conceptually and started to promote the notion of neurodiversity (see the earlier section), the contraposition between the neurotypical person and the alien autistic is leaving the arena for a more nuanced concept of a continuum of diversity across all humans (Kapp, 2020).

Autistic contribution has also been rich in visual culture; to give but one example, the image of the "puzzle," which had been a metaphor of autism with negative connotations (it was used in the logo of the National Autistic Society, with a crying child inside the puzzle piece), has been reappropriated in artistic projects that stress the ability of autistic people to invent themselves (see Figure 21.1).

The metaphor of the self-completing puzzle is ideal for leading to the last domain of this review, that of identity as self-understanding and self-invention. Before doing that, though, it must be mentioned that if the territory of autistic identifications is mainly occupied by the media, science, and autistic advocacy groups, the problem remains of how to give voice autistic people

---

[12] This was a point Asperger (1940) had much insisted on, especially in relation to the unreliability of formal assessments, and it is also the rationale for Lorna Wing settling on the word "spectrum" rather than "continuum" (Silberman, 2017).

Figure 21.1 *Sarah E. Vaughn, "Self Portrait," © Sarah E. Vaughn*

who are unable to join the public debate. While they have citizenship in the neurodiversity movement, their different circumstances mean that we know less of their relationship, and indeed acceptance, of the condition as part of who they are (Osteen, 2008). Lastly, we also still know little about how autism is impacted by social class and in general less privileged or minority positions in society (Davies, 2007).

21.2.3 Autistic Self: A Work in Progress

The third area that Brubaker and Cooper (2000) propose to dissolve the term "identity" into is "self-understanding." By this term they isolate uses of the word that refer to individuals' subjective sense of who they are and where they are socially located. Such understandings are not related, as for the identification processes that we just discussed, with discursive positions shaped by cultural forces; rather, they mean the experience and awareness of one's way of being and how that influences day-to-day actions and choices (Brubaker & Cooper, 2000, pp. 17–19). This area is of the utmost interest in autism, and easily one of the greatest opportunities psychology has ever had for advancing its knowledge of how the self is created and sustained.

As McDonagh (2008, p. 105) reminds us, Asperger himself had hypothesized a core experiential difference in autism: "Behind the originality of language formations stands the originality of experience. Autistic children have the ability to see things and events around them from a new point of view, which often shows surprising maturity" (Asperger, 1940/1991, p. 71).

How can we, though, get access to such experiences if not only they are discontinuous with those of others, but the language itself that could be used for describing them may not map onto that used by nonautistic people (Hacking, 2009)?

The differences in self-experience may be caused only by a divergent neurobiological setup, but also by the cumulative effects of that set-up throughout the years. For example, how do the first stages of self-development occur when, from infancy onward, the physical boundaries of one's own body are not always perceived, embodied agency is not always present, and the success of interpersonal communication not guaranteed? How does the sense of a coherent self-stabilize when narrative discourse is problematic?

Experimental research has gone down the deficit route in the area of the self as well, with paradoxical findings about both a weaker sense of self and a heightened egocentricity in people with autism (Lombardo & Baron-Cohen, 2010); because the research is again comparing autistic and nonautistic groups, the findings do not illuminate any specificity in the landscape of autistic self-understanding (see Fasulo, 2019 for a review).[13] From clinical sources and autobiographical accounts, however, at least three distinct areas of interest emerge. First, there are the negative self-attributions that derive from the clash with the peer group and the social world at large, particularly in individuals who do not get a diagnosis until late in their youth or adulthood. The constant sense of not fitting in, the communication breakdown, and often traumatic experiences of marginalization and bullying can make self-understanding elusive, fragmented, and lacking the sense of compactness and continuity that derive from sharing experiences with others and having them confirmed. Stress can lead to stress-release behaviors, which in turn can make the autistic person seem even more odd and pathological. For example, in Lloyd-Williams's words (2016):

> I was so tired all the time, but that's not the label you get. You don't get "tired." You get lazy . . . If other people aren't tired, then they must be right. I must be lazy. I'm bad. Which makes me sad and I can't chase the sadness away by watching the shadows the light casts on the ceiling. It only fades when I bang my head on the wall. I wonder if I'm mad. That's the sort of thing crazy people do.   (Lloyd-Williams, 2016)

Applying categories of self-understanding from outside in, as in the quote above, can determine a sense of self-estrangement and the lack of a unified sense of self that is often redressed when obtaining a diagnosis. This is why the diagnosis is such a pivotal moment, its value linked both to self-understanding

---

[13] Zahavi (2010) identifies two main issues with experimental research on self in autism: first, the conflation of the ability to access one's mental states with that of verbally reporting them; and secondly, the absence of robust theorization about the self behind experimental setups. From a philosophical point of view, Zahavi argues in favor of organizing the inquiry along the distinct areas of experiential, interpersonal, and a narrative self.

and to public announcements that will free the person from stigma (Bagatell, 2007). Here is an account of the moments after a diagnosis has been delivered:

> Sitting in my car in the parking lot after the last session, I felt an immense wave of relief wash over me as everything suddenly made sense. I looked back over my life, perhaps the way people do before they die, and thought of all the painful memories that could now be explained. Like someone making amends in a twelve-step program, I almost felt compelled to contact everyone who had ever been impacted by my autism – whether positively or negatively – and explain.   (Prince-Hughes, 2004, p. 174)

The diagnosis retrospectively makes things fall into place and frees the person from the responsibility for their difficulties. The process of creating a novel autobiographical narrative goes beyond redressing the negative self-attributions collected over the years; it can recast family relations and family lore about certain characters, and rewrite history backward. Such processes of reinterpretation still need to be investigated, including in terms of what differs when the diagnosis arrives at different ages (Fasulo, 2015).

A second interesting factor in self-understanding in autism is the bricolage nature of the self-understanding and self-presentation that transpires in many personal accounts. The self, at least according to certain psychological theorizations, is an illusion created by convergent psychological processes; such self-projections are mutable, but are bestowed unity by the same apparatus that generates them in the first place (Metzinger, 2003). In autism, fascinatingly, such illusions of unity and continuity do not always hold. Most typical people fabricate a self out of cultural suggestions, but such borrowings do not seem to blend in as naturally for people with autism, as if the memory and attention to details meant that the heterogeneous sources stay pristine in the interior psychological space, the different voices remaining distinct. For example, there are accounts of conjuring up a language for self-expression by borrowing material from pieces of TV programs and even advertisements (Williams, 1992), or from historical figures and personalities (Fasulo, Hunt & Isadore, 2015). Similarly, for young people, fictional characters can represent narrative shells onto which to mold a narrative persona. Reasons for such fragmentation in the self as experienced and presented are probably manyfold, but there are clues pointing to the scarcity of joint narrative interactions, from early infancy (Delafield-Butt & Trevarthen, 2015) and throughout life,[14] that may mean individuals resort to more idiosyncratic and less socially shared ways of constructing a self. A key role may be also played by the difficulties in establishing meaningful sentimental relationships, which in people with typical development inaugurate extensive processes of self-inquiry and

---

[14] The analysis of narratives of an autistic middle-aged man during counselling (Fasulo, 2019) showed a limited reliance on the conversational partner for the joint evaluation and conclusion of autobiographical episodes that Conversation Analysis demonstrated as the norm in personal storytelling (Sacks, 1992).

self-disclosure; Prince (2013) explicitly thematizes how she felt she had a collection of disparate social personae before they started to be recomposed through lengthy discussions about her feelings and perceptions with her first serious partner.

A third and final aspect that for me stands out – although there are surely others I may be overlooking – is the area of self-understanding that has to do with the perceived connections between the body and the external world, especially the natural world. In drawing a parallel between people with autism and the American native Navajo culture, Kapp (2011) notes the felt connection with animated and inanimate beings and the ability to find beauty and harmony in the natural world that unite both groups. From Grandin's uncanny understanding of cattle to Prince-Hughes's communication with gorillas, to McAnulty's and Thunberg's sense of personal involvement with nature and its preservation (Grandin, 2006; Prince-Hughes, 2004; McAnulty, 2020; Thunberg et al., 2020), there are many accounts that speak of a transitional self in which the boundaries between self and the exterior world are permeable, and therefore the individual feels engaged and preoccupied with the well-being of the environment. As in most things concerning autism, the same property that may be at the origin of difficulties – in this case altered proprio- and enteroceptive sensations – may be also creating at a psychological level an enriched ability of tuning in with nonhuman beings (Davidson & Smith, 2009). Rather than lack of empathy, it seems that for many autistic people there could be a widened commonality with the world of animate and inanimate objects, which could further dig a separation with fellow humans who demonstrate indifference toward other beings.

21.3 Conclusions

Understanding an identity that was born as a medical diagnosis and has become a narrative trope means following a dance in which all parts continuously change position and move each other along. It is common for all types of identity research to acknowledge the interdependence of their subject matter with cultural movements and socio-economic forces; however, autism can illustrate the complex interplay of such influences while also constituting a good case in point for the separation of different strands of research.

The very history of autism as a nosological category shows that changes in society prepared for the recognition and denomination of the syndrome; from the initial understanding exclusively in medical terms – disease and cure – the meaning of autism has been contested by advocacy movements fighting for its recognition as a permanent condition that needs to be managed, and not fought out of the person. From the beginning, autism reclaimed as a *collective identity* fostered the more radical shifts in the way the syndrome was to be talked about for generations to come. As these changes occurred, societies in the Western world developed a fascination with autism which meant that identity affordances were created – through processes of *identifications* – especially around the Asperger profile. The explosion of mediatic attention revealed how a novel cultural object can be affected by conventional means of representation. The canonical narrative curve imposed a resolution on stories that did not have one. The heterogeneity of the condition was sacrificed to the shaping of a literary and cinematographic type: the aloof but genial individual, perfect candidate for detective dramas and troubled love affairs, but offering little insight in terms of what being autistic can feel like. Autistic people themselves enter the arena of identifications not only with their autobiographies, but also with literary criticism, scientific inquiries, and the creation of networks in which the cultural work of autism-making is reflexively examined and exposed. Finally, we have discussed autistic identity as *self-understanding*. Being at odds with society and having different patterns of bodily sensations can generate types of subjectivities that we still know very little about, and conventional psychological research approaches based on one-to-one comparison with nonautistic individuals have not yet stepped up to the challenge.

The work of autistic scholars, and of researchers with a critical disability approach, promote innovative research paradigms that, starting from what autistic people have to say about their own condition, can build an understanding of autism in its own terms, and also develop instruments for lifelong support. Shifting the focus from deficits and impairments of autistic individuals to the exploration of autistic worlds-in-relation can ultimately build an enriched identity and create a welcoming environment for newborns into autism and for their families.

References

American Psychological Association. (1994). *Diagnostic and Statistical Manual of Mental Disorders: DSM-IV*. American Psychiatric Publishing.

Asperger, H. (1940/1991). "Autistic psychopathy" in childhood. In U. Frith (Ed.), *Autism and Asperger Syndrome* (pp. 1–36). Cambridge: Cambridge University press

Bagatell, N. (2007). Orchestrating voices: Autism, identity and the power of discourse. *Disability & Society*, 22(4), 413–426.

Barazzetti, A., Barbetta, P., Valtellina, E., & Pressato, P. (2017). Contextualising a pre-history of autism. Paper presented at the Critical Autism Conference, London, UK.

Baron-Cohen, S. (2011). *Zero Degrees of Empathy*. London: Penguin

Baron-Cohen, S. (1997). *Mindblindness: An essay on autism and theory of mind*. Cambridge, MA: MIT Press.

Belmonte, M. K. (2008). Does the experimental scientist have a "Theory of Mind"? *Review of General Psychology*, 12(2), 192–204.

Bendle, M. (2002). The crisis of identity in high modernity. *British Journal of Sociology, 53*(1), 1–18.

Block, D. (2006). Identity in applied linguistics. In Omoniyi, T. and White, G. (Eds.), *The Sociolinguistics of Identity* (pp. 34–49). London: Continuum.

Blommaert, J. & Rampton, B. (2011). Language and superdiversity. *Language and Superdiversities II, 13*(2), 1–22.

Blume, H. (1998, September). Neurodiversity: On the neurological underpinnings of geekdom. *The Atlantic*. Retrieved May 08, 2021, from www.theatlantic.com/magazine/archive/1998/09/neurodiversity/305909/.

Boldsen, S. (2018). Toward a phenomenological account of embodied subjectivity in autism. *Culture, Medicine, and Psychiatry, 42*(4), 893–913.

Briggs, C. L. (2002). Interviewing, power/knowledge and social inequality. In J. F. Gubrium, & J. A. Holstein (Eds.), *Handbook of Interview Research: Context and Method* (pp. 911–922). London: Sage.

Brubaker, R. & Cooper, F. (2000). Beyond "identity." *Theory and Society, 29*(1), 1–47.

Cameron, D. & Kulick, D. (2003). *Language and Sexuality*. Cambridge: Cambridge University Press.

Caniglia, E. (2013). Abbiamo veramente bisogno dell'identità? Alcune precauzioni per l'uso di un concetto ambiguo. [Do we really need identity? A few precautions for the use of an ambiguous concept]. *SocietàMutamentoPolitica, 4*(8), 201–217.

Craig, J. & Baron-Cohen, S. (1999). Creativity and imagination in autism and Asperger Syndrome. *Journal of Autism and Developmental Disorders, 29*, 319–326.

Davidson, J. & Smith, M. (2009). Autistic autobiographies and more-than-human emotional geographies. *Environment and Planning D: Society and Space, 27*(5), 898–916.

Davies, K. (2007). Are we hearing all the voices? *International Journal of Disability Development and Education, 54*(3), 3510355.

Davies, K. (2015). A troubled identity. Putting Butler to work on the comings and goings of Asperger's Syndrome. In T. Corcoran, J. White, & B. Whitburn (Eds.), *Disability Studies* (pp. 197–214). Leiden: Brill Sense.

Dekker, M. (2020). From exclusion to acceptance: Independent living on the autistic spectrum. In S. Kapp (Ed.), *Autistic Community and the Neurodiversity Movement. Stories from the Frontline* (pp. 40–49). Basingstoke: Palgrave Macmillan.

Delafield-Butt, J. T. & Trevarthen, C. (2015). The ontogenesis of narrative: From moving to meaning. *Frontiers in Psychology, 6*, article 1157.

Fasulo, A. (2015). History in waiting. Receiving a diagnosis of Asperger in midlife. In R. Piazza & A. Fasulo (Eds.), *Marked Identities* (pp. 170–191). Basingstoke: Palgrave Macmillan.

Fasulo, A. (2019). A different conversation: Psychological research and the problem of self in autism. *Integrative Psychological and Behavioral Science, 53*(4), 611–631.

Fasulo, A. & Fiore, F. (2007). A valid person: Non-competence as a conversational outcome. In A. Hepburn & S. Wiggins (Eds.), *Discursive Research in Practice* (pp. 224–246). Cambridge, Cambridge University Press.

Fasulo, A., Hunt, P. A., & Isadore, P. (2015). History in waiting: Receiving a diagnosis of Asperger in midlife. In R. Piazza and A. Fasulo (Eds.), *Marked Identities* (pp. 170–191). Basingstoke: Palgrave Macmillan.

Fasulo, A. & Piazza, R. (2015). Introduction. In R. Piazza and A. Fasulo (Eds.), *Marked Identities* (pp. 1–15). Basingstoke: Palgrave Macmillan.

Fein, E. (2015). Making meaningful worlds: Role-playing subcultures and the autism spectrum. *Culture, Medicine, and Psychiatry, 39*(2), 299–321.

Fletcher-Watson, S., Adams, J., Brook, K., Charman, T., Crane, L., Cusack, J., Leekam, S., Milton, D., Parr, J. R., & Pellicano, E. (2019). Making the future together: Shaping autism research through meaningful participation. *Autism, 23*(4), 943–953.

Frith, U. (Ed.). (1991). *Autism and Asperger Syndrome.* Cambridge: Cambridge University Press.

Frith, U. (2003). *Autism: Explaining the Enigma.* Oxford: Blackwell Publishing.

Goffman, E. (1963). *Stigma: Notes on the Management of Spoiled Identity.* Englewood Cliffs, NJ: Prentice Hall.

Grandin, T. (2006). *Thinking in Pictures: And Other Reports from My Life with Autism.* New York, NY: Vintage.

Grandin, T. & Scariano, M. (1986). *Emergence: Labeled Autistic.* Novato, CA: Arena Press.

Hacking, I. (2009a). Autistic autobiography. *Philosophical Transactions of the Royal Society B: Biological Sciences, 364*(1522), 1467–1473.

Hacking, I. (2009b). Humans, aliens and autism. *Daedalus, 138*(3), 44–59.

Higashida, N. (2013). *The Reason I Jump: The Inner Voice of a Thirteen-Year-Old Boy with Autism.* Toronto: Knopf.

Hughes, R. (2003). *Running with Walker.* London: Jessica Kingsley Publishers

Kanner, L. (1943). Autistic disturbances of affective contact. *Nervous Child, 2*, 217–250.

Kapp, S. K. (2011). Navajo and autism: The beauty of harmony, *Disability & Society, 26*(5), 583–595, doi:10.1080/09687599.2011.589192.

Kapp, S. K. (Ed.). (2020). *Autistic Community and the Neurodiversity Movement. Stories from the Frontline.* Basingstoke: Palgrave Macmillan, open access from www.palgrave.com/gp/book/9789811384363.

Karasik, P. & Karasik, J. (2003). *The Ride Together: A Brother and Sister's Memoir of Autism in the Family.* New York, NY: Washington Square.

Kulick, D. (2005). The importance of what gets left out. *Discourse Studies 7*(4–5), 615–624.

Limburg, J. (2017). *The Autistic Alice.* Hexham: Bloodaxe Books.

Lloyd-Williams, R. (2016). The Duck [Audio file]. Retrieved May 08, 2021, from https://autact.co.uk/audio/.

Lloyd-Williams, R. (2020). Autistic Pride. Retrieved May 08, 2021, from https://autistrhi.com.

Lombardo, M. V., & Baron-Cohen, S. (2010). Unraveling the paradox of the autistic self. *Wiley Interdisciplinary Reviews: Cognitive Science, 1*(3), 393–403.

López, B. (2015). Beyond modularisation: The need of a socio-neuro-constructionist model of autism. *Journal of Autism and Developmental Disorders, 45*(1), 31–41.

Markram, K. & Markram, H. (2010). The Intense World Theory: A unifying theory of the neurobiology of autism. *Frontiers in Human Neuroscience, 4*, 224, doi:10.3389/fnhum.2010.00224.

McAnulty, D. (2020). *Diary of a Young Naturalist*. Beaminster: Little Toller.

McDonagh, P. (2008). Autism and modernism: A genealogical exploration. In M. Osteen (Ed.), *Autism and Representation* (pp. 100–116). New York, NY: Routledge.

McGrath, J. (2017). *Naming Adult Autism: Culture, Science, Identity*. New York, NY: Rowman & Littlefield International.

Metzinger, T. (2003). *Being No One*. Cambridge, MA: MIT Press.

Milton, D. (2013). "Filling in the gaps": A micro-sociological analysis of autism. *Autonomy, the Critical Journal of Interdisciplinary Autism Studies, 1*(2). Retrieved May 08, 2021, from www.larry-arnold.net/Autonomy/index.php/autonomy/article/view/AR4/pdf.

Milton, D. (2014a). So what exactly are autism interventions intervening with? *Good Autism Practice, 15*(2), 6–14.

Milton, D. (2014b). Autistic expertise: A critical reflection on the production of knowledge in autism studies. *Autism, 18*(7), 794–802.

Morrall, C. (2008). *The Language of Others*. London: Sceptre.

Muratori, F. & Maestro, S. (2007). Autism as a downstream effect of primary difficulties in intersubjectivity interacting with abnormal development of brain connectivity. *International Journal for Dialogical Science, 2*(1), 93–118. Retrieved May 08, 2021, from http://ijds.lemoyne.edu/journal/2_1/index.html.

Muzikar, D. (2019). The autism puzzle piece: A symbol that's going to stay or go? *The Art of Autism*, April 20. Retrieved May 08, 2021, from www.theartofautism.com.

Nilsson, M., Handest, P., Nylander, L., Pedersen, L., Carlsson, J., & Arnfred, S. (2019). Arguments for a phenomenologically informed clinical approach to autism spectrum disorder. *Psychopathology, 52*(3), 153–160.

Ochs, E. & Solomon, O. (2010). Autistic sociality. *Ethos, 38*(1), 69–92.

Osteen, M. (Ed.). (2008). *Autism and Representation*. New York, NY: Routledge.

Osteen, M. (2013). Narrating autism. In J. Davidson & M. Orsini (Eds.), *Worlds of Autism. Across the Spectrum of Neurological Difference* (pp. 261–284). Minneapolis, MN: University of Minnesota Press.

Poe, C. A. (2019). *How To Be Autistic*. Oxford: Myriad.

Preiser, W. F., & Smith, K. H. (Eds.). (2011). *Universal Design Handbook*. New York, NY: McGraw-Hill.

Prince, D. E. (2013). "All the things I have ever been": Autoethnographic reflections on academic writing and autism. In J. Davidson & M. Orsini (Eds.), *Worlds of Autism: Across the Spectrum of Neurological Difference*, (pp. 319–330). Minneapolis, MN: University of Minnesota Press.

Prince-Hughes, D. (2004). *Songs of the Gorilla Nations. My Journey through Autism*. New York, NY: Three Rivers Press.

Pripas-Kapit, S. (2020). Historicizing Jim Sinclair's "Don't mourn for us": A cultural and intellectual history of neurodiversity's first manifesto. In Kapp, S. (Ed.), *Autistic Community and the Neurodiversity Movement. Stories from the*

Frontline. Basingstoke: Palgrave Macmillan, open access from www.palgrave .com/gp/book/9789811384363.

Robinson, J. E. (2019). Is autism becoming neurodiversity? When medical terms and community words converge. *Psychology Today*. Retrieved May 08, 2021, from www.psychologytoday.com/gb/blog/my-life-aspergers/201910/is-autism-becoming-neurodiversity.

Sacks, H. (1992). *Lectures on Conversation*, 2 vols. (Fall 1964–Spring 1972). Oxford: Blackwell.

Sacks, O. (1995). *An Anthropologist on Mars. Seven Paradoxical Tales*. London: Picador.

Scholiers, J. (n.d.). A less transparent self in autism. Unpublished manuscript.

Schwarz, P. (2008). Film as a vehicle for raising consciousness among autistic peers. In M. Osteen (Ed.), *Autism and Representation* (pp. 256–270). New York, NY: Routledge.

Silberman, S. (2017). *Neurotribes: The Legacy of Autism and How to Think Smarter about People Who Think Differently*. London: Atlantic Books.

Sinclair, J. (1993). Don't mourn for us. *Our Voice, 11*(3) [Autism Network International Newsletter]. Retrieved May 08, 2021, from www.autreat.com/dont_mourn.html.

Sinclair, J. (1992). Bridging the gaps: An inside-out view of autism. In E. Schopler & G. B. Mesibov, *High-Functioning Individuals with Autism*. New York, NY: Plenum Press, http://jisincla.mysite.syr.edu/bridgingnc.htm.

Sinclair, J. (1999). Why I dislike "person first" language. Retrieved May 08, 2021, from http://web.archive.org/web/20090210190652/http://web.syr.edu/~jisincla/person_first.htm.

Singer, J. (2019). There's a lot in a name – diversity vs. divergence. *Genius Within*, February 5. Retrieved May 08, 2021, from www.geniuswithin.co.uk/.

Sterponi, L., de Kirby, K., & Shankey, J. (2015). Rethinking language in autism. *Autism, 19*(5), 517–526.

Sterponi, L. & Fasulo, A. (2010). "How to go on": Intersubjectivity and progressivity in the communication of a child with autism. *Ethos, 38*(1), 116–142.

Thomas, R. E. (2020). Hannah Gadsby's Douglas is a second date disguised as stand-up. *Elle*, May 27. Retrieved May 08, 2021, from www.elle.com/culture/.

Thunberg, G., Thunberg, S., Ernman, M., & Ernman, B. (2020). *Our House Is on Fire: Scenes of a Family and a Planet in Crisis*. London: Penguin.

Trevarthen, C. & Delafield-Butt, J. T. (2013). Autism as a developmental disorder in intentional movement and affective engagement. *Frontiers in Integrative Neuroscience, 7*, 49, doi:10.3389/fnint.2013.00049.

Valtellina, E. (2018). A.S.: Classification, interpellation. In E. Fein and C. Rios (Eds.), *Autism in Translation, Culture, Mind and Society* (pp. 207–229). Cham: Palgrave Macmillan, doi:10.1007/978-3-319-93293-4_10.

Williams, D. (1992/2009). *Nobody Nowhere: The Remarkable Autobiography of an Autistic Girl*. London: Jessica Kingsley Publishers.

Wing, L. & Gould, J. (1979). Severe impairments of social interaction and associated abnormalities in children: Epidemiology and classification. *Journal of Autism and Developmental Disorders, 9*(1), 11–29.

Wolitzer, M. (2013). *The Interestings*. London: Vintage.

Woods, R., Milton, D., Arnold, L., & Graby, S. (2018). Redefining critical autism studies: A more inclusive interpretation. *Disability & Society*, *33*(6), 974–979.

Yergeau, M. (2013). Clinically significant disturbance: On theorists who theorize theory of mind. *Disability Studies Quarterly*, *33*(4), doi:10.18061/dsq. v33i4.3876.

Zahavi, D. (2010). Complexities of self. *Autism*, *14*(5), 547–551.

22 Gerontopsychology: Dementia and Identity

Lars-Christer Hydén

I don't know myself
I don't know at all
Oh, goodness gracious
What is it all.

These were the words of Auguste Deter in 1901 when her psychiatrist, Alois Alzheimer, asked her if she knew who she was (Maurer & Maurer, 2003). Obviously, Auguste Deter did not seem to recognize herself, but had become a stranger to herself. To the afterworld, her words have often been interpreted as if she lost her identity.

The notion of a close connection between memories and identity has been at the center for much of the writings about personal identity both in philosophy and psychology (Gallagher, 2011). Theoretically, the idea goes back to the British philosopher John Locke, as many have remarked (Matthews, 2006). Locke proposed that a person is the same self because they can remember their past experiences. In modern discussions about identity a connection between identity, episodic memories, autobiographical memories, as well as semantic memories (knowledge about self), is often suggested (see for instance, Bruner, 1994; Conway, 2005; Schechtman, 1996).

Dementia and in particular Alzheimer's disease (AD) challenge the connection between identity and memory. Persons with AD are often severely strained in both "encoding" or creating memories, as well as in "recalling" or remembering, and could hence not have or sustain an identity. As a result, it has been argued that persons with dementia "lose" their self and identity as they "lose" their autobiographical memories and knowledge (Fontana & Smith, 1989; Cohen & Eisdorfer, 1986). Thus, AD is a disorder that seems to highlight at least one of the central questions in the discussions around identity: Can persons that are challenged in using memories have an identity or are they doomed to be "empty vessels," a body without a soul (Fontana & Smith, 1989)?

The issue around memory and identity is further complicated by the fact that persons living with dementia also face challenges to their *linguistic* abilities, making it difficult for instance to tell stories and construct a narrative identity. The linguistic difficulties of persons living with dementia thus further challenges theories around the discursive construction of identities (Harré, 1998; Gergen, 1994; Bamberg, 2011), raising the question of the limits of linguistic contributions to the establishment, communication, and negotiation of identity.

The aim of this chapter is to make a contribution to the general discussion about personal identity by focusing on the specific issues that dementia raises, namely how challenges to the memory systems as well as the linguistic abilities affect the establishment, communication, and negotiation of identity. The discussion will be organized around five different theoretical ideas about identity that have been central in the discussions about self and identity in dementia:

(1) The relationship between *memory* (especially autobiographical memory) and *identity*: It is often claimed that identity is constructed or relies on the individual's knowledge and autobiographical memories. As people with dementia become challenged in both forming new memories as well as recalling past events, it is argued that identity is lost. This will be discussed starting in some experimental studies (Addis & Tippett, 2004), although it is an issue with relevance also for other conceptualizations of identity.

(2) A person's identity could be seen as an expression of the individual's experiences in a variety of forms of public interaction and discourse. Some of these experiences express a continuity of the person over time, while other expressions of identity are dependent on how others respond to the person's expressions: if others do not recognize the expressions of identity from the person living with dementia, there is a risk of de-personalization. How persons living with dementia creatively make use of their remaining cognitive and linguistic resources to express their identity and sense of self has been discussed by Sabat (2001).

(3) What is the role of *nonverbal* resources? As persons with dementia become increasingly challenged in using and understanding spoken language, bodily enactments as well as other forms of nonverbal communication become more important for establishing an identity. Thus, identity for these individuals will be based on pre-reflective interactions with the world and other people and is best thought of as an "embodied self" (Kontos, 2004).

(4) Although persons with dementia in later stages are challenged in their use of spoken language, they are still part of language-using communities and their experiences and biographies and identities are formed especially by *autobiographical storytelling*. This makes it interesting to investigate the possibilities of sustaining, presenting, developing, and revising narrative identities for persons with dementia (Beard, Knauss, & Moyer, 2009; Mills, 1998).

(5) It is obvious that spouses living together share many stories as well as autobiographical knowledge. This has resulted in the suggestion of

couples having a *shared identity*. This identity concept moves beyond the notion of the individual as the singular and unique "owner" of identities and personal knowledge. Further, when persons living with dementia become challenged in remembering events, they can use the personal knowledge and stories of spouses and carers in order to sustain their identities. This indicates that identities can be supported by socially distributed knowledge (Hydén & Forsblad, 2018).

A conceptual caveat: Although researchers frequently use the concepts "identity" and "self," these concepts are rarely defined or discussed, as Caddell and Clare (2010) noted. Sometimes the concept "self" is seen as an aspect of "personal identity," and at other times the concept "identity" refers to "social self." Most authors use the concepts identity and self as referring to a person's experience of and knowledge about him or herself. Often the term identity also refers to a person's experience of continuity over time. This means that in texts authors can use both the terms self and identity without much difference, while others have a preference for one term. In this text the term "identity" will be used, except when quoting authors who use the term "self." Identity as term – in contrast to the term self – is closely connected to an interactional theoretical and analytical approach to understanding individuals as engaged with each other in a more or less infinite number of social contexts: from private and informal ones to formal and institutional. All these contexts require, demand, and introduce various relevant identities to persons as private persons (father, parent, neighbor, etc.), as professionals (researcher, doctor, social worker), or as subjects in institutional contexts (patients, clients, pupils). Identity is related to issues around the continuity of a person over time and place and points out a specific individual in contrast to others as well as grounding an individual in a specific social context (cf. Bamberg, 2011). Identities can be challenged by disruptions pertaining either to the individual (illness, for instance) or to other changes.

In the following, a brief section will introduce the dementia diagnosis and the cognitive and communicative consequences of the various brain pathologies. This is followed by a presentation and discussion of the five different theoretical issues suggested above as well the empirical claims presented about identity in dementia. Finally, a concluding section sums up the positions and issues discussed.

22.1 What Is Dementia?

Dementia (or *major neurocognitive disorder*) is the name of a group of diseases that affect the individual's brain, primarily through either neurodegenerative processes or vascular changes, and result in certain cognitive symptoms. The neurodegenerative processes are progressive, starting in fairly specific places in the brain and then spreading globally. Vascular disorder may affect different parts of the brain, but generally also progresses.

Eventually, the disorder will result in the death of the person. The process has a gradual onset and progresses fairly slowly – with the exception of early onset dementia (before the age of 65), which is more rapid. Most people with a dementia diagnosis will live with the disease for many years – and will often continue to live at home for the better part of that time. In countries with general care systems, most people with dementia will spend the last period of the disorder at some kind of care facility. No cure for dementia is available at present, although some pharmacological treatments that help to stall symptoms temporarily seem to work for some individuals (Van der Linden & Juilerat Van der Linden, 2018).

Dementia specifically affects the individual's cognitive and linguistic abilities, resulting in cognitive, communicative, and social disabilities (Lezak et al., 2012). One of the main cognitive challenges in some forms of dementia is connected to the fact that several memory systems are affected by pathological brain processes: episodic and semantic memory, as well as working memory (Morris & Becker, 2004). This has consequences for other cognitive, linguistic, and communicative functions: challenges in word understanding, name finding, linguistic constructions, discursive organization, problem-solving, etc. As most of these cognitive, linguistic, and communicative functions are involved in forming, sustaining, presenting, and negotiating identity, the individual will face severe challenges; in particular autobiographical memories will be problematic, as well as taking part in conversations, and presenting and sustaining long held role identities.

As a result of cognitive and linguistic resources becoming challenged, dementia tends to disrupt the established everyday relations between identity, self, brain, body, and world. The challenges concern not only memory and social cognition but also the organization and performance of bodily actions and movements. Besides this, persons living with dementia often have other medical problems that might affect their everyday life, from hearing problems to cardiovascular issues (Bunn et al., 2014).

As the dementia progression is a fairly slow process, the changes are not sudden but rather slow and gradual. Persons living with dementia deal with the changes and try to compensate for the cognitive and linguistic challenges (Clare, 2008). Compensatory strategies range from using the remaining cognitive and linguistic resources productively (inventing new words, using narrative fragments) to using and engaging others in order to use their cognitive resources (memories and stories, for instance) in order to sustain, present, and negotiate identity (Hydén, 2018a).

22.2 Memory and Identity

Alzheimer's disease (AD) is one of several diseases that cause dementia. AD starts in the hippocampal area in the brain. This area is involved in creating and tracking in particular episodic memories. From this brain area, the degenerative processes then spread into other brain regions. The fact that the hippocampal area is affected by AD results in increasing memory challenges for people living with AD. Not only will new events not be remembered, but also memories of events in the past will be challenged. As the disease progresses, other memory systems will be affected (semantic memory, working memory, prospective memory) (Morris & Becker, 2004).

Although other forms of dementia than AD do not involve primary memory challenges (Lezak et al., 2012), it is the memory effects of AD that often have been seen as the typical case of dementia; it is also the most common dementia diagnosis. As a consequence, much of the discussions about dementia and identity has centered on the relation between identity and memory taking the symptoms of AD as the prototypical example of dementia.

As Brockmeier (2015) points out, memory is often defined as being some sort of "archive." This metaphor implies that memories or representations of events, experiences, or knowledge are *stored* somewhere in the brain and then retrieved when necessary through some kind of indexing system (as in old libraries). In dementia, this "archive" and the encoding and retrieval mechanisms become impaired. As a contrast to this metaphor – as will be discussed later in this chapter – memory systems can also be conceptualized without a central "archive" but rather as distributed neural networks involving all kinds of resources, from motor processes to visual imagination, to smell, touch, and verbal aspects. That is, memory processes could be seen as drawing on all kinds of distributed multimodal resources in the brain as well as in the environment (cf. Hydén, 2018b).

Given that memory often is conceptualized as an "archive" that is crucial for identity, it is interesting that there is not much empirical research about the connection between memory and identity. Case studies of amnesic persons indicate that although they did not create any new memories for decades, they still had a sense of self and an identity (see, for instance, Corkin, 2013). In the field of dementia, numerous clinical and experimental studies of the relation between dementia and changes in the memory system have been conducted. At the same time, few experimental and clinical studies have directly investigated the relation between changes of autobiographical memory and identity (although see Cohen-Mansfield, Golander, & Arnheim, 2000; Cohen-Mansfield, Parpura-Gilla, & Golander, 2006). If a strong relation exists between memory and identity, then this should show up in studies based on independent measures of autobiographical memory and identity.

In one of the few existing experimental studies about identity and autobiographical memory, Addis and Tippett (2004) found no relationship between measurements of autobiographical memory and strength of identity in persons with dementia. What they found was a weak trend toward a positive association between (a loss of) early adulthood memories and identity. In a replication of Addis and Tippetts's study, Naylor and Clare (2008) could not find any clear and simple relationship between autobiographical memory and identity in persons with dementia even when they weighted in measures for cognitive awareness:

> Autobiographical memory performance was not related to identity scores, suggesting that there was no straight-forward connection between impairment in autobiographical memory and self-report of identity. Autobiographical memory performance was, however, related to awareness of memory functioning, in that people with better recall of mid-life incidents showed greater awareness of memory functioning as indicated by lower discrepancies between self-ratings and informant reports. Awareness of memory functioning was also related to identity, in that people with lower awareness, as indicated by greater discrepancies between self-ratings and informant reports, also demonstrated a more positive and more definite sense of identity.   (Naylor & Clare, 2008, p. 601)

One possible interpretation of these results is that individuals with low awareness of changes in cognitive functions may resist acknowledging cognitive change and instead insist on their prior identity (ibid., p. 604).

A conclusion from these studies is that it seems likely that there is no clear and simple relation between loss of autobiographical memory and identity in persons with dementia. Although one should be very cautious in drawing conclusions from just two studies, they, together with other studies of people with brain injuries affecting their memory functions, indicate that identity is not primarily based on retrieval of autobiographical memories and personal knowledge. Rather, the studies indicate that persons seem to relate to their own memories as a resource they can either use or not use; or they can make use of a "prior identity." Thus, autobiographical memories and personal knowledge appear to be just one or two among several sources that persons reflexively can use when presenting an identity. This connects to theorizing about identity that stresses the constructive and situated aspects of identity (Bamberg, 2011; Mishler, 1999).

22.3 The Person's Identity

Much research since the early 1990s has been preoccupied with demonstrating that persons with dementia "have" a self and an identity (Caddell & Clare, 2010; Herskovits, 1995). Much of this research has been based on interviews with people living with dementia and aims to show that people living with dementia in early, as well as in mid- and late stages, have a sense of their self and identity, although they might have problems with verbally communicating and negotiating their identity. A central question has been to understand how these identities are constructed, presented, and negotiated.

In the early 1990s, the psychologist Tom Kitwood (1990; 1997) presented his work on personhood and dementia. He defined *personhood* in social psychological terms as "the status bestowed upon one human being, by others, in the context of social relationship and social being. It implies recognition, respect and trust" (Kitwood, 1997, p. 8). Kitwood's emphasis on the recognition of the person was taken up by the psychologist Steven Sabat (2001). Using the notion of personhood, Sabat together with colleagues in a number of articles went beyond the notion of personhood and argued that a person living with dementia still had a self (Sabat, 2002; Sabat & Harré, 1992, 1994; Sabat & Collins, 1999). According to Sabat and Harré (1992),

(1) there is a self, a personal singularity, that remains intact despite the debilitating effects of the disorder, and (2) there are other aspects of the person, the selves that are socially and publicly presented that can be lost, but only indirectly as a result of the disease. In the second case, the loss of self is directly related to nothing more than the ways in which others view and treat the AD sufferer. (p. 444)

Sabat and Harré (1992) argued that it is possible to differentiate between two different types of selves, while a third was added by Sabat (2002) later. Self 1, the "primary self," is the individual singularity, a formal, philosophical notion, indicating that persons are able to identify themselves as specific points in time and space and as agents. Thus, this kind of self is independent of, for instance, specific memories and has rather to do with the ability to refer to oneself in everyday talk by using pronouns like "I," "me," and "self" (cf. Small et al., 1998, for examples). Further, the primary self is also connected to agency and a sense of being the origin of actions (Sabat & Harré, 1992). This self basically never disappears even in the advanced stage of dementia: even when persons have lost their ability to use language and thus pronouns like "I" they can still experience themselves as the origin of actions.

Self 2 is made up of the person's physical and psychological attributes, and what can be called self-knowledge. It might be "one's height and weight, eye pigmentation, one's sense of humor, religious and political convictions, educational achievements, and vocational pursuits" (Sabat, 2002, p. 27). Some of these attributes have a long history going back to early childhood, while others have a recent origin. For persons living with dementia, much of the focus in social interaction will often turn to problems caused by the disease, while other cherished sides of the self will be in the background. Thus, the problematic sides tend to get more focus, and might also be connected to challenges in remembering.

Self 3, or the "social self," can be expressed as the many different selves or personae that the person presents in everyday interaction with others, for instance as characters in autobiographical stories (Sabat, 2002). The social roles that persons with dementia have occupied become challenged by the disease and if other persons tend to steer away from those social roles and attributes that the persons with dementia often value, few possibilities are left for the persons with dementia other than to retreat from social interaction.

Thus, Self 2 and Self 3 are sensitive to interaction with others, and malignant social interaction often results in the person with dementia becoming invalidated and depersonalized and thus "losing" their Selves 2 and 3 (Sabat, 2002; cf. Kitwood, 1990). At the same time, the social self can be upheld in many situations with the support of relatives and care providers (cf. Hedman et al., 2013).

Sabat's focus is on persons living with dementia and how these persons experience and define themselves – their selves – as well how others engage with these selves. Interaction become relevant to the degree it serves to recognize the self of the person living with dementia. As a consequence, identity is seen as an aspect of the self (in particular Self 2 and Self 3) and is expressed for instance as professional identity or in autobiographical stories. Thus, Sabat is less interested in how individuals living with dementia present and negotiate their identities in interaction, but rather in how their selves are expressed and recognized. The reason for this is that for Sabat, the self is not constituted in interaction, although it is dependent on interaction for its recognition and validation. The primary self (Self 1) is given as humans are natural agents and is expressed in interaction rather than emerging from interaction. The personal and social selves (Self 2 and 3) are expressed in the verbal interaction with other persons. Others are listeners and commentators on this verbal exchange, confirming, recognizing, challenging, or denying these personal expressions. Selves 2 and 3, like Self 1, do not emerge from interaction but are already constituted through the individual's experience of self.

Sabat's emphasis on the Self helps to describe and recognize agency as well as continuity in persons living with dementia and has convincingly demonstrated that people living with dementia do not "lose" their sense of self – they continue to experience themselves as persons. The fundamental theoretical limitation to this view is that Self and identity are primarily seen as expressing something already given in the person, rather than being constituted in and through interaction with other persons and the world.

22.4 The Embodied Self

Dementia is progressive, and at the advanced stages people living with dementia are severely challenged in using spoken language and thus in communicating verbally. These individuals are not the target group of Sabat's theory and would benefit more from a theoretical approach that stresses, for instance, nonverbal aspects of interaction. One of the few researchers who have tried to theorize and understand how persons with dementia express their self through their bodies, is Pia Kontos (2003, 2004, 2005). Instead of investigating the use of discursive tools for expressing identity and self, she has argued that the philosopher Maurice Merleau-Ponty's concept of *embodiment* is important in order to understand persons living with dementia (Merleau-Ponty, 2014).

Kontos argues that the theory of Sabat has a focus on interactional consequences – malignant social interaction – while leaving the body of the persons to one side and thus "not grant[ing] the lived experiential body in everyday life a significant role in the constitution and manifestation of selfhood" (Kontos, 2005, p. 555). Instead, she wants to take her starting point in the lived body. Her argument is that the origin of agency is found in pre-reflective experiences; specifically, in the body's interaction with the immediate physical and social environment. The importance of the lived body for identity formation is not specific for persons living with dementia but is rather something that is true for all individuals. However, this notion has special significance in the case of persons living with dementia, as other aspects and levels of identity – in particular, discursive aspects – are challenged as a consequence of the disease processes.

It is from the interaction with the immediate physical and social environment that the self emerges as a recurrent bodily pattern, as specific ways of moving the body, approaching the physical and social world: the way we walk, eat, and perform everyday chores, Kontos (2005) argues. Some of these patterns emerge from individual experiences, while others emerge as a result of the social and cultural habitus of interacting with the social physical world, as has been suggested by Bourdieu (1977). Thus, selfhood "consists in the dispositions and generative schemes of habitus" (Kontos, 2005, p. 563). This is what Kontos calls *the embodied selfhood*, which can be seen as

> a complex interrelationship between primordial and sociocultural characteristics of the body, all of which reside below the threshold of cognition, grounded in the pre-reflective level of experience, existing primarily in corporeal ways. (Kontos, 2005, p. 559)

The notion of embodied selfhood locates the self in the person as a "body-subject," rather than identifying an "inner" cognitive self. In contrast to Sabat (2001), the primary clinical and practical implication of Kontos's (2005) phenomenological approach to self and identity in persons living with dementia is more on noting the various ways the self is expressed in the pre-reflective body. The self is manifested in the ways "persons with dementia unthinkingly carry and project their bodies with coherence" (ibid., p. 566). It can be about the person's attention to appearance, cleanliness, or social etiquette, or the way the person knits or paints (Kontos, 2003). By paying attention to the embodied selfhood, carers could understand how "persons with dementia remain connected to the world" (Kontos, 2005, p. 566) and thus help to facilitate and support these connections.

Following the phenomenological approach, a person with dementia is thus not in a position to either have or not have a self and an identity. Instead, persons with dementia – like everyone else – express their subjectivity as an embodied self (cf. also Kontos, 2014; Phinney, 2014; Phinney & Chesla, 2003). It is also obvious that identity does not necessarily rely on verbal resources such as storytelling or categorizations. Identity can be shown rather than told: it is by their bodily engagement, by doing certain things in a specific way, that a person shows their identity. The phenomenological perspective thus highlights identity as part of the ways a person is connected to the world through practical engagement. A further step would be to show how "inter-embodied" selves and identities are based on *intercorporeality*, that is, a shared bodily presence in the socio-interactive environment (Jenkins, 2014; Meyer, Streeck, & Jordan, 2017). Such an approach would foster a dialogicality of selves and thus promote sharedness rather than individuality in dementia care (Jenkins, 2014).

22.5 Narrative Identity

A number of researchers have argued that stories both form and define identities: a person's identity develops and changes through a constant narrative elaboration and revision (Bamberg, 2011; Bamberg & Dege, Chapter 2 in this volume; Brockmeier, 2015; Brockmeier & Carbaugh, 2001; Bruner, 2002; Randall & McKim, 2004). Stories told by persons with dementia are often perceived to be *broken stories* because in contrast to other stories they are fragmented, partial, jumbled, and repetitive; they lack temporal and thematic coherence, and shift between characters, places, and times without any notice (Hydén & Brockmeier, 2008). The storyteller and the listeners tend to become *entangled* in broken stories: beginnings and endings are twisted together, interwoven with repetitions of the same event, resulting in shared states of narrative perplexity (Hydén, 2018a). Ultimately, the person with dementia will lose the ability to tell stories in conversational interaction, no longer giving voice to or authoring those stories where he or she features as a main character, and thus it is left to others to continue the telling.

The challenge in using autobiographical memories and the telling of broken stories has led many narrative researchers to argue that persons living with dementia cannot have a self or an identity. So, for instance, Jerome Bruner argued that it

> is through narrative that we create and re-create selfhood, that self is a product of our telling and not some essence to be delved for in the recesses of subjectivity. There is now evidence that if we lacked the capacity to make stories about ourselves, there would be no such thing as selfhood.
> (Bruner, 2002, pp. 85–86)

That is, *identity* is connected with *stories* which in turn are connected with *memories* – and if persons cannot remember the events and experiences of their lives, they cannot tell autobiographical stories, and as a consequence they will not have an identity.

As already discussed above, there does not seem to be any simple and direct relation between access to autobiographical memories and identity – thus questioning the narrative assumption about identity (cf. Brockmeier, 2014; Freeman, 2008). Above, it was also suggested that persons with dementia can use different resources – autobiographical memories being one of these – in order to construct and present an identity in different social settings. Further, a number of researchers have found that persons living with dementia can make use of autobiographical memories held by *other* persons, and then make use of these memories when presenting an identity. In a study based on interviews with people with dementia conducted with spouses present, Usita and her colleagues (1998) found that "participants with AD who were knowledgeable about their cognitive deficits" and recognized their losses "sought assistance, or stated their deficits" (p. 194). In practice this implied that persons with dementia who could not remember turned to their spouses for support and information. That is, if the persons living with dementia could not remember events from their past or could access knowledge about themselves on their own, and if they were aware of their challenges, they could ask for assistance and support. Thus, one possibility that persons with dementia can use in this situation is to ask their spouse or someone else who knows them for help with "remembering" an autobiographical event. This is something that was suggested by Mills (1997, 1998) in her study of persons with dementia talking part in reminiscence groups. She found that over time,

> as informants became more cognitively impaired by their disease there was an awareness, on the part of the interviewer, that they had bequeathed their narrative to another. It is argued that the sharing of such a narrative, within dementia care, reinforces carer attitudes of respect, understanding and acceptance. In this sense, therefore, the personal narrative of dementia sufferers is never lost. It continues its existence in the form of a valuable resource which can be returned to them, either verbally or non-verbally, during subsequent interactions. (Mills, 1998, p. 696)

This led Mills to argue that others – relatives or staff – can take over autobiographical memories of the individual and thus become "bearers" of these memories. Thus, when other persons around the person with dementia become holders of memories, the person with dementia can use these other persons as potential resources for "remembering" both events and personal knowledge. The person living with dementia can accomplish this by, for instance, requesting information from the healthy spouse and adding this to what he or she already "knows" and thus presenting an identity; or by letting other persons tell personal identity stories but claim ownership and responsibility of the stories and use them for presenting an identity (cf. Goodwin, 2004 on aphasia).

In most cases, couples, families, and friends have knowledge of each other's stories and share personal knowledge of each other because they have known each other for a long time and they also have shared experiences. In residential care settings, one way to expand the common ground between professional carers and persons with dementia is to systematically make use of life story work (McKeown, Clarke, & Repper, 2006). That is, the person with dementia and relatives share the individual's life stories with staff and hence help the staff to "know" the person with dementia by suggesting an interpretative context for that individual, making it easier to interact with the person (Surr, 2006).

One way to conceptualize the interaction between the person living with dementia and a healthy spouse or carer is to argue that the healthy partner creates "scaffolds" that can be used by the person living with dementia. Scaffolds can consist of projected turns formatted in such a way that it will be possible for the person with dementia to take on these turns (by using "yes/ no" questions, for instance). Scaffolds can also consist of often lengthy and complex search activities for words and linguistic expressions as well as for references to past events or persons. The use of these scaffolds will help the person with dementia to continue as an active participant and storyteller by making further contributions to the ongoing storytelling (Hydén, 2011). The narrative scaffolding becomes an integrated part of the ongoing collaboration as a means for upholding and presenting an identity through storytelling.

It is thus obvious from research about persons living with dementia and storytelling that they do not lose their ability to tell autobiographical stories as a way to present their identities – although these stories can be incomplete or broken, especially in the late-early and middle stages (Angus & Bowen, 2011; Beard et al., 2009; Beard, 2016; Phinney, 2002; Hamilton, 1996, 2008; Ramanathan, 1995). That is, the autobiographical stories do not live up to the taken-for-granted narrative norms, especially in terms of the discursive organization of the story, for instance coherence. This is an argument that at least partly disagrees with the idea that both self and identity remain more or less unaffected in persons with dementia, which is an idea that was presented by Steven Sabat and his colleagues (Sabat & Harré, 1992, 1994) in their articles about the self in dementia. The storytelling abilities are affected by dementia, so the autobiographical stories change as a result. Telling stories in new ways can be expected to result in new ways of experiencing self and others, and in particular the relationship between self, other, and the world. This also puts new demands on listeners to develop innovative ways of understanding and interpreting these autobiographical stories. Of particular importance is the ability to listen to autobiographical identity stories as poetic expressions, rather than literal descriptions of self and past events (Cheston, 1996). Thus, narrative identity is not about telling "true" autobiographical stories but rather about telling any story that can be used to understand who the teller claims to be or wants to be. In this way it also becomes possible for individuals living with dementia to change, develop, and revise their identities by, for instance, incorporating new narrative material irrespective of whether these stories are "true" or not.

22.6 Shared Identities

Identity is generally considered to be the expression of a specific individual. This notion is often supported by the use of a research design – individual interviews – that will produce exemplars of individual identities. If researchers change design and instead do interviews with couples or use observation and recording of interaction involving persons with dementia, this will often produce material that supports identity having features that are shared. During the last decade a number of studies of persons with dementia have been based on couple (dyadic) interviews or recorded interaction with couples starting from a narrative practice perspective (cf. Bamberg, 2011). As a consequence, these studies have discovered aspects of identity that are shared with a spouse, other significant others, or a broader community (Clare, Rowlands, & Quinn, 2008). Research investigating couples living with dementia have found that they expend considerable effort and ingenuity both in sustaining their relationship and in seeking to maintain the involvement of the person with dementia. Central to this collaborative story-telling practice is the care of a *shared identity* (Hernandez et al., 2019; Merrick, Camic, & O'Shaughnessy, 2016; Molyneaux et al., 2012; Robinson, Clare, & Evans, 2005), sometimes called a *we*-identity (Hydén & Nilsson, 2015), an *us*-identity (Davies, 2011), or *couplehood* (Hellström, Nolan & Lundh, 2005, 2007). The shared identity influences the individual identities so that the borders between the individual identities and the shared we-identity easily and often become blurred (Hernandez et al., 2019).

In presenting and negotiating shared identities, spouses must position themselves both *discursively* and *epistemically* as being able to claim part of the shared identity. They also organize their interaction in such a way that they can use each other's discursive and cognitive (epistemic) resources. Discursively, the spouses must position their individual *I*s as part of a collective *we* (Hydén & Nilsson, 2015). This is accomplished through a specific person-referencing practice where pronoun use makes it possible for the spouses to reference both individual *I*s and collective *we*s. The *we* can, for instance, function as an agent, as well as having mental states and attitudes, while the *I*s can be used for expressing disagreements.

Epistemically, shared identities are often established and pursued through the telling of *joint autobiographical stories*. Joint autobiographical stories portray the spouses as belonging together, as sharing experiences and values, as being something more than just two individual persons. Telling joint stories implies that the spouses must position themselves as being *knowledgeable* about each other and their couplehood (the we). This knowledge can be based on the spouses' shared experiences, on what one spouse told the other, or on inferences about the other spouse. That is, spouses develop and maintain a *common ground* (Clark, 1996) that consists of their shared experiences and knowledge about themselves as individual persons and about themselves as a pair. When the spouses do something together or when they tell stories about their individual experiences, they add to their common ground, but they also add their various versions and narrations of stories about their experiences and themselves.

The challenges that couples with dementia face have to do with the fact that the person with dementia gradually loses cognitive and linguistic resources and is presented with increasing challenges in everyday interaction. In everyday interaction these changes are manifested in the fact that the spouses' common ground starts to fragment as the person with dementia has increasing problems understanding what the healthy spouse refers to, but also in remembering shared events in the past and shared knowledge important in storytelling (names of children, date of marriage, etc.). These problems are recurrent and do not go away but will gradually increase as time goes by (Hydén, 2017).

This gradual loss of common ground challenges the shared identity as the spouses' shared experiences, knowledge, and previously told versions of stories have become much more difficult to use as a common resource when the spouses tell stories about themselves. The relationship between the spouses will become increasingly asymmetric as the healthy spouse must take responsibility for their shared identity and life. Eventually the healthy spouse must increasingly hold the spouse with dementia in person, as has been suggested by Lindemann (2014) and Zeiler (2014), as the person with dementia does not have the cognitive and linguistic resources needed to communicate an identity. This also implies that the healthy spouse eventually must function as a *vicarious voice* when the ability to take part in the shared identity work of the person with dementia is challenged even more as the disease progresses (Hydén, 2008).

Personal identities are thus not necessarily just individual as is often taken for granted: when persons live together, their individual identities become shared and based on a common ground. As mentioned above, this also may include intercorporeality, that is, a shared socio-interactive environment (Jenkins, 2014). The shared identity is challenged by the progressing dementia as the couple's common ground erodes and their mutual recognition gradually becomes difficult.

22.7 Concluding Discussion

What research about persons living with dementia shows is that although people living with dementia will face increasing cognitive and linguistic challenges, there is very little empirical evidence that they "lose" either a sense of self or their identities. Talking *with* persons living with dementia – not just *about* or *to* them (Hydén & Mishler, 1999) – will make it obvious that they have a subjectivity, present an identity, and participate as active agents in activities.

The changes brought about in the brain as a consequence of dementia imply an increase in the challenges the person living with dementia will face on his or her own: it will take longer to find words and construct utterances, as well as remembering events, and eventually no words are produced. In order to compensate for these challenges, the person with dementia can do several things. The person with dementia may *restructure* the cognitive and semiotic resources used to express and communicate identity. One possibility is a shift between verbal and other semiotic resources, especially bodily enactments. This implies that the discursive organization of utterances and in particular autobiographical stories will be affected, often including nonverbal substitutions, repetitions, and becoming more fragmented. As the agency of the person with dementia changes and becomes more bounded, the person becomes more dependent on others in presenting and communicating an identity. One possibility is to use the cognitive and linguistic resources of others, either directly, through support and information, or indirectly, through scaffolding where the healthy partner supports the person with dementia to communicate an identity.

Over time, there will be a shift in the *voice* of the person with dementia. In conversations as well as in storytelling, the person with dementia will be less able to take turns and tell stories. As the dementia progresses and the person with dementia can only make minimal communicative contributions, the person with dementia will be less considered as the originator of stories or information that might present and sustain identity. Thus, it will be others who tell those stories the person with dementia used to tell or submit certain information. That is, others will tell stories *about* the person with dementia, rather than together with the person with dementia. Ultimately, the person with dementia will thus be the subject or protagonist of the identity, but not its communicative origin. From a relational point of view, this often implies a change in the position of the person with dementia in joint activities like conversations. Many persons with dementia will go from having had a central position in joint activities to a peripheral position in terms of actions such as taking initiatives and introducing new topics in autobiographical storytelling.

These shifts in agency, uses of resources, and voice all contribute to changes in identity and sense of self: the power of the person with dementia to present different versions of events as well as of self diminishes over time. This will result in a less faceted identity. Obviously, certain aspects of identity will dominate over others as these aspects are more readily available. The person with dementia will further have less power to negotiate identity and self, and thus become more dependent on those stories that are available, or that are told by others. The unique voice of the person with dementia also becomes less pronounced. As this unique voice falters, something of what is typical of the teller will be lost (Freeman, 2008).

There are some general conclusions from the research on dementia and identity that have relevance for the discussion about personal identity.

First, it is obvious from this research that evidence does not support a close connection between autobiographical memory, knowledge, and identity. Rather, it seems that identity is a situated and opportunistic construction. That is, identities are constructed interactively by the use of a number of different available resources in the socio-interactive environment. Individuals living with dementia can, for instance, make use of others' utterances and stories in order to construct an identity; or knowledge and stories supplied by others can be used to present an identity. In this sense, identity construction is an opportunistic business. The disentanglement of memory and identity thus support interactive approaches to identity stressing creative, embodied, and situated aspects (De Fina, Schiffrin, & Bamberg, 2006).

Second, the dementia research shows that identities can be expressed, presented, negotiated, and acknowledged in many different ways and media: through the use of social categories, by telling autobiographical stories – individual as well as shared ones – and in embodied and enacted ways together with other bodies in intercorporeal relations (cf. Meyer, Streeck, & Jordan, 2017).

Thirdly, the research on dementia indicates that identities are not just an individual expression. Rather, identities are collaborative endeavors building on the various resources supplied by different participants in interactional situations. Further, establishment and negotiation of identities make use of shared stories owned together by families, friends, and communities, thus making identity a question of knowing these stories and having the right to tell them. This is an argument in favor of anti-individualistic conceptions of identity (cf. De Fina, 2013).

Fourthly, it is obvious that the researchers' decisions about study design and methods are quite consequential in constraining possible interpretations and conceptualizations of identity: individual interviews will exclude shared identities, while couple interviews or recorded interaction will help to understand collaborative aspects of identity as well as shared identities; an exclusive focus on spoken interaction will tend to miss the embodied aspects of identity which become more obvious when using video-recordings, and so on (cf. Ochs & Capps, 2001).

In conclusion, although dementia is often considered to be about loss, it is a disorder that results in a new being-in-the-world. As such, it is a disorder that at least partially displaces some of our most cherished notions about identity and shows that there are a number of possibilities to sustain and even revise and develop identities in a life with dementia. It is to be hoped that some of these possibilities will inform the general discussion about personal identity and make a contribution to our understanding of identity as a part of our shared socio-interactive environment.

References

Addis, D. R. & Tippett, L. J. (2004). Memory of myself: Autobiographical memory and identity in Alzheimer's disease. *Memory*, *12*, 56–74.

Angus, J. & Bowen, S. (2011). Quiet please, there's a lady on stage: Centering the person with dementia in life story narrative. *Journal of Aging Studies*, *25*, 110–117.

Bamberg, M. (2011). Who am I? Narration and its contribution to self and identity. *Theory and Psychology*, *21*(1), 3–24.

Beard, R. L. (2004). In their voices: Identity preservation and experiences of Alzheimer's disease. *Journal of Aging Studies*, *18*, 415–428.

Beard, R. L. (2016). *Living with Alzheimer's: Managing Memory Loss, Identity, and Illness*. New York, NY: New York University Press.

Beard, R. L., Knauss, J., & Moyer, D. (2009). Managing disability and enjoying life: How we reframe dementia through personal narratives. *Journal of Aging Studies*, *23*, 227–235.

Bourdieu, P. (1977). *Outline of a Theory of Practice*. Cambridge: Cambridge University Press.

Brockmeier, J. (2014). Questions of meaning: Memory, dementia, and the postauto-biographical perspective. In L. C. Hydén, H. Lindemann, & J. Brockmeier (Eds.), *Beyond Loss: Dementia, Identity, Personhood* (pp. 69–90). New York, NY: Oxford University Press.

Brockmeier, J. (2015). *Beyond the Archive: Memory, Narrative, and the Autobiographical Process*. New York, NY: Oxford University Press.

Brockmeier, J. & Carbaugh, D. (Eds.). (2001). *Narrative and Identity: Studies in Autobiography, Self and Culture*. Amsterdam: John Benjamins.

Bruner, J. (1994). The "remembered" self. In U. Neisser & R. Fivush (Eds.), *The Remembering Self: Construction and Accuracy in the Self-Narrative* (pp. 41–54). New York, NY: Cambridge University Press.

Bruner, J. (2002). *Making Stories: Law, Literature, Life*. New York, NY: Farrar, Straus and Giroux.

Bunn, H., Burn, A.-M., Goodman, C., Rait, G., Norton, S., Robinson, L., Schoeman, J., & Brayne, C. (2014). Comorbidity and dementia: A scoping review of the literature. *BMC Medicine*, *12*, 192. doi:10.1186/s12916-014-0192-4.

Caddell, L. S. & Clare, L. (2010). The impact of dementia on self and identity: A systematic review. *Clinical Psychology Review*, *30*, 113–126.

Cheston, R. (1996). Stories and metaphors: Talking about the past in a psychotherapy group for people with dementia. *Ageing and Society*, *16*, 576–602.

Clare, L. (2008). *Neuropsychological Rehabilitation and People with Dementia*. Hove: Psychology Press.

Clare, L., Rowlands, J. M., & Quinn, R. (2008). Collective strength. The impact of developing a shared social identity in early-stage dementia. *Dementia, 7,* 9–30.

Clark, H. H. (1996). *Using Language.* New York, NY: Cambridge University Press.

Cohen, D. & Eisdorfer, C. (1986). *The Loss of Self.* New York, NY: Norton.

Cohen-Mansfield, J., Golander, H., & Arnheim, G. (2000). Self-identity in older persons suffering from dementia: preliminary results. *Social Science and Medicine, 51,* 381–394.

Cohen-Mansfield, J., Parpura-Gilla, A., & Golander, H. (2006). Salience of self-identity roles in persons with dementia: Differences in perceptions among elderly persons, family members and caregivers. *Social Science & Medicine, 62,* 745–757.

Conway, M. A. (2005). Memory and the self. *Journal of Memory and Language, 53,* 594–628.

Corkin, S. (2013). *Permanent Present Tense: The Man with No Memory, and What He Taught the World.* London: Allen Lane.

Davies, J. C. (2011). Preserving the "us identity" through marriage commitment while living with early-stage dementia. *Dementia, 10,* 217–234.

Davis, D. H. J. (2004). Dementia: Sociological and philosophical constructions. *Social Science and Medicine, 58,* 369–378.

De Fina, A. (2013). Positioning level 3: Connecting local identity displays to macro social processes. *Narrative Inquiry, 23*(1), 40–61.

De Fina, A., Schiffrin, D., & Bamberg, M. (Eds.). (2006). *Discourse and Identity.* Cambridge: Cambridge University Press.

Fontana, A. & Smith, R. W. (1989). Alzheimer's disease victims: The "unbecoming" of self and the normalization of competence. *Sociological Perspectives, 32,* 35–46.

Freeman, M. (2008). Beyond narrative: Dementia's tragic promise. In L. C. Hydén & J. Brockmeier (Eds.), *Health, Illness, and Culture: Broken Narratives* (pp. 169–183). New York, NY: Routledge.

Gallagher, S. (2011). Introduction: A diversity of selves. In S. Gallagher (Ed.), *The Oxford Handbook of The Self* (pp. 1–29). Oxford: Oxford University Press.

Gergen, K. J. (1994). *Realities and Relationships: Soundings in Social Construction.* Cambridge, MA: Harvard University Press.

Goodwin, C. (2004). A competent speaker who can't speak: The social life of aphasia. *Journal of Linguistic Anthropology, 14,* 151–170.

Hamilton, H. E. (1996). Intratextuality, intertextuality, and the construction of identity as patient in Alzheimer's disease. *Text, 16,* 61–90.

Hamilton, H. E. (2008). Narrative as snapshot: Glimpses into the past in Alzheimer's discourse. *Narrative Inquiry, 18,* 53–82.

Harré, R. (1998). *The Singular Self: An Introduction to the Psychology of Personhood.* London: Sage.

Hedman, R., Hansebo, G., Ternstedt, B. M., Hellström, I., & Norberg, A. (2013). How people with Alzheimer's disease express their sense of self: Analysis using Rom Harré's theory of selfhood. *Dementia, 12,* 713–733.

Hellström, I., Nolan, M., & Lundh, U. (2005). We do things together: A case study of couplehood in dementia. *Dementia, 4,* 7–22.

Hellström, I., Nolan, M., & Lundh, U. (2007). Sustaining "couplehood": Spouses strategies for living positively with dementia. *Dementia, 6*, 383–409.

Hernandez, E., Spencer, B., Ingersoll-Dayton, B., Faber, A., & Ewert, A. (2019). "We are a team": Couple identity and memory loss. *Dementia, 18*, 1166–1180.

Herskovits, E. (1995). Struggling over subjectivity: Debates about the "self" and Alzheimer's disease. *Medical Anthropology Quarterly, 9*, 146–164.

Hydén, L. C. (2008). Broken and vicarious voices in narratives. In L. C. Hydén & J. Brockmeier (Eds.), *Health, Culture and Illness: Broken Narratives* (pp. 36–53). New York, NY: Routledge.

Hydén, L. C. (2011). Narrative collaboration and scaffolding in dementia. *Journal of Aging Studies, 25*, 339–347.

Hydén, L. C. (2017). Storytelling in dementia: Collaboration and common ground. In L. C. Hydén & E. Antelius (Eds.), *Living with Dementia: Relations, Responses and Agency in Everyday Life* (pp. 116–135). London: Palgrave.

Hydén, L. C. (2018a). *Entangled Narratives: Collaborative Storytelling and the Re-Imagining of Dementia*. New York, NY: Oxford University Press.

Hydén, L. C. (2018b). Dementia, embodied memories and the self. *Journal of Consciousness Studies, 25*, 225–241.

Hydén, L. C. & Brockmeier, J. (Eds.). (2008). *Health, Culture and Illness: Broken Narratives*. New York, NY: Routledge.

Hydén, L. C. & Forsblad, M. (2018). Collaborative remembering in dementia: The perspective from activity theory. In M. Meade, C. B. Harris, P. Van Bergen, J. Sutton, & A. J. Barnier (Eds.), *Collaborative Remembering: Theories, Research, and Applications* (pp. 436–455). Oxford: Oxford University Press.

Hydén, L. C. & Mishler, E. G. (1999). Medicine and language. *Annual Review of Applied Linguistics, 19*, 174–192.

Hydén, L. C. & Nilsson, E. (2015). Couples with dementia: Positioning the "we." *Dementia, 14*, 716–733.

Jenkins, N. (2014). Dementia and the inter-embodied self. *Social Theory & Health, 12*, 125–137.

Kitwood, T. (1990). The dialectics of dementia: With particular reference to Alzheimer's disease. *Ageing & Society, 10*, 177–196.

Kitwood, T. (1997). *Dementia Reconsidered: The Person Comes First*. Maidenhead: Open University Press.

Kontos, P. C. (2003). The painterly hand: Embodied consciousness and Alzheimer's disease. *Journal of Aging Studies, 17*, 151–170.

Kontos, P. C. (2004). Ethnographic reflections on selfhood, embodiment and Alzheimer's disease. *Ageing & Society, 24*, 829–849.

Kontos, P. C. (2005). Embodied selfhood in Alzheimer's disease: Rethinking person-centred care. *Dementia, 4*, 553–570.

Kontos, P. C. (2014). Musical embodiment, selfhood, and dementia. In L. C. Hydén, H. Lindemann, & J. Brockmeier (Eds.), *Beyond Loss: Dementia, Identity, Personhood* (pp. 107–119). New York, NY: Oxford University Press.

Lezak, M. D., Howieson, D. B., Bigler, E. D., & Tranel, D. (2012). *Neuropsychological Assessment, 5th Ed*. New York, NY: Oxford University Press.

Lindemann, H. (2014). *Holding and Letting Go: The Social Practice of Personal Identities*. New York, NY: Oxford University Press.

Matthews, E. (2006). Dementia and the identity of the person. In J. C. Hughes, S. J. Louw, & S. R. Sabat (Eds.), *Dementia: Mind, Meaning, and the Person* (pp. 163–177). Oxford: Oxford University Press.

Maurer, K. & Maurer, U. (2003). *Alzheimer: The Life of a Physician and the Career of a Disease*. New York, NY: Columbia University Press.

McKeown, J., Clarke, A., & Repper, J. (2006). Life story work in health and social care: Systematic literature review. *Journal of Advanced Nursing, 55,* 237–247.

Merleau-Ponty, M. (2014). *Phenomenology of Perception*. Milton Park: Routledge.

Merrick, K., Camic, P. M., & O'Shaughnessy, M. (2016). Couples constructing their experiences of dementia: A relational perspective. *Dementia, 15,* 34–50.

Meyer, C., Streeck, J., & Jordan, J. S. (Eds.). (2017). *Intercorporeality: Emerging Socialities in Interaction*. New York, NY: Oxford University Press.

Mills, M. A. (1997). Narrative identity and dementia: A study of emotion and narrative in older people with dementia. *Ageing and Society, 17,* 673–698.

Mills, M. A. (1998). *Narrative Identity and Dementia: A Study of Autobiographical Memories and Emotions*. Aldershot: Ashgate.

Mishler, E. G. (1999). *Storylines: Crafts Artists' Narratives of Identity*. Cambridge, MA: Harvard University Press.

Molyneaux, V. J., Butchard, S., Simpson, J., & Murray, C. (2012). The co-construction of couplehood in dementia. *Dementia, 11,* 483–502.

Morris, R. & Becker, J. (Eds.). (2004). *Cognitive Neuropsychology of Alzheimer's Disease, 2nd Ed*. Oxford: Oxford University Press.

Naylor, E. & Clare, L. (2008). Awareness of memory functioning, autobiographical memory and identity in early-stage dementia. *Neuropsychological Rehabilitation, 18,* 590–606.

Ochs, E. & Capps, L. (2001). *Living Narrative: Creating Lives in Everyday Storytelling*. Cambridge, MA: Harvard University Press.

Phinney, A. (2002). Fluctuating awareness and the breakdown of the illness narrative in dementia. *Dementia, 1,* 329–344.

Phinney, A. (2014). As the body speaks: Creative expression in dementia. In L. C. Hydén, H. Lindemann, & J. Brockmeier (Eds.), *Beyond Loss: Dementia, Identity, Personhood* (pp. 120–134). New York, NY: Oxford University Press.

Phinney, A. & Chesla, C. A. (2003). The lived body in dementia. *Journal of Aging Studies, 17,* 283–299.

Ramanathan, V. (1995). Narrative well-formedness in Alzheimer's discourse: An interactional examination across settings. *Journal of Pragmatics, 23,* 395–419.

Randall, W. L. & McKim, A. E. (2004). Towards a poetics of aging: The links between literature and life. *Narrative Inquiry, 14,* 235–260.

Robinson, L., Clare, L., & Evans, K. (2005). Making sense of dementia and adjusting to loss: Psychological reactions to a diagnosis of dementia in couples. *Aging & Mental Health, 9,* 337–347.

Sabat, S. R. (2001). *Experience of Alzheimer's Disease: Life through a Tangled Veil*. Oxford: Blackwell.

Sabat, S. R. (2002). Surviving manifestations of selfhood in Alzheimer's disease: A case study. *Dementia, 1,* 25–36.

Sabat, S. R. & Collins, M. (1999). Intact social, cognitive ability, and selfhood: A case study of Alzheimer's disease. *American Journal of Alzheimer's Disease and Other Dementia, 14*, 11–19.

Sabat, S. R. & Harré, R. (1992). The construction and deconstruction of self in Alzheimer's disease. *Ageing and Society, 12*, 443–461.

Sabat, S. R. & Harré, R. (1994). The Alzheimer's disease sufferer as a semiotic subject. *Philosophy, Psychology, Psychiatry, 1*, 145–160.

Saunders, P. A. (1998). "My brain's on strike": The construction of identity through memory accounts by dementia patients. *Research on Aging, 20*, 65–90.

Schechtman, M. (1996). *The Constitution of Selves*. Ithaca, NY: Cornell University Press.

Small, J. A., Geldart, K., Gutman, G., & Scott, M. A. C. (1998). The discourse of self in dementia. *Aging and Society, 18*, 291–316.

Surr, C. A. (2006). Preservation of self in people with dementia living in residential care: A socio-biographical approach. *Social Science and Medicine, 62*, 1720–1730.

Usita, P. M., Hyman, I. E., & Herman, K. C. (1998). Narrative intentions: Listening to life stories in Alzheimer's disease. *Journal of Aging Studies, 12*, 185–198.

Van der Linden, M. & Juilerat Van der Linden, A.-C. (2018). A life-course and multifactorial approach to Alzheimer's disease: Implications for research, clinical assessment and intervention practices. *Dementia, 17*, 880–895.

Zeiler, K. (2014). A philosophical defense of the idea that we can hold each other in personhood: intercorporeal personhood in dementia care. *Medical Health Care and Philosophy, 17*, 131–141.

23 The Study of Identity in Health Psychology

Abigail Locke and Jane Montague

In this chapter we consider the ways in which identities are studied within contemporary health psychology. Using exemplars from different aspects of health psychology research, we consider the enacted, situated, relational, and embodied nature of identities. We particularly emphasize identities in everyday contexts and the changes that can occur when encountering challenges to one's own or someone else's health. After outlining our definition of identity and considering how the topic has been approached within health psychology, our focus in the chapter moves to focusing on women's identities in healthcare contexts, noting also the gendered aspects and expectations within these contexts.

Drawing influence from social constructionist, social interactionist, and self-determination perspectives, our position is based in what is broadly known as sociological social psychology (SSP). Within this approach to self and identity the two are closely intertwined (Stets & Burke, 2005; Ryan & Deci, 2012): the self is theorized to emerge within complex and diverse social interactions through which identities (parts of the self) each become tied to specific aspects of our social structure (Howard, 2000). Rather than being conceptualized as purely internal constructs of the self, we argue that discrete identities are foregrounded at different times and in relation to specific contexts (Benwell & Stokoe, 2006; Antaki & Widdicombe, 1998); they reflect each of the different positions or role relationships related to an individual.

At points during the chapter we also refer to "roles." In our explication these are socially defined and recognized (such as doctor, lecturer, etc.) and designated through cultural expectations. Identity, within this chapter, is personally relevant and defined, and enables individuals to perform successfully within a number of defined roles by assuming the appropriate and expected behaviors.

23.1 Health Psychology and Identity

According to Matazarro (1980, as cited in Chamberlain & Murray, 2017), there are four main goals in health psychology:

(1) to promote and maintain health, ensuring and maintaining good health and positive health behaviors;

(2) to prevent and treat illness, usually focusing on people at risk of illness or those who are already ill;

(3) to examine the etiological and diagnostic correlates of health and illness, which involves research examining risk factors, role of loneliness/social relations, and psychological factors;

(4) to explore healthcare systems and healthcare policies, examining how health psychology can contribute to public health policy and initiatives, including behavioral insights to increase adherence to different policies and interactions with health professionals.

These four goals work across the wider discipline of health psychology and have formed the basis for more recent similar categorizations of health psychology. For example, Marks (2002) divided the work of health psychology as a whole across four categories: clinical, public, community, and critical.

The conventional view of health psychology, then, is as a multidisciplinary collection of ideas that brings together a number of areas of psychology and the social sciences (Morrison & Bennett, 2016). Influence is derived from such diverse fields as medical sociology, health economics, and behavioral medicine, which are coupled with concepts from social, cognitive, developmental, and biological psychology. One thing that all these areas have in common is that they mediate access to an objective world, taking a positivist approach to investigating health and illness (Murray, 2015). The influence of social psychology in particular has generated an approach in which models of health behavior are commonplace, e.g., the multidimensional health locus of control (Wallston et al., 1976), the theory of reasoned action (Fishbein & Ajzen, 1975), the theory of planned behavior (Ajzen, 1991), the transtheoretical model (Prochaska & Velicer, 1997), and the importance of self-efficacy on health behavior (Bandura, 1977).

In addition to applying a variety of social cognition models to understanding health, this mainstream approach adopts a biopsychosocial view of health behaviors and suggests that social norms influence us and help form our attitudes. It specifically focuses on how the individual is influenced to behave in "typical" ways in relation to their health and suggests that the uptake of and engagement with health behaviors can be affected by different characteristics of the individuals included in research. For example, some research suggests that men are more likely to engage in risky behaviors (Ogden, 2019), whereas other research shows that women might more regularly engage in health care-seeking behaviors (Thompson et al., 2016). In some arenas, this individualistic, apolitical perspective is called "mainstream" health psychology (MHP). Health psychology that operates from this mainstream perspective focuses, therefore, on an individualistic psychology exemplified by these models through which psychologists seek to change and influence behaviors with little to no mention of the role of identities in this endeavor.

It is important to note, however, that while at times there has been a separating out of health and social psychology within the mainstream approach, in more recent years there has been a coming together of "new approaches" in health research. In particular, along with the social prescribing model that appears in much health promotion work, prominent social psychologists such as Haslam and colleagues (Haslam et al., 2018; Jetten, Haslam, & Haslam, 2012) have been writing about the "social cure" and how social identities are key within health and well-being. This "social cure" work appears to be rooted within a more mainstream tradition of social (and health) psychology including the study of group identities, and social cognitive models, with the aim of applying the social identity approach and its processes. This work draws on Tajfel and Turner's (e.g., 1985) theories from social psychology to offer an understanding of health and well-being.

From the mid-1990s onwards, an alternative perspective arose: critical health psychology (CHP), developed across an international context and both authors' research is located within this approach. As Michelle Crossley (2000) noted, there are alternative classifications of ideas between the mainstream and critical approaches to health psychology, with mainstream taking a more conventional scientific approach that looks at measuring, predicting, and changing behaviors (Chamberlain & Murray, 2017). CHP in contrast, challenges assumptions and practices of MHP, arguing that people are "complex, changing and multifaceted" (Chamberlain & Murray, 2017, pp. 432–433). It challenges the mainstream approach in seeking to identify how individuals can be empowered or disenfranchised through knowledge of health contexts and implements a wider contextual consideration to attempts to change health behaviors. CHP integrates a wider sociocultural view including, for example, lifespan and socioeconomic factors in considering the ways in which precarity affects health and well-being (Gross et al., 2018). This attention to the ways in which wider social-psychological, sociopolitical, and sociocultural processes may influence the "choices" available to us in relation to our health and well-being practices, gives a more integrated view of the interplay between health and illness overall. CHP acknowledges the neoliberal political context in which many health behaviors and decisions are being made (Murray, 2015). Identity as a health psychology concern permeates the ways in which people adopt or change their behaviors. In many ways this can be seen to be an aspect of the prominence of the behavior change models currently so popular within health psychology and wider political agendas for many Global North settings (Barnes, 2015). It might also be prompted during a period of ill-health or a change in bodily or mental health status. In considering how health psychology has approached the study of identities, our examples illustrate two areas of impact on female identities. The first takes the "breast is best" health promotion campaign to illustrate how maternal identities are problematized within and negotiated through responses to such messages. The second focuses on the ways in which adjustment of women's identities is necessitated following a breast cancer diagnosis.

23.2 Identities as Enacted, Embodied, and Relational

We explore identities in two specific areas related to women. Firstly, we consider early motherhood and maternal identities. Much has been written in this area from a critical perspective, drawing heavily on work from other disciplines including sociology, media studies, and health. In this example, we discuss the work around maternal identities, in particular the way in which mothers orient around a "good mothering" discourse, considering the ways in which this has become bound up with debates around infant feeding practices. Second, we focus on a specific challenge to women's health and well-being: the changing identities encountered when negotiating a diagnosis of and treatment for breast cancer. Attention has been given to the increasing medicalization of the female body, e.g., in conception, pregnancy, birth, menstruation, or menopause (Ussher, 2006), and although oncological research is generally dominated by quantitative, biologically based methods, a growing body of qualitative work is beginning to explore the ways in which individuals experience the diagnostic and treatment processes through which their adjustment and recovery begins.

As we have previously stated, and will demonstrate through these two examples, we regard identities to be multifaceted within health psychology. Different analyses and approaches may treat identities as enacted and situated: how they are constructed in particular contexts or how they position people within those contexts. The enacting of these identities and their situated nature enables us to perform both macro and micro levels of analysis, exploring subtle changes in relation to various events and people. In addition, identities may be embodied: how the body is perceived by self and others and how it "works" within different contexts can affect the negotiation of resulting interactions. Finally, identities are viewed as relational, being enacted in relation to others, whether it is within the everyday business of life or when dealing with a challenge to one's "normal" circumstances. Taking identities as reflecting different aspects of the self, as discussed in our introduction to the chapter, these three features are explored in turn.

23.2.1 Enacted and Constructed Identities

As we mentioned previously, one way of thinking through the various identities that are displayed is to move away from considerations of identity as an essence that is somehow fixed and internal, to considering how identity is "performed," that is, how identities are constructed and enacted, including considerations of how identities are situated and vary in different settings. For example, we, the authors, can be variably constructed and enact identities within many categories, including "psychologists," "women," "mothers," "grandmothers," and so on. That is, identity can be seen "as a public phenomenon, a performance or construct that is interpreted by other people"

(Benwell & Stokoe, 2006, p. 4). In this sense, then, and in relation to health psychology, we can see how identities are constructed in health and illness, and how people are both being positioned and positioning themselves within wider discourses and narratives. Identities and the ways in which people construct themselves and others and how they enact certain roles and behaviors have been noted across the field of health and well-being. For example, in her work on myalgic encephalomyelitis (ME), Horton-Salway (2001) considered the ways in which patients constructed their changing identities following diagnoses of a "contested" illness. Similarly, Seymour-Smith (2008) considered the role of masculine identity in help-seeking, in particular the ways in which men accounted for seeking help and support during ill-health (see also Seymour-Smith, Wetherell, & Phoenix, 2002). By reaching an understanding of how identities are being constructed and/or how people are positioning themselves and being positioned in discourses around health and well-being, the tailoring of health interventions to account for these differences is enabled. Examining the construction of identities is only one aspect of considering identities in health psychology. We now move on to considering the role of embodiment and embodied identities.

23.2.2 Embodied Identities

Feminist scholars (e.g., Bordo, 2003) began to critique the mainstream viewpoint from a sociocultural frame arguing that constructions of body image, though made visible through physiological changes, are influenced through sociocultural discourses and practices. As Fredrickson and Roberts (1997, p. 174) state: "Bodies exist within social and cultural contexts." Locating these ideas within the SSP approach outlined at the beginning of this chapter, this viewpoint suggests that our identities are closely tied not only to our biological development and our physical appearance but also to interpretations of such features within society. Maintaining the outward appearance of someone who fits with societal expectations is important in order to be seen and to see oneself positively. As Goffman (1959) argued more than half a century ago, we will manage others' impressions of us in order to give the most positive view of ourselves and to "fit" with the expected norms surrounding us. In their experiences of breast cancer, for example, it is expected that women undergoing mastectomy will do their best to fit with the two-breasted world by choosing to reconstruct their breast. Any other choice positions them against the norm of being a woman – they are perceived as "other," i.e., as one-breasted and, in those instances, not conforming with the accepted social representation of the female body.

Negotiating the world as an embodied being means that effects are felt psychologically and are not simply only a matter of how we feel within ourselves but are reflected back to us through our interactions with others, some of which might contradict our feelings. Goffman suggests we instinctively seek positively valued identities through which we draw positive self-esteem and avoid psychological challenges such as anxiety and depression. However, research into physical difference in adulthood has highlighted difficulties in social encounters with others (e.g., Rumsey & Harcourt, 2005), focusing on aspects such as raised levels of anxiety and negative effects on self-esteem in relation to appearance (Reardon & Grogan, 2011) or leading to feelings of shame (Machlaclan, 2004): our consciousness of our own views of how others might perceive us (e.g., eating in public when overweight) can lead us to hiding behaviors and feeling stigmatized.

Phenomenological accounts of embodiment (Zeiler & Folkmarson Kall, 2015) emphasize lived experience and our agency to make decisions. They highlight the body as a unique site of identity through which we can express ourselves. We can choose particular "markers" related to our outward appearance (such as tattoos, hairstyles, clothing, etc.) through which our group memberships and individuality can be displayed; however, other aspects are less a matter of choice (sex, age, weight, race, and so on). These outward signs allow or hinder certain interactions and reactions, and each of them will affect our relationships with others (e.g., whether we approach them confidently or feel intimidated) and subsequently their reactions to us. In specific health contexts these different appearance markers might provide a source of information for medical practitioners, such as carrying information about the particular experiences of individuals in their care in relation to their life course, their cultural support needs, or their possible comorbid health conditions. Appearance markers also impact on relationships in other contexts; we explore relational identities in more depth below.

23.2.3 Relational Identities

By necessity within social interactions we do not act in isolation. Antaki and Widdicombe (1998) argue that behavior is always in response to others (relational) and our surrounding environment (situated). Within health contexts, such as those we discuss in this chapter, it is important to consider how our identities become constructed through such interactions and contexts. As we have previously discussed, our approach is to consider multiple identities, rather than identity being considered a singular concept. In relational terms, those identities we display within our interactions are always in response to others. An interaction where a health issue is discussed with a health professional is likely to be very different than one where it is discussed with a loved one, for example. In the case of maternal identities, mothers act and react in relation to infants and significant others, whether it be father, wider family, or interactions with health professionals. Identities are also always situated: coping with a health issue within a hospital context will draw on a different identity than coping with it at home in a familiar setting.

These relational and situated identities are linked to social identities in that we are led to identify with particular groups and communities (in this chapter, breastfeeding mothers and women with breast cancer). Similarly, they link to personal identities, i.e., in the ways that we adapt to or rebel against the expectations of us as individuals in any given context. These relational and situated social as well as personal identities are always performed (Goffman, 1959) in relation to others: at various times we might be parent, child, neighbor, health practitioner, student, etc.

Our relationships with others, and the contexts within which we are located, can affect our behaviors and our ability to follow our inclinations in numerous ways – they can be constrained or enabled within particular contexts and by those others we find ourselves interacting with. So, for example, a mother and baby come together in ways in which certain expectations and obligations are attributed to the mother in respect of what the baby needs; a patient and health practitioner come together in situations where the patient's behavior will determine the practitioners' ability to treat them (Benwell & Stokoe, 2006). These roles and accompanying identities are relevant only for the length of time that the relationship is pertinent; once that interaction is over, different identities will then become foregrounded. The relational and situated identities that we assume become questioned when they fail to fit the context appropriately, for example, when an individual begins to question their identity in the interaction. The relational and situated identities, and the ways in which the women on whom we focus conform with or disrupt these identities, will be discussed in more depth later in the chapter.

Rather than being viewed as separate entities for analysis, we regard all these different considerations of identities as interwoven, and the remainder of the chapter focuses closely on two areas of research that we have been involved in over the past few years. These both focus on how identities have been considered within areas relevant to critical health psychology. We first focus on maternal identities before moving to a challenge to health.

23.3 Maternal Identities and Health

Read any text related to parenting practices and early motherhood and a key theme running throughout is "good motherhood." As Sharon Hays noted in 1996 with the concept of "intensive mothering," contemporary mothering in Global North industrialized nations is overwhelmingly child-centered and self-sacrificial. This notion has been picked up and adapted by others in terms of parenting practices and renamed as "total" motherhood in relation to infant feeding practices (Wolf, 2010), "extensive" in terms of mothers in full-time work balancing their careers and childcare (Christopher, 2012), and "overzealous" with regards to the turn to the natural in terms of parenting practices (Badinter, 2013). It appears that to be classed as a "good mother" in this contemporary parenting ideology means that the mother needs to display certain behaviors and practices in order to be seen to inhabit this identity (Demuth, Keller, & Yovsi, 2012). These markers include the turn to the natural in terms of natural birth (Hallam et al., 2016, 2019) and method of infant feeding (Locke, 2018). There is also a wide literature within psychology and related disciplines that reflects and offers examples of how maternal identities become tied to different health practices in early parenting. Some examples include the timing of motherhood, where the "good mother" has her babies at an appropriate time, not when too young or too old in case of increased risk of complications. As Budds, Locke, and Burr (2013, 2016) noted, older mothers are typically portrayed in societal popular discourses as "selfish" and "leaving it too late" to have children due to them prioritizing their own identities over biological "realities." These "realities" include a loss of fertility with age and an increase in potential complications (Nwandison & Bewley, 2006). However, in contrast to these media accounts, Locke and Budds (2013) demonstrated how women were aware of the biological risks of delaying motherhood, but were not always able to become mothers earlier due to a myriad of other societal factors.

One of the key places where maternal identities come into sharp focus is through different practices of infant feeding. Research suggests that infant feeding methods are inextricably bound up with maternal identity (Earle, 2003), in particular the ways in which maternal identity is enacted, constructed, and, to some extent, embodied. Given that many health promotion campaigns have led with the problematic statement of "breast is best" (for example, in the UK from 1999), without unpacking the complexities and nuances of the infant feeding experience, this area continues to be contested. There has been a degree of morality tied up with infant feeding, such that "good mothers" are considered to be those who breastfeed (e.g., Lee, 2007, 2008; Murphy, 1999; Wall, 2001; Wolf, 2010), with mothers having the "moral imperative" to breastfeed (Crossley, 2009). As such, this may have moral implications for those women who may experience difficulties and, as a result, are unable to breastfeed, or alternatively those women who, for whatever reason, decide not to initiate breastfeeding. For example, Elizabeth Murphy (1999) has noted the moral accountability tied up with infant feeding, such that those women who bottle feed may be seen as deviating against the common mantra of "breast is best." Moreover, research suggests that women who formula-fed their children experienced guilt in doing so (Lee, 2007). The positioning of a simple dichotomy of breast formula is deeply problematic and ignores wider structural and intersectional concerns in infant feeding, not least that breastfeeding is a reproductive right and not a simple "choice" as it is framed in neoliberal health promotion discourses (Phipps, 2014). When we consider the identities of mothers within these settings, as we have seen from much of the literature, there is an underlying positioning of the breastfeeding mother as the "good mother." What then becomes apparent with maternal identities is how mothers account for their infant feeding practices, whether they are formula-feeding, mixed-feeding (a combination of formula and breast milk), or breastfeeding, and there is a literature to demonstrate the ways in which mothers are orienting around the "good mother" discourse while accounting for their individual decisions (e.g., Knaak, 2010; Lee, 2007, 2008; Locke, 2018). We can also see how "breast is best" is resisted for example, with the "Fed Is Best" Foundation, which contains information on infant feeding alongside mothers' stories. The tying of "good motherhood" to infant feeding is not only evident in breast/formula discourses but becomes evident as a wider discourse of activities marking "good motherhood" includes methods of weaning and responsiveness to the infant's needs (Locke, 2015). Infant feeding, in particular breastfeeding, can be considered an act of embodied neoliberalism (Cairns & Johnston, 2015) in which the bodily surveillance of the new mother is recognizable as a gendered practice, while also noting how new mothers are both positioned and positioning themselves and others in terms of maternal identities in these infant feeding discourses.

The simple "breast is best" trope does not work for all breastfeeding mothers, and it is here that the tensions in terms of gendered identities and expectations of the maternal and the feminine come into play, where breast-feeding mothers can also have to account for their maternal decision-making in terms of the length of time that they breastfeed for and the places in which they feed. The World Health Organization (WHO) guidelines are for continu-ing to give the infant breastmilk until two years of age or beyond,[1] but some studies report mothers who have adopted extended breastfeeding report feel-ing judged (Dowling, 2018), with some adopting a maternal identity of "mili-tant lactivism" (Faircloth, 2013). Others report the uncomfortable nature and shame of breastfeeding in public (Amir, 2014), where the "good mother" becomes the "good" feminine women and displays decorum and so is able to feed without showing the sexualized breast (Grant, 2016).

Previous research into experiences of breastfeeding demonstrates that women can experience a variety of complications with breastfeeding (e.g., Binns & Scott, 2002; Hoddinott & Pill, 1999). In her study of interviews with women in the United States, Kelleher (2006) found that many of the women she interviewed cited both short- and long-term difficulties with breastfeeding. Many women reported not being prepared for these negative experiences, which were completely unexpected. For example, women reported being surprised by the extent, intensity, and duration of the discomfort and pain they experienced in early breastfeeding, and some were concerned that these

---

[1] The WHO (2011, first paragraph of statement) recommends that "mothers worldwide ... [should] exclusively breastfeed infants for the child's first six months to achieve optimal growth, development and health. Thereafter, they should be given nutritious complementary foods and continue breastfeeding up to the age of two years or beyond."

experiences affected their relationship with their baby, thereby causing concern for their identities as mothers. Locke (2009, 2012) considered the ways in which breastfeeding was communicated to expectant mothers, noting the tensions inherent in the teaching of what is constructed as a natural skill (Locke, 2009) and one that was taught without considering some of the common early difficulties that may arise in breastfeeding practices (Locke, 2012). The impact of this on maternal identities is well reported if the mothers stop breastfeeding, perhaps due to unexpected difficulties, and experience guilt (Lee, 2007) and shame (Leeming, 2018; Smyth, 2018). The embodied nature of infant feeding is notably evident here for the mother, as in pregnancy, where maternal identity as well as being enacted as a "good mother" is also an embodied identity as "mother." The ways in which the body comes into maternal identity can be seen through the pain (Kelleher, 2006) and pleasure (Tugwell, 2019) that the mother may experience when feeding. This embodied identity is one aspect of the way in which a "good" maternal identity can be enacted. Note, though, how all of these different nuances in identity occur against a wider backdrop of societal norms and cultures of gender, mothering, and expectations of women.

A final aspect of identity that can be explored and demonstrated through infant feeding is relational identity. As we know from the literature, despite the encouragement for women to breastfeed, many experience issues that they were not expecting. Studies demonstrate the importance of support in breastfeeding and demonstrate that it often makes the difference between women continuing to breastfeed or not (Kelleher, 2006). However, there continue to be concerns about the advice and support available to women, with research suggesting that health professionals may have gaps in specific breastfeeding knowledge (e.g., Hall Moran et al., 2006). Elsewhere there have been reports of conflicting advice from health professionals, and this has been offered as an explanation for early cessation of feeding (Montalto et al., 2010). One aspect of breastfeeding that has, until relatively recently, not been considered is the relational aspect of feeding. This relationship is multifaceted (Leeming et al., 2013) – relationships with extended family and their perspectives on feeding, relationships with partner and changing dynamics after having a baby, relationships with health professionals, and finally and most important, the relationship with the infant (Grant, Mannay, & Marzella, 2018). The relationship between the mother and infant will have a profound impact on the feeding experiences for both, and this can manifest in a number of ways, e.g., whether the mother is suffering from postnatal depression (PND) and whether any difficulties in feeding impact on her identity as a mother and worsen her feelings of depression and inadequacy. The relational aspect of identity is key for a new mother as she is developing her maternal identity in the transition to and in early motherhood.

As this introduction to identity and infant feeding has demonstrated, maternal identity is multifaceted in contemporary parenting culture. We can see examples of the way that maternal identities are enacted (through particular displays of behaviors), embodied (through the experiences of becoming a mother and infant feeding), and relational (in the different relationships that the new mother is experiencing). All of this occurs against a wider backdrop of gender and society. In the following example, we explore another area of women's health: consideration of breast reconstruction surgery following treatment for breast cancer.

23.4 Negotiating Identities in Breast Cancer Care

In this part of the chapter we focus on a range of women's health and illness experiences, specifically illustrated through accounts of negotiating diagnosis of and treatment for breast cancer within the United Kingdom. We explore how the enacted, relational, and situated identities which the women inhabit enable them to change and adjust to their new circumstances. We also illustrate the ways in which taking an in-depth phenomenological approach, focusing on the richness of women's experiences, can bring new insights to health and illness concerns and, consequently, give a wider understanding of the effects on women's identities of the changes they encounter.

We start with a consideration of the context within which women are negotiating their health and illness identities. Cancer Research UK reported 55,213 new cases of invasive breast cancer between 2014 and 2016 in the UK, with 23 percent of those diagnosed in 2015 being preventable. The organization suggested that of those diagnosed across the time period in England and Wales, 78 percent survive for ten years or more. According to the charity Breast Cancer Care, this figure has doubled within the UK since the 1970s. Breast Cancer Care reported more than 80 percent of new cases of breast cancer each year as occurring in the over-50s, with one in seven women developing breast cancer at some point during their lifetime. Just 4 percent of new cases were reported as being in women aged 39 or under (around 2,200 cases overall); however, in 2013 within the UK the National Health Service (NHS) reported one in five women (equating to just over 10,000) diagnosed under the age of 50. Of those diagnosed, the majority will opt for surgery (approximately 90 percent of those under 50; Lawrence et al., 2011), with two-thirds of those opting for breast-conserving surgery and the remainder undergoing mastectomy with immediate or delayed reconstruction. However, this leaves a substantial number of women choosing not to reconstruct post-mastectomy even when a delayed option is available.

As discussed in the introduction to this chapter, people's lived, embodied experiences and identities are shaped in relation to people and environments; our existence as human beings is always intertwined and interconnected with others and influenced by the contexts we find ourselves inhabiting (De Boer, Zeiler, & Slatman, 2019; Fredrickson & Roberts, 1997). Fredrickson and

Roberts' (1997) objectification theory suggests females' assessment of their self-worth is linked to their perception of themselves (in the eyes of others) as sexual beings: the body is viewed as separate from the self (Maclachlan, 2004), although they both contribute to the construction of a woman's sexual identity. Further, it is proposed that sexual objectification is more common for women than for men. The effects of this view of women's bodies, or at least specific aspects of them, as being objectified or sexualized is illustrated by Grogan et al. (2013), whose research explores younger British women's choice of clothing. Participants were recorded while trying on dresses and were subsequently body-scanned and photographed in their chosen dress. Semi-structured interviews focusing on these visual images demonstrated that participants' ideal body shape was a balanced hour-glass where breast and hip size were comparable. Ideally, too, women suggested that their breasts (along with thighs and underwear) should not be on show, and they discounted some items as unwearable if this was perceived to be the case. This example from Grogan and colleagues suggests that, almost two decades after Fredrickson and Roberts's (1997) argument that all forms of sexual objectification view women "as bodies" whose value is in their use to others, this view is still prominent in women's self-reflections: bodies are constructed through our perception of the gaze of others, which in turn guides our appearance behaviors and our embodied identity.

One particular feature of women's bodies – the breast – has long been discussed as a key site for the public display of femininity (Millsted & Frith, 2003). Breasts have been described as the "primary things" in the objectification of women (Young, 1990, p. 90); they are emphasized culturally "as an essential part of being a woman" (Matlin, 2008, p. 364). This association of the breast with femininity has been contested through various media campaigns. The cultural and political movement "Topfreedom," for example, argue that women should be allowed to be topless in public places, publicizing their cause through events such as the Free the Nipple campaign (see, e.g., Rúdólfsdóttir & Jóhannsdóttir, 2018). In a Polish study drawing on Yalom's (1997) research, Zierkiewicz (2012) discusses the cultural meanings attributed to the breast beyond its link to femininity, positing meanings in relation to its erotic, domestic, political, sacred, commercialized, and medical positions.

The complexity of views surrounding women's breasts contributes to their objectification and the expectations attributed to women based on these views, as evidenced above. We see in the discussion of infant feeding above how the practice of breastfeeding has become bound up with maternal identities, for example. This focus on the breast and its varied meanings presents challenges to female identities when all is not as it should be, such as when negotiating the diagnosis and effects of breast cancer (Hallowell, 2000). Women are likely to be perceived as "less" female with the (partial) loss of a breast and as long ago as the 1980s, Audre Lorde (special edition, 1997) suggested that women were being socially encouraged to cover up their no- or one-breastedness.

More recently it has been argued that women are urged to conceal illness and distress related to their breasts (Wilkinson, 2001; Rubin & Tanenbaum, 2011). For these reasons, and similarly to the "Free the Nipple" campaign mentioned above, women have begun to protest hiding their identity as a no- or one-breasted woman (see Twitter's "Show Your Scar" or Stand Up to Cancer's "Mastectomy" campaigns).

Although a wealth of research details the effects of breast cancer from medical and nursing perspectives, a psychological focus on the effects of diagnosis, particularly on younger women (i.e., those under 50), is not readily apparent in the literature (though see, for example, Jagsi et al., 2014; Sisco et al., 2012; Holland et al., 2014). It is reported that women under 50 are more likely to be recommended to consider reconstruction (Alderman et al., 2007) and are often asked to make a decision about this at a time when they are processing a range of complex information imparted as part of the diagnostic process (Rumsey & Harcourt, 2005).

Cancer acts as a form of "biographical disruption" leading from a taken for granted assumption about the body and triggers re-evaluation of one's place in the world (Bury, 1982, p. 169). Arthur Frank (1995) describes this as an interruption of a "coherent life sequence" (p. 60): as cancer survivors are never completely cured, but are in a permanent state of potential recurrence of their cancer, this can affect feelings of "normality" and the ability to move on with life. Recently, however, a more positive slant has suggested that cancer can prompt re-embodiment/re-invention of the self (Williams, 1996; Gilbert et al., 2013) in which new identities can be formed. Individuals are not, therefore, merely passive victims of cancer but take practical and symbolic actions to claim these new identities.

Recent research from Fiona Holland and colleagues (Holland, Archer, & Montague, 2014; Archer, Holland, & Montague, 2016) has focused on the experiences of women under the age of 50 who had undergone mastectomy following a diagnosis of breast cancer and who had subsequently chosen not to reconstruct their breast. Holland et al.'s exploration of the women's decision-making processes highlighted their clear drive to survive where a very pragmatic view of their diseased breast was taken. The women in the study reported feeling that the diseased breast should be sacrificed in order to free themselves from cancer; their views of their diseased breasts were not of something erotic or sacred (Yalom, 1997), but something to "get rid of" (Holland et al., 2014, p. 4). The women interviewed by Holland and her colleagues recounted how many of their consultative conversations focused on reconstruction; although immediate reconstruction was not an option for some, future surgery was promoted as a normative process and even positioned as "expected," with a resulting feeling for some women of a pressure to comply with the medical professionals.

This expected nature of a desire to return to a two-breasted ideal was reportedly emphasized by some members of medical teams, who seemed to persistently promote a pro-reconstruction message. Often this was linked to the women's age, i.e., that being a young woman they would no doubt want to return to a "normal" appearance – a view that signified the breast as a key marker of their feminine identity (Harcourt & Rumsey, 2001). Their maintenance of the decision not to reconstruct, and their consistent need to defend it, left those women interviewed by Holland and colleagues feeling outside the norm. Even though statistically mastectomy without reconstruction across all age groups is commonplace (Alderman et al., 2007), the women's perception, particularly in relation to the push to reconstruction from some members of medical teams, was that they were going against the norm of maintaining a feminine ideal.

Women's cancer experiences encompass a range of challenges to body image, including aspects such as weight gain, hair loss, and scarring (Berterö & Wilmoth, 2007). Idealized views of femininity normalize women as thin, young, and sexually appealing. This categorization shapes many women's experience of embodiment, leading to them feeling a lack of femininity and an inability to accomplish the ideals attributed to their gender (see Gilbert et al., 2013; Parton, Ussher, & Perz, 2017). As we have outlined previously, for Fredrickson and Roberts (1997) objectification occurs when a woman's body or body parts become separated from her identity; in relation to women with breast cancer, their breasts became the site for "normality" as they relate to their "being-in-the-world" (Heidegger, 1927). Being one-breasted in a two-breasted world diminishes the perceived "value" as a woman (Berterö & Wilmoth, 2007; Holland et al., 2014; Archer et al., 2016). Psychologically, women treated as "objects" often adopt a similar perspective in relation to their own bodies. Their view of their bodies becomes internalized, leading to a heightened level of body monitoring. However, this is not the only way that women react, and the women who took part in Holland et al.'s research took on a more positive stance, discussing their "new normal" and reclaiming and celebrating their no- or one-breasted identities.

23.5 Summary

Returning to the call for this chapter, our aim was to outline the ways in which identity has been conceptualized within a health psychology context, considering how these concepts had been applied. Taking examples of our own research to illustrate this, we introduced two areas that regularly affect women: maternal identities in relation to infant feeding and the negotiation of identities following a breast cancer diagnosis. Through our two examples we draw attention to the multiplicity of identities in everyday life. Rather than viewing identity as a feature of individual development that is fixed by the time adulthood is reached, we have, instead, demonstrated how identities are played out in a variety of ways within different situations in life (Antaki &

Widdicombe, 1998). The concept of identity from this viewpoint, then, is realized through a number of approaches. It will be enacted and constructed in relation to the particular requirements of the context within which we find ourselves. Within our illustrative contexts certain obligations of women are foregrounded: to be a "good mother," there are expectations around how a child should be raised; similarly, to be a "good woman," the body should fit with the two-breasted norm. Similarly, identities are embodied: in certain circumstances the body is brought to conscious awareness, highlighting limitations that it can present to our negotiation of different circumstances. An obvious example can be seen in the discussion around breastfeeding in public; perhaps less obvious is the expectation that a (largely) symmetrical figure will be presented within which certain aspects will or will not be displayed (Grogan et al., 2013). Embodied identities, then, limit or enable particular actions for that individual. Finally, identities are also relational, constructed in conjunction with others and formed in response to the expectations others have of us but also that we have of ourselves.

As mentioned in the early part of this chapter, we, the authors, live many identities – "academics," "parents," "grandparents," and so on – that are enacted in relation to others. These identities foreground particular "ways of being" (Heidegger, 1927) depending on the context and circumstances. The women discussed in our examples encounter similar experiences. Their identities shift as their circumstances change, from pregnant woman to mother negotiating her mothering practices and identities against a backdrop of intensive parenting ideology and "good mothering" discourses. A two-breasted feminine norm – an embodied marker of appearance – becomes readily apparent to a woman who finds herself in the position of one- or no-breastedness. New ways of negotiating the world, and interacting with others, must be sought to manage these changes and to realize a "new normal" in her life (Archer et al., 2016).

Through our examples, then, there is a clear sense of the macro and micro: we focus on both levels of understanding. We also note the need, particularly when considering issues around health and well-being, to consider the embodied nature of identity, whether it be concerning appearance after ill-health or issues around pregnancy and early parenthood. Lastly, we added the frame of relational identity in that we need to consider the ways in which as relational beings our acts and experiences are always framed within a social and relational context. Our key message is that, just as there are a multiplicity of ways in which identities can be foregrounded for individuals, similarly there is no one way of researching these that sufficiently encompasses their complexity.

With that in mind, our chapter has explored the topic of identity/identities from a critical health psychology perspective. We postulate that identity has, at times, been overlooked by traditional/mainstream approaches, with inferences to identity rather than explicit references: however, we acknowledge that the recent move to the "social cure" work may address some of this gap. By contrast, and our reason for writing this chapter, we argue that identities should form a key area of study within critical health psychology, in particular to consider the differential effects and experiences of actors within social and health settings. Work in critical health psychology is constantly developing, and we see a move now toward a more intersectional analysis of identities, one where gendered, classed, racial, and other identities are considered for the ways that actors narrate and experience their lives.

References

Alderman, A. K., Kuhn, L. E., Lowery, J. C., & Wilkins, E. G. (2007). Does patient satisfaction with breast reconstruction change over time? Two-year results of the Michigan Breast Reconstruction Outcomes Study. *Journal of the American College of Surgeons, 204*(1), 7–12.

Ajzen, I. (1991). The theory of planned behavior. *Organizational Behavior and Human Decision Processes, 50*, 179–211.

Amir, L. H. (2014). Breastfeeding in public: "You can do it?" *International Breastfeeding Journal, 9*, article 187, doi:10.1186/s13006-014-0026-1.

Antaki, C. & Widdicombe, S. (Eds.). (1998). *Identities in Talk*. London: Sage.

Archer, S., Holland, F.G., & Montague, J. (2016). "Do you mean I'm not whole?" Exploring the role of support in women's experiences of mastectomy without reconstruction. *Journal of Health Psychology, 21*, 1–12, doi:10.1177/1359105316664135.

Ayo, N. (2012). Understanding health promotion in a neoliberal climate and the making of health conscious citizens. *Critical Public Health, 22*(1), 99–105.

Badinter, E. (2013). *The Conflict: How Modern Motherhood Undermines the Status of Women*. New York, NY: Saint Martin's Press.

Bandura, A. (1977). Self-efficacy: Toward a unifying theory of behavioral change. *Psychological Review, 84*(2), 191–215.

Barnes, B. (2015). Critiques of health behaviour change programs in the Global. *South African Journal of Psychology, 45*(4), 430–438.

Beck, U. (1992). *Risk Society*. London: Sage.

Benwell, B. & Stokoe, E. (2006). *Discourse and Identity*. Edinburgh: Edinburgh University Press.

Berterö, C. & Wilmoth, M. C. (2007). Breast cancer diagnosis and its treatment affecting the self: A meta-synthesis. *Cancer Nursing, 30*(3), 194–202.

Binns, C. W. & Scott, J. A. (2002). Using pacifiers: What are breastfeeding mothers doing? *Breastfeeding Review, 10*(2), 21–25.

Bordo, S. (2003). *Unbearable Weight: Feminism, Western Culture, and the Body, 10th Anniversary Ed*. Berkeley, CA: University of California Press.

Budds, K., Locke. A., & Burr, V. (2016). "For some people it isn't a choice, it's just how it happens": Accounts of "delayed" motherhood among middle-class women in the UK. *Feminism and Psychology, 26*(2), 170–187.

Budds, K., Locke. A., & Burr, V. (2013). Risky business. Constructing older mothers in the British Press. *Feminist Media Studies, 13*(1), 132–147.

Bury, M. (1982). Chronic illness as biographical disruption. *Sociology of Health and Illness*, *4*, 167–182.

Cairns, K. & Johnston, J. (2015). Choosing health: Embodied neoliberalism, postfeminism, and the "do-diet." *Theory and Society*, *44*(2), 153–175.

Chamberlain, K. & Murray, M. (2017). Health psychology. In C. Willig & W. Stainton-Rogers (Eds.), *The Sage Handbook of Qualitative Research in Psychology*, *2nd Ed.* (pp. 431–449). London: Sage.

Christopher, K. (2012). Extensive mothering: Employed mothers' constructions of the good mother. *Gender and Society*, *26*, 73–96.

Crossley, M. L. (2000). Narrative psychology, trauma and the study of self/identity. *Theory and Psychology*, *10*(4), 527–546.

Crossley, M. L. (2009). Breastfeeding as a moral imperative: An autoethnographic study. *Feminism & Psychology*, *19*, 71–87.

De Boer, M. Zeiler, K., & Slatman, J. (2019). Sharing lives, sharing bodies: Partners negotiating breast cancer experiences. *Medicine, Health Care and Philosophy*, *22*, 253–265, doi:10.1007/s11019-018-9866-6.

Demuth, C., Keller, H., & Yovsi, R. D. (2012). Cultural models in communication with infants: Lessons from Kikaikelaki, Cameroon and Muenster, Germany. *Journal of Early Childhood Research*, *10*(1), 70–87, doi:10.1177/1476718X11403993.

Dowling, S. (2018). "Betwixt and between": Women's experiences of breastfeeding long term. In S. Dowling, D. Pontin, & K. Boyer (Eds.), *Social Experiences of Breastfeeding: Building Bridges between Research, Policy and Practice* (pp. 55–70). Bristol: Policy Press.

Earle, S. (2003). Is breast best? Breastfeeding, motherhood and identity. In S. Earle & G. Letherby (Eds.), *Gender, Identity and Reproduction: Social Perspectives* (pp. 135–150). London: Palgrave.

Faircloth, C. (2013). *Militant Lactivism?: Attachment Parenting and Intensive Motherhood in the UK and France*. Oxford: Berghahn.

Fishbein, M. & Ajzen, I. (1975). *Belief, Attitude, Intention and Behavior*. Reading, MA: Addison-Wesley.

Frank, A. W. (1995). *The Wounded Storyteller. Body, Illness, and Ethics*. Chicago, IL: University of Chicago Press.

Fredrickson, B. L. & Roberts, T. A. (1997). Objectification theory: Toward understanding women's lived experiences and mental health risks. *Psychology of Women Quarterly*, *21*, 173–206.

Gilbert, E., Ussher, J. M., & Perz, J. (2013). Embodying sexual subjectivity after cancer: A qualitative study of people with cancer and intimate partners. *Psychology & Health*, *28*(6), 603–619.

Grant, A. (2016). "I ... don't want to see you flashing your bits around": Exhibitionism, othering and good motherhood in online perceptions of public breastfeeding. *Geoforum*, *71*, 52–61.

Goffman, E. (1959). *The Presentation of Self in Everyday Life*. New York, NY: Doubleday.

Grant, A., Mannay, D., & Marzella, R. (2018). "People try and police your behaviour": The impact of surveillance on mothers' and grandmothers' perceptions and experiences of infant feeding. *Families, Relationships and Societies*, *7*(3), 431–447, doi:10.1332/204674317X14888886530223.

Grogan, S., Gill, S., Brownbridge, K., Kilgariff, S., & Whalley, A. (2013). Dress fit and body image: A thematic analysis of women's accounts during and after trying on dresses. *Body Image*, *10*, 380–388.

Gross, S. Musgrave, G., Janciute, L. Barnett, S., Fuchs, C., Kavada, A., Kroeger, N., & Michalis, M. (2018). *Well-Being and Mental Health in the Gig Economy: Policy Perspectives on Precarity*. London: University of Westminster Press.

Hall Moran, V., Burt, S., Dykes, F., & Shuck, C. (2006). Breastfeeding support for adolescent mothers: similarities and differences in the approach of midwives and qualified breastfeeding supporters. *International Breastfeeding Journal*, *1*, 23, doi:10.1186/1746-4358-1-23.

Hallam, J., Howard, C., Locke, A., & Thomas, M. (2019). Empowering women through the positive birth movement. *Journal of Gender Studies*, *28*(3), 330–341.

Hallam, J., Howard, C., Locke, A., & Thomas, M. (2016). Communicating choice: an exploration of mothers' experiences of birth. *Journal of Reproductive and Infant Psychology*, *34*, 175–184, doi:10.1080/02646838.2015.1119260.

Hallowell, N. (2000). Reconstructing the body or reconstructing the woman? Perceptions of prophylactic mastectomy for hereditary breast cancer risk. In L. Potts (Ed.), *Ideologies of Breast Cancer: Feminist Perspectives* (pp. 153–180). Basingstoke: Palgrave Macmillan.

Harcourt D. & Rumsey, N. (2001). Psychological aspects of breast reconstruction: A review of the literature. *Journal of Advanced Nursing*, *35*(4), 477–487.

Haslam, C. Jetten, J., Cruwys, T., Dingle, G., & Haslam, A. (2018). *The New Psychology of Health: Unlocking the Social Cure*. Abingdon: Routledge Press.

Hays, S. (1996). *The Cultural Contradictions of Motherhood*. New Haven, CT: Yale University Press.

Heidegger, M. (1927). *Being and Time*, new edition translated by J. Macquarrie & E. Robinson, 1978. Oxford: Wiley-Blackwell.

Heyman, B., Alaszewski, A., Shaw, M., & Titterton, M. (2010). *Risk, Safety and Clinical Practice: Health Care through the Lens of Risk*. Oxford: Oxford University Press.

Hoddinott, P. & Pill, R. (1999). Nobody actually tells you: A study of infant feeding. *British Journal of Midwifery*, *7*(9), 558–565.

Holland, F. G., Archer, S., & Montague, J. (2014). Younger women's experiences of deciding against delayed breast reconstruction post-mastectomy following breast cancer: An interpretative phenomenological analysis. *Journal of Health Psychology*, *19*, 1–12.

Horton-Salway, M. (2001). Narrative identities and the management of personal accountability in talk about ME: A discursive approach to illness narrative. *Journal of Health Psychology*, *6*(2), 247–259.

Howard, J. A. (2000). Social psychology of identities. *Annual Review of Sociology*, *26*, 367–393.

Jagsi, R., Jiang, J., Momoh, A. O., Alderman, A., Giordano, S. H., Buchholz, T. A., Kronowitz, S. J., & Smith, B. D. (2014). Trends and variation in use of breast reconstruction in patients with breast cancer undergoing mastectomy in the

United States. *Journal of Clinical Oncology, 32*(9), 919–926, doi:10.1200/JCO.2013.52.2284.

Jetten, J., Haslam, C., & Haslam, A. (2012). *The Social Cure: Identity, Health and Well-being*. London: Psychology Press.

Kelleher, C. M. (2006). The physical challenges of early breastfeeding. *Social Science and Medicine, 63*, 2727–2738.

Knaak, S. (2010). Conceptualising risk, constructing choice: breastfeeding and good mothering in risk society. *Health, Risk and Society, 12*(4), 345–355.

Lawrence, G., Kearins, O., Lagord, C., Cheung, S., Sidhu, J., & Sagar, C. (2011). *The Second All Breast Cancer Report. Focussing on Inequalities: Variation in Breast Cancer Outcomes with Age and Deprivation*. London, UK: National Cancer Intelligence Network.

Lee, E. (2007). Health, morality, and infant feeding: British mothers' experiences of formula milk use in the early weeks. *Sociology of Health and Illness, 29*(7), 1075–1090.

Lee, E. (2008). Living with risk in the age of "intensive motherhood": Maternal identity and infant feeding. *Health, Risk & Society, 10*, 467–477.

Leeming, D. (2018). Managing the dynamics of shame in breastfeeding support. In S. Dowling, D. Pontin, & K. Boyer (Eds.), *Social Experiences of Breastfeeding: Building Bridges between Research, Policy and Practice* (pp. 23–38). Bristol: Policy Press.

Leeming, D., Williamson, I., Lyttle, S., & Johnson, S. (2013). Socially sensitive lactation: Exploring the social context of breastfeeding. *Psychology and Health, 28*, 450–468.

Lippman, A. (1999). Choice as a risk to women's health. *Health, Risk and Society, 1*, 281–291.

Locke, A. (2009). Natural versus taught: Competing discourses in antenatal Breastfeeding workshops. *Journal of Health Psychology, 14*(3), 435–446.

Locke, A. (2012). Preparing women to breastfeed: Teaching breastfeeding in prenatal classes in the United Kingdom. In P. Hall Smith, B. L. Hausman, & M. Labbok (Eds.), *Beyond Health, Beyond Choice: Breastfeeding Constraints and Realities* (pp. 110–119). Chapel Hill, NC: Rutgers Press.

Locke, A. (2015). Agency, "good motherhood" and "a load of mush": Constructions of baby-led weaning in the press. *Women's Studies International Forum, 53*, 139–146.

Locke, A. (2018). Parenting ideologies, infant feeding and popular culture. In S. Dowling, D. Pontin, & K. Boyer (Eds.), *Social Experiences of Breastfeeding: Building Bridges between Research, Policy and Practice* (pp. 147–162). Bristol: Policy Press.

Locke, A. & Budds, K. (2013). "We thought if it's going to take two years then we need to start that now": Age, probabilistic reasoning and the timing of pregnancy in older first-time mothers. *Health, Risk and Society, 15*(6–7), 525–542.

Lorde, A. (1997). *The Cancer Journals: Special Edition*. San Francisco, CA: Aunt Lute Books.

Lupton, D. (1999). *Risk*. London: Routledge.

Maclachlan, M. (2004). *Embodiment: Clinical, Critical and Cultural Perspectives on Health and Illness*. Milton Keynes: Open University Press.

Marks, D. (2002). *The Health Psychology Reader*. London: Sage.

Matarazzo, J. D. (1980). Behavioral health and behavioral medicine: Frontiers for a new health psychology. *American Psychologist*, *35*(9), 807–817, doi:10.1037/0003-066X.35.9.807.

Matlin, M. W. (2008). *The Psychology of Women, 6th Ed*. Belmont, CA: Thomson Wadsworth.

Millsted, R. & Frith, H. (2003). Being large-breasted: Women negotiating embodiment. *Women's Studies International Forum*, *26*(5), 455–465.

Montalto, S. A., Borg, H., Buttigieg-Said, M., & Clemmer, E. J. (2010). Incorrect advice: The most significant negative determinant on breast feeding in Malta. *Midwifery*, *26*(1), e6–e13.

Morrison, V. & Bennett, P. (2016). *An Introduction to Health Psychology, 4th Ed*. Harlow: Pearson.

Murphy, E. (1999). "Breast is best": Infant feeding and maternal deviance. *Sociology of Health and Illness*, *21*, 187–208.

Murray, M. (2015). *Critical Health Psychology, 2nd Ed*. Basingstoke: Palgrave Macmillan.

National Health Service (September, 2019). www.nhs.uk/conditions/breast-cancer/.

Nwandison, M. & Bewley, S. (2006). What is the right age to reproduce? *Fetal and Maternal Medicine Review*, *17*, 185–204.

Ogden, J. (2019). *Health Psychology, 6th Ed*. New York, NY: McGraw-Hill Education.

Parton, C., Ussher, J. M., & Perz, J. (2017). Women's constructions of heterosex and sexual embodiment after cancer. *Feminism & Psychology*, *27*(3), 298–317.

Phipps, A. (2014). *The Politics of the Body: Gender in a Neoliberal and Neoconservative Age*. Cambridge: Polity Press.

Prochaska, J. O. & Velicer, W. F. (1997). The transtheoretical model of health behavior change. *American Journal of Health Promotion*, *12*, 38–48.

Reardon, R. & Grogan, S. (2011). Women's reasons for seeking breast reduction: A qualitative investigation. *Journal of Health Psychology*, *16*, 31–41.

Rubin, L. R. & Tanenbaum, M. (2011). "Does that make me a woman?" Breast cancer, mastectomy, and breast reconstruction decisions among sexual minority women. *Psychology of Women Quarterly*, *35*(3), 401–414.

Rúdólfsdóttir, A. G. & Jóhannsdóttir, Á. (2018). Fuck patriarchy! An analysis of digital mainstream media discussion of the #FreetheNipple activities in Iceland in March 2015. *Feminism & Psychology*, *28*(1), 133–151.

Rumsey, N. & Harcourt, D. (2005). *The Psychology of Appearance*. Milton Keynes: Open University Press.

Ryan, R. M. & Deci, E. L. (2012). Multiple identities within a single self: A self-determination theory perspective on internalization within contexts and cultures. In M. R. Leary & J. P. Tangney (Eds.), *Handbook of Self and Identity* (p. 225–246). New York, NY: Guilford Press.

Seymour-Smith, S. (2008). "Blokes don't like that sort of thing": Men's negotiation of a "troubled" self-help group identity. *Journal of Health Psychology*, *13*(6), 785–797.

Seymour-Smith, S., Wetherell, M., & Phoenix, A. (2002). "My wife ordered me to come!" A discursive analysis of doctors' and nurses' accounts of men's use of general practitioners. *Journal of Health Psychology*, *7*(3), 253–267.

Sisco, M., Du, H., Warner, J. P., Howard, M. A., Winchester, D. P., & Yao, K. (2012). Have we expanded the equitable delivery of postmastectomy breast reconstruction in the new millennium? Evidence from the National Cancer Database. *Journal of the American College of Surgeons, 215*, 658–666.

Smyth, L. (2018). Breastfeeding's emotional intensity: The moral politics of health promotion. In S. Dowling, D. Pontin, & K. Boyer (Eds.), *Social Experiences of Breastfeeding: Building Bridges between Research, Policy and Practice* (pp. 39–54). Bristol: Policy Press.

Stets, J. E. & Burke, P. J. (2005). Identity theory and social identity theory. *Social Psychology Quarterly, 63*(3), 224–237.

Tajfel, H. & Turner, J. C. (1985). The social identity theory of intergroup behaviour. In S. Worchel & W. G. Austin (Eds.), *Psychology of Intergroup Relations* (pp. 7–24). Chicago, IL: Nelson-Hall.

Thompson, A. E., Anisimowicz, Y., Miedema, B., Hogg, W., Wodchis, W. P., & Aubrey-Bassler, K. (2016). The influence of gender and other patient characteristics on health care-seeking behaviour: A QUALICOPC study. *BMC Family Practice, 17*, article 38, doi:10.1186/s12875-016-0440-0.

Tugwell, S. (2019). Breastfeeding selfies as relational practice: Becoming a maternal subject in the digital age: a single case study. *International Breastfeeding Journal, 14*, article 23, doi:10.1186/s13006-019-0218-9.

Ussher, J. (2006). *Managing the Monstrous Feminine: Regulating the Reproductive Body*. London: Routledge.

Wall, G. (2001). Moral constructions of motherhood in breastfeeding discourse. *Gender and Society, 15*, 592–610.

Wallston, B. S., Wallston, K. A., Kaplan, G. D., et al. (1976). The development and validation of the health related locus of control (HLC) scale. *Journal of Consulting and Clinical Psychology, 44*, 580–585.

Wilkinson, S. (2001). Breast cancer: Feminism, representations and resistance – a commentary on Dorothy Broom's "Reading breast cancer." *Health, 5*(2), 269–277.

Williams, S. J. (1996). The vicissitudes of embodiment across the chronic illness trajectory. *Body and Society, 2*, 23–47.

Wolf, J. B. (2007). Is breast really best? Risk and total motherhood in the national breastfeeding awareness campaign. *Journal of Health, Politics, Policy and Law, 32*, 595–636.

Wolf, J. B. (2010). *Is Breast Best? Taking on the Breastfeeding Experts and the New High Stakes of Motherhood*. New York, NY: NYU Press.

Yalom, M. (1997). *A History of the Breast*. New York, NY: Alfred A. Knopf.

Young, I. M. (1990). Breasted experience: The look and feeling. In I. M. Young (Ed.), *Throwing Like a Girl and Other Essays on Feminist Philosophy and Social Theory* (pp. 189–209). Bloomington, IN: Indiana University Press.

Zeiler, K. & Folkmarson Kall, L. (2015). *Feminist Phenomenology and Medicine*. New York, NY: New York Press.

Zierkiewicz, E. (2012). Mastectomy scars: Stigma, emblem or sign of disability? Analysis of principal meanings of the loss of a breast. *Fizjoterapia, 20*(2), 32–42.

24 Identity Scholarship in Educational Psychology: Toward a Complex Dynamic Systems Perspective

Avi Kaplan, Hanoch Flum, Ishwar Bridgelal, and Joanna K. Garner

Educational psychology is a field of inquiry that involves the application of psychological science to the investigation and improvement of educational phenomena and, reciprocally, to the enhancement of psychological science itself. The traditional focal phenomena in educational psychology have been learning, motivation, and achievement in educational settings, and the research in the field has investigated the cultural factors, contextual characteristics, organizational practices, social dynamics, and individual differences that undergird these processes. With roots going back over a century to William James, G. Stanley Hall, and John Dewey, and with the scholarship of numerous psychologists harnessing theories from cognitive, personality, developmental, social, and cultural psychology, the field of educational psychology has been highly diverse and inclusive in its collective aim to understand and improve human phenomena in formal and informal educational settings (Alexander, 2018).

One would expect, therefore, that the popular concept of *identity* would be of high interest to educational psychologists. Surprisingly, until relatively recently, the concept has been practically missing from the extensive educational psychological literature (Wigfield & Wagner, 2005).[1] Much more common has been the use of the related concept *self*, reflecting diverging theoretical traditions that identity scholars and educational psychologists have drawn upon during the second half of the twentieth century (Roeser, Peck, & Nasir, 2006). Throughout the field's long history, conceptions of the person in educational psychology drew primarily on social-cognitive perspectives, like those proffered by James (1890), Bandura (1977), Harter (1983), and Markus (1977). However, this has

---

[1] A cursory search in PsychInfo with the term "Identity" in the title or abstract of articles in the field's flagship journal – the *Journal of Educational Psychology* – returned a mere twenty-seven results throughout the 110 years of the journal's publications. Only nineteen of these articles used the term identity to refer to people's sense of who they are. The other eight used the term to refer to "Phoneme Identity" – students' ability to recognize the same sound in different words.

been changing in the past couple of decades, with identity scholarship from various disciplines and domains increasingly informing educational psychological theory, research, and interventions, and manifesting in high visibility educational psychology publications, including special issues (e.g., Kaplan & Flum, 2009, 2012), conceptual articles (e.g., Hand & Gresalfi, 2015; Penuel & Wertzch, 1995), handbook chapters (e.g., Master, Cheryan, & Meltzoff., 2016; Nasir, Rowley, & Perez, 2016; Roeser, Peck, & Nasir, 2006), literature reviews (e.g., Verhoeven, Poorthuis, & Volman, 2019), and edited volumes (e.g., Schutz, Hong, & Cross Francis, 2018).

Not surprisingly, as with the general identity literature (cf. Schwartz, Luyckx, & Vignoles, 2011), the identity scholarship in educational psychology has been epistemologically and methodologically diverse, and framed by different theoretical perspectives. Research from the different perspectives has meaningfully contributed to understanding particular facets of identity and its role in educational psychological phenomena. Additionally, such diversity demonstrates the broad application of identity processes to educational psychology. However, it has also introduced a plethora of different terms that refer to identity but reflect different definitions, foci, and assumptions about the nature of identity and its formation. Terms such as personal identity, social identity, ethnic and racial identity, gender identity, religious identity, disability identity, student or academic identity, and mathematics, science, and reading identities have joined a literature already saturated with self-related terms such as self-schema, self-concept, self-efficacy, possible selves, and self-regulation. The proliferation of identity-related constructs has created great challenges for synthesizing findings to better capture the comprehensive nature of identity processes and their role in learning, motivation, and achievement in educational settings (Roeser et al., 2006).

In the current chapter, we provide a framework that aspires to harmonize the discordant voices on identity in educational psychology. We begin by briefly reviewing three different perspectives on identity and their foci in educational psychological research. We follow by describing an emerging integrative perspective of identity as a complex dynamic system and its application in educational psychological scholarship. We conclude by noting several emergent areas of identity research in educational psychology, and we emphasize the potential of identity research to bridge educational psychological scholarship with educational practice and policy.

24.1 Complementary Foci in Educational Psychological Identity Research

Throughout its history, the societal project of education has centered on the development of students into certain kinds of people, irrespective of how that development was defined in any particular era for a particular group of students.

It is not surprising, therefore, that scholars have considered identity to be intertwined with educational processes. Erikson (1968), who is credited with bringing the concept of identity to the scientific domain (Gleason, 1983), identified schooling as a paramount cultural context for the identity formation of young people. Later on, several identity scholars from diverse fields contextualized their research in educational settings (e.g., Berzonsky & Kuk, 2005; Crocetti, Rubini, & Meeus, 2008; Dreyer, 1994; Lannegrand-Willems & Bosma, 2006; Schachter & Rich, 2011; Wenger, 1998). In turn, educational researchers have used identity as a frame for investigating a variety of educational phenomena such as students' learning, motivation, and achievement (Verhoeven et al., 2019), teachers' professional development (Schutz et al., 2018), and institutional structures and practices that promote the normalization, exclusion, and valuation of particular ways of being a person (Apple, 2014; Gee, 2000).

This chapter focuses on the scholarship that involves the application of psychological perspectives on identity to educational psychological research on the motivation, learning, and achievement of youth in educational settings. The identity literature reflects a variety of theoretical frameworks from different scholarly traditions, including social-cognitive, social psychological, psychosocial, and social cultural perspectives, as well as their combinations (Verhoeven et al., 2019). While these perspectives share many assumptions, they also differ in their definitions of identity, primary unit of analysis, and preferred methodologies (Penuel & Wertsch, 1995; Vignoles, Schwartz, & Luyckx, 2011). Notably, each perspective itself is also diverse, and includes sub-perspectives that differ in assumptions, constructs, and emphases (for more extensive reviews of these perspectives and their various strands see Côté & Levine, 2002; Kroger, 2004; Schwartz et al., 2011, and chapters in the current volume). As the literature is vast, we pursue our purpose of clarifying central conceptual tenets in educational psychology identity research by highlighting three overarching and complementary research foci: identity content, identity structure and formation processes, and the role of culture in identity. While all identity perspectives include assumptions concerning the role of culture, and consider identity's content, structure, and process, research from different perspectives tends to foreground certain aspects. Correspondingly, in the three sections below, we review educational psychological research on identity from the following perspectives and their main foci: (1) social cognitive and social psychological perspectives that foreground identity content; (2) psychosocial perspectives that foreground identity structure and formation processes; and (3) social cultural perspectives that foreground the role of culture in identity and its formation.

24.1.1 Social Cognitive and Social Psychological Research on Identity Content in Education

The most prevalent application of identity concepts in educational psychology has focused on the *content* of people's identities, referring to what Gee (2000) has defined as "[b]eing recognized as a certain 'kind of person'" (p. 99). Arguably, most educational psychology scholarship that has focused on identity content is based on social cognitive and social psychological perspectives that highlight the individual's self-perceptions and self-definitions regarding personal and social attributes. Notably, throughout most of educational psychology's history, scholars have employed the term *self* when referring to people's self-perceptions and self-definitions (Roeser et al., 2006), but more recently, researchers have also been employing the terms *self/identity* (Roeser et al., 2006) and *identities* for these constructs (Master et al., 2016; Oyserman, 2015; Oyserman & James, 2011).

Social cognitive and social psychological perspectives on identity draw on an early distinction by William James (1890) between the "I-self" and the "me-self." The I-self refers to the person's awareness and regulatory phenomenological experience (the "subject," the "knower"), and the me-self refers to the collection of self-perceived personal and social categories and attributes (the "object," the "known") (Roeser et al., 2006). The me-self – a network of cognitive-emotive self-knowledge that constitutes the self-schema (Markus, 1977) – comprises the self-perceptions and self-definitions by which individuals construct their personal and social identities. Personal identities refer to the content of self-perceptions of individual attributes (e.g., smart, curious, sensitive, thin, interested in science), and social identities refer to the content of self-definitions regarding social-collective attributes, social roles, and group memberships (e.g., female, Latina, student, debate team member) (Master et al., 2016).[2]

Social cognitive and social psychological scholarship on identity content in education has investigated the relations between students' particular self-perceptions on personal attributes (e.g., ability, interest), or their self-definitions on social attributes (e.g., race, ethnicity, gender, language proficiency, affiliation with a subject matter community), with their motivation, engagement, and achievement (Master et al., 2016; Nasir et al., 2016). The predominant methodologies employed in this research have been experimental studies and quantitative correlational studies using students' self-reported data collected through summated-scales questionnaires.

Perhaps the most frequently studied identity content in educational psychology has been students' self-concept of ability. A large body of research has demonstrated the positive reciprocal relations between students' self-perceptions of having high ability in a domain and their motivation and achievement (Marsh et al., 2017; Usher, 2016). Another central personal identity in educational psychological research has been students' self-perceptions of having high and enduring personal interest in a subject

---

[2] See Gee (2000) for a more elaborate categorization of different types of content identities as based in assumptions about their source in "nature," "institution," "discourse," and "social affinity."

domain, with research supporting the positive reciprocal relations between students' individual interest and their level and quality of engagement, learning, and achievement in that subject domain (Harackiewicz & Knogler, 2017; Renninger, 2009). The valuation of these self-perceptions in a domain, and the degree to which they are central to the student's self-concept, are held to reflect the student's level of "identification" with the academic subject. High levels of identification correlate positively with the student's motivation, continued learning, and performance (Osborne & Jones, 2011).

Social cognitive and social psychological research on students' self-definitions on social attributes, categories, and group memberships includes subject matter identities, most commonly in Science, Technology, Engineering and Mathematics (STEM) domains, including "mathematics identity," "science identity," or an overall "STEM identity" (Kim, Sinatra, & Seyranian, 2018), as well as gender, ethnic, and language identities (Master et al., 2016). The relations of distinct social identities with the students' motivation and achievement are moderated by the social-contextual meanings and stereotypes associated with particular social groups or categories. Research has demonstrated, for example, that students' gender identities frame girls' and boys' differential perceived competence and expectancies for success, value, and perceived costs of engagement in stereotypically masculine or feminine academic domains. These antecedents of motivation, in turn, have been related to gendered patterns of choice, effort, and academic success in the same stereotyped domains (Eccles et al., 1983; Wigfield, Rosenzweig, & Eccles, 2017). Research has also found that students at different intersections of gender and ethnic identities expressed different degrees of identifications (e.g., "I am a physics person," Hazari, Sadler, & Sonnert, 2013), and held different perceived values, costs, and expectancies for success in different academic domains and tasks (Wigfield et al., 2017).

Social psychological research has also investigated the relationships between students' self-worth concerns regarding their social identities and their motivation and engagement in academic tasks (Master et al., 2016). Self-worth concerns regarding gender or ethnicity have been associated with engaging in schoolwork with the goals of demonstrating high ability and avoiding demonstrating low ability in order to protect self-worth – a motivational profile associated with impaired learning and performance (Kaplan, 2004). A related phenomenon that has received significant scholarly attention involves "stereotype threat" – a concern with affirming a negative stereotype about one's social identity (e.g., low academic achievement of African Americans, low achievement of women in math and engineering, Steele & Aronson, 1995). Research has demonstrated that the heightened self-worth concerns associated with stereotype threat undermine motivation and performance (Cohen & Garcia, 2008; Ryan & Ryan, 2005; Steele, Spencer, & Aronson, 2002).

Social cognitive and social psychological research has also investigated the role of the educational context in the relations of personal and social identity content with students' motivation, learning, and achievement (Master et al., 2016; Nasir et al., 2016; Verhoeven et al., 2019). Educational contexts that emphasize social comparison and hinge students' self-worth on high performance have been found to prime social identities (Kaplan, 2004), enhance stereotype threat (Ryan & Ryan, 2005), and trigger intergroup perceptions that negatively impact students' motivation and willingness to collaborate across social groups (Kaplan, 2004; Tossman, Kaplan, & Assor, 2008).

Social Cognitive and Social Psychological Identity Interventions in Education

Social cognitive and social psychological identity interventions in education have targeted personal or social identity content assumed to hinder student engagement (Master et al., 2016). Such interventions have aimed to promote perceived connections between people's individual or social identities and academic tasks, to reduce self-worth concerns associated with personal and social identities, and to enhance perceptions that these identities belong in the academic context. Such identity interventions have commonly employed experimental designs and sought to identify practices that may be scaled up across contexts and students. For example, interventions targeting students' self-concept of ability have featured pedagogical strategies that aim to enhance students' academic skills (indirect strategies to affect their self-concept) and deliver feedback that emphasizes effort, strategy use, and improvement (direct strategies to affect self-concept) (O'Mara et al., 2006). Interventions that target students' perceived value and personal interest in academic domains have used pedagogies that build on students' existing interests and engage them in meaningful problem-solving. Alternatively, these interventions have prompted students to write about the connection of academic content to their lives, about what they learned, and what they want to continue to learn in a subject domain (Harackiewicz, Smith, & Priniski, 2016; Renninger et al., 2014).

Intervention research targeting students' social identities has also employed experiments to test practices that aim to associate a particular social identity with academic success, reduce its negative association with schoolwork, and assure students that this social identity is not an academic liability (Master et al., 2016). For example, interventions have involved presenting students of different genders with information about their gender's success (e.g., girls' higher graduation rates, boys' higher income levels) to promote associations between the particular gender identity and academic success (Elmore & Oyserman, 2012). Strategies have also included prompting students to describe the congruence between their ethnicity and academic success, to write about a value that is important to them in ways that affirm their self-worth, and to listen to older students from the same ethnic group assure them that their sense of belonging to the academic context will improve (Oyserman et al., 2017; Walton & Cohen, 2011).

Summary: Social Cognitive and Social Psychological Research on Identity Content in Education

Social cognitive and social psychological research on identity content in education defines identity as a person's focal self-perception or self-definition concerning a personal or a social attribute. According to this definition, people have multiple identities – one for each personal and social attribute, domain, or category – but most studies have focused on a single identity that is either "chronically" primed or triggered by the situation (Master et al., 2016; for an exception, see Oyserman et al., 2006). The research has investigated the relations between students' self-perceptions and self-definitions of these personal and social attributes, self-worth concerns related to this identity content, and their motivation, achievement, sense of belonging, and overall well-being. Social cognitive and social psychological perspectives consider these identities to be malleable through experiences that modify self-perceptions of these personal or social attributes. Correspondingly, identity interventions have aimed to reframe the identity content perceived to hinder adaptive engagement by associating it with academic success, reducing self-worth concerns, and promoting a sense of belonging to the academic context. The predominantly quantitative and experimental methods in this scholarship stem from assumptions that the findings and interventions can be generalized across contexts, although recent findings suggest that the effects may be, in fact, contextualized (Walton & Yeager, 2020).

24.1.2 Psychosocial Research in Education Foregrounding Identity Structure and Formation Processes

Research from psychosocial perspectives on identity in education has focused primarily on the structure and formation processes of students' identity, and their role in students' learning, motivation, and achievement. Following Erikson's (1950, 1968) conception of identity, psychosocial perspectives define identity as an individual's comprehensive, deep, and mostly unconscious mental structure that includes an intricate network of identity commitments in life: worldview and ideology, self-perceptions and self-definitions, purpose and goals, and ways of acting in different life domains. Yet while psychosocial perspectives on identity acknowledge this identity content, they consider the deep psychological structure that organizes this content to be the important identity feature for explaining the person's motivation, development, and overall well-being (Kroger & Marcia, 2011, Chapter 10 in this volume).

Most psychosocial identity research in education has focused on variability in the types of identity structures and the processes of their formation. Erikson (1968) viewed different types of identity structure to reflect different unconscious resources, or ego strengths and vulnerabilities, which, in turn, underlie different orientations toward engagement in normative cultural tasks and social interactions, coping with change and challenges, and sense of sameness, continuity, purpose in life, and well-being (Marcia, 1980). Whereas this variability may manifest in various dimensions, perhaps the most central structural dimension is degree of integration across identity commitments in the various life domains. Yet, according to psychosocial perspectives, normative youth in school, and even in college, are not expected to have had the time, context, and physiological maturity to form comprehensive, well-integrated identity structures. Thus, most psychosocial research with youth in education has focused on identity structures and identity formation processes that correspond to the developmental stages of adolescence and emerging adulthood.

In the most influential psychosocial research framework on identity formation in adolescence, Marcia (1966, 1993) conceptualized different types of identity structures by combining two dimensions: absence or presence of identity commitments, and low or high engagement in identity exploration. The combination of the two dimensions generates four structure–process statuses that reflect different sources of the identity content, and different processes of incorporating this content into the identity structure: Identity Achievement, Foreclosure, Moratorium, and Diffused. The Identity Achievement status refers to an identity structure with a relatively integrated set of identity commitments that were self-constructed through identity exploration. Identity exploration is an agentic, internally driven identity formation process by which the individual examines and questions identifications; gathers information and considers alternative worldviews, self-perceptions, goals, and actions; experiments with different roles; negotiates the meaning of different identity commitments with others in the cultural milieu; and integrates identity content in different life domains and across roles and situations (Grotevant, 1987). The Foreclosure status refers to a structure with strong identity commitments; however, unlike in the Identity Achievement status, these commitments were adopted through mostly unquestioned identification with significant others like parents, role models, or idealized cultural groups, with little engagement in identity exploration. Consequently, the Foreclosed identity structure is commonly rigid and not well integrated. The Moratorium status refers to a relatively inchoate identity structure with few current identity commitments, but the individual is engaged in a high level of identity exploration to form such commitments. Finally, the Diffused status refers to a similarly fragmented structure with few identity commitments, but the individual has not engaged in identity exploration and instead adopts uncritically the momentary identity content (e.g., perceptions, values, goals, and actions) evinced by other people, mostly peers or charismatic figures, in the immediate situation.[3]

Several studies investigated the relations between students' identity statuses with their motivation, learning, and achievement. This research, in which most studies used quantitative correlational designs with students' self-report on summated scales, and a smaller set of studies that used interviews, mostly corroborated findings from the general literature on the benefits of the Identity Achievement status and the developmental potential of the Moratorium status (Kaplan & Flum, 2010). Research has found positive relations between the Achieved Identity status in the education domain with students' perceived competence; accuracy in assessing their academic standing; the value assigned to a domain; low perceived cost of pursuing a major; use of effective learning strategies; and perceived fulfillment of psychological needs for autonomy, competence, and relatedness. Identity Achievement status was also inversely related to the use of self-handicapping strategies in school (Chorba, Was, & Isaacson, 2012; Lange & Byrd, 2002; Luyckx et al., 2009; Perez, Cromley, & Kaplan, 2014). In comparison, the Diffuse status, and sometimes also the Moratorium status, were associated with less effective learning strategies, less accuracy in assessing students' own performance, higher use of self-handicapping strategies, and unfulfilled needs for autonomy, competence, and relatedness (Chorba et al., 2012; Lange & Byrd, 2002; Luyckx et al., 2009). The Foreclosure status presented a mixed profile of findings: this identity status was positively associated with students' uses of effective learning strategies, self-assessed academic standing, satisfaction of the need for relatedness, and lower use of self-handicapping strategies (Chorba et al., 2012; Lange & Byrd, 2002). However, Foreclosure was also associated with lower satisfaction of the needs for autonomy and competence, higher perceived costs of pursuing a major, and higher intentions to leave the major (Luyckx et al., 2009; Perez et al., 2014). Research also suggests that, in the long run, psychological need satisfaction and academic achievement may influence students' identity status. That is, higher need satisfaction and higher achievement may strengthen identity commitments, while high need satisfaction facilitates identity exploration, and low grades spur reconsideration of identity commitments in the domain of education (Luyckx et al., 2009; Pop et al., 2016).

Researchers have also investigated the identity processing strategies and styles that people employ when confronting identity issues, life problems, and

---

[3] Research has identified several additional statuses as well as sub-types of the four original identity statuses, has characterized a variety of exploration phenomena, has pointed to the developmental appropriateness of seemingly less adaptive statuses in certain ages and contexts, and has noted patterns of shifts among identity statuses along time as well as cycles in identity exploration and commitment making (Crocetti, 2017; Kroger & Marcia, 2011, Chapter 10 in this volume; Luyckx et al., 2011; Meeus, 2011; Negru-Subtirica & Klimstra, Chapter 18 in this volume).

important decisions (Berzonsky, 2011; Flum, 1994; Kerpelman, Pittman, & Lamke, 1997). Berzonsky (2011) identified three identity processing styles that correspond with the different identity statuses: informational, normative, and diffuse-avoidant.[4] The informational identity processing style characterizes people in the Identity Achievement and Moratorium statuses and is akin to engaging in identity exploration. This style involves assuming agency in proactively seeking, evaluating, and synthesizing self-relevant information, and it has been associated with openness to experience, cognitive complexity, introspection, a sense of autonomy and independence, and problem-focused coping. The normative identity processing style characterizes people in the Foreclosure status. This style involves confronting identity information in a reactive way through conforming to normative expectations, and it has been associated with high need for structure, resistance to information incompatible with already held beliefs and values, and coping strategies that rely on support from significant others. The diffuse-avoidant identity processing style characterizes people in the Diffuse status. This style involves avoiding dealing with identity issues and decisions or relying ad hoc on transitory situational guides, and it has been associated with low self-awareness, maladaptive attributions, avoidant and emotion-focused coping, self-handicapping strategies, and depression (Berzonsky, 2011).

Studies investigating relations between students' identity processing styles and their motivation and performance have found that students' reports of employing the informational processing style were associated with high academic and social functioning, high levels of academic autonomy, sense of educational purpose, and academic achievement. Students' reports of relying on the normative processing style were associated with clear educational purpose and achievement as well, but also with a lower level of autonomy and lower openness to different ideas. Reports of using the diffuse-avoidant processing style were associated with a negative profile of these outcomes (Berzonsky & Kuk, 2005; Cadely et al., 2011). Correspondingly, research has found that students' engagement and experience of burnout in school predicted their later identity processing style, with engagement positively predicting the informational processing style and burnout positively predicting the normative and diffuse-avoidant processing styles (Erentaitė et al., 2018).

Psychosocial scholarship has also emphasized the role of the school context and of educators in students' psychosocial identity formation (Lannegrand-Willems & Bosma, 2006; Flum & Kaplan, 2006; Harrell-Levy & Kerpelman, 2010; Schachter & Rich, 2011; Verhoeven et al., 2019). This research, which used diverse methodologies, including surveys, observations, interviews, and ethnographic case studies, highlighted how schools and teachers affect

---

[4] Youth in each identity status may use strategies from all three of the identity processing styles at different times, but they also demonstrate a preference for certain identity processing strategies that correspond with their identity formation status.

students' psychosocial identity processes. These agents extend meaningful opportunities for students to connect the academic material to their lives; create a supportive social climate in which students feel safe to explore different beliefs and experiment with different roles; communicate to students the legitimacy of making mistakes; and facilitate mutual peer support and encouragement for personal expression and exploration (Verhoeven et al., 2019).

Psychosocial Identity Interventions in Education

Probably due to early attempts that did not bear success, and the assumption that identity statuses are relatively stable and, hence, that psychosocial interventions in identity would require lengthy and deep processes (Kroger & Marcia, 2011), there have been only very few psychosocial interventions that aim to promote youth identity development (Archer, 1994, 2008; Eichas et al., 2015; Montgomery, Hernandez, & Ferrer-Wreder, 2008). Interventions in school are even rarer (Dreyer, 1994; Schachter & Rich, 2011).[5] But this state of affairs might be changing. Recently, Schachter and Rich (2011) have argued for the intentional application of the psychosocial identity perspective to "Identity Education" (IdEd) – "the deliberate active involvement of educators with the psychosocial processes and practices that are involved in students' identity development" (p. 224). Flum and Kaplan (2006; Kaplan, Garner, & Brock, 2019) have also argued that promoting students' confidence and skills in identity exploration should become a primary educational goal, particularly in light of the uncertain and rapidly changing nature of life in the twenty-first century.

Building on these ideas, Kaplan, Sinai, and Flum (2014) developed one of the few interventions that pursue IdEd by integrating identity exploration practices into the academic curriculum. The intervention employs a design-based research approach that translates four psychosocial conceptual principles into the design of educational activities: promoting perceived self-relevance, triggering identity exploration, facilitating a sense of safety, and scaffolding identity exploration strategies. Promoting perceived self-relevance refers to encouraging students to self-construct connections between aspects of the educational environment (e.g., a concept in the curriculum) with an aspect of their identity (e.g., values or goals). Triggering identity exploration involves designing for experiences of discrepancy from current identity commitments, such as novelty, uncertainty, or lack of self-knowledge. Facilitating a sense of safety refers to practices that reduce the perceived psychological risks of identity exploration by allowing diversity of private or public expressions and fostering a supportive classroom climate. Finally, scaffolding identity

---

[5] However, certain progressive instructional approaches can be conceptualized as harnessing psychosocial identity formation processes that encourage students to explore their identity.

exploration strategies involves designing educational activities that guide students to engage in different identity exploration strategies, such as generating self-relevant content, introspection, role play, and reflective social interactions with peers and adults. Research in literacy and mathematics secondary and college classrooms, science museums, and digital educational games suggests that the approach can be used to promote students' identity exploration, and that exploration is associated with more adaptive motivation for studying the academic content (D'Antonio, 2020; Garner, Kaplan, & Pugh, 2016; Garner et al., in press; Foster & Shah, 2016; Shah, Foster, & Barany, 2017; Heffernan et al., 2017; Kaplan et al., 2014; Sinai, Kaplan, & Flum, 2012).

Summary: Psychosocial Research on Identity Structure and Process in Education

Psychosocial identity research in educational settings defines identity as an individual's deep and comprehensive mental structure that organizes a network of identity content (beliefs, values, self-perceptions, goals, actions) in various major life domains (e.g., education, relationships, career). According to the psychosocial perspective, a person has a single overarching identity whose type of structure undergirds the person's motivation, learning, development, coping with change and challenges, and well-being. As people pursue the developmental task of forming a coherent identity structure, they negotiate identity issues with different identity processing styles that reflect different identity structures. Most psychosocial research in educational settings has focused on the relations of different identity structure–process statuses and identity formation styles with students' motivation, performance, and overall educational functioning. With few exceptions, most psychosocial research in educational settings has employed quantitative methods that seek generalized patterns of relations between particular identity structures and formation processes with educational outcomes, with less attention to the role of culture and context in these processes. Though change in identity status does occur, such shifts are relatively slow, as an individual's identity status may persist for months or even years. Nevertheless, the nascent literature on psychosocial identity interventions in educational settings highlights the potential for promoting students' identity exploration and, consequently, their identity development in ways that intertwine with adaptive academic engagement.

24.1.3 Social Cultural Research in Education on Identity as a Cultural Product

Research from social cultural perspectives on identity in education has focused primarily on the role of culture in students' identity content and formation processes. There are numerous social cultural perspectives, and they differ in emphasis on the scale and stability of the cultural meanings that shape people's identities (Côté & Levine, 2002). Some perspectives emphasize cultural meanings embedded in relatively stable historical social structures that position people in very established roles that frame their sense of who they are and how they should act. Other perspectives emphasize the dynamical, moment-by-moment, situated interpretations and negotiations around the meanings of social positions and roles in particular contexts and cultural activities. There are also social cultural perspectives that integrate assumptions regarding meanings based in broad social structures with the situated interpretations and dynamic negotiations of meaning about inhabiting a role in a particular activity. Such different emphases notwithstanding, the shared underlying assumption among social cultural perspectives on identity is that people's sense of who they are and how they may or should act are based in the cultural meanings that are relayed, negotiated, imagined, and adopted through participation in activities in particular social cultural contexts (Burke & Stets, 2009; Holland & Lachicotte, 2007).

Most social cultural identity research in education has drawn on perspectives informed by Vygotsky's (1978) cultural-historical theory of human development (Hickey, 2003; Hand & Gresalfi, 2015; McCaslin, 2009; Nolen, Ward, & Horn, 2011; Penuel & Wertsch, 1995). These perspectives conceptualize identity as based in the culturally derived meanings of a person's actions. Cultural meanings of situated actions integrate broad historical and cultural meanings about the nature and value of situations and personal attributes, institutional and social-contextual affordances and constraints, and semiotic and tangible cultural tools available in the situation that mediate an actor's pursuit of the purpose and goals of a cultural activity. As people participate in a particular activity, the meanings of their actions signify who they are to others and to themselves. Identity formation, then, involves the dynamic shift in a person's culturally significant actions that occur during continuous participation in activities. Such shifts take place within the person's zone of proximal development (ZPD). That is, culturally mediated identities emerge in social interaction between people who have different levels of cultural knowledge and skills and who co-regulate their actions through the mutual appropriation, negotiation, and transformation of cultural tools and modes of participation (McCaslin, 2009).

A conceptually similar strand of social cultural identity research in education has drawn on symbolic interactionist perspectives (Burke & Stets, 2009; Holland & Lachicotte, 2007; Serpe & Stryker, 2011). Symbolic interactionism, which originated in the writing of Mead (1934) and Cooley (1902), views identities as based in the cultural meanings of people's social positions and roles, both formal (e.g., student, teacher, principal) and informal (e.g., friend, colleague, pedestrian). In this perspective, a person's identity emerges from the social positions and roles they occupy and the manners in which they enact them. Identity formation thus occurs by transitioning to new social positions and roles and infusing roles with new meanings through social interaction and negotiation while participating in cultural activities (Burke & Stets, 2009;

Holland & Lachicotte, 2007). As both neo-Vygotskian and Symbolic Interactionist perspectives view identities as based in the cultural meaning of a person's particular actions, they consider motivation for action as inseparable from identity formation, and accordingly, they affirm the key contributions to identity of learning new knowledge and skills.

Social cultural research on identity in education has focused on the way that meanings embedded in historical structures, contextual practices, and conceptual and tangible tools frame and mediate students' actions, motivation, learning, and sense of who they are and can be. Social cultural research in education has highlighted, for example, the ways by which societal and organizational structures that provide differential educational opportunities to students from different social groups frame those students' self-definitions, sense of agency, perceived competence, and goal-setting (McCaslin, 2009; McCaslin & Lavigne, 2010). Social cultural research has also demonstrated how classroom contexts and educational practices that manifest different meanings (e.g., reflected in didactic versus discussion-based instruction) shape students' conceptions of learning the subject matter, sense of what it means to be a member of the subject matter community, self-perceptions and personal sense of belonging to the community, and motivation and learning of the content (Boaler & Greeno, 2000; Nolen et al., 2011; Sfard & Prusak, 2005). Social cultural research has also described how students appropriate and negotiate their identities through different modes of participation in activities, such as engaging in full participation, legitimate peripheral participation, peripheral and marginal nonparticipation, as well as different trajectories toward or away from participation. Different modes of participation reflect and frame students' identities by mediating their sense of belonging to the context and academic community, perceived efficacy to succeed in the academic activities, perceived options for themselves in the community, and motivation for participation in future educational activities (Hickey, 2003; Nolen et al., 2015; Wenger, 1998).

Social cultural research has highlighted, for example, how cultural practices and negotiations around interpretation of students' social behavior in school shape students' self-perceptions as more or less academically able (Gresalfi, 2009). Research has also demonstrated how cultural meanings in the school context regarding characteristics of boys and girls, and contextual criteria for competence in mathematics and in language arts, frame boys' and girls' different modes of participation in classroom activities, interpretation of these experiences, and perceptions of themselves and of others as more and less able in the subject domain (Hand & Gresalfi, 2015; Hickey, 2003). Similarly, social cultural research showed how school practices, such as ability grouping that correspond with different racial representation and curricula that include or exclude reference to different racial groups, framed different meanings of students' racial identity, and how these meanings related to the students' engagement and achievement (Nasir, McLaughlin, & Jones, 2009; Nasir et al., 2016).

Social Cultural Educational Identity Interventions in Education

The social cultural conception of identity as anchored in participation in educational activities renders education itself an identity intervention. This conception views identities as framed by the network of cultural meanings regarding the purpose of schooling, the nature of learning and motivation, and the value of different modes of assessment and achievement. Accordingly, social cultural interventions aim to modify social structures, interpersonal interactions, discourses, and other cultural tools that mediate participation. By reconstructing the meanings within which students construe their identities, social cultural interventions evoke students' engaged participation (Cobb, Gresalfi, & Hodge, 2009; Faircloth, 2009; Nolen et al., 2015).

The most prevalent approach to social cultural identity interventions in educational settings involve designing educational contexts and activities that aim to socialize students into the classroom's community of practice (Lave & Wenger, 2001). Such interventions are designed to establish zones of proximal development within which students engage in a series of progressive activities, and, like apprentices, appropriate the goals, cultural tools, and modes of action of particular academic communities, such as mathematicians, scientists, or writers (e.g., Deane & Song, 2015). Another type of social cultural identity intervention focuses on designing activities that encourage students whose identities dispose them to nonparticipation and disengagement to reframe the meaning of participation in educational activities. The social cultural design aims to modify the purpose of the educational activities from simply learning the academic content and achieving high grades to learning through meaningful incorporation of diverse students' personal interests, self-perceptions and definitions, and lived experiences (e.g., culturally relevant pedagogy; Faircloth, 2009; Kim, Sinatra, & Seyranian, 2018). In this respect, these social cultural interventions differ from social psychological interventions that aim to enhance perceived relevance or belonging, as the latter design special activities to specifically trigger these desirable perceptions, while the former involve redesigning the core educational activities through which students learn the academic content as well as develop a sense of identity as members of the academic community.

A third type of social cultural identity intervention goes beyond socialization and inclusive participation to promote students' agency in critiquing and recreating the educational activity. These interventions commonly involve addressing activities and practices that reflect social problems of concern to the school community, and they employ collaborative and participatory designs that involve the students, other members of the school, and even members of the broader community in transforming the activities, the nature and meaning of educational participation, and, correspondingly, students' identities and educational engagement (Gutiérrez, Engeström, & Sannino, 2016).

Summary: Social Cultural Research in Education on Identity as a Cultural Product

Social cultural identity research in educational settings defines identity as emerging from students' participation in educational activities in particular social cultural contexts. According to these perspectives, people have many identities that reflect the numerous social cultural positions and roles they inhabit in different contexts and activities. Social cultural perspectives consider these identities to be intertwined with the particular cultural context and activity, and most research has gone beyond the individual to focus on the cultural-contextual meanings and tangible and semiotic cultural tools that mediate students' participation and, thus, mediate the formation and enactment of their identities. Correspondingly, social cultural interventions focus on modifying educational activity systems in ways that frame the integrated emergence of desirable identities, motivation, and learning. With its primary focus on meaning and the nature of contextual activities, most social cultural research has employed ethnographic-qualitative methods to describe, investigate, and transform students' identities in particular contexts.

24.1.4 Identity Perspectives on Educational Psychological Processes: An Interpretive Summary

Identity research in educational psychology has generated a substantial body of knowledge regarding the relations between students' sense of who they are and their motivation, learning, and achievement in educational settings. This research represents a diversity of theoretical perspectives, foci, and methodologies. Social cognitive and social psychological research on identity content contributed to understanding the relations between students' self-perceptions and self-definitions with self-worth concerns, sense of belonging, motivation, and achievement. Psychosocial research revealed patterns relating different overarching identity structures and identity formation processes with sense of purpose, orientations to learning, and well-being. Social cultural research has shed light on the way cultural meanings embedded in educational contexts and activities mediate students' interpretations of their academic ability, motivation and perceived action possibilities in school, and sense of membership in the academic community. Thus, research from the different perspectives captures certain facets of identity while placing other facets – those highlighted by other perspectives – in the background.

The different perspectives harbor some divergent assumptions about identity. Social cognitive and social psychological perspectives define identity as one social cognitive element among others within the individual's self-schema, view the activation of such identities as both internal to the individual and as primed by the context, and consider identities malleable in response to contextual cues. Quite differently, psychosocial perspectives consider identity to be an individual's comprehensive and mostly unconscious mental framework that reflects the status of a lengthy negotiation between the person and their context. In comparison, social cultural perspectives define identity as the cultural meaning of the person's enactment of a social role, integrating the person with their context and activity and predicating the malleability of identity on changes in the social cultural environment. Such differing assumptions have instigated decades-old debates regarding the nature of identity: whether it is stable or malleable, individual or social-collective, personal or contextual, conscious or unconscious, agentic or reactive, and epigenetic or discursive (Côté & Levine, 2002; Gergen, 1991; Holland & Lachicotte, 2007).

In recent years, however, researchers have called for integrating the different perspectives. Clearly, people's identities integrate content, structure, process, and cultural meanings. Furthermore, identity phenomena may defy neat categorization and instead exhibit properties of both ends of the aforementioned dialectics; they manifest both stability and change, individual and social-collective attributes, personal and contextual characteristics, conscious and unconscious processes, agentic and reactive sources of change, and epigenetic as well as discursive patterns of development. These realizations, and the growing recognition that different identity perspectives hold complementary strengths and limitations, have spurred attempts to formulate integrative identity models (Galliher, Rivas-Drake, & Dubow, 2017; Penuel & Wertsch, 1995; Schwartz et al., 2011). However, designing integrative models is very challenging, since it requires incorporating diverging assumptions into a coherent epistemological framework. In the section below, we describe one such integrative model that has been applied in educational psychological research. The Dynamic Systems Model of Role Identity (DSMRI) (Kaplan & Garner, 2017) integrates the diverse identity perspectives into a coherent framework by building on assumptions of Complex Dynamic Systems (CDS) (Guastello, Koopmans, & Pincus, 2009; Kunnen & Van Geert, 2012).

24.2 A Complex Dynamic Systems Perspective on Identity: The Dynamic Systems Model of Role Identity (DSMRI)

The Dynamic Systems Model of Role Identity (DSMRI) integrates insights about the multiplicity and transience of identity content from social cognitive and social psychological perspectives, the various relatively enduring structural and formation processes from psychosocial perspectives, and the cultural mediation of identity from social cultural perspectives, into a unified framework that captures the diversity of identity phenomena (for elaboration on the DSMRI, see Garner & Kaplan, 2019; Kaplan & Garner, 2017;

Kaplan & Garner, 2018; Kaplan, Garner, & Brock, 2019). To do so, the DSMRI relies on a conceptualization of identity as a Complex Dynamic System (CDS) (Kunnen & Van Geert, 2012; cf. Overton, 2013). The CDS approach has been developed to conceptualize a variety of natural and social phenomena whose diverse behaviors defy linear cause–effect explanations and manifest patterns across traditional dichotomies such as stable–malleable, specific–general, and inherent–contextualized. Examples of such phenomena include the weather, the brain, ecosystems, the economy, language, organizations, personality, emotion, cognition, motivation, and development. In order to capture and model such diversity of behavior, the CDS approach conceptualizes the phenomenon as a network of interdependent elements embedded in varying contextual dimensions that continuously interact to give rise to the system's dynamic behavior (explication of the ontological and epistemological assumptions of the CDS approach can be found in Bar-Yam, 1997; Guastello & Leibovitch, 2009; Kaplan, Katz, & Flum, 2012; Koopmans & Stamovlasis, 2016; Overton, 2013; Waldrop, 1992).

24.2.1 Role Identity as the Unit of Analysis

The DSMRI builds on CDS assumptions to define the primary unit of analysis for identity as the mental framework that gives rise to the experience and action of interest. The model draws on symbolic interactionist perspectives to define this mental framework as based in the social-cultural role that the person occupies in a particular situation (Burke & Stets, 2009). The cultural meanings of the social role (e.g., a student) integrate with the person's unique characteristics, history, and social positioning to give rise to that person's idiosyncratic interpretation of who they are in that role in the particular situation – the person's role identity. The DSMRI proposes that it is this role identity that frames the situated emergence of the person's interpretation of events, motivation, and actions. This role identity can refer to any social cultural role, whether formal (e.g., teacher, student, counselor, principal), informal (e.g., friend, colleague, pedestrian, workshop participant), or unlabeled (e.g., the role of a person getting up in the morning), and can range from the very specific (e.g., an urban high school freshman taking a mathematics exam) to the very general (e.g., an adolescent contemplating the meaning of life). The relevant role identity for explaining a person's experiences and actions is the one that frames the person's subjective, and most commonly implicit, understanding, of the role they are occupying in the particular situation. As a CDS, the role identity cannot be captured by reducing it to any of its individual components, its behavior is most often nonlinear and not completely predictable, and its continuous emergence is dependent both on the social-cultural context and on the system's history of emergent states. Figure 24.1 presents a scheme of the DSMRI.

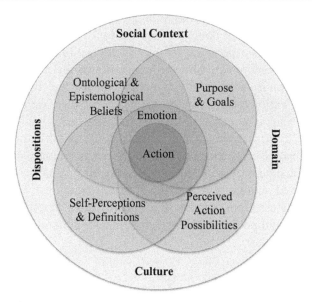

Figure 24.1 *The Dynamic Systems Model of role identity (adapted from Kaplan & Garner, 2017)*

24.2.2 Role Identity Content, Structure, and Process

The basic assumption underlying the DSMRI is that, in any situation, the role identity system frames the person's actions toward salient goals in light of their interpretations of the situation and of themselves in that situation. Correspondingly, the model conceptualizes the content of the role identity system to be organized into four interdependent, multi-element, components drawn from social cognitive and social psychological theories of identity and motivation: Ontological and Epistemological Beliefs, Purpose and Goals, Self-Perceptions and Self-Definitions, and Perceived Action Possibilities (Bandura, 1997; Dweck, 2006; Eccles, 2009; Maehr & Braskamp, 1986; Oyserman & James, 2011; Weiner, 2010). Ontological and Epistemological Beliefs refer to the person's working model of the world relevant to the role and situation – formal and informal knowledge held to be true regarding the nature of the world (ontological beliefs), assumptions about the certainty and complexity of this knowledge (epistemological beliefs), and emotions associated with these beliefs. Purpose and Goals refer to the person's overall purpose in their social cultural role, their more concrete goals, and the emotions tied to these purpose and goals. Self-Perceptions and Self-Definitions concern the person's self-perceptions regarding personal characteristics and self-definitions regarding social characteristics, and the emotions that are tied to these perceptions and definitions. Perceived Action Possibilities refer to the behaviors that the person perceives as available and unavailable for the pursuit of their purpose and goals in light of ontological and epistemological beliefs and self-perceptions and self-definitions, as well as the emotions tied to such behaviors. In any situation, the contents from the four components integrate to give rise to the person's experiences, emotions, and actions.

The role identity structure can vary in the breadth of the its content, the depth and type of connections among content elements, and the nature of connections among various role identities within the person's overall identity system. A psychosocial assumption in the DSMRI that corresponds with the nature of complex dynamic systems is that the role identity structure aspires toward states of relative coherence of the identity content within and across components (e.g., a state of alignment among ontological beliefs, goals, self-perceptions, perceived actions, and their emotional associations). Stability in the role identity structure is nevertheless dynamic, reflecting repeating convergences of contextual and personal factors that manifests in iterations that are very similar to one another.

Role identity processes may manifest upon change to any feature of the system, including the breadth and the centrality of content, and the depth, nature, and affective valence of structural connections. Whereas the identity system aspires toward coherence, its trajectory of change would depend on its history and structure at any point in time, as well as on the impact of situated events. Role identity formation processes may manifest movement toward enhanced coherence and integration, or toward increased entropy and misalignment (Kunnen & Van Geert, 2012). Shifts in systemic formation processes may reflect the actor's agency, which could manifest as a top-down systemic process in which a higher-order role identity assumes an I-self position to reflect, explore, or regulate a lower level role identity; or a bottom-up systemic process, in which experiences in lower level role identities instigate shifts in higher-order role identities. Different sources and types of the systemic change processes correspond to different psychosocial and social-cognitive identity formation strategies. The individual may engage in agentic identity exploration, rely on normative external or internal content, or yield to shifting situational triggers and influences.

24.2.3 Culture in Role Identity

Role identity content, structure, and processes of exploration and formation are inevitably shaped and mediated by social-cultural meanings and practices. The DSMRI specifies four factors that serve as the role identity system's control parameters and frame its emergence: the mediating cultural means; the social context and its relational affordances; the person's physical and psychological dispositions (e.g., height, weight, agility, temperament, implicit needs, self-worth concerns, and emotional contingencies); and the role's subject domain (such as home life, school life, work life) and subject (such as mathematics, social studies, sports, law). These four factors integrate into a unique configuration in any situation to frame the continuous emergence of the role identity content. (Elaboration on the DSMRI can be found in Kaplan & Garner, 2017, 2018; Kaplan, Garner, & Brock, 2019; Kaplan, Neuber, & Garner, 2019).

24.2.4 DSMRI Research in Education

Whereas research and interventions using the DSMRI are at an early stage, a growing number of studies suggest its promise for pursuing integrative research questions concerning identity in educational psychological processes. For example, one DSMRI study employed narrative interviewing to study undergraduate honor students' academic role identities as mediated by cultural meanings of smartness, and how role identities reflecting different configurations of ontological beliefs of smartness, self-perceptions as "being smart," academic goals, and perceived action possibilities manifested in different emotions, actions, and well-being (Kaplan et al., 2019; Neuber, 2019). Other DSMRI studies using interviews investigated the role identity change of science teachers who participated in a professional development institute (Garner & Kaplan, 2019; Hathcock, Garner, & Kaplan, 2020), and how the role identities of educational policymakers framed their decision-making (Brock & Kaplan, 2020). Other applications of the DSMRI have included: an analysis of reflective writing to investigate change in teaching role identity and motivation for college teaching among graduate students who participated in a semester-long teaching course (Gunersel et al., 2016); a year-long collaborative case study of the dynamic shifts in teaching role identity, motivation, and instructional practice of a teacher during his first-year of teaching (Vedder-Weiss et al., 2018); collaborative interventions in an undergraduate mathematics course and a high school mathematics class to promote students' identity exploration of their mathematics student role identity, motivation, and engagement (Heffernan et al., 2017; Heffernan & Newton, 2019); a semester-long intervention in the student role identity of community college remedial writers (D'Antonio, 2020); and case studies involving reflective written products and narrative interviews to study the professional identity development of pre-service school counselors (Sinai, Tossman, & Kaplan, 2017) and pre-service Non-Formal educators (Tossman et al., 2018).

24.3 Emerging Identity Topics in Educational Psychology Research

Despite its relatively short history, identity research in educational psychology has made important strides. In addition to the scholarship reviewed above, identity research in educational psychology has ventured into additional research domains highly relevant to educational practice. Below, we note four such emerging areas of inquiry: identity in digital learning environments, teacher identity, identity in informal educational environments, and collective identity of teams and organizations.

24.3.1 Identity in Digital Learning Environments

A burgeoning area of inquiry in educational psychology concerns students' learning, motivation, and achievement in digital learning environments (Mishra, Koehler, & Greenhow, 2016). For example, educational psychologists have been investigating students' learning and motivation in fully online learning environments, immersive digital educational games, and virtual reality contexts. Much of this research has been framed by social cognitive and social cultural perspectives and their intersection, and it has focused on students' self-perceptions and actions in relation to learning while using digital technology and how these are mediated by contextual meanings and tools in virtual educational activity systems. Some of this research has applied identity perspectives. For example, researchers studying students' experiences in immersive digital education games have studied the way students project their identities onto game avatars. These researchers explore the meaning of students' experiences as avatars for their academic identities (Foster & Shah, 2016). Such research has also begun to investigate the game features that facilitate engagement in constructive identity exploration (Shah, Foster, & Barany, 2017). With the increasing incorporation of digital technologies in education, identity-focused educational psychology research could provide important contributions to inform technological design and educational practice and policy.

24.3.2 Teacher Identity

Throughout its history, educational psychological scholarship has focused almost exclusively on students. In the past couple of decades, however, researchers have also begun to attend to the motivation, learning, performance, and professional development of teachers. Much of this research has drawn on social cognitive perspectives, and early research focused primarily on teachers' self-efficacy (Klassen et al., 2011; Tschannen-Moran et al., 1998). More recently, the research has expanded to consider teachers' achievement goals, values, and perceived costs (Fives & Buehl, 2012; Richardson, Karabenick, & Watt, 2014). In parallel, education researchers have adopted the concept of identity, mostly from social cultural perspectives, to investigate teacher professional development (Beijaard, Meijer, & Verloop, 2004). In recent years, this scholarship has influenced educational psychologists, who currently entertain a diversity of perspectives on teacher identity (Schutz et al., 2018). The educational psychological research on teacher identity is nascent, and many inquiries are ripe with promise, among them questions about the role of identity in teacher learning, motivation, practice, professional development, sense of community, and well-being (Kaplan & Garner, 2018; Yang, Shu, & Yin, 2021).

24.3.3 Identity in Informal Educational Environments

Most educational psychological scholarship, including research on identity in educational settings, has focused on formal, K-16 educational contexts. Recently, however, educational psychologists have begun to investigate learning and motivation in informal educational environments such as out-of-school programs, youth movements, sports teams, and museums (Barron & Bell, 2016). Much of this research has been framed by social cultural perspectives and has sought to investigate how informal environmental arrangements and activities frame students' participation, emerging identities, motivation, learning, and development. Burgeoning topics in this area of research involve understanding the characteristics of environments, exhibits, and activities that promote adaptive identity exploration and formation, the role of peers, and the contributions of interactions with mentors and role models to identity formation (Barron & Bell, 2016; Garner, Kaplan, & Pugh, 2016; Garner et al., in press).

24.3.4 Collective Identities: Teams and Organizations

Whereas the traditional emphasis in educational psychology has been on motivation, learning, and achievement at the level of the individual, some scholarship has attended to educational psychological processes at the collective level. Probably the most familiar collective concept in educational psychology is "collective efficacy" (Bandura, 2000) – "[p]eople's shared beliefs in their collective power to produce desired results" (p. 75). Research has investigated collective efficacy in relation to teams' motivation and performance in education, business, sports, and the military (Bandura, 2000). Research has also investigated other collective-self concepts, such as group norms and goals (Feldman, 1984) and group perceptions and collective action (Habbershon & Astrachan, 1997). The notion that people who belong to a collective can share the collective's goals, self-definitions, and beliefs and engage in collective action has been captured by collective identity concepts such as a "team identity" and "organizational identity" (Albert & Whetten, 1985; Gioia, Schultz, & Corley, 2000; Haslam & Ellemers, 2011). As with personal identity, the literature on collective identities is diverse and involves different definitions and theoretical perspectives, with diverging assumptions about the nature of collective identity phenomena and how they relate to the identities, motivation, and action of individual members. Attention to group-level phenomena has been growing in educational psychology, and research has explored teachers' collective efficacy, students' shared perceptions of their classroom, and student groups' pursuit of shared goals (Bardach et al., 2018; Klassen, Usher, & Bong, 2010; Rogat, Linnenbrink-Garcia, & DiDonato, 2013). A collective identity perspective may be fruitful for integrating different lines of educational psychological research on the agency, beliefs, motivation, learning, and action of collectives in education. In particular, a complex dynamic system perspective on identity that assumes a self-similar (fractal) hierarchical structure and dynamic influences across hierarchical levels in the identity system provides a promising framework for integrating identity processes at the collective and individual levels (Garner et al., 2021; Kaplan & Garner, 2017).

24.4 Conclusion: Educational Psychology Identity Research, Practice, and Policy

Educational psychology scholarship has made tremendous contributions to understanding students' engagement as well as the supportive and detrimental characteristics of educational environments and instructional practices. However, throughout much of the field's history, studies on students' cognition, motivation, emotion, peer interactions, classroom climate, and home environments have constituted mostly distinct lines of inquiry (Pintrich, Marx, & Boyle, 1993). Increasingly, scholars have been attempting to integrate these different literatures into models that better capture the complexity of students' authentic experiences in educational situations (Sinatra & Seyranian, 2016). The concept of identity as a complex dynamic system with content, structure, and processes that are framed by social cultural contexts and activities can provide an integrative framework for a variety of educational psychological concepts and guide such efforts (Hand & Gresalfi, 2015; Garner & Kaplan, 2019; Kim et al., 2018; Nolen et al., 2015).

Importantly, applying identity frameworks to conceptualize current educational psychological understandings may not suffice. Most research in educational psychology has been conducted in educational systems with structures, instructional practices, and academic tasks designed for the industrial era. In the twenty-first century, global environmental, economic, political, and technological forces have created new circumstances, transformed the world of work, and increased volatility, uncertainty, complexity, and ambiguity (Bennett & Lemoine, 2014; Flum & Kaplan, 2006). Lamentably, two decades into the century, the impact of these trends on structures and practices in public education has been relatively minor – but this may soon change. The onset of the COVID-19 pandemic during the writing of this chapter dramatically reshaped all aspects of life, including education. In a matter of weeks, education from the earliest grades through graduate and professional school was thrown into disarray. Schools were closed, and instruction moved online for months. Students, teachers, and parents had to reformulate their role identities and negotiate teaching and learning with others who were experiencing similar identity disruptions. At present there is still great uncertainty regarding the future of educational practices across preschool through graduate education following the pandemic. These experiences accentuate the need for educational systems to heed their role in preparing students for a world of rapid change and an uncertain future. Education in the twenty-first century can and should be designed to enhance students' confidence and skills in confronting change and uncertainty, and educators can claim this mantle by engaging students in individually and collectively gathering information about the world and themselves, reflecting on and reconsidering current identity commitments, and adopting new and flexible beliefs, self-perceptions and self-definitions, goals, and actions. In other words, contemporary students are likely to benefit from repeated identity exploration under the auspices of supportive educators (Flum & Kaplan, 2006). Such Identity Education (Schachter & Rich, 2011) would require substantial changes in educational policy regarding curriculum standards and goals, instructional strategies, pre-service and in-service teacher professional development, and assessment and accountability practices. It is clear, however, that such changes to educational policy and practice will be needed to promote students' adaptive identities, learning, motivation, and resilience. Intentional support for identity exploration will equip students to thrive in the twenty-first century, but even more importantly, it may renew the transformational promise of education (Kaplan, Garner, & Brock, 2019).

References

Albert, S. & Whetten, D. A. (1985). Organizational identity. *Research in Organizational Behavior, 7*, 263–295.

Alexander, P. A. (2018). Past as prologue: Educational psychology's legacy and progeny. *Journal of Educational Psychology, 110*(2), 147–162.

Apple, M. W. (2014). *Official Knowledge: Democratic Education in a Conservative Age, 3rd Ed.* New York, NY: Routledge.

Archer, S. L. (Ed.). (1994). *Interventions for Adolescent Identity Development.* Thousand Oaks, CA: Sage.

Archer, S. L. (2008). Identity and interventions: An introduction. *Identity: An International Journal of Theory and Research, 8*(2), 89–94.

Bandura, A. (1977). Self-efficacy: Toward a unifying theory of behavioral change. *Psychological Review, 84*(2), 191–215.

Bandura, A. (1997). *Self-efficacy: The Exercise of Control.* New York, NY: Freeman.

Bandura, A. (2000). Exercise of human agency through collective efficacy. *Current Directions in Psychological Science, 9*(3), 75–78.

Bar-Yam, Y. (1997). *Dynamics of Complex Systems.* New York, NY: Perseus Press.

Bardach, L., Yanagida, T., Schober, B., & Lüftenegger, M. (2018). Within-class consensus on classroom goal structures: Relations to achievement and achievement goals in mathematics and language classes. *Learning and Individual Differences, 67*, 78–90.

Barron, B. & Bell, P. (2016). Learning environments in and out of school. In L. Corno & E. Anderman (Eds.), *Handbook of Educational Psychology* (pp. 337–350). London: Routledge.

Baumeister, R. F. & Muraven, M. (1996). Identity as adaptation to social, cultural, and historical context. *Journal of Adolescence, 19*(5), 405–416.

Beijaard, D., Meijer, P. C., & Verloop, N. (2004). Reconsidering research on teachers' professional identity. *Teaching and Teacher Education, 20*(2), 107–128.

Bennett, N. & Lemoine, G. J. (2014). What a difference a word makes: Understanding threats to performance in a VUCA world. *Business Horizons, 57*(3), 311–317.

Berzonsky, M. D. (2011). A social-cognitive perspective on identity construction. In S. J. Schwartz, K. Luyckx & V. Vignoles (Eds.), *Handbook of Identity Theory and Research, Vol. 1* (pp. 55–76). New York, NY: Springer.

Berzonsky, M. D. & Adams, G. R. (1999). Reevaluating the identity status paradigm: Still useful after 35 years. *Developmental Review, 19*, 557–590.

Berzonsky, M. D. & Kuk, L. S. (2005). Identity style, psychosocial maturity, and academic performance. *Personality and Individual Differences, 39*(1), 235–247.

Boaler, J. & Greeno, J. G. (2000). Identity, agency, and knowing in mathematics worlds. In J. Boaler (Ed.), *Multiple Perspectives on Mathematics Teaching and Learning* (pp. 171–200). Westport, CT: Ablex.

Brock, B. & Kaplan, A. (2020, August). Education policymakers' identity and decision making in an increasingly complex world. Poster presented at the annual convention of the American Psychological Association, Washington, DC.

Burke, P. J. & Stets, J. E. (2009). *Identity Theory.* New York, NY: Oxford University Press.

Cadely, H. S. E., Pittman, J. F., Kerpelman, J. L., & Adler-Baeder, F. (2011). The role of identity styles and academic possible selves on academic outcomes for high school students. *Identity, 11*(4), 267–288.

Chorba, K., Was, C. A., & Isaacson, R. M. (2012). Individual differences in academic identity and self-handicapping in undergraduate college students. *Individual Differences Research, 10*(2), 60–68.

Cobb, P., Gresalfi, M., & Hodge, L. L. (2009). An interpretive scheme for analyzing the identities that students develop in mathematics classrooms. *Journal for Research in Mathematics Education, 40*(1), 40–68.

Cohen, G. L. & Garcia, J. (2008). Identity, belonging, and achievement. *Current Directions in Psychological Science, 17*(6), 365–370.

Cooley, C. H. (1902/1972). Looking-glass self. In J. G. Manis & B. N. Melzer (Eds.), *Symbolic Interaction: A Reader in Social Psychology, 2nd Ed.* (pp. 231–233). Boston, MA: Allyn and Bacon.

Côté, J. E. & Levine, C. (2002). *Identity Formation, Agency, and Culture: A Social Psychological Synthesis.* Mahwah, NJ: Erlbaum.

Crocetti, E. (2017). Identity formation in adolescence: The dynamic of forming and consolidating identity commitments. *Child Development Perspectives, 11*(2), 145–150.

Crocetti, E., Rubini, M., & Meeus, W. (2008). Capturing the dynamics of identity formation in various ethnic groups: Development and validation of a three-dimensional model. *Journal of Adolescence, 31*(2), 207–222.

D'Antonio, M. (2020). Pedagogy and identity in the community college developmental writing classroom: A qualitative study in three cases. *Community College Journal of Research and Practice, 44*(1), 30–51.

Deane, P. & Song, Y. (2015). The key practice, discuss and debate ideas: Conceptual framework, literature review, and provisional learning progressions for argumentation. *ETS Research Report Series, 2015*(2), 1–21.

Dreyer, P. H. (1994). Designing curricular identity interventions for secondary schools. In S. L. Archer (Ed.), *Interventions for Adolescent Identity Development* (pp. 121–140). Thousand Oaks, CA: Sage.

Dweck, C. S. (2006). *Mindset: How We Can Learn to Fulfill our Potential.* New York, NY: Random.

Eccles, J. (2009). Who am I and what am I going to do with my life? Personal and collective identities as motivators of action. *Educational Psychologist, 44,* 78–89.

Eccles, J., Adler, T. F., Futterman, R., Goff, S. B., Kaczala, C. M., Meece, J. L., & Midgley, C. (1983). Expectancies, values, and academic behaviors. In J. T. Spence (Ed.), *Achievement and Achievement Motives: Psychological and Sociological Approaches* (pp. 75–146). San Francisco, CA: Freeman.

Eichas, K., Meca, A., Montgomery, M. J., & Kurtines, W. M. (2015). Identity and positive youth development: Advances in developmental intervention science. In K. C. McLean, & M. Syed (Eds.), *The Oxford Handbook of Identity Development* (pp. 337–354). New York, NY: Oxford University Press.

Elmore, K. C. & Oyserman, D. (2012). If "we" can succeed, "I" can too: Identity-based motivation and gender in the classroom. *Contemporary Educational Psychology, 37,* 176–185, doi:10.1016/j.cedpsych.2011.05.003.

Erentaitė, R., Vosylis, R., Gabrialavičiūtė, I., & Raižienė, S. (2018). How does school experience relate to adolescent identity formation over time? Cross-lagged associations between school engagement, school burnout and identity processing styles. *Journal of Youth and Adolescence, 47*(4), 760–774.

Erikson, E. H. (1950). *Childhood and Society.* New York, NY: Norton.

Erikson, E. H. (1968). *Identity: Youth and Crisis.* New York, NY: Norton.

Faircloth, B. S. (2009). Making the most of adolescence: Harnessing the search for identity to understand classroom belonging. *Journal of Adolescent Research, 24*(3), 321–348.

Feldman, D. C. (1984). The development and enforcement of group norms. *Academy of Management Review, 9*(1), 47–53.

Fives, H. & Buehl, M. (2012). Spring cleaning for the messy construct of teachers' beliefs: What are they? Which have been examined? What can they tell us? In K. R. Harris, S. Graham & T. Urdan (Eds.), *APA Educational Psychology Handbook: Vol. 2. Individual Differences and Cultural and Contextual Factors* (pp. 471–499). Washington, DC: American Psychological Association.

Flum, H. (1994). Styles of identity formation in early and middle adolescence. *Genetic, Social, and General Psychology Monographs, 120*(4), 437–467.

Flum, H. & Kaplan, A. (2006). Exploratory orientation as an educational goal. *Educational Psychologist, 41,* 99–110.

Foster, A. & Shah, M. (2016). Knew me and new me: Facilitating student identity exploration and learning through game integration. *International Journal of Gaming and Computer Mediated Simulations, 8*(3), 39–58.

Galliher, R., Rivas-Drake, D., & Dubow, E. (2017). Identity development process and content: Toward an integrated and contextualized science of identity. *Developmental Psychology*, *53*(11), 2009–2010.

Garner, J. K., Hathcock, S., Vasinda, S., & Brienen, R. (2021). Situated action as collective identity exploration in an informal science education project. Presented at the Annual Meeting of the American Educational Research Association.

Garner, J. K. & Kaplan, A. (2019). A complex dynamic systems perspective on teacher learning and identity formation: An instrumental case. *Teachers and Teaching*, *25*(1), 7–33.

Garner, J. K., Kaplan, A., & Pugh, K. (2016). Museums as contexts for transformative experiences and identity development. *Journal of Museum Education*, *41*(4), 341–352.

Garner, J. K., Rutledge, A., Matheny, E., & Kuhn, M. (in press). Invention education as a context for children's identity exploration. *Journal of STEM Outreach*.

Gee, J. P. (2000). Identity as an analytic lens for research in education. *Review of Research in Education*, *25*, 99–125.

Gergen, K. J. (1991). *The Saturated Self: Dilemmas of Identity in Contemporary Life*. New York, NY: Basic Books.

Gioia, D. A., Schultz, M., & Corley, K. G. (2000). Organizational identity, image, and adaptive instability. *Academy of Management Review*, *25*(1), 63–81.

Gleason, P. (1983). Identifying identity: A semantic history. *Journal of American History*, *69*(4), 910–931.

Gregg, A. P., Sedikides, C., & Gebauer, J. E. (2011). Dynamics of identity: Between self-enhancement and self-assessment. In S. J. Schwartz, K. Luyckx, & V. Vignoles (Eds.), *Handbook of Identity Theory and Research* (pp. 305–328). New York, NY: Springer.

Gresalfi, M. S. (2009). Taking up opportunities to learn: Constructing dispositions in mathematics classrooms. *Journal of the Learning Sciences*, *18*(3), 327–369.

Grotevant, H. D. (1987). Toward a process model of identity formation. *Journal of Adolescent Research*, *2*(3), 203–222.

Guastello, S. J., Koopmans, M., & Pincus, D. (2009). *Chaos and Complexity in Psychology*. New York, NY: Cambridge University Press.

Guastello, S. J. & Leibovitch, L. S. (2009). Introduction to nonlinear dynamics and complexity. In S. J. Guastello, M. Koopmans, & D. Pincus (Eds.), *Chaos and Complexity in Psychology* (pp. 1–40). New York, NY: Cambridge University Press.

Gunersel, A. B., Kaplan, A., Barnett, P., Etienne, M., & Ponnock, A. R. (2016). Profiles of change in motivation for teaching in higher education at an American research university. *Teaching in Higher Education*, *21*(6), 628–643.

Gutiérrez, K. D., Engeström, Y., & Sannino, A. (2016). Expanding educational research and interventionist methodologies. *Cognition and Instruction*, *34*(3), 275–284.

Habbershon, T. G. & Astrachan, J. H. (1997). Perceptions are reality: How family meetings lead to collective action. *Family Business Review*, *10*(1), 37–52.

Hand, V. & Gresalfi, M. (2015). The joint accomplishment of identity. *Educational Psychologist*, *50*(3), 190–203, doi:10.1080/00461520.2015.1075401.

Harackiewicz, J. M., Smith, J. L., & Priniski, S. J. (2016). Interest matters: The importance of promoting interest in education. *Policy Insights from the Behavioral and Brain Sciences, 3*(2), 220–227.

Harackiewicz, J. M. & Knogler, M. (2017). *Interest: Theory and application.* In A. J. Elliot, C. S. Dweck, & D. S. Yeager (Eds.), *Handbook of Competence and Motivation: Theory and Application* (pp. 334–352). New York, NY: Guilford Press.

Harrell-Levy, M. K. & Kerpelman, J. L. (2010). Identity process and transformative pedagogy: Teachers as agents of identity formation. *Identity: An International Journal of Theory and Research, 10*(2), 7–91.

Harter, S. (1983). Developmental perspectives on the self-system. In E. M. Hetherington (Ed.), *Handbook of Child Psychology: Vol. 4. Socialization, Personality, and Social Development* (pp. 275–385). New York, NY: Wiley.

Haslam, S. A. & Ellemers, N. (2011). Identity processes in organizations. In S. J. Schwartz, K. Luyckx, & V. Vignoles (Eds.), *Handbook of Identity Theory and Research* (pp. 715–744). New York, NY: Springer.

Hathcock, S. J., Garner, J. K., & Kaplan, A. (2020). Examining micro-change within and among science teachers' identities: A multiple case study. *Science Education, 104,* 827–856.

Hazari, Z., Sadler, P. M., & Sonnert, G. (2013). The science identity of college students: Exploring the intersection of gender, race, and ethnicity. *Journal of College Science Teaching, 42*(5), 82–91.

Heffernan, K., Kaplan, A., Peterson, S., & Newton Jones, K. (2017). Integrating identity formation and subject matter learning: Math concepts as tools for identity exploration. In E. Lyle (Ed.), *At the Intersection of Selves and Subject: Exploring the Curricular Landscape of Identity* (pp. 53–62). Rotterdam: Sense.

Heffernan, K. & Newton, K. J. (2019). Exploring mathematics identity: An intervention of early childhood preservice teachers. *Journal of Early Childhood Teacher Education, 40*(3), 296–324.

Hickey, D. T. (2003). Engaged participation versus marginal nonparticipation: A stridently sociocultural approach to achievement motivation. *The Elementary School Journal, 103*(4), 401–429.

Holland, D. & Lachicotte Jr., W. (2007). Vygotsky, Mead, and the new sociocultural studies of identity. In H. Daniels, M. Cole, & J. V. Wertsch (Eds.), *The Cambridge Companion to Vygotsky* (pp. 101–135). New York, NY: Cambridge University Press.

James, W. (1890). *The Principles of Psychology, 2 Vols.* New York, NY: Henry Holt.

Josselson, R. (1994). Identity and relatedness in the life cycle. In H. A. Bosma, T. L. G. Graafsma, H. D. Grotevant, & D. J. de Levita (Eds.), *Identity and Development: An Interdisciplinary Approach* (p. 81–102). Thousand Oaks, CA: Sage Publications, Inc.

Kaplan, A. (2004). Achievement goals and intergroup relations. In P. R. Pintrich & M. L. Maehr (Eds.), *Advances in Research on Motivation and Achievement: Vol. 13: Motivating Students, Improving Schools: The Legacy of Carol Midgley* (pp. 97–136). Oxford: Elsevier.

Kaplan, A. & Flum, H. (2009). Motivation and identity: The relations of action and development in educational contexts. *Educational Psychologist, 44*(2), 73–77.

Kaplan, A. & Flum, H. (2010). Achievement goal orientations and identity formation styles. *Educational Research Review*, *5*(1), 50–67.

Kaplan, A. & Flum, H. (2012). Identity formation in educational settings. *Contemporary Educational Psychology*, *37*(3), 171–175, 240–245.

Kaplan, A. & Garner, J. K. (2017). A complex dynamic systems perspective on identity and its development: The dynamic systems model of role identity. *Developmental Psychology*, *53*(11), 2036–2051.

Kaplan, A. & Garner, J. K. (2018). Teacher identity and motivation: The dynamic systems model of role identity. In P. Schutz, J. Hong, & D. Cross (Eds.), *Research on Teacher Identity and Motivation: Mapping Challenges and Innovations* (pp. 71–82). New York, NY: Springer Publishing.

Kaplan, A., Garner, J. K., & Brock, B. (2019). Identity and motivation in a changing world: A complex dynamic systems perspective. In E. Gonida & M. Lemos (Eds.), *Advances in Motivation and Achievement (Vol. 20): Motivation in Education at a Time of Global Change: Theory, Research, and Implications for Practice* (pp. 101–127). Bingley: Emerald.

Kaplan, A., Katz, I., & Flum, H. (2012). Motivation theory in educational practice: Knowledge claims, challenges, and future directions. In K. R. Harris, S. G. Graham, & T. Urdan (Eds.), *APA Educational Psychology Handbook, Vol. 2: Individual Differences, Cultural Considerations, and Contextual Factors in Educational Psychology* (pp. 165–194). Washington, DC: American Psychological Association.

Kaplan, A., Neuber, A., & Garner, J. K. (2019). An identity systems perspective on high ability in self-regulated learning. *High Ability Studies*, *30*(1–2), 53–78.

Kaplan, A., Sinai, M., & Flum, H. (2014). Design-based interventions for promoting students' identity exploration within the school curriculum. In S. Karabenick & T. Urdan (Eds.), *Advances in Motivation and Achievement, Vol. 18* (pp. 247–295). Bingley: Emerald.

Kerpelman, J. L., Pittman, J. F., & Lamke, L. K. (1997). Toward a microprocess perspective on adolescent identity development: An identity control theory approach. *Journal of Adolescent Research*, *12*(3), 325–346.

Kim, A. Y., Sinatra, G. M., & Seyranian, V. (2018). Developing a STEM identity among young women: A social identity perspective. *Review of Educational Research*, *88*(4), 589–625.

Klassen, R. M., Tze, V. M., Betts, S. M., & Gordon, K. A. (2011). Teacher efficacy research 1998–2009: Signs of progress or unfulfilled promise? *Educational Psychology Review*, *23*(1), 21–43.

Klassen, R. M., Usher, E. L., & Bong, M. (2010). Teachers' collective efficacy, job satisfaction, and job stress in cross-cultural context. *Journal of Experimental Education*, *78*(4), 464–486.

Koopmans, M. & Stamovlasis, D. (Eds.). (2016). *Complex Dynamical Systems in Education: Concepts, Methods and Applications*. Cham: Springer.

Kroger, J. (2004). *Identity in Adolescence: The Balance between Self and Other, 3rd Ed.* New York, NY: Routledge.

Kroger, J. & Marcia, J. E. (2011). The identity statuses: Origins, meanings, and interpretations. In S. J. Schwartz, K. Luyckx, & V. L. Vignoles (Eds.), *Handbook of Identity Theory and Research* (pp. 31–53). New York, NY: Springer.

Kunnen, S. & Van Geert, P. (2012). A dynamic system approach to adolescent development. In S. Kunnen (Ed.), *A Dynamic Systems Approach to Adolescent Development* (pp. 3–14). London: Routledge/Psychology Press.

Lange, C. & Byrd, M. (2002). Differences between students' estimated and attained grades in a first-year introductory psychology course as a function of identity development. *Adolescence, 37*(145), 93–107.

Lannegrand-Willems, L. & Bosma, H. A. (2006). Identity development-in-context: The school as an important context for identity development. *Identity, 6*(1), 85–113.

Lave, J. & Wenger, E. (2001). Legitimate peripheral participation in communities of practice. In J. Clarke, A. Hanson, R. Harrison, & F. Reeve (Eds.), *Supporting Lifelong Learning* (pp. 121–126). London: Routledge.

Luyckx, K., Schwartz, S. J., Goossens, L., Beyers, W., & Missotten, L. (2011). Processes of personal identity formation and evaluation. In S. J. Schwartz, K. Luyckx, & V. Vignoles (Eds.), *Handbook of Identity Theory and Research* (pp. 77–98). New York, NY: Springer.

Luyckx, K., Vansteenkiste, M., Goossens, L., & Duriez, B. (2009). Basic need satisfaction and identity formation: Bridging self-determination theory and process-oriented identity research. *Journal of Counseling Psychology, 56*(2), 276–288.

Maehr, M. L. & Braskamp, L. A. (1986). *The Motivation Factor: A Theory of Personal Investment*. Lexington, MA: Lexington Books.

Marcia, J. E. (1966). Development and validation of ego-identity status. *Journal of Personality and Social Psychology, 3*, 551–558.

Marcia, J. E. (1980). Identity in adolescence. In J. Adelson (Ed.), *Handbook of Adolescent Psychology* (pp. 159–187). New York, NY: Wiley.

Marcia, J. E. (1993a). The ego identity status approach to ego identity. In J. E. Marcia, A. S. Waterman, D. R. Matteson, S. L. Archer, & J. L. Orlofsky (Eds.), *Ego Identity: A Handbook for Psychosocial Research* (pp. 1–21). New York, NY: Springer.

Markus, H. (1977). Self-schemata and processing information about the self. *Journal of Personality and Social Psychology, 35*(2), 63–78.

Markus, H. & Kitayama, S. (1991). Culture and the self: Implications for cognition, emotion, and motivation. *Psychological Review, 98*, 224–253.

Marsh, H. W., Martin, A. J., Yeung, A. S., & Craven, R. G. (2017). Competence self-perceptions. In A. J. Elliot, C. S. Dweck, & D. Yeager (Eds.), *Handbook of Competence and Motivation, 2nd Ed.* (pp. 85–115). New York, NY: Guilford Press.

Master, A., Cheryan, S., & Meltzoff, A. (2016). Motivation and identity. In K. Wentzel & D. Miele (Eds.), *Handbook of Motivation at School, 2nd Ed.* (pp. 300–319). New York, NY: Routledge.

McCaslin, M. (2009). Co-regulation of student motivation and emergent identity. *Educational Psychologist, 44*(2), 137–146, doi:10.1080/00461520902832384.

McCaslin, M. & Lavigne, A. L. (2010). Social policy, educational opportunity, and classroom practice: A co-regulation approach to research on student motivation and achievement. In T. Urdan & S. Karabenick (Eds.), *Advances in Motivation and Achievement: Vol. 16B. The Decade Ahead: Applications and Contexts of Motivation and Achievement* (pp. 211–249). Bingley: Emerald.

Mead, G. H. (1934). *Mind, Self and Society, from the Standpoint of a Social Behaviorist*, ed. by C. W. Morris. Chicago, IL: University of Chicago Press.

Meeus, W. (2011). The study of adolescent identity formation 2000–2010: A review of longitudinal research. *Journal of Research on Adolescence, 21*(1), 75–94.

Mishra, P., Koehler, M. J., & Greenhow, C. (2016). The work of educational psychologists in a digitally networked world. In L. Corno & E. Anderman (Eds.), *Handbook of Educational Psychology, 3rd Ed.* (pp. 29–40). New York, NY: Routledge.

Montgomery, M. J., Hernandez, L., & Ferrer-Wreder, L. (2008). Identity development and intervention studies: The right time for a marriage? *Identity: An International Journal of Theory and Research, 8,* 173–182.

Nasir, N. I. S., McLaughlin, M. W., & Jones, A. (2009). What does it mean to be African American? Constructions of race and academic identity in an urban public high school. *American Educational Research Journal, 46*(1), 73–114.

Nasir, N. S., Rowley, S. J., & Perez, W. (2016). Culture, racial/ethnic, and linguistic diversity, and identity. In L. Corno & E. Anderman (Eds.), *Handbook of Educational Psychology, 3rd Ed.* (pp. 186–198). New York, NY: Routledge.

Neuber, A. (2019). The meaning of being smart: An identity study of first-year honors college students. Doctoral dissertation, Temple University, Philadelphia, PA.

Nolen, S. B., Horn, I. S., & Ward, C. J. (2015). Situating motivation. *Educational Psychologist, 50*(3), 234–247, doi:10.1080/00461520.2015.1075399.

Nolen, S. B., Ward, C. J., & Horn, I. S. (2011). Motivation, engagement, and identity: Opening a conversation. In D. McInerney, R. Walker, & G. A. D. Liem (Eds.), *Sociocultural Theories of Learning and Motivation: Looking Back, Looking Forward* (pp. 109–135). Greenwich, CT: Information Age.

O'Mara, A. J., Marsh, H. W., Craven, R. G., & Debus, R. L. (2006). Do self-concept interventions make a difference? A synergistic blend of construct validation and meta-analysis. *Educational Psychologist, 41*(3), 181–206.

Osborne, J. W. & Jones, B. D. (2011). Identification with academics and motivation to achieve in school: How the structure of the self influences academic outcomes. *Educational Psychology Review, 23*(1), 131–158.

Overton, W. F. (2013). A new paradigm for developmental science: Relationism and relational-developmental systems. *Applied Developmental Science, 17*(2), 94–107.

Oyserman, D. (2015). Identity-based motivation. In R. Scott & S. Kosslyn (Eds.), *Emerging Trends in the Behavioral and Social Sciences* (pp. 1–11). Hoboken, NJ: Wiley.

Oyserman, D. (2017). Culture three ways: Culture and subcultures within countries. *Annual Review of Psychology, 68,* 435–463.

Oyserman, D., Bybee, D., & Terry, K. (2006). Possible selves and academic outcomes: How and when possible selves impel action. *Journal of Personality and Social Psychology, 91,* 188–204.

Oyserman, D. & James, L. (2011). Possible identities. In S. J. Schwartz, K. Luyckx, & V. L. Vignoles (Eds.), *Handbook of Identity Theory and Research* (pp. 117–145). New York, NY: Springer.

Oyserman, D., Lewis Jr., N. A., Yan, V. X., Fisher, O., O'Donnell, S. C., & Horowitz, E. (2017). An identity-based motivation framework for self-regulation. *Psychological Inquiry, 28*(2–3), 139–147.

Penuel, W. R. & Wertsch, J. V. (1995). Vygotsky and identity formation: A sociocultural approach. *Educational Psychologist, 30*(2), 83–92.

Perez, R., Cromley, J. G., & Kaplan, A. (2014). The role of identity development, values, and costs in college STEM retention. *Journal of Educational Psychology, 106*(1), 315–329.

Pintrich, P. R., Marx, R. W., & Boyle, R. A. (1993). Beyond cold conceptual change: The role of motivational beliefs and classroom contextual factors in the process of conceptual change. *Review of Educational Research, 63*(2), 167–199.

Pop, E. I., Negru-Subtirica, O., Crocetti, E., Opre, A., & Meeus, W. (2016). On the interplay between academic achievement and educational identity: A longitudinal study. *Journal of Adolescence, 47*, 135–144.

Renninger, K. A. (2009). Interest and identity development in instruction: An inductive model. *Educational Psychologist, 44*(2), 105–118.

Renninger, K. A., Austin, L., Bachrach, J. E., Chau, A., Emmerson, M. S., King, B. R., & Stevens, S. (2014). Going beyond the "Whoa! That's cool!" of inquiry: Achieving science interest and learning with the ICAN intervention. *Motivational Interventions, 18*, 107–138.

Richardson, P. W., Watt, H. M. G., & Karabenick, S. A. (2014). *Teacher Motivation: Theory and Practice.* New York, NY: Routledge

Roeser, R. W., Peck, S. C., & Nasir, N. S. (2006). Self and identity processes in school motivation, learning, and achievement. In P. A. Alexander & P. H. Winne (Eds.), *Handbook of Educational Psychology, 2nd Ed.* (pp. 391–424). Mahwah, NJ: Lawrence Erlbaum.

Rogat, T. K., Linnenbrink-Garcia, L., & DiDonato, N. (2013). Motivation in collaborative groups. In C. E. Hmelo-Silver, C. A. Chinn, C. K. K. Chan, & A. M. O'Donnell (Eds.), *The International Handbook of Collaborative Learning* (pp. 250–267). New York, NY: Routledge.

Ryan, K. E. & Ryan, A. M. (2005). Psychological processes underlying stereotype threat and standardized math test performance. *Educational Psychologist, 40*(1), 53–63.

Schachter, E. P. & Rich, Y. (2011). Identity education: A conceptual framework for educational researchers and practitioners. *Educational Psychologist, 46*, 222–238.

Schutz, P., Hong, J. Y., & Cross Francis, D. (Eds.). (2018). *Research on Teacher Identity: Mapping Challenges and Innovations.* New York, NY: Springer.

Schwartz, S. J., Luyckx, K., & Vignoles, V. L. (Eds.). (2011). *Handbook of Identity Theory and Research.* New York, NY: Springer.

Serpe, R. T. & Stryker, S. (2011). The symbolic interactionist perspective and identity theory. In S. J. Schwartz, K. Luyckx, V. L. Vignoles (Eds.), *Handbook of Identity Theory and Research* (pp. 225–248). New York, NY: Springer.

Sfard, A. & Prusak, A. (2005). Telling identities: In search of an analytic tool for investigating learning as a culturally shaped activity. *Educational Researcher, 34*(4), 14–22.

Shah, M., Foster, A., & Barany, A. (2017). Facilitating learning as identity change through game-based learning. In Y. Baek (Ed.), *Game-Based Learning:*

Theory, Strategies and Performance Outcomes (pp. 257–278). New York, NY: Nova.

Sinai, M., Kaplan, A., & Flum, H. (2012). Promoting identity exploration within the school curriculum: A design-based study in a junior high literature lesson in Israel. *Contemporary Educational Psychology, 37*, 195–205.

Sinai, M., Tossman, I., & Kaplan, A. (2017, August). Interplay of the personal and pedagogical in the identity formation of preservice school counselors. Poster presented at the annual meeting of the American Psychological Association, Washington DC.

Sinatra, G. M. & Seyranian, V. (2016). Warm change about hot topics: The role of motivation and emotion in attitude and conceptual change about controversial science topics. In L. Corno & E. Anderman (Eds.), *Handbook of Educational Psychology, 3rd Ed.* (pp. 245–246). New York, NY: Routledge.

Steele, C. M. (1988). The psychology of self-affirmation: Sustaining the integrity of the self. In L. Berkowitz (Ed.), *Advances in Experimental Social Psychology, Vol. 21* (pp. 261–302). New York, NY: Academic Press.

Steele, C. M. (1997). A threat in the air: How stereotypes shape intellectual identity and performance. *American Psychologist, 52*, 613–629.

Steele, C. M. & Aronson, J. (1995). Stereotype threat and the intellectual test performance of African-Americans. *Journal of Personality and Social Psychology, 68*, 797–811.

Steele, C. M., Spencer, S. J., & Aronson, J. (2002). Contending with group image: The psychology of stereotype and social identity threat. In M. Zanna (Ed.), *Advances in Experimental Social Psychology, Vol. 34* (pp. 379–440). New York, NY: Academic Press.

Tajfel, H. & Turner, J. C. (1986). The social identity theory of intergroup behavior. In S. Worchel & W. G. Austin (Eds.), *Psychology of Intergroup Relations* (pp. 7–24). Chicago, IL: Nelson-Hall.

Tossman, I., Kaplan, A., & Assor, A. (2008). Academic achievement goal structures and young adolescents' biased preferences for peers as cooperation partners: A longitudinal study. *International Review of Social Psychology, 21*, 183–217.

Tossman, I., Sinai, M., Cohen-Malayev, M., & Kaplan, A. (2018, May). Professional identity formation in an unstructured profession: A qualitative investigation of non-formal education students. Paper presented at the annual meeting of the Society for the Study of Emerging Adulthood, Cluj-Napoca, Romania.

Tschannen-Moran, M., Woolfolk Hoy, A., & Hoy, W. K. (1998). Teacher efficacy: Its meaning and measure. *Review of Educational Research, 68*, 202–248.

Turner, J. C. & Reynolds, K. J. (2001). The social identity perspective in intergroup relations: Theories, themes, and controversies. In R. Brown & S. L. Gaertner (Eds.), *Blackwell Handbook of Social Psychology: Intergroup Processes* (pp. 133–152). Malden, MA: Blackwell.

Usher, E. L. (2016). Personal capability beliefs. In L. Corno & E. Anderman (Eds.), *Handbook of Educational Psychology, 3rd Ed.* (pp. 146–159). New York, NY: Taylor and Francis.

Vedder-Weiss, D., Biran, L., Kaplan A., & Garner, J. K. (2018). Reflexive inquiry as a scaffold for teacher identity exploration during the first year of teaching. In E.

Lyle (Ed.), *The Negotiated Self: Employing Reflexive Inquiry to Explore Teacher Identity* (pp. 227–237). Rotterdam: Sense.

Verhoeven, M., Poorthuis, A. M., & Volman, M. (2019). The role of school in adolescents' identity development. A literature review. *Educational Psychology Review, 31*(1), 35–63.

Vignoles, V. L., Schwartz, S. J., & Luyckx, K. (2011). Introduction: Toward an integrative view of identity. In S. J. Schwartz, K. Luyckx, & V. L. Vignoles (Eds.), *Handbook of Identity Theory and Research* (pp. 1–27). New York, NY: Springer.

Vygotsky, L. S. (1978). *Mind in Society: The Development of Higher Mental Processes.* Cambridge, MA: Harvard University Press.

Waldrop, M. M. (1992). *Complexity: The Emerging Science at the Edge of Order and Chaos.* New York, NY: Touchstone.

Walton, G. M. & Cohen, G. L. (2011). A brief social-belonging intervention improves academic and health outcomes of minority students. *Science, 331*(6023), 1447–1451.

Walton, G. M. & Yeager, D. S. (2020). Seed and soil: Psychological affordances in contexts help to explain where wise interventions succeed or fail. *Current Directions in Psychological Science, 29*(3), 219–226.

Weiner, B. (2010). The development of an attribution-based theory of motivation: A history of ideas. *Educational Psychologist, 45*(1), 28–36.

Wenger, E. (1998). *Communities of Practice: Learning, Meaning and Identity.* Cambridge: Cambridge University Press.

Wigfield, A., Rosenzweig, E. Q., & Eccles, J. (2017). Achievement values: Interactions, interventions, and future directions. In A. Elliot, C. Dweck, & D. Yeager (Eds.), *Handbook of Competence and Motivation: Theory and Application, 2nd Ed.* (pp. 116–135). New York, NY: Guilford Press.

Wigfield, A. & Wagner, A. L. (2005). Competence, motivation and identity development during adolescence. In A. J. Elliot & C. S. Dweck (Eds.), *Handbook of Competence and Motivation* (pp. 222–239). New York, NY: Guilford.

Yang, S., Shu, D., & Yin, H. (2021). Frustration drives me to grow: Unraveling EFL teachers' emotional trajectory interacting with identity development. *Teaching and Teacher Education, 105*. https://doi.org/10.1016/j.tate.2021.103420

25 Political Psychology: Identity Development in a Traumatic Environment

David Becker

Over the last fifteen years, I have been working in the Middle East as a consultant for German and Swiss development cooperation activities, focusing on psychosocial projects for and with the Palestinian population in the region. This involved spending a great deal of time in the Gaza Strip, the West Bank, Jordan, and in Lebanon. For the last five years, I have helped develop a staff and self-care system for UNRWA Syria,[1] meeting with frontline staff regularly in Beirut, discussing and reflecting with them on survival strategies in the middle of war. Although I have been working with and thinking about the issues discussed in this chapter for many years, my current outlook is very much shaped by my experience with Palestinians, by trying to help colleagues set up and carry out projects under chronic conditions of war.

Realities to consider:

- A ten-year-old child, growing up in the Gaza Strip, who survived several wars, is used to frequent bombing strikes – a life in which threats, insecurities, fear, violence and death are normal ingredients of everyday experience.
- Palestinians growing up in Lebanon are forced to live in camps that have existed for many years, with high levels of poverty, unemployment, and often armed violence. From the 1970s to the 1990s, Lebanon endured a civil war, which included Syrian and Israeli incursions. 2006 was the year of the second Lebanon war. Since the beginning of the war in Syria, there has been an enormous influx of refugees, including Palestinians from Syria, which made the situation in the camps even more difficult. Currently (2020), Lebanon is a country in political turmoil, facing a terrible economic crisis.
- Palestinians in Syria were comparatively well integrated. With the start of the civil war, their situation deteriorated significantly. The history of the

---

[1] UNRWA = United Nations Relief and Works Agency for Palestine Refugees in the Near East. UNRWA Syria has about 3,500 staff in Syria, who are in charge of about 438,000 Palestinian refugees currently still living there.

Yarmouk Camp makes the disaster that struck Palestinians in Syria palpable. Before the war, over 100,000 Palestinians lived in Yarmouk. By 2014, due to the intense fighting, about 90,000 were forced to flee. After the Syrian government reconquered the city, about 200 residents remain, and the city has been mostly destroyed.

In realities like these, people try to defend the capacity to lead normal lives, but in fact must adapt to chronic destruction. They experience chronic fear, which means that the normal mechanism which supports human beings to react and protect themselves against threats becomes a permanent psychological feature of personhood, persisting long after the threats may have disappeared and actually weakening self-protection.

Trauma in such a context is not a single terrible event; it is an ongoing and permanent reality. Ruptures shape people's lives so deeply that they simply become part of their way of living and shaping relationships. One tries to develop friendships, feel close to others, and develop some trust, but one also expects that everything can be destroyed at any time. Today, we can be friends; tomorrow we might kill each other. We do not know what is going to happen, and the best way to survive is to not even try to know. If something good happens, take it, but never expect that it will continue.

Destruction and death are omnipresent. In more normal circumstances, people do not think about death every day. In a war region, death becomes a conscious and permanent part of the psychic structure. However, the innumerable deaths and the excessive violence associated with them renders the psychologically necessary task of mourning a tough and often impossible endeavor. People get caught between two bad alternatives: either they grieve and risk being overcome by overwhelming sadness and depression, or they try to avoid grieving but then risk dehumanizing completely, being unable to feel anything.

In war people do not only endure injustice, they are also perpetual witnesses to injustice against others. In both situations people are usually powerless to do anything. So, beyond the direct suffering, they experience deep impotence and are often left with an anger on which they cannot act. Rather, they must suppress it and carry on. This recurrent experience can lead to resentment and to the projection of the anger onto others who have no relation to the perpetuating of injustice.

People growing up under conditions of war and persecution are thus not just psychologically afflicted by the reality in which they live, but, in fact, their core features of identity, of selfhood, and of their outlook on past, present, and future are deeply shaped by their experiences of chronic threat, destruction, loss, and severe injustice. Mead's (1973) notions of *I* and *me* constitute paradigmatic features of identity that both leave room for fragile and ever-changing senses of selfhood and social processes (Mead, 1973) and still always imply some degree of continuity, some degree of achievable individual and social coherence within a specific historic context. Must we thus assume that identity development for people growing up under conditions of war does not require continuity? Or should we believe that destruction and breakdown can become a core aspect of identity when it happens to be the social norm under which people grow up? And if that is true, how would such an identity respond when war comes to an end?

The concept of trauma is probably the concept in psychology most focused on the contrary: on issues of destruction, of individual and social breakdown, of ruptures and discontinuities. Trauma has become a modern buzzword, used as a kind of omnipresent adjective to emphasize the severity of one or another kind of suffering. Nevertheless, it has also become a scientific concept that, for the first time, globally acknowledges the fact that certain social realities have a severely destructive effect on the mental health and the social well-being of human beings. Although definitions in the world of psychology, psychiatry, and social sciences vary widely and range from rather narrow individual medicalized or psychotherapeutic concepts (APA, 1980) to very broad socio-political theories in which entire collectives are understood as traumatized (Kühner, 2007), overall the term has become a key element in recognizing, valuing, and dealing with extreme human suffering. But if it is true that millions of people existing in conditions of war, conflict, and extreme economic hardship not only suffer from trauma, but actually live and develop in continually traumatizing social contexts, then a series of theoretical and practical issues arise that put many key assumptions of trauma theory into doubt: Is the consequence of trauma really a mental illness? If not, do we not run the risk of trivializing extreme suffering once again? Could we recognize and describe the role of traumatic environment for identity development without reverting to theories like post-traumatic growth (Ernst, 2007; Tedeschi & Calhoun, 2004)?

Trauma theory and identity development theory are usually not discussed simultaneously. By doing just that, in this chapter, I propose to explore the potential of recognizing and acknowledging extreme suffering and all the fragility and discontinuity it necessarily implies, while at the same time, understanding that trauma very often is not a mental illness, but rather a social reality that shapes people's lives and constructs very specific kinds of vulnerabilities and challenges. In this view, trauma as a social reality is ultimately at the core of identity construction where continuity is the continuity of terror and where the prospect of change exists as a faint hope, sometimes deeply buried, but always a key perspective. Attempting this joint deconstruction, so to speak, trying to critically interface identity theories with trauma concepts, and trauma theories with identity concepts, is not easy, because the theories in question are themselves contradictory and constitute contested fields of scientific discussion. As a first step, I will discuss trauma theory more in depth, highlighting the double feature of trauma as a complex psychosocial process of extreme suffering and as a social discourse about suffering and the associated social value judgments. I will try to show how what I regard as the most suitable trauma concept, sequential traumatization (Keilson, 1978; Becker, 2014), provides an interesting framework for understanding how identity is not only threatened by trauma but shaped by it, becoming a key factor not only for the perpetuation of individual and social suffering, but also for perspectives of transformation and social change. In a second step, I will discuss identity theory, first introducing some thoughts by Brubaker and Cooper (2000) and then focusing on Krappmann's (1971) approach to identity and the relevance of the key competences he defines, namely, the capacity for role distance, role-taking and empathy, tolerance of ambiguity and, finally, self- or what Krappmann calls identity-presentation. These competences seem to me a much better way of assessing the ways in which people deal with trauma, than, for example, through diagnosis of post-traumatic stress disorder (PTSD) diagnosis. In my view, these competences allow the problem of trauma to be situated where it belongs, not exclusively in the person or only outside of the person, but inside *and* between people, in the psychosocial realm. As a third and final step, and with this background in mind, I will focus specifically on what it means to survive in a world "gone crazy," dealing with the permanent psychosocial realities of threat and fear, destruction and trauma, loss and grief, injustice and impotent anger, and once again refer to my experience in the Middle East. Specifically, I will discuss the complexities of developing a capacity to defend resilience and vulnerability as well as the enormous need for recognition, paired with the fear of what that might imply on a personal and social level. I will conclude with an argument in favor of Krappmann's competences as excellent indicators to help us deal with trauma in the social field.

25.1 Trauma Theory and Some Implications for Identity Concepts

French sociologists Didier Fassin and Richard Rechtmann (2009) explain convincingly that the development of trauma theory can only be understood within the framework of a double genealogy. They reflect on the historic change in trauma theory, which initially did not especially validate victims' experiences, which in contemporary theory, are placed squarely in the center of attention:

> It is all the more remarkable that psychic trauma should become the locus for this validation of victims' stories, because nothing in the development of

psychopathological concepts would have predicted such an outcome. Indeed, it is not in advances in psychiatry and psychology that we should seek the reason for this transformation. On the contrary, it was changes in the social order and social values that, if they did not actually produce the clinical innovations, at least made them possible. We therefore argue that the reconfiguration of the relationship between trauma and victim, in which the victim gains legitimacy as trauma comes to attest to the truth of his or her version, has a dual genealogy – on the one hand scientific, based on the definition of trauma, and on the other hand moral, focused around the acknowledgment of the victim.   (Fassin & Rechtmann, 2009, p. 29)

The authors believe that when analyzing trauma and trying to understand the historic change it has brought about in the social discourse on victims, one has to study two processes: one needs to describe the trauma concept as it developed in the scientific field, specifically psychiatry and psychology in the last two centuries and, simultaneously, one has to look at changing moral discourses in societies, which in turn are informed by specific societal conflicts and their outcomes, as for instance during World War II and the Holocaust. In this sense, Fassin and Rechtmann (2009) do not only understand trauma within a double genealogy, but actually suggest two very different meanings or qualities of trauma, one of which is the clinical concept and the other being the moral discourse which always accompanies and surrounds this topic.

Following Fassin's and Rechtmann's thinking, one can trace the development of trauma conceptualizations as scientific developments and as shifts in moral discourses. As scientific developments, simplifying slightly and naming just a few important contributions, one can start with the early English theory of "railway spine" (Erichsen, 1867) taking nerve damage as an explanation for psychological symptoms appearing after having survived train accidents, moving through the early psychoanalytical theories (Breuer & Freud 1895), which offered a more psychological explanation, hypothesizing that traumatic experiences were experiences too overpowering for the psychic structure to resist and using hypnosis as treatment strategy, ending up with the theory of "shell shock" in World War I (Myers, 1915), where attempts to account for the severe psychic and physical reactions of soldiers who had survived prolonged shelling focused on the issue of unconscious avoidance and fear. One could then continue with the later psychanalytical theories (Freud, 1926; Ferenczi, 1988; Balint, 1966; Winnicott, 1965) that changed the focus of trauma theory from the overpowering event to the traumatic situation, thus giving more importance to the relational context of trauma. Next, the post-Holocaust trauma theories could be examined, e.g., Bettelheim's (1943) concept of extreme traumatization, Niederland's (1961) concept of survivor syndrome, and Keilson's (1978) theory of sequential traumatization, which will be discussed more in depth below. Finally, one would arrive at the concept of PTSD as first defined in the DSM III of the American Psychiatric

Association (1980), and the deeply political concept of psychosocial trauma coined by Latin-American social psychologist Martin-Baró (1990).

As moral discourses about victims, about perpetrators, guilt, responsibility, etc. have shifted, one could state the following. First a rather negative approach to victims prevailed. Early theories were preoccupied with potential insurance fraud (e.g., train accidents in England in the nineteenth century), supposed secondary gains of the victims through their symptoms (for example, the belief that workers who suffered a traumatic incident simply did not want to work), and what can be seen in the development of aversive psychiatric treatments in Germany at the beginning of the twentieth century. During and after World War I, so-called shell-shocked soldiers were actually perceived by many as cowards. However, following the Holocaust, a very different, more benevolent attitude toward victims began to emerge. The crimes against humanity committed by the Nazis could only be brought to justice if victims were taken seriously, that is, that although they were hurt and mutilated, they were, nevertheless, the only witnesses besides the perpetrators themselves who could provide evidence of the intended genocide. It is in this context, that the reality of the traumatic experience became important, not as something to doubt, but as evidence of the crimes of the perpetrators.

When, in the 1980s, PTSD was first conceptualized (American Psychiatric Association, 1980), it was in direct response to the situation of Vietnam War veterans who needed help but had already been released from military service. Interestingly, what then became important in trauma theory were the symptoms and proof of their linkage to events in the past, while the specific nature and context of these events became less important. In a certain way, PTSD brought about final global recognition of victims of trauma, but it also rendered trauma theory less concerned with morals, with context, and with politics than it had been in the aftermath of the Holocaust. Within the concept of PTSD, the traumatic experiences of traffic accidents, bullying in the workplace, surviving torture or a concentration camp, or having been an American soldier in Vietnam became all the same: they can be summed up in terms of victims having been exposed to overpowering life-threatening stressors.

In the so-called Third World, the colonies striving for independence (Algeria, for example), the Latin-American countries where wars and dictatorships raged for so many years, and also South Africa fighting apartheid began to produce their own outlooks on trauma. These perspectives took the political as the clear focus of trauma, centering the social reality of repression and dehumanization, as can be seen, for example, in Fanon's *The Wretched of the Earth* (1963), where he develops theories of trauma in the context of Algeria's war for independence, and in Martin-Baró's *Psicología social de la guerra* (1990), focusing on trauma in the context of the civil war in El Salvador. Thus, since its beginnings, trauma theory has never been only a clinical psychological concept. It has always been simultaneously part of ongoing social conflicts, value discussions, and political discourses. In fact, simply by following any given trauma theory's double genealogy, it becomes apparent that the core issue this concept deals with is essentially psychosocial. Such a concept thus needs to grasp and analyze specific psychological processes, while at the same time understanding the broader dimensions; how they form part of social discourses about these very processes, specifically about suffering; and how those who suffer are valued by the whole of society. When the editors of this handbook first invited me to participate, the topic was envisioned as part of a discussion of identity within the frame of health psychology. Later, it was decided that it might fit better within the frame of political psychology. In my opinion, this is an excellent illustration of the issues described above: trying to conceive of trauma confined to the realm of clinical psychology does not only not do justice to the social dimensions involved, but actually ignores the reality that an exclusively clinical perspective is, in itself, a political statement. The writer and concentration camp survivor Jean Améry (1977/1966) was one of the first to heavily criticize the tendency to label victims as mentally ill, to conceive of them as suffering from a syndrome, when their suffering was, in fact, the essence of the political system of the Nazis. Nevertheless, viewing that suffering only on a broad political level risks forgetting and negating the material bodies, the victims who have to accept, as part of their psychic structure, the most terrible experience possible, as Améry was also keenly aware. Trauma, from that perspective, belongs to the clinical and the political. Extreme suffering as a product and as constituting part of a given political reality is an experience, or a series of experiences, within people and, at the same time, between people in the sphere of society. Thus, the aftermath of trauma is necessarily also a question of morality and of ethical conflict in society.

Looking at the history of the trauma concept and its two intertwined but essentially different characteristics, we can see that two very different aspects are constantly in play: on one side, the massive psychological destruction attributed to the traumatic experience, the central focus on rupture, discontinuity, fragmentation, dissociation; and, on the other side, a complex set of changing social attributions and value judgments, defining victims as good or bad, heroes or parasites, sick or healthy – fundamentally a discussion on a societal level of the meaning of justice, of how to deal with perpetrators and victims, of guilt and responsibility, of how to confront a history of destruction on the level of society. Trauma theory shows how deeply identity can be destroyed by certain experiences, but also how identities are simultaneously constructed through these experiences. Probably the first professional to describe this connection between destruction and construction of identity was Frantz Fanon in his book *Black Skin, White Masks* (1986/1952). His topic is the colonial reality of whites defining and actually inventing "black" identity and the difficulty of overcoming this profound alienation. Although he does not use the word trauma here, he speaks from inside the traumatic experience. In very direct and moving words, breaking the conventions of *scientific* language, he shows how violent these racist attributions and projections are, how much they are based on not seeing or acknowledging the other, and how difficult it is to escape the trap: If, in your essence, you are defined as what you are not, how can you define who you are, how can you become yourself? The problem here is that even if you discover the alienation, even if you reject it, your new self-affirmation is still constructed as an answer to the worldview forced on you by the colonialists, and thus maintains a certain degree of dependency.

Trauma theory, in its purely clinical formulation, describes a set of relevant symptoms, but also constructs something very similar to what Fanon (1986) explained in reference to colonialism: By decontextualizing, individuals who suffered trauma are mutilated again. They are attributed the identity of destroyed, sick persons, who might be healed by a good therapist, but whose suffering has, in the end, very little to do with the society around them. The *illness*, the *disorder* recognizes something real, but at the same time severs the link between individual and social process and makes the relationship unrecognizable and unsurmountable. As Hamber et al. (2015) correctly point out, PTSD "tells us little about the context of violence, its cultural specificities, and how dealing with violence is linked with a social economic, political and cultural context" (p. 4). PTSD conceptualization pathologizes a social phenomenon and "drives thinking toward homogeneity, as if all of the experiences of violence have the same outcome or need the same treatment" (Hamber et al., 2015, p. 4). While PTSD gives a rather clear description of individual suffering, it completely ignores context and social reality. Instead of making a connection between the victim and the social cause of suffering, it deepens the divide, transforming a societal issue into a personal illness. Other trauma concepts, like Martin-Baró's psychosocial trauma (1990) or my own first conceptualization of extreme traumatization (Becker, 1992), which built on Bettelheim (1943), emphasize the social dimension, but possibly do not fully grasp the profoundness of the individual wound. Today it would seem that the concept of *sequential traumatization* by Hans Keilson (1978) is probably the best integrative understanding of trauma, respecting and acknowledging individual suffering, while simultaneously valuing its social characteristic and avoiding the individualized labeling problem.

Keilson (1978) developed the term in reference to Jewish war orphans in the Netherlands. As a psychoanalyst, who was also a former resistance activist and clear political thinker, he was interested in the inner psychic processes of his clients, but he always understood that the key definition of trauma had to refer to the external context. He also understood that trauma in a political context is not a one-time event, but a process. The idea of sequence is the key to his trauma concept, which, at the same time, preserves the idea of intrapsychic breakdown, of total powerlessness, so central to most other trauma definitions. Keilson originally defined three sequences, focusing on the beginning of persecution, the time of direct terror, and the postwar situation.

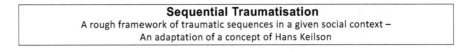

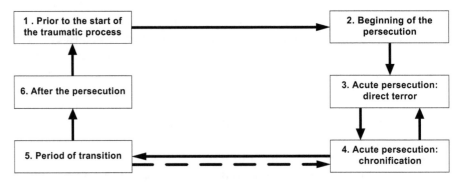

Figure 25.1 *Sequential traumatization: A basic framework of traumatic sequences in a given social context (Becker, 2016)*

Building on Keilson's work, Barbara Weyermann and I (Becker & Weyermann, 2006; Becker 2014) extended the idea of sequences from three to six in order to construct a trauma framework that can be used as a contextualized approach in different cultural settings. This approach foregrounds the process character of trauma and stresses that the specific characteristics of suffering cannot be universally predefined, but must be described and understood in the different circumstances in which they come to exist (see Figure 25.1).

To decide what is prior to the traumatic process is not easy and is a decision to be taken consciously. The so-called normality before the official beginning of war or persecution in itself contains a history with more or less traumatic realities that play a role later on. In Bosnia and Herzegovina, for example, this sequence might be defined as the time before 1992, when Yugoslavia still existed and when war had not broken out. But this Yugoslavia was built on the traumatic experiences of World War II, which later on, during the war from 1992 to 1995, became very present again. The definition of the first sequence is thus, on the one hand, a pragmatic one, but, on the other hand, also a recognition of the power and importance of history. The second sequence sums up the beginning of persecution, before it becomes absolutely overpowering. In Bosnia, this would be the last years before the break-up from Yugoslavia, the developing nationalist discourse, the beginning of hostilities, the months leading up to open war; then followed by the sequences 3 and 4 (see Figure 25.1), which describe the times of *direct and acute terror*. War, however, does not play out as in a film, where years are summed up in a few hours. In war and conflict, times of direct terror alternate with moments of relative calm, where normality seems to return, while people wait for the next moment of acute destruction. These two types of sequences are differentiated here. During direct terror people suffer terribly and are essentially focused on survival. Under such conditions, they might not notice their traumatization. But then follows the sequence of *chronification*, the time of partial normalization. In this sequence, people are under less acute threat, but notice their suffering increasingly. Fear is omnipresent. Both sequences alternate continuously with each other. Sequence 5 then is the period of transition, which can last for a longer or a shorter time period. In Bosnia, this started with the Dayton Agreement in 1995, a truce through which the active war was stopped, but through which peace was not achieved. Finally, the sixth sequence is the time after conflict in which, as Keilson (1978) demonstrated convincingly, the trauma does not end, but continues as a more or less pathology-provoking process, depending on how power relationships develop and how a given society deals with its victims and with its history of destruction. Germany has been in this sequence for many years and, as the current conflicts with right-wing and neo-Nazi parties and complex East–West dynamics show, is still very actively involved in working through it.

These sequences do not determine or suggest specific interpretations of the intrapsychic dynamics of trauma, but they establish the direct linkage between suffering and specific social contexts, and, they facilitate an understanding of the traumatic process as a complex amalgam of experiences of rupture, destruction, and partial reconstruction. Their continuous presence and development in later time sequences does not depend just on intrapsychic processes but also on relational societal realities. Thus, trauma is not, as PTSD would suggest, a limited psychic experience of breakdown, of being totally overpowered, and then developing specific symptoms corresponding to the mental illness of post-traumatic stress in the aftermath. Quite the contrary, the experience of breakdown, of being existentially overpowered, stays linked to the social environment and develops according to the changing relationships in this environment. Trauma is not something that happens and then is part of the past. Trauma is always in the past and simultaneously in the present. Keilson (1978), for example, was able to show that children who had suffered terribly in the second sequence, the sequence of Nazi terror, of concentration camps, and of separation from their parents, still ended up being comparably healthy adults, if, in the third sequence, the postwar period, they experienced a good and emotionally supportive social environment. Children who suffered comparably less in sequence 2, but suffered a lot in sequence 3, ended up having relevant psychological problems as adults. This demonstrates that it is never only the severity of the initial traumatic event that determines the degree of psychic suffering, but it is basically its social destiny and the new traumatic experiences in later time sequences. The severity of apparent trauma symptoms of a refugee from Syria does not depend only on their experiences in Syria, but also a lot on what happens in their host country, offering or not offering asylum, treating or not treating the refugee with respect and benevolence. An Argentinian family, where the pregnant daughter and her husband were disappeared during the dictator-ship, will be more or less healthy according to the way their society deals with these crimes in the course of history: Will the perpetrators be punished or not? Will the disappeared be unburied or not? Will they find the child born in custody and return it to its real family or not? Although it is true that every traumatic experience leaves its marks, that it constitutes a deep psychic wound, its medium- and long-range quality of psychic illness will fundamen-tally depend on the relationship between the victim and the surrounding environment. Trauma thus begins with an experience of total impotence, of deep suffering, of being overwhelmed and psychologically destroyed, but it then continues, in partial reconstructions, new experiences of terror, and long processes of more or less meaning-giving or meaning-destruction, social recognition and integration or social marginalization and reopening and deepening of old wounds. Although psychopathologies may develop as a result of trauma, trauma should not be conceptualized as a psychopathology (which, unfortunately, it is in 90 percent of current publications). Trauma should be conceptualized as a deep psychosocial process of wounding, which may or may not lead to psychopathology, but which always shapes and centrally structures people's identities and which is the result and the expres-sion of a specific social process.

Traumatized people are not either ill or healthy, broken or whole. In fact, these dichotomies represent exactly what is wrong with trauma theory. The parameters of suffering, which in these cases are always individual and social, should actually refer much more to identity development than to psychic disorders. Persons who suffer traumatic processes are continuously constructing their sense of selfhood and social belonging, the way they perceive themselves and how others perceive them, in an ongoing and dynamic identity development process, just like everybody else. But this process is also distinct in the centrality of the linkage between the individual suffering of the traumatized person and the way society deals with this suffering. People are more or less traumatized depending on the way society deals with them, and their identities are more or less dominated by destruc-tion depending on the degree to which their context is willing not only to overcome destruction, but actually acknowledge and contain the suffering it has created in the past and in the present. Identity from the perspective of trauma is neither rigid and obtained once and for all, nor ever-flexible and completely different in response to a changing environment. Traumatic issues remain and continue to be relevant over time – in fact, throughout a lifetime. In that sense, they constitute a deep and continuous moral conflict: of belonging and not belonging, of hurt and recognition, of the space in society for vulnerability, of the search for a life that will discontinue the continuity of destruction, and of the capacity of societies to work toward that goal not only in general, but also very specifically, in reference to the traumatized persons.

25.2 Searching for Identity Concepts That Could Help Deal With Trauma More Adequately

Identity is a highly contested concept, increasingly difficult to discern what the term really is supposed to mean (see, for example, Bamberg & Dege, Chapter 2, and Freeman, Chapter 4 in this volume). Assumptions have evolved considerably since Erikson (1959) developed his ideas on identity, defining it as something that develops in the psychosocial process of growing up and which is ultimately something one has acquired, a kind of coronation of the individual development process. Although Erikson's model of development was rather interesting and contained the idea of personality development as a result of confrontations and complementation between psychic processes and social experiences, the end result of identity development was, nevertheless, a rather static and rigid one, something you achieve once and for all and that stays with you for the rest of life. Relying only on Erikson's conceptualization, we would end up having to define traumatized persons as never really developing an identity as a result of too much break down, too much existential change.

Brubaker and Cooper (2000), surveying a considerably extended field of identity theories by psychologists, sociologists, and philosophers, correctly distinguish between at least five very different ways of defining this term:

(1) "Understood as a ground or basis of social or political action, 'identity' is often opposed to 'interest' in an effort to highlight and conceptualize *noninstrumental* modes of social and political action" (Brubaker & Cooper, 2000, p. 6). In this context, one might refer either to more particularistic categorical attributes, like race, ethnicity, gender, and sexual orientation, or to more universally conceived social structures, like position in the market, occupational structure, or the mode of production.
(2) Identity is understood as a collective phenomenon in which a group is characterized by a fundamental sameness either subjectively felt or objectively given. "This sameness is expected to manifest itself in solidarity, in shared dispositions and consciousness, or in collective action" (ibid., p. 7).
(3) Identity is understood as a core aspect of selfhood and points "to something allegedly *deep, basic, abiding, or foundational*" (ibid., p. 7). A lot of psychological theory focuses on this aspect. Erikson (1959) would be included in this group.
(4) Identity is understood as a product of social or political action, i.e., as the "*processual, interactive* development of the kind of collective self-understanding, solidarity, or 'groupness' that can make collective action possible" (Brubaker & Cooper, 2000, p. 7).
(5) And, finally, identity is invoked in highlighting the "*unstable, multiple, fluctuating, and fragmented* nature of the contemporary 'self'" (ibid., p. 8).

In this sense, it is like a negative mirror of the Eriksonian construction, since the key focus is on deconstruction.

In order to manage these multiple possibilities of talking about identity, Brubaker and Cooper (2000) suggest differentiating between strong and weak identity concepts. They imply that identity always means too much or too little. Strong conceptions are those that underline the commonsense meaning of the term that places emphasis on sameness over time or across persons. In this context, they state that identity seems to be something that all people "have, or ought to have, or are searching for … something people (and groups) can have without being aware of it" (p. 10). A weak definition of identity consciously breaks with the everyday meaning of the term, emphasizing rather that identity is "multiple, unstable, influx, contingent, fragmented, constructed, negotiated, and so on" (p. 11).

Looking at Brubaker's and Cooper's proposals from a trauma perspective, some issues become more palpable. For example, in reference to the first two categories outlined above, it is interesting to see how, in the framework of war and political persecution, groups and identities are constructed that did not exist before and that do, in a certain way, reflect a reality, but in another way always do injustice to the people they refer to. For example, being a refugee undoubtedly constitutes such a group identity, but always eliminates other key aspects, like education, the profession one had, gender, family culture, etc. This is even more problematic when considering the term *victim* or *survivor*. Being a Holocaust survivor might become a necessary definition of a person's identity, and socially it may even imply a key act of recognition, but it is always also a stigmatization, a reduction (see for example Améry, 1977/1966; Brunner, 2020). And finally, to suppose that all victims share the same political interest would clearly be erroneous. In reference to the third category, one might consider how deeply the selfhood of traumatized persons is shaped by their suffering and how much change is still possible. Using the sequential approach outlined above, it is clear that identity is never shaped in such a rigid way, and that it will and can change according to the social surrounding. Looking at category (4), one must ask how many victims of war and persecution are active parties to the conflict and how many of them are forced into a collective self-understanding they did not choose. Palestinian and Israeli identities have, for example, strongly developed as part of and within the conflict of the last 100 years (see Adwan, Bar-On, & Naveh, 2015). Category (5) is invoked as a category of identity deconstruction. From a trauma perspective it probably makes sense to see it the other way around: this is what identity sometimes is based on. Fragmentation does not mean many selves, but a conflicted structure. Finally, taking Brubaker's and Cooper's argument about strong and weak identity concepts into account, these different perspectives suggest that only an amalgam of the two will do justice to the reality of traumatized people.

Based on a useful and compelling discussion and linkage of Mead (1973), Erikson (1959), and especially Goffman (1959, 1961a, 1961b), Krappmann's (1971) conceptualization of identity offers a different approach that potentially overcomes the apparent dichotomy between strong and weak identity concepts. Krappmann (1971) picks up on Mead's I and me differentiation, refers to Erikson's description of the need for *self-identity*, and draws on Goffman (1959, 1961a, 1961b) when describing a very clear perception of the continuous social construction of identity. While personal sameness and corresponding competences are emphasized as a necessary capacity for social interaction, theorizing within the realm of symbolic interactionism, he consistently highlights the simultaneous social construction, reconstruction, and change of this sameness. Krappmann states that a series of social and individual conditions need to be met in order to enable the individual to develop sufficient ego identity (*Ich-Identität*), which is necessary for the successful development of processes of interaction. On the level of society, he describes the need for flexible systems of norms, which leave room for subjective interpretation and shaping of behavior, for *role-making*. He emphasizes the need for the diminishing of social repression, which assures that the re- and new interpretation of norms is not sanctioned negatively. On the level of the individual, active capacities like anticipation of expectations of others, interpretation of norms, and presentation of one's own expectations, as well as passive capacities like tolerance for discrepancies of expectations and incomplete satisfaction of needs and wishes, are necessary. But these capacities are not seen by Krappmann (1971) as personality traits to be achieved, but are understood as necessary structural ingredients of developing processes of interaction which can be threatened, changed, destroyed, constructed, or reconstructed. He defines four key competences which, on one side, are preconditions for successful social interaction, but, on the other, are in fact constructed only in and through social interaction: role distance, role-taking/empathy, ambiguity tolerance, and self-presentation.

Role distance implies the capacity of the individual to act toward norms in a reflective and interpretative way. Norms need to have been internalized in a way that allows for a reflective process on them, in spite of internalization. Individuals need to be able to pick up on the expectations of others and explain their own intentions, showing in which way they interpret these norms on the basis of their biography and participation in other systems of interaction (Krappmann, 1971, p. 142).

Role distance is a condition for *role-taking or empathy*, which, according to Mead (1973) is the cognitive capacity to pick up the expectations of the person with whom one is interacting. Krappmann (1971) quotes Couto (1951), who defines the term as "the symbolic process by which a person momentarily pretends to himself that he is another person, projects himself into the perceptual field of the other person, imaginatively 'puts himself in the other's place,' in order that he may get an insight into the other person's probable behaviour in a given situation" (p. 142). Krappmann discusses psychoanalytical thoughts on empathy and concludes that this symbolic process is cognitive and emotional and requires ego identity while, at the same time, it helps to construct it. I cannot be I without the capacity to anticipate the other's expectations, or, to put it differently, without the experience of mutual processes of role-taking and role distance.

Krappmann (1971, p. 167) defines *ambiguity tolerance* as possibly the most decisive variable, because identity development requires repeated synthesis of conflictive identifications. Without ambiguity tolerance, the individual is unable to act in face of the ambiguities that unavoidably appear in interactions because of the need to adapt to different systems and relationships to which one belongs, while simultaneously protecting a personal biographic continuity. Without ambiguity tolerance, no ego identity is thinkable, because it has to articulate itself balancing the expectations of satisfying individual needs with the common frame of a joint system of symbols and norms. The individual is forced to continuously confront the fact that expectations and needs do not match, that there is a breach between personal experiences and broader available categories of social reality. The construction of ego identity depends on conflicts and ambiguities. When alternatives of action, inconsistencies, and incompatibilities are repressed or denied, the individual lacks the capacity to express their special position in reference to specific conflicts.

This leads to the fourth and last competence, which Krappmann (1971), in accordance with Goffman (1959) calls *self-presentation*. He explains that an identity that an individual arguably has, if not introduced into the process of interaction, does not come into effect, either toward itself or toward others. The capacity to present identity is a precondition and consequence of ego identity (Krappmann 1971, p. 168). Again referring to Goffman (1959), Krappmann explains that, on the one hand, identity is never the property of the individual and rather a product of mutual control of interaction, while, on the other hand, the individual undertakes persistent efforts to protect and defend identity against destruction by others, institutional controls, and blows of fate, although it acquired this identity in interaction.

All four competencies, understood as abilities that are a result of and a precondition for successful interaction, are interesting concepts when trying to understand identity constructions under the conditions of war and persecution. All of these competences are very much threatened, put in doubt, or maybe even destroyed in chronically traumatic conditions. Obviously self and identity-presentation might not be a very good survival strategy when living under political repression, with huge military, police, and secret service control of the population. Ambiguity tolerance might be psychologically useful but difficult to sustain when authoritarian regimes tend to paint reality very much in black and white, dividing the world in good and bad, and giving themselves the right to punish those they consider bad. Also, on a personal level, when experiences of injustice, death, and destruction are everyday experiences, it might become rather difficult to stay tolerant toward inner and outer contradictions. Empathy might be more important than ever under such circumstances, but also very dangerous, as it will imply the connection to terrible and totally overpowering feelings. Finally, role distance might very quickly turn into a permanent feature of dissociation and splitting as a healthy survival mechanism, but at a high price. In short, it makes sense to take Krappmann's competences and describe in greater depth how interactions under traumatic conditions are shaped by direct and permanent attacks against these competences, and how, nevertheless, in these circumstances, individuals develop and defend capacities to interact and to sustain a sense of identity. These competences are not achieved once and for all, and then available for use by the individual. They are not inner or outer processes alone, but always both. They are a part of social interaction, which is why they might help us to assess traumatic reality, not as a psychic illness, but as a psychosocial process.

25.3 Developing Identity under Traumatic Circumstances

Looking at these conditions of life and identity development in terms of Krappmann's general outlook (1971), we can infer that all four competences of identity development are shaped, if not harmed by this reality of fear, trauma, grief, and anger. In war, respectful human norms are not valid anymore. Under threat, one cannot openly negotiate mutual expectations. Basically, one must mistrust everyone, and one needs to be very careful in expressing what one really thinks and feels. The permanent situation of threat makes it difficult to accept and link up to expectations of others. One has to worry about oneself all the time. Furthermore, traumatic experiences make it even more difficult to know and feel *who I am*, who others are, what the acceptable norms between us could be, and, as a result, the capacity to negotiate roles is extremely limited. Role distance therefore is difficult, and role-taking in consequence even more so. As one yearns for the empathy of others, one is increasingly vulnerable and less capable of providing such empathy. On one side, one needs to be empathetic in order to judge adequately what *the enemy* (whoever that is) might do to oneself. But this is not empathy in terms of feeling for the other and establishing a relationship. It is a defense, a form of self-protection. Empathy with friends also becomes complicated, because since everybody is at risk of being emotionally overwhelmed, people begin to empathetically help each other to not be empathetic. We both are very sad. We both need to cry. We both are afraid of crying because we are not sure we can ever stop again. Therefore, one or both of us make a stupid joke to ensure that we do not talk about what is really going on.

Ambiguity tolerance requires minimal basic security and a world in which contradictions are allowed. But in war and conflict, social reality is shaped by absolutes. Things are about life or death, belonging to one or another group, being strong or weak, having power or being powerless. At the same time, the need for ambiguity tolerance increases dramatically. The basic situations of life are extremely contradictory and require an ongoing capacity to deal with contradictions within oneself and in relationship to others. In particular, the permanent reality of being vulnerable leads to the desire to be permanently strong and resistant. Of course, nobody is strong and resistant twenty-four hours a day. Thus, in these circumstances, ambiguity tolerance becomes very difficult, and, at the same time, even more necessary. The fourth of Krappmann's competences, the capacity of self-presentation, also changes under the conditions of persecution and violence. Self-presentation becomes an exercise of self-hiding. It becomes very difficult, even toward oneself, to defend a convincing ego identity. Feelings of extreme impotence and weakness coexist with dreams of being strong and a wish for a different world. All of this is accompanied by underlying feelings of dread and insecurity and a deep frustration with not feeling recognized by anybody.

A good example of the problems just described can be observed in Palestinian schools. These are extremely authoritarian. Physical violence against children is frequent; teaching is frontal and focused on repetition. Nevertheless, whenever the teacher asks a question, all the children always raise their hands and try to make the teacher call on them. Most of them do not know the answer, and may not even have heard the question, because they started to raise their hands way before the question was finished. From my perspective, it seems that these children are just using every minimal chance to be recognized by someone, even if that might result in punishment later.

The difficulties of identity development under circumstances of war and persecution are further illustrated with an experience I had with Palestinians in Lebanon. I carried out a three-day workshop about fear, trauma, and grief with young Palestinian adults in Lebanon who were supposed to develop social initiatives with other youths in their camp. The goal here was not to offer clinical training, but to facilitate a prolonged group conversation in reference to their lives and work experiences. While discussing fear, one of the partici-pants asked me about my opinion in reference to the fact that he had wanted to kill someone, but, in the end, had not done it, because his wife had convinced him not to. He had felt something strange inside himself and wanted to know if I thought this had something to do with fear. When he explained the story behind this question a little more, it became clear that he and his family had a leading role in the camp in which they lived. He had gotten into an escalating conflict with a neighbor who had publicly attacked him and insulted his wife. As this continued one night, he decided to shoot the neighbor. But then his wife convinced him otherwise. Thereafter, he had felt himself diminished, and a female neighbor had even called him a coward. When we enacted this situation in a role play, he explained with strong emotion that the decision not to kill had emerged while his wife was talking and he was looking at his little son. In the discussion, the group expressed solidarity with him and his decision. But it was also clear that, according to their own rules or beliefs, he had not really acted as he should have. I expressed that I felt that his son had had a victory of life over death that night. The next day, the discussion about violence and violent fights continued. One group member shared a photo of a cat he had loved, but which someone had shot. Someone else shared his love for pigeon doves and the fact that many of the ones he kept had recently died. Thinking that the neighbor's cat was responsible, he beat the cat severely, which then jumped off the balcony and died. He called this suicide. Then his mother told him that the pigeons had probably eaten rat poison, and now he felt guilty for the death of the cat.

The situations depicted here may seem rather absurd. However, they have so much to do with death and dying, with killing or being killed, somehow rather unclearly shifting between human beings and animals, between cat-love and political fights. There is not enough room here to describe the whole discussion in detail, but it was in fact a very serious and honest discussion in a group of people struggling with the omnipresence of violence, their participation in this violence, and their wish to reflect about roots and causes. This group had been working together for a longer time, and had begun to reflect deeply on who they were and who they wanted to be. It became clear that in their everyday life there is very little chance to reflect on these issues. They have to act quickly. Thinking is often not really an option. But when given the chance to really sit down and take some time, as in this training, it became visible not only how much they needed such a space, but also how able they were to use it. In other words, although we can suppose that all of these young people have developed their identities under traumatic conditions, and although we can see that Krappmann's competences have been severely jeopardized, we can also see how they can be socially reactivated.

In a certain way, our discussion was proof of the deep suffering they had all experienced, but it also showed how ambiguity tolerance (I want to kill/I don't want to kill/I can think about it and take a decision), empathy (looking at the son, discussing how all had similar contradictory experiences about violence), role-taking (I discuss my leadership role in the group), role distancing (if we want to help each other, it cannot be all about pride), and self-presentation (I am strong/I am weak/ All together we are both) reappeared as competences in each and every one of them. They are people who have suffered a lot, but they are not mentally ill, and they have a quite healthy capacity to reflect. As Krappmann (1971) correctly pointed out, these competences are not something that people have or do not have, but they are facilitated and constructed within changing social realities.

25.4 Conclusions

People who survive in the middle of war suffer, and in many ways have been hurt and damaged, but they are also specialists in survival. They have learned to deal with incredible situations. They find answers and solutions to unsolvable problems. The essence of their identities is contradiction: traumatized but survival specialists, victims of violence and violent themselves, hopeful and lovers of life, and hopeless, despaired, and fixated on death. They have a huge capacity to adapt to new situations, and they are rigid and unable to really discuss something that allows for multiple alternatives. They are empathetic and completely closed up. Much too early, as children, they had to become adults. As adults, they sometimes seem very much like children. These people are not either/or, they are both. Thus, in certain situations, like the one described above, they will engage in a very reflective discussion in which a lot of empathy and a lot of ambiguity tolerance become apparent. Initially, in such discussions, a lot of chaos and confusion may appear, but then the participants themselves rather quickly begin to work productively with the issues that have come up, provided that they feel recognized and accepted and perceive that a real and durable relationship is being offered to them. I believe that trauma is not a mental illness, but a social and political reality in many parts of the world. It implies a history of deep wounds and ongoing deep vulnerability with the corresponding mechanisms of dissociation and repression. But it also implies a strong capacity to survive, to creatively invent answers to difficult situations, and to positively use chances of change if they are offered. If traumatic experiences become psychopathology, it is not so much as a consequence of a destroyed identity within the framework of trauma, but of the lack of ambiguity tolerance of the social environment.

A group of mental health professionals of the national academy of sciences, in Leopoldina, Germany, have recently published a text on refugees and the traumatic processes in which they maintain that traumatized persons, especially men, are basically ticking time bombs if they do not receive adequate trauma treatment (Leopoldina, 2018). I would think this is a confusion of cause and effect. If the social environment is willing to understand that people who have suffered extremely throughout their lives are both healthy and ill, fragmented and whole, and thus fundamentally contradictory, then possibly they can establish a relationship in which these people can flourish and develop, with identities that embody their pain, but also their creativity, their capacity to participate and lead meaningful and socially rich lives. If we insist on a black or white definition, then it is us who turn these people into time bombs.

The development of ego identity under the conditions of war and persecution is difficult. The social environment of persecution often does not allow for expression of these identities that is not self-destructive. But we must also recognize that all people growing up under these circumstances have a fierce, burning, and legitimate wish to develop identity, to be someone, to show that they are alive, that they did not disappear or become totally destroyed because of their traumatization. From that point of view, it is important to understand that whatever we might think theoretically about identity, on the practical level, hard identity concepts are a need and a wish for people. The ego identity people develop in war is about the discontinuities, the ruptures, and the losses. It is also about the need to find environments which enhance the expression and the tolerance for contradictions. I am strongly convinced that we could make 70 percent of trauma therapy unnecessary, if we were willing to enhance recognition of traumatic identity and focus on developing the social conditions to strengthen Krappmann's competences.

References

Adwan, S., Bar-On, D., & Naveh, E. (Eds.). (2015). *Die Geschichte des Anderen kennen lernen* [Getting to know each other's history]. Frankfurt/New York: Campus Verlag.

American Psychiatric Association. (1980). *Diagnostical and Statistical Manual, 3rd Ed.* Washington, DC: American Psychiatric Association.

Améry, J. (1977/1966). *Jenseits von Schuld und Sühne* [Beyond guilt and atonement]. Stuttgart: Klett-Cotta.

Balint, M. (1966). *Die Urformen der Liebe und die Technik der Psychoanalyse* [Primary love and psychoanalytic technique]. Stuttgart: Klett Verlag.

Becker, D. (1992). *Ohne Haß keine Versöhnung. Das Trauma der Verfolgten* [No reconciliation without hatred: The trauma of the persecuted]. Freiburg: Kore Verlag.

Becker, D. (2014). *Die Erfindung des Traumas – Verflochtene Geschichten* [The invention of trauma – Entangled histories]. Gießen: Psychosozial-Verlag.

Becker, D. (2016). Working on the psychosocial gap: Challenges, hopes, perspectives. In B. Austin & M. Fischer (Eds.), *Transforming War-Related Identities: Individual and Social Approaches to Healing and Dealing with the Past. Berghof Handbook Dialogue Series No. 11* (pp. 33–40). Berlin: Berghof Foundation.

Becker, D. & Weyermann, B. (2006). *Gender, conflict transformation and the psychosocial approach.* Retrieved on May 11, 2021, from www.erweiterungsbeitrag.admin.ch/dam/deza/en/documents/themen/gender/91135-arbeitshilfe-gender-konflikttrans-psychosoz-ansatz_EN.pdf.

Bettelheim, B. (1943). Individual and mass behaviour in extreme situations. *Journal of Abnormal and Social Psychology, 4*(38), 417–452.

Breuer, J. & Freud, S. (1895). *Studien über Hysterie* [Studies in hysteria]. Leipzig/Vienna: Franz Deuticke.

Brubaker, R. & Cooper, F. (2000). Beyond "identity." *Theory and Society, 29*(1), 1–47.

Brunner, B. (2020). Contested manhood: Autobiographical reflections of German Protestant theologians after World War II. In B. Krondorfer & O. Creangă (Eds.), *The Holocaust and Masculinities: Critical Inquiries into the Presence and Absence of Men* (pp. 203–220). Albany, NY: State University of New York Press.

Erichsen, J. E. (1867). *On Railway and Other Injuries of the Nervous System.* Philadelphia, PA: Henry C. Lea.

Erikson, E. (1959). *Identity and the Life Cycle.* New York, NY: International Universities Press.

Ernst, H. (2007). *Wenn der Schmerz nachlässt* [When the pain becomes less]. *Psychologie Heute, 10*(7). Retrieved January 7, 2009, from www.psychologie-heute.de/editorials/heft0710.html.

Fanon. F. (1963). *The Wretched of the Earth.* New York, NY: Grove.

Fanon. (1986/1952). *Black Skin, White Masks,* translated by C. L. Markmann. London: Pluto Press.

Fassin, D. & Rechtmann, R. (2009). *The Empire of Trauma.* Princeton, NJ: Princeton University Press

Ferenczi, S. (1988). *Ohne Sympathie keine Heilung – Das klinische Tagebuch von 1932* [Without sympathy no cure – The clinical diary of 1932]. Frankfurt: S. Fischer.

Freud, S. (1926). *Hemmung, Symptom und Angst* [Inhibition, symptom and anxiety]. Vienna: Internationaler Psychoanalytischer Verlag.

Goffman, E. (1959). *The Presentation of Self in Everyday Life.* New York, NY: Doubleday.

Goffman, E. (1961a). *Asylums: Essays on the Social Situation of Mental Patients and Other Inmates.* New York, NY: Double Day.

Goffman, E. (1961b). *Encounters.* Indianapolis, IN: Bobbs-Merril.

Hamber, B. & Gallagher, E. (Eds.). (2015). *Psychosocial Perspectives on Peacebuilding.* New York, NY: Springer.

Hamber, B., Gallagher, E., Weine, S.M., Agger, I., Bava, S., Gaborit, M., Murthy, R.S., & Saul, J. (2015). Exploring how context matters in addressing the impact of armed conflict. In B. Hamber & E. Gallagher (Eds.), *Psychosocial Perspectives on Peacebuilding* (pp. 1–31). New York, NY: Springer.

Keilson, H. (1978). *Sequentielle Traumatisierung bei Kindern* [Sequential traumatization in children]. Stuttgart: Enke.

Krappmann, L. (1971). *Soziologische Dimensionen der Identität: Strukturelle Bedingungen für die Teilnahme an Interaktionsprozessen* [Sociological dimensions of identity: Structural requirements for the participation in the process of interaction]. Stuttgart: Klett Verlag.

Kühner, A. (2007). *Kollektive Traumata: Konzepte, Argumente, Perspektiven.* [Collective traumas: Concepts, arguments, pespectives] Gießen: Psychosozial-Verlag.

Leopoldina Nationale Akademie der Wissenschaften. (2018). *Traumatisierte Füchtlinge – Schnelle Hilfe ist jetzt nötig* [Traumatized refugees – Quick help is necessary now]. Retrieved May 11, 2021, from www.leopoldina.org/uploads/tx_leopublication/2018_Stellungnahme_traumatisierte_Fluechtlinge.pdf.

Martin-Baró, I. (Ed.). (1990). *Psicología social de la guerra: Trauma y terapia* [Social psychology of war: Trauma and therapy]. San Salvador: UCA Editores.

Mead, G. H. (1973). *Geist, Identität und Gesellschaft aus der Sicht des Sozialbehaviorismus* [Mind, self and society]. Frankfurt: Suhrkamp.

Myers, C. S. (1915). A contribution to the study of shell shock: Being an account of three cases of loss of memory, vision, smell, and taste, Admitted into the Duchess of Westminster's War Hospital, Le Touquet. *The Lancet, 185,* 316–320.

Niederland, W.G. (1961). The problem of the survivor. *Journal of the Hillside Hospital, 10,* 233–247.

Tedeschi, R. & Calhoun, L. (2004). Posttraumatic growth: A new perspective on psychotraumatology. *Psychiatric Times, 21*(4), 58–60.

Winnicott, D. W. (1965). *The Maturational Processes and the Facilitating Environment.* London: Hogarth Press.

26 Organizational Psychology: When, Why, and How Is Identity Work (Less) Important in Organizational Life?

Stefan Sveningsson, Susann Gjerde, and Mats Alvesson

Identity is often viewed among organizational scholars as one of the most important concepts to help understand life in contemporary organizations. For example, studies of identity among organizational members in roles such as manager, professional, consultant, and priest have provided valuable insights around managerial and professional work, motivation, change, leadership, control, and gender (Alvesson, Ashcraft, & Thomas, 2008; Brown, 2019). While drawing on many of these studies, this chapter offers a somewhat contrasting view. We examine *if* identity is as important as is often claimed, and as a consequence, *when* and *why* concerns of identity are triggered in working life, and we do so through a constructionist identity perspective. In the chapter, we argue that many people do not necessarily engage with their identities most of the time (Alvesson & Robertson, 2016) and explore why they do in *certain* kinds of jobs and in *particular* situations while in others identity is neither present nor salient, at least not as a major issue. The chapter aims to cut down the identity concept in size and suggests that a more focused view on identity may help us come to better grips with what on one level *is* of great societal concern – identity-related struggle, tension, and confusion in people's working lives – without adding too much to another concern: a (re) production of unwanted narcissism in our already narcissistic time of age (Foley, 2010; Lasch, 1979).

26.1 On Identity

The study of identities in organizations is very popular among management and organizational scholars (Brown, 2019; Corlett, 2017) and there exists a vast number of interpretations and definitions. We align our understanding of identity with a growing consensus in organization studies and some other disciplines (e.g., Cerulo, 1997) as to the *meanings* people attribute to themselves as they seek to answer questions of who they are and consequently how they should *act* (Alvesson, Ashcraft & Thomas, 2008; Alvesson & Willmott, 2002; Brown, 2015). Implications for action may be vague, but these self-in-role meanings make some paths seem more reasonable than others, such as "a leader leads."

Proceeding from an individual perspective, we conceptualize identity as the conscious efforts to respond to the abovementioned questions in addition to others, such as: "What are my key beliefs, values, and priorities?"; "In what ways am I similar to/different from other people?"; "Which groups do I identify with?"; "What do I stand for?"; and "What is important to me?" (Sveningsson & Alvesson, 2003). Questions may also point to what we do *not* value or identify with. For example, managers have been found to frequently stress that they are *not* authoritarian, controlling, or dominating as a basis for constructing more positive identities (Lundberg, 2019; Sveningsson & Alvesson, 2016). Thus identity is seen as representing a subjectivity which forms emotions, thoughts, values, and actions in a particular direction that are related to relevant contexts, including interactions with various others.

Identities are constructed as external and internal forces are woven together into stories that occasionally can be seen as narratives that join the past, present, and future of people's self-understanding. External forces may be organizational cultures, professional standards, societal discourses, general ideals, and recipes for conduct and social roles (e.g., what a manager should look like) that provide input into people's identity construction process and regulate how people come to understand themselves, their priorities, and behavior (Alvesson & Sveningsson, 2011; Clarke, Brown, & Hope Hailey, 2009; Knights & Clarke, 2014; Koveshnikov, Vaara, & Ehrnrooth, 2016). Internal forces may be personality traits, bodily and individual experiences which also leave their imprint on individuals' self-understanding. This interpretation of identity and how narratives are woven together into our self-in-role meanings overlaps with what McAdams (1993) conceptualizes as a "life story." This is a central dimension in identity and something that potentially integrates the diversity of role expectations common in modern life. It points to the creation of a more integrative identity as people work to align potentially contrasting and divergent demands and expectations.

Compared to McAdams we would, in line with our more situational and dynamic view, emphasize the narrating and re-narrating of a life story – or various versions of it – depending on the specific context triggering identity work, and deemphasize a "fixed" life story. The past, present, and future offer a wealth of varied material for the construction of narratives. Identity triggering events and interactions vary and generate very different responses depending on how they relate to gender, age, being a superior, a subordinate, an employee in general, a person with a certain profession (e.g., engineering), a family person, having a certain ethnicity, religion, sexual orientation, or ethic conviction (e.g., being an environmentalist), etc.

Since both external and internal inputs contribute to the constructions of people's self-meaning, we see identities as "social products" that are "symbolic and reflexive in character" (Burke & Reitzes, 1981, p. 84), or as Kuhn (2006) defines it, "the conception of the self reflexively and discursively understood" (p. 1340). This means identities are an amalgamation of socially, occupationally, and organizationally related orientations with more idiosyncratic issues such as personal life history and individual cognitions and emotions (McCall & Simmons, 1978). Our identity perspective also overlaps with the concept of self-identity, which is often understood as a reflexively organized narrative resulting from different discourses and various experiences (Giddens, 1991). These *reflexive constructions* of the self are built out of language, symbols, culture, values, etc. that result from a variety of social interactions and exposure to messages and ideals produced and distributed by, e.g., educational agencies, mass media, or leadership developers.

Following this reasoning, identity constructions are dependent on a variety of situational contingencies that are often seen as more or less ongoing in contrast to more essentialist views that understand identity as more unitary and static. As life in modern organizations is seen as continuously turbulent and changing, many studies assume that people are now, more often than ever, engaged in more or less continuous constructions of identity in order to sustain temporary stability and coherence. Having a fairly consistent, coherent, enduring, and integrative identity may be helpful in organizational life, since it provides a relatively stable platform for orienting oneself (Ashforth, 2016). But in a fragmented world, with ideals and demands which are at times contradictory, individuals will occasionally work intensively with identity (Knights & Clarke 2014; Petriglieri, Ashford, & Wrzesniewski, 2019; Sennett, 1998).

When flexibility and negotiation are called for and effort and ambition are significant, answers to who we believe we are and what we should do may be less straightforward (Collinson, 2003). And so in many cases, identities may be less integrated, consistent, and clear, which sometimes calls for active efforts on behalf of the individual to work on their identities. This process of engaging in forming, repairing, maintaining, strengthening, or revising identity is commonly understood as *identity work* (Alvesson & Willmott, 2002; Sveningsson & Alvesson, 2003). The intensification of identity work will vary between people in different occupations/roles. In this chapter, we explore this by focusing on *if*, *when*, and *why* it differs. This means we acknowledge that identity concerns are both limited and widespread among organizational members, at times significant and sometimes less so.

Our constructionist understanding of identity differs from social identity theory (SIT) and social category theory (SCT) (Ashforth, 2016; Tajfel, 1978). While SIT (Ashforth & Mael, 1989) and SCT are concerned with shared attributes of category members, "prototypes," "in-groups," "out-groups" (Tajfel & Turner, 1986), and people's perceptions of "oneness with or belongingness to a social category or role" (Ashforth, 2001, p. 25), we are interested in the self as reflexively understood in a social, discursive, and organizational context. We acknowledge that social categories and prototype attributes often feed into these, but our emphasis is on how people reflect upon and understand themselves in relation to these. Our identity understanding also differs from a psychoanalytic interpretation of identity. The psychoanalytic focus emphasizes inner psychological processes, based on early development, life history, and the unconscious (Erikson, 1968), as central to how work life is experienced. We are interested in the open, situational, discursive, and social nature of human subjectivity rather than psychological issues contingent upon early identifications.

26.2 What Is (Less) Identity Work?

Identity work is a metaphor that refers to ways people at work attempt to shape, repair, maintain, and revise constructions of who they are in order to – at least temporarily – produce relatively coherent and distinct views of themselves (Alvesson & Willmott, 2002; Brown, 2015; Snow & Anderson, 1987; Sveningsson & Alvesson, 2003; Watson, 2009). More explicitly, identity work takes place through discursive, dramaturgical, symbolic, socio-cognitive, and psychodynamic approaches, during which self-meanings are "worked on" (Brown, 2017, p. 296). We see the identity work metaphor as generally valuable in all nonstatic contexts, including in contemporary society with its multitude of groups, affiliations, values, recipes, demands, and expectations (Giddens, 1991). These pluralistic and dynamic aspects are often pronounced in workplace contexts, in particular in large organizations and in service work, with strong requirements for people to be adaptable and responsive to many different people, sometimes triggering identity work.

There are different forms of identity work. A typology that builds upon the kind of tension and friction people experience between ideals and organizational complexities suggests five forms: three rather complicated and negative and two less problematic and positive ones (Sveningsson & Alvesson, 2016). The more complicated form of identity work – "identity juggling," "identity wrestling," "identity clash"– are the result of more explicit and complicated tensions and frictions between self-views and reality. In these cases people struggle to maintain a positive self-view in an environment that is less confirming of their identity claims or even hostile toward the identity claims. During such situations where one is not confirmed by others over time, it is quite hard to maintain a consistent self-view. Two other forms of identity work – "identity adjustment" and "identity expression" – do not entail struggle but more positive identity work, as there are less tensions and friction. Identity adjustment suggests some feel required to adapt their self-view only marginally, and in the case of expression, identities are actively reproduced to some extent.

The question about the extent to which identity work takes place in contemporary organizations and the intensity at which it occurs are an ongoing discussion in organization studies. Some researchers assume identity work is a constant and continuous process which happens without much consideration, while others argue the metaphor should only be used to address concentrated and punctuated efforts of *work* (Alvesson & Willmott, 2002; Brown, 2015).

We align with the latter, stricter understanding and see identity work as a particular form of identity construction during which conscious and focused effort is directed at maintenance, repair, or revision of identities (as self-in-role meaning). This interpretation cuts the concept of identity work down in size and suggests that "most people do not engage in identity work most of the time" but typically only during occasional and periodic episodes (Alvesson & Robertson, 2016, p. 17). It is important to use concepts so that they cover less and reveal more (Geertz, 1973) and, as we will soon see, this may be more helpful in letting us understand organizational life from the inside out and how the outside affects people. We will take a closer look at these episodes, why they trigger identity work, and who in particular is triggered (i.e., what occupational roles may be triggered more often than others). But before we do, a few words on the importance (and lack thereof) of identity.

26.3 Identity Is (Less) Important

Identity functions as a powerful sense-making (Weick, 1995) and dynamic motivational device, as it shapes people's understanding of the world (Markus & Wurf, 1987). Identities influence our *intrapersonal* processes impacting how we process information, feelings, and motivation, and our *interpersonal* processes affecting the situations we are drawn toward, how we perceive and interact with others, and how we respond to their feedback (Markus & Nurius, 1987). Having a fairly clear sense of who we are may help us situate ourselves in changing local contexts and attribute meaning to what we experience, think, and feel, giving us a sense of control as contexts change (Ashforth, 2001). Some even believe that identity is so vital that individuals "cannot act meaningfully without a situated sense of who they are and who their fellow actors are" (Ashforth, 2016, p. 361).

However, organizations consist of roles, cultures, values, power relations, and hierarchical structures that will also mediate and regulate people's meaning-making, motivations, and interactions. And although the vast amounts of identity research may suggest identity is particularly important in contemporary working life, it could very well be that "not everyone engages in the kind of reflexivity that academics expect them to" (Garrety, 2008, p. 98). Identity work by definition involves some reflexivity, (semi-)conscious reflection on who I am and how this affects me; i.e., it is not entirely unconscious. It calls for a mobilization of reinterpretations of disturbing experiences and phenomena, or the memory search of or reasoning about a subject matter so that a favorable self-understanding is restored or arrived at.

In some occupations where work activities are routine or standardized (i.e., more "identity neutral"), there will be less need to involve one's identities, weaker identity tensions, and consequently less triggering of identity work. In some work contexts people may even be uninterested in identity matters. When work tasks are repetitive and without ambiguous elements that trigger people to reflect upon who they are, people may simply follow imperatives and instructions without frequent identity concerns. Issues of status, boredom, and lack of confirmation may of course potentially trigger identity reflections in highly routinized jobs, but less so than when tasks and social roles are more ambiguous (e.g., What does a "good manager/leader" look like?. Why am I doing research?).

Still, people in complex jobs such as finance may also be less concerned about identity than we may otherwise be led to believe. For example, Alvesson and Robertson (2016) followed a group of investment banking professionals over a year, and found that they went about their daily working lives without giving much explicit thought to who they were or what this meant for how they should act, even if they experienced rude and sexist clients and ruthless employers. Such incidents should perhaps jolt people into identity reflections. Nevertheless, potentially insulting interactions were trivialized (more than denied), as people referred to "obvious" cultural aspects of this industry, such as (huge) payments and bonuses, as much more significant. For these bankers, potential identity threats simply bounced off, and the authors, somewhat surprised, referred to this as "teflonic identity maneuvering."

A conscious self-understanding may of course always be active on some level, but working life often implies more focus on getting the job done while interacting with others and following policies, rules, and conventions, and less on expressions of identity. It is only during certain circumstances that identity matters are brought to the fore of people's attention. This is usually when people experience open-decision situations that give no clear direction for their actions or decisions, situations that have significance for their subjectivity, and/or threats and challenges to and ruptures in their self-understandings. These are the times when people really start to reflect more consciously upon their identities and attempt to maintain, repair, strengthen, or revise self-meanings (Brown, 2015; Knights & Clarke, 2014; Sveningsson & Alvesson, 2003). It is during these identity-invoking situations that we are able to catch a glimpse of identities that go beyond matter-of-fact descriptions of who they are and can truly catch identity work in flight.

From a methodological point of view, it is thus important to acknowledge that not everything a person says in an interview reflects identity or identity work. Sometimes it simply reflects the following of available social scripts, impression management, and contingencies of the interview situation where gender, age, affiliation, personal style, interests, mood, and the words used by the researcher, for example, may trigger a specific idiosyncratic response (Alvesson, 2011). We will come back to this in the discussion of occupation and roles.

26.4 When and Why Is Identity Work Triggered?

Most research on identity suggests that identity questions are generally triggered during times of change, uncertainty, complexity, and development. Specific events, encounters, transitions, and surprises, as well as constant strains, all serve to heighten awareness of the constructed quality of self-identity and to compel more concentrated identity work. Specific identity-sensitive disruptions start processes of identity constructions. A typical example of change is related to role transition, e.g., as people move from junior to senior roles (Ibarra, 1999), from professional (nurse) to managerial roles (Croft, Currie, & Lockett, 2015), or from one senior managerial role to the next (Gjerde & Ladegard, 2019). Role transitions imply that people have to engage with a new set of tasks, role sets (subordinates, superiors, and peers), relations, and functions, in addition to changing cultures, values, and ideals. And as people feel these new demands, expectations, and the content of their work shift, it can be difficult to maintain a coherent picture of who they are and what they can do.

Even if the degree of change may at times be exaggerated in the literature, it appears that demands for rapid and conflicting changes, and consequently some fragmentation of working conditions, are rather salient elements of modern working life. Change is often accompanied by complexity, which can make it difficult to create continuity and coherence in our existence (Sennett, 1998). In such situations, identities become more challenged and fragile (Brown & Coupland, 2015). The experienced uncertainty and feelings of inadequacy and anxiety that often follow change may lead to a more active search for stability in the form of a reconstructed identity. Sometimes people experience change as an "identity threat," i.e., they appraise the situation "as indicating potential harm to the value, meanings, or enactment of an identity" (Petriglieri, 2011, p. 641). But threats may also come in the form of dilemmas, existential crisis, lack of confirmation, or social conflicts at work that the individual perceives as hindering them from freely and consistently expressing their identities.

Other challenges to a stable and coherent identity may come as people experience a discrepancy between the *ideals and standards* of their job or role and their actual or perceived performance (Stets & Burke, 2003). Managers are up against this challenge quite often due to widespread "contradictory demands and unreasonable ideals" (Sveningsson & Alvesson, 2016, p. 249). Managers cannot simply "be themselves" at work, but have to act as the "voice of their corporation" and be seen as knowledgeable and "in control," while presenting themselves as "credible human individuals" (Watson, 2008, p. 122). They are expected to be good role models and lead the way for change, and to show increased flexibility and renewal in general. It is not always easy to "make the best of it" (Nyberg & Sveningsson, 2014).

There is an increasingly intensive promotion of a variety of ideals in education, mass media, and work organizations, available not only for managers but for anyone at work, that one may easily buy into. These represent seductive images of how one should behave and develop in different occupations and work roles (Foley, 2010; Knights & Clarke, 2014); e.g., people are expected (or claimed) to do knowledge work, personnel administration is portrayed as strategic human resource management, supervisors are referred to as leaders, and there is a lot of interest in corporate vision and brand which promises something remarkable (Alvesson, 2013). Furthermore, ideals such as gender equality, diversity management, environmentalism, career optimization, customer orientation, and a variety of leadership ideals (being transformative, authentic, humble, servant, etc.) put strong imprints on social and organizational life.

This multitude of changeable and sometimes *contradictory standards* and ideals occasionally contributes to making identity an ongoing and fragmented project. The grandiose fantasies that float around and which are integrated into people's identities will frequently clash with the imperfections of organizational life (Knights & Vurdubakis, 1994; Nyberg & Sveningsson, 2014). It is of course possible that variation and incoherence in terms of ideals and discourses can be combined and balanced and thus lead to a form of stability. As Clarke et al. (2009) write, "people tend to employ multiple competing and often inconsistent sensemaking frameworks to explain chronic problems and to rationalize inconsistent policies and beliefs. Thus, identities may be stable without being coherent, and consist of core statement but not be unified" (p. 341). Nevertheless, this is hardly unproblematic, and tensions are difficult to avoid. And so, rather than offer more coherent and realistic meanings that potentially provide some stability, at least during certain phases of our lives, the vast majority of ideals and discourses provide organizational members engaging in ambiguous service work with more tension than ease.

The need for *confirmation* or validation is important for status and self-esteem and is quite naturally also an important aspect of identity work. People develop stories about who they are, on their own and through interaction with others, which form a meaningful and coherent context that integrate the past, present, and future in a time context (Giddens, 1991; McAdams, 1996). When such "an edited past, a preferred present and desired future" (Wright, Nyberg, & Grant, 2012, p.1471) are confirmed by others, identities become reinforced. There are, however, occasions when identity claims are not confirmed, and the narratives may be challenged, rejected, or simply ignored by others. As DeRue and Ashford (2010) describe in their conceptual paper, it is not enough to simply claim an identity as, e.g., a leader or follower. Such claims need to be relationally recognized and, with time, collectively endorsed for a leader or a follower identity to take shape, and for the leader–follower relationships that uphold such identities to develop.

Middle managers are a group who are rarely left in peace with their identity constructions by others (Sims, 2003). They may, for example, happily see themselves as central leading figures, while more senior managers or their subordinates may see them as administrators who implement orders from above and therefore challenge their self-understanding through words and actions that go counter to this self-view. Challenges to their self-view from role demands, superiors, subordinates, and peers may trigger attempts to uphold favored identities, as researchers found in a study where the "heroine" in their case study engaged in massive identity work. She attempted to hold on to a self-view as a Leader and corporate culture Change Agent. But this was an identity the people around her would not validate, since they saw her as being in charge of administration and technical support (Sveningsson & Alvesson, 2003). For new managers, the situation may be particularly fragile, and so uncertainty about who they are is common (Ibarra, 1999) and they may be hugely dependent on confirmation from their environment. Furthermore, attempts to establish, maintain, and gain acknowledgment for a particular leadership style often fail, which can be very upsetting (Wenglén, 2005).

26.5 Who and Where: Roles and Occupations

It has been suggested throughout the chapter that the increasing importance of identity can be understood against the background of uncertain, changing, and complex times and a loss of authority and traditional norms in modern society (Giddens, 1991). As traditional identity anchors such as class, family, and society, but possibly also craftmanship and professionalism, have lost some of their former relevance, people search for new ways to understand themselves (Kuhn, 2006). Modernity has brought an increased narcissism (Bauman, 2000; Lasch, 1979) fueled by consumerism, mass media, and a therapeutically oriented culture that encourages people to devote much energy to emotions and identity (Sveningsson & Larsson, 2006).

But not all work roles and occupations are equally preoccupied with identity. In certain jobs and during certain periods, organizational members may be no more influenced by identity than personality, knowledge, habits, the following of norms, and social flow, and the myriad of things that affect us, from cultural templates to policies, rules, labor processes, and various requirements from significant and insignificant others. We have previously mentioned that people who perform routine and nonambiguous jobs often experience less need for identity work. Those who perform work where the expected outcome is quite *concrete*, say that of a farmer or a mail officer as opposed to that of a brand manager or a diversity management expert, may also engage in their work without too much identity reflection.

Jobs that lack clear material grounding and are high on ambiguity (in terms of what knowledge is needed, what work should be done, and what counts as good performance), may experience more frequent episodes of identity work (Alvesson, 2004). Given ambiguity and uncertainty about work content, intangible work tasks may require some symbolic work that involves the person. This means that work activities become more identity-involving and consequently more tension-ridden with identity work. Examples of positions and occupations that demand some form of identity involvement are managers and professionals, who have been a favored target for studies of identity among management and organizational scholars (Brown, 2019). Thus, we find studies of leaders (Sinclair, 2011), priests (Kreiner, Hollensbe, & Sheep, 2006), business school deans (Brown 2019), consultants (Alvesson & Sveningsson, 2011), marketing managers (Ellis & Ybema, 2010), middle managers (Gjerde & Alvesson, 2020; Watson, 2009), and sustainability managers (Wright et al., 2012) engaging in identity work. But also so-called independent workers (Petriglieri et al., 2019), public sector workers (Thomas & Davies, 2005), and academics (Knights & Clarke, 2014) are groups that face ambiguity and lack of a clear grounding, and so have been explored through an identity lens.

It is important to recognize that work positions – professional, organizational, social – are not a given but are interpreted and shaped by people (Knights & Clarke, 2014). Thus, people are dependent upon some form of validation to know if and how they are meeting expectations in order to build self-understanding in relation to what they do. Validation comes as people interact, but identities may also be threatened and undermined during social interaction (Sluss & Ashforth, 2007). If identity claims are not confirmed, people may experience that their identities are questioned, which in turn may trigger identity work (Knights & Clarke, 2014). Confirmation or lack thereof may also come in the form of performance measures and audit mechanisms that may trigger identity work. For example, a study on academic life at UK business schools has shown how the increased performance pressure stemming from a variety of measures, such as student satisfaction surveys, quality assessment audits, the research excellence framework, and ideal images of what it means to be a successful academic, has intensified identity work substantially (Knight & Clarke, 2014).

Social and occupational ideals of what it means to be, e.g., a manager, leader, consultant, or professional feed into how people see themselves in today's workplaces. Such ideals are found in most occupations, but managers are faced with a particularly long list. For a number of years they have been targeted by a large number of leader idealizations of how they *should* be: from strong to humble, strategic to operative (i.e., available for others), result-oriented to sociable, demanding to therapist, moral role model to business-like, and so on (Alvesson & Spicer, 2011; Koot & Sabelis, 2002; Sinclair, 2011).

From an identity perspective, some ideals are attractive, as managers can portray themselves as morally good, strategic, and make use of other seductive terms (Alvesson & Spicer, 2012). But many of the (often contrasting) ideals may also make it difficult for managers to maintain a stable identity that can form a platform for self-esteem and self-confidence. Apart from representing contrasting ideals, difficulties also occur when complex situations, demands, and expectations in organizations do not comply very well with many of the ideals.

This clashing of ideals with reality is described in a book by Sveningsson and Alvesson (2016). Their descriptions are based upon a number of in-depth studies (repeat-interviews and observations) of managers from a variety of industries at work in interactions with subordinates and superiors. Their studies suggest that managers who identify with different leader ideals often engage in identity work in order to maintain a positive self-view, as their identities are often at odds with organizational demands, expectations from colleagues, and contradictory leader ideals. They suggest that two leader ideals in particular offer templates for manager (or preferably leader) identity: the *strategic leader* ideal (visons, strategies, etc.) and the *understander of human nature* ideal (humanist, listening, therapist, etc.). Related to the ideals is the overall notion that managers as leaders should act authentically (i.e., remain true to themselves), which suggests a strong identity involvement in relation to the ideals. Identifying with and trying to enact these ideals in complex organizations sets the managers up in a constant crossfire filled with ambiguous and contradictory expectations. Thus, tensions build as the managers are unable to match their self-view with their practice or views among people around them. This causes doubt, frustration, and uncertainty, and as a result, managers are triggered into identity work in terms of adjustments, modifications, repairs, radical change, and, in some cases, even exits. The identity maintenance work needed to avoid cracks in the managerial identity project becomes a mechanism to deal with these tensions. Still, despite identity work efforts, the tensions never really go away, and some managers encounter existential crises.

Attempting to perform popular leader ideals, such as being a strategist, change agent, people-improver, or coach, may be problematic and occasionally undermine the possibility of maintaining a coherent self-view (Sveningsson & Alvesson, 2016). Real-life organizational complexities and the strong pressures to do administration, use technical expertise, and simply act as a subordinate who implements policies and decisions from senior levels, as well as the unwillingness of many employees to be followers, make it difficult to form managerial work according to a particular leadership template and keep a positive self-view. People eager to work with strategy and leadership generally find themselves in a position which involves a great deal of work with bureaucracy, a lot of traditional management, and strong demands to adapt to imperatives and requests from seniors, subordinates, and colleagues. And their environment is not always a great source of confirmation. Colleagues may even directly reject an individual's claim of who they are and what they do, e.g., they may not be impressed by a manager who claims to be an excellent coach or a superior authentic person (Sveningsson & Alvesson, 2016). And so, many leadership ideals could be seen as traps rather than as facilitators of well-functioning managerial work and smooth leader–follower relations. These traps create tensions for people who start engaging in identity work as a means to free themselves, or at least reduce pain and frustration, through engaging in hopeful thinking, fantasies, and rationalizations.

26.6 Conclusion

Identity is a popular concept in work and organization studies, and like other fashionable terms, it is often used in a wide and unclear way. It is easy to refer to identities through sociological factsheet categories, such as occupation, position, or gender, that seem to be rather stable and easily accessible as a representation. This means a static, essentialistic view (one which is often conflated with self-categories or social role, e.g., being a mother, manager, or doctor). We find that it is more interesting, in particular in a work and organizational context, to study identity as "identity work," the situations and processes where people address and perhaps struggle with ideas of who they are and how they should react and act. Identity work is a more sliced term than identity construction or simply identity, which allows us to consider identity issues in flux when identity concerns emerge in a situational context. Identity is, then, a process or a verb, and not a fixed state.

Identity studies can help us understand parts of contemporary organizational life. Issues around power, compliance, organizational cultures, ethics, etc. can be productively studied through investigations of identity issues. The focus is then not on identity per se, but on identity as an entrance to gain insights into contemporary organizational phenomena and what they mean for people at work. Meetings may, for example, be seen less as a matter of dealing with issues, information sharing, and decision-making and more as arenas where people attempt to clarify, confirm, or revise who they are (Kärreman & Alvesson, 2001). Leadership can, for example, be understood as a discourse that is used less as a guide to or summary of managerial people practices, and more as a vehicle for identity work, including a way to boost the self-esteem and legitimacy of managers who imagine themselves as "leaders" (Alvesson & Sveningsson, 2003).

We believe that exploring identity issues, triggered by and made accessible through investigations of identity work, is important for understanding people in their organizations, their decision-making, priorities, motivation, and leadership. At the same time, we need to acknowledge that often other media (e.g., bureaucracy and incentives) and logics other than identity are central for people's acting; for example, people's motivation may be less concerned with what is personally meaningful for them than with the following of instructions, routines, and incentives. It is therefore important to consider identity vs. other phenomena/concepts, and to not assume that identity and identity work are prevalent with everyone and at every occasion. We see a clear tendency to overuse identity and identity work in organizational research in order to say something about most aspects of organizational behavior (Alvesson & Gjerde, 2020b). Still, as long as the term is not overstretched or misused or colonizes our understandings of experiences and subjectivities in workplaces, we find that identity work allows for many an insight.

In this chapter, we have employed a fairly strict understanding of the term identity work to describe and explain when, why, and where identity work is typically triggered. We have argued that routine, or occasional episodes of lack of, confirmation of identity, does not call for identity work. Our strict use of the identity work concept suggests it should involve an element of conscious work effort to form, repair, maintain, strengthen, or revise identities hence, the identity *work* metaphor (Brown, 2017). We have shown why and where identity work happens as people face a choice at work that includes some personal aspect (since the situation is ambiguous or needs use of self to be addressed) and/or some disruption of existence and self-understanding due to changes in role, tasks, and relations, or unexpected and challenging interaction, which forces them to become more consciously aware of who they are. This can be when ideals are forced upon organizational members in a way that creates ruptures in self-understanding, clashing or pulling these in opposite directions, or when confirmation is needed but is lacking due to the ambiguous nature of many modern jobs. As a result, people may be prompted into identity work as a defense against negative signals or self-doubts, or in an attempt to stabilize a contextual understanding of self from which to act.

Understanding the typical identity work triggers and mechanisms may be theoretically helpful for understanding other phenomena, such as meetings and leadership. And the many examples of identity work provided in this chapter give us a glimpse into people's experiences in organizational life from the inside out. The chapter may also be of value from a practical point of view as it provides people who find themselves in jobs, roles, and situations that typically spark identity work with insights as to why it happens and how to deal with it when it does. Due to our strict understanding of the term, we do not suggest everyone in organizational life will or should attend to their identities all or most of the time. This will hopefully avoid the inspiration of unnecessary (and unwanted) preoccupation with identity among people who are blissfully ignorant of who they are and what this means for the job they do. This should leave them with more time to focus on the job at hand and let them be led by the many other elements that will guide and organize their working life.

References

Alvesson, M. (2004). *Knowledge Work and Knowledge-Intensive Firms*. Oxford: Oxford University Press.

Alvesson, M. (2011). *Interpreting Interviews*. London: Sage.

Alvesson, M. (2013). *The Triumph of Emptiness*. Oxford: Oxford University Press.

Alvesson, M., Ashcraft, K., & Thomas, R. (2008). Identity matters: Reflections on the construction of identity scholarship in organization studies. *Organization, 15*, 5–28.

Alvesson, M. & Gjerde, S. (2020a). Meddling in the middle: The middle manager Yo-yo on a constant move. In Z. Jaser (Ed.), *The Connecting Leader: Serving Concurrently as a Leader and a Follower* (pp.131–151). Charlotte, NC: Information Age Publishing.

Alvesson, M. & Gjerde, S. (2020b). On the scope and limits of identity. In A. Brown (Ed.), *The Oxford Handbook of Identities in Organizations* (pp. 35–50). Oxford: Oxford University Press.

Alvesson, M. & Robertson, M. (2016). Money matters: Teflonic identity manoeuvring in the investment banking sector. *Organization Studies, 37*, 7–34.

Alvesson, M. & Spicer, A. (Eds.). (2011). *Metaphors We Lead By*. London: Routledge.

Alvesson, M. & Spicer, A. (2012). A stupidity-based theory of organizations. *Journal of Management Studies, 49*(7), 1194–1220.

Alvesson, M. & Sveningsson, S. (2003). The good visions, the bad micro-management and the ugly ambiguity: Contradictions of (non-)leadership in a knowledge-intensive company. *Organization Studies, 24*(6), 961–988.

Alvesson, M. & Sveningsson, S. (2011). Identity work in consultancy projects: Ambiguity and distribution of credit and blame. In C. Candlin & J. Crichton (Eds.), *Discourses of Deficit* (pp. 159–174). London: Palgrave.

Alvesson, M. & Willmott H. (2002). Producing the appropriate individual. Identity regulation as organizational control. *Journal of Management Studies, 39*, 619–644.

Ashforth, B. E. (2001). *Role Transitions in Organizational Life: An Identity-Based Perspective*. Mahwah, NJ: Lawrence Erlbaum Associates.

Ashforth, B. E. (2016). Exploring identity and identification in organizations: Time for some course corrections. *Journal of Leadership & Organizational Studies, 23*(4), 361–373.

Ashforth, B. E. & Kreiner, G. E. (1999). "How can you do it?": Dirty work and the challenge of constructing a positive identity. *Academy of Management Review, 24*(3), 413–434.

Ashforth, B. E. & Mael, F. (1989). Social identity theory and the organization. *Academy of Management Review, 14*(1), 20–39.

Bauman, Z. (2000). *Liquid Modernity*. Cambridge: Polity Press.

Brown, A. D. (2015). Identities and identity work in organizations. *International Journal of Management Reviews, 17*, 20–40.

Brown, A. D. (2017). Identity work and organizational identification. *International Journal of Management Reviews, 19*, 296–317.

Brown, A. D. (2019). Identities in organization studies. *Organization Studies, 40*(1), 7–21.

Brown, A. D. & Coupland, C. (2015). Identity threats, identity work and elite professionals. *Organization Studies, 36,* 1315–1336.

Brown A. D., Lewis, M.A., & Oliver, N. (2019). Identity work, loss and preferred identities: A study of UK business school deans. *Organization Studies, 2019,* doi:10.1177%2F0170840619857464.

Burke, P. J. & Reitzes, D. C. (1981). The link between identity and role performance. *Social Psychology Quarterly, 44*(2), 83–92.

Burke, P. J. & Reitzes, D. C. (1991). An identity theory approach to commitment. *Social Psychology Quarterly, 43*(1), pp 18–29.

Cerulo, K. (1997). Identity construction: New issues, new directions. *Annual Review of Sociology, 23,* 385–409.

Clarke, C., Brown, A., & Hope Hailey, V. (2009). Working identities? Antagonistic discursive resources and managerial identity. *Human Relations, 62*(3), 323–352.

Collinson, D. (2003). Identities and insecurities. *Organization, 10,* 527–547.

Corlett, S., McInnes, P., Coupland, C., & Sheep, M. (2017). Exploring the registers of identity research. *International Journal of Management Reviews, 19,* 261–272. doi:10.1111/ijmr.12149.

Coupland, C. & Brown, A. D. (2012). Identities in action: Processes and outcomes. *Scandinavian Journal of Management, 28,* 1–4.

Croft, C., Currie, G., & Lockett, A. (2015). The impact of emotionally important social identities on the construction of a managerial leader identity: A challenge for nurses in the English National Health Service. *Organization Studies, 36,* 113–131.

Day, D. V. & Harrison, M. M. (2007). A multilevel, identity-based approach to leadership development. *Human Resource Management Review, 17*(4), 360–373.

DeRue, D. S. & Ashford, S. J. (2010). Who will lead and who will follow? A social process of leadership identity construction in organizations. *Academy of Management Review, 35*(4), 627–647.

Driver, M. (2013). The lack of power or the power of lack in leadership as a discursively constructed identity. *Organization Studies, 34,* 407–422.

Ellis, N. & Ybema, S. (2010). Marketing identities: Shifting circles of identification in inter-organizational relationships. *Organization Studies, 31,* 279–305.

Epitropaki, O., Kark, R., Mainemelis, C., & Lord, R. G. (2017). Leadership and followership identity processes: A multilevel review. *The Leadership Quarterly, 28*(1), 104–129.

Erikson, E. H. (1968). *Identity: Youth and Crisis.* New York, NY: Norton.

Foley, M. (2010). *The Age of Absurdity.* London: Simon & Schuster.

Gabriel, Y., Gray, D. E., & Goregaokar, H. (2010). Temporary derailment or the end of the line? Managers coping with unemployment at 50. *Organization Studies, 31,* 1687–1712.

Garrety, K. H. (2008). Organisational control and the self: Critiques and normative expectations. *Journal of Business Ethics, 82*(1), 93–106.

Geertz, C. (1973). *The Interpretation of Cultures: Selected Essays.* New York, NY: Basic Books.

Giddens, A. (1991). *Modernity and Self-Identity.* Cambridge: Polity Press.

Gjerde, S. & Alvesson, M. (2020). Sandwiched: Exploring role and identity of middle managers in the genuine middle. *Human Relations, 73*(1), 124–151.

Gjerde, S. & Ladegard, G. (2019). Leader role crafting and the functions of leader role identities. *Journal of Leadership & Organizational Studies, 26*(1), 44–59.

Haslam, S. A., Reicher, S. D., & Platow, M. J. (2011). *The New Psychology of Leadership: Identity, Influence and Power.* New York, NY: Psychology Press.

Ibarra, H. (1999). Provisional selves: Experimenting with image and identity in professional adaptation. *Administrative Science Quarterly, 44*(4), 764–791.

Ibarra, H., Wittman, S., Petriglieri, G., & Day, D. (2014). Leadership and identity: An examination of three theories and new research directions. In D. Day (Ed.), *The Oxford Handbook of Leadership and Organizations* (pp. 285–301). Oxford: Oxford University Press.

Kärreman, D. & Alvesson, M. (2001). Making newsmakers. *Conversational identity at work. Organization Studies, 22*(1), 59–89.

Knights, D. & Clarke, C. A. (2014). It's a bittersweet symphony, this life: Fragile academic selves and insecure identities at work. *Organization Studies, 35,* 335–357.

Knights, D. & Clarke, C. A. (2017). Pushing the boundaries of amnesia and myopia: A critical review of the literature on identity in management and organization studies. *International Journal of Management Reviews, 19,* 337–356.

Knights, D. & Vurdubakis, T. (1994). Foucault, power, resistance and all that. In J. M. Jermier, D. Knights & W. R. Nord (eds.), *Resistance and Power in Organizations* (pp. 167–198). London: Routledge.

Koot, W. & Sabelis, I. (2002). *Beyond Complexity: Paradoxes and Coping Strategies in Managerial Life.* Amsterdam: Rozenberg.

Koveshnikov, A., Vaara, E., & Ehrnrooth, M. (2016). Stereotype-based managerial identity work in multinational corporations. *Organization Studies, 37,* 1353–1379.

Kreiner, G. E., Hollensbe, E. C., & Sheep, M. L. (2006). Where is the "me" among the "we"? Identity work and the search for optimal balance. *Academy of Management Journal, 49*(5), 1031–1057.

Kuhn, T. (2006). A "demented work ethic" and a "lifestyle firm": Discourse, identity, and workplace time commitments. *Organization Studies, 27,* 1339–1358.

Lasch, C. (1979). *The Culture of Narcissism: American Life in an Age of Diminishing Expectations.* New York, NY: Norton.

Lok, J. (2010). Institutional logics as identity projects. *Academy of Management Journal, 53,* 1305–1335.

Lord, R. G. & Hall, R. J. (2005). Identity, deep structure and the development of leadership skill. *The Leadership Quarterly, 16*(4), 591–615.

Lundberg, M. (2019). Trust and self-trust in leadership identity constructions: A qualitative exploration of narrative ecology in the discursive aftermath of heroic discourse. Doctoral dissertation, Copenhagen Business School.

Markus, H. & Nurius, P. (1986). Possible selves. *American Psychologist, 41,* 954–969.

Markus, H. & Wurf, E. (1987). The dynamic self-concept: A social psychological perspective. *Annual Review of Psychology, 38,* 299–337.

McAdams, D. P. (1993). *The Stories We Live By: Personal Myths and the Making of the Self.* New York, NY: Guilford Press.

McAdams, D. P. (1996). Personality, modernity, and the storied self: A contemporary framework for studying persons. *Psychological Inquiry*, *7*(4), 295–321.

McCall, G. J. & Simmons, J. L. (1978). *Identities and Interactions: An Examination of Associations in Everyday Life, Revised Ed.* New York, NY: Free Press.

Nyberg, D. & Sveningsson, S. (2014). Paradoxes of authentic leadership: Leader identity struggles. *Leadership*, *10*(4), 437–455.

Petriglieri, J. L. (2011). Under threat: Responses to and the consequences of threats to individuals' identities. *Academy of Management Review*, *36*(4), 641–662, doi:10.5465/amr.2009.0087.

Petriglieri, G., Ashford, S., & Wrzesniewski, A. (2019). Agony and ecstasy in the gig economy: Cultivating holding environments for precarious and personalized work identities. *Administrative Science Quarterly*, *64*(1), 124–170.

Sennett, R. (1998). *The Corrosion of Character*. New York, NY: Norton.

Sims, D. (2003). Between the millstones: A narrative account of the vulnerability of middle managers' storying. *Human Relations*, *56*, 1195–1211.

Sinclair, A. (2011). Being leaders: Identity and identity work. In A. Bryman, D. Collinson, K. Grint, B. Jackson, & M. Uhl-Bien (Eds.), *The Sage Handbook of Leadership* (pp. 508–517). London: Sage.

Sluss, D. & Ashforth, B. (2007). Relational identity and identification: Defining ourselves through work relationships. *Academy of Management Review*, *32*(1), 9–32.

Snow, D. A. & Anderson, L. (1987). Identity work among the homeless: The verbal construction and avowal of personal identities. *American Journal of Sociology*, *92*(6), 1336–1371.

Stets, J. E. & Burke, P. J. (2003). A sociological approach to self and identity. In M. R. Leary & J. P. Tangney (Eds.), *Handbook of Self and Identity* (pp. 128–152). New York, NY: The Guilford Press.

Sveningsson, S. & Alvesson, M. (2003). Managing managerial identities: Organizational fragmentation, discourse and identity struggle. *Human Relations*, *56*, 1163–1193.

Sveningsson, S. & Alvesson, M. (2016). *Managerial Lives*. Cambridge: Cambridge University.

Sveningsson, S. & Larsson, M. (2006). Fantasies of leadership: Identity work. *Leadership*, *2*(2), 203–224.

Tajfel, H. (Ed.). (1978). *Differentiation between Social Groups: Studies in the Social Psychology of Intergroup Relations*. London: Academic Press.

Tajfel, H. & Turner, J. C. (1986). The social identity theory of intergroup behavior. In S. Worchel & W. G. Austin (Eds.), *Psychology of Intergroup Relations* (pp. 7–24). Chicago, IL: Nelson-Hall.

Thomas, R. & Davies, A. (2005). Theorizing the micro-politics of resistance: New public management and managerial identities in the UK public services. *Organization Studies*, *26*, 683–706.

Thornborrow, T. & Brown, A. D. (2009). "Being regimented": Aspiration, discipline and identity work in the British parachute regiment. *Organization Studies*, *30*, 355–376.

Watson, T. (2008). Managing identity: Identity work, personal predicaments and structural circumstances. *Organisation*, *15*(1), 121–143.

Watson, T. (2009). Narrative, life-story and the management of identity: A case study in autobiographical identity work. *Human Relations, 62*(3), 425–452.

Weick, K. E. (1995). *Sensemaking in Organizations*. Thousand Oaks, CA: Sage.

Wenglén, R. (2005). *Från dum till klok? En studie av mellanchefers lärande. Lund, Studies in Economics and Management, 81*. Lund: Lund Business Press.

Wright, C., Nyberg, D., & Grant, D. (2012). "Hippies on the third floor": Climate change, narrative identity and the micro-politics of corporate environmentalism. *Organization Studies, 33*, 1451–1475.

27 Conceptualizing the Multiple Levels of Identity and Intersectionality

Leoandra Onnie Rogers and Moin Syed

Kimberlé Crenshaw put forth the term "intersectionality" in the 1989 Stanford Law Review to provide an accessible metaphor to describe the discrimination that Black women face in society. Discrimination, Crenshaw argues, is not an event that happens on a single route of oppression, such as racial *or* gender discrimination, or even along parallel routes (race *and* gender); rather, Black women experience discrimination at the *intersection* of multiple routes of oppression – race × gender × social class – creating a uniquely compounded reality. The term intersectionality is now used within U.S. scholarship to refer to the systems of power, privilege, and oppression that are built into a society's laws, policies, values, and practices, which interlock to give meaning to social categories; namely, race, gender, social class, and sexuality (Cole, 2009; Crenshaw, 1991; Shields, 2008). With disciplinary roots in legal studies and Black feminist scholarship (Collins, 1999; Crenshaw, 1991; hooks, 1989), intersectionality takes a bird's-eye view of society – a structural lens. Yet, as the construct of intersectionality has gained traction and moved across disciplines (Carbado et al., 2013) to encompass a much broader sociodemographic group (beyond adult Black women), new questions have been asked of the construct and additional perspectives have come into view.

Psychological perspectives on intersectionality have centered on questions (and tensions) about how to apply intersectionality in the study of identity – that is, whether and how intersectionality informs how individuals come to understand who they are ("Who am I?") and who they are in relation to others ("Who are we?") (Ruble et al., 2004; Rogers, 2018). Identity is an obvious link to intersectionality because the categories of difference/inequality that comprise intersectionality are also the identity groups that we frequently study (e.g., racial identity, gender identity). At the same time, identity is (mostly conceived to be) a personal-level construct, which seems to stand in opposition, or at least pose a conflict, to the structural lens that defines intersectionality.

With growing interest in intersectionality, it has been a struggle to define what "counts" as intersectionality research, especially in psychology (Bowleg, 2008; Collins, 1999). As Syed (2010) pointed out, intersectionality "*was not, and is not*, a scientific theory used to generate predictions about human behavior or mental processes" (p. 61). However, the application of intersectionality across disciplinary lines offers an opportunity to test basic assumptions of psychological processes through an intersectional lens. In this chapter, we consider what the study of identity reveals to us about intersectionality as a psychological process. While many conversations on this topic focus on the points of disconnect between psychology and intersectionality and the resultant difficulties of integrating intersectionality into psychological research (which we discuss below), less attention has been paid to what a psychological perspective might bring to intersectionality. Identity is a useful psychological process to examine, because it is experienced broadly and may reveal some of the nuances of intersectionality that are less visible from the vantage point of structures. Understanding the psychology of intersectionality may position us to imagine strategies to redress intersectional inequalities not only from the systems and structural levels but also from the more intimate levels of individuals and relationships.

We first situate our approach to identity by drawing on Erikson's psychosocial identity theory (1968) and frame our developmental focus. Next, we discuss the core challenges that identity researchers in psychology often face when integrating intersectionality: the disciplinary emphasis on individual-level processes, discrete variables, and linear associations (Cole, 2009; Bowleg, 2008; Syed & Ajayi, 2018). We then present an analytical framework, based on our empirical analysis of the race × gender identities among Black and White adolescents in the United States, to conceptualize identity and intersectionality as phenomena that can be measured and analyzed at multiple levels – *personal*, *relational*, and *structural*. We conclude that a multilevel perspective provides psychologists a new way to "see" intersectionality in identity development.

27.1 Conceptualization of Identity

Identity is conceptualized and defined in a myriad of ways both within and across disciplines (Brubaker & Cooper, 2000; Hammack, 2015; Syed, DeYoung, & Tiberius, 2020), and thus it is important to establish the conceptualization of identity in which we ground our discussion of intersectionality from the beginning. As cultural-developmental psychologists we align theoretically with Erik Erikson's (1963, 1968) psychosocial theory of lifespan development, which characterized human development by a series of eight psychosocial tensions (or "crises"). Each of the tensions is present to varying degrees throughout ontogeny, but developmental demands due to maturation and environment (society, culture) bring different tensions to the fore at different points of the lifespan (see Syed & McLean, 2018).

At the fulcrum of childhood and adulthood is the tension of *identity vs. role confusion*, corresponding to the need for individuals to understand who they are and how they fit into society. Erikson provided many – and at times contradictory – definitions of identity (Waterman, 2015), but at the most general level he defined identity as an inner sense of *sameness and continuity*. "Sameness and continuity" does not mean "static and unchanging." Rather, continuity pertains to the ability of individuals to make meaning of how their identities have changed over time and/or how they are different across contexts, and perhaps, by extension, across and at the intersection of multiple social identity groups (e.g., race × gender × sexuality).

The Eriksonian view of identity clearly has a strong intrapsychic component. From this perspective, identity is something that people "have"; that is, identity corresponds to cognitive representations of the self that individuals take with them from context to context. This perspective, however, is not at odds with a sociocultural or structural view of identity. Identities are created and modified within cultures and contexts, in relation to others (McLean, 2016; Schachter & Ventura, 2008), and can be fleeting and contradictory (De Fina, 2015). This sociocultural perspective, represented for example by discursive approaches to identity (e.g., Bamberg, 2004; Korobov, 2015) and social psychological approaches focused on salience (e.g., Sellers et al., 1998), sheds light on the moment-to-moment and day-to-day aspects of identity. Such a view has been well integrated with more long-term aspects of identity both theoretically (McLean, Pasupathi, & Pals, 2007; Schachter, 2015; Thorne, 2004) and empirically (Yip, 2014).

Erikson's intrapsychic emphasis can also fit with a structural perspective of identity that attends to power, privilege, oppression, and hierarchy. Erikson's strong attention to structural constraints and opportunities is an under-recognized fact (Way & Rogers, 2015; Rogers, 2018) and was scrubbed from subsequent models of identity in developmental psychology (Syed & Fish, 2018). Indeed, Erikson (1968) argued that we cannot "separate" self from society, "because the two help to define each other and are truly relative to each other" (p. 23). The inextricable link between the internal and structural factors associated with identity development allows us to reject simplistic models that emphasize boundless individual agency (e.g., Waterman, 2015), as well as models that specify only top-down sociocultural influences on identity (e.g., Markus & Kitayama, 1991). Rather, the Eriksonian view highlights a dynamic interaction between the two. It is this perspective that we have attempted to elaborate in our recent and ongoing work (e.g., McLean & Syed, 2015; Rogers & Way, 2018). This perspective of identity also gives space for intersectionality and its relevance for psychosocial development.

The *developmental* focus of our approach to identity speaks to process and change and is also relevant to the discussion of intersectionality. In general, the study of identity development has focused more on the "crisis" period that most typifies adolescence/emerging adulthood than on the roots and processes that precede it (Rogers, 2018; Schachter & Ventura, 2008). However, identity is an ongoing psychological phenomenon that matures over the life course. The early adolescent years (12–14 years old) bring new and increasingly complex cognitive and social competencies that are crucial to the task of identity and intensify the relevance of the social self across multiple groups, such as race and gender. Because identity experiences are cumulative, it makes sense to investigate how youth understand and structure their identities during these formative years. Although longitudinal analyses offer an optimal window into development, the investigation of a developmental construct, such as identity, at different developmental periods is also of great value in that it provides insight into what is known during certain time frames and how such manifestations might align or misalign with what is known of other developmental periods. In this regard, we know more about how intersectionality shows up in the identity experiences of adults but less about its presence during the adolescent years (Rogers & Nelson, 2019). Very few studies of intersectionality to date have examined intersectionality among adolescents (14 years +), and even fewer during the preadolescent years (see Ghavami & Peplau, 2018, for an exception). Listening to the perspective of early adolescents offers a novel window into identity and intersectionality.

27.2 Intersectionality in Psychology

We acknowledge first that the concept of intersectionality was developed and refined within the United States, rooted in its particular histories of social group stratification, power, and hierarchies, specifically from an American Black feminist perspective. Accordingly, some of the ideas and foci might not directly translate to other cultural contexts (Walgenbach, 2012). Indeed, in many Western European countries, "race" is not explicitly discussed, and much of the social discussion and political rhetoric focuses on migration background (Moffitt, Juang, & Syed, 2020). As a result, intersectional scholarship within such contexts would need to engage in a power-based analysis of oppression and privilege with respect to the cultural conception of *immigrants* rather than *race* as is primary in the United States. This difference in application highlights the way in which intersectionality has the potential to be broadly applicable; it is not a framework for specific groups, social identities, or experiences, but rather a framework or lens for conceptualizing and analyzing the power dynamics of societies and systems (see Moffitt et al., 2020 for more details on applications to the European context). Extended to the psychological realm, it is a framework for understanding how local (and global) power dynamics are embedded in psychological phenomena. As US-based scholars, we apply intersectionality from within this cultural boundary. However, that is not to say that intersectionality as a concept, nor the ideas advanced in this chapter, are limited to the US context. Within these constraints, there are a number of issues still to be examined if we are to integrate intersectionality into the psychological study of identity. Here we highlight three key concerns: interdisciplinarity, methodology, and theory.

27.2.1 Interdisciplinary Concerns

The uptake of intersectionality perspectives in identity scholarship, specifically, has led to a number of reviews and commentaries concerning why
intersectionality matters and recommendations for how to use it (Bowleg,
2008; Cole, 2009), as well as cautions about how not to use it (Syed &
McLean, 2016) in identity research. In particular, scholars have underscored
the need for appropriate definitions of intersectionality within an identity
framework. For example, Syed and McLean (2016) distinguish between different forms or configurations of "multiple identities" as a useful structure for
identity scholars to classify their research. A focus on alignment or congruence
between identities, for example, is one approach but rather distinct from a
focus on the relative importance of multiple identity groups (e.g., race compared to gender compared to religion; Kiang, Fuligni, & Yip, 2008). Syed
and McLean underscore that while there are various approaches to the study
of multiple identities, not all necessarily align with an intersectionality
perspective.

A major lingering question is how much of the original conceptualization of
intersectionality must be preserved as it moves into different disciplines. Is
"conceptual purity" necessary or even desirable? There is no doubt that the
concept of intersectionality will have to change in some way for it to be
integrated with psychology. As an empirical science, psychology asks different
questions and has different expectations for what concepts and theories provide compared to the humanistic origins of intersectionality (Syed, 2010; Syed
& Ajayi, 2018). The question is how intersectionality can be successfully
integrated into the psychology of identity without losing its essential meaning.
Indeed, there are better and worse changes vis-à-vis the original concept. As
noted, a sole focus on multiple identities – how individuals configure and
manage their many potential competing identities – is not sufficient to be
labeled an intersectional inquiry. From the original lens of critical Black
feminist intersectionality, any intersectional inquiry must recognize and attend
to the structural context. To be "doing intersectionality," in other words, there
must be attention to complexities of privilege and oppression and how they
intersect to contour the lives of multiply marginalized individuals. But how
does an individually focused field such as psychology successfully incorporate
this kind of structural perspective in its theoretical and empirical work? We
describe one potential approach later in this chapter.

27.2.2 Methodological Concerns

A second issue involves methodological and analytical approaches. The
assumptions of many psychological methods and statistical techniques are
simply incongruent with the assumptions of intersectionality. For example,
the very notion of variables as discrete entities contrasts with the notion of

complex, overlapping social categories. All of the intersections matter, but how then do we measure everything without measuring nothing at all? Analytical models similarly rely on specification of which variable predicts another in a linear fashion. However, intersectionality is cyclical and context-ually embedded. As a result, some scholars fall on the side of arguing for strictly qualitative methods, arguing that in-depth interviewing is the only accurate approach to measure intersectionality. Yet, even in qualitative approaches, the question of definition (raised above) comes into play. As Bowleg (2008) illustrated, how one poses the interview question matters for the type of data and answers we receive. Asking about being "Black and female" is not the same as asking about "being lesbian, as a Black female," which differs still from the "experience of Black lesbians."

Moreover, asking individuals directly about intersectionality may not always yield accurate insights into how intersectionality has structured the contexts that influence their lives. For example, Azmitia, Syed, and Radmacher (2008) found that asking college students directly about the intersections of race, class, and gender often led to unelaborated responses. Rather, it was when discussing contexts of their lives – family, peers, school, work – that they would unwittingly describe intersectional experiences. This methodological issue raises an important conceptual issue for the integration of intersectionality into the psychological study of identity, namely that inter-sectionality may operate outside of individuals' conscious experience and that inquiries must be grounded in the contexts of individuals' lives.

27.2.3 Theoretical Concerns

There are multiple possible theoretical concerns that could be raised regarding the integration of intersectionality in psychology. Here we draw attention to two that we believe are particularly relevant for the study of identity: (1) integration with development and (2) employing multiple levels of analysis.

One issue unearthed in the psychological commentary on intersectionality concerns issues of moving across social groups and developmental stages (Ghavami, Kastiaficas, & Rogers, 2016; Hershberg & Johnson, 2019; Syed & Ajayi, 2018). Intersectionality is a concept and construct developed from legal studies and focused on explaining discrimination among adult Black women. What does it mean to shift this construction into the field of psych-ology, and more specifically developmental psychology, which focuses on stability and change over time, and often studies diverse and younger popula-tions? Indeed, much of the developmental research that draws from intersec-tionality has examined emerging adults (Azmitia, Radmacher, & Syed, 2008; Kuper, Wright, & Mustanski, 2018), but what about younger kids? Developmental considerations include cognitive capacities, abstract thinking, and early formations of identity (e.g., Ghavami et al., 2016). We know that youth have social identities and experience discrimination with regard to what it means to be girl or boy (Brown, 2017; Rogers & Meltzoff, 2017). What is less clear is when and how youth perceive these processes at the intersection of social categories: race × gender, or sexuality × gender, or race × social class. Ghavami and colleagues (Ghavami & Peplau, 2018; Ghavami & Mistry, 2019) are leading the way into this territory with person perception research on the stereotypes that early adolescents ascribe to their peers at the intersection of identities: What stereotypes apply to Black gay boys versus White gay boys? Recognizing that intersectionality surfaces in young people's identity processes is an important step for pursuing developmental questions about how such processes emerge and change over time.

A second theoretical tension centers on the unit of analysis, which refers to where researchers implicitly (or explicitly) locate the issue or problem of study. In psychology, the unit of analysis is most often the individual, and in identity scholarship (theory and research) we most often measure individuals to describe the human experience as a feature of the individual psyche. Intersectionality views the structure as the unit of analysis, the site where discrimination and inequality operate. Herein lies the crux of the disconnect. Psychologists typically enter (and remain) at the personal level, whereas intersectionality theory enters and (often remains) at the structural level. What both perspectives often lack is a multilevel view – a recognition that both individuals and systems contribute each with a valuable vantage point. From a single-level perspective, these visual fields are unlikely to ever converge; but with a multilevel view, one can ask and begin to see how and where these perspectives intersect.

We consider here that intersectionality and identity operate at multiple levels simultaneously – personal, relational, structural – and individuals may enter (or exit) these conversations at these various access points. For example, being a "White girl" may not matter *personally*, but the individual may still recognize that being a White girl matters *relationally* with others and within the larger *structural* realities of society. From a psychological perspective, this "White girl" may differ in consequential ways from a "White girl" who also does not place any importance on this identity, but moreover does not recognize that race and gender positions matter in society broadly, and perhaps differ still from a "White girl" who claims a strong personal significance of her intersectional identity, but views it as *only* relevant to herself and inconsequential for how others perceive and interact with her (relational), or how society affords her privileges based on her intersectional identity location (structural). In this way, the levels of identity and intersectionality are both experiential and empirical; they capture the range of ways that individuals might engage with relevant social categories and a research tool, or level of analysis, for the empirical study of such processes. Moreover, these levels are nested, or related to each other. A multilevel framework, as we illustrate with empirical examples below, allows us to see the complexity of identity and intersectionality across levels of the human experience.

We recognize the general tendency of psychology to privilege individuals and individual-level variables over systems and structures of oppression as a notable limitation for conducting research from an intersectionality frame. However, psychology also brings the psyche and subjective experience into the structural conversation. Rather than choosing sides, we adopt a *transactional approach* in which self and society are mutually constituted, recognizing that systems indeed structure the experiences of individuals and that individuals have agency to respond, and by virtue of doing so, to alter those structures (Hammack, 2008; Rogers, 2018). In this way, we hold space for multiple perspectives to coexist as we consider what the psychological perspective of identity might reveal to us about intersectionality.

27.3 Intersectionality and Identity at Multiple Levels: Personal, Relational, Structural

Our multilevel view of identity and intersectionality emerged through listening to the ways in which young people described the meaning and significance of their race × gender identities – what it means to be a Black girl or a White boy. The data we present here are drawn from a larger longitudinal, mixed-method study of children's self-perceptions and social relationships (see Rogers, 2020; Rogers & Meltzoff, 2017). The analysis is based on interview data from a sub-sample of Black and White adolescents, aged 9–14 years old (N = 63; M_{age} = 12.51 years; SD = 1.55). There were seventeen Black girls, ten Black boys, sixteen White girls, and twenty White boys. Each adolescent was individually interviewed using a semi-structured interview protocol designed to capture how young people reason about their race × gender identities.

Our intent in probing how young people make sense of intersectionality in this way is not to "test" whether or not intersectionality exists; the structural reality of intersectional inequality is robustly evident in societal stratifications along multiple dimensions (Collins, 1991; Suárez-Orozco, Yoshikawa, & Tseng, 2015). Our curiosity here concerns how intersectionality is *experienced*, *perceived*, and *rationalized* by young people who are in the process of learning what it means to occupy these intersectional identity locations. What does it mean to be a Black girl or a White boy? How do youth make sense of their memberships within these social groups?

Exploring the psychology of intersectionality during early adolescence is new for the field. Nearly all of the extant empirical work on intersectional identities focuses on emerging adult and adult populations (Azmitia et al., 2008; Kiang et al., 2008; Rogers & Nelson, 2019). However, examining intersectionality from the perspective of young people offers a window into the *process* (Ghavami et al., 2016; Syed & Ajayi, 2018). Early adolescence marks the beginning of the period of the "identity crisis," a time when youth are actively exploring their identities, interpreting and integrating past experiences with current social roles and expectations, and imagining future possibilities. Early adolescents are very aware of their multiple social group memberships, such as race and gender, forming a clear sense of "we-ness" with members of their social groups, "we" boys, for example (Frable, 1997; Ruble et al., 2004). But, do youth have a sense of "we-ness" with their intersectional group identities, such as "we" Black girls or "we" White boys? Moreover, early adolescents are aware of the social structures and stereotypes that define multiple social groups (Brown et al. 2011; Way et al., 2013); they know how others are perceived by society and among their peer groups, and can recognize how they themselves fit into (or deviate from) the social expectations.

Our data analysis is based on verbatim transcripts from adolescent interviews. We employed an axial coding procedure (Wolcott, 1994) with two organizing factors that emerged from the open-coding analysis: *significance* and *reasoning* (see Table 27.1).

Significance refers to how much importance individuals place on their intersectional identities (e.g., "How important is being a Black girl?") and whether they believed anything would change as a result of being in a different identity position (e.g., "How would things change if you were a *White* girl?"). The second factor, *reasoning*, concerned the explanation or rationalization provided. This is where the multilevel perspective surfaced, as adolescents spontaneously reasoned about these intersectional identity positions from the "personal," "relational," and "structural" levels. These were not mutually exclusive in our conceptualizing or coding of the data.

The multilevel framing of the analysis emerged from listening to the data. Certainly, multilevel or systems perspectives are not themselves novel to developmental research. However, in thinking about how to make sense of intersectionality, this lens was especially useful. The initial coding of the interview data focused primarily on *content* – what themes, ideas, and concepts young people raised when discussing their intersectional identities. Beyond the content, however, we noticed patterns in how young people reasoned about the relevance of intersectional identities, and more specifically that there were distinct ways of engaging this conversation. These distinctions were made visible by incorporating the terminology of ecological systems theory – which we termed the individual, relational, and structural levels of the ecosystem. Within this frame, our analysis shifted from which adolescents said what to *how* and at *which level* of the system young people were having the discussion. For some, it was a personal, individual-level conversation, and for others intersectionality was inextricable from social and relational realities. Acknowledging "where" young people entered this conversation allowed for deeper interpretation beyond "how much" or "how often" a theme was mentioned; it allowed for both the structural and psychological realities of intersectionality to coexist.

Table 27.1 *Levels of intersectionality: Significance and reasoning about intersectional identities*

Reasoning	Significance	
	Consequential	Inconsequential
Personal • Who *I* am • *I* don't care • Pride	White girl, 8th grade: I: Like how important is it to you, being a white girl? R: [clears throat] It's weird because these are like my most proud of and least proud of paired up together. Um, I don't think it's that important.	Black girl, 7th grade: R: It doesn't matter at all! I: How do you think things might be different if you were um, a white girl? R: Well then obviously my hair would be different. It'd be way easier . . .
Relational • Family, peers, teachers • Differential treatment	Black girl, 4th grade: Well then I wouldn't have the same family and I probably wouldn't have the same feeling at home probably not the same friends or school and stuff and my church because I really like my church and stuff.	White girl, 8th grade: Not at all important, but like, at my lunch table, there's like, cause all my friends are White. But that's cause, they're just – that's just who I met. So that's just cause of their personalities. Like, I couldn't care less if they were all Black, if I was Black. I couldn't care less. But at our lunch table, though, it's just a bunch of White girls and one White guy.
Structural • Discrimination • General stereotypes	Black boy, 7th grade: Yeah dealing with all these people that don't like Black people . . . Uh some of the cops I thought were okay, but some of these other cops don't have to kill people. But some of them kill them for no reason just like because they don't like Black people.	White boy, 8th grade: Um, Not much . . . Like maybe a few decades ago with the civil rights stuff it would of mattered, but now a days it doesn't matter that much.

A primary motivation for including a data-based perspective in this chapter is to shift the conversation from only theorizing about how intersectionality fits into psychology to examining what we might learn about the psychology of intersectionality empirically. In our experiences of discussing intersectionality with our colleagues, we find that the ideas resonate but they are unsure of what incorporating intersectionality would look like in their empirical work. We hope this empirically based approach responds to the call for guidance, and believe it is useful for other researchers – it can inform one's research design, questions, analysis. Here we provide some qualitative excerpts to help illustrate the broader theoretical points (A more detailed discussion of the data analysis and findings can be found in Rogers & Syed, 2021).

27.3.1 Personal-Level Intersectionality

On a personal level, intersectionality centers the individual but often only the individual – how the individual describes and feels about identity, how phenotypic and microlevel experiences figure into the (in)significance of identity for the self. As psychologists, the personal level is the most familiar. Identity constructs such as "centrality," which measures how important a given social group is to the self, or rating scales that assess how positively or negatively one feels about their identity (Sellers et al., 1998), are examples of a personal-level view that centers the individual as the unit of analysis. When moving into the realm of intersectionality, psychologists have largely maintained the same lens, measuring how individuals rate their *multiple* identities and the extent to which those ratings differ across identity categories (e.g., Kiang et al., 2008), for example, labeling the self as a "Black female" or "White male," or ranking the importance of one's "Lesbian" identity relative to "Black" and "Female" identities.

This level of analysis is valuable. It provides a subjective view of a structural process, homing in on how an individual understands or makes sense of themselves within a stratified society. Our own empirical example drew from very similar questions:

QUESTION (Q):   All right so we put Black and boy together, how important is being a Black boy to you, not much, a little or a lot?

ANSWER (A):   Not much because everybody is like – every boy is kind of the same, I mean it doesn't really – I don't really go off my skin color; I don't care about skin color.

Q: Okay and why don't you care about skin color?

A: Because a boy, if he is White or if he is Black, if he's Black I mean he's still a boy, you've got just different skin color. (Black Boy, 8th grade)

Q: How would things change if you were a Black girl?

A: I would still be the same person I am today, so I just – I don't really see how it matters that much; it's just that you're a boy or you're a girl. (White Girl, 8th grade)

From a psychological perspective, these responses are interesting and identity-relevant. The limitation, however, is that the question, interpretation, and conclusion focus only on the individual without situating the individual within a sociocultural context. That is, for these young people, intersectional identities are *not* important. But other adolescents view intersectionality as a highly significant aspect of their sense of self: "I like it [being a Black girl] a lot!

I love that I have really thick hair [laughter] … and I love when my hair's curly cuz I just feel really great" (Black Girl, 8th grade). Emphasizing a uniquely racialized and gendered feature of her Black girl identity, hair style/texture (Cielto & Rogers, 2019), this young girl perceives and integrates race and gender holistically and positively into her sense of self. And still for others, this explicit intersectional identity is quite a mixed bag:

> Well, being a girl is a lot and I guess being a white girl – I guess it would be in-between them … A little. (White Girl, 6th grade)

> Because I said it was a little bit important that I was girl but um, and I said it was a lot about being black, the fact that I'm a Black girl really just circles back to being black, not really being a girl. (Black Girl, 6th grade)

Q: How about being a White boy, how important is that to you?
A: Um a boy, a lot; White, not … So, not much. (White Boy, 8th grade)

These are interesting micro- or personal-level explanations of intersectional identities that reveal the subjectivity of intersectionality as part of an identity process. And, as represented in these example quotes, one could conduct group comparisons to evaluate which intersectional groups, Black girls compared to White girls, for example, rate their intersectional identities, on average, as more or less important (Rogers & Syed, 2021).

Where the personal-level analysis falls short, however, that it is often taken to be the sole level of analysis. This is not to say that psychology, particularly social psychology, is unaware that racial and gender categories are *social* constructs that organize social groups, rather that the unit of analysis is individuals rather than structures. Recognizing this tendency, two prominent social psychologists recently urged the field to don "hierarchy-shaped glasses" (Kteily & Richeson, 2017, p. 327) in order to see how phenomena observed at the personal and group levels are indeed reflections of the broader societal hierarchy. Acknowledging the level of analysis has important implications for interpretation. That is, what do these findings about identity importance mean for interpreting the significance of intersectionality? Does it mean that intersectionality is not relevant to all early adolescents, or to certain groups (White adolescents), or that adolescents are unaware of intersectionality? It would be neither appropriate nor useful to conclude from these findings that intersectionality is meaningless – or to question whether intersectionality exists. Rather, we ought to use the findings as a springboard to ask what psychological motivations may drive this personal interpretation of intersectionality.

Acknowledging that the personal level is only one level of intersectionality reframes our interpretation and helps bridge the disciplinary and theoretical gap. Our axial coding approach allows us to see how personal-level intersectionality is often employed to explain why intersectional identities are inconsequential, to downplay significance, and that this strategy can be an intentional one – one that is inextricably tied to relational and structural realities beyond the individual (Rogers & Syed, 2021). Holding these other levels in view while examining the personal allows us to draw conclusions that are more congruent with the original aims of intersectionality. It also allows for the incongruence that often defines the human psyche; that is, that humans can, and often do, hold contradicting beliefs. As we illustrate below, sometimes the same individuals who disclaim the importance of intersectionality personally also acknowledge the relational and structural implications of these identities.

27.3.2 Relational-Level Intersectionality

We also observe identity and intersectionality at the level of relationships and social interactions. From this view, intersectionality exists not as a feature or construct for the self, but as one that can be used to interpret processes between people and among groups: within relationships and interactions with peers, teachers, family, and colleagues. From this level of analysis and interpretation, we hear how intersectionality and identity are intimately tied to the perceptions of and interactions with others, making the unit of analysis the relationship rather than the individual. From this lens, the meaning of identity and intersectionality is socially constructed, maintained, and disrupted in the context of relationships. In our data, adolescents sometimes could only make sense of or explain their own intersectional identities – why they mattered or did not matter – by describing their relational worlds.

Friendships and one's social circle were sometimes referenced as evidence for the *insignificance* of these identities. For example:

Q: Okay. How about being a White boy, if we put those two together, how important is that to you, not much, a little or a lot?
A: Hum no, not much.
Q: Not much? Do you think things would be different if you were a Black boy?
A: Not really. I mean because a couple of my friends from [elementary school] were Black and I still hung out with them and they were good, so. (White Boy, 7th grade)

The idea of having a diverse social group – attending a diverse school, church or community events, having friends or family members of varying racial/gender backgrounds, living in a diverse neighborhood – as evidence for or explanation of the insignificance of intersectional identities is an interesting psychological process, and it offers a means for understanding how and why individuals rationalize the structural intersectional inequality.

At the relational level, individuals might find the perspective they need to speak about intersectionality beyond the self. In our data, more often than not, the adolescents engaged the relational sphere to state the obvious relevance of intersectionality, but in a way that shifted the responsibility from the individual to the shared interaction; these were not personal beliefs but artifacts of the relational or social context. For example, when adolescents were explicitly asked whether anything else would change if their race/gender changed, they most frequently discussed how their relationships would change:

> Well then I wouldn't have the same family and I probably wouldn't have the same feeling at home, probably not the same friends or school.   (Black Girl, 4th grade)

> Um it would be like how you act and your group of friends and all that stuff.   (White Boy, 8th grade)

What is telling from these narratives is how "master narratives" – widely shared and culturally sanctioned stories and stereotypes – are invoked in the meaning-making (McLean & Syed, 2015). Whereas the reasoning at the individual level rarely elicits the cultural context, when individuals reason about intersectionality through relationships, the sociocultural realities come to the surface. Adolescents said things like: being a girl (instead of a boy) would make you "nicer," and being Black (instead of White) would change "how you act 100 percent" at school and the types of "movies" you watch and the types of "sports" you play. The evidence of this relational or shared story also comes through when listening to youth speak about the "other." The following quotes are from two girls who illustrate the shared reality of intersectionality:

Q: Why would you get in less trouble if you were a White girl?
A: Uh because they always be like – they always think that Black people will be doing everything and I'm like yeah, sometimes we are bad-ish and they think we always be doing stuff, so that's why. (Black Girl, 7th grade)

> It's kind of like racist but, I feel like they're [teachers are] more trusting of like the White girls than they are of like a Black girl or something.   (White Girl, 8th grade)

From their respective social locations in the US racial hierarchy, these early adolescent girls speak the same "truth" and experience of intersectional positionality.

The relational level of intersectionality also seems to offer, and perhaps reveal, the contradictions embedded in the psychological processing of intersectionality, and particularly with regard to oppression and privilege. The notion of intersectionality existing as a transaction between people rather than within individuals, differs from the structural level (discussed below) in that the focus is on specific people and relationships rather than cultural systems. But, the tensions of the self, the other, and society are salient through relational lens:

Q: Do you think things would change if you were Black?
A: Um probably in some ways. Like I, I'd like to think like in my mind it shouldn't matter, but a lot of – to a lot of people it does matter. So, like, if

I'm – when I would be around those people they would – yeah, it would be different than it is now.

Q: Even if it didn't matter ...?

A: Yeah, it didn't matter to me but it still matters to some other people. So ... (White Boy, 8th grade)

Making explicit the division and contradiction at the personal ("in my mind") and the relational ("but to a lot of people") levels, he suggests that the relational trumps the personal, because if it matters to everyone else, then "it still matters." Another example is a White girl who explained:

> I don't think anything would be different [if race or gender changed] but that would be up to like my friends and family and stuff ... I don't think my friends would change but I would love to see how they would react! And my family, I'd really doubt they would, but like I said, I'd see how they'd react.   (White Girl, 8th grade)

Both of these examples make visible the relational level of analysis on identity – and intersectionality. The relational level acknowledges that "others" (and even society) structure and give meaning to identity. Indeed, if society did not stratify and assign value to individuals on the basis of social groups, then it really would matter much less – or differently than it does. At the same time, offloading responsibility *only* to "others" may have the effect of undermining one's sense of agency and motivation to create change. In order to move forward we must recognize that personal identity narratives often function to maintain the societal master narrative and the inequalities it supports (McLean & Syed, 2015). In other words, both the personal and the social (and structural) are necessary for change. Recognizing that it is up to us – our families, our schools, our communities – whether and how these social positions matter is an important perspective for imagining how identity can function as a lever for social change (Rogers, 2018).

27.3.3 Structural-Level Intersectionality

The structural level is the quintessential or original level at which intersectionality operates – built into societal structures and systems (Crenshaw, 1991). This is also the level psychological research most frequently ignores. The absence of structural-level analyses is both theoretical and methodological – psychological theories and measures of identity have not, traditionally, been designed to explain structural processes. However, in the past decade we see a concerted effort to address this limitation through theory and empirical research that centers structures and inequalities in identity scholarship (Galliher, McLean, & Syed, 2017; McLean & Syed, 2015; Rogers, 2018; Rogers & Way, 2018). With these frameworks we are better positioned to engage with intersectionality at the structural level.

The importance of the structural level cannot be understated. If we are to understand the conditions under which humans develop and form relationships with themselves and others, we must take seriously the sociocultural oppressions and inequalities that regulate everyday human interactions and experiences. At the same time, to only privilege the structure without attending to the ways that individuals experience and make meaning of and negotiate these cultural rhythms, is to miss the psychology of it (Hammack, 2008; McLean & Syed, 2015; Rogers & Way, 2018). Listening for structure in the narratives, we can hear adolescents' awareness of the ways that societal stereotypes, discrimination, and inequalities systematically organize these identity locations and filter into their relational and personal levels of experience. In these data, we capture this structural awareness by asking young people to *imagine* their experiences through the identity lens of another. For example, a White girl (8th grade) reflects on how things would change if she were a Black girl: "Probably would have less privilege because a lot of White people are racist so I'd probably have less privilege and I think that's the only thing that would really change." Asked to reflect on a change to her gender identity, she replied: "Um I'd have a ton of privilege; I'd be like the top of the food chain; I'd have so much privilege and I'd be like – yeah." Recognizing the privilege afforded to (White) males in a patriarchal society, as a White girl she can see the notch above her own race/gender positionality. Through these two perspectives, we can hear that she has a conception of both racial and gender inequality, and her own (race) privilege and (gender) oppression within this hierarchy. A Black girl (8th grade) reflected on the same questions:

> Um, I think if I was a White a girl, like [pause] how it would be different. Um, I think people wouldn't like judge me on certain things like because people say like when they met me I look rude, so probably if I was White, they would probably be like – uh, excuse me – not, um, dang. I think I wouldn't get judged as much as if I was White.

These quotes exemplify the structural level because they state (a) that judgment and bias are tied to these social groups and (b) that these judgments are part of society. As one White girl (8th grade) explained, as a boy "you probably get treated more fairly, honestly. By everyone." It is "everyone" rather than the select individuals in one's immediate environment (parents, peers). We can also visualize the nuances of intersectional oppression from the subjective perspective. The quotes by the White girls recognize the gender privilege afforded to (White) boys, whereas the second quote from a Black girl underscores the racial privilege afforded to Whiteness more comprehensively. Although asking young people to imagine what it is like to be part of another racial and gender group may pull for generalities that align with stereotypes, which is evident in some of the answers young people provide, their responses reveal, in a way, how the personal and master narratives interweave to forge identity.

Furthermore, these responses reveal a critical awareness of the societal structures that come into view when two identity categories are brought into relationship with each other – the unique opportunities of being White *and* male, and the challenges of being Black *and* female in this society.

It is also important to note that the structural level is not distal, but intimately experienced at the personal level of experiences and expectations. This again underscores the value of a multilevel lens for analyzing and interpreting intersectionality within psychology:

> If I was a White girl, I would probably get treated – I probably wouldn't get treated any way [be]cause they only say anything bad about Black – I mean I don't know what they say about White girls [be]cause I'm not White. But um, I would feel – probably I would probably like being White more than Black because I always like their hair and their body shapes and um, since they're White, they get more jobs, so they have more money and so I would enjoy having more money. Or at least my mom might have more money. So, I'd be fine with it, if I was White.   (Black Girl, 8th grade)

This Black girl's description of White privilege is both about structures that privilege Whiteness and wealth and beauty standards of White femininity but also about access to employment and familial wealth and the personal/phenotypic features of hair texture and skin tone. At each of these levels, we hear how her awareness of and engagement with an intersectionality influences how she sees herself and others.

If the structural is the only level of analysis, the individual is merely a passive recipient of these realities of discrimination and inequality. A multilevel view affords us the perspective to simultaneously listen to and interpret how individuals also respond to and engage with these structures. That is, we can hear how the psychology of intersectionality plays out in their identity formation. One way individuals may engage with the structural level of intersectionality is through accommodation, or aligning themselves with the master narrative and viewing their identities in accordance with it. For example, when a Black boy (7th grade) imagined what it would be like if he were a White boy, he responded: "Not being good at sports." Likewise, when a Black girl (7th grade) imagined being a Black boy (a change to gender), she replied: "I'd probably be like an athlete or something or I'd probably be into football."

Another way that individuals respond to the structures of intersectionality is through resistance – constructing their identities in ways that challenge, disrupt, or deviate from society's expectations (McLean et al., 2018; Rogers & Way, 2018). For example, when Black girls claim their intersectional identity as highly important because they "get to prove people wrong" and affirm that they are worthy of "respect" and value, they are responding to and resisting the master narrative that positions them as inferior on the basis of their identities: "Like, being a girl and being Black, those are kind of two precious things because they [other people] kind of expect more from you and like they kind of expect less at the same time" (Black Girl, 7th grade). Embedded in the realities of oppression and low expectations, these young Black girls understand their identities and positionalities from a stance of resistance, embracing both the good and the bad as "precious." Their response to the intersecting oppression of society is to challenge the structure that threatens to undermine their identities and find wholeness at intersection: "If you can't love yourself in one section, how are you supposed to love yourself in other?" (Black Girl, 8th grade). Our empirical or theoretical considerations of intersectional identity need to make space for such wholeness, or our conclusions are woefully incomplete.

27.4 Conclusion

The purpose of this chapter was to consider what the study of identity reveals to us about intersectionality as a psychological process. Our conceptualization of identity, rooted within Erikson's (1968) lifespan developmental theory, shows how "traditional" psychological notions of identity can be merged with structural considerations, which is not often the provenance of psychological research. The concept of intersectionality provides a powerful tool for analyzing and understanding the nature and consequences of interlocking oppression and privilege. Intersectionality offers a lens for understanding systemic oppression and inequality, and identity is a psychosocial process that unfolds within the sociocultural context. Bringing these together allows for much deeper and more complex theorizing about both identity and social structures.

In this chapter, we considered intersectionality in identity through an empirical lens. Rather than urge our discipline to shift the entire focus to the structural level of systemic inequality at the loss of phenomenology and subjectivity, psychology can leverage its disciplinary strength of prioritizing individual experience to interlace the personal and relational with the structural. Assuming that identity and intersectionality function at multiple levels of experience allows for more meaningful questions, analyses, and interpretations of identity processes. It creates a prism of realities, where structures, relationships, and individuals coexist and interact and, from different angles, shine a different light on the complexities of identity and intersectionality. A prism is not neatly divided into equal parts or pieces, and no single piece or angle of prism could ever meaningfully capture the light to reflect a rainbow as a full prism does. Psychology is drawn to intersectionality because it more accurately describes the phenomena related to justice and equality that our field cares about deeply (Killen, Rutland, & Yip, 2016). As a field, we will not see the impact of an intersectionality perspective without embracing a more nuanced and contextually embedded set of prism lenses.

References

Anyon, J. (1984). Intersections of gender and class: Accommodation and resistance by working-class and affluent females to contradictory sex role ideologies. *Journal of Education, 166*, 25–48.

Azmitia, M., Radmacher, K., & Syed, M. (2008). On the intersection of personal and social identities: Introduction and evidence from a longitudinal study of emerging adults. *New Directions for Child and Adolescent Development, 120*, 1–16, doi:10.1002/cd.212.

Bamberg, M. (2004). Form and functions of "slut bashing" in male identity constructions in 15-year-olds. *Human Development, 47*(6), 331–353.

Bowleg, L. (2008). When Black + lesbian + woman ≠ Black lesbian woman: The methodological challenges of qualitative and quantitative intersectionality research. *Sex Roles, 59*, 312–325, doi:10.1007/s11199-008-9400-z.

Braun, V. & Clarke, V. (2006). Using thematic analysis in psychology. *Qualitative Research in Psychology, 3*, 77–101, doi:10.1191/1478088706qp063oa.

Brown, C. S. (2017). *Discrimination in Childhood and Adolescence: A Developmental Intergroup Approach*. New York, NY: Psychology Press.

Brown, C. S., Alabi, B. O., Huynh, V. W., & Masten, C. L. (2011). Ethnicity and gender in late childhood and early adolescence: Group identity and awareness of bias. *Developmental Psychology, 47*, 463–471, doi:10.1037/a0021819.

Brubaker, R. & Cooper, F. (2000). Beyond "identity." *Theory and Society, 29*(1), 1–47.

Carbado, D. W., Crenshaw, K. W., Mays, V. M., & Tomlinson, B. (2013). Intersectionality: Mapping the movements of a theory. *Du Bois Review: Social Science Research on Race, 10*(2), 303–312.

Cielto, J. & Rogers, L. O. (2019, February). Does hair matter? How Black girls integrate physical features in their social identities. Poster presented at the annual meeting of the Society for Personality and Social Psychology, Portland, OR.

Cole, E. R. (2009). Intersectionality and research in psychology. *American Psychologist, 64*, 170–180, doi:10.1037/a0014564.

Collins, P. H. (1991). Black women and motherhood. In V. Held (Ed.), *Justice and Care: Essential Readings in Feminist Ethics* (pp. 117–137). New York, NY: Routledge.

Collins, P. H. (1999). Moving beyond gender: Intersectionality and scientific knowledge. In M. F. Ferree (Ed.), *Revisioning Gender* (pp. 261–284). Thousand Oaks, CA: Sage.

Crenshaw, K. (1991). Mapping the margins: Intersectionality, identity politics, and violence against women of color. *Stanford Law Review, 43*, 1241–1299.

De Fina, A. (2015). Narrative and identities. In A. De Fina & A. Georgakopoulou (Eds.), *The Handbook of Narrative Analysis* (pp. 351–368). Oxford: Wiley.

Erikson, E. H. (1963). *Childhood and Society, 2nd Ed.* New York, NY: Norton.

Erikson, E. H. (1968). *Identity: Youth and Crisis*. New York, NY: Norton.

Frable, D. E. (1997). Gender, racial, ethnic, sexual, and class identities. *Annual Review of Psychology, 48*, 139–162, doi:10.1146/annurev.psych.48.1.139.

Galliher, R. V., McLean, K. C., & Syed, M. (2017). An integrated developmental model for studying identity content in context. *Developmental Psychology, 53* (11), 2011–2022, doi:10.1037/dev0000299.

Ghavami, N., Kastiaficas, D., & Rogers, L. O. (2016). Toward an intersectional approach in developmental science: The role of race, gender, sexual orientation, and immigrant status. In S. S. Horn, M. D. Ruck, & L. S. Liben (Eds.), *Advances in Child Development and Behavior* (pp. 31–73). Burlington: Academic Press, doi:10.1016/bs.acdb.2015.12.001.

Ghavami, N. & Mistry, R. S. (2019). Urban ethnically diverse adolescents' perceptions of social class at the intersection of race, gender, and sexual orientation. *Developmental Psychology*, 55, 457–470.

Ghavami, N. & Peplau, L. A. (2018). Urban middle school students' stereotypes at the intersection of sexual orientation, ethnicity, and gender. *Child Development*, 89, 881–896.

Hammack, P. L. (2008). Narrative and the cultural psychology of identity. *Personality and Social Psychology Review*, 12, 222–247.

Hammack, P. L. & Toolis, E. E. (2015). Putting the social into personal identity: The master narrative as root metaphor for psychological and developmental science. *Human Development*, 58, 350–364.

Hershberg, R. M. & Johnson, S. K. (2019). Critical reflection about socioeconomic inequalities among White young men from poor and working-class backgrounds. *Developmental Psychology*, 55, 562–573.

hooks, b. (1989). *Talking Back: Thinking Feminist, Thinking Black*. Boston, MA: South End Press.

Kiang, L., Fuligni, A. J., & Yip, T. (2008). Multiple social identities and adjustment in young adults from ethnically diverse backgrounds. *Journal of Research on Adolescence*, 18(4), 643–670, doi:10.1111/j.1532-7795.2008.00575.x.

Killen, M., Rutland, A., & Yip, T. (2016). Equity and justice in developmental science: Discrimination, social exclusion, and intergroup attitudes. *Child Development*, 87, 1317–1336, doi:10.1111/cdev.12593.

Korobov, N. (2015). Identities as an interactional process. In K. C. McLean, & M. Syed (Eds.), *The Oxford Handbook of Identity Development* (pp. 562–583). New York, NY: Oxford University Press.

Kteily, N. S. & Richeson, J. A. (2016). Perceiving the world through hierarchy-shaped glasses: On the need to embed social identity effects on perception within the broader context of intergroup hierarchy. *Psychological Inquiry*, 27, 327–334.

Kuper, L. E., Wright, L., & Mustanski, B. (2018). Gender identity development among transgender and gender nonconforming emerging adults: An intersectional approach. *International Journal of Transgenderism*, 19(4), 436–455.

Markus, H. R. & Kitayama, S. (1991). Culture and the self: Implications for cognition, emotion, and motivation. *Psychological Review*, 98, 224–253.

McAdams, D. P. & McLean, K. C. (2013). Narrative identity. *Current Directions in Psychological Science*, 22, 233–238.

McLean, K. C. (2016). *The Co-authored Self: Family Stories and the Construction of Personal Identity*. New York, NY: Oxford University Press.

McLean, K. C., Lilgendahl, J. P., Fordham, C., Alpert, E., Marsden, E., Szymanowski, K., & McAdams, D. P. (2018). Identity development in cultural context: The role of deviating from master narratives. *Journal of Personality*, 86, 631–651.

McLean, K. C., Pasupathi, M., & Pals, J. L. (2007). Selves creating stories creating selves: A process model of self-development. *Personality and Social Psychology Review*, *11*, 262–278.

McLean, K. C. & Syed, M. (2015). Personal, master, and alternative narratives: An integrative framework for understanding identity development in context. *Human Development*, *58*, 318–349, doi:10.1159/000445817.

Moffitt, U., Juang, L. P., & Syed, M. (2020). Intersectionality and youth identity development research in Europe. *Frontiers in Psychology*, *11*, 1–14, doi:10.3389/fpsyg.2020.00078.

Rogers, L. O. (2020). "I'm kind of a feminist": Using master narratives to analyze gender identity in middle childhood. *Child Development*, *91*, 179–196, doi:10.1111/cdev.13142?af=R.

Rogers, L. O. (2018). Who am I, who are we? Erikson and a transactional approach to identity research. *Identity*, *18*(4), 284–294, doi:10.1080/15283488.2018.1523728.

Rogers, L. O. & Meltzoff, A. N. (2017). Is gender more important and meaningful than race? An analysis of racial and gender identity among Black, White, and mixed-race children. *Cultural Diversity and Ethnic Minority Psychology*, *23*, 323–334, doi:10.1037/cdp0000125.

Rogers, L. O. & Nelson, E. P. (2019, February). Who, what, and how: A systematic literature review of identity intersectionality research in psychology. Poster presented at the annual meeting for Society for Personality and Social Psychology, Portland, OR.

Rogers, L. O. & Syed, M. (2021). "I'm just a girl; not a White girl": Intersectionality and early adolescents' race-×-gender identities. *OSF Preprints*: 10.31219/osf.io/3kau6

Rogers, L. O. & Way, N. (2018). Reimagining social and emotional development: Accommodation and resistance to dominant ideologies in the identities and friendships of boys of color. *Human Development*, *61*(6), 311–331, doi:10.1159/000493378.

Ruble, D. N., Alvarez, J., Bachman, M., Cameron, J., Fuligni, A., Coll, C. G., & Rhee, E. (2004). The development of a sense of "we": The emergence and implications of children's collective identity. In M. Bennett & F. Sani (Eds.), *The Development of the Social Self* (p. 29–76). New York, NY: Psychology Press.

Schachter, E. P. (2015). Integrating "internal," "interactional," and "external" perspectives: Identity process as the formulation of accountable claims regarding selves. In K. C. McLean, & M. Syed (Eds.), *The Oxford Handbook of Identity Development* (pp. 228–245). New York, NY: Oxford University Press.

Schachter, E. P. & Ventura, J. J. (2008). Identity agents: Parents as active and reflective participants in their children's identity formation. *Journal of Research on Adolescence*, *18*(3), 449–476.

Sellers, R. M., Smith, M. A., Shelton, J. N., Rowley, S. A., & Chavous, T. M. (1998). Multidimensional model of racial identity: A reconceptualization of African American racial identity. *Personality and Social Psychology Review*, *2*, 18–39.

Settles, I. H. (2006). Use of an intersectional framework to understand Black women's racial and gender identities. *Sex Roles, 54,* 589–601.

Shields, S. A. (2008). Gender: An intersectionality perspective. *Sex Roles, 59,* 301–311.

Suárez-Orozco, C., Yoshikawa, H., & Tseng, V. (2015). *Intersecting Inequalities: Research to Reduce Inequality for Immigrant-Origin Children and Youth.* New York, NY: William T. Grant Foundation.

Syed, M. (2010). Disciplinarity and methodology in intersectionality theory and research. *American Psychologist, 65,* 61–62, doi:10.1037/a0017495.

Syed, M. & Ajayi, A. A. (2018). Promises and pitfalls in the integration of intersectionality with development science. In C. E. Santos & R. B. Toomey (Eds.), *Envisioning the Integration of an Intersectionality Lens in Development Science: New Directions for Child and Adolescent Development* (pp. 109–117). San Francisco, CA: Jossey-Bass.

Syed, M., DeYoung, C. G., & Tiberius, V. (2020). Self, motivation, and virtue, or: How we learned to stop worrying and love deep integration. In N. E. Snow & D. Narvaez (Eds.), *Self, Motivation, and Virtue: Innovative Interdisciplinary Research* (pp. 7–24). New York, NY: Routledge.

Syed, M. & Fish, J. (2018). Revisiting Erik Erikson's legacy on culture, race, and ethnicity. *Identity, 18,* 274–283.

Syed, M. & McLean, K. C. (2016). Understanding identity integration: Theoretical, methodological, and applied issues. *Journal of Adolescence, 47,* 109–118.

Syed, M. & McLean, K. C. (2018). Erikson's theory of psychosocial development. In E. Braaten (Ed.), *The Sage Encyclopedia of Intellectual and Developmental Disorders* (pp. 578–581). Thousand Oaks, CA: Sage.

Thorne, A. (2004). Putting the person into social identity. *Human Development, 47,* 361–365.

Turner, K. L. & Brown, C. S. (2007). The centrality of gender and ethnic identities across individuals and contexts. *Social Development, 16,* 700–719.

Walgenbach, K. (2012). *Intersektionalität – eine Einführung* [Intersectionality: An introduction]. Retrieved May 13, 2021, from http://portal-intersektionalitaet .de/theoriebildung/schluesseltexte/walgenbacheinfuehrung/.

Waterman, A. S. (2015). Identity as internal processes: How the "I" comes to define the "Me." In K. C. McLean & M. Syed (Eds.), *The Oxford Handbook of Identity Development* (pp. 195–209). Oxford: Oxford University Press.

Way, N., Hernández, M. G., Rogers, L. O., & Hughes, D. L. (2013). "I'm not going to become no rapper": Stereotypes as a context of ethnic and racial identity development. *Journal of Adolescent Research, 28,* 407–430. doi:10.1177/ 0743558413480836.

Way, N. & Rogers, L. O. (2015). "[T]hey say Black men won't make it, but I know I'm gonna make it": Identity development in the context of cultural stereotypes. In M. Syed & K. McLean (Eds.), *Oxford Handbook of Identity Development* (pp. 269–285). New York, NY: Oxford University Press.

Williams, C. D., Byrd, C. M., Quintana, S. M., Anicama, C., Kiang, L., Umaña-Taylor, A. J, Calzada, E. J., Gautier, M. P., Ejesi, K., Tuitt, N. R., Martinez-

Fuentes, S., White, L., Marks, A., Rogers, L. O., & Whitesell, N. (2020). A lifespan model of ethnic-racial identity. *Child Development, 17*, 99–129.

Wolcott, H. F. (1994). *Transforming Qualitative Data: Description, Analysis, and Interpretation*. Thousand Oaks, CA: Sage.

Yip, T. (2014). Ethnic identity in everyday life: The influence of identity development status. *Child Development, 85*, 205–219.

PART V

Where Is Identity?

28 Where Is Identity? Reflections on Identity Conceptualizations, Dimensions, and Implications

Carolin Demuth and Meike Watzlawik

I'm Not There (2007) is the title of a movie about the life of singer, songwriter, and poet Bob Dylan. In the film, the role of Dylan is played by six different actors (including Cate Blanchett), each of whom depicts, in turn, the various facets of his persona (poet, prophet, outlaw, fake, superstar, rock-and-roll martyr, born-again Christian – seven identities braided together). While the title *I'm Not There* refers to one of Dylan's songs,[1] the movie can be seen as an exploration of identity, whose title hints at the fleeting nature of self that scholars seem to struggle with. We may also – somewhat provocatively – apply the statement "I'm not there" to the concept of identity in the sense that it might not be just where it has been assumed to reside, as defined by *Western* academia. Thus, in the following, we will try to approach the question, "Where *is* identity?" from various angles, and point out future directions for identity studies.

Theories of identity – like theories in general, along with the empirical work and applications for which they form a basis – always need to be understood within the historical and sociocultural context in which they emerge. Over the past ten years, as we have tried to argue (see Watzlawik, Demuth, & Bamberg, Chapter 1 in this volume), the field of identity research has undergone a number of upheavals – and is still changing rapidly. We have therefore tried to clarify the cultural and historical context in which this handbook has emerged, and what we conceive to be state-of-the-art for contemporary identity research and theory.

Our aim was to assess whether current research on identity centers around one or a small number of key notions. This led us to realize that the field is still disjointed and diverse, which may be related to the fact that identity research spans a wide range of transdisciplinary fields, including psychology, sociology,

We would like to express our gratitude to Michael Bamberg for his comments on a previous version of this chapter.

[1] The title of the film is taken from the 1967 Dylan Basement Tapes recording of "I'm Not There," a song that had not been officially released until it appeared on the film's soundtrack album.

linguistics, anthropology, organizational studies, political science, and neuro-science, and is rooted in a variety of theoretical and epistemological traditions. Despite all these differences, there are also clear commonalities concerning the issues of *what* identity is, *where* it is, and *how* it is constituted. They can be characterized as follows:

First, continuity and change as well as sameness and difference remain of central concern in identity studies, albeit understood somewhat differently by individual scholars (cf. Bamberg & Dege, Chapter 2 in this volume). Identity is, however, increasingly conceived as a dynamic and fluid process, rather than as an essentialist or stable entity across contexts.

Second, we also see a tendency to move away from (only) investigating interiorities as the central place for identity constructions, and a turning toward relational approaches that study discursive practices in social interaction.

Third, while there has been a wide agreement that *language* is constitutive of identity, we have recently seen a shift away from language, or rather, an invitation to go beyond it (Calder-Dawe & Martinussen, Chapter 6 in this volume; Freeman, Chapter 4 in this volume; Hydén, Chapter 22 in this volume), to rethink our common ideas of what language is, calling for a more complex, contextualized, and embodied understanding of language as well as identity (Bertau, Chapter 8 in this volume). In maintaining the notion that language is central for identity construction, we may first pose the question, "Where is language?" before addressing the question, "Where is identity?"

28.1 Where Is Language?

A number of researchers have called for a corrective to the dominant and largely tacitly held view that language, in its essence, is a referential system and a reflection of the individual's cognition. Mostly drawing on Wittgensteinian and Bakhtinian but also ethnomethodological traditions, they have put forward alternative views on language as an interactive (Duranti & Goodwin, 1992), dialogical (Linell, 2009), and largely spontaneous (Shotter, 2008; see also Demuth & Glaveanu, 2016) phenomenon, and ask for a redef-inition of language in terms of dynamic, dialogical, material, and cultural activity, inseparably interwoven with the cultural fabric of life (Brockmeier, 2013). While the body of studies within this field also addresses nonverbal aspects of language practices in terms of gesture, mimicry, and intonation, there are important aspects of social interaction, such as the *material* world in which interactions take place (Goodwin, 2000, 2003), as well as phenomeno-logical aspects of *experiencing* language practices (Bertau, 2014a, 2014b; Cresswell & Teucher, 2011; Ochs, 2012) that need to be addressed, and that have so far received little attention. Language is more than a symbolic medium that, because it stands apart from experience, allows us to represent it. Language is also a constitutive component of our experience.

Our apprehension of things in the world includes the very experiencing of those things as having certain linguistic denotations (Bertau, 2014a, 2014b), or as being parts of certain language "games" (Wittgenstein, 1953/2009). Accordingly, studies on identity need to take into account the phenomeno-logical and dialogical nature of language (e.g., Bertau, Chapter 8 in this volume; Larrain & Haye, 2020). Likewise, we may ask: Is language based on verbal content and paraverbal elements only? Or, as Demuth, Raudaskoski, and Raudaskoski (2020) have queried: Is identity a co-construction of otherwise separated and ahistoric individuals, independent of the material environment?

In her book, *Where Is Language?* (2015), Ruth Finnegan argues that language is central to human experience and our understanding of who we are. But she also asks: What is language, and where does it reside? She challenges the predominant Western view of pitting "literate, rational, scien-tific, civilized, Western, modern" concepts against those that are "communal, emotional, non-scientific, traditional, ... and oral" (p. 5), which, in academia, has led to an understanding of language as abstract sign system and rational means of *expressing* some hidden mental entities in the mind (e.g., identity). What are commonly described as paralinguistic (e.g., volume, pitch, and intonation) or extralinguistic (e.g., gesture, mimicry, body posture, and body movement) elements are in fact, she argues, not supplementary extras attached to language, but intrinsic to how we communicate. She puts forward a view of language as a multidimensional and multiparticipant *performance* that may be written, spoken, or sung. Communication is seen as comprising multisensory elements, including the auditory, visual, tactile, and somatic, and as happening in a material environment, i.e., within specific physical settings and spatial arrangements. We may likewise ask, "*Where* is identity?" and we will do so with different foci in the subsequent paragraphs of this chapter.

28.2 Where Is Identity Located?

The question, "Where is identity located?" will be addressed on two levels: with regard to the *internal–external* distinction and the *temporal* dimension.

28.2.1 Internal or External?

Current research points to an increasing recognition, among identity scholars from various theoretical backgrounds, that identity neither resides within the individual nor is it purely external (in other words, constructed or assigned to us by others). Scholars in the field of psychology and linguistics agree that psychological concepts such as remembering, identity, and self need to be understood as *dynamic processes* that are *dialogically* intertwined with the social world, meaning that they are *locally situated* in social interaction and embedded in the *phenomenological, bodily*, and *material* world as well as in historical time and place (e.g., Bamberg & Dege, Chapter 2; Bertau, Chapter 8; Calder-Dawe & Martinussen, Chapter 6; Norris & Matelau-Doherty, Chapter 14, all this volume; Brockmeier, 2015; Demuth, Raudaskoski, & Raudaskoski, 2020). Hence the question "Where is identity located?" points to a decentered view that goes beyond the individual and social interaction between individuals, but requires taking into account material aspects of the environment in which identity construction is at work.

The question about internality versus externality brings up further questions about reflection and consciousness (Bamberg & Dege, Chapter 2; Freeman, Chapter 4, both this volume), as well as agency and intentionality. It also raises a question as to how people with cognitive and language impairments construct identity. Research on people with dementia has shown that those suffering from the condition draw on other people's resources to construct identity through self-remembering if they themselves no longer have the resources to do so (Brockmeier, 2015; Hydén, Chapter 22 in this volume). Fasulo (Chapter 21 in this volume) makes a similar argument for people diagnosed with autistic spectrum disorder (see also Bamberg & Demuth, 2016 for a comment on deaf people). Referring to Brubaker and Cooper (2000), she points out that identity in terms of self-understanding refers to "the experience and awareness of one's way of being and how that influences day-to-day actions and choices" (Fasulo, this volume, **p. 477**). As such, identity thus defined may not require discursive positions shaped by cultural forces in the same way as assumed in discursive approaches to identity.

Lastly, the question "Where is identity located?" also addresses identity constructions that go beyond the individual in terms of *collective identity* (Murakami, 2012, 2018; Wagoner, 2018). Identity, here, is placed within the social organization of remembering, i.e., the social practices of remembering historic events (e.g., through storytelling, public memorial sites, and public ceremonies) that located identity within the interdependency of public and private memory (see also Gonzalez Rial & Guimarães, Chapter 7 in this volume).

28.2.2 Temporal Dimension

Several contributions in this handbook have addressed the dimension of continuity and change over time. Across the various approaches, we find increasing acknowledgment of understanding identity as a constantly and dynamically evolving process, albeit within different epistemologies. While narrative has often been considered to be the via regia through which we can study these temporal dimensions (e.g., Bamberg, 2011, 2012; Brockmeier & Carbaugh, 2001; Freeman, Chapter 4 in this volume; Giaxoglou & Georgakopoulou, Chapter 11 in this volume), we also find approaches that try to capture these dimensions by means of questionnaires and standardized interview studies that are in line with Eriksonian tradition (e.g., Kroger & Marcia, Chapter 10, Negru-Subtirica & Klimstra, Chapter 18, both this volume; see also Habermas & Kemper, Chapter 9 in this volume).

The question "Where is identity?" may also be asked in a different way, namely: "Where (and when) is identity *relevant?*"

28.3 Where (and When) Is Identity (Made) Relevant?

As Sveningsson, Gjerde, and Alvesson (Chapter 26 in this volume) argue, many people do not necessarily engage with their identities intact most of the time, even though "[m]odernity has brought an increased narcissism ... fuelled by consumerism, mass media, and a therapeutically oriented culture which encourages people to devote much energy to emotions and identity" (ibid., **p. 594**). An interesting question that arises from there is *why* identity becomes relevant in particular situations. In a similar vein, conversation analytical work also investigates when and where identity is made relevant (cf. Wilkes & Speer, Chapter 12 in this volume), rather than assuming its omnipresence across space and time.

Interestingly, taken into account rather less in current identity research are aspects of how, for instance, the material home can favor identity constructions (Giorgi & Fasulo, 2013), and how changes of residence, and with them, a sense of belonging, affects identities and the stories we tell (Taylor, 2010). Likewise, issues such as personal lifestyle, hairstyle, clothing, and body decoration, as well as the aesthetic preferences for one's residence, which all can be considered relevant to identity (construction), are prominent in other disciplines such as gender studies, consumer studies, and anthropology, but less likely to be featured under the header of *identity* research. This possibly points to a general problem in (identity) research, namely that similar constructs and concepts are discussed across disciplines with differing vocabularies, such that an exchange is made difficult (but not impossible).

28.4 Where Is Identity When Looking beyond "Western" Theories?

Bamberg and Dege (Chapter 2 in this volume) have laid out a thorough picture of how the concept of identity has historically evolved under so-called Western modernity (see also Bertau, Chapter 8 in this volume). Likewise, methodologies that go along with dominant identity research need to be seen as outcomes of these historical processes. Critical scholars invite us to rethink core concepts such as culture, self, and identity (Bhatia, 2007) and to decolonize psychology from dominant Euro-American understandings of these concepts (e.g., Bhatia & Priya, 2018; Gonzalez Rial & Guimarães, Chapter 7 in this volume).[2] This also implies the use of appropriate methodological procedures in identity research, including ethnographic approaches. Ethnographic methods are also crucial in research across different cultural communities (Demuth & Fasulo, 2021; Gonzalez Rial & Guimarães, Chapter 7 in this volume). Rethinking research along these lines also brings to the fore some of its ethical aspects, including the question, "Who is entitled to study whom, or whose identity?" (see also Fasulo, Chapter 22 in this volume, with a similar argument regarding studying and making claims about people diagnosed with autism). How should different populations be addressed? Do we do research *on* these populations or rather *with* them? (See, for example, Vincent, 2018, on recommendations for *ethical* recruitment (for more details see LINK) and collaboration with transgender participants.) How do we, for example, deal with often quite personal information in identity research (cf. Berry, Chapter 15 in this volume)? Who benefits from the research results? For what purposes are they used, and by whom (cf. Mazur, Chapter 20 in this volume)? When it was discussed, for example, whether sexual identities might be more fluid than assumed, this provided an argument for some that conversion therapies are possible after all – yet it has been proven that they do more harm than good (cf. Watzlawik, 2014).

In this context, such power relationships need to be critically reflected upon, and dissolved. Having developed over the course of history (cf. Bamberg & Dege, Chapter 2 in this volume), they have become so routine that they feel almost "natural." We, as researchers, need to critically question ourselves so as to determine to what extent each one of us contributes to maintaining these discriminating structures.

28.5 Where Is the Future of Identity Research?

The question "Where is the future of identity research?" is closely linked with how societies change, and what challenges these changes will entail for questions of identity. We may see various challenges in the near future.

On a global level, we are faced with larger migration movements. Along with politically forced and economically motivated relocations, climate change is sure to bring about further migration movements in the future (Brown, 2008). Local displacement and rupture, issues of belonging, coping with uncertainty, and a growing internationalization will become increasingly

[2] It is noteworthy here to mention the recent founding of the Association for European Qualitative Researchers in Psychology (EQuiP), with the aim to foster qualitative research approaches (developed) outside of the dominant Anglo-American academic realm (www.equipsy.org).

important issues for identity studies. Along with these developments, we see increasing populist movements and issues of racism in many countries.

The 2020 pandemic, but also the current political and climatological changes, alerts us to the fact that we will have to learn to live with uncertainties – whether caused by a virus, natural catastrophes, or political upheavals – in new ways, as these uncertainties affect us more directly in our everyday experience.

Technological advancements have brought about a range of new possibilities and unique opportunities for online social interaction. Accordingly, locating identity construction in situated social interaction has taken on new forms (cf. Giaxoglou & Georgakopoulou, Chapter 11 in this volume). On a more general level, artificial intelligence and increasing digitalization open up new fields of identity research: for instance, the range of possibilities to invent various (online) identities, including multiple avatars, as well as human–robot interaction (e.g., Krummheuer, 2016, or Saase, 2020, and Murstein, 2018, on cyborg identities and intersectionality). Identity studies may also, however, focus on consumers' perceived *threats* from artificial intelligence, and the need to *protect* one's identity from the algorithms of the dominant online commerce giants. Certainly, future identity research will also be affected by current neoliberal trends that dominate the academic world, turning more and more universities into manufacturing concerns (Szulevicz & Feilberg, 2018), and forcing researchers to serve the market rather than the broader notion of the public good. Under such conditions, economic factors rather than intellectual reasoning determine what kind of research will be funded, so that researchers will need to find ways to pursue academic freedom (Valsiner et al., 2021). A further field for identity research lies in the effects of neoliberalism in contemporary consumer societies on human moral identity (Brinkmann, Chapter 5 in this volume).

In light of the societal and political developments we have only glimpsed in the sections above, we may finally ask the question: Where do we go from here?

28.6 Where Do We Go from Here?

Identity remains a fascinating concept for study. Within the different research traditions presented in this handbook, we find a number of new and promising developments that are not only made visible via theoretical advancements that conceptualize identity as a complex, contextualized, situated, *dynamic*, and embodied *process*, but also through innovative methodological approaches: multimodality, for example, which has entered the field of identity research (Giaxoglou & Georgakopoulou, Chapter 11; Norris & Matelau-Doherty, Chapter 14, both this volume). Multimodal approaches to studying social interaction have been proposed by scholars such as Mondada (e.g., 2013), Goodwin (2000, 2003), and Streeck (e.g., Streeck, Goodwin, & LeBaron, 2011), and are presently experiencing an upsurge within studies on social interaction (Cekaite & Mondada, 2020), as well as in discursive psychology (Wiggins & Osvaldsson Cromdal, 2021; Demuth, 2021). Identity researchers who work within a socially interactive approach can take up these developments, and apply microanalytic study to multimodal components of communication (voice effects, gestures, posture, etc.) and the material environment, including how sensorial and material dimensions of autobiographical remembering contribute to identity constructions.

At the same time, more traditional approaches have been further developed to capture change over time, aiming to describe dynamic processes of identity development/construction in larger samples, with the help of, for example, longitudinal designs. Researchers have also discussed how this approach permits individual valuation of which *life domains* are central for identity construction (cf. Negru-Subtirica & Klimstra, Chapter 18 in this volume). Across the various methodological approaches, capturing *dynamics* is a major issue that will remain a challenge in the future.

When constructs such as *intersectionality* (cf. Rogers & Syed, Chapter 27 in this volume) are taken seriously – in the sense of recognizing that roles, categories, (self-)positionings, I-positions, and the like are all interconnected – microanalytical analyses, in particular, offer one way of investigating how these *interdependencies* reflect the complex interactions within dominance relations. El-Tayeb (2003, as cited in Walgenbach, 2012) even stresses, with regard to the interdependence of *race* and gender, the *impossibility* of adequately analyzing one without the other.

Having said all this, if we really aim at understanding a phenomenon in flux, one that hides behind many names and definitions, one that is *dynamically* and *dialogically* intertwined with the social world, that is *locally situated* and embedded in the *phenomenological*, *bodily*, and *material* world, as well as in a historical time and place, we will probably need to select what specific cases we want to study, and then dissect which domains and facets we want to look at specifically. This will lead and has led to fragmentation in research (e.g., Valsiner, 2006), fragments that we should aim to put back together, as we have tried to do in this handbook. The importance of continuing this project while grasping the complexity of human phenomena becomes especially clear and tangible when we actively and appreciatively engage with those embraced by our research. With a world population of 7.8 billion individuals as of January 2021, there should be ample opportunities to do so.

References

Bamberg, M. (2011). Who am I? Narration and its contribution to self and identity. *Theory & Psychology, 21*(1), 1–22.

Bamberg, M. (2012). Narrative analysis. In H. Cooper, P. M. Camic, D. L. Long, A. T. Panter, D. Rindskopf, & K. Sher (Eds.), *APA Handbook of Research Methods in Psychology, Vol. 2* (pp. 85–102). Washington, DC: American Psychological Association.

Bamberg, M. & Demuth, C. (2016). Narrative inquiry: An interview with Michael Bamberg. *Europe's Journal of Psychology*, *12*(1), 14–28.

Bertau, M. C. (2014a). Introduction: The self within the space–time of language performance. *Theory & Psychology*, *24*(4), 433–441.

Bertau, M. C. (2014b). Exploring language as the "in-between." *Theory & Psychology*, *24*(4), 524–541.

Bhatia, S. (2007). Rethinking culture and identity in psychology: Towards a transnational cultural psychology. *Journal of Theoretical and Philosophical Psychology*, *27*–28(2–1), 301–321.

Bhatia, S. & Priya, K. R. (2018). Decolonizing culture: Euro-American psychology and the shaping of neoliberal selves in India. *Theory & Psychology*, *28*(5), 645–668.

Brockmeier, J. (2013). Afterword: The monkey wrenches of narrative. In M. Andrews, C. Squire, & M. Tamboukou (Eds.), *Doing Narrative Research, 2nd Ed.* (pp. 161–170). London: Sage.

Brockmeier, J. (2015). *Beyond the Archive. Memory, Narrative, and the Autobiographical Process*. New York, NY: Oxford University Press.

Brockmeier, J. & Carbaugh, D. (Eds.). (2001). *Narrative and Identity: Studies in Autobiography, Self and Culture*. Philadelphia, PA: John Benjamins.

Brown, O. (2008). *Migration and Climate Change 31, IOM Migration Series*. Geneva: International Organization for Migration.

Brubaker, R. & Cooper, F. (2000). Beyond "Identity." *Theory and Society*, *29*(1), 1–47.

Cekaite, A. & Mondada, L. (Eds.). (2020). *Touch in Social Interaction: Touch, Language, and Body*. London: Routledge.

Cresswell, J. & Teucher, U. (2011). The body and language: M. M. Bakhtin on ontogenetic development. *New Ideas in Psychology*, *29*, 106–118.

Demuth, C. (2021). Socializing accountability in classroom interactions: embodied discursive practices in a North Indian preschool. In S. Wiggins & K. Osvaldsson Cromdal (Eds.), *Discursive Psychology and Embodiment: Beyond Subject–Object Binaries* (pp. 81–111). London: Palgrave Macmillan.

Demuth, C. & Fasulo, A. (forthcoming). Comparative qualitative designs in cultural psychology. In U. Flick (Ed.), *Sage Handbook of Qualitative Research Design*. London: Sage.

Demuth, C. & Glaveanu, V. P. (2016). Language. In V. P. Glaveanu, L. Tanggaard Pedersen, & C. Wegener (Eds.), *Creativity: A New Vocabulary* (pp. 14–28). London: Palgrave Macmillan.

Demuth, C., Raudaskoski, P., & Raudaskoski, S. (Eds.). (2020). *Lived Culture and Psychology: Sharedness and Normativity as Discursive, Embodied and Affective Engagements with the World in Social Interaction*. Lausanne: Frontiers Media SA.

Duranti, A. & Goodwin, C. (Eds.). (1992). *Rethinking Context: Language as an Interactive Phenomenon*. Cambridge: Cambridge University Press.

Finnegan, R. (2015). *Where Is Language? An Anthropologist's Questions on Language, Literature and Performance*. London: Bloomsbury.

Giorgi, S. & Fasulo, A. (2013). Transformative homes: Squatting and furnishing as sociocultural projects. *Home Cultures, 10*(2), 111–133.

Goodwin, C. (2000). Action and embodiment within situated human interaction. *Journal of Pragmatics, 32*, 1489–1522.

Goodwin, C. (2003). The body in action. In J. Coupland & R. Gwyn (Eds.), *Discourse, the Body and Identity* (pp. 19–42). New York, NY: Palgrave Macmillan.

Krummheuer, A. L. (2016). Who am I? What are you? Identity construction in encounters between a teleoperated robot and people with acquired brain injury. In A. Agah, J.J. Cabibihan, A. Howard, M. Salichs & H. He (Eds.), *Social Robotics. ICSR 2016. Lecture Notes in Computer Science, Vol. 9979* (pp. 880–889), Cham: Springer.

Larrain, A. & Haye, A. (2020). Self as an aesthetic effect. In C. Demuth, P. Raudaskoski, & S. Raudaskoski (Eds.), *Lived Culture and Psychology: Sharedness and Normativity as Discursive, Embodied and Affective Engagements with the World in Social Interaction* (pp. 57–66). Lausanne: Frontiers Media.

Linell, P. (2009). *Rethinking Language, Mind, and World Dialogically*. Charlotte, NC: Information Age.

Mondada, L. (2013). *Multimodal interaction*. In C. Müller, A. J. Cienki, E. Fricke, S. H. Ladewig, D. McNeil, & S. Teßendorf (Eds.), *Body – Language – Communication: An International Handbook on Multimodality in Human Interaction* (pp. 577–589). Berlin: De Gruyter.

Murakami, K. (2012). *Identities in Action: Discursive Psychology of Remembering and Reconciliation* (pp. 75–98). Hauppauge, NY: Nova Science Publishers.

Murakami, K. (2018). Materiality of memory: The case of the remembrance poppy. In. B. Wagoner (Ed.), *Handbook of Culture and Memory* (pp. 117–132). Oxford: University Press.

Murstein, M. (2018). *I'm a Queerfeminist Cyborg, That's Okay: Gedankensammlung zu Anti/Ableismus*. Berlin: Edition Assemblage.

Ochs, E. (2012). Experiencing language. *Anthropological Theory, 12*(2), 142–160.

Saase, S. (2020). Privilegien 5.0 – Cyborgs und Psyborgs mit intersektionalem Privilegienbewusstsein? [Privileges 5.0 – Cyborgs and psyborgs with intersectional privilege awareness?] In K.-J. Bruder, C. Bialluch, J. Günther, B. Nielsen, & R. Zimmering (Eds.), *"Digitalisierung" – Sirenengesänge oder Schlachtruf einer kannibalistischen Weltordnung* ["Digitization" – Siren song or battle cry of a cannibalistic world order] (pp. 221–234). Frankfurt am Main: Westend.

Shotter, J. (2008). *Conversational Realities Revisited: Life, Language, Body and World*. Chagrin Falls, OH: Taos Institute.

Streeck, J., Goodwin, C., & LeBaron, C. (2011). *Embodied Interaction: Language and Body in the Material World*. New York, NY: Cambridge University Press.

Szulevicz, T. & Feilberg, K. (2018). What has happened to quality? In J. Valsiner, A. Lutsenko, & A. Antoniouk (Eds.), *Sustainable Futures for Higher Education, Cultural Psychology of Education 7* (pp. 313–326). Cham: Springer International.

Taylor, S. (2010). *Narratives of Identity and Place*. New York, NY: Routledge.

Valsiner, J. (2006). Dangerous curves in knowledge construction within psychology: Fragmentation of methodology. *Theory & Psychology*, *16*(5), 597–612.

Valsiner, J., Demuth, C., Wagoner, B., & Allesoe, B. (forthcoming). A talk with Jaan Valsiner about the future of cultural psychology. *Europe's Journal of Psychology*.

Vincent, B. W. (2018). Studying trans: Recommendations for ethical recruitment and collaboration with transgender participants in academic research. *Psychology & Sexuality*, *9*(3), 1–15.

Wagoner, B. (2018). *Handbook of Culture and Memory*. Oxford: Oxford University Press.

Walgenbach, K. (2012). *Intersektionalität – eine Einführung* [Intersectionality: An introduction]. Retrieved May 13, 2021, from http://portal-intersektionalitaet .de/theoriebildung/schluesseltexte/walgenbacheinfuehrung/.

Watzlawik, M. (2014). Homo-, bi- oder heterosexuell? Identitätsfindung in, zwischen und außerhalb der Norm [Homosexual, bi-sexual or heterosexual? Finding identity in, between and outside the norm]. *Zeitschrift für Inklusion*, *3*. Retrieved May 13, 20201, from www.inklusion-online.net/index.php/inklu sion-online/article/view/227.

Wiggins, S. & Osvaldsson Cromdal, K. (Eds.). (2021). *Discursive Psychology and Embodiment: Beyond Subject–Object Ninaries*. London: Palgrave Macmillan.

Wittgenstein, L. (1953/2009). *Philosophical Investigations, 4th Revised Ed.* Chichester: Wiley-Blackwell.

Author Index

Subject Index

Lightning Source UK Ltd.
Milton Keynes UK
UKHW050824191121
394234UK00004B/45